Blackstone's Statutes on

INTELLECTUAL PROPERTY

Blackstone's Statutes on
INTELLECTUAL PROPERTY

Fourth Edition

Edited by

Andrew Christie
BSc, LLB (Hons)(Melb), LLM (Lond), PhD (Cantab)
Associate Professor, Law School, University of Melbourne

and

Stephen Gare
MA (Cantab), MA (Business Law)
Partner in Rowe & Maw, London

BLACKSTONE
PRESS LIMITED

First published in Great Britain 1992 by Blackstone Press Limited,
Aldine Place, London W12 8AA. Telephone 0181-740 2277

© Andrew Christie and Stephen Gare, 1992

ISBN: 1 85431 871 3

First edition, 1992
Second edition, 1995
Third edition, 1997
Fourth edition, 1998

British Library cataloguing in Publication Data
A CIP catalogue record for this book is available from the British Library

Typeset by Montage Studios Limited, Horsmonden, Kent
Printed by Ashford Colour Press, Gosport, Hampshire

CONTENTS

EDITORS' PREFACE

Although only 20 months have passed since publication of the previous edition, we feel the amount of new legislative material produced in that period warrants a new edition of this work.

At the national level, we have included in Part I the Plant Varieties Act 1997 (which effectively replaces the Plant Variety and Seeds Act 1964) and the Copyright and Rights in Databases Regulations 1997. All of the remaining material in Part I has been updated to include legislative amendments made as of 1 July 1998.

The EC material introduced into Part II of this edition is the long-awaited Biotechnology Directive.

We have taken the opportunity of this new edition to supplement the International legislative material in Part III, in the following manner. We have added the Integrated Circuits Treaty (which, although not yet in force, has relevance by virtue of the TRIPS Agreement), the Satellite Convention and the Lisbon Agreement for the Protection of Appellations of Origin. We have also added the Agreed Statements concerning both the WIPO Copyright Treaty and the WIPO Performances and Phonograms Treaty. Finally, we have introduced those articles in Part III of the TRIPS Agreement not previously included, as well as Part VII of the same, thereby providing a complete version of this important treaty.

As with the previous editions, this volume seeks to provide a comprehensive and affordable collection of materials satisfying the needs of students of the discipline. Accordingly, we have deleted material of a procedural nature, where this is unlikely to be referred to in a course concerned primarily with principles of the law. We have continued our past practice of setting out material first, by the jurisdiction to which it applies (the UK, the European Community and the international community), and secondly, by the date of first enactment.

We are grateful to the following organisations for consenting to the reproduction of extracts of their respective publications in Part III of the book:

UN   Rio Convention on Biological Diversity 1992

UNESCO   Universal Copyright Convention 1952 (1971 revision)

UPOV   UPOV Convention for the Protection of New Varieties of Plants 1961 (1991 revision)

WIPO   Paris Convention for the Protection of Industrial Property 1883 (1967 revision with 1979 amendments)

          Berne Convention for the Protection of Literary and Artistic Works 1886 (1971 revision with 1979 amendments))

          Madrid Agreement concerning the International Registration of Marks 1891 (1967 revision with 1979 amendments) and 1989 Protocol

          Lisbon Agreement for the Protection of Appellations of Origin 1958 (1967 revision with 1979 amendments)

Rome Convention for the Protection of Performers, Producers of Phonograms and Broadcasting Organisations 1961

Geneva Convention for the Protection of Producers of Phonograms Against Unauthorised Duplication of their Phonograms 1971

Convention Relating to the Distribution of Programme-Carrying Signals Transmitted by Satellite 1974

Treaty on Intellectual Property in Respect of Integrated Circuits 1989

WIPO Copyright Treaty 1996 and Agreed Statements

WIPO Performances and Phonograms Treaty 1996 and Agreed Statements

WTO   TRIPS Agreement 1994

We also acknowledge Crown Copyright in the UK legislation included in this book.

We are pleased to acknowledge the helpful suggestions of Professor Gerald Dworkin and the contribution of Dr Karen Cleaver of Rowe & Maw to the preparation of this publication.

Andrew Christie
Stephen Gare
September 1998

PART I UK LEGISLATION

THE REGISTERED DESIGNS ACT 1949 (AS AMENDED)

An Act to consolidate certain enactments relating to registered designs. Amended by Copyright, Design and Patents Act 1988. [16 December 1949]

Registrable designs and proceedings for registration

1 Designs registrable under Act

(1) In this Act "design" means features of shape, configuration, pattern or ornament applied to an article by any industrial process, being features which in the finished article appeal to and are judged by the eye, but does not include—

    (a)   a method or principle of construction, or

    (b)   features of shape or configuration of an article which—

        (i)   are dictated solely by the function which the article has to perform, or

        (ii)   are dependent upon the appearance of another article of which the article is intended by the author of the design to form an integral part.

(2) A design which is new may, upon application by the person claiming to be the proprietor, be registered under this Act in respect of any article, or set of articles, specified in the application.

(3) A design shall not be registered in respect of an article if the appearance of the article is not material, that is, if aesthetic considerations are not normally taken into account to a material extent by persons acquiring or using articles of that description, and would not be so taken into account if the design were to be applied to the article.

(4) A design shall not be regarded as new for the purposes of this Act if it is the same as a design—

    (a)   registered in respect of the same or any other article in pursuance of a prior application, or

    (b)   published in the United Kingdom in respect of the same or any other article before the date of the application,

or if it differs from such a design only in immaterial details or in features which are variants commonly used in the trade.

This subsection has effect subject to the provisions of sections 4, 6 and 16 of this Act.

(5) The Secretary of State may by rules provide for excluding from registration under this Act designs for such articles of a primarily literary or artistic character as the Secretary of State thinks fit.

(6) A design shall not be registered if it consists of or contains a controlled representation within the meaning of the Olympic Symbol etc. (Protection) Act 1995 unless it appears to the registrar—

    (a)   that the application is made by the person for the time being appointed under section 1(2) of the Olympic Symbol etc. (Protection) Act 1995 (power of Secretary of State to appoint a person as the proprietor of the Olympics association right), or

    (b)   that consent has been given by or on behalf of the person mentioned in paragraph (a) of this subsection.

2 Proprietorship of designs

(1) The author of a design shall be treated for the purposes of this Act as the original proprietor of the design, subject to the following provisions.

(1A) Where a design is created in pursuance of a commission for money or money's worth, the person commissioning the design shall be treated as the original proprietor of the design.

(1B) Where, in a case not falling within subsection (1A), a design is created by an employee in the course of his employment, his employer shall be treated as the original proprietor of the design.

(2)   Where a design, or the right to apply a design to any article, becomes vested, whether by assignment, transmission or operation of law, in any person other than the original proprietor, either alone or jointly with the original proprietor, that other person, or as the case may be the original proprietor and that other person, shall be treated for the purposes of this Act as the proprietor of the design or as the proprietor of the design in relation to that article.

(3)   In this Act the "author" of a design means the person who creates it.

(4)   In the case of a design generated by computer in circumstances such that there is no human author, the person by whom the arrangements necessary for the creation of the design are made shall be taken to be the author.

3   Proceedings for registration

(1)   An application for the registration of a design shall be made in the prescribed form and shall be filed at the Patent Office in the prescribed manner.

(2)   An application for the registration of a design in which design right subsists shall not be entertained unless made by the person claiming to be the design right owner.

(3)   For the purpose of deciding whether a design is new, the registrar may make such searches, if any, as he thinks fit.

. . .

4   Registration of same design in respect of other articles, etc.

(1)   Where the registered proprietor of a design registered in respect of any article makes an application—

(a)   for registration in respect of one or more other articles, of the registered design, or

(b)   for registration in respect of the same or one or more other articles, of a design consisting of the registered design with modifications or variations not sufficient to alter the character or substantially to affect the identity thereof,

the application shall not be refused and the registration made on that application shall not be invalidated by reason only of the previous registration or publication of the registered design:

Provided that the right in a design registered by virtue of this section shall not extend beyond the end of the period, and any extended period, for which the right subsists in the original registered design.

(2)   Where any person makes an application for the registration of a design in respect of any article and either—

(a)   that design has been previously registered by another person in respect of some other article; or

(b)   the design to which the application relates consists of a design previously registered by another person in respect of the same or some other article with modifications or variations not sufficient to alter the character or substantially to affect the identity thereof,

then, if at any time while the application is pending the applicant becomes the registered proprietor of the design previously registered, the foregoing provisions of this section shall apply as if at the time of making the application the applicant had been the registered proprietor of that design.

5   Provisions for secrecy of certain designs

(1)   Where, either before or after the commencement of this Act, an application for the registration of a design has been made, and it appears to the registrar that the design is one of a class notified to him by the Secretary of State as relevant for defence purposes, he may give directions for prohibiting or restricting the publication of information with respect to the design, or the communication of such information to any person or class of persons specified in the directions.

. . .

6 Provisions as to confidential disclosure, etc.

(1) An application for the registration of a design shall not be refused, and the registration of a design shall not be invalidated, by reason only of—

(a) the disclosure of the design by the proprietor to any other person in such circumstances as would make it contrary to good faith for that other person to use or publish the design;

(b) the disclosure of the design in breach of good faith by any person other than the proprietor of the design; or

(c) in the case of a new or original textile design intended for registration, the acceptance of a first and confidential order for goods bearing the design.

(2) An application for the registration of a design shall not be refused and the registration of a design shall not be invalidated by reason only—

(a) that a representation of the design, or any article to which the design has been applied, has been displayed, with the consent of the proprietor of the design, at an exhibition certified by the Secretary of State for the purposes of this subsection;

(b) that after any such display as aforesaid, and during the period of the exhibition, a representation of the design or any such article as aforesaid has been displayed by any person without the consent of the proprietor; or

(c) that a representation of the design has been published in consequence of any such display as is mentioned in paragraph (a) of this subsection,

if the application for registration of the design is made not later than six months after the opening of the exhibition.

(3) An application for the registration of a design shall not be refused, and the registration of a design shall not be invalidated, by reason only of the communication of the design by the proprietor thereof to a government department or to any person authorised by a government department to consider the merits of the design, or of anything done in consequence of such a communication.

(4) Where an application is made by or with the consent of the owner of copyright in an artistic work for the registration of a corresponding design, the design shall not be treated for the purposes of this Act as being other than new by reason only of any use previously made of the artistic work, subject to subsection (5).

(5) Subsection (4) does not apply if the previous use consisted of or included the sale, letting for hire or offer or exposure for sale or hire of articles to which had been applied industrially—

(a) the design in question, or

(b) a design differing from it only in immaterial details or in features which are variants commonly used in the trade,

and that previous use was made by or with the consent of the copyright owner.

(6) The Secretary of State may make provision by rule as to the circumstances in which a design is to be regarded for the purposes of this section as "applied industrially" to articles, or any description of articles.

Effect of registration, &c.

7 Right given by registration

(1) The registration of a design under this Act gives the registered proprietor the exclusive right—

(a) to make or import—

(i) for sale or hire, or

(ii) for use for the purposes of a trade or business, or

(b) to sell, hire or offer or expose for sale or hire,

an article in respect of which the design is registered and to which that design or a design not substantially different from it has been applied.

(2)   The right in the registered design is infringed by a person who without the licence of the registered proprietor does anything which by virtue of subsection (1) is the exclusive right of the proprietor.

(3)   The right in the registered design is also infringed by a person who, without the licence of the registered proprietor makes anything for enabling any such article to be made, in the United Kingdom or elsewhere, as mentioned in subsection (1).

(4)   The right in the registered design is also infringed by a person who without the licence of the registered proprietor—

(a)   does anything in relation to a kit that would be an infringement if done in relation to the assembled article (see subsection (1)), or

(b)   makes anything for enabling a kit to be made or assembled, in the United Kingdom or elsewhere, if the assembled article would be such an article as is mentioned in subsection (1);

and for this purpose a "kit" means a complete or substantially complete set of components intended to be assembled into an article.

(5)   No proceedings shall be taken in respect of an infringement committed before the date on which the certificate of registration of the design under this Act is granted.

(6)   The right in a registered design is not infringed by the reproduction of a feature of the design which, by virtue of section 1(1)(b), is left out of account in determining whether the design is registrable.

8   Duration of right in registered design

(1)   The right in a registered design subsists in the first instance for a period of five years from the date of the registration of the design.

(2)   The period for which the right subsists may be extended for a second, third, fourth and fifth period of five years, by applying to the registrar for an extension and paying the prescribed renewal fee.

(3)   If the first, second, third or fourth period expires without such application and payment being made, the right shall cease to have effect; and the registrar shall, in accordance with rules made by the Secretary of State, notify the proprietor of that fact.

(4)   If during the period of six months immediately following the end of that period an application for extension is made and the prescribed renewal fee and any prescribed additional fee is paid, the right shall be treated as if it had never expired, with the result that—

(a)   anything done under or in relation to the right during that further period shall be treated as valid,

(b)   an act which would have constituted an infringement of the right if it had not expired shall be treated as an infringement, and

(c)   an act which would have constituted use of the design for the services of the Crown if the right had not expired shall be treated as such use.

(5)   Where it is shown that a registered design—

(a)   was at the time it was registered a corresponding design in relation to an artistic work in which copyright subsists, and

(b)   by reason of a previous use of that work would not have been registrable but for section 6(4) of this Act (registration despite certain prior applications of design),

the right in the registered design expires when the copyright in that work expires, if that is earlier than the time at which it would otherwise expire, and it may not thereafter be renewed.

(6)   The above provisions have effect subject to the proviso to section 4(1) (registration of same design in respect of other articles, &c.) and, in the case of the right of the Secretary of State in any design forming part of the British mercantile marine

uniform registered under this Act, to the right's subsisting so long as the design remains on the register.

...

9 Exemption of innocent infringer from liability for damages

(1)   In proceedings for the infringement of the right in a registered design damages shall not be awarded against a defendant who proves that at the date of the infringement he was not aware, and had no reasonable ground for supposing, that the design was registered; and a person shall not be deemed to have been aware or to have had reasonable grounds for supposing as aforesaid by reason only of the marking of an article with the word "registered" or any abbreviation thereof, or any word or words expressing or implying that the design applied to the article has been registered, unless the number of the design accompanied the word or words or the abbreviation in question.

(2)   Nothing in this section shall affect the power of the court to grant an injunction in any proceedings for infringement of the right in a registered design.

10 Compulsory licence in respect of registered design

(1)   At any time after a design has been registered any person interested may apply to the registrar for the grant of a compulsory licence in respect of the design on the ground that the design is not applied in the United Kingdom by any industrial process or means to the article in respect of which it is registered to such an extent as is reasonable in the circumstances of the case; and the registrar may make such order on the application as he thinks fit.

(2)   An order for the grant of a licence shall, without prejudice to any other methods of enforcement, have effect as if it were a deed executed by the registered proprietor and all other necessary parties, granting a licence in accordance with the order.

(3)   No order shall be made under this section which would be at variance with any treaty, convention, arrangement or engagement applying to the United Kingdom and any convention country.

(4)   An appeal shall lie from any order of the registrar under this section.

11 Cancellation of registration

(1)   The registrar may, upon a request made in the prescribed manner by the registered proprietor, cancel the registration of a design.

(2)   At any time after a design has been registered any person interested may apply to the registrar for the cancellation of the registration of the design on the ground that the design was not, at the date of the registration thereof, new ..., or on any other ground on which the registrar could have refused to register the design; and the registrar may make such order on the application as he thinks fit.

(3)   At any time after a design has been registered, any person interested may apply to the registrar for the cancellation of the registration on the ground that—

(a)   the design was at the time it was registered a corresponding design in relation to an artistic work in which copyright subsisted, and

(b)   the right in the registered design has expired in accordance with section 8(4) of this Act (expiry of right in registered design on expiry of copyright in artistic work); and the registrar may make such order on the application as he thinks fit.

(4)   A cancellation under this section takes effect—

(a)   in the case of cancellation under subsection (1), from the date of the registrar's decision,

(b)   in the case of cancellation under subsection (2), from the date of registration,

(c)   in the case of cancellation under subsection (3), from the date on which the right in the registered design expired,

or, in any case, from such other date as the registrar may direct.

(5)   An appeal lies from any order of the registrar under this section.

11A   Powers exercisable for protection of the public interest
(1)   Where a report of the Monopolies and Mergers Commission has been laid before parliament containing conclusions to the effect—
(a)   on a monopoly reference, that a monopoly situation exists and facts found by the Commission operate or may be expected to operate against the public interest,
(b)   on a merger reference, that a merger situation qualifying for investigation has been created and the creation of the situation, or particular elements in or consequences of it specified in the report, operate or may be expected to operate against the public interest,
(c)   on a competition reference, that a person was engaged in an anti-competitive practice which operated or may be expected to operate against the public interest, or
(d)   on a reference under section 11 of the Competition Act 1980 (reference of public bodies and certain other persons), that a person is pursuing a course of conduct which operates against the public interest,
the appropriate Minister or Ministers may apply to the registrar to take action under this section.
(2)   Before making an application the appropriate Minister or Ministers shall publish, in such manner as he or they think appropriate, a notice describing the nature of the proposed application and shall consider any representations which may be made within 30 days of such publication by persons whose interests appear to him or them to be affected.
(3)   If on an application under this section it appears to the registrar that the matters specified in the Commission's report as being those which in the Commission's opinion operate, or operated or may be expected to operate, against the public interest include—
(a)   conditions in licences granted in respect of a registered design by its proprietor restricting the use of the design by the licensee or the right of the proprietor to grant other licences, or
(b)   a refusal by the proprietor of a registered design to grant licences on reasonable terms,
he may by order cancel or modify any such conditions or may, instead or in addition, make an entry in the register to the effect that licences in respect of the design are to be available as of right.
(4)   The terms of a licence available by virtue of this section shall, in default of agreement, be settled by the registrar on an application by the person requiring the licence; and terms so settled shall authorise the licensee to do everything which would be an infringement of the right in the registered design in the absence of a licence.
(5)   Where the terms of a licence are settled by the registrar, the licence has effect from the date on which the application to him was made.
(6)   An appeal lies from any order of the registrar under this section.
(7)   In this section "the appropriate Minister or Ministers" means the Minister or Ministers to whom the report of the Monopolies and Mergers Commission was made.

11B   Undertaking to take licence of right in infringement proceedings
(1)   If in proceedings for infringement of the right in a registered design in respect of which a licence is available as of right under section 11A of this Act the defendant undertakes to take a licence on such terms as may be agreed or, in default of agreement, settled by the registrar under that section—
(a)   no injunction shall be granted against him, and
(b)   the amount recoverable against him by way of damages or on an account of profits shall not exceed double the amount which would have been payable by him as

licensee if such a licence on those terms had been granted before the earliest infringement.

(2)　An undertaking may be given at any time before final order in the proceedings, without any admission of liability.

(3)　Nothing in this section affects the remedies available in respect of an infringement committed before licences of right were available.

12　Use for services of the Crown

The provisions of the First Schedule to this Act shall have effect with respect to the use of registered designs for the services of the Crown and the rights of third parties in respect of such use.

International Arrangements

13　Orders in Council as to convention countries

(1)　His Majesty may, with a view to the fulfilment of a treaty, convention, arrangement or engagement, by Order in Council declare that any country specified in the Order is a convention country for the purposes of this Act:

Provided that a declaration may be made as aforesaid for the purposes either of all or of some only of the provisions of this Act, and a country in the case of which a declaration made for the purposes of some only of the provisions of this Act is in force shall be deemed to be a convention country for the purposes of those provisions only.

(2)　His Majesty may by Order in Council direct that any of the Channel Islands, any colony, ... shall be deemed to be a convention country for the purposes of all or any of the provisions of this Act; and an Order made under this subsection may direct that any such provisions shall have effect, in relation to the territory in question, subject to such conditions or limitations, if any, as may be specified in the Order.

(3)　For the purposes of subsection (1) of this section, every colony, protectorate, territory subject to the authority or under the suzerainty of another country, and territory administered by another country ... under the trusteeship system of the United Nations, shall be deemed to be a country in the case of which a declaration may be made under that subsection.

14　Registration of design where application for protection in convention country has been made

(1)　An application for registration of a design in respect of which protection has been applied for in a convention country may be made in accordance with the provisions of this Act by the person by whom the application for protection was made or his personal representative or assignee:

Provided that no application shall be made by virtue of this section after the expiration of six months from the date of the application for protection in a convention country or, where more than one such application for protection has been made, from the date of the first application.

(2)　Where an application for registration of a design is made by virtue of this section, the application shall be treated, for the purpose of determining whether that or any other design is new, as made on the date of the application for protection in the convention country or, if more than one such application was made, on the date of the first such application.

(3)　Subsection (2) shall not be construed as excluding the power to give directions under section 3(4) of this Act in relation to an application made by virtue of this section.

(4)　Where a person has applied for protection for a design by an application which—

　　(a)　in accordance with the terms of a treaty subsisting between two or more convention countries, is equivalent to an application duly made in any one of those convention countries; or

(b)   in accordance with the law of any convention country, is equivalent to an application duly made in that convention country,
he shall be deemed for the purposes of this section to have applied in that convention country.
...

Register of designs, etc.

17   Register of designs
   (1)   The registrar shall maintain the register of designs, in which shall be entered—
      (a)   the names and addresses of proprietors of registered designs;
      (b)   notices of assignments and of transmissions of registered designs; and
      (c)   such other matters as may be prescribed or as the registrar may think fit.
   (2)   No notice of any trust, whether express, implied or constructive, shall be entered in the register of designs, and the registrar shall not be affected by any such notice.
...

18   Certificate of registration
   (1)   The registrar shall grant a certificate of registration in the prescribed form to the registered proprietor of a design when the design is registered.
...

19   Registration of assignments, etc.
   (1)   Where any person becomes entitled by assignment, transmission or operation of law to a registered design or to a share in a registered design, or becomes entitled as mortgagee, licensee or otherwise to any other interest in a registered design, he shall apply to the registrar in the prescribed manner for the registration of his title as proprietor or co-proprietor or, as the case may be, of notice of his interests, in the register of designs.
...

   (4)   Subject to any rights vested in any other person of which notice is entered in the register of designs, the person or persons registered as proprietor of a registered design shall have power to assign, grant licences under, or otherwise deal with the design, and to give effectual receipts for any consideration for any such assignment, licence or dealing.
   Provided that any equities in respect of the design may be enforced in like manner as in respect of any other personal property.
   (5)   Except for the purposes of an application to rectify the register under the following provisions of this Act, a document in respect of which no entry has been made in the register of designs under subsection (3) of this section shall not be admitted in any court as evidence of the title of any person to a registered design or share of or interest in a registered design unless the court otherwise directs.

20   Rectification of register
(1)   The court may, on the application of any person aggrieved, order the register of designs to be rectified by the making of any entry therein or the variation or deletion of any entry therein.
...

22   Inspection of registered designs
   (1)   Where a design has been registered under this Act, there shall be open to inspection at the Patent Office on and after the day on which the certificate of registration is issued—
      (a)   the representation or specimen of the design, and
      (b)   any evidence filed in support of the applicant's contention that the appearance of an article is material (for the purposes of section 1(3) of this Act).

This subsection has effect subject to the following provisions of this section and to any rules made under section 5(2) of this Act.

...

Legal proceedings and appeals

25 Certificate of contested validity of registration

(1)   If in any proceedings before the court the validity of the registration of a design is contested, and it is found by the court that the design is validly registered, the court may certify that the validity of the registration of the design was contested in those proceedings.

(2)   Where any such certificate has been granted, then if in any subsequent proceedings before the court for infringement of the right in the registered design or for cancellation of the registration of the design, a final order or judgment is made or given in favour of the registered proprietor, he shall, unless the court otherwise directs, be entitled to his costs as between solicitor and client:

Provided that this subsection shall not apply to the costs of any appeal in any such proceedings as aforesaid.

26 Remedy for groundless threats of infringement proceedings

(1)   Where any person (whether entitled to or interested in a registered design or an application for registration of a design or not) by circulars, advertisements or otherwise threatens any other person with proceedings for infringement of the right in a registered design, any person aggrieved thereby may bring an action against him for any such relief as is mentioned in the next following subsection.

(2)   Unless in any action brought by virtue of this section the defendant proves that the acts in respect of which proceedings were threatened constitute or, if done, would constitute, an infringement of the right in a registered design the registration of which is not shown by the plaintiff to be invalid, the plaintiff shall be entitled to the following relief, that is to say:—

(a)   a declaration to the effect that the threats are unjustifiable;

(b)   an injunction against the continuance of the threats; and

(c)   such damages, if any, as he has sustained thereby.

(2A)   Proceedings may not be brought under this section in respect of a threat to bring proceedings for an infringement alleged to consist of the making or importing of anything.

(3)   For the avoidance of doubt it is hereby declared that a mere notification that a design is registered does not constitute a threat of proceedings within the meaning of this section.

...

Rules

...

35 Fine for falsely representing a design as registered

(1)   If any person falsely represents that a design applied to any article sold by him is registered in respect of that article, he shall be liable on summary conviction to a fine not exceeding level 3 on the standard scale; and for the purposes of this provision a person who sells an article having stamped, engraved or impressed thereon or otherwise applied thereto the word "registered", or any other word expressing or implying that the design applied to the article is registered, shall be deemed to represent that the design applied to the article is registered in respect of that article.

(2)   If any person, after the right in a registerd design has expired, marks any article to which the design has been applied with the word "registered", or any word or words implying that there is a subsisting right in the design under this Act, or causes any such

article to be so marked, he shall be liable on summary conviction to a fine not exceeding level 1 on the standard scale.

35A   Offence by body corporate: liability of officers

(1)   Where an offence under this Act committed by a body corporate is proved to have been committed with the consent or connivance of a director, manager, secretary or other similar officer of the body, or a person purporting to act in any such capacity, he as well as the body corporate is guilty of the offence and liable to be proceeded against and punished accordingly.

(2)   In relation to a body corporate whose affairs are managed by its members "director" means a member of the body corporate.

. . .

Supplemental

. . .

43   Savings

(1)   Nothing in this Act shall be construed as authorising or requiring the registrar to register a design the use of which would, in his opinion, be contrary to law or morality.

(2)   Nothing in this Act shall affect the right of the Crown or of any person deriving title directly or indirectly from the Crown to sell or use articles forfeited under the laws relating to customs or excise.

44   Interpretation

(1)   In this Act, except where the context otherwise requires, the following expressions have the meanings hereby respectively assigned by them, that is to say—

"Appeal Tribunal" means the Appeal Tribunal constituted and acting in accordance with section 28 of this Act as amended by the Administration of Justice Act 1969;

"article" means any article of manufacture and includes any part of an article if that part is made and sold separately;

"artistic work" has the same meaning as in Part I of the Copyright, Designs and Patents Act 1988;

"assignee" includes the personal representative of a deceased assignee, and references to the assignee of any person include references to the assignee of the personal representative or assignee of that person;

"author", in relation to a design, has the meaning given by section 2(3) and (4);

. . .

"corresponding design", in relation to an artistic work, means a design which if applied to an article would produce something which would be treated for the purposes of Part I of the Copyright, Designs and Patents Act 1988 as a copy of that work;

"the court" shall be construed in accordance with section 27 of this Act;

"design" has the meaning assigned to it by section 1(1) of this Act;

"employee", "employment" and "employer" refer to employment under a contract of service or of apprenticeship;

. . .

"prescribed" means prescribed by rules made by the Secretary of State under this Act;

"proprietor" has the meaning assigned to it by section two of this Act;

"registered proprietor" means the person or persons for the time being entered in the register of designs as proprietor of the design;

"registrar" means the Comptroller-General of Patents Designs and Trade Marks;

"set of articles" means a number or articles of the same general character ordinarily on sale or intended to be used together, to each of which the same design, or the same design with modifications or variations not sufficient to alter the character or substantially to affect the identity thereof, is applied.

(2)   Any reference in this Act to an article in respect of which a design is registered shall, in the case of a design registered in respect of a set of articles, be construed as a reference to any article of that set.

(3)   Any question arising under this Act whether a number of articles constitute a set of articles shall be determined by the registrar; and notwithstanding anything in this Act any determination of the registrar under this subsection shall be final.

(4)   For the purposes of subsection (1) of section 14 and of section 16 of this act, the expression "personal representative", in relation to a deceased person, includes the legal representative of the deceased appointed in any country outside the United Kingdom.

...

PATENTS ACT 1977
(1977, c. 37)

An Act to establish a new law of patents applicable to future patents and applications of patents; to amend the law of patents applicable to existing patents and applications for patents; to give effect to certain international conventions on patents; and for connected purposes.

[29 July 1977]

...

PART I   NEW DOMESTIC LAW
Patentability

1   Patentable inventions

(1)   A patent may be granted only for an invention in repect of which the following conditions are satisfied, that is to say—

  (a)   the invention is new;
  (b)   it involves an inventive step;
  (c)   it is capable of industrial application;
  (d)   the grant of a patent for it is not excluded by subsections (2) and (3) below;
and references in this Act to a patentable invention shall be construed accordingly.

(2)   It is hereby declared that the following (among other things) are not inventions for the purposes of this Act, that is to say, anything which consists of—

  (a)   a discovery, scientific theory or mathematical method;
  (b)   a literary, dramatic, musical or artistic work or any other aesthetic creation whatsoever;
  (c)   a scheme, rule or method for performing a mental act, playing a game or doing business, or a program for a computer;
  (d)   the presentation of information;
but the foregoing provision shall prevent anything from being treated as an invention for the purposes of this Act only to the extent that a patent or application for a patent relates to that thing as such.

(3)   A patent shall not be granted—

  (a)   for an invention the publication or exploitation of which would be generally expected to encourage offensive, immoral or anti-social behaviour;
  (b)   for any variety of animal or plant or any essentially biological process for the production of animals or plants, not being a micro-biological process or the product of such a process.

(4)   For the purposes of subsection (3) above behaviour shall not be regarded as offensive, immoral or anti-social only because it is prohibited by any law in force in the United Kingdom or any part of it.

(5)   The Secretary of State may by order vary the provisions of subsection (2) above for the purpose of maintaining them in conformity with developments in science and technology; and no such order shall be made unless a draft of the order has been laid before, and approved by resolution of, each House of Parliament.

2 Novelty

(1)   An invention shall be taken to be new if it does not form part of the state of the art.

(2)   The state of the art in the case of an invention shall be taken to comprise all matter (whether a product, a process, information about either, or anything else) which has at any time before the priority date of that invention been made available to the public (whether in the United Kingdom or elsewhere) by written or oral description, by use or in any other way.

(3)   The state of the art in the case of an invention to which an application for a patent or a patent relates shall be taken also to comprise matter contained in an application for another patent which was published on or after the priority date of that invention, if the following conditions are satisfied, that is to say—

(a)   that matter was contained in the application for that other patent both as filed and as published; and

(b)   the priority date of that matter is earlier than that of the invention.

(4)   For the purposes of this section the disclosure of matter constituting an invention shall be disregarded in the case of a patent or an application for a patent if occurring later than the beginning of the period of six months immediately preceding the date of filing the application for the patent and either—

(a)   the disclosure was due to, or made in consequence of, the matter having been obtained unlawfully or in breach of confidence by any person—

(i)   from the inventor or from any other person to whom the matter was made available in confidence by the inventor or who obtained it from the inventor because he or the inventor believed that he was entitled to obtain it; or

(ii)   from any other person to whom the matter was made available in confidence by any person mentioned in sub-paragraph (i) above or in this sub-paragraph or who obtained it from any person so mentioned because he or the person from whom he obtained it believed that he was entitled to obtain it;

(b)   the disclosure was made in breach of confidence by any person who obtained the matter in confidence from the inventor or from any other person to whom it was made available, or who obtained it, from the inventor; or

(c)   the disclosure was due to, or made in consequence of the inventor displaying the invention at an international exhibition and the applicant states, on filing the application, that the invention has been so displayed and also, within the prescribed period, files written evidence in support of the statement complying with any prescribed conditions.

(5)   In this section references to the inventor include references to any proprietor of the invention for the time being.

(6)   In the case of an invention consisting of a substance or composition for use in a method of treatment of the human or animal body by surgery or therapy or of diagnosis practised on the human or animal body, the fact that the substance or composition forms part of the state of the art shall not prevent the invention from being taken to be new if the use of the substance or composition in any such method does not form part of the state of the art.

3 Inventive step

An invention shall be taken to involve an inventive step if it is not obvious to a person skilled in the art, having regard to any matter which forms part of the state of the art by virtue only of section 2(2) above (and disregarding section 2(3) above).

4 Industrial application

(1) Subject to subsection (2) below, an invention shall be taken to be capable of industrial application if it can be made or used in any kind of industry, including agriculture.

(2) An invention of a method of treatment of the human or animal body by surgery or therapy or of diagnosis practised on the human or animal body shall not be taken to be capable of industrial application.

(3) Subsection (2) above shall not prevent a product consisting of a substance or composition being treated as capable of industrial application merely because it is invented for use in any such method.

5 Priority date

(1) For the purposes of this Act the priority date of an invention to which an application for a patent relates and also of any matter (whether or not the same as the invention) contained in any such application is, except as provided by the following provisions of this Act, the date of filing the application.

(2) If in or in connection with an application for a patent (the application in suit) a declaration is made, whether by the applicant or any predecessor in title of his, complying with the relevant requirements of rules and specifying one or more earlier relevant applications for the purposes of this section made by the applicant or a predecessor in title of his and each having a date of filing during the period of twelve months immediately preceding the date of filing the application in suit, then—

(a) if an invention to which the application in suit relates is supported by matter disclosed in the earlier relevant application or applications, the priority date of that invention shall instead of being the date of filing the application in suit be the date of filing the relevant application in which that matter was disclosed or, if it was disclosed in more than one relevant application, the earliest of them;

(b) the priority date of any matter contained in the application in suit which was also disclosed in the earlier relevant application or applications shall be the date of filing the relevant application in which that matter was disclosed or, if it was disclosed in more than one relevant application, the earliest of them.

(3) Where an invention or other matter contained in the application in suit was also disclosed in two earlier relevant applications filed by the same applicant as in the case of the application in suit or a predecessor in title of his and the second of those relevant applications was specified in or in connection with the application in suit, the second of those relevant applications shall, so far as concerns that invention or matter, be disregarded unless—

(a) it was filed in or in respect of the same country as the first; and

(b) not later than the date of filing the second, the first (whether or not so specified) was unconditionally withdrawn, or was abandoned or refused, without—

(i) having been made available to the public (whether in the United Kingdom or elsewhere);

(ii) leaving any rights outstanding; and

(iii) having served to establish a priority date in relation to another application, wherever made.

(4) The foregoing provisions of this section shall apply for determining the priority date of an invention for which a patent has been granted as they apply for determining the priority date of an invention to which an application for that patent relates.

(5)   In this section "relevant application" means any of the following applications which has a date of filing, namely—
(a)   an application for a patent under this Act;
(b)   an application in or for a convention country (specified under section 90 below) for protection in respect of an invention or an application which, in accordance with the law of a convention country or a treaty or international convention to which a convention country is a party, is equivalent to such an application.

6   Disclosure of matter, etc., between earlier and later applications

(1)   It is hereby declared for the avoidance of doubt that where an application (the application in suit) is made for a patent and a declaration is made in accordance with section 5(2) above in or in connection with the application specifying an earlier relevant application, the application in suit and any patent granted in pursuance of it shall not be invalidated by reason only of relevant intervening acts.
(2)   In this section—
"relevant application" has the same meaning as in section 5 above; and
"relevant intervening acts" means acts done in relation to matter disclosed in an earlier relevant application between the dates of the earlier relevant application and the application in suit, as for example, filing another application for the invention for which the earlier relevant application was made, making information available to the public about the invention or that matter or working that invention, but disregarding any application, or the disclosure to the public of matter contained in any application, which is itself to be disregarded for the purposes of section 5(3) above.

Right to apply for and obtain a patent and be mentioned as inventor

7   Right to apply for and obtain a patent

(1)   Any person may make an application for a patent either alone or jointly with another.
(2)   A patent for an invention may be granted—
(a)   primarily to the inventor or joint inventors;
(b)   in preference to the foregoing, to any person or persons who, by virtue of any enactment or rule of law, or any foreign law or treaty or international convention, or by virtue of an enforceable term of any agreement entered into with the inventor before the making of the invention, was or were at the time of the making of the invention entitled to the whole of the property in it (other than equitable interests) in the United Kingdom;
(c)   in any event, to the successor or successors in title of any person or persons mentioned in paragraph (a) or (b) above or any person so mentioned and the successor or successors in title of another person so mentioned;
and to no other person.
(3)   In this Act "inventor" in relation to an invention means the actual deviser of the invention and "joint inventor" shall be construed accordingly.
(4)   Except so far as the contrary is established, a person who makes an application for a patent shall be taken to be the person who is entitled under subsection (2) above to be granted a patent and two or more persons who make such an application jointly shall be taken to be the persons so entitled.

8   Determination before grant of questions about entitlement to patents, etc.

(1)   At any time before a patent has been granted for an invention (whether or not an application has been made for it)—
(a)   any person may refer to the comptroller the question whether he is entitled to be granted (alone or with any other persons) a patent for the invention or has or would have any right in or under any patent so granted or any application for such a patent; or

(b)   any of two or more co-proprietors of an application for a patent for that invention may so refer the question whether any right in or under the application should be transferred or granted to any other person;
and the comptroller shall determine the question and may make such order as he thinks fit to give effect to the determination.

. . .

9   Determination after grant of questions referred before grant

If a question with respect to a patent or application is referred by any person to the comptroller under section 8 above, whether before or after the making of an application for the patent, and is not determined before the time when the application is first in order for a grant of a patent in pursuance of the application, that fact shall not prevent the grant of a patent, but on its grant that person shall be treated as having referred to the comptroller under section 37 below any question mentioned in that section which the comptroller thinks appropriate.

10   Handling of application by joint applicants

If any dispute arises between joint applicants for a patent whether or in what manner the application should be proceeded with, the comptroller may, on a request made by any of the parties, give such directions as he thinks fit for enabling the application to proceed in the name of one or more of the parties alone or for regulating the manner in which it shall be proceeded with, or for both those purposes, according as the case may require.

. . .

12   Determination of questions about entitlement to foreign and convention patents, etc.

(1)   At any time before a patent is granted for an invention in pursuance of an application made under the law of any country other than the United Kingdom or under any treaty or international convention (whether or not that application has been made)—

(a)   any person may refer to the comptroller the question whether he is entitled to be granted (alone or with any other persons) any such patent for that invention or has or would have any right in or under any such patent or an application for such a patent; or

(b)   any of two or more co-proprietors of an application for such a patent for that invention may so refer the question whether any right in or under the application should be transferred or granted to any other person;
and the comptroller shall determine the question so far as he is able to and may make such order as he thinks fit to give effect to the determination.

. . .

13   Mention of inventor

(1)   The inventor or joint inventors of an invention shall have a right to be mentioned as such in any patent granted for the invention and shall also have a right to be so mentioned if possible in any published application for a patent for the invention and, if not so mentioned, a right to be so mentioned in accordance with rules in a prescribed document.

(2)   Unless he has already given the Patent Office the information hereinafter mentioned, an applicant for a patent shall within the prescribed period file with the Patent Office a statement—

(a)   identifying the person or persons whom he believes to be the inventor or inventors; and

(b)   where the applicant is not the sole inventor or the applicants are not the joint inventors, indicating the derivation of his or their right to be granted the patent;
and, if he fails to do so, the application shall be taken to be withdrawn.

(3)   Where a person has been mentioned as sole or joint inventor in pursuance of this section, any other person who alleges that the former ought not to have been so mentioned may at any time apply to the comptroller for a certificate to that effect, and the comptroller may issue such a certificate; and if he does so, he shall accordingly rectify any undistributed copies of the patent and of any documents prescribed for the purposes of subsection (1) above.

Applications

14   Making of application

(1)   Every application for a patent—
    (a)   shall be made in the prescribed form and shall be filed at the Patent Office in the prescribed manner; and
    (b)   shall be accompanied by the fee prescribed for the purposes of this subsection (hereinafter in this Act referred to as the filing fee).

(2)   Every application for a patent shall contain—
    (a)   a request for the grant of a patent;
    (b)   a specification containing a description of the invention, a claim or claims and any drawing referred to in the description or any claim; and
    (c)   an abstract;
but the foregoing provision shall not prevent an application being initiated by documents complying with section 15(1) below.

(3)   The specification of an application shall disclose the invention in a manner which is clear enough and complete enough for the invention to be performed by a person skilled in the art.

(4)   (repealed)

(5)   The claim or claims shall—
    (a)   define the matter for which the applicant seeks protection;
    (b)   be clear and concise;
    (c)   be supported by the description; and
    (d)   relate to one invention or to a group of inventions which are so linked as to form a single inventive concept.

(6)   Without prejudice to the generality of subsection (5)(d) above, rules may provide for treating two or more inventions as being so linked as to form a single inventive concept for the purposes of this Act.

(7)   The purpose of the abstract is to give technical information and on publication it shall not form part of the state of the art by virtue of section 2(3) above, and the comptroller may determine whether the abstract adequately fulfils its purpose and, if it does not, may reframe it so that it does.

(8)   (repealed)

(9)   An application for a patent may be withdrawn at any time before the patent is granted and any withdrawal of such an application may not be revoked.

15   Date of filing application

(1)   The date of filing an application for a patent shall, subject to the following provisions of this Act, be taken to be the earliest date on which the following conditions are satisfied in relation to the application, that is to say—
    (a)   the documents filed at the Patent Office contain an indication that a patent is sought in pursuance of the application;
    (b)   those documents identify the applicant or applicants for the patent;
    (c)   those documents contain a description of the invention for which a patent is sought (whether or not the description complies with the other provisions of this Act and with any relevant rules); and
    (d)   the applicant pays the filing fee.

. . .

(4)   Where, after an application for a patent has been filed and before the patent is granted, a new application is filed by the original applicant or his successor in title in accordance with rules in respect of any part of the matter contained in the earlier application and the conditions mentioned in subsection (1) above are satisfied in relation to the new application (without the new application contravening section 76 below) the new application shall be treated as having, as its date of filing, the date of filing the earlier application.

(5)   An application which has a date of filing by virtue of the foregoing provisions of this section shall be taken to be withdrawn at the end of the relevant prescribed period, unless before that end the applicant—

(a)   files at the Patent Office one or more claims for the purposes of the application and also the abstract; and

(b)   makes a request for a preliminary examination and search under the following provisions of this Act and pays the search fee.

16   Publication of application

(1)   Subject to section 22 below, where an application has a date of filing, as soon as possible after the end of the prescribed period, the comptroller shall, unless the application is withdrawn or refused before preparations for its publication have been completed by the Patent Office, published it as filed (including not only the original claims but also any amendments of those claims and new claims subsisting immediately before the completion of those preparations) and he may, if so requested by the applicant, publish it as aforesaid during that period, and in either event shall advertise the fact and date of its publication in the journal.

(2)   The comptroller may omit from the specification of a published application for a patent any matter—

(a)   which in his opinion disparages any person in a way likely to damage him, or

(b)   the publication or exploitation of which would in his opinion be generally expected to encourage offensive, immoral or anti-social behaviour.

Examination and search

17   Preliminary examination and search

(1)   Where an application for a patent has a date of filing and is not withdrawn, and before the end of the prescribed period—

(a)   a request is made by the applicant to the Patent Office in the prescribed form for a preliminary examination and a search; and

(b)   the prescribed fee is paid for the examination and search (the search fee); the comptroller shall refer the application to an examiner for a preliminary examination and search, except that he shall not refer the application for a search until it includes one or more claims.

(2)   On a preliminary examination of an application the examiner shall determine whether the application complies with those requirements of this Act and the rules which are designated by the rules as formal requirements for the purposes of this Act and shall report his determination to the comptroller.

. . .

18   Substantive examination and grant or refusal of patent

(1)   Where the conditions imposed by section 17(1) above for the comptroller to refer an application to an examiner for a preliminary examination and search are satisfied and at the time of the request under that subsection or within the prescribed period—

(a)   a request is made by the applicant to the Patent Office in the prescribed form for a substantive examination; and

(b)   the prescribed fee is paid for the examination;
the comptroller shall refer the application to an examiner for a substantive examination; and if no such request is made or the prescribed fee is not paid within that period, the application shall be treated as having been withdrawn at the end of that period.
...

(2)   On a substantive examination of an application the examiner shall investigate, to such extent as he considers necessary in view of any examination and search carried out under section 17 above, whether the application complies with the requirements of this Act and the rules and shall determine that question and report his determination to the comptroller.

(3)   If the examiner reports that any of those requirements are not complied with, the comptroller shall give the applicant an opportunity within a specified period to make observations on the report and to amend the application so as to comply with those requirements (subject, however, to section 76 below), and if the applicant fails to satisfy the comptroller that those requirements are complied with, or to amend the application so as to comply with them, the comptroller may refuse the application.

(4)   If the examiner reports that the application, whether as originally filed or as amended in pursuance of section 17 above, this section or section 19 below, complies with those requirements at any time before the end of the prescribed period, the comptroller shall notify the applicant of that fact and, subject to subsection (5) and sections 19 and 22 below and on payment within the prescribed period of any fee prescribed for the grant, grant him a patent.

(5)   Where two or more applications for a patent for the same invention having the same priority date and filed by the same applicant or his successor in title, the comptroller may on that ground refuse to grant a patent in pursuance of more than one of the applications.

19   General power to amend application before grant

(1)   At any time before a patent is granted in pursuance of an application the applicant may, in accordance with the prescribed conditions and subject to section 76 below, amend the application of his own volition.

(2)   The comptroller may, without an application being made to him for the purpose, amend the specification and abstract contained in an application for a patent so as to acknowledge a registered trade mark.

20   Failure of application

(1)   If it is not determined that an application for a patent complies before the end of the prescribed period with all the requirements of this Act and the rules, and application shall be treated as having been refused by the comptroller at the end of that period, and section 97 below shall apply accordingly.
...

21   Observations by third party on patentability

(1)   Where an application for a patent has been published but a patent has not been granted to the applicant, any other person may make observations in writing to the comptroller on the question whether the invention is a patentable invention, stating reasons for the observations, and the comptroller shall consider the observations in accordance with rules.

(2)   It is hereby declared that a person does not become a party to any proceedings under this Act before the comptroller by reason only that he makes observations under this section.

Security and safety

22 Information prejudicial to defence of realm or safety of public

(1)   Where an application for a patent is filed in the Patent Office (whether under this Act or any treaty or international convention to which the United Kingdom is a party and whether before or after the appointed day) and it appears to the comptroller that the application contains information of a description notified to him by the Secretary of State as being information the publication of which might be prejudicial to the defence of the realm, the comptroller may give directions prohibiting or restricting the publication of that information or its communication to any specified person or description of persons.

(2)   If it appears to the comptroller that any application so filed contains information the publication of which might be prejudicial to the safety of the public, he may give directions prohibiting or restricting the publication of that information or its communication to any specified person or description of persons until the end of a period not exceeding three months from the end of the period prescribed for the purposes of section 16 above.

. . .

23 Restrictions on applications abroad by United Kingdom residents

(1)   Subject to the following provisions of this section, no person resident in the United Kingdom shall, without written authority granted by the comptroller, file or cause to be filed outside the United Kingdom an application for a patent for an invention unless—

(a)   an application for a patent for the same invention has been filed in the Patent Office (whether before, on or after the appointed day) not less than six weeks before the application outside the United Kingdom; and

(b)   either no directions have been given under section 22 above in relation to the application in the United Kingdom or all such directions have been revoked.

(2)   Subsection (1) above does not apply to an application for a patent for an invention for which an application for a patent has first been filed (whether before or after the appointed day) in a country outside the United Kingdom by a person resident outside the United Kingdom.

. . .

Provisions as to patents after grant

24 Publication and certificate of grant

(1)   As soon as practicable after a patent has been granted under this Act the comptroller shall publish in the journal a notice that it has been granted.

. . .

(3)   The comptroller shall, at the same time as he publishes a notice under subsection (1) above in relation to a patent publish the specification of the patent, the names of the proprietor and (if different) the inventor and any other matters constituting or relating to the patent which in the comptroller's opinion it is desirable to publish.

25 Term of patent

(1)   A patent granted under this Act shall be treated for the purposes of the following provisions of this Act as having been granted, and shall take effect, on the date on which notice of its grant is published in the journal and, subject to subsection (3) below, shall continue in force until the end of the period of 20 years beginning with the date of filing the application for the patent or with such other date as may be prescribed.

. . .

26 Patent not to be impugned for lack of unity

No person may in any proceeding object to a patent or to an amendment of a specification of a patent on the ground that the claims contained in the specification of the patent, as they stand or, as the case may be, as proposed to be amended, relate—
    (a)   to more than one invention, or
    (b)   to a group of inventions which are not so linked as to form a single inventive concept.

27 General power to amend specification after grant

(1)   Subject to the following provisions of this section and to section 76 below, the comptroller may, on an application made by the proprietor of a patent, allow the specification of the patent to be amended subject to such conditions, if any, as he thinks fit.

. . .

28 Restoration of lapsed patents

(1)   Where a patent has ceased to have effect by reason of a failure to pay any renewal fee, an application for the restoration of the patent may be made to the comptroller within the prescribed period.

. . .

(2)   An application under this section may be made by the person who was the proprietor of the patent or by any other person who would have been entitled to the patent if it had not ceased to have effect; and where the patent was held by two or more persons jointly, the application may, with the leave of the comptroller, be made by one or more of them without joining the others.

(2A)   Notice of the application shall be published by the comptroller in the prescribed manner.

(3)   If the comptroller is satisfied that—
    (a)   the proprietor of the patent took reasonable care to see that any renewal fee was paid within the prescribed period or that that fee and any prescribed additional fee were paid within the six months immediately following the end of that period,
the comptroller shall by order restore the patent on payment of any unpaid renewal fee and any prescribed additional fee.

. . .

28A Effect of order for restoration of patent

(1)   The effect of an order for the restoration of a patent is as follows.

(2)   Anything done under or in relation to the patent during the period between expiry and restoration shall be treated as valid.

(3)   Anything done during that period which would have constituted an infringement if the patent had not expired shall be treated as an infringement—
    (a)   if done at a time when it was possible for the patent to be renewed under section 25(4), or
    (b)   if it was a continuation or repetition of an earlier infringing act.

(4)   If after it was no longer possible for the patent to be so renewed, and before publication of notice of the application for restoration, a person—
    (a)   began in good faith to do an act which would have constituted an infringement of the patent if it had not expired, or
    (b)   made in good faith effective and serious preparations to do such an act,
he has the right to continue to do the act or, as the case may be, to do the act, notwithstanding the restoration of the patent; but this right does not extend to granting a licence to another person to do the act.

(5)   If the act was done, or the preparations were made, in the course of a business, the person entitled to the right conferred by subsection (4) may—

(a)   authorise the doing of that act by any partners of his for the time being in that business, and

(b)   assign that right, or transmit it on death (or in the case of a body corporate on its dissolution), to any person who acquires that part of the business in the course of which the act was done or the preparations were made.

(6)   Where a product is disposed of to another in exercise of the rights conferred by subsection (4) or (5), that other and any person claiming through him may deal with the product in the same way as if it had been disposed of by the registered proprietor of the patent.

(7)   The above provisions apply in relation to the use of a patent for the services of the Crown as they apply in relation to infringement of the patent.

29   Surrender of patents

(1)   The proprietor of a patent may at any time by notice given to the comptroller offer to surrender his patent.

. . .

Property in patents and applications, and registration

30   Nature of, and transactions in, patents and applications for patents

(1)   Any patent or application for a patent is personal property (without being a thing in action), and any patent or any such application and rights in or under it may be transferred, created or granted in accordance with subsections (2) to (7) below.

(2)   Subject to section 36(3) below, any patent or any such application, or any right in it, may be assigned or mortgaged.

(3)   Any patent or any such application or right shall vest by operation of law in the same way as any other personal property and may be vested by an assent of personal representatives.

(4)   Subject to section 36(3) below, a licence may be granted under any patent or any such application for working the invention which is the subject of the patent or the application; and—

(a)   to the extent that the licence so provides, a sub-licence may be granted under any such licence and any such licence or sub-licence may be assigned or mortgaged; and

(b)   any such licence or sub-licence shall vest by operation of law in the same way as any other personal property and may be vested by an assent of personal representatives.

(5)   Subsections (2) to (4) above shall have effect subject to the following provisions of this Act.

(6)   Any of the following transactions, that is to say—

(a)   any assignment or mortgage of a patent or any such application, or any right in a patent or any such application;

(b)   any assent relating to any patent or any such application or right;

shall be void unless it is in writing and is signed by or on behalf of the parties to the transaction (or, in the case of an assent or other transaction by a personal representative, by or on behalf of the personal representative) or in the case of a body corporate is so signed or is under the seal of that body.

(7)   An assignment of a patent or any such application or a share in it, and an exclusive licence granted under any patent or any such application, may confer on the assignee or licensee the right of the assignor or licensor to bring proceedings by virtue of section 61 or 69 below for a previous infringement or to bring proceedings under section 58 below for a previous act.

. . .

32   Register of patents etc.

(1)   The comptroller shall maintain the register of patents, which shall comply with rules made by virtue of this section and shall be kept in accordance with such rules.

(2)   Without prejudice to any other provision of this Act or rules, rules may make provisions with respect to the following matters, including provision imposing requirements as to any of those matters—

(a)   the registration of patents and of published applications for patents;

(b)   the registration of transactions, instruments or events affecting rights in or under patents and applications;

(c)   the furnishing to the comptroller of any prescribed documents or description of documents in connection with any matter which is required to be registered;

(d)   the correction of errors in the register and in any documents filed at the Patent Office in connection with registration; and

(e)   the publication and advertisement of anything done under this Act or rules in relation to the register.

(3)   Notwithstanding anything in subsection (2)(b) above, no notice of any trust, whether express, implied or constructive, shall be entered in the register and the comptroller shall not be affected by any such notice.

. . .

33   Effect of registration, etc., on rights in patents

(1)   Any person who claims to have acquired the property in a patent or application for a patent by virtue of any transaction, instrument or event to which this section applies shall be entitled as against any other person who claims to have acquired that property by virtue of an earlier transaction, instrument or event to which this section applies if, at the time of the later transaction, instrument or event—

(a)   the earlier transaction, instrument or event was not registered, or

(b)   in the case of any application which has not been published, notice of the earlier transaction, instrument or event had not been given to the comptroller, and

(c)   in any case, the person claiming under the later transaction, instrument or event, did not know of the earlier transaction, instrument or event.

(2)   Subsection (1) above shall apply equally to the case where any person claims to have acquired any right in or under a patent or application for a patent, by virtue of a transaction, instrument or event to which this section applies, and that right is incompatible with any such right acquired by virtue of an earlier transaction, instrument or event to which this section applies.

(3)   This section applies to the following transactions, instruments and events:—

(a)   the assignment or assignation of a patent or application for a patent, or a right in it;

(b)   the mortgage of a patent or application or the granting of security over it;

(c)   the grant, assignment or assignation of a licence or sub-licence, or mortgage of a licence or sub-licence, under a patent or application;

(d)   the death of the proprietor or one of the proprietors of any such patent or application or any person having a right in or under a patent or application and the vesting by an assent of personal representatives of a patent, application or any such right; and

(e)   any order or directions of a court or other competent authority—

(i)   transferring a patent or application or any right in or under it to any person; or

(ii)   that an application should proceed in the name of any person;

and in either case the event by virtue of which the court or authority had power to make any such order or give any such directions.

(4)   Where an application for the registration of a transaction, instrument or event has been made, but the transaction, instrument or event has not been registered, then, for the purposes of subsection (1)(a) above, registration of the application shall be treated as registration of the transaction, instrument or event.

34   Rectification of register

(1)   The court may, on the application of any person aggrieved, order the register to be rectified by the making, or the variation or deletion, of any entry in it.

...

36   Co-ownership of patents and applications for patents

(1)   Where a patent is granted to two or more persons, each of them shall, subject to any agreement to the contrary, be entitled to an equal undivided share in the patent.

(2)   Where two or more persons are proprietors of a patent, then, subject to the provisions of this section and subject to any agreement to the contrary—

(a)   each of them shall be entitled, by himself or his agents, to do in respect of the invention concerned, for his own benefit and without the consent of or the need to account to the other or others, any act which would apart from this subsection and section 55 below, amount to an infringement of the patent concerned; and

(b)   any such act shall not amount to an infringement of the patent concerned.

(3)   Subject to the provisions of sections 8 and 12 above and section 37 below and to any agreement for the time being in force, where two or more persons are proprietors of a patent one of them shall not without the consent of the other or others grant a licence under the patent or assign or mortgage a share in the patent or in Scotland cause or permit security to be granted over it.

(4)   Subject to the provisions of those sections, where two or more persons are proprietors of a patent, anyone else may supply one of those persons with the means, relating to an essential element of the invention, for putting the invention into effect, and the supply of those means by virtue of this subsection shall not amount to an infringement of the patent.

(5)   Where a patented product is disposed of by any of two or more proprietors to any person, that person and any other person claiming through him shall be entitled to deal with the product in the same way as if it had been disposed of by a sole registered proprietor.

(6)   Nothing in subsection (1) or (2) above shall affect the mutual rights or obligations of trustees or of the personal representatives of a deceased person, or their rights or obligations as such.

(7)   The foregoing provisions of this section shall have effect in relation to an application for a patent which is filed as they have effect in relation to a patent and—

(a)   references to a patent and a patent being granted shall accordingly include references respectively to any such application and to the application being filed; and

(b)   the reference in subsection (5) above to a patented product shall be construed accordingly.

37   Determination of right to patent after grant

(1)   After a patent has been granted for an invention any person having or claiming a proprietary interest in or under the patent may refer to the comptroller the question—

(a)   who is or are the true proprietor or proprietors of the patent,

(b)   whether the patent should have been granted to the person or persons to whom it was granted, or

(c)   whether any right in or under the patent should be transferred or granted to any other person or persons;

and the comptroller shall determine the question and make such order as he thinks fit to give effect to the determination.

...

(5)   On any such reference no order shall be made under this section transferring the patent to which the reference relates on the ground that the patent was granted to a person not so entitled, and no order shall be made under subsection (4) above on that ground, if the reference was made after the end of the period of two years beginning with

the date of the grant, unless it is shown that any person registered as a proprietor of the patent knew at the time of the grant or, as the case may be, of the transfer of the patent to him that he was not entitled to the patent.

(6)   An order under this section shall not be so made as to affect the mutual rights or obligations of trustees or of the personal representatives of a deceased person, or their rights or obligations as such.

...

Employees' inventions

39   Right to employees' inventions

(1)   Notwithstanding anything in any rule of law, an invention made by an employee shall, as between him and his employer, be taken to belong to his employer for the purposes of this Act and all other purposes if—

(a)   it was made in the course of the normal duties of the employee or in the course of duties falling outside his normal duties, but specifically assigned to him, and the circumstances in either case were such that an invention might reasonably be expected to result from the carrying out of his duties; or

(b)   the invention was made in the course of the duties of the employee and, at the time of making the invention, because of the nature of his duties and the particular responsibilities arising from the nature of his duties he had a special obligation to further the interests of the employer's undertaking.

(2)   Any other invention made by an employee shall, as between him and his employer, be taken for those purposes to belong to the employee.

(3)   Where by virtue of this section an invention belongs, as between him and his employer, to an employee, nothing done—

(a)   by or on behalf of the employee or any person claiming under him for the purposes of pursuing an application for a patent, or

(b)   by any person for the purpose of performing or working the invention,

shall be taken to infringe any copyright or design right to which, as between him and his employer, his employer is entitled in any model or document relating to the invention.

40   Compensation of employees for certain inventions

(1)   Where it appears to the court or the comptroller on an application made by an employee within the prescribed period that the employee has made an invention belonging to the employer for which a patent has been granted, that the patent is (having regard among other things to the size and nature of the employer's undertaking) of outstanding benefit to the employer and that by reason of those facts it is just that the employee should be awarded compensation to be paid by the employer, the court or the comptroller may award him such compensation of an amount determined under section 41 below.

(2)   Where it appears to the court or the comptroller on an application made by an employee within the prescribed period that—

(a)   a patent has been granted for an invention made by and belonging to the employee;

(b)   his rights in the invention, or in any patent or application for a patent for the invention, have since the appointed day been assigned to the employer or an exclusive licence under the patent or application has since the appointed day been granted to the employer;

(c)   the benefit derived by the employee from the contract of assignment, assignation or grant or any ancillary contract ("the relevant contract") is inadequate in relation to the benefit derived by the employer from the patent; and

(d)   by reason of those facts it is just that the employee should be awarded compensation to be paid by the employer in addition to the benefit derived from the relevant contract;

the court or the comptroller may award him such compensation of an amount determined under section 41 below.

(3)   Subsections (1) and (2) above shall not apply to the invention of an employee where a relevant collective agreement provides for the payment of compensation in respect of inventions of the same description as that invention to employees of the same description as that employee.

(4)   Subsection (2) above shall have effect notwithstanding anything in the relevant contract or any agreement applicable to the invention (other than any such collective agreement).

(5)   If it appears to the comptroller on an application under this section that the application involves matters which would more properly be determined by the court, he may decline to deal with it.

(6)   In this section—

"the prescribed period", in relation to proceedings before the court, means the period prescribed by rules of court, and

"relevant collective agreement" means a collective agreement within the meaning of the Trade Union and Labour Relations (Consolidation) Act 1992 made by or on behalf of a trade union to which the employee belongs, and by the employer or an employers' association to which the employer belongs which is in force at the time of the making of the invention.

(7)   References in this section to an invention belonging to an employer or employee are references to it so belonging as between the employer and the employee.

41   Amount of compensation

(1)   An award of compensation to an employee under section 40(1) or (2) above in relation to a patent for an invention shall be such as will secure for the employee a fair share (having regard to all the circumstances) of the benefit which the employer has derived, or may reasonably be expected to derive, from the patent or from the assignment, assignation or grant to a person connected with the employer of the property or any right in the invention or the property in, or any right in or under, an application for that patent.

(2)   For the purposes of subsection (1) above the amount of any benefit derived or expected to be derived by an employer from the assignment, assignation or grant of—

(a)   the property in, or any right in or under, a patent for the invention or an application for such a patent; or

(b)   the property or any right in the invention;

to a person connected with him shall be taken to be the amount which could reasonably be expected to be so derived by the employer if that person had not been connected with him.

(3)   Where the Crown or a Research Council in its capacity as employer assigns or grants the property in, or any right in or under, an invention, patent or application for a patent to a body having among its functions that of developing or exploiting inventions resulting from public research and does so for no consideration or only a nominal consideration, any benefit derived from the invention, patent or application by that body shall be treated for the purposes of the foregoing provisions of this section as so derived by the Crown or, as the case may be, Research Council.

In this subsection "Research Council" means a body which is a Research Council for the purposes of the Science and Technology Act 1965.

(4)   In determining the fair share of the benefit to be secured for an employee in respect of a patent for an invention which has always belonged to an employer, the court or the comptroller shall, among other things, take the following matters into account, that is to say—

(a) the nature of the employee's duties, his remuneration and the other advantages he derives or has derived from his employment or has derived in relation to the invention under this Act;

(b) the effort and skill which the employee has devoted to making the invention;

(c) the effort and skill which any other person has devoted to making the invention jointly with the employee concerned, and the advice and other assistance contributed by any other employee who is not a joint inventor of the invention; and

(d) the contribution made by the employer to the making, developing and working of the invention by the provision of advice, facilities and other assistance, by the provision of opportunities and by his managerial and commercial skill and activities.

(5) In determining the fair share of the benefit to be secured for an employee in respect of a patent for an invention which originally belonged to him, the court or the comptroller shall, among other things, take the following matters into account, that is to say—

(a) any conditions in a licence or licences granted under this Act or otherwise in respect of the invention or the patent;

(b) the extent to which the invention was made jointly by the employee with any other person; and

(c) the contribution made by the employer to the making, developing and working of the invention as mentioned in subsection (4)(d) above.

(6) Any order for the payment of compensation under section 40 above may be an order for the payment of a lump sum or for periodical payment, or both.

(7) Without prejudice to section 32 of the Interpretation Act 1889 (which provides that a statutory power may in general be exercised from time to time), the refusal of the court or the comptroller to make any such order on an application made by an employee under section 40 above shall not prevent a further application being made under that section by him or any successor in title of his.

(8) Where the court or the comptroller has made any such order, the court or he may on the application of either the employer or the employee vary or discharge it or suspend any provision of the order and revive any provision so suspended, and section 40(5) above shall apply to the application as it applies to an application under that section.

...

42 Enforceability of contracts relating to employees' inventions

(1) This section applies to any contract (whenever made) relating to inventions made by an employee, being a contract entered into by him—

(a) with the employer (alone or with another); or

(b) with some other person at the request of the employer or in pursuance of the employee's contract of employment.

(2) Any term in a contract to which this section applies which diminishes the employee's rights in inventions of any description made by him after the appointed day and the date of the contract, or in or under patents for those inventions or applications for such patents, shall be unenforceable against him to the extent that it diminishes his rights in an invention of that description so made, or in or under a patent for such an invention or an application for any such patent.

(3) Subsection (2) above shall not be construed as derogating from any duty of confidentiality owed to his employer by an employee by virtue of any rule of law or otherwise.

(4) This section applies to any arrangement made with a Crown employee by or on behalf of the Crown as his employer as it applies to any contract made between an employee and an employer other than the Crown, and for the purposes of this section "Crown employee" means a person employed under or for the purposes of a

government department or any officer or body exercising on behalf of the Crown functions conferred by any enactment or a person serving in the naval, military or air forces of the Crown.

43 Supplementary

(1) Sections 39 to 42 above shall not apply to an invention made by an employee unless at the time he made the invention one of the following conditions was satisfied in his case, that is to say—

(a) he was mainly employed in the United Kingdom; or

(b) he was not mainly employed anywhere or his place of employment could not be determined, but his employer had a place of business in the United Kingdom to which the employee was attached, whether or not he was also attached elsewhere.

(3) In sections 39 to 42 above and this section, except so far as the context otherwise requires, references to the making of an invention by an employee are references to his making it alone or jointly with any other person, but do not include references to his merely contributing advice or other assistance in the making of an invention by another employee.

(4) Any references in sections 39 to 42 above to a patent and to a patent being granted are respectively references to a patent or other protection and to its being granted whether under the law of the United Kingdom or the law in force in any other country or under any treaty or international convention.

(5) For the purposes of sections 40 and 41 above the benefit derived or expected to be derived by an employer from a patent shall, where he dies before any award is made under section 40 above in respect of the patent, include any benefit derived or expected to be derived from the patent by his personal representatives or by any person in whom it was vested by their assent.

(6) Where an employee dies before an award is made under section 40 above in respect of a patented invention made by him, his personal representatives or their successors in title may exercise his right to make or proceed with an application for compensation under subsection (1) or (2) of that section.

(7) In sections 40 and 41 above and this section "benefit" means benefit in money or money's worth.

(8) Section 533 of the Income and Corporation Taxes Act 1970* (definition of connected persons) shall apply for determining for the purposes of section 41(2) above whether one person is connected with another as it applies for determining that question for the purposes of the Tax Acts.

---

*[now contained in s. 839 of the Income and Corporation Taxes Act 1988]

Contracts as to patented products, etc.

44 Avoidance of certain restrictive conditions

(1) Subject to the provisions of this section, any condition or term of a contract for the supply of a patented product or of a licence to work a patented invention, or of a contract relating to any such supply or licence, shall be void in so far it purports—

(a) in the case of a contract for supply, to require the person supplied to acquire from the supplier, or his nominee, or prohibit him from acquiring from any specified person, or from acquiring except from the supplier or his nominee, anything other than the patented product;

(b) in the case of a licence to work a patented invention, to require the licensee to acquire from the licensor or his nominee, or prohibit him from acquiring from any specified person, or from acquiring except from the licensor or his nominee, anything other than the product which is the patented invention or (if it is a process) other than any product obtained directly by means of the process or to which the process has been applied;

(c)   in either case, to prohibit the person supplied or licensee from using articles (whether patented products or not) which are not supplied by, or any patented process which does not belong to, the supplier or licensor, or his nominee, or to restrict the right of the person supplied or licensee to use any such articles or process.

(2)   Subsection (1) above applies to contracts and licences whether made or granted before or after the appointed day, but not to those made or granted before 1 January 1950.

(3)   In proceedings against any person for infringement of a patent it shall be a defence to prove that at the time of the infringement there was in force a contract relating to the patent made by or with the consent of the plaintiff or pursuer or a licence under the patent granted by him or with his consent and containing in either case a condition or term void by virtue of this section.

(4)   A condition or term of a contract or licence shall not be void by virtue of this section if—

(a)   at the time of the making of the contract or granting of the licence the supplier or licensor was willing to supply the product, or grant a licence to work the invention, as the case may be, to the person supplied or licensee, on reasonable terms specified in the contract or licence and without any such condition or term as is mentioned in subsection (1) above; and

(b)   the person supplied or licensee is entitled under the contract or licence to relieve himself of his liability to observe the condition or term on giving to the other party three months' notice in writing and subject to payment to that other party of such compensation (being, in the case of a contract to supply, a lump sum or rent for the residue of the term of the contract and, in the case of a licence, a royalty for the residue of the term of the licence) as may be determined by an arbitrator or arbiter appointed by the Secretary of State.

(5)   If in any proceeding it is alleged that any condition or term of a contract or licence is void by virtue of this section it shall lie on the supplier or licensor to prove the matters set out in paragraph (a) of subsection (4) above.

(6)   A condition or term of a contract or licence shall not be void by virtue of this section by reason only that it prohibits any person from selling goods other than those supplied by a specific person or, in the case of a contract for the hiring of or licence to use a patented product, that it reserves to the bailor (or, in Scotland, hirer) or licensor, or his nominee, the right to supply such new parts of the patented product as may be required to put or keep it in repair.

45   Determination of parts of certain contracts

(1)   Any contract for the supply of a patented product or licence to work a patented invention, or contract relating to any such supply or licence, may at any time after the patent or all the patents by which the product or invention was protected at the time of the making of the contract or granting of the licence has or have ceased to be in force, and notwithstanding anything to the contrary in the contract or licence or in any other contract, be determined, to the extent (and only to the extent) that the contract or licence relates to the product or invention, by either party on giving three months' notice in writing to the other party.

(2)   In subsection (1) above "patented product" and "patented invention" include respectively a product and an invention which is the subject of an application for a patent, and that subsection shall apply in relation to a patent by which any such product or invention was protected and which was granted after the time of the making of the contract or granting of the licence in question, on an application which had been filed before that time, as it applies to a patent in force at that time.

(3)   If, on an application under this subsection made by either party to a contract or licence falling within subsection (1) above, the court is satisfied that, in consequence of the patent or patents concerned ceasing to be in force, it would be unjust to require the

applicant to continue to comply with all the terms and conditions of the contract or licence, it may make such order varying those terms or conditions as, having regard to all the circumstances of the case, it thinks just as between the parties.

(4)   Without prejudice to any other right of recovery, nothing in subsection (1) above shall be taken to entitle any person to recover property bailed under a hire-purchase agreement (within the meaning of the Consumer Credit Act 1974).

(5)   The foregoing provisions of this section apply to contracts and licences whether made before or after the appointed day.

(6)   The provisions of this section shall be without prejudice to any rule of law relating to the frustration of contracts and any right of determining a contract or licence exercisable apart from this section.

Licences of right and compulsory licences

46   Patentee's application for entry in register that licences are available as of right

(1)   At any time after the grant of a patent its proprietor may apply to the comptroller for an entry to be made in the register to the effect that licences under the patent are to be available as of right.

(2)   Where such an application is made, the comptroller shall give notice of the application to any person registered as having a right in or under the patent and, if satisfied that the proprietor of the patent is not precluded by contract from granting licences under the patent, shall make the entry.

(3)   Where such an entry is made in respect of a patent—

(a)   any person shall, at any time after the entry is made, be entitled as of right to a licence under the patent on such terms as may be settled by agreement or, in default of agreement, by the comptroller on the application of the proprietor of the patent or the person requiring the licence;

(b)   the comptroller may, on the application of the holder of any licence granted under the patent before the entry was made, order the licence to be exchanged for a licence of right on terms so settled;

(c)   if in proceedings for infringement of the patent (otherwise than by the importation of any article) from a country which is not a member State of the European Economic Community the defendant or defender undertakes to take a licence on such terms, no injunction or interdict shall be granted against him and the amount (if any) recoverable against him by way of damages shall not exceed double the amount which would have been payable by him as licensee if such a licence on those terms had been granted before the earliest infringement;

(d)   the renewal fee payable in respect of the patent after the date of entry shall be half the fee which would be payable if the entry had not been made.

(3A)   An undertaking under subsection (3)(c) above may be given at any time before final order in the proceedings, without any admission of liability.

(4)   The licensee under a licence of right may (unless, in the case of a licence the terms of which are settled by agreement, the licence otherwise expressly provides) request the proprietor of the patent to take proceedings to prevent any infringement of the patent; and if the proprietor refuses or neglects to do so within two months after being so requested, the licensee may institute proceedings for the infringement in his own name as if he were proprietor, making the proprietor a defendant or defender.

(5)   A proprietor so added as defendant or defender shall not be liable for any costs or expenses unless he enters an appearance and takes part in the proceedings.

47   Cancellation of entry made under s. 46

(1)   At any time after an entry has been made under section 46 above in respect of a patent, the proprietor of the patent may apply to the comptroller for cancellation of the entry.

. . .

48 Compulsory licences

(1)   At any time after the expiration of three years, or of such other period as may be prescribed, from the date of the grant of a patent, any person may apply to the comptroller on one or more of the grounds specified in subsection (3) below—

(a)   for a licence under the patent,

(b)   for an entry to be made in the register to the effect that licences under the patent are to be available as of right, or

(c)   where the applicant is a government department, for the grant to any person specified in the application of a licence under the patent.

. . .

(3)   The grounds are:—

(a)   where the patented invention is capable of being commercially worked in the United Kingdom, that it is not being so worked or is not being so worked to the fullest extent that is reasonably practicable;

(b)   where the patented invention is a product, that a demand for the product in the United Kingdom—

(i)   is not being met on reasonable terms, or

(ii)   is being met to a substantial extent by importation;

(c)   where the patented invention is capable of being commercially worked in the United Kingdom, that it is being prevented or hindered from being so worked—

(i)   where the invention is a product, by the importation of the product,

(ii)   where the invention is a process, by the importation of a product obtained directly by means of the process or to which the process has been applied;

(d)   that by reason of the refusal of the proprietor of the patent to grant a licence or licences on reasonable terms—

(i)   a market for the export of any patented product made in the United Kingdom is not being supplied, or

(ii)   the working or efficient working in the United Kingdom of any other patented invention which makes a substantial contribution to the art is prevented or hindered, or

(iii)   the establishment or development of commercial or industrial activities in the United Kingdom is unfairly prejudiced;

(e)   that by reason of conditions imposed by the proprietor of the patent on the grant of licences under the patent, or on the disposal or use of the patented product or on the use of the patented process, the manufacture, use or disposal of materials not protected by the patent, or the establishment or development of commercial or industrial activities in the United Kingdom, is unfairly prejudiced.

(4)   Subject to the provisions of subsections (5) to (7) below, if he is satisfied that any of those grounds are established, the comptroller may—

(a)   where the application is under subsection (1)(a) above, order the grant of a licence to the applicant on such terms as the comptroller thinks fit;

(b)   where the application is under subsection (1)(b) above, make such an entry as is there mentioned;

(c)   where the application is under subsection (1)(c) above, order the grant of a licence to the person specified in the application on such terms as the comptroller thinks fit.

(5)   Where the application is made on the ground that the patented invention is not being commercially worked in the United Kingdom or is not being so worked to the fullest extent that is reasonably practicable, and it appears to the comptroller that the time which has elapsed since the publication in the journal of a notice of the grant of the patent has for any reason been insufficient to enable the invention to be so worked, he

may by order adjourn the application for such period as will in his opinion give sufficient time for the invention to be so worked.

(6) No entry shall be made in the register under this section on the ground mentioned in subsection (3)(d)(i) above, and any licence granted under this section on that ground shall contain such provisions as appear to the comptroller to be expedient for restricting the countries in which any product concerned may be disposed of or used by the licensee.

(7) No order or entry shall be made under this section in respect of a patent (the patent concerned) on the ground mentioned in subsection (3)(d)(ii) above unless the comptroller is satisfied that the proprietor of the patent for the other invention is able and willing to grant to the proprietor of the patent concerned and his licensees a licence under the patent for the other invention on reasonable terms.

(8) An application may be made under this section in respect of a patent notwithstanding that the applicant is already the holder of a licence under the patent; and no person shall be estopped or barred from alleging any of the matters specified in subsection (3) above by reason of any admission made by him, whether in such a licence or otherwise, or by reason of his having accepted such a licence.

49 Provisions about licences under s. 48

(1) Where the comptroller is satisfied, on an application made under section 48 above in respect of a patent, that the manufacture, use or disposal of materials not protected by the patent is unfairly prejudiced by reason of conditions imposed by the proprietor of the patent on the grant of licences under the patent, or on the disposal or use of the patented product or the use of the patented process, he may (subject to the provisions of that section) order the grant of licences under the patent to such customers of the applicant as he thinks fit as well as to the applicant.

(2) Where an application under section 48 above is made in respect of a patent by a person who holds a licence under the patent, the comptroller—

(a) may, if he orders the grant of a licence to the applicant, order the existing licence to be cancelled, or

(b) may, instead of ordering the grant of a licence to the applicant, order the existing licence to be amended.

(3) (repealed)

(4) Section 46(4) and (5) above shall apply to a licence granted in pursuance of an order under section 48 above and to a licence granted by virtue of an entry under that section as it applies to a licence granted by virtue of an entry under section 46 above.

50 Exercise of powers on applications under s. 48

(1) The powers of the comptroller on an application under section 48 above in respect of a patent shall be exercised with a view to securing the following general purposes:—

(a) that inventions which can be worked on a commercial scale in the United Kingdom and which should in the public interest be so worked shall be worked there without undue delay and to the fullest extent that is reasonably practicable;

(b) that the inventor or other person beneficially entitled to a patent shall receive reasonable remuneration having regard to the nature of the invention;

(c) that the interests of any person for the time being working or developing an invention in the United Kingdom under the protection of a patent shall not be unfairly prejudiced.

(2) Subject to subsection (1) above, the comptroller shall, in determining whether to make an order or entry in pursuance of such an application, take account of the following matters, that is to say—

(a)   the nature of the invention, the time which has elapsed since the publication in the journal of a notice of the grant of the patent and the measures already taken by the proprietor of the patent or any licensee to make full use of the invention;

(b)   the ability of any person to whom a licence would be granted under the order concerned to work the invention to the public advantage; and

(c)   the risks to be undertaken by that person in providing capital and working the invention if the application for an order is granted,

but shall not be required to take account of matters subsequent to the making of the application.

51   Powers exercisable in consequence of report of Monopolies and Mergers Commission

(1)   Where a report of the Monopolies and Mergers Commission has been laid before Parliament containing conclusions to the effect—

(a)   on a monopoly reference, that a monopoly situation exists and facts found by the Commission operate or may be expected to operate against the public interest,

(b)   on a merger reference, that a merger situation qualifying for investigation has been created and the creation of the situation, or particular elements in or consequences of it specified in the report, operate or may be expected to operate against the public interest,

(c)   on a competition reference, that a person was engaged in an anti-competitive practice which operated or may be expected to operate against the public interest, or

(d)   on a reference under section 11 of the Competition Act 1980 (reference of public bodies and certain other persons), that a person is pursuing a course of conduct which operates against the public interest,

the appropriate Minister or Ministers may apply to the comptroller to take action under this section.

(2)   Before making an application the appropriate Minister or Ministers shall publish, in such manner as he or they think appropriate, a notice describing the nature of the proposed application and shall consider any representations which may be made within 30 days of such publication by persons whose interests appear to him or them to be affected.

(3)   If on an application under this section it appears to the comptroller that the matters specified in the Commission's report as being those which in the Commission's opinion operate, or operated or may be expected to operate, against the public interest include—

(a)   conditions in licences granted under a patent by its proprietor restricting the use of the invention by the licensee or the right of the proprietor to grant other licences, or

(b)   a refusal by the proprietor of a patent to grant licences on reasonable terms he may by order cancel or modify any such condition or may, instead or in addition, make an entry in the register to the effect that licences under the patent are to be available as of right.

(4)   In this section "the appropriate Minister or Ministers" means the Minister or Ministers to whom the report of the Commission was made.

52   Opposition, appeal and arbitration

(1)   The proprietor of the patent concerned or any other person wishing to oppose an application under sections 48 to 51 above may, in accordance with rules, give to the comptroller notice of opposition; and the comptroller shall consider the opposition in deciding whether to grant the application.

. . .

53   Compulsory licences; supplementary provisions

. . .

(4)   An entry made in the register under sections 48 to 51 above shall for all purposes have the same effect as an entry made under section 46 above.

(5)   No order or entry shall be made in pursuance of an application under sections 48 to 51 above which would be at variance with any treaty or international convention to which the United Kingdom is a party.

. . .

Use of patented inventions for services of the Crown

55   Use of patented inventions for services of the Crown

(1)   Notwithstanding anything in this Act, any government department and any person authorised in writing by a government department may, for the services of the Crown and in accordance with this section, do any of the following acts in the United Kingdom in relation to a patented invention without the consent of the proprietor of the patent, that is to say—

(a)   where the invention is a product, may—

(i)   make, use, import or keep the product, or sell or offer to sell it where to do so would be incidental or ancillary to making, using, importing or keeping it; or

(ii)   in any event, sell or offer to sell it for foreign defence purposes or for the production or supply of specified drugs and medicines, or dispose or offer to dispose of it (otherwise than by selling it) for any purpose whatever;

(b)   where the invention is a process, may use it or do in relation to any product obtained directly by means of the process anything mentioned in paragraph (a) above;

(c)   without prejudice to the foregoing, where the invention or any product obtained directly by means of the invention is a specified drug or medicine, may sell or offer to sell the drug or medicine;

(d)   may supply or offer to supply to any person any of the means, relating to an essential element of the invention, for putting the invention into effect;

(e)   may dispose or offer to dispose of anything which was made, used, imported or kept in the exercise of the powers conferred by this section and which is no longer required for the purpose for which it was made, used, imported or kept (as the case may be),

and anything done by virtue of this subsection shall not amount to an infringement of the patent concerned.

. . .

56   Interpretation, etc., of provisions about Crown use

(1)   Any reference in section 55 above to a patented invention, in relation to any time, is a reference to an invention for which a patent has before that time been, or is subsequently, granted.

(2)   In this Act, except so far as the context otherwise requires, "the services of the Crown" includes—

(a)   the supply of anything for foreign defence purposes;

(b)   the production or supply of specified drugs and medicines; and

(c)   such purposes relating to the production or use of atomic energy or research into matters connected therewith as the Secretary of State thinks necessary or expedient;

and "use for the services of the Crown" shall be construed accordingly.

. . .

57   Rights of third parties in respect of Crown use

(1)   In relation to—

(a)   any use made for the services of the Crown of an invention by a government department, or a person authorised by a government department, by virtue of section 55 above, or

(b)   anything done for the services of the Crown to the order of a government department by the proprietor of a patent in respect of a patented invention or by the proprietor of an application in respect of an invention for which an application for a patent has been filed and is still pending,
the provisions of any licence, assignment, assignation or agreement to which this subsection applies shall be of no effect so far as those provisions restrict or regulate the working of the invention, or the use of any model, document or information relating to it, or provide for the making of payments in respect of, or calculated by reference to, such working or use; and the reproduction or publication of any model or document in connection with the said working or use shall not be deemed to be an infringement of any copyright or design right subsisting in the model or document or of any topography right.

(2)   Subsection (1) above applies to a licence, assignment, assignation or agreement which is made, whether before or after the appointed day, between (on the one hand) any person who is a proprietor of or an application for the patent, or anyone who derives title from any such person or from whom such person derives title, and (on the other hand) any person whatever other than a government department.

. . .

57A   Compensation for loss of profit

(1)   Where use is made of an invention for the services of the Crown, the government department concerned shall pay—

(a)   to the proprietor of the patent, or

(b)   if there is an exclusive licence in force in respect of the patent, to the exclusive licensee,
compensation for any loss resulting from his not being awarded a contract to supply the patented product or, as the case may be, to perform the patented process or supply a thing made by means of the patented process.

(2)   Compensation is payable only to the extent that such a contract could have been fulfilled from his existing manufacturing or other capacity; but is payable notwithstanding the existence of circumstances rendering him ineligible for the award of such contract.

(3)   In determining the loss, regard shall be had to the profit which would have been made on such a contract and to the extent to which any manufacturing or other capacity was under-used.

(4)   No compensation is payable in respect of any failure to secure contracts to supply the patented product or, as the case may be, to perform the patented process or supply a thing made by means of the patented process, otherwise than for the services of the Crown.

(5)   The amount payable shall, if not agreed between the proprietor or licensee and the government department concerned with the approval of the Treasury, be determined by the court on a reference under section 58, and is in addition to any amount payable under section 55 or 57.

(6)   In this section "the government department concerned', in relation to any use of an invention for the services of the Crown, means the government department by whom or on whose authority the use was made.

(7)   In the application of this section to Northern Ireland, the reference in subsection (5) above to the Treasury shall, where the government department concerned is a department of the Government of Northern Ireland, be construed as a reference to the Department of Finance and Personnel.

58   References of disputes as to Crown use

(1)   Any dispute as to—

(a)   the exercise by a government department, or a person authorised by a government department, of the powers conferred by section 55 above,

(b)   terms for the use of an invention for the services of the Crown under that section,

(c)   the right of any person to receive any part of a payment made in pursuance of subsection (4) of that section, or

(d)   the right of any person to receive a payment under section 57A,

may be referred to the court by either party to the dispute after a patent has been granted for the invention.

(2)   If in such proceedings any question arises whether an invention has been recorded or tried as mentioned in section 55 above, and the disclosure of any document recording the invention, or of any evidence of the trial thereof, would in the opinion of the department be prejudicial to the public interest, the disclosure may be made confidentially to counsel for the other party or to an independent expert mutually agreed upon.

...

Infringement

60   Meaning of infringement

(1)   Subject to the provisions of this section, a person infringes a patent for an invention if, but only if, while the patent is in force, he does any of the following things in the United Kingdom in relation to the invention without the consent of the proprietor of the patent, that is to say—

(a)   where the invention is a product, he makes, disposes of, offers to dispose of, uses or imports the product or keeps it whether for disposal or otherwise;

(b)   where the invention is a process, he uses the process or he offers it for use in the United Kingdom when he knows, or it is obvious to a reasonable person in the circumstances, that its use there without the consent of the proprietor would be an infringement of the patent;

(c)   where the invention is a process, he disposes of, offers to dispose of, uses or imports any product obtained directly by means of that process or keeps any such product whether for disposal or otherwise.

(2)   Subject to the following provisions of this section, a person (other than the proprietor of the patent) also infringes a patent for an invention if, while the patent is in force and without the consent of the proprietor, he supplies or offers to supply in the United Kingdom a person other than a licensee or other person entitled to work the invention with any of the means, relating to an essential element of the invention, for putting the invention into effect when he knows, or it is obvious to a reasonable person in the circumstances, that those means are suitable for putting, and are intended to put, the invention into effect in the United Kingdom.

(3)   Subsection (2) above shall not apply to the supply or offer of a staple commercial product unless the supply or the offer is made for the purpose of inducing the person supplied or, as the case may be, the person to whom the offer is made to do an act which constitutes an infringement of the patent by virtue of subsection (1) above.

...

(5)   An act which, apart from this subsection, would constitute an infringement of a patent for an invention shall not do so if—

(a)   it is done privately and for purposes which are not commercial;

(b)   it is done for experimental purposes relating to the subject-matter of the invention;

(c)   it consists of the extemporaneous preparation in a pharmacy of a medicine for an individual in accordance with a prescription given by a registered medical or dental practitioner or consists of dealing with a medicine so prepared;

(d)   it consists of the use, exclusively for the needs of a relevant ship, of a product or process in the body of such a ship or in its machinery, tackle, apparatus or other accessories, in a case where the ship has temporarily or accidentally entered the internal or territorial waters of the United Kingdom;

(e)   it consists of the use of a product or process in the body or operation of a relevant aircraft, hovercraft or vehicle which has temporarily or accidentally entered or is crossing the United Kingdom (including the air space above it and its territorial waters) or the use of accessories for such a relevant aircraft, hovercraft or vehicle;

(f)   it consists of the use of an exempted aircraft which has lawfully entered or is lawfully crossing the United Kingdom as aforesaid or of the importation into the United Kingdom, or the use or storage there, of any part or accessory for such an aircraft.

(6)   For the purposes of subsection (2) above a person who does an act in relation to an invention which is prevented only by virtue of paragraph (a), (b) or (c) of subsection (5) above from constituting an infringement of a patent for the invention shall not be treated as a person entitled to work the invention, but—

(a)   the reference in that subsection to a person entitled to work an invention includes a reference to a person so entitled by virtue of section 55 above, and

(b)   a person who by virtue of section 28A(4) or (5) above or section 64 below is entitled to do an act in relation to the invention without it constituting such an infringement shall, so far as concerns that act, be treated as a person entitled to work the invention.

(7)   In this section—

"relevant ship" and "relevant aircraft, hovercraft or vehicle" mean respectively a ship and an aircraft, hovercraft or vehicle registered in, or belonging to, any country, other than the United Kingdom, which is a party to the Convention for the Protection of Industrial Property signed at Paris on 20 March 1883; and

"exempted aircraft" means an aircraft to which section 89 of the Civil Aviation Act 1982 (aircraft exempted from seizure in respect of patent claims) applies.

61   Proceedings for infringement of patent

(1)   Subject to the following provisions of this Part of this Act, civil proceedings may be brought in the court by the proprietor of a patent in respect of any act alleged to infringe the patent and (without prejudice to any other jurisdiction of the court) in those proceedings a claim may be made—

(a)   for an injunction or interdict restraining the defendant or defender from any apprehended act of infringement;

(b)   for an order for him to deliver up or destroy any patented product in relation to which the patent is infringed or any article in which that product is inextricably comprised;

(c)   for damages in respect of the infringement;

(d)   for an account of the profits derived by him from the infringement;

(e)   for a declaration or declarator that the patent is valid and has been infringed by him.

(2)   The court shall not, in respect of the same infringement, both award the proprietor of a patent damages and order that he shall be given an account of the profits.

(3)   The proprietor of a patent and any other person may by agreement with each other refer to the comptroller the question whether that other person has infringed the patent and on the reference the proprietor of the patent may make any claim mentioned in subsection (1)(c) or (e) above.

(4)   Except so far as the context requires, in the following provisions of this Act—

(a)   any reference to proceedings for infringement and the bringing of such proceedings includes a reference to a reference under subsection (3) above and the making of such a reference;

(b)   any reference to a plaintiff or pursuer includes a reference to the proprietor of the patent; and

(c)   any reference to a defendant or defender includes a reference to any other party to the reference.

(5)   If it appears to the comptroller on a reference under subsection (3) above that the question referred to him would more properly be determined by the court, he may decline to deal with it and the court shall have jurisdiction to determine the question as if the reference were proceedings brought in the court.

(6)   Subject to the following provisions of this part of this Act, in determining whether or not to grant any kind of relief claimed under this section and the extent of the relief granted the court or the comptroller shall apply the principles applied by the court in relation to that kind of relief immediately before the appointed day.

62   Restrictions on recovery of damages for infringement

(1)   In proceedings for infringement of a patent damages shall not be awarded, and no order shall be made for an account of profits, against a defendant or defender who proves that at the date of the infringement he was not aware, and had no reasonable grounds for supposing, that the patent existed; and a person shall not be taken to have been so aware or to have had reasonable grounds for so supposing by reason only of the application to a product of the word "patent" or "patented", or any word or words expressing or implying that a patent has been obtained for the product, unless the number of the patent accompanied the word or words in question.

(2)   In proceedings for infringement of a patent the court or the comptroller may, if it or he thinks fit, refuse to award any damages or make any such order in respect of an infringement committed during any further period specified under section 25(4) above, but before the payment of the renewal fee and any additional fee prescribed for the purposes of that subsection.

(3)   Where an amendment of the specification of a patent has been allowed under any of the provisions of this Act, no damages shall be awarded in proceedings for an infringement of the patent committed before the decision to allow the amendment unless the court or the comptroller is satisfied that the specification of the patent as published was framed in good faith and with reasonable skill and knowledge.

63   Relief for infringement of partially valid patent

(1)   If the validity of a patent is put in issue in proceedings for infringement of the patent and it is found that the patent is only partially valid, the court or the comptroller may, subject to subsection (2) below, grant relief in respect of that part of the patent which is found to be valid and infringed.

(2)   Where in any such proceedings it is found that a patent is only partially valid, the court or the comptroller shall not grant relief by way of damages, costs or expenses, except where the plaintiff or pursuer proves that the specification for the patent was framed in good faith and with reasonable skill and knowledge, and in that event the court or the comptroller may grant relief in respect of that part of the patent which is valid and infringed, subject to the discretion of the court or the comptroller as to costs or expenses and as to the date from which damages should be reckoned.

(3)   As a condition of relief under this section the court or the comptroller may direct that the specification of the patent shall be amended to its or his satisfaction upon an application made for the purpose under section 75 below, and an application may be so made accordingly, whether or not all other issues in the proceedings have been determined.

64   Right to continue use begun before priority date.

(1)   Where a patent is granted for an invention, a person who in the United Kingdom before the priority date of the invention—

(a)   does in good faith an act which would constitute an infringement of the patent if it were in force, or

(b)   makes in good faith effective and serious preparations to do such an act,
has the right to continue to do the act or, as the case may be, to do the act, notwithstanding the grant of the patent; but this right does not extend to granting a licence to another person to do the act.

(2)   If the act was done, or the preparations were made, in the course of a business, the person entitled to the right conferred by subsection (1) may—

(a)   authorise the doing of that act by any partners of his for the time being in that business, and

(b)   assign that right, or transmit it on death (or in the case of a body corporate on its dissolution), to any person who acquires that part of the business in the course of which the act was done or the preparations were made.

(3)   Where a product is disposed of to another in exercise of the rights conferred by subsection (1) or (2), that other and any person claiming through him may deal with the product in the same way as if it had been disposed of by the registered proprietor of the patent.

65   Certificate of contested validity of patent

(1)   If in any proceedings before the court or the comptroller the validity of a patent to any extent is contested and that patent is found by the court or the comptroller to be wholly or partially valid, the court or the comptroller may certify the finding and the fact that the validity of the patent was so contested.

(2)   Where a certificate is granted under this section, then, if in any subsequent proceedings before the court or the comptroller for infringement of the patent concerned or for revocation of the patent a final order or judgment or interlocutor is made or given in favour of the party relying on the validity of the patent as found in the earlier proceedings, that party shall, unless the court or the comptroller otherwise directs, be entitled to his costs or expenses as between solicitor and own client (other than the costs or expenses of any appeal in the subsequent proceedings).

66   Proceedings infringement by a co-owner

(1)   In the application of section 60 above to a patent of which there are two or more joint proprietors the reference to the proprietor shall be construed—

(a)   in relation to any act, as a reference to that proprietor or those proprietors who, by virtue of section 36 above or any agreement referred to in that section, is or are entitled to do that act without its amounting to an infringement; and

(b)   in relation to any consent, as a reference to that proprietor or those proprietors who, by virtue of section 36 above or any such agreement, is or are the proper person or persons to give the requisite consent.

(2)   One of two or more joint proprietors of a patent may without the concurrence of the others bring proceedings in respect of an act alleged to infringe the patent, but shall not do so unless the others are made parties to the proceedings; but any of the others made a defendant or defender shall not be liable for any costs or expenses unless he enters an appearance and takes part in the proceedings.

67   Proceedings for infringement by exclusive licensee

(1)   Subject to the provisions of this section, the holder of an exclusive licence under a patent shall have the same right as the proprietor of the patent to bring proceedings in respect of any infringement of the patent committed after the date of the licence; and references to the proprietor of the patent in the provisions of this Act relating to infringement shall be construed accordingly.

(2)   In awarding damages or granting any other relief in any such proceedings the court or the comptroller shall take into consideration any loss suffered or likely to be suffered by the exclusive licensee as such as a result of the infringement, or, as the case

may be, the profits derived from the infringement, so far as it constitutes an infringement of the rights of the exclusive licensee as such.

(3) In any proceedings taken by an exclusive licensee by virtue of this section the proprietor of the patent shall be made a party to the proceedings, but if made a defendant or defender shall not be liable for any costs or expenses unless he enters an appearance and takes part in the proceedings.

68   Effect of non-registration on infringement proceedings

Where by virtue of a transaction, instrument or event to which section 33 above applies a person becomes the proprietor or one of the proprietors or an exclusive licensee of a patent and the patent is subsequently infringed, the court or the comptroller shall not award him damages or order that he be given an account of the profits in respect of which a subsequent infringement occurring before the transaction, instrument or event is registered unless—

(a)   the transaction, instrument or event is registered within the period of six months beginning with its date; or

(b)   the court or the comptroller is satisfied that it was not practicable to register the transaction, instrument or event before the end of that period and that it was registered as soon as practicable thereafter.

69   Infringement of rights conferred by publication of application

(1)   Where an application for a patent for an invention is published, then, subject to subsections (2) and (3) below, the applicant shall have, as from the publication and until the grant of the patent, the same right as he would have had, if the patent had been granted on the date of the publication of the application, to bring proceedings in the court or before the comptroller for damages in respect of any act which would have infringed the patent; and (subject to subsections (2) and (3) below) references in sections 60 to 62 and 66 to 68 above to a patent and the proprietor of a patent shall be respectively construed as including references to any such application and the applicant, and references to a patent being in force, being granted, being valid or existing shall be construed accordingly.

(2)   The applicant shall be entitled to bring proceedings by virtue of this section in respect of any act only—

(a)   after the patent has been granted; and

(b)   if the act would, if the patent had been granted on the date of the publication of the application, have infringed not only the patent, but also the claims (as interpreted by the description and any drawings referred to in the description or claims) in the form in which they were contained in the application immediately before the preparations for its publication were completed by the Patent Office.

(3)   Section 62(2) and (3) above shall not apply to an infringement of the rights conferred by this section, but in considering the amount of any damages for such an infringement, the court or the comptroller shall consider whether or not it would have been reasonable to expect, from a consideration of the application as published under section 16 above, that a patent would be granted conferring on the proprietor of the patent protection from an act of the same description as that found to infringe those rights, and if the court or the comptroller finds that it would not have been reasonable, it or he shall reduce the damages to such an amount as it or he thinks just.

70   Remedy for groundless threats of infringement proceedings

(1)   Where a person (whether or not the proprietor of, or entitled to any right in, a patent) by circulars, advertisements or otherwise threatens another person with proceedings for any infringement of a patent, a person aggrieved by the threats (whether or not he is the person to whom the threats are made) may, subject to subsection (4)

below, bring proceedings in the court against the person making the threats, claiming any relief mentioned in subsection (3) below.

(2)   In any such proceedings the plaintiff or pursuer shall, if he proves that the threats were so made and satisfies the court that he is a person aggrieved by them, be entitled to the relief claimed unless—

(a)   the defendant or defender proves that the acts in respect of which proceedings were threatened constitute or, if done, would constitute an infringement of a patent; and

(b)   the patent alleged to be infringed is not shown by the plaintiff or pursuer to be invalid in a relevant respect.

(3)   The said relief is—

(a)   a declaration or declarator to the effect that the threats are unjustifiable;

(b)   an injunction or interdict against the continuance of the threats; and

(c)   damages in respect of any loss which the plaintiff or pursuer has sustained by the threats.

(4)   Proceedings may not be brought under this section for a threat to bring proceedings for an infringement alleged to consist of making or importing a product for disposal or of using a process.

(5)   It is hereby declared that a mere notification of the existence of a patent does not constitute a threat of proceedings within the meaning of this section.

71   Declaration or declarator as to non-infringement

(1)   Without prejudice to the court's jurisdiction to make a declaration or declarator apart from this section, a declaration or declarator that an act does not, or a proposed act would not, constitute an infringement of a patent may be made by the court or the comptroller in proceedings between the person doing or proposing to do the act and the proprietor of the patent, notwithstanding that no assertion to the contrary has been made by the proprietor, if it is shown—

(a)   that that person has applied in writing to the proprietor for a written acknowledgment to the effect of the declaration or declarator claimed, and has furnished him with full patriculars in writing of the act in question; and

(b)   that the proprietor has refused or failed to give any such acknowledgment.

(2)   Subject to section 72(5) below, a declaration made by the comptroller under this section shall have the same effect as a declaration or declarator by the court.

Revocation of patents

72   Power to revoke patents on application

(1)   Subject to the following provisions of this Act, the court or the comptroller may on the application of any person by order revoke a patent for an invention on (but only on) any of the following grounds, that is to say—

(a)   the invention is not a patentable invention;

(b)   that the patent was granted to a person who was not entitled to be granted that patent;

(c)   the specification of the patent does not disclose the invention clearly enough and completely enough for it to be performed by a person skilled in the art;

(d)   the matter disclosed in the specification of the patent extends beyond that disclosed in the application for the patent, as filed, or, if the patent was granted on a new application filed under section 8(3), 12 or 37(4) above or as mentioned in section 15(4) above, in the earlier application, as filed;

(e)   the protection conferred by the patent has been extended by an amendment which should not have been allowed.

(2)   An application for the revocation of a patent on the ground mentioned in subsection (1)(b) above—

(a)   may only be made by a person found by the court in an action for a declaration or declarator, or found by the court or the comptroller on a reference under section 37 above, to be entitled to be granted that patent or to be granted a patent for part of the matter comprised in the specification of the patent sought to be revoked; and

(b)   may not be made if that action was commenced or that reference was made after the end of the period of two years beginning with the date of the grant of the patent sought to be revoked, unless it is shown that any person registered as a proprietor of the patent knew at the time of the grant or of the transfer of the patent to him that he was not entitled to the patent.

. . .

(5)   A decision of the comptroller or on appeal from the comptroller shall not estop any party to civil proceedings in which infringement of a patent is in issue from alleging invalidity of the patent on any of the grounds referred to in subsection (1) above, whether or not any of the issues involved were decided in the said decision.

. . .

73   Comptroller's power to revoke patents on his own initiative

(1)   If it appears to the comptroller that an invention for which a patent has been granted formed part of the state of the art by virtue only of section 2(3) above, he may on his own initiative by order revoke the patent, but shall not do so without giving the proprietor of the patent an opportunity of making any observations and of amending the specification of the patent so as to exclude any matter which formed part of the state of the art as aforesaid without contravening section 76 below.

. . .

Putting validity in issue

74   Proceedings in which validity of patent may be put in issue

(1)   Subject to the following provisions of this section, the validity of a patent may be put in issue—

(a)   by way of defence, in proceedings for infringement of the patent under section 61 above or proceedings under section 69 above for infringement of rights conferred by the publication of an application;

(b)   in proceedings under section 70 above;

(c)   in proceedings in which a declaration in relation to the patent is sought under section 71 above;

(d)   in proceedings before the court or the comptroller under section 72 above for the revocation of the patent;

(e)   in proceedings under section 58 above.

(2)   The validity of a patent may not be put in issue in any other proceedings and, in particular, no proceedings may be instituted (whether under this Act or otherwise) seeking only a declaration as to the validity or invalidity of a patent.

(3)   The only grounds on which the validity of a patent may be put in issue (whether in proceedings for revocation under section 72 above or otherwise) are the grounds on which the patent may be revoked under that section.

(4)   No determination shall be made in any proceedings mentioned in subsection (1) above on the validity of a patent which any person puts in issue on the ground mentioned in section 72(1)(b) above unless—

(a)   it has been determined in entitlement proceedings commenced by that person or in the proceedings in which the validity of the patent is in issue that the patent should have been granted to him and not some other person; and

(b)   except where it has been so determined in entitlement proceedings, the proceedings in which the validity of the patent is in issue are commenced before the end of the period of two years beginning with the date of the grant of the patent or it is shown that any person registered as a proprietor of the patent knew at the time of the grant or of the transfer of the patent to him that he was not entitled to the patent.

(5)   Where the validity of a patent is put in issue by way of defence or counterclaim the court or the comptroller shall, if it or he thinks it just to do so, give the defendant an opportunity to comply with the condition in subsection (4)(a) above.

(6)   In subsection (4) above "entitlement proceedings", in relation to a patent, means a reference under section 37(1) above on the ground that the patent was granted to a person not entitled to it or proceedings for a declaration or declarator that it was so granted.

(7)   Where proceedings with respect to a patent are pending in the court under any provision of this Act mentioned in subsection (1) above, no proceedings may be instituted without the leave of the court before the comptroller with respect to that patent under section 61(3), 69, 71 or 72 above.

(8)   It is hereby declared that for the purposes of this Act the validity of a patent is not put in issue merely because the comptroller is considering its validity in order to decide whether to revoke it under section 73 above.

General provisions as to amendment of patents and applications

75   Amendment of patent in infringement or revocation proceedings

(1)   In any proceedings before the court or the comptroller in which the validity of a patent is put in issue the court or, as the case may be, the comptroller may, subject to section 76 below, allow the proprietor of the patent to amend the specification of the patent in such manner, and subject to such terms as to advertising the proposed amendment and as to costs, expenses or otherwise, as the court or comptroller thinks fit.

(2)   A person may give notice to the court or the comptroller of his opposition to an amendment proposed by the proprietor of the patent under this section, and if he does so the court or the comptroller shall notify the proprietor and consider the opposition in deciding whether the amendment or any amendment should be allowed.

(3)   An amendment of a specification of a patent under this section shall have effect and be deemed always to have had effect from the grant of the patent.

(4)   Where an application for an order under this section is made to the court, the applicant shall notify the comptroller, who shall be entitled to appear and be heard and shall appear if so directed by the court.

76   Amendments of applications and patents not to include added matter

(1)   An application for a patent which—

(a)   is made in respect of matter disclosed in an earlier application, or in the specification of a patent which has been granted, and

(b)   discloses additional matter, that is, matter extending beyond that disclosed in the earlier application, as filed, or the application for the patent, as filed,

may be filed under section 8(3), 12 or 37(4) above, or as mentioned in section 15(4) above, but shall not be allowed to proceed unless it is amended so as to exclude the additional matter.

(2)   No amendment of an application for a patent shall be allowed under section 17(3), 18(3) or 19(1) if it results in the application disclosing matter extending beyond that disclosed in the application as filed.

(3)   No amendment of the specification of a patent shall be allowed under section 27(1), 73 or 75 if it—

(a)   results in the specification disclosing additional matter, or

(b)   extends the protection conferred by the patent.

PART II   PROVISIONS ABOUT INTERNATIONAL CONVENTIONS

European patents and patent applications

77   Effect of European patent (UK)

(1)   Subject to the provisions of this Act, a European patent (UK) shall, as from the publication of the mention of its grant in the European Patent Bulletin, be treated for the purposes of Parts I and III of this Act as if it were a patent under this Act granted in pursuance of an application made under this Act and as if notice of the grant of the patent had, on the date of that publication, been published under section 24 above in the journal; and—

(a)   the proprietor of a European patent (UK) shall accordingly as respects the United Kingdom have the same rights and remedies, subject to the same conditions, as the proprietor of a patent under this Act;

(b)   references in Parts I and III of this Act to a patent shall be construed accordingly; and

(c)   any statement made and any certificate filed for the purposes of the provision of the convention corresponding to section 2(4)(c) above shall be respectively treated as a statement made and written evidence filed for the purposes of the said paragraph (c).

(2)   Subsection (1) above shall not affect the operation in relation to a European patent (UK) of any provisions of the European Patent Convention relating to the amendment or revocation of such a patent in proceedings before the European Patent Office.

(3)   Where in the case of a European patent (UK)—

(a)   proceedings for infringement, or proceedings under section 58 above, have been commenced before the court or the comptroller and have not been finally disposed of, and

(b)   it is established in proceedings before the European Patent Office that the patent is only partially valid,

the provisions of section 63 or, as the case may be, of subsections (7) to (9) of section 58 apply as they apply to proceedings in which the validity of a patent is put in issue and in which it is found that the patent is only partially valid.

(4)   Where a European patent (UK) is amended in accordance with the European Patent Convention, the amendment shall have effect for the purposes of Parts I and III of this Act as if the specification of the patent had been amended under this Act; but subject to subsection (6)(b) below.

(4A)   Where a European patent (UK) is revoked in accordance with the European Patent Convention, the patent shall be treated for the purposes of Parts I and III of this Act as having been revoked under this Act.

. . .

(6)   While this subsection is in force—

(a)   subsection (1) above shall not apply to a European patent (UK) the specification of which was published in French or German, unless a translation into English of the specification as amended is filed at the Patent Office and the prescribed fee is paid before the end of the prescribed period;

(b)   subsection (4) above shall not apply to an amendment made in French or German unless a translation of the amendment into English is filed at the Patent Office and the prescribed fee is paid before the end of the prescribed period.

(7)   Where such a translation is not filed, the patent shall be treated as always having been void.

(8)   The comptroller shall publish any translation filed at the Patent Office under subsection (6) above.

. . .

78   Effect of filing an application for a European patent (UK)

(1)   Subject to the provisions of this Act, an application for a European patent (UK) having a date of filing under the European Patent Convention shall be treated for the purposes of the provisions of this Act to which this section applies as an application for a patent under this Act having that date as its date of filing and having the other incidents listed in subsection (3) below, but subject to the modifications mentioned in the following provisions of this section.

(2)   This section applies to the following provisions of this Act:—

section 2(3) and so much of section 14(7) as relates to section 2(3);

section 5;

section 6;

so much of section 13(3) as relates to an application for and issue of a certificate under that subsection;

sections 30 to 33;

section 36;

sections 55 to 69;

section 74, so far as relevant to any of the provisions mentioned above;

section 111; and

section 125.

(3)   The incidents referred to in subsection (1) above in relation to an application for a European patent (UK) are as follows:—

(a)   any declaration of priority made in connection with the application under the European Patent Convention shall be treated for the purposes of this Act as a declaration made under section 5(2) above;

(b)   where a period of time relevant to priority is extended under that convention, the period of twelve months specified in section 5(2) above shall be so treated as altered correspondingly;

(c)   where the date of filing an application is re-dated under that convention to a later date, that date shall be so treated as the date of filing the application;

(d)   the application, if published in accordance with that convention, shall, subject to subsection (7) and section 79 below, be so treated as published under section 16 above;

(e)   any designation of the inventor under that convention or any statement under it indicating the origin of the right to a European patent shall be treated for the purposes of section 13(3) above as a statement filed under section 13(2) above;

(f)   registration of the application in the register of European patents shall be treated as registration under this Act.

. . .

(5)   Subsections (1) to (3) above shall cease to apply to an application for a European patent (UK), except as mentioned in subsection (5A) below, if—

(a)   the application is refused or withdrawn or deemed to be withdrawn, or

(b)   the designation of the United Kingdom in the application is withdrawn or deemed to be withdrawn,

but shall apply again if the rights of the applicant are re-established under the European Patent Convention, as from their re-establishment.

(5A)   The occurrence of any of the events mentioned in subsection (5)(a) or (b) shall not affect the continued operation of section 2(3) above in relation to matter contained in an application for a European patent (UK) which by virtue of that provision has become part of the state of the art as regards other inventions.

. . .

(7)   While this subsection is in force, an application for a European patent (UK) published by the European Patent Office under the European Patent Convention in French or German shall be treated for the purposes of sections 55 and 69 above as

published under section 16 above when a translation into English of the claims of the specification of the application has been filed at and published by the Patent Office and the prescribed fee has been paid, but an applicant—

(a)   may recover a payment by virtue of section 55(5) above in respect of the use of the invention in question before publication of that translation; or

(b)   may bring proceedings by virtue of section 69 above in respect of an act mentioned in that section which is done before publication of that translation;

if before that use or the doing of that act he has sent by post or delivered to the government department who made use or authorised the use of the invention, or, as the case may be, to the person alleged to have done the act, a translation into English of those claims.

. . .

79   Operation of s. 78 in relation to certain European patent applications

(1)   Subject to the following provisions of this section, section 78 above, in its operation in relation to an international application for a patent (UK) which is treated by virtue of the European Patent Convention as an application for a European patent (UK), shall have effect as if any reference in that section to anything done in relation to the application under the European Patent Convention included a reference to the corresponding thing done under the Patent Co-operation Treaty.

(2)   Any such international application which is published under that treaty shall be treated for the purposes of section 2(3) above as published only when a copy of the application has been supplied to the European Patent Office in English, French or German and the relevant fee has been paid under that convention.

(3)   Any such international application which is published under that treaty in a language other than English, French or German shall, subject to section 78(7) above, be treated for the purposes of sections 55 and 69 above as published only when it is re-published in English, French and German by the European Patent Office under that convention.

. . .

PART III   MISCELLANEOUS AND GENERAL

. . .

Offences

. . .

110   Unauthorised claim of patent rights

(1)   If a person falsely represents that anything disposed of by him for value is a patented product he shall, subject to the following provisions of this section, be liable on summary conviction to a fine not exceeding level 3 on the standard scale.

(2)   For the purposes of subsection (1) above a person who for value disposes of an article having stamped, engraved or impressed on it or otherwise applied to it the word "patent" or "patented" or anything expressing or implying that the article is a patented product, shall be taken to represent that the article is a patented product.

(3)   Subsection (1) above does not apply where the representation is made in respect of a product after the patent for that product or, as the case may be, the process in question has expired or been revoked and before the end of a period which is reasonably sufficient to enable the accused to take steps to ensure that the representation is not made (or does not continue to be made).

(4)   In proceedings for an offence under this section it shall be a defence for the accused to prove that he used due diligence to prevent the commission of the offence.

111   Unauthorised claim that patent has been applied for
(1)   If a person represents that a patent has been applied for in respect of any particle disposed of for value by him and—
    (a)   no such application has been made, or
    (b)   any such application has been refused or withdrawn,
he shall, subject to the following provisions of this section, be liable on summary conviction to a fine not exceeding level 3 on the standard scale.
(2)   Subsection (1)(b) above does not apply where the representation is made (or continues to be made) before the expiry of a period which commences with the refusal or withdrawal and which is reasonably sufficient to enable the accused to take steps to ensure that the representation is not made (or does not continue to be made).
(3)   For the purposes of subsection (1) above a person who for value disposes of an article having stamped, engraved or impressed on it or otherwise applied to it the words "patent applied for" or "patent pending", or anything expressing or implying that a patent has been applied for in respect of the article, shall be taken to represent that a patent has been applied for in respect of it.
(4)   In any proceedings for an offence under this section it shall be a defence for the accused to prove that he used due diligence to prevent the commission of such an offence.
. . .

Supplemental

. . .

125   Extent of invention
(1)   For the purposes of this Act an invention for a patent for which an application has been made or for which a patent has been granted shall, unless the context otherwise requires, be taken to be that specified in a claim of the specification of the application or patent, as the case may be, as interpreted by the description and any drawings contained in that specification, and the extent of the protection conferred by a patent or application for a patent shall be determined accordingly.
(2)   It is hereby declared for the avoidance of doubt that where more than one invention is specified in any such claim, each invention may have a different priority date under section 5 above.
(3)   The Protocol on the Interpretation of Article 69 of the European Patent Convention (which Article contains a provision corresponding to subsection (1) above) shall, as for the time being in force, apply for the purposes of subsection (1) above as it applies for the purposes of that Article.

125A   Disclosure of invention by specification: availability of samples of micro-organisms
(1)   Provision may be made by rules prescribing the circumstances in which the specification of an application for a patent, or of a patent, for an invention which requires for its performance the use of a micro-organism is to be treated as disclosing the invention in a manner which is clear enough and complete enough for the invention to be performed by a person skilled in the art.
(2)   The rules may in particular require the applicant or patentee—
    (a)   to take such steps as may be prescribed for the purposes of making available to the public samples of the micro-organism, and
    (b)   not to impose or maintain restrictions on the uses to which such samples may be put, except as may be prescribed.
(3)   The rules may provide that, in such cases as may be prescribed, samples need only be made available to such persons or descriptions of persons as may be prescribed;

and the rules may identify a description of persons by reference to whether the comptroller has given his certificate as to any matter.

(4)   An application for revocation of the patent under section 72(1)(c) above may be made if any of the requirements of the rules cease to be complied with.

...

130   Interpretation

(1)   In this Act, except so far as the context otherwise requires—

"application for a European patent (UK)" and "international application for a patent (UK)" each mean an application of the relevant description which, on its date of filing, designates the United Kingdom;

"appointed day", in any provision of this Act, means the day appointed under section 132 below for the coming into operation of that provision;

"Community Patent Convention" means the Convention for the European Patent for the Common Market and "Community patent" means a patent granted under that convention;

"comptroller" means the Comptroller-General of Patents, Designs and Trade Marks;

"Convention on International Exhibitions" means the Convention relating to International Exhibitions signed in Paris on 22 November 1928, as amended or supplemented by any protocol to that convention which is for the time being in force;

"court" means

(a)   as respects England and Wales, the High Court or any patents county court having jurisdiction by virtue of an order under section 287 of the Copyright, Designs and Patents Act 1988;

(b)   as respects Scotland, the Court of Session;

(c)   as respects Northern Ireland, the High Court in Northern Ireland;

"date of filing" means—

(a)   in relation to an application for a patent made under this Act, the date which is the date of filing that application by virtue of section 15 above; and

(b)   in relation to any other application, the date which, under the law of the country where the application was made or in accordance with the terms of a treaty or convention to which that country is a party, is to be treated as the date of filing that application or is equivalent to the date of filing an application in that country (whatever the outcome of the application);

"designate" in relation to an application or a patent, means designate the country or countries (in pursuance of the European Patent Convention or the Patent Co-operation Treaty) in which protection is sought for the invention which is the subject of the application or patent;

"employee" means a person who works or (where the employment has ceased) worked under a contract of employment or in employment under or for the purposes of a government department or a person who serves (or served) in the naval, military or air forces of the Crown;

"employer", in relation to an employee, means the person by whom the employee is or was employed;

"European Patent Convention" means the Convention on the Grant of European Patents, "European patent" means a patent granted under that convention, "European patent (UK)" means a European patent designating the United Kingdom, "European Patent Bulletin" means the bulletin of that name published under that convention, and "European Patent Office" means the office of that name established by that convention;

"exclusive licence" means a licence from the proprietor of or applicant for a patent conferring on the licensee, or on him and persons authorised by him, to the exclusion of all other persons (including the proprietor or applicant), any right in respect of the invention to which the patent or application relates, and "exclusive licensee" and "non-exclusive licence" shall be construed accordingly;

"filing fee" means the fee prescribed for the purposes of section 14 above;

"formal requirements" means those requirements designated as such by rules made for the purposes of section 17 above;

"international application for a patent" means an application made under the Patent Co-operation Treaty;

"International Bureau" means the secretariat of the World Intellectual Property Organisation established by a convention signed at Stockholm on 14 July 1967;

"international exhibition" means an official or officially recognised international exhibition falling within the terms of the Convention on International Exhibitions or falling within the terms of any subsequent treaty or convention replacing that convention;

"inventor" has the meaning assigned to it by section 7 above;

"journal" has the meaning assigned to it by section 123(6) above;

"mortgage", when used as a noun, includes a charge for securing money or money's worth and, when used as a verb, shall be construed accordingly;

"1949 Act" means the Patents Act 1949;

"patent" means a patent under this Act;

"Patent Co-operation Treaty" means the treaty of that name signed at Washington on 19 June 1970;

"patented invention" means an invention for which a patent is granted and "patented process" shall be construed accordingly;

"patented product" means a product which is a patented invention or, in relation to a patented process, a product obtained directly by means of the process or to which the process has been applied;

"prescribed" and "rules" have the meanings assigned to them by section 123 above;

"priority date" means the date determined as such under section 5 above;

"published" means made available to the public (whether in the United Kingdom or elsewhere) and a document shall be taken to be published under any provision of this Act if it can be inspected as of right at any place in the United Kingdom by members of the public, whether on payment of a fee or not; and "republished" shall be construed accordingly;

"register" and cognate expressions have the meanings assigned to them by section 32 above;

"relevant convention court", in relation to any proceedings under the European Patent Convention, the Community Patent Convention or the Patent Co-operation Treaty, means that court or other body which under that convention or treaty has jurisdiction over those proceedings, including (where it has such jurisdiction) any department of the European Patent Office;

"right", in relation to any patent or application, includes an interest in the patent or application and, without prejudice to the foregoing, any reference to a right in a patent includes a reference to a share in the patent;

"search fee" means the fee prescribed for the purposes of section 17(1) above;

"services of the Crown" and "use for the services of the Crown" have the meanings assigned to them by section 56(2) above, including, as respects any period of emergency within the meaning of section 59 above, the meanings assigned to them by the said section 59.

(2)   Rules may provide for stating in the journal that an exhibition falls within the definition of international exhibition in subsection (1) above and any such statement shall be conclusive evidence that the exhibition falls within that definition.

(3)   For the purposes of this Act matter shall be taken to have been disclosed in any relevant application within the meaning of section 5 above or in the specification of a patent if it was either claimed or disclosed (otherwise than by way of disclaimer or acknowledgment of prior art) in that application or specification.

(4)   References in this Act to an application for a patent, as filed, are references to such an application in the state it was on the date of filing.

(5)   References in this Act to an application for a patent being published are references to its being published under section 16 above.

(6)   References in this Act to any of the following conventions, that is to say—
   (a)   The European Patent Convention;
   (b)   The Community Patent Convention;
   (c)   The Patent Co-operation Treaty; are references to that convention or any other international convention or agreement replacing it, as amended or supplemented by any convention or international agreement (including in either case any protocol or annex), or in accordance with the terms of any such convention or agreement, and include references to any instrument made under any such convention or agreement.

(7)   Whereas by a resolution made on the signature of the Community Patent Convention the governments of the member states of the European Economic Community resolved to adjust their laws relating to patents so as (among other things) to bring those laws into conformity with the corresponding provisions of the European Patent Convention, the Community Patent Convention and the Patent Co-operation Treaty, it is hereby declared that the following provisions of this Act, that is to say, sections 1(1) to (4), 2 to 6, 14(3), (5) and (6), 37(5), 54, 60, 69, 72(1) and (2), 74(4), 82, 83, 100 and 125, are so framed as to have, as nearly as practicable, the same effects in the United Kingdom as the corresponding provisions of the European Patent Convention, the Community Patent Convention and the Patent Co-operation Treaty have in the territories to which those Conventions apply.

(8)   Part I of the Arbitration Act 1996 shall not apply to any proceedings before the comptroller under this Act.

(9)   Except so far as the context otherwise requires, any reference in this Act to any enactment shall be construed as a reference to that enactment as amended or extended by or under any other enactment, including this Act.
. . .

COPYRIGHT, DESIGNS AND PATENTS ACT 1988
AS AMENDED
(1988, c. 48)

An Act to restate the law of copyright, with amendments; to make fresh provision as to the rights of performers and others in performances; to confer a design right in original designs; to amend the Registered Designs Act 1949; to make provision with respect to patent agents and trade mark agents; to confer patents and designs jurisdiction on certain county courts; to amend the law of patents; to make provision with respect to devices designed to circumvent copy-protection of works in electronic form; to make fresh provision penalising the fraudulent application or use of a trade mark an offence; to make provision for the benefit of the Hospital for Sick Children, Great Ormond Street, London; to enable financial assistance to be given to certain international bodies; and for connected purposes.   [15 November 1988]

. . .

PART I   COPYRIGHT

CHAPTER I   SUBSISTENCE, OWNERSHIP AND DURATION OF COPYRIGHT

Introductory

1   Copyright and copyright works

(1)   Copyright is a property right which subsists in accordance with this Part in the following descriptions of work—

(a)   original literary, dramatic, musical or artistic works,

(b)   sound recordings, films, broadcasts or cable programmes, and

(c)   the typographical arrangement of published editions.

(2)   In this Part "copyright work" means a work of any of those descriptions in which copyright subsists.

(3)   Copyright does not subsist in a work unless the requirements of this Part with respect to qualification for copyright protection are met (see section 153 and the provisions referred to there).

2   Rights subsisting in copyright works

(1)   The owner of the copyright in a work of any description has the exclusive right to do the acts specified in Chapter II as the acts restricted by the copyright in a work of that description.

(2)   In relation to certain descriptions of copyright work the following rights conferred by Chapter IV (moral rights) subsist in favour of the author, director or commissioner of the work, whether or not he is the owner of the copyright—

(a)   section 77 (right to be identified as author or director),

(b)   section 80 (right to object to derogatory treatment of work), and

(c)   section 85 (right to privacy of certain photographs and films).

Descriptions of work and related provisions

3   Literary, dramatic and musical works

(1)   In this Part—

"literary work" means any work, other than a dramatic or musical work, which is written, spoken or sung, and accordingly includes—

(a)   a table or compilation other than a database,

(b)   a computer program,

(c)   preparatory design material for a computer program, and

(d)   a database;

"dramatic work" includes a work of dance or mime; and

"musical work" means a work consisting of music, exclusive of any words or action intended to be sung, spoken or performed with the music.

(2)   Copyright does not subsist in a literary, dramatic or musical work unless and until it is recorded, in writing or otherwise; and references in this Part to the time at which such a work is made are to the time at which it is so recorded.

(3)   It is immaterial for the purposes of subsection (2) whether the work is recorded by or with the permission of the author; and where it is not recorded by the author, nothing in that subsection affects the question whether copyright subsists in the record as distinct from the work recorded.

3A   Databases

(1)   In this Part "database" means a collection of independent works, data or other materials which—

(a)   are arranged in a systematic or methodical way, and

(b)   are individually accessible by electronic or other means.

(2)   For the purposes of this Part a literary work consisting of a database is original if, and only if, by reason of the selection or arrangement of the contents of the database the database constitutes the author's own intellectual creation.

4   Artistic works
(1)   In this Part "artistic work" means—
   (a)   a graphic work, photograph, sculpture or collage, irrespective of artistic quality,
   (b)   a work of architecture being a building or a model for a building, or
   (c)   a work of artistic craftsmanship.
(2)   In this Part—
"building" includes any fixed structure, and a part of a building or fixed structure;
"graphic work" includes—
   (a)   any painting, drawing, diagram, map, chart or plan, and
   (b)   any engraving, etching, lithograph, woodcut or similar work;
"photograph" means a recording of light or other radiation on any medium on which an image is produced or from which an image may by any means be produced, and which is not part of a film;
"sculpture" includes a cast or model made for purposes of sculpture.

5A   Sound recordings
(1)   In this Part "sound recording" means—
   (a)   a recording of sounds, from which the sounds may be reproduced, or
   (b)   a recording of the whole or any part of a literary, dramatic or musical work, from which sounds reproducing the work or part may be produced,
regardless of the medium on which the recording is made or the method by which the sounds are reproduced or produced.
(2)   Copyright does not subsist in a sound recording which is, or to the extent that it is, a copy taken from a previous sound recording.

5B   Films
(1)   In this Part "film" means a recording on any medium from which a moving image may by any means be produced.
(2)   The sound track accompanying a film shall be treated as part of the film for the purposes of this Part.
(3)   Without prejudice to the generality of subsection (2), where that subsection applies—
   (a)   references in this Part to showing a film include playing the film sound track to accompany the film, and
   (b)   references to playing a sound recording do not include playing the film sound track to accompany the film.
(4)   Copyright does not subsist in a film which is, or to the extent that it is, a copy taken from a previous film.
(5)   Nothing in this section affects any copyright subsisting in a film sound track as a sound recording.

6   Broadcasts
(1)   In this Part a "broadcast" means a transmission by wireless telegraphy of visual images, sounds or other information which—
   (a)   is capable of being lawfully received by members of the public, or
   (b)   is transmitted for presentation to members of the public;
and references to broadcasting shall be construed accordingly.
(2)   An encrypted transmission shall be regarded as capable of being lawfully received by members of the public only if decoding equipment has been made available to members of the public by or with the authority of the person making the transmission or the person providing the contents of the transmission.

(3)   References in this Part to the person making a broadcast, broadcasting a work, or including a work in a broadcast are—
    (a)   to the person transmitting the programme, if he has responsibility to any extent for its contents, and
    (b)   to any person providing the programme who makes with the person transmitting it the arrangements necessary for its transmission;
and references in this Part to a programme, in the context of broadcasting, are to any item included in a broadcast.

(4)   For the purposes of this Part, the place from which a broadcast is made is the place where, under the control and responsibility of the person making the broadcast, the programme-carrying signals are introduced into an uninterrupted chain of communication (including, in the case of a satellite transmission, the chain leading to the satellite and down towards the earth).

(4A)   Subsections (3) and (4) have effect subject to section 6A (safeguards in case of certain satellite broadcasts).

(5)   References in this Part to the reception of a broadcast include reception of a broadcast relayed by means of a telecommunications system.

(6)   Copyright does not subsist in a broadcast which infringes, or to the extent that it infringes, the copyright in another broadcast or in a cable programme.

6A   Safeguards in case of certain satellite broadcasts

(1)   This section applies where the place from which a broadcast by way of satellite transmission is made is located in a country other than an EEA State and the law of that country fails to provide at least the following level of protection—
    (a)   exclusive rights in relation to broadcasting equivalent to those conferred by section 20 (infringement by broadcasting) on the authors of literary, dramatic, musical and artistic works, films and broadcasts;
    (b)   a right in relation to live broadcasting equivalent to that conferred on a performer by section 182(1)(b) (consent required for live broadcast of performance); and
    (c)   a right for authors of sound recordings and performers to share in a single equitable remuneration in respect of the broadcasting of sound recordings.

(2)   Where the place from which the programme-carrying singals are transmitted to the satellite ("the uplink station") is located in an EEA State—
    (a)   that place shall be treated as the place from which the broadcast is made, and
    (b)   the person operating the uplink station shall be treated as the person making the broadcast.

(3)   Where the uplink station is not located in an EEA State but a person who is established in an EEA State has commissioned the making of the broadcast—
    (a)   that person shall be treated as the person making the broadcast, and
    (b)   the place in which he has his principal establishment in the European Economic Area shall be treated as the place from which the broadcast is made.

7   Cable programmes

(1)   In this Part—
    "cable programme" means any item included in a cable programme service; and
    "cable programme service" means a service which consists wholly or mainly in sending visual images, sounds or other information by means of a telecommunications system, otherwise than by wireless telegraphy, for reception—
    (a)   at two or more places (whether for simultaneous reception or at different times in response to requests by different users), or
    (b)   for presentation to members of the public,
and which is not, or so far as it is not, excepted by or under the following provisions of this section.

(2)   The following are excepted from the definition of "cable programme service"—

(a)   a service or part of a service of which it is an essential feature that while visual images, sounds or other information are being conveyed by the person providing the service there will or may be sent from each place of reception, by means of the same system or (as the case may be) the same part of it, information (other than signals sent for the operation or control of the service) for reception by the person providing the service or other persons receiving it;

(b)   a service run for the purposes of a business where—

(i)   no person except the person carrying on the business is concerned in the control of the apparatus comprised in the system,

(ii)   the visual images, sounds or other information are conveyed by the system solely for purposes internal to the running of the business and not by way of rendering a service or providing amenities for others, and

(iii)   the system is not connected to any other telecommunications system;

(c)   a service run by a single individual where—

(i)   all the apparatus comprised in the system is under his control,

(ii)   the visual images, sounds or other information conveyed by the system are conveyed solely for domestic purposes of his, and

(iii)   the system is not connected to any other telecommunications system;

(d)   services where—

(i)   all the apparatus comprised in the system is situated in, or connects, premises which are in single occupation, and

(ii)   the system is not connected to any other telecommunications system, other than services operated as part of the amenities provided for residents or inmates of premises run as a business;

(e)   services which are, or to the extent that they are, run for persons providing broadcasting or cable programme services or providing programmes for such services.

(3)   The Secretary of State may by order amend subsection (2) so as to add or remove exceptions, subject to such transitional provision as appears to him to be appropriate.

(4)   An order shall be made by statutory instrument; and no order shall be made unless a draft of it has been laid before and approved by resolution of each House of Parliament.

(5)   References in this Part to the inclusion of a cable programme or work in a cable programme service are to its transmission as part of the service; and references to the person including it are to the person providing the service.

(6)   Copyright does not subsist in a cable programme—

(a)   if it is included in a cable programme service by reception and immediate re-transmission of a broadcast, or

(b)   if it infringes, or to the extent that it infringes, the copyright in another cable programme or in a broadcast.

8   Published editions

(1)   In this Part "published edition", in the context of copyright in the typographical arrangement of a published edition, means a published edition of the whole or any part of one or more literary, dramatic or musical works.

(2)   Copyright does not subsist in the typographical arrangement of a published edition if, or to the extent that, it reproduces the typographical arrangement of a previous edition.

Authorship and ownership of copyright

9   Authorship of work

(1)   In this Part "author", in relation to a work, means the person who creates it.

(2)   That person shall be taken to be—

(aa)   in the case of a sound recording, the producer;

(ab)   in the case of a film, the producer and the principal director;

(b)   in the case of a broadcast, the person making the broadcast (see section 6(3)) or, in the case of a broadcast which relays another broadcast by reception and immediate re-transmission, the person making that other broadcast;

(c)   in the case of a cable programme, the person providing the cable programme service in which the programme is included;

(d)   in the case of the typographical arrangement of a published edition, the publisher.

(3)   In the case of a literary, dramatic, musical or artistic work which is computer-generated, the author shall be taken to be the person by whom the arrangements necessary for the creation of the work are undertaken.

(4)   For the purposes of this Part a work is of "unknown authorship" if the identity of the author is unknown or, in the case of a work of joint authorship, if the identity of none of the authors is known.

(5)   For the purposes of this Part the identity of an author shall be regarded as unknown if it is not possible for a person to ascertain his identity by reasonable inquiry; but if his identity is once known it shall not subsequently be regarded as unknown.

10   Works of joint authorship

(1)   In this Part a "work of joint authorship" means a work produced by the collaboration of two or more authors in which the contribution of each author is not distinct from that of the other author or authors.

(1A)   A film shall be treated as a work of joint authorship unless the producer and the principal director are the same person.

(2)   A broadcast shall be treated as a work of joint authorship in any case where more than one person is to be taken as making the broadcast (see section 6(3)).

(3)   References in this Part to the author of a work shall, except as otherwise provided; be construed in relation to a work of joint authorship as references to all the authors of the work.

11   First ownership of copyright

(1)   The author of a work is the first owner of any copyright in it, subject to the following provisions.

(2)   Where a literary, dramatic, musical or artistic work, or a film, is made by an employee in the course of his employment, his employer is the first owner of any copyright in the work subject to any agreement to the contrary.

(3)   This section does not apply to Crown copyright or Parliamentary copyright (see sections 163 and 165) or to copyright which subsists by virtue of section 168 (copyright of certain international organisations).

Duration of copyright

12   Duration of copyright in literary, dramatic, musical or artistic works

(1)   The following provisions have effect with respect to the duration of copyright in a literary, dramatic, musical or artistic work.

(2)   Copyright expires at the end of the period of 70 years from the end of the calendar year in which the author dies, subject as follows.

(3)   If the work is of unknown authorship, copyright expires—

(a)   at the end of the period of 70 years from the end of the calendar year in which the work was made, or

(b)   if during that period the work is made available to the public, at the end of the period of 70 years from the end of the calendar year in which it is first so made available, subject as follows.

(4)   Subsection (2) applies if the identity of the author becomes known before the end of the period specified in paragraph (a) or (b) of subsection (3).

(5)   For the purposes of subsection (3) making available to the public includes—
  (a)   in the case of a literary, dramatic or musical work—
     (i)   performance in public, or
     (ii)   being broadcast or included in a cable programme service;
  (b)   in the case of an artistic work—
     (i)   exhibition in public,
     (ii)   a film including the work being shown in public, or
     (iii)   being included in a broadcast or cable programme service;
but in determining generally for the purposes of that subsection whether a work has been made available to the public no account shall be taken of any unauthorised act.

(6)   Where the country of origin of the work is not an EEA state and the author of the work is not a national of an EEA state, the duration of copyright is that to which the work is entitled in the country of origin, provided that does not exceed the period which would apply under subsections (2) to (5).

(7)   If the work is computer-generated the above provisions do not apply and copyright expires at the end of the period of 50 years from the end of the calendar year in which the work was made.

(8)   The provisions of this section are adapted as follows in relation to a work of joint authorship—
  (a)   the reference in subsection (2) to the death of the author shall be construed—
     (i)   if the identity of all the authors is known, as a reference to the death of the last of them to die, and
     (ii)   if the identity of one or more of the authors is known and the identity of one or more others is not, as a reference to the death of the last whose identity is known;
  (b)   the reference in subsection (4) to the identity of the author becoming known shall be construed as a reference to the identity of any of the authors becoming known;
  (c)   the reference in subsection (6) to the author not being a national of an EEA state shall be construed as a reference to none of the authors being a national of an EEA state.

(9)   This section does not apply to Crown copyright or Parliamentary copyright (see sections 163 to 166) or to copyright which subsists by virtue of section 168 (copyright of certain international organisations).

13A   Duration of copyright in sound recordings

(1)   The following provisions have effect with respect to the duration of copyright in a sound recording.

(2)   Copyright expires—
  (a)   at the end of the period of 50 years from the end of the calendar year in which it is made, or
  (b)   if during that period it is released, 50 years from the end of the calendar year in which it is released;
subject as follows.

(3)   For the purposes of subsection (2) a sound recording is "released" when it is first published, played in public, broadcast or included in a cable programe service; but in determining whether a sound recording has been released no account shall be taken of any unauthorised act.

(4)   Where the author of a sound recording is not a national of an EEA state, the duration of copyright is that to which the sound recording is entitled in the country of which the author is a national, provided that does not exceed the period which would apply under subsections (2) and (3).

(5)   If or to the extent that the application of subsection (4) would be at variance with an international obligation to which the United Kingdom became subject prior to 29th October 1993, the duation of copyright shall be as specified in subsections (2) and (3).

13B   Duration of copyright in films

(1)   The following provisions have effect with respect to the duration of copyright in a film.

(2)   Copyright expires at the end of the period of 70 years from the end of the calendar year in which the death occurs of the last to die of the following persons—
   (a)   the principal director,
   (b)   the author of the screenplay,
   (c)   the author of the dialogue, or
   (d)   the composer of music specially created for and used in the film;
subject as follows.

(3)   If the identity of one or more of the persons referred to in subsection (2)(a) to (d) is known and the identity of one or more others is not, the reference in that subsection to the death of the last of them to die shall be construed as a reference to the death of the last whose identity is known.

(4)   If the identity of the persons referred to in subsection (2)(a) to (d) is unknown, copyright expires at—
   (a)   the end of the period of 70 years from the end of the calendar year in which the film was made, or
   (b)   if during that period the film is made available to the public, at the end of the period of 70 years from the end of the calendar year in which it is first so made available.

(5)   Subsections (2) and (3) apply if the identity of any of those persons becomes known before the end of the period specified in paragraph (a) or (b) of subsection (4).

(6)   For the purposes of subsection (4) making available to the public includes—
   (a)   showing in public, or
   (b)   being broadcast or included in a cable programme service;
but in determining generally for the purposes of that subsection whether a film has been made available to the public no account shall be taken of any unauthorised act.

(7)   Where the country of origin is not an EEA state and the author of the film is not a national of an EEA state, the duration of copyright is that to which the work is entitled in the country of origin, provided that does not exceed the period which would apply under subsections (2) to (6).

(8)   In relation to a film of which there are joint authors, the reference in subsection (7) to the author not being a national of an EEA state shall be construed as a reference to none of the authors being a national of an EEA state.

(9)   If in any case there is no person falling within paragraphs (a) to (d) of subsection (2), the above provisions do not apply and copyright expires at the end of the period of 50 years from the end of the calendar year in which the film was made.

(10)   For the purposes of this section the identity of any of the persons referred to in subsection (2)(a) to (d) shall be regarded as unknown if it is not possible for a person to ascertain his identity by reasonable inquiry; but if the identity of any such person is once known it shall not subsequently be regarded as unknown.

14   Duration of copyright in broadcasts and cable programmes

(1)   The following provisions have effect with respect to the duration of copyright in a broadcast or cable programme.

(2)   Copyright in a broadcast or cable programme expires at the end of the period of 50 years from the end of the calendar year in which the broadcast was made or the programme was included in a cable programme service, subject as follows.

(3)   Where the author of the broadcast or cable programme is not a national of an EEA state, the duration of copyright in the broadcast or cable programme is that to which it is entitled in the country of which the author is a national, provided that does not exceed the period which would apply under subsection (2).

(4)   If or to the extent that the application of subsection (3) would be at variance with an international obligation to which the United Kingdom became subject prior to 29th October 1993, the duration of copyright shall be as specified in subsection (2).

(5)   Copyright in a repeat broadcast or cable programme expires at the same time as the copyright in the original broadcast or cable programme; and accordingly no copyright arises in respect of a repeat broadcast or cable programme which is broadcast or included in a cable programme service after the expiry of the copyright in the original broadcast or cable programme.

(6)   A repeat broadcast or cable programme means one which is a repeat either of a broadcast previously made or of a cable programme previously included in a cable programme service.

15   Duration of copyright in typographical arrangement of published editions

Copyright in the typographical arrangement of a published edition expires at the end of the period of 25 years from the end of the calendar year in which the edition was first published.

15A   Meaning of country of origin

(1)   For the purposes of the provisions of this Part relating to the duration of copyright the country of origin of a work shall be determined as follows.

(2)   If the work is first published in a Berne Convention country and is not simultaneously published elsewhere, the country of origin is that country.

(3)   If the work is first published simultaneously in two or more countries only one of which is a Berne Convention country, the country of origin is that country.

(4)   If the work is first published simultaneously in two or more countries of which two or more are Berne Convention countries, then—

(a)   if any of those countries is an EEA state, the country of origin is that country; and

(b)   if none of those countries is an EEA state, the country of origin is the Berne Convention country which grants the shorter or shortest period of copyright protection.

(5)   If the work is unpublished or is first published in a country which is not a Berne Convention country (and is not simultaneously published in a Berne Convention country), the country of origin is—

(a)   if the work is a film and the maker of the film has his headquarters in, or is domiciled or resident in a Berne Convention country, that country;

(b)   if the work is—

(i)   a work of architecture constructed in a Berne Convention country, or

(ii)   an artistic work incorporated in a building or other structure situated in a Berne Convention country,

that country;

(c)   in any other case, the country of which the author of the work is a national.

(6)   In this section—

(a)   a "Berne Convention country" means a country which is a party to any Act of the International Convention for the Protection of Literary and Artistic Works signed at Berne on 9th September 1886; and

(b)   references to simultaneous publication are to publication within 30 days of first publication.

CHAPTER II   RIGHTS OF COPYRIGHT OWNER

The acts restricted by copyright

16   The acts restricted by copyright in a work

(1)   The owner of the copyright in a work has, in accordance with the following provisions of this Chapter, the exclusive right to do the following acts in the United Kingdom—

(a)   to copy the work (see section 17);

(b)   to issue copies of the work to the public (see section 18);

(ba)   to rent or lend the work to the public (see Section 18A);

(c)   to perform, show or play the work in public (see section 19);

(d)   to broadcast the work or include it in a cable programme service (see section 20);

(e)   to make an adaptation of the work or do any of the above in relation to an adaptation (see section 21);

and those acts are referred to in this Part as the "act restricted by the copyright".

(2)   Copyright in a work is infringed by a person who without the licence of the copyright owner does, or authorises another to do, any of the acts restricted by the copyright.

(3)   References in this Part to the doing of an act restricted by the copyright in a work are to the doing of it—

(a)   in relation to the work as a whole or any substantial part of it, and

(b)   either directly or indirectly;

and it is immaterial whether any intervening acts themselves infringe copyright.

(4)   This Chapter has effect subject to—

(a)   the provisions of Chapter III (acts permitted in relation to copyright works), and

(b)   the provisions of Chapter VII (provisions with respect to copyright licensing).

17   Infringement of copyright by copying

(1)   The copying of the work is an act restricted by the copyright in every description of copyright work; and references in this Part to copying and copies shall be construed as follows.

(2)   Copying in relation to a literary, dramatic, musical or artistic work means reproducing the work in any material form.

This includes storing the work in any medium by electronic means.

(3)   In relation to an artistic work copying includes the making of a copy in three dimensions of a two-dimensional work and the making of a copy in two dimensions of a three-dimensional work.

(4)   Copying in relation to a film, television broadcast or cable programme includes making a photograph of the whole or any substantial part of any image forming part of the film, broadcast or cable programme.

(5)   Copying in relation to the typographical arrangement of a published edition means making a facsimile copy of the arrangement.

(6)   Copying in relation to any description of work includes the making of copies which are transient or are incidental to some other use of the work.

18   Infringement by issue of copies to the public

(1)   The issue to the public of copies of the work is an act restricted by the copyright in every description of copyright work.

(2)   References in this Part to the issue to the public of copies of a work are to—

(a)   the act of putting into circulation in the EEA copies not previously put into circulation in the EEA by or with the consent of the copyright owner, or

(b)   the act of putting into circulation outside the EEA copies not previously put into circulation in the EEA or elsewhere.

(3)   References in this Part to the issue to the public of copies of a work do not include—

(a)   any subsequent distribution, sale, hiring or loan of those copies previously put into circulation (but see section 18A: infringement by rental or lending), or

(b)   any subsequent importation of such copies into the United Kingdom or another EEA state,

except so far as paragraph (a) of subsection (2) applies to putting into circulation in the EEA copies previously put into circulation outside the EEA.

(4)   References in this Part to the issue of copies of a work include the issue of the original.

18A   Infringement by rental or lending of work to the public

(1)   The rental or lending of copies of the work to the public is an act restricted by the copyright in—

(a)   a literary, dramatic or musical work,

(b)   an artistic work, other than—

(i)   a work of architecture in the form of a building or a model for a building, or

(ii)   a work of applied art, or

(c)   a film or a sound recording.

(2)   In this Part, subject to the following provisions of this section—

(a)   "rental" means making a copy of the work available for use, on terms that it will or may be returned, for direct or indirect economic or commercial advantage, and

(b)   "lending" means making a copy of the work available for use, on terms that it will or may be returned, otherwise than for direct or indirect economic or commercial advantage, through an establishment which is accessible to the public.

(3)   The expressions "rental" and "lending" do not include—

(a)   making available for the purpose of public performance, playing or showing in public, broadcasting or inclusion in a cable programme service;

(b)   making available for the purpose of exhibition in public; or

(c)   making available for on-the-spot reference use.

(4)   The expression "lending" does not include making available between establishments which are accessible to the public.

(5)   Where lending by an establishment accessible to the public gives rise to a payment the amount of which does not go beyond what is necessary to cover the operating costs of the establishment, there is no direct or indirect economic or commercial advantage for the purposes of this section.

(6)   References in this Part to the rental or lending of copies of a work include the rental or lending of the original.

19   Infringement by performance, showing or playing of work in public

(1)   The performance of the work in public is an act restricted by the copyright in a literary, dramatic or musical work.

(2)   In this Part "performance", in relation to a work—

(a)   includes delivery in the case of lectures, addresses, speeches and sermons, and

(b)   in general, includes any mode of visual or acoustic presentation, including presentation by means of a sound recording, film, broadcast or cable programme of the work.

(3)   The playing or showing of the work in public is an act restricted by the copyright in a sound recording, film, broadcast or cable programme.

(4)   Where copyright in a work is infringed by its being performed, played or shown in public by means of apparatus for receiving visual images or sounds conveyed by electronic means, the person by whom the visual images or sounds are sent, and in the

case of a performance the performers, shall not be regarded as responsible for the infringement.

20 Infringement by broadcasting or inclusion in a cable programme service
The broadcasting of the work or its inclusion in a cable programme service is an act restricted by the copyright in—
  (a)   a literary, dramatic, musical or artistic work,
  (b)   a sound recording or film, or
  (c)   a broadcast or cable programme.

21 Infringement by making adaptation or act done in relation to adaptation
  (1)   The making of an adaptation of the work is an act restricted by the copyright in a literary, dramatic or musical work.
For this purpose an adaptation is made when it is recorded, in writing or otherwise.
  (2)   The doing of any of the acts specified in sections 17 to 20, or subsection (1) above, in relation to an adaptation of the work is also an act restricted by the copyright in a literary, dramatic or musical work.
For this purpose it is immaterial whether the adaptation has been recorded, in writing or otherwise, at the time the act is done.
  (3)   In this Part "adaptation"—
     (a)   in relation to a literary work, other than a computer program or a database, or in relation to a dramatic work, means—
        (i)   a translation of the work;
        (ii)   a version of a dramatic work in which it is converted into a non-dramatic work or, as the case may be, of a non-dramatic work in which it is converted into a dramatic work;
        (iii) a version of the work in which the story or action is conveyed wholly or mainly by means of pictures in a form suitable for reproduction in a book, or in a newspaper, magazine or similar periodical;
     (ab)   in relation to a computer program, means an arrangement or altered version of the program or a translation of it;
     (ac)   in relation to a database, means an arrangement or altered version of the database or a translation of it;
     (b)   in relation to a musical work, means an arrangement or transcription of the work.
  (4)   In relation to a computer program a "translation" includes a version of the program in which it is converted into or out of a computer language or code or into a different computer language or code.
  (5)   No inference shall be drawn from this section as to what does or does not amount to copying a work.

Secondary infringement of copyright

22 Secondary infringement: importing infringing copy
The copyright in a work is infringed by a person who, without the licence of the copyright owner, imports into the United Kingdom, otherwise than for his private and domestic use, an article which is, and which he knows or has reason to believe is, an infringing copy of the work.

23 Secondary infringement: possessing or dealing with infringing copy
The copyright in a work is infringed by a person who, without the licence of the copyright owner—
  (a)   possesses in the course of a business,
  (b)   sells or lets for hire, or offers or exposes for sale or hire,
  (c)   in the course of a business exhibits in public or distributes, or

(d)   distributes otherwise than in the course of a business to such an extent as to affect prejudicially the owner of the copyright,
an article which is, and which he knows or has reason to believe is, an infringing copy of the work.

24   Secondary infringement: providing means for making infringing copies

(1)   Copyright in a work is infringed by a person who, without the licence of the copyright owner—
(a)   makes,
(b)   imports into the United Kingdom,
(c)   possesses in the course of a business, or
(d)   sells or lets for hire, or offers or exposes for sale or hire,
an article specifically designed or adapted for making copies of that work, knowing or having reason to believe that it is to be used to make infringing copies.

(2)   Copyright in a work is infringed by a person who without the licence of the copyright owner transmits the work by means of a telecommunications system (otherwise than by broadcasting or inclusion in a cable programme service), knowing or having reason to believe that infringing copies of the work will be made by means of the reception of the transmission in the United Kingdom or elsewhere.

25   Secondary infringement: permitting use of premises for infringing performance

(1)   Where the copyright in a literary, dramatic or musical work is infringed by a performance at a place of public entertainment, any person who gave permission for that place to be used for the performance is also liable for the infringement unless when he gave permission he believed on reasonable grounds that the performance would not infringe copyright.

(2)   In this section "place of public entertainment" includes premises which are occupied mainly for other purposes but are from time to time made available for hire for the purposes of public entertainment.

26   Secondary infringement: provision of apparatus for infringing performance, &c.

(1)   Where copyright in a work is infringed by a public performance of the work, or by the playing or showing of the work in public, by means of apparatus for—
(a)   playing sound recordings,
(b)   showing films, or
(c)   receiving visual images or sounds conveyed by electronic means,
the following persons are also liable for the infringement.

(2)   A person who supplied the apparatus, or any substantial part of it, is liable for the infringement if when he supplied the apparatus or part—
(a)   he knew or had reason to believe that the apparatus was likely to be so used as to infringe copyright, or
(b)   in the case of apparatus whose normal use involves a public performance, playing or showing, he did not believe on reasonable grounds that it would not be so used as to infringe copyright.

(3)   An occupier of premises who gave permission for the apparatus to be brought onto the premises is liable for the infringement if when he gave permission he knew or had reason to believe that the apparatus was likely to be so used as to infringe copyright.

(4)   A person who supplied a copy of a sound recording or film used to infringe copyright is liable for the infringement if when he supplied it he knew or had reason to believe that what he supplied, or a copy made directly or indirectly from it, was likely to be so used as to infringe copyright.

Infringing copies

27 Meaning of "infringing copy"

(1)   In this Part "infringing copy", in relation to a copyright work, shall be construed in accordance with this section.

(2)   An article is an infringing copy if its making constituted an infringement of the copyright in the work in question.

(3)   An article is also an infringing copy if—

    (a)   it has been or is proposed to be imported into the United Kingdom, and

    (b)   its making in the United Kingdom would have constituted an infringement of the copyright in the work in question, or a breach of an exclusive licence agreement relating to that work.

(4)   Where in any proceedings the question arises whether an article is an infringing copy and it is shown—

    (a)   that the article is a copy of the work, and

    (b)   that copyright subsists in the work or has subsisted at any time,

it shall be presumed until the contrary is proved that the article was made at a time when copyright subsisted in the work.

(5)   Nothing in subsection (3) shall be construed as applying to an article which may lawfully be imported into the United Kingdom by virtue of any enforceable Community right within the meaning of section 2(1) of the European Communities Act 1972.

(6)   In this Part "infringing copy" includes a copy falling to be treated as an infringing copy by virtue of any of the following provisions—

    section 32(5) (copies made for purposes of instruction or examination),

    section 35(3) (recordings made by educational establishments for educational purposes),

    section 36(5) (reprographic copying by educational establishments for purposes of instruction),

    section 37(3)(b) (copies made by librarian or archivist in reliance on false declaration),

    section 56(2) (further copies, adaptations, &c. of work in electronic form retained on transfer of principal copy),

    section 63(2) (copies made for purpose of advertising artistic work for sale),

    section 68(4) (copies made for purpose of broadcast or cable programme), or

    any provision of an order under section 141 (statutory licence for certain reprographic copying by educational establishments).

CHAPTER III   ACTS PERMITTED IN RELATION TO COPYRIGHT WORKS

Introductory

28 Introductory provisions

(1)   The provisions of this Chapter specify acts which may be done in relation to copyright works notwithstanding the subsistence of copyright; they relate only to the question of infringement of copyright and do not affect any other right or obligation restricting the doing of any of the specified acts.

(2)   Where it is provided by this Chapter that an act does not infringe copyright, or may be done without infringing copyright, and no particular description of copyright work is mentioned, the act in question does not infringe the copyright in a work of any description.

(3)   No inference shall be drawn from the description of any act which may by virtue of this Chapter be done without infringing copyright as to the scope of the acts restricted by the copyright in any description of work.

(4)   The provisions of this Chapter are to be construed independently of each other, so that the fact that an act does not fall within one provision does not mean that it is not covered by another provision.

General

29 Research and private study

(1)   Fair dealing with a literary work, other than a database, or a dramatic, musical or artistic work for the purposes of research or private study does not infringe any copyright in the work or, in the case of a published edition, in the typographical arrangement.

(1A)   Fair dealing with a database for the purposes of research or private study does not infringe any copyright in the database provided that the source is indicated.

(2)   Fair dealing with the typographical arrangement of a published edition for the purposes mentioned in subsection (1) does not infringe any copyright in the arrangement.

(3)   Copying by a person other than the researcher or student himself is not fair dealing if—

(a)   in the case of a librarian, or a person acting on behalf of a librarian, he does anything which regulations under section 40 would not permit to be done under section 38 or 39 (articles or parts of published works: restriction on multiple copies of same material), or

(b)   in any other case, the person doing the copying knows or has reason to believe that it will result in copies of substantially the same material being provided to more than one person at substantially the same time and for substantially the same purpose.

(4)   It is not fair dealing—

(a)   to convert a computer program expressed in a low level language into a version expressed in a higher level language, or

(b)   incidentally in the course of so converting the program to copy it,

(these acts being permitted if done in accordance with section 50B (decompilation)).

(5)   The doing of anything in relation to a database for the purposes of research for a commercial purpose is not fair dealing with the database.

30 Criticism, review and news reporting

(1)   Fair dealing with a work for the purpose of criticism or review, of that or another work or of a performance of a work, does not infringe any copyright in the work provided that it is accompanied by a sufficient acknowledgement.

(2)   Fair dealing with a work (other than a photograph) for the purpose of reporting current events does not infringe any copyright in the work provided that (subject to subsection (3)) it is accompanied by a sufficient acknowledgement.

(3)   No acknowledgement is required in connection with the reporting of current events by means of a sound recording, film, broadcast or cable programme.

31 Incidental inclusion of copyright material

(1)   Copyright in a work is not infringed by its incidental inclusion in an artistic work, sound recording, film, broadcast or cable programme.

(2)   Nor is the copyright infringed by the issue to the public of copies, or the playing, showing broadcasting or inclusion in a cable programme service, of anything whose making was, by virtue of subsection (1), not an infringement of the copyright.

(3)   A musical work, words spoken or sung with music, or so much of a sound recording, broadcast or cable programme as includes a musical work or such words, shall not be regarded as incidentally included in another work if it is deliberately included.

Education

32 Things done for purposes of instruction or examination

(1)   Copyright in a literary, dramatic, musical or artistic work is not infringed by its being copied in the course of instruction or of preparation for instruction, provided the copying—

    (a)   is done by a person giving or receiving instruction, and

    (b)   is not by means of a reprographic process.

(2)   Copyright in a sound recording, film, broadcast or cable programme is not infringed by its being copied by making a film or film sound-track in the course of instruction, or of preparation for instruction, in the making of films or film sound-tracks, provided the copying is done by a person giving or receiving instruction.

(3)   Copyright is not infringed by anything done for the purposes of an examination by way of setting the questions, communicating the questions to the candidates or answering the questions.

(4)   Subsection (3) does not extend to the making of a reprographic copy of a musical work for use by an examination candidate in performing the work.

(5)   Where a copy which would otherwise be an infringing copy is made in accordance with this section but is subsequently dealt with, it shall be treated as an infringing copy for the purpose of that dealing, and if that dealing infringes copyright for all subsequent purposes.

For this purpose "dealt with" means sold or let for hire or offered or exposed for sale or hire.

33   Anthologies for educational use

(1)   The inclusion of a short passage from a published literary or dramatic work in a collection which—

    (a)   is intended for use in educational establishments and is so described in its title, and in any advertisements issued by or on behalf of the publisher, and

    (b)   consists mainly of material in which no copyright subsists,

does not infringe the copyright in the work if the work itself is not intended for use in such establishments and the inclusion is accompanied by a sufficient acknowledgement.

(2)   Subsection (1) does not authorise the inclusion of more than two excerpts from copyright works by the same author in collections published by the same publisher over any period of five years.

(3)   In relation to any given passage the reference in subsection (2) to excerpts from works by the same author—

    (a)   shall be taken to include excerpts from works by him in collaboration with another, and

    (b)   if the passage in question is from such a work, shall be taken to include excerpts from works by any of the authors, whether alone or in collaboration with another.

(4)   References in this section to the use of a work in an educational establishment are to any use for the educational purposes of such an establishment.

34   Performing, playing or showing work in course of activities of educational establishment.

(1)   The performance of a literary, dramatic or musical work before an audience consisting of teachers and pupils at an educational establishment and other persons directly connected with the activities of the establishment—

    (a)   by a teacher or pupil in the course of the activities of the establishment, or

    (b)   at the establishment by any person for the purposes of instruction,

is not a public performance for the purposes of infringement of copyright.

(2)   The playing or showing of a sound recording, film, broadcast or cable programme before such an audience at an educational establishment for the purposes of instruction is not a playing or showing of the work in public for the purposes of infringement of copyright.

(3)   A person is not for this purpose directly connected with the activities of the educational establishment simply because he is the parent of a pupil at the establishment.

35   Recording by educational establishments of broadcasts and cable programmes

(1)   A recording of a broadcast or cable programme, or a copy of such a recording, may be made by or on behalf of an educational establishment for the educational purposes of that establishment without thereby infringing the copyright in the broadcast or cable programme, or in any work included in it.

(2)   This section does not apply if or to the extent that there is a licensing scheme certified for the purposes of this section under section 143 providing for the grant of licences.

(3)   Where a copy which would otherwise be an infringing copy is made in accordance with this section but is subsequently dealt with, it shall be treated as an infringing copy for the purposes of that dealing, and if that dealing infringes copyright for all subsequent purposes.

For this purpose "dealt with" means sold or let for hire or offered or exposed for sale or hire.

36   Reprographic copying by educational establishments of passages from published works

(1)   Reprographic copies of passages from published literary, dramatic or musical works may, to the extent permitted by this section, be made by or on behalf of an educational establishment for the purposes of instruction without infringing any copyright in the work, or in the typographical arrangement.

(2)   Not more than one per cent. of any work may be copied by or on behalf of an establishment by virtue of this section in any quarter, that is, in any period 1 January to 31 March, 1 April to 30 June, 1 July to 30 September or 1 October to 31 December.

(3)   Copying is not authorised by this section if, or to the extent that licences are available authorising the copying in question and the person making the copies knew or ought to have been aware of that fact.

(4)   The terms of a licence granted to an educational establishment authorising the reprographic copying for the purposes of instruction of passages from published literary, dramatic or musical works are of no effect so far as they purport to restrict the proportion of a work which may be copied (whether on payment or free of charge) to less than that which would be permitted under this section.

(5)   Where a copy which would otherwise be an infringing copy is made in accordance with this section but is subsequently dealt with, it shall be treated as an infringing copy for the purposes of that dealing, and if that dealing infringes copyright for all subsequent purposes.

For this purpose "dealt with" means sold or let for hire or offered or exposed for sale or hire.

36A   Lending of copies by educational establishments

Copyright in a work is not infringed by the lending of copies of the work by an educational establishment.

Libraries and archives

37   Libraries and archives: introductory

(1)   In sections 38 to 43 (copying by librarians and archivists)—

(a)   references in any provision to a prescribed library or archive are to a library or archive of a description prescribed for the purposes of that provision by regulations made by the Secretary of State; and

(b)   references in any provision to the prescribed conditions are to the conditions so prescribed.

(2)   The regulations may provide that, where a librarian or archivist is required to be satisfied as to any matter before making or supplying a copy of a work—

(a)   he may rely on a signed declaration as to that matter by the person requesting the copy, unless he is aware that it is false in a material particular, and

(b)   in such cases as may be prescribed, he shall not make or supply a copy in the absence of a signed declaration in such form as may be prescribed.

(3)   Where a person requesting a copy makes a declaration which is false in a material particular and is supplied with a copy which would have been an infringing copy if made by him—

(a)   he is liable for infringement of copyright as if he had made the copy himself, and

(b)   the copy shall be treated as an infringing copy.

(4)   The regulations may make different provision for different descriptions of libraries or archives and for different purposes.

(5)   Regulations shall be made by statutory instrument which shall be subject to annulment in pursuance of a resolution of either House of Parliament.

(6)   References in this section, and in sections 38 to 43, to the librarian or archivist include a person acting on his behalf.

38   Copying by librarians: articles in periodicals

(1)   The librarian of a prescribed library may, if the prescribed conditions are complied with, make and supply a copy of an article in a periodical without infringing any copyright in the text, in any illustrations accompanying the text or in the typographical arrangement.

(2)   The prescribed conditions shall include the following—

(a)   that copies are supplied only to persons satisfying the librarian that they require them for purposes of research or private study, and will not use them for any other purpose;

(b)   that no person is furnished with more than one copy of the same article or with copies of more than one article contained in the same issue of a periodical; and

(c)   that persons to whom copies are supplied are required to pay for them a sum not less than the cost (including a contribution to the general expenses of the library) attributable to their production.

39   Copying by librarians: parts of published works

(1)   The librarian of a prescribed library may, if the prescribed conditions are complied with, make and supply from a published edition a copy of part of a literary, dramatic or musical work (other than an article in a periodical) without infringing any copyright in the work, in any illustrations accompanying the work or in the typographical arrangement.

(2)   The prescribed conditions shall include the following—

(a)   that copies are supplied only to persons satisfying the librarian that they require them for purposes of research or private study, and will not use them for any other purpose;

(b)   that no person is furnished with more than one copy of the same material or with a copy of more than a reasonable proportion of any work; and

(c)   that persons to whom copies are supplied are required to pay for them a sum not less than the cost (including a contribution to the general expenses of the library) attributable to their production.

40   Restriction on production of multiple copies of the same material

(1)   Regulations for the purposes of sections 38 and 39 (copying by librarian of article or part of published work) shall contain provision to the effect that a copy shall be supplied only to a person satisfying the librarian that his requirement is not related to any similar requirement of another person.

(2)   The regulations may provide—

(a)   that requirements shall be regarded as similar if the requirements are for copies of substantially the same material at substantially the same time and for substantially the same purpose; and

(b)   that requirements of persons shall be regarded as related if those persons receive instruction to which the material is relevant at the same time and place.

40A   Lending of copies by libraries or archives

(1)   Copyright in a work of any description is not infringed by the lending of a book by a public library if the book is within the public lending right scheme.
For this purpose—

(a)   "the public lending right scheme" means the scheme in force under section 1 of the Public Lending Right Act 1979, and

(b)   a book is within the public lending right scheme if it is a book within the meaning of the provisions of the scheme relating to eligibility, whether or not it is in fact eligible.

(2)   Copyright in a work is not infringed by the lending of copies of the work by a prescribed library or archive (other than a public library) which is not conducted for profit.

41   Copying by librarians: supply of copies to other libraries

(1)   The librarian of a prescribed library may, if the prescribed conditions are complied with, make and supply to another prescribed library a copy of—

(a)   an article in a periodical, or

(b)   the whole or part of a published edition of a literary, dramatic or musical work,
without infringing any copyright in the text of the article or, as the case may be, in the work, in any illustrations accompanying it or in the typographical arrangement.

(2)   Subsection (1)(b) does not apply if at the time the copy is made the librarian making it knows, or could by reasonable inquiry ascertain, the name and address of a person entitled to authorise the making of the copy.

42   Copying by librarians or archivists: replacement copies of works

(1)   The librarian or archivist of a prescribed library or archive may, if the prescribed conditions are complied with, make a copy from any item in the permanent collection of the library or archive—

(a)   in order to preserve or replace that item by placing the copy in its permanent collection in addition to or in place of it, or

(b)   in order to replace in the permanent collection of another prescribed library or archive an item which has been lost, destroyed or damaged,
without infringing the copyright in any literary, dramatic or musical work, in any illustrations accompanying such a work or, in the case of a published edition, in the typographical arrangement.

(2)   The prescribed conditions shall include provision for restricting the making of copies to cases where it is not reasonably practicable to purchase a copy of the item in question to fulfil that purpose.

43   Copying by librarians or archivists: certain unpublished works

(1)   The librarian or archivist of a prescribed library or archive may, if the prescribed conditions are complied with, make and supply a copy of the whole or part of a literary, dramatic or musical work from a document in the library or archive without infringing any copyright in the work or any illustrations accompanying it.

(2)   This section does not apply if—

(a)   the work had been published before the document was deposited in the library or archive, or

(b)   the copyright owner has prohibited copying of the work,
and at the time the copy is made the librarian or archivist making it is, or ought to be,
aware of that fact.
(3)   The prescribed conditions shall include the following—
(a)   that copies are supplied only to persons satisfying the librarian or archivist that
they require them for purposes of research or private study and will not use them for any
other purpose;
(b)   that no person is furnished with more than one copy of the same material; and
(c)   that persons to whom copies are supplied are required to pay for them a sum
not less than the cost (including a contribution to the general expenses of the library or
archive) attributable to their production.

44   Copy of work required to be made as condition of export
If an article of cultural or historical importance or interest cannot lawfully be exported
from the United Kingdom unless a copy of it is made and deposited in an appropriate
library or archive, it is not an infringement of copyright to make that copy.

Public administration

45   Parliamentary and judicial proceedings
(1)   Copyright is not infringed by anything done for the purposes of parliamentary
or judicial proceedings.
(2)   Copyright is not infringed by anything done for the purposes of reporting such
proceedings; but this shall not be construed as authorising the copying of a work which
is itself a published report of the proceedings.

46   Royal Commissions and statutory inquiries
(1)   Copyright is not infringed by anything done for the purposes of the proceedings
of a Royal Commission or statutory inquiry.
(2)   Copyright is not infringed by anything done for the purpose of reporting any
such proceedings held in public; but this shall not be construed as authorising the
copying of a work which is itself a published report of the proceedings.
(3)   Copyright in a work is not infringed by the issue to the public of copies of the
report of a Royal Commission or statutory inquiry containing the work or material from
it.
(4)   In this section—
"Royal Commission" includes a Commission appointed for Northern Ireland by
the Secretary of State in pursuance of the prerogative powers of Her Majesty
delegated to him under section 7(2) of the Northern Ireland Constitution Act
1973; and
"statutory inquiry" means an inquiry held or investigation conducted in pursuance
of a duty imposed or power conferred by or under an enactment.

47   Material open to public inspection or on official register
(1)   Where material is open to public inspection pursuant to a statutory requirement, or is on a statutory register, any copyright in the material as a literary work is not
infringed by the copying of so much of the material as contains factual information of
any description, by or with the authority of the appropriate person, for a purpose which
does not involve the issuing of copies to the public.
(2)   Where material is open to public inspection pursuant to a statutory requirement, copyright is not infringed by the copying or issuing to the public of copies of the
material, by or with the authority of the appropriate person, for the purpose of enabling
the material to be inspected at a more convenient time or place or otherwise facilitating
the exercise of any right for the purpose of which the requirement is imposed.

(3)   Where material which is open to public inspection pursuant to a statutory requirement, or which is on a statutory register, contains information about matters of general scientific, technical, commercial or economic interest, copyright is not infringed by the copying or issuing to the public of copies of the material, by or with the authority of the appropriate person, for the purpose of disseminating that information.

(4)   The Secretary of State may by order provide that subsection (1), (2) or (3) shall, in such cases as may be specified in the order, apply only to copies marked in such manner as may be so specified.

(5)   The Secretary of State may by order provide that subsections (1) to (3) apply, to such extent and with such modifications as may be specified in the order—
  (a)   to material made open to public inspection by—
     (i)   an international organisation specified in the order, or
     (ii)   a person so specified who has functions in the United Kingdom under an international agreement to which the United Kingdom is party, or
  (b)   to a register maintained by an international organisation specified in the order,
as they apply in relation to material open to public inspection pursuant to a statutory requirement or to a statutory register.

(6)   In this section—
  "appropriate person" means the person required to make the material open to public inspection or, as the case may be, the person maintaining the register;
  "statutory register" means a register maintained in pursuance of a statutory requirement; and
  "statutory requirement" means a requirement imposed by provision made by or under an enactment.

(7)   An order under this section shall be made by statutory instrument which shall be subject to annulment in pursuance of a resolution of either House of Parliament.

48   Material communicated to the Crown in the course of public business

(1)   This section applies where a literary, dramatic, musical or artistic work has in the course of public business been communicated to the Crown for any purpose, by or with the licence of the copyright owner and a document or other material thing recording or embodying the work is owned by or in the custody or control of the Crown.

(2)   The Crown may, for the purpose for which the work was communicated to it, or any related purpose which could reasonably have been anticipated by the copyright owner, copy the work and issue copies of the work to the public without infringing any copyright in the work.

(3)   The Crown may not copy a work, or issue copies of a work to the public, by virtue of this section if the work has previously been published otherwise than by virtue of this section.

(4)   In subsection (1) "public business" includes any activity carried on by the Crown.

(5)   This section has effect subject to any agreement to the contrary between the Crown and the copyright owner.

(6)   In this section "the Crown" includes a health service body, as defined in section 60(7) of the National Health Service and Community Care Act 1990, and a National Health Service trust established under Part I of that Act or the National Health Service (Scotland) Act 1978 and also includes a health and social services body, as defined in Article 7(6) of the Health and Personal Social Services (Northern Ireland) Order 1991, and a Health and Social Services trust established under that Order; and the reference in subsection (1) above to public business shall be construed accordingly.

49   Public records

Material which is comprised in public records within the meaning of the Public Records Act 1958, the Public Records (Scotland) Act 1937 or the Public Records Act (Northern

Ireland) 1923 which are open to public inspection in pursuance of that Act, may be copied, and a copy may be supplied to any person, by or with the authority of any officer appointed under that Act, without infringement of copyright.

50 Acts done under statutory authority

(1)   Where the doing of a particular act is specifically authorised by an Act of Parliament, whenever passed, then, unless the Act provides otherwise, the doing of that act does not infringe copyright.

(2)   Subsection (1) applies in relation to an enactment contained in Northern Ireland legislation as it applies in relation to an Act of Parliament.

(3)   Nothing in this section shall be construed as excluding any defence of statutory authority otherwise available under or by virtue of any enactment.

Computer programs: lawful users

50A Back up copies

(1)   It is not an infringement of copyright for a lawful user of a copy of a computer program to make any back up copy of it which it is necessary for him to have for the purposes of his lawful use.

(2)   For the purposes of this section and sections 50B and 50C a person is a lawful user of a computer program if (whether under a licence to do any acts restricted by the copyright in the program or otherwise), he has a right to use the program.

(3)   Where an act is permitted under this section, it is irrelevant whether or not there exists any term or condition in an agreement which purports to prohibit or restrict the act (such terms being, by virtue of section 296A, void).

50B Decompilation

(1)   It is not an infringement of copyright for a lawful user of a copy of a computer program expressed in a low level language—

(a)   to convert it into a version expressed in a higher level language, or

(b)   incidentally in the course of so converting the program, to copy it,

(that is, to "decompile" it), provided that the conditions in subsection (2) are met.

(2)   The conditions are that—

(a)   it is necessary to decompile the program to obtain the information necessary to create an independent program which can be operated with the program decompiled or with another program ("the permitted objective"); and

(b)   the information so obtained is not used for any purpose other than the permitted objective.

(3)   In particular, the conditions in subsection (2) are not met if the lawful user—

(a)   has readily available to him the information necessary to achieve the permitted objective;

(b)   does not confine the decompiling to such acts as are necessary to achieve the permitted objective;

(c)   supplies the information obtained by the decompiling to any person to whom it is not necessary to supply it in order to achieve the permitted objective; or

(d)   uses the information to create a program which is substantially similar in its expression to the program decompiled or to do any act restricted by copyright.

(4)   Where an act is permitted under the section, it is irrelevant whether or not there exists any term or condition in an agreement which purports to prohibit or restrict the act (such terms being, by virtue of section 296A, void).

50C Other acts permitted to lawful users

(1)   It is not an infringement of copyright for a lawful user of a copy of a computer program to copy or adapt it, provided that the copying or adapting—

(a)   is necessary for his lawful use; and

(b)   is not prohibited under any term or condition of an agreement regulating the circumstances in which his use is lawful.

(2)   It may, in particular, be necessary for the lawful use of a computer program to copy it or adapt it for the purpose of correcting errors in it.

(3)   This section does not apply to any copying or adapting permitted under section 50A or 50B.

50D   Acts permitted in relation to databases

(1)   It is not an infringement of copyright in database for a person who has a right to use the database or any part of the database, (whether under a licence to do any of the acts restricted by the copyright in the database or otherwise) to do, in the exercise of that right, anything which is necessary for the purposes of access to and use of the contents of the database or of that part of the database.

(2)   Where an act which would otherwise infringe copyright in a database is permitted under this section, it is irrelevant whether or not there exists any term or condition in any agreement which purports to prohibit or restrict the act (such terms being, by virtue of section 296B, void).

Designs

51   Design documents and models

(1)   It is not an infringement of any copyright in a design document or model recording or embodying a design for anything other than an artistic work or a typeface to make an article to the design or to copy an article made to the design.

(2)   Nor is it an infringement of the copyright to issue to the public, or include in a film, broadcast or cable programme service, anything the making of which was, by virtue of subsection (1), not an infringement of that copyright.

(3)   In this section—

"design" means the design of any aspect of the shape or configuration (whether internal or external) of the whole or part of an article, other than surface decoration; and

"design document" means any record of a design, whether in the form of a drawing, a written description, a photograph, data stored in a computer or otherwise.

52   Effect of exploitation of design derived from artistic work

(1)   This section applies where an artistic work has been exploited, by or with the licence of the copyright owner, by—

(a)   making by an industrial process articles falling to be treated for the purposes of this Part as copies of the work, and

(b)   marketing such articles, in the United Kingdom or elsewhere.

(2)   After the end of the period of 25 years from the end of the calendar year in which such articles are first marketed, the work may be copied by making articles of any description, or doing anything for the purpose of making articles of any description, and anything may be done in relation to articles so made, without infringing copyright in the work.

(3)   Where only part of an artistic work is exploited as mentioned in subsection (1), subsection (2) applies only in relation to that part.

(4)   The Secretary of State may by order make provision—

(a)   as to the circumstances in which an article, or any description of article, is to be regarded for the purposes of this section as made by an industrial process;

(b)   excluding from the operation of this section such articles of a primarily literary or artistic character as he thinks fit.

(5)   An order shall be made by statutory instrument which shall be subject to annulment in pursuance of a resolution of either House of Parliament.

(6)   In this section—

(a)   references to articles do not include films; and

(b)   references to the marketing of an article are to its being sold or let for hire or offered or exposed for sale or hire.

53   Things done in reliance on registration of design

(1)   The copyright in an artistic work is not infringed by anything done—

(a)   in pursuance of an assignment or licence made or granted by a person registered under the Registered Designs Act 1949 as the proprietor of a corresponding design, and

(b)   in good faith in reliance on the registration and without notice of any proceedings for the cancellation of the registration or for rectifying the relevant entry into the register of designs;

and this is so notwithstanding that the person registered as the proprietor was not the proprietor of the design for the purposes of the 1949 Act.

(2)   In subsection (1) a "corresponding design", in relation to an artistic work, means a design within the meaning of the 1949 Act which if applied to an article would produce something which would be treated for the purposes of this Part as a copy of the artistic work.

Typefaces

54   Use of typeface in ordinary course of printing

(1)   It is not an infringement of copyright in an artistic work consisting of the design of a typeface—

(a)   to use the typeface in the ordinary course of typing, composing text, typesetting or printing.

(b)   to possess an article for the purpose of such use, or

(c)   to do anything in relation to material produced by such use;

and this is so notwithstanding that an article is used which is an infringing copy of the work.

(2)   However, the following provisions of this Part apply in relation to persons making, importing or dealing with articles specifically designed or adapted for producing material in a particular typeface, or possessing such articles for the purpose of dealing with them, as if the production of material as mentioned in subsection (1) did infringe copyright in the artistic work consisting of the design of the typeface—

section 24 (secondary infringement: making, importing, possessing or dealing with article for making infringing copy),

sections 99 and 100 (order for delivery up and right of seizure),

section 107(2) (offence of making or possessing such an article), and

section 108 (order for delivery up in criminal proceedings).

(3)   The references in subsection (2) to "dealing with" an article are to selling, letting for hire, or offering or exposing for sale or hire, exhibiting in public, or distributing.

55   Articles for producing material in particular typeface

(1)   This section applies to the copyright in an artistic work consisting of the design of a typeface where articles specifically designed or adapted for producing material in that typeface have been marketed by or with the licence of the copyright owner.

(2)   After the period of 25 years from the end of the calendar year in which the first such articles are marketed, the work may be copied by making further such articles, or doing anything for the purpose of making such articles, and anything may be done in relation to articles so made, without infringing copyright in the work.

(3)   In subsection (1) "marketed" means sold, let for hire or offered or exposed for sale or hire, in the United Kingdom or elsewhere.

Works in electronic form

56 Transfers of copies of works in electronic form

(1) This section applies where a copy of a work in electronic form has been purchased on terms which, expressly or impliedly or by virtue of any rule of law, allow the purchaser to copy the work, or to adapt it or make copies of an adaptation, in connection with his use of it.

(2) If there are no express terms—

(a) prohibiting the transfer of the copy by the purchaser, imposing obligations which continue after a transfer, prohibiting the assignment of any licence or terminating any licence on a transfer, or

(b) providing for the terms on which a transferee may do the things which the purchaser was permitted to do,

anything which the purchaser was allowed to do may also be done without infringement of copyright by a transferee; but any copy, adaptation or copy of an adaptation made by the purchaser which is not also transferred shall be treated as an infringing copy for all purposes after the transfer.

(3) The same applies where the original purchased copy is no longer usable and what is transferred is a further copy used in its place.

(4) The above provisions also apply on a subsequent transfer, with the substitution for references in subsection (2) to the purchaser of references to the subsequent transferor.

Miscellaneous: literary, dramatic, musical and artistic works

57 Anonymous or pseudonymous works: acts permitted on assumptions as to expiry of copyright or death of author.

(1) Copyright in a literary, dramatic, musical or artistic work is not infringed by an act done at a time when, or in pursuance of arrangements made at a time when—

(a) it is not possible by reasonable inquiry to ascertain the identity of the author, and

(b) it is reasonable to assume—

(i) that copyright has expired, or

(ii) that the author died 70 years or more before the beginning of the calendar year in which the act is done or the arrangements are made.

(2) Subsection (1)(b)(ii) does not apply in relation to—

(a) a work in which Crown copyright subsists, or

(b) a work in which copyright originally vested in an international organisation by virtue of section 168 and in respect of which an Order under that section specifies a copyright period longer than 70 years.

(3) In relation to a work of joint authorship—

(a) the reference in subsection (1) to its being possible to ascertain the identity of the author shall be construed as a reference to its being possible to ascertain the identity of any of the authors, and

(b) the reference in subsection (1)(b)(ii) to the author having died shall be construed as a reference to all the authors having died.

58 Use of notes or recordings of spoken words in certain cases

(1) Where a record of spoken words is made, in writing or otherwise, for the purpose—

(a) of reporting current events, or

(b) of broadcasting or including in a cable programme service the whole or part of the work,

it is not an infringement of any copyright in the words as a literary work to use the record or material taken from it (or to copy the record, or any such material, and use the copy) for that purpose, provided the following conditions are met.

(2)   The conditions are that—

(a)   the record is a direct record of the spoken words and is not taken from a previous record or from a broadcast or cable programme;

(b)   the making of the record was not prohibited by the speaker and, where copyright already subsisted in the work, did not infringe copyright;

(c)   the use made of the record or material taken from it is not of a kind prohibited by or on behalf of the speaker or copyright owner before the record was made; and

(d)   the use is by or with the authority of a person who is lawfully in possession of the record.

59   Public reading or recitation

(1)   The reading or recitation in public by one person of a reasonable extract from a published literary or dramatic work does not infringe any copyright in the work if it is accompanied by a sufficient acknowledgement.

(2)   Copyright in a work is not infringed by the making of a sound recording, or the broadcasting or inclusion in a cable programme service, of a reading or recitation which by virtue of subsection (1) does not infringe copyright in the work, provided that the recording, broadcast or cable programme consists mainly of material in relation to which it is not necessary to rely on that subsection.

60   Abstracts of scientific or technical articles

(1)   Where an article on a scientific or technical subject is published in a periodical accompanied by an abstract indicating the contents of the article, it is not an infringement of copyright in the abstract, or in the article, to copy the abstract or issue copies of it to the public.

(2)   This section does not apply if or to the extent that there is a licensing scheme certified for the purposes of this section under section 143 providing for the grant of licences.

61   Recordings of folksongs

(1)   A sound recording of a performance of a song may be made for the purpose of including it in an archive maintained by a designated body without infringing any copyright in the words as a literary work or in the accompanying musical work, provided the conditions in subsection (2) below are met.

(2)   The conditions are that—

(a)   the words are unpublished and of unknown authorship at the time the recording is made,

(b)   the making of the recording does not infringe any other copyright, and

(c)   its making is not prohibited by any performer.

(3)   Copies of a sound recording made in reliance on subsection (1) and included in an archive maintained by a designated body may, if the prescribed conditions are met, be made and supplied by the archivist without infringing copyright in the recording or the works included in it.

(4)   The prescribed conditions shall include the following—

(a)   that copies are only supplied to persons satisfying the archivist that they require them for purposes of research or private study and will not use them for any other purpose, and

(b)   that no person is furnished with more than one copy of the same recording.

(5)   In this section—

(a)   "designated" means designated for the purposes of this section by order of the Secretary of State, who shall not designate a body unless satisfied that it is not established or conducted for profit,

(b)   "prescribed" means prescribed for the purposes of this section by order of the Secretary of State, and

(c) references to the archivist include a person acting on his behalf.

(6) An order under this section shall be made by statutory instrument which shall be subject to annulment in pursuance of a resolution of either House of Parliament.

62 Representation of certain artistic works on public display

(1) This section applies to—

(a) buildings, and

(b) sculptures, models for buildings and works of artistic craftsmanship, if permanently situated in a public place or in premises open to the public.

(2) The copyright in such a work is not infringed by—

(a) making a graphic work representing it,

(b) making a photograph or film of it, or

(c) broadcasting or including in a cable programme service a visual image of it.

(3) Nor is the copyright infringed by the issue to the public of copies, or the broadcasting or inclusion in a cable programme service, of anything whose making was, by virtue of this section, not an infringement of the copyright.

63 Advertisement of sale of artistic work

(1) It is not an infringement of copyright in an artistic work to copy it, or to issue copies to the public, for the purpose of advertising the sale of the work.

(2) Where a copy which would otherwise be an infringing copy is made in accordance with this section but is subsequently dealt with for any other purpose, it shall be treated as an infringing copy for the purposes of that dealing, and if that dealing infringes copyright for all subsequent purposes.

For this purpose "dealt with" means sold or let for hire, offered or exposed for sale or hire, exhibited in public or distributed.

64 Making of subsequent works by same artist

Where the author of an artistic work is not the copyright owner, he does not infringe the copyright by copying the work in making another artistic work, provided he does not repeat or imitate the main design of the earlier work.

65 Reconstruction of buildings

Anything done for the purposes of reconstructing a building does not infringe any copyright—

(a) in the building, or

(b) in any drawings or plans in accordance with which the building was, by or with the licence of the copyright owner, constructed.

Miscellaneous: lending of works and playing of sound recordings

66 Lending to public of copies of certain works

(1) The Secretary of State may by order provide that in such cases as may be specified in the order the lending to the public of copies of literary, dramatic, musical or artistic works, sound recordings or films shall be treated as licensed by the copyright owner subject only to the payment of such reasonable royalty or other payment as may be agreed or determined in default of agreement by the Copyright Tribunal.

(2) No such order shall apply if, or to the extent that, there is a licensing scheme certified for the purposes of this section under section 143 providing for the grant of licences.

(3) An order may make different provision for different cases and may specify cases by reference to any factor relating to the work, the copies lent, the lender or the circumstances of the lending.

(4) An order shall be made by statutory instrument; and no order shall be made unless a draft of it has been laid before and approved by a resolution of each House of Parliament.

(5)   Nothing in this section affects any liability under section 23 (secondary infringement: possessing or dealing with infringing copy) in respect of the lending of infringing copies.

Miscellaneous: films and sound recordings

66A   Films: acts permitted on assumptions as to expiry of copyright, &c.
(1)   Copyright in a film is not infringed by an act done at a time when, or in pursuance of arrangements made at a time when—
(a)   it is not possible by reasonable inquiry to ascertain the identity of any of the persons referred to in section 13B(2)(a) to (d) (persons by reference to whose life the copyright period is ascertained), and
(b)   it is reasonable to assume—
(i)   that copyright has expired, or
(ii)   that the last to die of those persons died 70 years or more before the beginning of the calendar year in which the act is done or the arrangements are made.
(2)   Subsection (1)(b)(ii) does not apply in relation to—
(a)   a film in which Crown copyright subsists, or
(b)   a film in which copyright originally vested in an international organisation by virtue of section 168 and in respect of which an Order under that section specifies a copyright period longer than 70 years.

67   Playing of sound recordings for purposes of club, society, &c.
(1)   It is not an infringement of the copyright in a sound recording to play it as part of the activities of, or for the benefit of, a club, society or other organisation if the following conditions are met.
(2)   The conditions are—
(a)   that the organisation is not established or conducted for profit and its main objects are charitable or are otherwise concerned with the advancement of religion, education or social welfare, and
(b)   that the proceeds of any charge for admission to the place where the recording is to be heard are applied solely for the purposes of the organisation.

Miscellaneous: broadcasts and cable programmes

68   Incidental recording for purposes of broadcast or cable programme
(1)   This section applies where by virtue of a licence or assignment of copyright a person is authorised to broadcast or include in a cable programme service—
(a)   a literary, dramatic or musical work, or an adaptation of such a work,
(b)   an artistic work, or
(c)   a sound recording or film.
(2)   He shall by virtue of this section be treated as licensed by the owner of the copyright in the work to do or authorise any of the following for the purposes of the broadcast or cable programme—
(a)   in the case of a literary, dramatic or musical work, or an adaptation of such a work, to make a sound recording or film of the work or adaptation;
(b)   in the case of an artistic work, to take a photograph or make a film of the work;
(c)   in the case of a sound recording or film, to make a copy of it.
(3)   That licence is subject to the condition that the recording, film, photograph or copy in question—
(a)   shall not be used for any other purpose, and
(b)   shall be destroyed within 28 days of being first used for broadcasting the work or, as the case may be, including it in a cable programme service.
(4)   A recording, film, photograph or copy made in accordance with this section shall be treated as an infringing copy—

(a)   for the purposes of any use in breach of the condition mentioned in subsection (3)(a), and

(b)   for all purposes after that conditon or the condition mentioned in subsection (3)(b) is broken.

69   Recording for purposes of supervision and control of broadcasts and cable programmes

(1)   Copyright is not infringed by the making or use by the British Broadcasting Corporation, for the purpose of maintaining supervision and control over programmes broadcast by them, of recordings of those programmes.

(2)   Copyright is not infringed by anything done in pursuance of—

(a)   section 11(1), 95(1) or 167(1) of the Broadcasting Act 1990 or section 115(4) or (6), 116(5) or 117 of the Broadcasting Act 1996;

(b)   a condition which, by virtue of section 11(2) or 95(2) of the Broadcasting Act 1990, is included in a licence granted under Part I or III of that Act or Part I or II of the Broadcasting Act 1996; or

(c)   a direction given under section 109(2) of the Broadcasting Act 1990 (power of Radio Authority to require production of recordings etc.).

(3)   Copyright is not infringed by—

(a)   the use by the Independent Television Commission or the Radio Authority, in connection with the performance of any of their functions under the Broadcasting Act 1990 or the Broadcasting Act 1996, of any recording, script or transcript which is provided to them under or by virtue of any provision of those Acts; or

(b)   the use by the Broadcasting Standards Commission, in connection with any complaint made to them under the Broadcasting Act 1996, of any recording or transcript requested or required to be provided to them, and so provided, under section 115(4) or (6) or 116(5) of that Act.

70   Recording for purposes of time-shifting

The making for private and domestic use of a recording of a broadcast or cable programme solely for the purpose of enabling it to be viewed or listened to at a more convenient time does not infringe any copyright in the broadcast or cable programme or in any work included in it.

71   Photographs of television broadcasts or cable programmes

The making for private and domestic use of a photograph of the whole or any part of an image forming part of a television broadcast or cable programme, or a copy of such a photograph, does not infringe any copyright in the broadcast or cable programme or in any film included in it.

72   Free public showing or playing of broadcast or cable programme

(1)   The showing or playing in public of a broadcast or cable programme to an audience who have not paid for admission to the place where the broadcast or programme is to be seen or heard does not infringe any copyright in—

(a)   the broadcast or cable programme, or

(b)   any sound recording or film included in it.

(2)   The audience shall be treated as having paid for admission to a place—

(a)   if they have paid for admission to a place of which that place forms part; or

(b)   if goods or services are supplied at that place (or a place of which it forms part)—

(i)   at prices which are substantially attributable to the facilities afforded for seeing or hearing the broadcast or programme, or

(ii)   at prices exceeding those usually charged there and which are partly attributable to those facilities.

(3)   The following shall not be regarded as having paid for admission to a place—

(a)   persons admitted as residents or inmates of the place;

(b)   persons admitted as members of a club or society where the payment is only for membership of the club or society and the provision of facilities for seeing or hearing broadcasts or programmes is only incidental to the main purposes of the club or society.

(4)   Where the making of the broadcast or inclusion of the programme in a cable programme service was an infringement of the copyright in a sound recording or film, the fact that it was heard or seen in public by the reception of the broadcast or programme shall be taken into account in assessing the damages for that infringement.

73   Reception and re-transmission of broadcast in cable programme service

(1)   This section applies where a broadcast made from a place in the United Kingdom is, by reception and immediate re-transmission, included in a cable programme service.

(2)   The copyright in the broadcast is not infringed—

(a)   if the inclusion is in pursuance of a relevant requirement, or

(b)   if and to the extent that the broadcast is made for reception in the area in which the cable programme service is provided and forms part of a qualifying service.

(3)   The copyright in any work included in the broadcast is not infringed if and to the extent that the broadcast is made for reception in the area in which the cable programme service is provided; but where the making of the broadcast was an infringement of the copyright in the work, the fact that the broadcast was re-transmitted as a programme in a cable programme service shall be taken into account in assessing the damages for that infringement.

(4)   Where—

(a)   the inclusion is in pursuance of a relevant requirement, but

(b)   to any extent, the area in which the cable programme service is provided ("the cable area") falls outside the area for reception in which the broadcast is made ("the broadcast area"),

the inclusion in the cable programme service (to the extent that it is provided for so much of the cable area as falls outside the broadcast area) of any work included in the broadcast shall, subject to subsection (5), be treated as licensed by the owner of the copyright in the work, subject only to the payment to him by the person making the broadcast of such reasonable royalty or other payment in respect of the inclusion of the broadcast in the cable programme service as may be agreed or determined in default of agreement by the Copyright Tribunal.

(5)   Subsection (4) does not apply if, or to the extent that, the inclusion of the work in the cable programme service is (apart from that subsection) licensed by the owner of the copyright in the work.

(6)   In this section "qualifying service" means, subject to subsection (8), any of the following services—

(a)   a regional or national Channel 3 service,

(b)   Channel 4, Channel 5 and S4C,

(c)   the teletext service referred to in section 49(2) of the Broadcasting Act 1990,

(d)   the service referred to in section 57(1A)(a) of that Act (power of S4C to provide digital service), and

(e)   the television broadcasting services and teletext service of the British Broadcasting Corporation;

and expressions used in this subsection have the same meaning as in Part I of the Broadcasting Act 1990.

(7)   In this section "relevant requirement" means a requirement imposed under—

(a)   section 78A of the Broadcasting Act 1990 (inclusion of certain services in local delivery services provided by digital means), or

(b)   paragraph 4 of Part III of Schedule 12 to that Act (inclusion of certain services in diffusion services originally licensed under the Cable and Broadcasting Act 1984).

(8)   The Secretary of State may by order amend subsection (6) so as to add any service to, or remove any service from, the definition of "qualifying service".

(9)   The Secretary of State may also by order—

(a)   provide that in specified cases subsection (3) is to apply in relation to broadcasts of a specified description which are not made as mentioned in that subsection, or

(b)   exclude the application of that subsection in relation to broadcasts of a specified description made as mentioned in that subsection.

(10)   Where the Secretary of State exercises the power conferred by subsection (9)(b) in relation to broadcasts of any description, the order may also provide for subsection (4) to apply, subject to such modifications as may be specified in the order, in relation to broadcasts of that description.

(11)   An order under this section may contain such transitional provision as appears to the Secretary of State to be appropriate.

(12)   An order under this section shall be made by statutory instrument which shall be subject to annulment in pursuance of a resolution of either House of Parliament.

73A   Royalty or other sum payable in pursuance of section 73(4)

(1)   An application to settle the royalty or other sum payable in pursuance of subsection (4) of section 73 (reception and re-transmission of broadcast in cable programme service) may be made to the Copyright Tribunal by the copyright owner or the person making the broadcast.

(2)   The Tribunal shall consider the matter and make such order as it may determine to be reasonable in the circumstances.

(3)   Either party may subsequently apply to the Tribunal to vary the order, and the Tribunal shall consider the matter and make such order confirming or varying the original order as it may determine to be reasonable in the circumstances.

(4)   An application under subsection (3) shall not, except with the special leave of the Tribunal, be made within twelve months from the date of the original order or of the order on a previous application under that subsection.

(5)   An order under subsection (3) has effect from the date on which it is made or such later date as may be specified by the Tribunal.

74   Provision of sub-titled copies of broadcast or cable programme

(1)   A designated body may, for the purpose of providing people who are deaf or hard of hearing, or physically or mentally handicapped in other ways, with copies which are sub-titled or otherwise modified for their special needs, make copies of television broadcasts or cable programmes and issue copies to the public, without infringing any copyright in the broadcasts or cable programmes or works included in them.

(2)   A "designated body" means a body designated for the purposes of this section by order of the Secretary of State, who shall not designate a body unless he is satisfied that it is not established or conducted for profit.

(3)   An order under this section shall be made by statutory instrument which shall be subject to annulment in pursuance of a resolution of either House of Parliament.

(4)   This section does not apply if, or to the extent that, there is a licensing scheme certified for the purposes of this section under section 143 providing for the grant of licences.

75   Recording for archival purposes

(1)   A recording of a broadcast or cable programme of a designated class, or a copy of such a recording, may be made for the purpose of being placed in an archive maintained by a designated body without thereby infringing any copyright in the broadcast or cable programme or in any work included in it.

(2)   In subsection (1) "designated" means designated for the purposes of this section by order of the Secretary of State, who shall not designate a body unless he is satisfied that it is not established or conducted for profit.

(3)   An order under this section shall be made by statutory instrument which shall be subject to annulment in pursuance of a resolution of either House of Parliament.

Adaptations

76   Adaptations

An act which by virtue of this Chapter may be done without infringing copyright in a literary, dramatic or musical work does not, where that work is an adaptation, infringe any copyright in the work from which the adaptation was made.

CHAPTER IV   MORAL RIGHTS

Right to be identified as author or director

77   Right to be identified as author or director

(1)   The author of a copyright literary, dramatic, musical or artistic work, and the director of a copyright film, has the right to be identified as the author or director of the work in the circumstances mentioned in this section; but the right is not infringed unless it has been asserted in accordance with section 78.

(2)   The author of a literary work (other than words intended to be sung or spoken with music) or a dramatic work has the right to be identified whenever—

(a)   the work is published commercially, performed in public, broadcast or included in a cable programme service; or

(b)   copies of a film or sound recording including the work are issued to the public;

and that right includes the right to be identified whenever any of those events occur in relation to an adaptation of the work as the author of the work from which the adaptation was made.

(3)   The author of a musical work, or a literary work consisting of words intended to be sung or spoken with music, has the right to be identified whenever—

(a)   the work is published commercially;

(b)   copies of a sound recording of the work are issued to the public; or

(c)   a film of which the sound-track includes the work is shown in public or copies of such a film are issued to the public;

and that right includes the right to be identified whenever any of those events occur in relation to an adaptation of the work as the author of the work from which the adaptation was made.

(4)   The author of an artistic work has the right to be identified whenever—

(a)   the work is published commercially or exhibited in public, or a visual image of it is broadcast or included in a cable programme service;

(b)   a film including a visual image of the work is shown in public or copies of such a film are issued to the public; or

(c)   in the case of a work of architecture in the form of a building or a model for a building, a sculpture or a work of artistic craftsmanship, copies of a graphic work representing it, or of a photograph of it, are issued to the public.

(5)   The author of a work of architecture in the form of a building also has the right to be identified on the building as constructed or, where more than one building is constructed to the design, on the first to be constructed.

(6)   The director of a film has the right to be identified whenever the film is shown in public, broadcast or included in a cable programme service or copies of the film are issued to the public.

(7)   The right of the author or director under this section is—

(a)   in the case of commercial publication or the issue to the public of copies of a film or sound recording, to be identified in or on each copy or, if that is not appropriate, in some other manner likely to bring his identity to the notice of a person acquiring a copy,

(b)   in the case of identification on a building, to be identified by appropriate means visible to persons entering or approaching the building, and

(c)   in any other case, to be identified in a manner likely to bring his identity to the attention of a person seeing or hearing the performance, exhibition, showing, broadcast or cable programme in question;

and the identification must in each case be clear and reasonably prominent.

(8)   If the author or director in asserting his right to be identified specifies a pseudonym, initials or some other particular form of identification, that form shall be used; otherwise any reasonable form of identification may be used.

(9)   This secton has effect subject to section 79 (exceptions to right).

78   Requirement that right be asserted

(1)   A person does not infringe the right conferred by section 77 (right to be identified as author or director) by doing any of the acts mentioned in that section unless the right has been asserted in accordance with the following provisions so as to bind him in relation to that act.

(2)   The right may be asserted generally, or in relation to any specified act or description of acts—

(a)   on an assignment of copyright in the work, by including in the instrument effecting the assignment a statement that the author or director asserts in relation to that work his right to be identified, or

(b)   by instrument in writing signed by the author or director.

(3)   The right may also be asserted in relation to the public exhibition of an artistic work—

(a)   by securing that when the author or other first owner of copyright parts with possession of the original, or of a copy made by him or under his direction or control, the author is identified on the original or copy, or on a frame, mount or other thing to which it is attached, or

(b)   by including in a licence by which the author or other first owner of copyright authorises the making of copies of the work a statement signed by or on behalf of the person granting the licence that the author asserts his right to be identified in the event of the public exhibition of a copy made in pursuance of the licence.

(4)   The persons bound by an assertion of the right under subsection (2) or (3) are—

(a)   in the case of an assertion under subsection (2)(a), the assignee and anyone claiming through him, whether or not he has notice of the assertion;

(b)   in the case of an assertion under subsection (2)(b), anyone to whose notice the assertion is brought;

(c)   in the case of an assertion under subsection (3)(a), anyone into whose hands that original or copy comes, whether or not the identification is still present or visible;

(d)   in the case of an assertion under subsection (3)(b), the licensee and anyone into whose hands a copy made in pursuance of the licence comes, whether or not he has notice of the assertion.

(5)   In an action for infringement of the right the court shall, in considering remedies, take into account any delay in asserting the right.

79   Exceptions to right

(1)   The right conferred by section 77 (right to be identified as author or director) is subject to the following exceptions.

(2)   The right does not apply in relation to the following descriptions of work—

(a)   a computer program;

(b)   the design of a typeface;

(c)   any computer-generated work.

(3)   The right does not apply to anything done by or with the authority of the copyright owner where copyright in the work originally vested—

(a)   in the author's employer by virtue of section 11(2) (works produced in course of employment), or

(b)   in the director's employer by virtue of section 9(2)(a) (person to be treated as author of film).

(4)   The right is not infringed by an act which by virtue of any of the following provisions would not infringe copyright in the work—

(a)   section 30 (fair dealing for certain purposes), so far as it relates to the reporting of current events by means of a sound recording, film, broadcast or cable programme;

(b)   section 31 (incidental inclusion of work in an artistic work, sound recording, film, broadcast or cable programme);

(c)   section 32(3) (examination questions);

(d)   section 45 (parliamentary and judicial proceedings);

(e)   section 46(1) or (2) (Royal Commissions and statutory inquiries);

(f)   section 51 (use of design documents and models);

(g)   section 52 (effect of exploitation of design derived from artistic work);

(h)   section 57 or 66A (acts permitted on assumptions as to expiry of copyright, etc.).

(5)   The right does not apply in relation to any work made for the purpose of reporting current events.

(6)   The right does not apply in relation to the publication in—

(a)   a newspaper, magazine or similar periodical, or

(b)   an encyclopaedia, dictionary, yearbook or other collective work of reference, of a literary, dramatic, musical or artistic work made for the purposes of such publication or made available with the consent of the author for the purposes of such publication.

(7)   The right does not apply in relation to—

(a)   a work in which Crown copyright or Parliamentary copyright subsists, or

(b)   a work in which copyright originally vested in an international organisation by virtue of section 168,

unless the author or director has previously been identified as such in or on published copies of the work.

Right to object to derogatory treatment of work

80   Right to object to derogatory treatment of work

(1)   The author of a copyright literary, dramatic, musical or artistic work, and the director of a copyright film, has the right in the circumstances mentioned in this section not to have his work subjected to derogatory treatment.

(2)   For the purposes of this section—

(a)   "treatment" of a work means any addition to, deletion from or alteration to or adaptation of the work, other than—

(i)   a translation of a literary or dramatic work, or

(ii)   an arrangement or transcription of a musical work involving no more than a change of key or register; and

(b)   the treatment of a work is derogatory if it amounts to distortion or mutilation of the work or is otherwise prejudicial to the honour or reputation of the author or director;

and in the following provisions of this section references to a derogatory treatment of a work shall be construed accordingly.

(3)   In the case of a literary, dramatic or musical work the right is infringed by a person who—

(a)   publishes commercially, performs in public, broadcasts or includes in a cable programme service a derogatory treatment of the work; or

(b)   issues to the public copies of a film or sound recording of, or including, a derogatory treatment of the work.

(4)   In the case of an artistic work the right is infringed by a person who—

(a)   publishes commercially or exhibits in public a derogatory treatment of the work, or broadcasts or includes in a cable programme service a visual image of a derogatory treatment of the work,

(b)   shows in public a film including a visual image of a derogatory treatment of the work or issues to the public copies of such a film, or

(c)   in the case of—

(i)   a work of architecture in the form of a model for a building,

(ii)   a sculpture, or

(iii)   a work of artistic craftsmanship,

issues to the public copies of a graphic work representing, or of a photograph of, a derogatory treatment of the work.

(5)   Subsection (4) does not apply to a work of architecture in the form of a building; but where the author of such a work is identified on the building and it is the subject of derogatory treatment he has the right to require the identification to be removed.

(6)   In the case of a film, the right is infringed by a person who—

(a)   shows in public, broadcasts or includes in a cable programme service a derogatory treatment of the film; or

(b)   issues to the public copies of a derogatory treatment of the film.

(7)   The right conferred by this section extends to the treatment of parts of a work resulting from a previous treatment by a person other than the author or director, if those parts are attributed to, or are likely to be regarded as the work of, the author or director.

(8)   This section has effect subject to sections 81 and 82 (exceptions to and qualifications of right).

81   Exceptions to right

(1)   The right conferred by section 80 (right to object to derogatory treatment of work) is subject to the following exceptions.

(2)   The right does not apply to a computer program or to any computer-generated work.

(3)   The right does not apply in relation to any work made for the purpose of reporting current events.

(4)   The right does not apply in relation to the publication in—

(a)   a newspaper, magazine or similar periodical, or

(b)   an encyclopaedia, dictionary, yearbook or other collective work of reference,

of a literary, dramatic, musical or artistic work made for the purposes of such publication or made available with the consent of the author for the purposes of such publication.

Nor does the right apply in relation to any subsequent exploitation elsewhere of such a work without any modification of the published version.

(5)   The right is not infringed by an act which by virtue of section 57 or 66A (acts permitted on assumptions as to expiry of copyright, etc.) would not infringe copyright.

(6)   The right is not infringed by anything done for the purpose of—

(a)   avoiding the commission of an offence,

(b)   complying with a duty imposed by or under an enactment, or

(c)   in the case of the British Broadcasting Corporation, avoiding the inclusion in a programme broadcast by them of anything which offends against good taste or decency or which is likely to encourage or incite to crime or to lead to disorder or to be offensive to public feeling,
provided, where the author or director is identified at the time of the relevant act or has previously been identified in or on published copies of the work, that there is a sufficient disclaimer.

82   Qualification of right in certain cases

(1)   This section applies to—
(a)   works in which copyright originally vested in the author's employer by virtue of section 11(2) (works produced in course of employment) or in the director's employer by virtue of section 9(2)(a) (person to be treated as author of film),
(b)   works in which Crown copyright or Parliamentary copyright subsists, and
(c)   works in which copyright originally vested in an international organisation by virtue of section 168.
(2)   The right conferred by section 80 (right to object to derogatory treatment of work) does not apply to anything done in relation to such a work by or with the authority of the copyright owner unless the author or director—
(a)   is identified at the time of the relevant act, or
(b)   has previously been identified in or on published copies of the work;
and where in such a case the right does apply, it is not infringed if there is a sufficient disclaimer.

83   Infringement of right by possessing or dealing with infringing article

(1)   The right conferred by section 80 (right to object to derogatory treatment of work) is also infringed by a person who—
(a)   possesses in the course of a business, or
(b)   sells or lets for hire, or offers or exposes for sale or hire, or
(c)   in the course of a business exhibits in public or distributes, or
(d)   distributes otherwise than in the course of a business so as to affect prejudicially the honour or reputation of the author or director,
an article which is, and which he knows or has reason to believe is, an infringing article.
(2)   An "infringing article" means a work or a copy of a work which—
(a)   has been subjected to derogatory treatment within the meaning of section 80, and
(b)   has been or is likely to be the subject of any of the acts mentioned in that section in circumstances infringing that right.

False attribution of work

84   False attribution of work

(1)   A person has the right in the circumstances mentioned in this section—
(a)   not to have a litarary, dramatic, musical or artistic work falsely attributed to him as author, and
(b)   not to have a film falsely attributed to him as director;
and in this section an "attribution", in relation to such a work, means a statement (express or implied) as to who is the author or director.
(2)   The right is infringed by a person who—
(a)   issues to the public copies of a work of any of those descriptions in or on which there is a false attribution, or
(b)   exhibits in public an artistic work, or a copy of an artistic work, in or on which there is a false attribution.

(3)   The right is also infringed by a person who—

(a)   in the case of a literary, dramatic or musical work, performs the work in public, broadcasts it or includes it in a cable programme service as being the work of a person, or

(b)   in the case of a film, shows it in public, broadcasts it or includes it in a cable programme service as being directed by a person,

knowing or having reason to believe that the attribution is false.

(4)   The right is also infringed by the issue to the public or public display of material containing a false attribution in connection with any of the acts mentioned in subsection (2) or (3).

(5)   The right is also infringed by a person who in the course of a business—

(a)   possesses or deals with a copy of a work of any of the descriptions mentioned in subsection (1) in or on which there is a false attribution, or

(b)   in the case of an artistic work, possesses or deals with the work itself when there is a false attribution in or on it,

knowing or having reason to believe that there is such an attribution and that it is false.

(6)   In the case of an artistic work the right is also infringed by a person who in the course of a business—

(a)   deals with a work which has been altered after the author parted with possession of it as being the unaltered work of the author, or

(b)   deals with a copy of such a work as being a copy of the unaltered work of the author,

knowing or having reason to believe that that is not the case.

(7)   References in this section to dealing are to selling or letting for hire, offering or exposing for sale or hire, exhibiting in public, or distributing.

(8)   This section applies where, contrary to the fact—

(a)   a literary, dramatic or musical work is falsely represented as being an adaptation of the work of a person, or

(b)   a copy of an artistic work is falsely represented as being a copy made by the author of the artistic work,

as it applies where the work is falsely attributed to a person as author.

Right to privacy of certain photographs and films

85   Right to privacy of certain photographs and films

(1)   A person who for private and domestic purposes commissions the taking of a photograph or the making of a film has, where copyright subsists in the resulting work, the right not to have—

(a)   copies of the work issued to the public,

(b)   the work exhibited or shown in public, or

(c)   the work broadcast or included in a cable programme service;

and, except as mentioned in subsection (2), a person who does or authorises the doing of any of those acts infringes that right.

(2)   The right is not infringed by an act which by virtue of any of the following provisions would not infringe copyright in the work—

(a)   section 31 (incidental inclusion of work in an artistic work, film, broadcast or cable programme);

(b)   section 45 (parliamentary and judicial proceedings);

(c)   section 46 (Royal Commissions and statutory inquiries);

(d)   section 50 (acts done under statutory authority);

(e)   section 57 or 66A (acts permitted on assumptions as to expiry of copyright, etc.).

Supplementary

86   Duration of rights

(1)   The rights conferred by section 77 (right to be identified as author or director), section 80 (right to object to derogatory treatment of work) and section 85 (right to privacy of certain photographs and films) continue to subsist so long as copyright subsists in the work.

(2)   The right conferred by section 84 (false attribution) continues to subsist until 20 years after a person's death.

87   Consent and waiver of rights

(1)   It is not an infringement of any of the rights conferred by this Chapter to do any act to which the person entitled to the right has consented.

(2)   Any of those rights may be waived by instrument in writing signed by the person giving up the right.

(3)   A waiver—

(a)   may relate to a specific work, to works of a specified description or to works generally, and may relate to existing or future works, and

(b)   may be conditional or unconditional and may be expressed to be subject to revocation;

and if made in favour of the owner or prospective owner of the copyright in the work or works to which it relates, it shall be presumed to extend to his licensees and successors in title unless a contrary intention is expressed.

(4)   Nothing in this Chapter shall be construed as excluding the operation of the general law of contract or estoppel in relation to an informal waiver or other transaction in relation to any of the rights mentioned in subsection (1).

88   Application of provisions to joint works

(1)   The right conferred by section 77 (right to be identified as author or director) is, in the case of a work of joint authorship, a right of each joint author to be identified as a joint author and must be asserted in accordance with section 78 by each joint author in relation to himself.

(2)   The right conferred by section 80 (right to object to derogatory treatment of work) is, in the case of a work of joint authorship, a right of each joint author and his right is satisfied if he consents to the treatment in question.

(3)   A waiver under section 87 of those rights by one joint author does not affect the rights of the other joint authors.

(4)   The right conferred by section 84 (false attribution) is infringed, in the circumstances mentioned in that section—

(a)   by any false statement as to the authorship of a work of joint authorship, and

(b)   by the false attribution of joint authorship in relation to a work of sole authorship;

and such a false attribution infringes the right of every person to whom authorship of any description is, whether rightly or wrongly, attributed.

(5)   The above provisions also apply (with any necessary adaptations) in relation to a film which was, or is alleged to have been, jointly directed, as they apply to a work which is, or is alleged to be, a work of joint authorship.

A film is "jointly directed" if it is made by the collaboration of two or more directors and the contribution of each director is not distinct from that of the other director or directors.

(6)   The right conferred by section 85 (right to privacy of certain photographs and films) is, in the case of a work made in pursuance of a joint commission, a right of each person who commissioned the making of the work, so that—

(a)   the right of each is satisfied if he consents to the act in question, and

(b) a waiver under section 87 by one of them does not affect the rights of the others.

89 Application of provisions to parts of works

(1) The rights conferred by section 77 (right to be identified as author or director) and section 85 (right to privacy of certain photographs and films) apply in relation to the whole or any substantial part of a work.

(2) The rights conferred by section 80 (right to object to derogatory treatment of work) and section 84 (false attribution) apply in relation to the whole or any part of a work.

CHAPTER V   DEALINGS WITH RIGHTS IN COPYRIGHT WORKS

Copyright

90 Assignment and licences

(1) Copyright is transmissible by assignment, by testamentary disposition or by operation of law, as personal or moveable property.

(2) An assignment or other transmission of copyright may be partial, that is, limited so as to apply—

(a) to one or more, but not all, of the things the copyright owner has the exclusive right to do;

(b) to part, but not the whole, of the period for which the copyright is to subsist.

(3) An assignment of copyright is not effective unless it is in writing signed by or on behalf of the assignor.

(4) A licence granted by a copyright owner is binding on every successor in title to his interest in the copyright, except a purchaser in good faith for valuable consideration and without notice (actual or constructive) of the licence or a person deriving title from such a purchaser; and references in this Part to doing anything with, or without, the licence of the copyright owner shall be construed accordingly.

91 Prospective ownership of copyright

(1) Where by an agreement made in relation to future copyright, and signed by or on behalf of the prospective owner of the copyright, the prospective owner purports to assign the future copyright (wholly or partially) to another person, then if, on the copyright coming into existence, the assignee or another person claiming under him would be entitled as against all other persons to require the copyright to be vested in him, the copyright shall vest in the assignee or his successor in title by virtue of this subsection.

(2) In this Part—

"future copyright" means copyright which will or may come into existence in respect of a future work or class or works or on the occurrence of a future event; and "prospective owner" shall be construed accordingly, and includes a person who is prospectively entitled to copyright by virtue of such an agreement as is mentioned in subsection (1).

(3) A licence granted by a prospective owner of copyright is binding on every successor in title to his interest (or prospective interest) in the right, except a purchaser in good faith for valuable consideration and without notice (actual or constructive) of the licence or a person deriving title from such a purchaser; and references in this Part to doing anything with, or without the licence of the copyright owner shall be construed accordingly.

92 Exclusive licences

(1) In this Part an "exclusive licence" means a licence in writing signed by or on behalf of the copyright owner authorising the licensee to the exclusion of all other

persons, including the person granting the licence, to exercise a right which would otherwise be exercisable exclusively by the copyright owner.

(2)   The licensee under an exclusive licence has the same rights against a successor in title who is bound by the licence as he has against the person granting the licence.

93   Copyright to pass under will with unpublished work

Where under a bequest (whether specific or general) a person entitled, beneficially or otherwise, to—

(a)   an original document or other material thing recording or embodying a literary, dramatic, musical or artistic work which was not published before the death of the testator, or

(b)   an original material thing containing a sound recording or film which was not published before the death of the testator,

the bequest shall, unless a contrary intention is indicated in the testator's will or a codicil to it, be construed as including the copyright in the work in so far as the testator was the owner of the copyright immediately before his death.

93A   Presumption of transfer of rental right in case of film production agreement

(1)   Where an agreement concerning film production is concluded between an author and a film producer, the author shall be presumed, unless the agreement provides to the contrary, to have transferred to the film producer any rental right in relation to the film arising by virtue of the inclusion of a copy of the author's work in the film.

(2)   In this section "author" means an author, or prospective author, of a literary, dramatic, musical or artistic work.

(3)   Subsection (1) does not apply to any rental right in relation to the film arising by virtue of the inclusion in the film of the screenplay, the dialogue or music specifically created for and used in the film.

(4)   Where this section applies, the absence of signature by or on behalf of the author does not exclude the operation of section 91(1) (effect of purported assignment of future copyright).

Right to equitable remuneration where rental right transferred

93B   Right to equitable remuneration where rental right transferred

(1)   Where an author to whom this section applies has transferred his rental right concerning a sound recording or a film to the producer of the sound recording or film, he retains the right to equitable remuneration for the rental.

The authors to whom this section applies are—

(a)   the author of a literary, dramatic, musical or artistic work, and

(b)   the principal director of a film.

(2)   The right to equitable remuneration under this section may not be assigned by the author except to a collecting society for the purpose of enabling it to enforce the right on his behalf.

The right is, however, transmissible by testamentary disposition or by operation of law as personal or moveable property; and it may be assigned or further transmitted by any person into whose hands it passes.

(3)   Equitable remuneration under this section is payable by the person for the time being entitled to the rental right, that is, the person to whom the right was transferred or any successor in title of his.

(4)   The amount payable by way of equitable remuneration is as agreed by or on behalf of the persons by and to whom it is payable, subject to section 93C (reference of amount to Copyright Tribunal).

(5)   An agreement is of no effect in so far as it purports to exclude or restrict the right to equitable remuneration under this section.

(6)   References in this section to the transfer of rental right by one person to another include any arrangement having that effect, whether made by them directly or through intermediaries.

(7)   In this section a "collecting society" means a society or other organisation which has as its main object, or one of its main objects, the exercise of the right to equitable remuneration under this section on behalf of more than one author.

93C   Equitable remuneration: reference of amount to Copyright Tribunal

(1)   In default of agreement as to the amount payable by way of equitable remuneration under section 93B, the person by or to whom it is payable may apply to the Copyright Tribunal to determine the amount payable.

(2)   A person to or by whom equitable remuneraton is payable under that section may also apply to the Copyright Tribunal—
    (a)   to vary any agreement as to the amount payable, or
    (b)   to vary any previous determination of the Tribunal as to that matter;
but except with the special leave of the Tribunal no such application may be made within twelve months from the date of a previous determination.

An order made on an application under this subsection has effect from the date on which it is made or such later date as may be specified by the Tribunal.

(3)   On an application under this section the Tribunal shall consider the matter and make such order as to the method of calculating and paying equitable remuneration as it may determine to be reasonable in the circumstances, taking into account the importance of the contribution of the author to the film or sound recording.

(4)   Remuneration shall not be considered inequitable merely because it was paid by way of a single payment or at the time of the transfer of the rental right.

(5)   An agreement is of no effect in so far as it purports to prevent a person questioning the amount of equitable remuneration or to restrict the powers of the Copyright Tribunal under this section.

Moral rights

94   Moral rights not assignable
The rights conferred by Chapter IV (moral rights) are not assignable.

95   Transmission of moral rights on death

(1)   On the death of a person entitled to the right conferred by section 77 (right to identification of author or director), section 80 (right to object to derogatory treatment of work) or section 85 (right to privacy of certain photographs and films)—
    (a)   the right passes to such person as he may by testamentary disposition specifically direct,
    (b)   if there is no such direction but the copyright in the work in question forms part of his estate, the right passes to the person to whom the copyright passes, and
    (c)   if or to the extent that the right does not pass under paragraph (a) or (b) it is exercisable by his personal representatives.

(2)   Where copyright forming part of a person's estate passes in part to one person and in part to another, as for example where a bequest is limited so as to apply—
    (a)   to one or more, but not all, of the things the copyright owner has the exclusive right to do or authorise, or
    (b)   to part, but not the whole, of the period for which the copyright is to subsist,
any right which passes with the copyright by virtue of subsection (1) is correspondingly divided.

(3)   Where by virtue of subsection (1)(a) or (b) a right becomes exercisable by more than one person—

    (a) it may, in the case of the right conferred by section 77 (right to identification of author or director), be asserted by any of them;

    (b) it is, in the case of the right conferred by section 80 (right to object to derogatory treatment of work) or section 85 (right to privacy of certain photographs and films), a right exercisable by each of them and is satisfied in relation to any of them if he consents to the treatment or act in question; and

    (c) any waiver of the right in accordance with section 87 by one of them does not affect the rights of the others.

    (4) A consent or waiver previously given or made binds any person to whom a right passes by virtue of subsection (1).

    (5) Any infringement after a person's death of the right conferred by section 84 (false attribution) is actionable by his personal representatives.

    (6) Any damages recovered by personal representatives by virtue of this section in respect of an infringement after a person's death shall devolve as part of his estate as if the right of action had subsisted and been vested in him immediately before his death.

CHAPTER VI   REMEDIES FOR INFRINGEMENT

Rights and remedies of copyright owner

96   Infringement actionable by copyright owner

    (1) An infringement of copyright is actionable by the copyright owner.

    (2) In an action for infringement of copyright all such relief by way of damages, injunctions, accounts or otherwise is available to the plaintiff as is available in respect of the infringement of any other property right.

    (3) This section has effect subject to the following provisions of this Chapter.

97   Provisions as to damages in infringement action

    (1) Where in an action for infringement of copyright it is shown that at the time of the infringement the defendant did not know, and had no reason to believe, that copyright subsisted in the work to which the action relates, the plaintiff is not entitled to damages against him, but without prejudice to any other remedy.

    (2) The court may in an action for infringement of copyright having regard to all the circumstances, and in particular to—

    (a) the flagrancy of the infringement, and

    (b) any benefit accruing to the defendant by reason of the infringement,

award such additional damages as the justice of the case may require.

98   Undertaking to take licence of right in infringement proceedings

    (1) If in proceedings for infringement of copyright in respect of which a licence is available as of right under section 144 (powers exercisable in consequence of report of Monopolies and Mergers Commission) the defendant undertakes to take a licence on such terms as may be agreed or, in default of agreement, settled by the Copyright Tribunal under that section—

    (a) no injunction shall be granted against him,

    (b) no order for delivery up shall be made under section 99, and

    (c) the amount recoverable against him by way of damages or on an account of profits shall not exceed double the amount which would have been payable by him as licensee if such a licence on those terms had been granted before the earliest infringement.

    (2) An undertaking may be given at any time before final order in the proceedings, without any admission of liability.

    (3) Nothing in this section affects the remedies available in respect of an infringement committed before licences of right were available.

99 Order for delivery up

(1) Where a person—

(a) has an infringing copy of a work in his possession, custody or control in the course of a business, or

(b) has in his possession, custody or control an article specifically designed or adapted from making copies of a particular copyright work, knowing or having reason to believe that it has been or is to be used to make infringing copies,

the owner of the copyright in the work may apply to the court for an order that the infringing copy or article be delivered up to him or to such other person as the court may direct.

. . .

100 Right to seize infringing copies and other articles

(1) An infringing copy of a work which is found exposed or otherwise immediately available for sale or hire, and in respect of which the copyright owner would be entitled to apply for an order under section 99, may be seized and detained by him or a person authorised by him.

The right to seize and detain is exercisable subject to the following conditions and is subject to any decision of the court under section 114.

(2) Before anything is seized under this section notice of the time and place of the proposed seizure must be given to a local police station.

(3) A person may for the purpose of exercising the right conferred by this section enter premises to which the public have access but may not seize anything in the possession, custody or control of a person at a permanent or regular place of business of his, and may not use any force.

(4) At the time when anything is seized under this section there shall be left at the place where it was seized a notice in the prescribed form containing the prescribed particulars as to the person by whom or on whose authority the seizure is made and the grounds on which it is made.

(5) In this section—

"premises" includes land, buildings, moveable structures, vehicles, vessels, aircraft and hovercraft; and

"prescribed" means prescribed by order of the Secretary of State.

(6) An order of the Secretary of State under this section shall be made by statutory instrument which shall be subject to annulment in pursuance of a resolution of either House of Parliament.

Rights and remedies of exclusive licensee

101 Rights and remedies of exclusive licensee

(1) An exclusive licensee has, except against the copyright owner, the same rights and remedies in respect of matters occurring after the grant of the licence as if the licence had been an assignment.

(2) His rights and remedies are concurrent with those of the copyright owner; and references in the relevant provisions of this Part to the copyright owner shall be construed accordingly.

(3) In an action brought by an exclusive licensee by virtue of this section a defendant may avail himself of any defence which would have been available to him if the action had been brought by the copyright owner.

102 Exercise of concurrent rights

(1) Where an action for infringement of copyright brought by the copyright owner or an exclusive licensee relates (wholly or partly) to an infringement in respect of which they have concurrent rights of action, the copyright owner or, as the case may be, the

exclusive licensee may not, without the leave of the court, proceed with the action unless the other is either joined as a plaintiff or added as a defendant.

. . .

(3)   The above provisions do not affect the granting of interlocutory relief on an application by a copyright owner or exclusive licensee alone.

. . .

Remedies for infringement of moral rights

103   Remedies for infringement of moral rights
(1)   An infringement of a right conferred by Chapter IV (moral rights) is actionable as a breach of statutory duty owed to the person entitled to the right.
(2)   In proceedings for infringement of the right conferred by section 80 (right to object to derogatory treatment of work) the court may, if it thinks it is an adequate remedy in the circumstances, grant an injunction on terms prohibiting the doing of any act unless a disclaimer is made, in such terms and in such manner as may be approved by the court, dissociating the author or director from the treatment of the work.

Presumptions

104   Presumptions relevant to literary, dramatic, musical and artistic works
(1)   The following presumptions apply in proceedings brought by virtue of this Chapter with respect to a literary, dramatic, musical or artistic work.
(2)   Where a name purporting to be that of the author appeared on copies of the work as published or on the work when it was made, the person whose name appeared shall be presumed, until the contrary is proved—
(a)   to be the author of the work;
(b)   to have made it in circumstances not falling within section 11(2), 163, 165 or 168 (works produced in course of employment, Crown copyright, Parliamentary copyright or copyright of certain international organisations).
(3)   In the case of a work alleged to be a work of joint authorship, subsection (2) applies in relation to each person alleged to be one of the authors.
(4)   Where no name purporting to be that of the author appeared as mentioned in subsection (2) but—
(a)   the work qualifies for copyright protection by virtue of section 155 (qualification by reference to country of first publication), and
(b)   a name purporting to be that of the publisher appeared on copies of the work as first published,
the person whose name appeared shall be presumed, until the contrary is proved, to have been the owner of the copyright at the time of publication.
(5)   If the author of the work is dead or the identity of the author cannot be ascertained by reasonable inquiry, it shall be presumed, in the absence of evidence to the contrary—
(a)   that the work is an original work, and
(b)   that the plaintiff's allegations as to what was the first publication of the work and as to the country of first publication are correct.

105   Presumptions relevant to sound recordings and films
(1)   In proceedings brought by virtue of this Chapter with respect to a sound recording, where copies of the recording as issued to the public bear a label or other mark stating—
(a)   that a named person was the owner of copyright in the recording at the date of issue of the copies, or
(aa)   that a named person was the principal director, the author of the screenplay, the author of the dialogue or the composer of music specifically created for and used in the film,

(b)   that the recording was first published in a specified year or in a specified country,
the label or mark shall be admissible as evidence of the fact stated and shall be presumed to be correct until the contrary is proved.

(2)   In proceedings brought by virtue of this Chapter with respect to a film, where copies of the film as issued to the public bear a statement—

(a)   that a named person was the director or producer of the film,

(b)   that a named person was the owner of copyright in the film at the date of issue of the copies, or

(c)   that the film was first published in a specified year or in a specified country,
the statement shall be admissible as evidence of the facts stated and shall be presumed to be correct until the contrary is proved.

(3)   In proceedings brought by virtue of this Chapter with respect to a computer program, where copies of the program are issued to the public in electronic form bearing a statement—

(a)   that a named person was the owner of copyright in the program at the date of issue of the copies, or

(b)   that the program was first published in a specified country or that copies of it were first issued to the public in electronic form in a specified year,
the statement shall be admissible as evidence of the facts stated and shall be presumed to be correct until the contrary is proved.

(4)   The above presumptions apply equally in proceedings relating to an infringement alleged to have occurred before the date on which the copies were issued to the public.

(5)   In proceedings brought by virtue of this Chapter with respect to a film, where the film as shown in public, broadcast or included in a cable programme service bears a statement—

(a)   that a named person was the director or producer of the film, or

(aa)   that a named person was the principal director of the film, the author of the screenplay, the author of the dialogue or the composer of music specifically created for and used in the film, or,

(b)   that a named person was the owner of copyright in the film immediately after it was made,
the statement shall be admissible as evidence of the facts stated and shall be presumed to be correct until the contrary is proved.

(6)   For the purposes of this section, a statement that a person was the director of a film shall be taken, unless a contrary indication appears, as meaning that he was the principal director of the film.

This presumption applies equally in proceedings relating to an infringement alleged to have occurred before the date on which the film was shown in public, broadcast or included in a cable programme service.

106   Presumptions relevant to works subject to Crown copyright

In proceedings brought by virtue of this Chapter with respect to a literary, dramatic or musical work in which Crown copyright subsists, where there appears on printed copies of the work a statement of the year in which the work was first published commercially, that statement shall be admissible as evidence of the fact stated and shall be presumed to be correct in the absence of evidence to the contrary.

Offences

107   Criminal liability for making or dealing with infringing articles, &c.

(1)   A person commits an offence who, without the licence of the copyright owner—

(a)   makes for sale or hire, or

(b)　imports into the United Kingdom otherwise than for his private and domestic use, or

(c)　possesses in the course of a business with a view to committing any act infringing the copyright, or

(d)　in the course of a business—
　　(i)　sells or lets for hire, or
　　(ii)　offers or exposes for sale or hire, or
　　(iii)　exhibits in public, or
　　(iv)　distributes, or

(e)　distributes otherwise than in the course of a business to such an extent as to affect prejudicially the owner of the copyright,

an article which is, and which he knows or has reason to believe is, an infringing copy of a copyright work.

(2)　A person commits an offence who—

(a)　makes an article specifically designed or adapted for making copies of a particular copyright work, or

(b)　has such an article in his possession,

knowing or having reason to believe that it is to be used to make infringing copies for sale or hire or for use in the course of a business.

(3)　Where copyright is infringed (otherwise than by reception of a broadcast or cable programme)—

(a)　by the public performance of a literary, dramatic or musical work, or

(b)　by the playing or showing in public of a sound recording or film,

any person who caused the work to be so performed, played or shown is guilty of an offence if he knew or had reason to believe that copyright would be infringed.

(4)　A person guilty of an offence under subsection (1)(a), (b), (d)(iv) or (e) is liable—

(a)　on summary conviction to imprisonment for a term not exceeding six months or a fine not exceeding the statutory maximum, or both;

(b)　on conviction on indictment to a fine or imprisonment for a term not exceeding two years, or both.

(5)　A person guilty of any other offence under this section is liable on summary conviction to imprisonment for a term not exceeding six months or a fine not exceeding level 5 on the standard scale, or both.

(6)　Sections 104 to 106 (presumptions as to various matters connected with copyright) do not apply to proceedings for an offence under this section; but without prejudice to their application in proceedings for an order under section 108 below.

107A　Enforcement by local weights and measures authority

(1)　It is the duty of every local weights and measures authority to enforce within their area the provisions of section 107.

(2)　The following provisions of the Trade Descriptions Act 1968 apply in relation to the enforcement of that section by such an authority as in relation to the enforcement of that Act—

　　section 27 (power to make test purchases),
　　section 28 (power to enter premises and inspect and seize goods and documents),
　　section 29 (obstruction of authorised officers), and
　　section 33 (compensation for loss, &c. of goods seized).
. . .

108　Order for delivery up in criminal proceedings

(1)　The court before which proceedings are brought against a person for an offence under section 107 may, if satisfied that at the time of his arrest or charge—

(a)　he had in his possession, custody or control in the course of a business an infringing copy of a copyright work, or

(b)   he had in his possession, custody or control an article specifically designed or adapted for making copies of a particular copyright work, knowing or having reason to believe that it had been or was to be used to make infringing copies,
order that the infringing copy or article be delivered up to the copyright owner or to such other person as the court may direct.

. . .

110   Offence by body corporate: liability of officers

(1)   Where an offence under section 107 committed by a body corporate is proved to have been committed with the consent or connivance of a director, manager, secretary or other similar officer of the body, or a person purporting to act in any such capacity, he as well as the body corporate is guilty of the offence and liable to be proceeded against and punished accordingly.

(2)   In relation to a body corporate whose affairs are managed by its members "director" means a member of the body corporate.

Provision for preventing importation of infringing copies

111   Infringing copies may be treated as prohibited goods

(1)   The owner of the copyright in a published literary, dramatic or musical work may give notice in writing to the Commissioners of Customs and Excise—
(a)   that he is the owner of the copyright in the work, and
(b)   that he requests the Commissioners, for a period specified in the notice, to treat as prohibited goods printed copies of the work which are infringing copies.

(2)   The period specified in a notice under subsection (1) shall not exceed five years and shall not extend beyond the period for which copyright is to subsist.

(3)   The owner of the copyright in a sound recording or film may give notice in writing to the Commissioners of Customs and Excise—
(a)   that he is the owner of the copyright in the work,
(b)   that infringing copies of the work are expected to arrive in the United Kingdom at a time and a place specified in the notice, and
(c)   that he requests the Commissioners to treat the copies as prohibited goods.

(3A)   The Commissioners may treat as prohibited goods only infringing copies of works which arrive in the United Kingdom—
(a)   from outside the European Economic Area, or
(b)   from within that Area but not having been entered for free circulation.

(3B)   This section does not apply to goods entered, or expected to be entered, for free circulation, export, re-export or for a suspensive procedure in respect of which an application may be made under Article 3(1) of Council Regulation (EC) No. 3295/94 laying down measures to prohibit the release for free circulation, export, re-export or entry for a suspensive procedure of counterfeit and pirated goods.

(4)   When a notice is in force under this section the importation of goods to which the notice relates, otherwise than by a person for his private and domestic use, subject to subsections (3A) and (3B), is prohibited; but a person is not by reason of the prohibition liable to any penalty other than forfeiture of the goods.

. . .

Supplementary

. . .

114   Order as to disposal of infringing copy or other article

(1)   An application may be made to the court for an order that an infringing copy or other article delivered up in pursuance of an order under section 99 or 108, or seized and detained in pursuance of the right conferred by section 100, shall be—
(a)   forfeited to the copyright owner, or

(b)   destroyed or otherwise dealt with as the court may think fit,
or for a decision that no such order should be made.
. . .

CHAPTER VII   COPYRIGHT LICENSING

Licensing schemes and licensing bodies

116   Licensing schemes and licensing bodies
(1)   In this Part a "licensing scheme" means a scheme setting out—
   (a)   the classes of case in which the operator of the scheme, or the person on whose behalf he acts, is willing to grant copyright licences, and
   (b)   the terms on which licences would be granted in those classes of case;
and for this purpose a "scheme" includes anything in the nature of a scheme, whether described as a scheme or as a tariff or by any other name.
(2)   In this Chapter a "licensing body" means a society or other organisation which has as its main object, or one of its main objects, the negotiation or granting, either as owner or prospective owner of copyright or as agent for him, of copyright licences, and whose objects include the granting of licences covering works of more than one author.
(3)   In this section "copyright licences" means licences to do, or authorise the doing of, any of the acts restricted by copyright.
(4)   References in this Chapter to licences or licensing schemes covering works of more than one author do not include licences or schemes covering only—
   (a)   a single collective work or collective works of which the authors are the same, or
   (b)   works made by, or by employees of or commissioned by, a single individual, firm, company or group of companies.
For this purpose a group of companies means a holding company and its subsidiaries, within the meaning of section 736 of the Companies Act 1985.

References and applications with respect to licensing schemes

117   Licensing schemes to which following sections apply
Sections 118 to 123 (references and applications with respect to licensing schemes) apply to licensing schemes which are operated by licensing bodies and cover works of more than one author, so far as they relate to licences for—
   (a)   copying the work,
   (b)   rental or lending of copies of the work to the public,
   (c)   performing, showing or playing the work in public, or
   (d)   broadcasting the work or including it in a cable programme service;
and references in those sections to a licensing scheme shall be construed accordingly.

118   Reference of proposed licensing scheme to tribunal
(1)   The terms of a licensing scheme proposed to be operated by a licensing body may be referred to the Copyright Tribunal by an organisation claiming to be representative of persons claiming that they require licences in cases of a description to which the scheme would apply, either generally or in relation to any description of case.
(2)   The Tribunal shall first decide whether to entertain the reference, and may decline to do so on the ground that the reference is premature.
(3)   If the Tribunal decides to entertain the reference it shall consider the matter referred and make such order, either confirming or varying the proposed scheme, either generally or so far as it relates to cases of the description to which the reference relates, as the Tribunal may determine to be reasonable in the circumstances.
(4)   The order may be made so as to be in force indefinitely or for such period as the Tribunal may determine.

119   Reference of licensing scheme to tribunal

(1)   If while a licensing scheme is in operation a dispute arises between the operator of the scheme and—

(a)   a person claiming that he requires a licence in a case of a description to which the scheme applies, or

(b)   an organisation claiming to be representative of such persons,

that person or organisation may refer the scheme to the Copyright Tribunal in so far as it relates to cases of that description.

(2)   A scheme which has been referred to the Tribunal under this section shall remain in operation until proceedings on the reference are concluded.

(3)   The Tribunal shall consider the matter in dispute and make such order, either confirming or varying the scheme so far as it relates to cases of the description to which the reference relates, as the Tribunal may determine to be reasonable in the circumstances.

(4)   The order may be made so as to be in force indefinitely or for such period as the Tribunal may determine.

. . .

121   Application for grant of licence in connection with licensing scheme

(1)   A person who claims, in a case covered by a licensing scheme, that the operator of the scheme has refused to grant him or procure the grant to him of a licence in accordance with the scheme, or has failed to do so within a reasonable time after being asked, may apply to the Copyright Tribunal.

(2)   A person who claims, in a case excluded from a licensing scheme, that the operator of the scheme either—

(a)   has refused to grant him a licence or procure the grant to him of a licence, or has failed to do so within a reasonable time of being asked, and that in the circumstances it is unreasonable that a licence should not be granted, or

(b)   proposes terms for a licence which are unreasonable,

may apply to the Copyright Tribunal.

(3)   A case shall be regarded as excluded from a licensing scheme for the purposes of subsection (2) if—

(a)   the scheme provides for the grant of licences subject to terms excepting matters from the licence and the case falls within such an exception, or

(b)   the case is so similar to those in which licences are granted under the scheme that it is unreasonable that it should not be dealt with in the same way.

(4)   If the Tribunal is satisfied that the claim is well-founded, it shall make an order declaring that, in respect of the matters specified in the order, the applicant is entitled to a licence on such terms as the Tribunal may determine to be applicable in accordance with the scheme or, as the case may be, to be reasonable in the circumstances.

(5)   The order may be made so as to be in force indefinitely or for such period as the Tribunal may determine.

. . .

123   Effect of order of tribunal as to licensing scheme

(1)   A licensing scheme which has been confirmed or varied by the Copyright Tribunal—

(a)   under section 118 (reference of terms of proposed scheme), or

(b)   under section 119 or 120 (reference of existing scheme to Tribunal),

shall be in force or, as the case may be, remain in operation, so far as it relates to the description of case in respect of which the order was made, so long as the order remains in force.

(2)   While the order is in force a person who in a case of a class to which the order applies—

    (a)   pays to the operator of the scheme any charges payable under the scheme in respect of a licence covering the case in question or, if the amount cannot be ascertained, gives an undertaking to the operator to pay them when ascertained, and

    (b)   complies with the other terms applicable to such a licence under the scheme, shall be in the same position as regards infringement of copyright as if he had at all material times been the holder of a licence granted by the owner of the copyright in question in accordance with the scheme.

...

    (5)   Where the Tribunal has made an order under section 121 (order as to entitlement to licence under licensing scheme) and the order remains in force, the person in whose favour the order is made shall if he—

    (a)   pays to the operator of the scheme any charges payable in accordance with the order or, if the amount cannot be ascertained, gives an undertaking to pay the charges when ascertained, and

    (b)   complies with the other terms specified in the order,

be in the same position as regards infringement of copyright as if he had at all material times been the holder of a licence granted by the owner of the copyright in question on the terms specified in the order.

References and applications with respect to licensing by licensing bodies

124 Licences to which following sections apply

Sections 125 to 128 (references and applications with respect to licensing by licensing bodies) apply to licences which are granted by a licensing body otherwise than in pursuance of a licensing scheme and cover works of more than one author, so far as they authorise—

    (a)   copying the work,

    (b)   rental or lending of copies of the work to the public,

    (c)   performing, showing or playing the work in public, or

    (d)   broadcasting the work or including it in a cable programme service;

and references in those sections to a licence shall be construed accordingly.

125 Reference to tribunal of proposed licence

    (1)   The terms on which a licensing body proposes to grant a licence may be referred to the Copyright Tribunal by the prospective licensee.

...

    (3)   If the Tribunal decides to entertain the reference it shall consider the terms of the proposed licence and make such order, either confirming or varying the terms, as it may determine to be reasonable in the circumstances.

...

126 Reference to tribunal of expiring licence

    (1)   A licensee under a licence which is due to expire, by effluxion of time or as a result of notice given by the licensing body, may apply to the Copyright Tribunal on the ground that it is unreasonable in the circumstances that the licence should cease to be in force.

...

    (4)   If the Tribunal finds the application well-founded, it shall make an order declaring that the licensee shall continue to be entitled to the benefit of the licence on such terms as the Tribunal may determine to be reasonable in the circumstances.

...

128 Effect of order of tribunal as to licence

    (1)   Where the Copyright Tribunal has made an order under section 125 or 126 and the order remains in force, the person entitled to the benefit of the order shall if he—

(a)   pays to the licensing body any charges payable in accordance with the order or, if the amount cannot be ascertained, gives an undertaking to pay the charges when ascertained, and

(b)   complies with the other terms specified in the order,

be in the same position as regards infringement of copyright as if he had at all material times been the holder of a licence granted by the owner of the copyright in question on the terms specified in the order.

(2)   The benefit of the order may be assigned—

(a)   in the case of an order under section 125, if assignment is not prohibited under the terms of the Tribunal's order; and

(b)   in the case of an order under section 126, if assignment was not prohibited under the terms of the original licence.

. . .

Factors to be taken into account in certain classes of case

129   General considerations: unreasonable discrimination

In determining what is reasonable on a reference or application under this Chapter relating to a licensing scheme or licence, the Copyright Tribunal shall have regard to—

(a)   the availability of other schemes, or the granting of other licences, to other persons in similar circumstances, and

(b)   the terms of those schemes or licences,

and shall exercise its powers so as to secure that there is no unreasonable discrimination between licensees, or prospective licensees, under the scheme or licence to which the reference or application relates and licensees under other schemes operated by, or other licences granted by, the same person.

. . .

135   Mention of specific matters not to exclude other relevant considerations

The mention in sections 129 to 134 of specific matters to which the Copyright Tribunal is to have regard in certain classes of case does not affect the Tribunal's general obligation in any case to have regard to all relevant considerations.

. . .

Royalty or other sum payable for lending of certain works

142   Royalty or other sum payable for lending of certain works

(1)   An application to settle the royalty or other sum payable in pursuance of section 66 (lending of copies of certain copyright works) may be made to the Copyright Tribunal by the copyright owner or the person claiming to be treated as licensed by him.

. . .

Certification of licensing schemes

143   Certification of licensing schemes

(1)   A person operating or proposing to operate a licensing scheme may apply to the Secretary of State to certify the scheme for the purposes of—

(a)   section 35 (educational recording of broadcasts or cable programmes),

(b)   section 60 (abstracts of scientific or technical articles),

(c)   section 66 (lending to public of copies of certain works),

(d)   section 74 (sub-titled copies of broadcasts or cable programmes for people who are deaf or hard of hearing), or

(e)   section 141 (reprographic copying of published works by educational establishments).

. . .

Compulsory collective administration of certain rights

144A   Collective exercise of certain rights in relation to cable re-transmission
(1)   This section applies to the right of the owner of copyright in a literary, dramatic, musical or artistic work, sound recording or film to grant or refuse authorisation for cable re-transmission of a broadcast from another EEA member state in which the work is included.
That right is referred to below as "cable re-transmission right".
(2)   Cable re-transmission right may be exercised against a cable operator only through a licensing body.
(3)   Where a copyright owner has not transferred management of his cable re-transmission right to a licensing body, the licensing body which manages rights of the same category shall be deemed to be mandated to manage his right.
Where more than one licensing body manages rights of that category, he may choose which of them is deemed to be mandated to manage his right.
(4)   A copyright owner to whom subsection (3) applies has the same rights and obligations resulting from any relevant agreement between the cable operator and the licensing body as have copyright owners who have transferred management of their cable re-transmission right to that licensing body.
(5)   Any rights to which a copyright owner may be entitled by virtue of subsection (4) must be claimed within the period of three years beginning with the date of the cable re-transmission concerned.
(6)   This section does not affect any rights exercisable by the maker of the broadcast, whether in relation to the broadcast or a work included in it.
(7)   In this section—
"cable operator" means a person providing a cable programme service; and
"cable re-transmission" means the reception and immediate re-transmission by way of a cable programme service of a broadcast.
. . .

Jurisdiction and procedure

149   Jurisdiction of the Tribunal
The Copyright Tribunal has jurisdiction under this Part to hear and determine proceedings under—
(za)   section 73 (determination of royalty or other remuneration to be paid with respect to re-transmission of broadcast including work);
(zb)   section 93C (application to determine amount of equitable remuneration under section 93B);
(a)   section 118, 119, or 120 (reference of licensing scheme);
(b)   section 121 or 122 (application with respect to entitlement to licence under licensing scheme);
(c)   section 125, 126 or 127 (reference or application with respect to licensing by licensing body);
(cc)   section 135D or 135E (application or reference with respect to use as of right of sound recordings in broadcasts or cable programme services);
(d)   section 139 (appeal against order as to coverage of licensing scheme or licence);
(e)   section 142 (application to settle royalty or other sum payable for lending of certain works);
(f)   section 144(4) (application to settle terms of copyright licence available as of right);
. . .

CHAPTER IX   QUALIFICATION FOR AND EXTENT OF COPYRIGHT PROTECTION

Qualification for copyright protection

153   Qualification for copyright protection

(1)   Copyright does not subsist in a work unless the qualification requirements of this Chapter are satisfied as regards—
  (a)   the author (see section 154), or
  (b)   the country in which the work was first published (see section 155), or
  (c)   in the case of a broadcast or cable programme, the country from which the broadcast was made or the cable programme was sent (see section 156).

(2)   Subsection (1) does not apply in relation to Crown copyright or Parliamentary copyright (see sections 163 to 166) or to copyright subsisting by virtue of section 168 (copyright of certain international organisations).

(3)   If the qualification requirements of this Chapter, or section 163, 165 or 168, are once satisfied in respect of a work, copyright does not cease to subsist by reason of any subsequent event.

154   Qualification by reference to author

(1)   A work qualifies for copyright protection if the author was at the material time a qualifying person, that is—
  (a)   a British citizen, a British Dependent Territories citizen, a British National (Overseas), a British Overseas citizen, a British subject or a British protected person within the meaning of the British Nationality Act 1981, or
  (b)   an individual domiciled or resident in the United Kingdom or another country to which the relevant provisions of this Part extend, or
  (c)   a body incorporated under the law of a part of the United Kingdom or of another country to which the relevant provisions of this Part extend.

(2)   Where, or so far as, provision is made by Order under section 159 (application of this Part to countries to which it does not extend), a work also qualifies for copyright protection if at the material time the author was a citizen or subject of, an individual domiciled or resident in, or a body incorporated under the law of, a country to which the Order relates.

(3)   A work of joint authorship qualifies for copyright protection if at the material time any of the authors satisfies the requirements of subsection (1) or (2); but where a work qualifies for copyright protection only under this section, only those authors who satisfy those requirements shall be taken into account for the purposes of—
  section 11(1) and (2) (first ownership of copyright; entitlement of author or author's employer),
  section 12 (duration of copyright), and section 9(4) (meaning of "unknown authorship") so far as it applies for the purposes of section 12, and
  section 57 (anonymous or pseudonymous works: acts permitted on assumptions as to expiry of copyright or death of author).

(4)   The material time in relation to a literary, dramatic, musical or artistic work is—
  (a)   in the case of an unpublished work, when the work was made or, if the making of the work extended over a period, a substantial part of that period;
  (b)   in the case of a published work, when the work was first published or, if the author had died before that time, immediately before his death.

(5)   The material time in relation to other descriptions of work is as follows—
  (a)   in the case of a sound recording or film, when it was made;
  (b)   in the case of a broadcast, when the broadcast was made;

(c)   in the case of a cable programme, when the programme was included in a cable programme service;

(d)   in the case of the typographical arrangement of a published edition, when the edition was first published.

155   Qualification by reference to country of first publication

(1)   A literary, dramatic, musical or artistic work, a sound recording or film, or the typographical arrangement of a published edition, qualifies for copyright protection if it is first published—

(a)   in the United Kingdom, or

(b)   in another country to which the relevant provision of this Part extend.

(2)   Where, or so far as, provision is made by Order under section 159 (application of this Part to countries to which it does not extend), such a work also qualifies for copyright protection if it is first published in a country to which the Order relates.

(3)   For the purposes of this section, publication in one country shall not be regarded as other than the first publication by reason of simultaneous publication elsewhere; and for this purpose publication elsewhere within the previous 30 days shall be treated as simultaneous.

156   Qualification by reference to place of transmission

(1)   A broadcast qualifies for copyright protection if it is made from, and a cable programme qualifies for copyright protection if it is sent from, a place in—

(a)   the United Kingdom, or

(b)   another country to which the relevant provisions of this Part extend.

(2)   Where, or so far as, provision is made by Order under section 159 (application of this Part to countries to which it does not extend), a broadcast or cable programme also qualifies for copyright protection if it is made from or, as the case may be, sent from a place in a country to which the Order relates.

Extent and application of this Part

157   Countries to which this Part extends

(1)   This Part extends to England and Wales, Scotland and Northern Ireland.

(2)   Her Majesty may by Order in Council direct that this Part shall extend, subject to such exceptions and modifications as may be specified in the Order to—

(a)   any of the Channel Islands,

(b)   the Isle of Man, or

(c)   any colony.

(3)   That power includes power to extend, subject to such exceptions and modifications as may be specified in the Order, any Order in Council made under the following provisions of this Chapter.

(4)   The legislature of a country to which this Part has been extended may modify or add to the provisions of this Part, in their operation as part of the law of that country, as the legislature may consider necessary to adapt the provisions to the circumstances of that country—

(a)   as regards procedure and remedies, or

(b)   as regards works qualifying for copyright protection by virtue of a connection with that country.

(5)   Nothing in this section shall be construed as restricting the extent of paragraph 36 of Schedule 1 (transitional provisions: dependent territories where the Copyright Act 1956 or the Copyright Act 1911 remains in force) in relation to the law of a dependent territory to which this Part does not extend.

. . .

159   Application of this Part to countries to which it does not extend

(1)   Her Majesty may by Order in Council make provision for applying in relation to a country to which this Part does not extend any of the provisions of this Part specified in the Order, so as to secure that those provisions—

(a)   apply in relation to persons who are citizens or subjects of that country or are domiciled or resident there, as they apply to persons who are British citizens or are domiciled or resident in the United Kingdom, or

(b)   apply in relation to bodies incorporated under the law of that country as they apply in relation to bodies incorporated under the law of a part of the United Kingdom, or

(c)   apply in relation to works first published in that country as they apply in relation to works first published in the United Kingdom, or

(d)   apply in relation to broadcasts made from or cable programmes sent from that country as they apply in relation to broadcasts made from or cable programmes sent from the United Kingdom.

(2)   An Order may make provision for all or any of the matters mentioned in subsection (1) and may—

(a)   apply any provisions of this Part subject to such exceptions and modifications as are specified in the Order; and

(b)   direct that any provisions of this Part apply either generally or in relation to such classes of works, or other classes of case, as are specified in the Order.

(3)   Except in the case of a Convention country or another member State of the European Economic Community, Her Majesty shall not make an Order in Council under this section in relation to a country unless satisfied that provision has been or will be made under the law of that country, in respect of the class of works to which the Order relates, giving adequate protection to the owners of copyright under this Part.

(4)   In subsection (3) "Convention country" means a country which is a party to a Convention relating to copyright to which the United Kingdom is also a party.

(5)   A statutory instrument containing an Order in Council under this section shall be subject to annulment in pursuance of a resolution of either House of Parliament.

160   Denial of copyright protection to citizens of countries not giving adequate protection to British works

(1)   If it appears to Her Majesty that the law of a country fails to give adequate protection to British works to which this section applies, or to one or more classes of such works, Her Majesty may make provision by Order in Council in accordance with this section restricting the rights conferred by this Part in relation to works of authors connected with that country.

(2)   An Order in Council under this section shall designate the country concerned and provide that, for the purposes specified in the Order, works first published after a date specified in the Order shall not be treated as qualifying for copyright protection by virtue of such publication if at that time the authors are—

(a)   citizens or subjects of that country (not domiciled or resident in the United Kingdom or another country to which the relevant provisions of this Part extend), or

(b)   bodies incorporated under the law of that country;

and the Order may make such provision for all the purposes of this Part or for such purposes as are specified in the Order, and either generally or in relation to such class of cases as are specified in the Order, having regard to the nature and extent of that failure referred to in subsection (1).

(3)   This section applies to literary, dramatic, musical and artistic works, sound recordings and films; and "British works" means works of which the author was a qualifying person at the material time within the meaning of section 154.

(4)   A statutory instrument containing an Order in Council under this section shall be subject to annulment in pursuance of a resolution of either House of Parlaiment.

Supplementary

161   Territorial waters and the continental shelf
(1)   For the purposes of this Part the territorial waters of the United Kingdom shall be treated as part of the United Kingdom.
(2)   This Part applies to things done in the United Kingdom sector of the continental shelf on a structure or vessel which is present there for purposes directly connected with the exploration of the sea bed or subsoil or the exploitation of their natural resources as it applies to things done in the United Kingdom.
(3)   The United Kingdom sector of the continental shelf means the areas designated by order under section 1(7) of the Continental Shelf Act 1964.

162   British ships, aircraft and hovercraft
(1)   This Part applies to things done on a British ship, aircraft or hovercraft as it applies to things done in the United Kingdom.
(2)   In this section—
    "British ship" means a ship which is a British ship for the purposes of the Merchant Shipping Act 1995 otherwise than by virtue of registration in a country outside the United Kingdom; and
    "British aircraft" and "British hovercraft" mean an aircraft or hovercraft registered in the United Kingdom.

CHAPTER X   MISCELLANEOUS AND GENERAL

Crown and Parliamentary copyright

163   Crown copyright
(1)   Where a work is made by Her Majesty or by an officer or servant of the Crown in the course of his duties—
    (a)   the work qualifies for copyright protection notwithstanding section 153(1) (ordinary requirement as to qualification for copyright protection), and
    (b)   Her Majesty is the first owner of any copyright in the work.
(2)   Copyright in such a work is referred to in this Part as "Crown copyright", notwithstanding that it may be, or have been, assigned to another person.
(3)   Crown copyright in a literary, dramatic, musical or artistic work continues to subsist—
    (a)   until the end of the period of 125 years from the end of the calendar year in which the work was made, or
    (b)   if the work is published commercially before the end of the period of 75 years from the end of the calendar year in which it was made, until the end of the period of 50 years from the end of the calendar year in which it was first so published.
(4)   In the case of a work of joint authorship where one or more but not all of the authors are persons falling within subsection (1), this section applies only in relation to those authors and the copyright subsisting by virtue of their contribution to the work.
(5)   Except as mentioned above, and subject to any express exclusion elsewhere in this Part, the provisions of this Part apply in relation to Crown copyright as to other copyright.
(6)   This section does not apply to a work if, or to the extent that, Parliamentary copyright subsists in the work (see sections 165 and 166).

164   Copyright in Acts and Measures
(1)   Her Majesty is entitled to copyright in every Act of Parliament or Measure of the General Synod of the Church of England.

(2)   The copyright subsists from Royal Assent until the end of the period of 50 years from the end of the calendar year in which Royal Assent was given.

(3)   References in this Part to Crown copyright (except in section 163) include copyright under this section; and, except as mentioned above, the provisions of this Part apply in relation to copyright under this section as to other Crown copyright.

(4)   No other copyright, or right in the nature of copyright, subsists in an Act or Measure.

165   Parliamentary copyright

(1)   Where a work is made by or under the direction or control of the House of Commons or the House of Lords—

(a)   the work qualifies for copyright protection notwithstanding section 153(1) (ordinary requirement as to qualification for copyright protection), and

(b)   the House by whom, or under whose direction or control, the work is made is the first owner of any copyright in the work, and if the work is made by or under the direction or control of both Houses, the two Houses are joint first owners of copyright.

(2)   Copyright in such a work is referred to in this Part as "Parliamentary copyright", notwithstanding that it may be, or have been, assigned to another person.

(3)   Parliamentary copyright in a literary, dramatic, musical or artistic work continues to subsist until the end of the period of 50 years from the end of the calendar year in which the work was made.

(4)   For the purposes of this section, works made by or under the direction or control of the House of Commons or the House of Lords include—

(a)   any work made by an officer or employee of that House in the course of his duties, and

(b)   any sound recording, film, live broadcast or live cable programme of the proceedings of that House;

but a work shall not be regarded as made by or under the direction or control of either House by reason only of its being commissioned by or on behalf of that House.

(5)   In the case of a work of joint authorship where one or more but not all of the authors are acting on behalf of, or under the direction or control of, the House of Commons or the House of Lords, this section applies only in relation to those authors and the copyright subsisting by virtue of their contribution to the work.

(6)   Except as mentioned above, and subject to any express exclusion elsewhere in this Part, the provisions of this Part apply in relation to Parliamentary copyright as to other copyright.

(7)   The provisions of this section also apply, subject to any exceptions or modifications specified by Order in Council, to works made by or under the direction or control of any other legislative body of a country to which this Part extends; and references in this Part to "Parliamentary copyright" shall be construed accordingly.

(8)   A statutory instrument containing an Order in Council under subsection (7) shall be subject to annulment in pursuance of a resolution of either House of Parliament.

166   Copyright in Parliamentary Bills

(1)   Copyright in every Bill introduced into Parliament belongs, in accordance with the following provisions, to one or both of the Houses of Parliament.

(2)   Copyright in a public Bill belongs in the first instance to the House into which the Bill is introduced, and after the Bill has been carried to the second House to both Houses jointly, and subsists from the time when the text of the Bill is handed in to the House in which it is introduced.

(3)   Copyright in a private Bill belongs to both Houses jointly and subsists from the time when a copy of the Bill is first deposited in either House.

(4)   Copyright in a personal Bill belongs in the first instance to the House of Lords, and after the Bill has been carried to the House of Commons to both Houses jointly, and subsists from the time when it is given a First Reading in the House of Lords.

(5)   Copyright under this section ceases—

(a)   on Royal Assent, or

(b)   if the Bill does not receive Royal Assent, on the withdrawal or rejection of the Bill or the end of the Session:

Provided that, copyright in a Bill continues to subsist notwithstanding its rejection in any Session by the House of Lords if, by virtue of the Parliament Acts 1911 and 1949, it remains possible for it to be presented for Royal Assent in that Session.

(6)   References in this Part to Parliamentary copyright (except in section 165) include copyright under this section; and, except as mentioned above, the provisions of this Part apply in relation to copyright under this section as to other Parliamentary copyright.

(7)   No other copyright, or right in the nature of copyright, subsists in a Bill after copyright has once subsisted under this section; but without prejudice to the subsequent operation of this section in relation to a Bill which, not having passed in one Session, is reintroduced in a subsequent Session.

167   Houses of Parliament: supplementary provisions with respect to copyright

(1)   For the purposes of holding, dealing with and enforcing copyright, and in connection with all legal proceedings relating to copyright, each House of Parliament shall be treated as having the legal capacities of a body corporate, which shall not be affected by a prorogation or dissolution.

(2)   The functions of the House of Commons as owner of copyright shall be exercised by the Speaker on behalf of the House; and if so authorised by the Speaker, or in case of a vacancy in the office of Speaker, those functions may be discharged by the Chairman of Ways and Means or a Deputy Chairman.

(3)   For this purpose a person who on the dissolution of Parliament was Speaker of the House of Commons, Chairman of Ways and Means or a Deputy Chairman may continue to act until the corresponding appointment is made in the next Session of Parliament.

(4)   The functions of the House of Lords as owner of copyright shall be exercised by the Clerk of the Parliaments on behalf of the House; and if so authorised by him, or in case of a vacancy in the office of Clerk of the Parliaments, those functions may be discharged by the Clerk Assistant or the Reading Clerk.

(5)   Legal proceedings relating to copyright—

(a)   shall be brought by or against the House of Commons in the name of "The Speaker of the House of Commons"; and

(b)   shall be brought by or against the House of Lords in the name of "The Clerk of the Parliaments".

Other miscellaneous provisions

168   Copyright vesting in certain international organisations

(1)   Where an original literary, dramatic, musical or artistic work—

(a)   is made by an officer or employee of, or is published by, an international organisation to which this section applies, and

(b)   does not qualify for copyright protection under section 154 (qualification by reference to author) or section 155 (qualification by reference to country of first publication),

copyright nevertheless subsists in the work by virtue of this section and the organisation is first owner of that copyright.

(2)   The international organisations to which this section applies are those as to which Her Majesty has by Order in Council declared that it is expedient that this section should apply.

(3)   Copyright of which an international organisation is first owner by virtue of this section continues to subsist until the end of the period of 50 years from the end of the calendar year in which the work was made or such longer period as may be specified by Her Majesty by Order in Council for the purpose of complying with the international obligations of the United Kingdom.

(4)   An international organisation to which this section applies shall be deemed to have, and to have had at all material times, the legal capacities of a body corporate for the purpose of holding, dealing with and enforcing copyright and in connection with all legal proceedings relating to copyright.

(5)   A statutory instrument containing an Order in Council under this section shall be subject to annulment in pursuance of a resolution of either House of Parliament

169   Folklore, &c.: anonymous unpublished works

(1)   Where in the case of an unpublished literary, dramatic, musical or artistic work of unknown authorship there is evidence that the author (or, in the case of a joint work, any of the authors) was a qualifying individual by connection with a country outside the United Kingdom, it shall be presumed until the contrary is proved that he was such a qualifying individual and that copyright accordingly subsists in the work, subject to the provisions of this Part.

(2)   If under the law of that country a body is appointed to protect and enforce copyright in such works, Her Majesty may by Order in Council designate that body for the purposes of this section.

(3)   A body so designated shall be recognised in the United Kingdom as having authority to do in place of the copyright owner anything, other than assign copyright, which it is empowered to do under the law of that country; and it may, in particular, bring proceedings in its own name.

(4)   A statutory instrument containing an Order in Council under this section shall be subject to annulment in pursuance of a resolution of either House of Parliament.

(5)   In subsection (1) a "qualifying individual" means an individual who at the material time (within the meaning of section 154) was a person whose works qualified under that section for copyright protection.

(6)   This section does not apply if there has been an assignment of copyright in the work by the author of which notice has been given to the designated body; and nothing in this section affects the validity of an assignment of copyright made, or licence granted, by the author or a person lawfully claiming under him.

Transitional provisions and savings

170   Transitional provisions and savings

Schedule 1 contains transitional provisions and savings relating to works made, and acts or events occurring, before the commencement of this Part, and otherwise with respect to the operation of the provisions of this Part.

171   Rights and privileges under other enactments or the common law

(1)   Nothing in this Part affects—

(a)   any right or privilege of any person under any enactment (except where the enactment is expressly repealed, amended or modified by this Act);

(b)   any right or privilege of the Crown subsisting otherwise than under an enactment;

(c)   any right or privilege of either House of Parliament;

(d)   the right of the Crown or any person deriving title from the Crown to sell, use or otherwise deal with articles forfeited under the laws relating to customs and excise;

(e)   the operation of any rule of equity relating to breaches of trust or confidence.

(2)   Subject to those savings, no copyright or right in the nature of copyright shall subsist otherwise than by virtue of this Part or some other enactment in that behalf.

(3)   Nothing in this Part affects any rule of law preventing or restricting the enforcement of copyright, on grounds of public interest or otherwise.

(4)   Nothing in this Part affects any right of action or other remedy, whether civil or criminal, available otherwise than under this Part in respect of acts infringing any of the rights conferred by Chapter IV (moral rights).

(5)   The savings in subsection (1) have effect subject to section 164(4) and section 166(7) (copyright in Acts, Measures and Bills: exclusion of other rights in the nature of copyright).

Interpretation

172   General provisions as to construction

(1)   This Part restates and amends the law of copyright, that is, the provisions of the Copyright Act 1956, as amended.

(2)   A provision of this Part which corresponds to a provision of the previous law shall not be construed as departing from the previous law merely because of a change of expression.

(3)   Decisions under the previous law may be referred to for the purpose of establishing whether a provision of this Part departs from the previous law, or otherwise for establishing the true construction of this Part.

172A   Meaning of EEA and related expressions

(1)   In this Part—
   "the EEA" means the European Economic Area;
   "EEA national" means a national of an EEA state; and
   "EEA state" means a state which is a contracting party to the EEA Agreement.

173   Construction of references to copyright owner

(1)   Where different persons are (whether in consequence of a partial assignment or otherwise) entitled to different aspects of copyright in a work, the copyright owner for any purpose of this Part is the person who is entitled to the aspect of copyright relevant for that purpose.

(2)   Where copyright (or any aspect of copyright) is owned by more than one person jointly, references in this Part to the copyright owner are to all the owners, so that, in particular, any requirement of the licence of the copyright owner requires the licence of all of them.

174   Meaning of "educational establishment" and related expressions

(1)   The expression "educational establishment" in a provision of this Part means—
   (a)   any school, and
   (b)   any other description of educational establishment specified for the purposes of this Part, or that provision, by order of the Secretary of State.

(2)   The Secretary of State may by order provide that the provisions of this Part relating to educational establishments shall apply, with such modifications and adaptations as may be specified in the order, in relation to teachers who are employed by a local education authority to give instruction elsewhere to pupils who are unable to attend an educational establishment.

(3)   In subsection (1)(a) "school"—
   (a)   in relation to England and Wales, has the same meaning as in the Education Act 1996;

(b)   in relation to Scotland, has the same meaning as in the Education (Scotland) Act 1962, except that it includes an approved school within the meaning of the Social Work (Scotland) Act 1968; and

(c)   in relation to Northern Ireland, has the same meaning as in the Education and Libraries (Northern Ireland) Order 1986.

(4)   An order under subsection (1)(b) may specify a description of educational establishment by reference to the instruments from time to time in force under any enactment specified in the order.

(5)   In relation to an educational establishment the expressions "teacher" and "pupil" in this Part include, respectively, any person who gives and any person who receives instruction.

(6)   References in this Part to anything being done "on behalf of" an educational establishment are to its being done for the purposes of that establishment by any person.

(7)   An order under this section shall be made by statutory instrument which shall be subject to annulment in pursuance of a resolution of either House of Parliament.

175   Meaning of publication and commercial publication

(1)   In this Part "publication", in relation to a work—

(a)   means the issue of copies to the public, and

(b)   includes, in the case of a literary, dramatic, musical or artistic work, making it available to the public by means of an electronic retrieval system; and related expressions shall be construed accordingly.

(2)   In this Part "commercial publication", in relation to a literary, dramatic, musical or artistic work means—

(a)   issuing copies of the work to the public at a time when copies made in advance of the receipt of orders are generally available to the public, or

(b)   making the work available to the public by means of an electronic retrieval system; and related expressions shall be construed accordingly.

(3)   In the case of a work of architecture in the form of a building, or an artistic work incorporated in a building, construction of the building shall be treated as equivalent to publication of the work.

(4)   The following do not constitute publication for the purposes of this Part and references to commercial publication shall be construed accordingly—

(a)   in the case of a literary, dramatic or musical work—

(i)   the performance of the work, or

(ii)   the broadcasting of the work or its inclusion in a cable programme service (otherwise than for the purposes of an electronic retrieval system);

(b)   in the case of an artistic work—

(i)   the exhibition of the work,

(ii)   the issue to the public of copies of a graphic work representing, or of photographs of, a work of architecture in the form of a building or a model for a building, a sculpture or a work of artistic craftsmanship,

(iii)   the issue to the public of copies of a film including the work, or

(iv)   the broadcasting of the work or its inclusion in a cable programme service (otherwise than for the purposes of an electronic retrieval system);

(c)   in the case of a sound recording or film—

(i)   the work being played or shown in public, or

(ii)   the broadcasting of the work or its inclusion in a cable programme service.

(5)   References in this Part to publication or commercial publication do not include publication which is merely colourable and not intended to satisfy the reasonable requirements of the public.

(6)   No account shall be taken for the purposes of this section of any unauthorised act.

176   Requirement of signature: application in relation to body corporate

(1)   The requirement in the following provisions that an instrument be signed by or on behalf of a person is also satisfied in the case of a body corporate by the affixing of its seal—

section 78(3)(b) (assertion by licensor of right to identification of author in case of public exhibition of copy made in pursuance of the licence),

section 90(3) (assignment of copyright),

section 91(1) (assignment of future copyright),

section 92(1) (grant of exclusive licence).

(2)   The requirement in the following provisions that an instrument be signed by a person is satisfied in the case of a body corporate by signature on behalf of the body or by the affixing of its seal—

section 78(2)(b) (assertion by instrument in writing of right to have author identified),

section 87(2) (waiver of moral rights).

...

178   Minor definitions

In this Part—

"article", in the context of an article in a periodical, includes an item of any description;

"business" includes a trade or profession;

"collective work" means—

(a)   a work of joint authorship, or

(b)   a work in which there are distinct contributions by different authors or in which works or parts of works of different authors are incorporated;

"computer-generated", in relation to a work, means that the work is generated by computer in circumstancs such that there is no human author of the work;

"country" includes any territory;

"the Crown" includes the Crown in right of Her Majesty's Government in Northern Ireland or in any country outside the United Kingdom to which this Part extends;

"electronic" means actuated by electric, magnetic, electro-magnetic, electro-chemical or electro-mechanical energy, and "in electronic form" means in a form usable only by electronic means;

"employed", "employee", "employer" and "employment" refer to employment under a contract of service or of apprenticeship;

"facsimile copy" includes a copy which is reduced or enlarged in scale;

"international organisation" means an organisation the members of which include one or more states;

"judicial proceedings" includes proceedings before any court, tribunal or person having authority to decide any matter affecting a person's legal rights or liabilities;

"parliamentary proceedings" includes proceedings of the Northern Ireland Assembly or of the European Parliament;

"producer", in relation to a sound recording or a film, means the person by whom the arrangements necessary for the making of the sound recording or film are undertaken;

"public library" means a library administered by or on behalf of—

(a)   in England and Wales, a library authority within the meaning of the Public Libraries and Museums Act 1964;

(b)   in Scotland, a statutory library authority within the meaning of the Public Libraries (Scotland) Act 1955;

(c)   in Northern Ireland, an Education and Library Board within the meaning of the Education and Libraries (Northern Ireland) Order 1986;

"rental right" means the right of a copyright owner to authorise or prohibit the rental of copies of the work (see section 18A);

"reprographic copy" and "reprographic copying" refer to copying by means of a reprographic process;

"reprographic process" means a process—

(a)   for making facsimile copies, or

(b)   involving the use of an appliance for making multiple copies,

and includes, in relation to a work held in electronic form, any copying by electronic means, but does not include the making of a film or sound recording;

"sufficient acknowledgement" means an acknowledgement identifying the work in question by its title or other description, and identifying the author unless—

(a)   in the case of a published work, it is published anonymously;

(b)   in the case of an unpublished work, it is not possible for a person to ascertain the identity of the author by reasonable inquiry;

"sufficient disclaimer", in relation to an act capable of infringing the right conferred by section 80 (right to object to derogatory treatment of work), means a clear and reasonably prominent indication—

(a)   given at the time of the act, and

(b)   if the author or director is then identified, appearing along with the identification,

that the work has been subjected to treatment to which the author or director has not consented;

"telecommunications system" means a system for conveying visual images, sounds or other information by electronic means;

"typeface" includes an ornamental motif used in printing;

"unauthorised", as regards anything done in relation to a work, means done otherwise than—

(a)   by or with the licence of the copyright owner, or

(b)   if copyright does not subsist in the work, by or with the licence of the author or, in a case where section 11(2) would have applied, the author's employer or, in either case, persons lawfully claiming under him, or

(c)   in pursuance of section 48 (copying, &c. of certain material by the Crown);

"wireless telegraphy" means the sending of electro-magnetic energy over paths not provided by a material substance constructed or arranged for that purpose but does not include the transmission of microwave energy between terrestrial fixed points;

"writing" includes any form of notation or code, whether by hand or otherwise and regardless of the method by which, or medium in or on which, it is recorded, and "written" shall be construed accordingly.

179   Index of defined expressions

The following Table shows provisions defining or otherwise explaining expressions used in this Part (other than provisions defining or explaining an expression used only in the same section)—

account of profits and accounts (in Scotland)	section 177
acts restricted by copyright	section 16(1)
adaptation	section 21(3)
archivist (in sections 37 to 43)	section 37(6)
article (in a periodical)	section 178
artistic work	section 4(1)
assignment (in Scotland)	section 177
author	sections 9 and 10(3)
broadcast (and related expressions)	section 6

building	section 4(2)
business	section 178
cable programme, cable programme service (and related expressions)	section 7
collective work	section 178
commencement (in Schedule 1)	paragraph 1(2) of that Schedule
commercial publication	section 175
computer-generated	section 178
copy and copying	section 17
copyright (generally)	section 1
copyright (in Schedule 1)	paragraph 2(2) of that Schedule
copyright owner	sections 101(2) and 173
Copyright Tribunal	section 145
copyright work	section 1(2)
costs (in Scotland)	section 177
country	section 178
country of origin	section 15A
the Crown	section 178
Crown copyright	sections 163(2) and 164(3)
database	section 3A(1)
defendant (in Scotland)	section 177
delivery up (in Scotland)	section 177
dramatic work	section 3(1)
educational establishment	sections 174(1) to (4)
EEA, EEA national and EEA state	section 172A
electronic and electronic form	section 178
employed, employee, employer and employment	section 178
exclusive licence	section 92(1)
existing works (in Schedule 1)	paragraph 1(3) of that Schedule
facsimile copy	section 178
film	section 5B
future copyright	section 91(2)
general licence (in sections 140 and 141)	section 140(7)
graphic work	section 4(2)
infringing copy	section 27
injunction (in Scotland)	section 177
interlocutory relief (in Scotland)	section 177
international organisation	section 178
issue of copies to the public	section 18
joint authorship (work of)	sections 10(1) and (2)
judicial proceedings	section 178
lawful user (in sections 50A to 50C)	section 50A(2)
lending	section 18A(2) to (6)
librarian (in sections 37 to 43)	section 37(6)
licence (in sections 125 to 128)	section 124
licence of copyright owner	sections 90(4), 91(3) and 173
licensing body (in Chapter VII)	section 116(2)
licensing scheme (generally)	section 116(1)

licensing scheme (in sections 118 to 121)	section 117
literary work	section 3(1)
made (in relation to a literary, dramatic or musical work)	section 3(2)
musical work	section 3(1)
needletime	section 135A
the new copyright provisions (in Schedule 1)	paragraph 1(1) of that Schedule
the 1911 Act (in Schedule 1)	paragraph 1(1) of that Schedule
the 1956 Act (in Schedule 1)	paragraph 1(1) of that Schedule
on behalf of (in relation to an educational establishment)	section 174(5)
original (in relation to a database)	section 3A(2)
Parliamentary copyright	sections 165(2) and (7) and 166(6)
parliamentary proceedings	section 178
performance	section 19(2)
photograph	section 4(2)
plaintiff (in Scotland)	section 177
prescribed conditions (in sections 38 to 43)	section 37(1)(b)
prescribed library or archive (in sections 38 to 43)	section 37(1)(a)
producer (in relation to a sound recording or film)	section 178
programme (in the context of broadcasting)	section 6(3)
prospective owner (of copyright)	section 91(2)
publication and related expressions	section 175
public library	section 178
published edition (in the context of copyright in the typographical arrangement)	section 8
pupil	section 174(5)
rental	section 18A(2) to (6)
rental right	section 178
reprographic copies and reprographic copying	section 178
reprographic process	section 178
sculpture	section 4(2)
signed	section 176
sound recording	sections 5A and 135A
sufficient acknowledgement	section 178
sufficient disclaimer	section 178
teacher	section 174(5)
telecommunications system	section 178
terms of payment	section 135A
typeface	section 178
unauthorised (as regards things done in relation to a work)	section 178
unknown (in relation to the author of a work)	section 9(5)
unknown authorship (work of)	section 9(4)
wireless telegraphy	section 178
work (in Schedule 1)	paragraph 2(1) of that Schedule
work of more than one author (in Chapter VII)	section 116(4)
writing and written	section 178

PART II   RIGHTS IN PERFORMANCES

Introductory

180   Rights conferred on performers and persons having recording rights

(1)   This Part confers rights—

(a)   on a performer, by requiring his consent to the exploitation of his performances (see sections 181 to 184), and

(b)   on a person having recording rights in relation to a performance, in relation to recordings made without his consent or that of the performer (see sections 185 to 188), and creates offences in relation to dealing with or using illicit recordings and certain other related acts (see sections 198 and 201).

(2)   In this Part—

"performance" means—

(a)   a dramatic performance (which includes dance and mime),

(b)   a musical performance,

(c)   a reading or recitation of a literary work, or

(d)   a performance of a variety act or any similar presentation,

which is, or so far as it is, a live performance given by one or more individuals; and "recording", in relation to a performance, means a film or sound recording—

(a)   made directly from the live performance,

(b)   made from a broadcast of, or cable programme including, the performance, or

(c)   made, directly or indirectly, from another recording of the performance.

(3)   The rights conferred by this Part apply in relation to performances taking place before the commencement of this Part; but no act done before commencement, or in pursuance of arrangements made before commencement, shall be regarded as infringing those rights.

(4)   The rights conferred by this Part are independent of—

(a)   any copyright in, or moral rights relating to, any work performed or any film or sound recording of, or broadcast or cable programme including, the performance, and

(b)   any other right or obligation arising otherwise than under this Part.

Performers' rights

181   Qualifying performances

A performance is a qualifying performance for the purposes of the provisions of this Part relating to performers' rights if it is given by a qualifying individual (as defined in section 206) or takes place in a qualifying country (as so defined).

182   Consent required for recording, &c. of live performance

(1)   A performer's rights are infringed by a person who, without his consent—

(a)   makes a recording of the whole or any substantial part of a qualifying performance directly from the live performance,

(b)   broadcasts live, or includes live in a cable programme service, the whole or any substantial part of a qualifying performance,

(c)   makes a recording of the whole or any substantial part of a qualifying performance directly from a broadcast of, or cable programme including, the live performance.

(2)   A performer's rights are not infringed by the making of any such recording by a person for his private and domestic use.

(3)   In an action for infringement of a performer's rights brought by virtue of this section damages shall not be awarded against a defendant who shows that at the time of the infringement he believed on reasonable grounds that consent had been given.

182A Consent required for copying of recording

(1)   A performer's rights are infringed by a person who, without his consent, makes, otherwise than for his private and domestic use, a copy of a recording of the whole or any substantial part of a qualifying performance.

(2)   It is immaterial whether the copy is made directly or indirectly.

(3)   The right of a performer under this section to authorise or prohibit the making of such copies is referred to in this Part as "reproduction right".

182B Consent required for issue of copies to public

(1)   A performer's rights are infringed by a person who, without his consent, issues to the public copies of a recording of the whole or any substantial part of a qualifying performance.

(2)   References in this Part to the issue to the public of copies of a recording are to—

(a)   the act of putting into circulation in the EEA copies not previously put into circulation in the EEA by or with the consent of the performer, or

(b)   the act of putting into circulation outside the EEA copies not previously put into circulation in the EEA or elsewhere.

(3)   References in this Part to the issue to the public of copies of a recording do not include—

(a)   any subsequent distribution, sale, hiring or loan of copies previously put into circulation (but see section 182C: consent required for rental or lending), or

(b)   any subsequent importation of such copies into the United Kingdom or another EEA state,

except so far as paragraph (a) of subsection (2) applies to putting into circulation in the EEA copies previously put into circulation outside the EEA.

(4)   References in this Part to the issue of copies of a recording of a performance include the issue of the original recording of the live performance.

(5)   The right of a performer under this section to authorise or prohibit the issue of copies to the public is referred to in this Part as "distribution right".

182C Consent required for rental or lending of copies to public

(1)   A performer's rights are infringed by a person who, without his consent, rents or lends to the public copies of a recording of the whole or any substantial part of a qualifying performance.

(2)   In this Part, subject to the following provisions of this section—

(a)   "rental" means making a copy of a recording available for use, on terms that it will or may be returned, for direct or indirect economic or commercial advantage, and

(b)   "lending" means making a copy of a recording available for use, on terms that it will or may be returned, otherwise than for direct or indirect economic or commercial advantage, through an establishment which is accessible to the public.

(3)   The expressions "rental" and "lending" do not include—

(a)   making available for the purpose of public performance, playing or showing in public, broadcasting or inclusion in a cable programme service;

(b)   making available for the purpose of exhibition in public; or

(c)   making available for on-the-spot reference use.

(4)   The expression "lending" does not include making available between establishments which are accessible to the public.

(5)   Where lending by an establishment accessible to the public gives rise to a payment the amount of which does not go beyond what is necessary to cover the operating costs of the establishment, there is no direct or indirect economic or commercial advantage for the purposes of this section.

(6)   References in this Part to the rental or lending of copies of a recording of a performance include the rental or lending of the original recording of the live performance.

(7)   In this Part—
"rental right" means the right of a performer under this section to authorise or prohibit the rental of copies to the public, and
"lending right" means the right of a performer under this section to authorise or prohibit the lending of copies to the public.

182D   Right to equitable remuneration for exploitation of sound recording

(1)   Where a commercially published sound recording of the whole or any substantial part of a qualifying performance—
(a)   is played in public, or
(b)   is included in a broadcast or cable programme service,
the performer is entitled to equitable remuneration from the owner of the copyright in the sound recording.

(2)   The right to equitable remuneration under this section may not be assigned by the performer except to a collecting society for the purpose of enabling it to enforce the right on his behalf.
The right is, however, transmissible by testamentary disposition or by operation of law as personal or moveable property; and it may be assigned or further transmitted by any person into whose hands it passes.

(3)   The amount payable by way of equitable remuneration is as agreed by or on behalf of the persons by and to whom it is payable, subject to the following provisions.

(4)   In default of agreement as to the amount payable by way of equitable remuneration, the person by or to whom it is payable may apply to the Copyright Tribunal to determine the amount payable.

(5)   A person to or by whom equitable remuneration is payable may also apply to the Copyright Tribunal—
(a)   to vary any agreement as to the amount payable, or
(b)   to vary any previous determination of the Tribunal as to that matter;
but except with the special leave of the Tribunal no such application may be made within twelve months from the date of a previous determination.
An order made on an application under this subsection has effect from the date on which it is made or such later date as may be specified by the Tribunal.

(6)   On an application under this section the Tribunal shall consider the matter and make such order as to the method of calculating and paying equitable remuneration as it may determine to be reasonable in the circumstances, taking into account the importance of the contribution of the performer to the sound recording.

(7)   An agreement is of no effect in so far as it purports—
(a)   to exclude or restrict the right to equitable remuneration under this section, or
(b)   to prevent a person questioning the amount of equitable remuneration or to restrict the powers of the Copyright Tribunal under this section.

183   Infringement of performer's rights by use of recording made without consent

A performer's rights are infringed by a person who, without his consent—
(a)   shows or plays in public the whole or any substantial part of a qualifying performance, or
(b)   broadcasts or includes in a cable programme service the whole or any substantial part of a qualifying performance,
by means of a recording which was, and which that person knows or has reason to believe was, made without the performer's consent.

184   Infringement of performer's rights by importing, possessing or dealing with illicit recording

(1)   A performer's rights are infringed by a person who, without his consent—

(a)   imports into the United Kingdom otherwise than for his private and domestic use, or

(b)   in the course of a business possesses, sells or lets for hire, offers or exposes for sale or hire, or distributes,

a recording of a qualifying performance which is, and which that person knows or has reason to believe is, an illicit recording.

(2)   Where in an action for infringement of a performer's rights brought by virtue of this section a defendant shows that the illicit recording was innocently acquired by him or a predecessor in title of his, the only remedy available against him in respect of the infringement is damages not exceeding a reasonable payment in respect of the act complained of.

(3)   In subsection (2) "innocently acquired" means that the person acquiring the recording did not know and had no reason to believe that it was an illicit recording.

Rights of person having recording rights

185   Exclusive recording contracts and persons having recording rights

(1)   In this Part an "exclusive recording contract" means a contract between a performer and another person under which that person is entitled to the exclusion of all other persons (including the performer) to make recordings of one or more of his performances with a view to their commercial exploitation.

(2)   References in this Part to a "person having recording rights", in relation to a performance, are (subject to subsection (3)) to a person—

(a)   who is party to and has the benefit of an exclusive recording contract to which the performance is subject, or

(b)   to whom the benefit of such a contract has been assigned,

and who is a qualifying person.

(3)   If a performance is subject to an exclusive recording contract but the person mentioned in subsection (2) is not a qualifying person, references in this Part to a "person having recording rights" in relation to the performance are to any person—

(a)   who is licensed by such a person to make recordings of the performance with a view to their commercial exploitation, or

(b)   to whom the benefit of such a licence has been assigned,

and who is a qualifying person.

(4)   In this section "with a view to commercial exploitation" means with a view to the recordings being sold or let for hire, or shown or played in public.

186   Consent required for recording of performance subject to exclusive contract

(1)   A person infringes the rights of a person having recording rights in relation to a performance who, without his consent or that of the performer, makes a recording of the whole or any substantial part of the performance, otherwise than for his private and domestic use.

(2)   In an action for infringement of those rights brought by virtue of this section damages shall not be awarded against a defendant who shows that at the time of the infringement he believed on reasonable grounds that consent had been given.

187   Infringement of recording rights by use of recording made without consent

(1)   A person infringes the rights of a person having recording rights in relation to a performance who, without his consent or, in the case of a qualifying performance, that of the performer—

(a)   shows or plays in public the whole or any substantial part of the performance, or

(b)   broadcasts or includes in a cable programme service the whole or any substantial part of the performance, by means of a recording which was, and which that person knows or has reason to believe was, made without the appropriate consent.

(2)   The reference in subsection (1) to "the appropriate consent" is to the consent of—

(a)   the performer, or

(b)   the person who at the time the consent was given had recording rights in relation to the performance (or, if there was more than one such person, of all of them).

188   Infringement of recording rights by importing, possessing or dealing with illicit recording

(1)   A person infringes the rights of a person having recording rights in relation to a performance who, without his consent or, in the case of a qualifying performance, that of the performer—

(a)   imports into the United Kingdom otherwise than for his private and domestic use, or

(b)   in the course of a business possesses, sells or lets for hire, offers or exposes for sale or hire, or distributes,

a recording of the performance which is, and which that person knows or has reason to believe is, an illicit recording.

(2)   Where in an action for infringement of those rights brought by virtue of this section a defendant shows that the illicit recording was innocently acquired by him or a predecessor in title of his, the only remedy available against him in respect of the infringement is damages not exceeding a reasonable payment in respect of the act complained of.

(3)   In subsection (2) "innocently acquired" means that the person acquiring the recording did not know and had no reason to believe that it was an illicit recording.

Exceptions to rights conferred

189   Acts permitted notwithstanding rights conferred by this Part

The provisions of Schedule 2 specify acts which may be done notwithstanding the rights conferred by this Part, being acts which correspond broadly to certain of those specified in Chapter III of Part I (acts permitted notwithstanding copyright).

190   Power of tribunal to give consent on behalf of performer in certain cases

(1)   The Copyright Tribunal may, on the application of a person wishing to make a copy of a recording of a performance, give consent in a case where the identity or whereabouts of the person entitled to the reproduction right cannot be ascertained by reasonable inquiry.

(2)   Consent given by the Tribunal has effect as consent of the person entitled to the reproduction right for the purposes of—

(a)   the provisions of this Part relating to performers' rights, and

(b)   section 198(3)(a) (criminal liability: sufficient consent in relation to qualifying performances),

and may be given subject to any conditions specified in the Tribunal's order.

(3)   The Tribunal shall not give consent under subsection (1)(a) except after the service or publication of such notices as may be required by rules made under section 150 (general procedural rules) or as the Tribunal may in any particular case direct.

. . .

(5)   In any case the Tribunal shall take into account the following factors—

(a)   whether the original recording was made with the performer's consent and is lawfully in the possession or control of the person proposing to make the further recording;

(b)   whether the making of the further recording is consistent with the obligations of the parties to the arrangements under which, or is otherwise consistent with the purposes for which, the original recording was made.

(6)   Where the Tribunal gives consent under this section it shall, in default of agreement between the applicant and the person entitled to the reproduction right, make such order as it thinks fit as to the payment to be made to that person in consideration of consent being given.

Duration of rights

191   Duration of rights

(1)   The following provisions have effect with respect to the duration of the rights conferred by this Part.

(2)   The rights conferred by this Part in relation to a performance expire—

(a)   at the end of the period of 50 years from the end of the calendar year in which the performance takes place, or

(b)   if during that period a recording of the performance is released, 50 years from the end of the calendar year in which it is released,

subject as follows.

(3)   For the purposes of subsection (2) a recording is "released" when it is first published, played or shown in public, broadcast or included in a cable programme service; but in determining whether a recording has been released no account shall be taken of any unauthorised act.

(4)   Where a performer is not a national of an EEA state, the duration of the rights conferred by this Part in relation to his performance is that to which the performance is entitled in the country of which he is a national, provided that does not exceed the period which would apply under subsections (2) and (3).

(5)   If or to the extent that the application of subsection (4) would be at variance with an international obligation to which the United Kingdom became subject prior to 29th October 1993, the duration of the rights conferred by this Part shall be as specified in subsections (2) and (3).

191A   Performers' property rights

(1)   The following rights conferred by this Part on a performer—

reproduction right (section 182A),

distribution right (section 182B),

rental right and lending right (section 182C),

are property rights ("a performer's property rights").

(2)   References in this Part to the consent of the performer shall be construed in relation to a performer's property rights as references to the consent of the rights owner.

(3)   Where different persons are (whether in consequence of a partial assignment or otherwise) entitled to different aspects of a performer's property rights in relation to a performance, the rights owner for any purpose of this Part is the person who is entitled to the aspect of those rights relevant for that purpose.

(4)   Where a performer's property rights (or any aspect of them) is owned by more than one person jointly, references in this Part to the rights owner are to all the owners, so that, in particular, any requirement of the licence of the rights owner requires the licence of all of them.

191B   Assignment and licences

(1)   A performer's property rights are transmissible by assignment, by testamentary disposition or by operation of law, as personal or moveable property.

(2)   An assignment or other transmission of a performer's property rights may be partial, that is, limited so as to apply—

(a)   to one or more, but not all, of the things requiring the consent of the rights owner;

(b)   to part, but not the whole, of the period for which the rights are to subsist.

(3)   An assignment of a performer's property rights is not effective unless it is in writing signed by or on behalf of the assignor.

(4) A licence granted by the owner of a performer's property rights is binding on every successor in title to his interest in the rights, except a purchaser in good faith for valuable consideration and without notice (actual or constructive) of the licence or a person deriving title from such a purchaser; and references in this Part to doing anything with, or without, the licence of the rights owner shall be construed accordingly.

191C Prospective ownership of a performer's property rights

(1) This section applies where by an agreement made in relation to a future recording of a performance, and signed by or on behalf of the performer, the performer purports to assign his performer's property rights (wholly or partially) to another person.

(2) If on the rights coming into existence the assignee or another person claiming under him would be entitled as against all other persons to require the rights to be vested in him, they shall vest in the assignee or his successor in title by virtue of this subsection.

(3) A licence granted by a prospective owner of a performer's property rights is binding on every successor in title to his interest (or prospective interest) in the rights, except a purchaser in good faith for valuable consideration and without notice (actual or constructive) of the licence or a person deriving title from such a purchaser. References in this Part to doing anything with, or without, the licence of the rights owner shall be construed accordingly.

(4) In subsection (3) "prospective owner" in relation to a performer's property rights means a person who is prospectively entitled to those rights by virtue of such an agreement as is mentioned in subsection (1).

191D Exclusive licences

(1) In this Part an "exclusive licence" means a licence in writing signed by or on behalf of the owner of a performer's property rights authorising the licensee to the exclusion of all other persons, including the person granting the licence, to do anything requiring the consent of the rights owner.

(2) The licensee under an exclusive licence has the same rights against a successor in title who is bound by the licence as he has against the person granting the licence.

191E Performer's property right to pass under will with unpublished original recording

Where under a bequest (whether general or specific) a person is entitled beneficially or otherwise to any material thing containing an original recording of a performance which was not published before the death of the testator, the bequest shall, unless a contrary intention is indicated in the testator's will or a codicil to it, be construed as including any performer's rights in relation to the recording to which the testator was entitled immediately before his death.

191F Presumption of transfer of rental right in case of film production agreement

(1) Where an agreement concerning film production is concluded between a performer and a film producer, the performer shall be presumed, unless the agreement provides to the contrary, to have transferred to the film producer any rental right in relation to the film arising from the inclusion of a recording of his performance in the film.

(2) Where this section applies, the absence of signature by or on behalf of the performer does not exclude the operation of section 191C (effect of purported assignment of future rights).

(3) The reference in subsection (1) to an agreement concluded between a performer and a film producer includes any agreement having effect between those persons, whether made by them directly or through intermediaries.

(4) Section 191G (right to equitable remuneration on transfer of rental right) applies where there is a presumed transfer by virtue of this section as in the case of an actual transfer.

191G   Right to equitable remuneration where rental right transferred

(1)   Where a performer has transferred his rental right concerning a sound recording or a film to the producer of the sound recording or film, he retains the right to equitable remuneration for the rental.

The reference above to the transfer of rental right by one person to another includes any arrangement having that effect, whether made by them directly or through intermediaries.

(2)   The right to equitable remuneration under this section may not be assigned by the performer except to a collecting society for the purpose of enabling it to enforce the right on his behalf.

The right is, however, transmissible by testamentary disposition or by operation of law as personal or moveable property; and it may be assigned or further transmitted by any person into whose hands it passes.

(3)   Equitable remuneration under this section is payable by the person for the time being entitled to the rental right, that is, the person to whom the right was transferred or any successor in title of his.

(4)   The amount payable by way of equitable remuneration is as agreed by or on behalf of the persons by and to whom it is payable, subject to section 191H (reference of amount to Copyright Tribunal).

(5)   An agreement is of no effect in so far as it purports to exclude or restrict the right to equitable remuneration under this section.

(6)   In this section a "collecting society" means a society or other organisation which has as its main object, or one of its main objects, the exercise of the right to equitable remuneration on behalf of more than one performer.

191H   Equitable remuneration: reference of amount to Copyright Tribunal

(1)   In default of agreement as to the amount payable by way of equitable remuneration under section 191G, the person by or to whom it is payable may apply to the Copyright Tribunal to determine the amount payable.

(2)   A person to or by whom equitable remuneration is payable may also apply to the Copyright Tribunal—

(a)   to vary any agreement as to the amount payable, or

(b)   to vary any previous determination of the Tribunal as to that matter;

but except with the special leave of the Tribunal no such application may be made within twelve months from the date of a previous determination.

An order made on an application under this subsection has effect from the date on which it is made or such later date as may be specified by the Tribunal.

(3)   On an application under this section the Tribunal shall consider the matter and make such order as to the method of calculating and paying equitable remuneration as it may determine to be reasonable in the circumstances, taking into account the importance of the contribution of the performer to the film or sound recording.

(4)   Remuneration shall not be considered inequitable merely because it was paid by way of a single payment or at the time of the transfer of the rental right.

(5)   An agreement is of no effect in so far as it purports to prevent a person questioning the amount of equitable remuneration or to restrict the powers of the Copyright Tribunal under this section.

191I   Infringement actionable by rights owner

(1)   An infringement of a performer's property rights is actionable by the rights owner.

(2)   In an action for infringement of a performer's property rights all such relief by way of damages, injunctions, accounts or otherwise is available to the plaintiff as is available in respect of the infringement of any other property right.

(3)   This section has effect subject to the following provisions of this Part.

191J   Provisions as to damages in infringement action

(1)   Where in an action for infringement of a performer's property rights it is shown that at the time of the infringement the defendant did not know, and had no reason to believe, that the rights subsisted in the recording to which the action relates, the plaintiff is not entitled to damages against him, but without prejudice to any other remedy.

(2)   The court may in an action for infringement of a performer's property rights having regard to all the circumstances, and in particular to—

(a)   the flagrancy of the infringement, and

(b)   any benefit accruing to the defendant by reason of the infringement, award such additional damages as the justice of the case may require.

191K   Undertaking to take licence of right in infringement proceedings

(1)   If in proceedings for infringement of a performer's property rights in respect of which a licence is available as of right under paragraph 17 of Schedule 2A (powers exercisable in consequence of competition report) the defendant undertakes to take a licence on such terms as may be agreed or, in default of agreement, settled by the Copyright Tribunal under that paragraph—

(a)   no injunction shall be granted against him,

(b)   no order for delivery up shall be made under section 195, and

(c)   the amount recoverable against him by way of damages or on an account of profits shall not exceed double the amount which would have been payable by him as licensee if such a licence on those terms had been granted before the earliest infringement.

(2)   An undertaking may be given at any time before final order in the proceedings, without any admission of liability.

(3)   Nothing in this section affects the remedies available in respect of an infringement committed before licences of right were available.

191L   Rights and remedies for exclusive licensee

(1)   An exclusive licensee has, except against the owner of a performer's property rights, the same rights and remedies in respect of matters occurring after the grant of the licence as if the licence had been an assignment.

(2)   His rights and remedies are concurrent with those of the rights owner; and references in the relevant provisions of this Part to the rights owner shall be construed accordingly.

(3)   In an action brought by an exclusive licensee by virtue of this section a defendant may avail himself of any defence which would have been available to him if the action had been brought by the rights owner.

191M   Exercise of concurrent rights

(1)   Where an action for infringement of a performer's property rights brought by the rights owner or an exclusive licensee relates (wholly or partly) to an infringement in respect of which they have concurrent rights of action, the rights owner or, as the case may be, the exclusive licensee may not, without the leave of the court, proceed with the action unless the other is either joined as plaintiff or added as a defendant.

(2)   A rights owner or exclusive licensee who is added as a defendant in pursuance of subsection (1) is not liable for any costs in the action unless he takes part in the proceedings.

(3)   The above provisions do not affect the granting of interlocutory relief on an application by the rights owner or exclusive licensee alone.

(4)   Where an action for infringement of a performer's property rights is brought which relates (wholly or partly) to an infringement in respect of which the rights owner and an exclusive licensee have or had concurrent rights of action—

(a)   the court shall in assessing damages take into account—

      (i)   the terms of the licence, and

      (ii)   any pecuniary remedy already awarded or available to either of them in respect of the infringement;

     (b)   no account of profits shall be directed if an award of damages has been made, or an account of profits has been directed, in favour of the other of them in respect of the infringement; and

     (c)   the court shall if an account of profits is directed apportion the profits between them as the court considers just, subject to any agreement between them;
and these provisions apply whether or not the rights owner and the exclusive licensee are both parties to the action.

    (5)   The owner of a performer's property rights shall notify any exclusive licensee having concurrent rights before applying for an order under section 195 (order for delivery up) or exercising the right conferred by section 196 (right of seizure); and the court may on the application of the licensee make such order under section 195 or, as the case may be, prohibiting or permitting the exercise by the rights owner of the right conferred by section 196, as it thinks fit having regard to the terms of the licence.

Non-property rights

192A Performers' non-property rights

    (1)   The rights conferred on a performer by—

section 182 (consent required for recording, &c. of live performance),

section 183 (infringement of performer's rights by use of recording made without consent), and

section 184 (infringement of performer's rights importing, possessing or dealing with illicit recording),

are not assignable or transmissible, except to the following extent.

They are referred to in this Part as "a performer's non-property rights".

    (2)   On the death of a person entitled to any such right—

     (a)   the right passes to such person as he may by testamentary disposition specifically direct, and

     (b)   if or to the extent that there is no such direction, the right is exercisable by his personal representatives.

    (3)   References in this Part to the performer, in the context of the person having such right, shall be construed as references to the person for the time being entitled to exercise those rights.

    (4)   Where by virtue of subsection (2)(a) a right becomes exercisable by more than one person, it is exercisable by each of them independently of the other or others.

    (5)   Any damages recovered by personal representatives by virtue of this section in respect of an infringement after a person's death shall devolve as part of his estate as if the right of action had subsisted and been vested in him immediately before his death.

192B Transmissibility of rights of person having recording rights

    (1)   The rights conferred by this Part on a person having recording rights are not assignable or transmissible.

    (2)   This does not affect section 185(2)(b) or (3)(b), so far as those provisions confer rights under this Part on a person to whom the benefit of a contract or licence is assigned.

193 Consent

    (1)   Consent for the purposes of this Part by a person having a performer's non-property rights, or by a person having recording rights, may be given in relation to a specific performance, a specified description of performances or performances generally, and may relate to past or future performances.

(2) A person having recording rights in a performance is bound by any consent given by a person through whom he derives his rights under the exclusive recording contract or licence in question, in the same way as if the consent had been given by him.

(3) Where a performer's non-property right passes to another person, any consent binding on the person previously entitled binds the person to whom the right passes in the same way as if the consent had been given by him.

194 Infringement actionable as breach of statutory duty

An infringement of—

(a) a performer's non-property rights, or

(b) any right conferred by this Part on a person having recording rights,

is actionable by the person entitled to the right as a breach of statutory duty.

Delivery up or seizure of illicit recordings

195 Order for delivery up

(1) Where a person has in his possession, custody or control in the course of a business an illicit recording of a performance, a person having performer's rights or recording rights in relation to the performance under this Part may apply to the court for an order that the recording be delivered up to him or to such other person as the court may direct.

(2) An application shall not be made after the end of the period specified in section 203; and no order shall be made unless the court also makes, or it appears to the court that there are grounds for making, an order under section 204 (order as to disposal of illicit recording).

(3) A person to whom a recording is delivered up in pursuance of an order under this section shall, if an order under section 204 is not made, retain it pending the making of an order, or the decision not to make an order, under that section.

(4) Nothing in this section affects any other power of the court.

196 Right to seize illicit recordings

(1) An illicit recording of a performance which is found exposed or otherwise immediately available for sale or hire, and in respect of which a person would be entitled to apply for an order under section 195, may be seized and detained by him or a person authorised by him.

The right to seize and detain is exercisable subject to the following conditions and is subject to any decision of the court under section 204 (order as to disposal of illicit recording).

(2) Before anything is seized under this section notice of the time and place of the proposed seizure must be given to a local police station.

(3) A person may for the purpose of exercising the right conferred by this section enter premises to which the public have access but may not seize anything in the possession, custody or control of a person at a permanent or regular place of business of his and may not use any force.

(4) At the time when anything is seized under this section there shall be left at the place where it was seized a notice in the prescribed form containing the prescribed particulars as to the person by whom or on whose authority the seizure is made and the grounds on which it is made.

(5) In this section—

"premises" includes land, buildings, fixed or move able structures, vehicles, vessels, aircraft and hovercraft; and

"prescribed" means prescribed by order of the Secretary of State.

(6) An order of the Secretary of State under this section shall be made by statutory instrument which shall be subject to annulment in pursuance of a resolution of either House of Parliament.

197   Meaning of "illicit recording"
(1)   In this Part "illicit recording", in relation to a performance, shall be construed in accordance with this section.
(2)   For the purposes of a performer's rights, a recording of the whole or any substantial part of a performance of his is an illicit recording if it is made, otherwise than for private purposes, without his consent.
(3)   For the purposes of the rights of a person having recording rights, a recording of the whole or any substantial part of a performance subject to the exclusive recording contract is an illicit recording if it is made, otherwise than for private purposes, without his consent or that of the performer.
(4)   For the purposes of sections 198 and 199 (offences and orders for delivery up in criminal proceedings), a recording is an illicit recording if it is an illicit recording for the purposes mentioned in subsection (2) or subsection (3).
(5)   In this Part "illicit recording" includes a recording falling to be treated as an illicit recording by virtue of any of the following provisions of Schedule 2—
   paragraph 4(3) (recordings made for purposes of instruction or examination),
   paragraph 6(2) (recordings made by educational establishments for educational purposes),
   paragraph 12(2) (recordings of performance in electronic form retained on transfer of principal recording), or
   paragraph 16(3) (recordings made for purposes of broadcast or cable programme),
but otherwise does not include a recording made in accordance with any of the provisions of that Schedule.
(6)   It is immaterial for the purposes of this section where the recording was made.

Offences

198   Criminal liability for making, dealing with or using illicit recordings
(1)   A person commits an offence who without sufficient consent—
   (a)   makes for sale or hire, or
   (b)   imports into the United Kingdom otherwise than for his private and domestic use, or
   (c)   possesses in the course of a business with a view to committing any act infringing the rights conferred by this Part, or
   (d)   in the course of a business—
      (i)   sells or lets for hire, or
      (ii)   offers or exposes for sale or hire, or
      (iii) distributes,
a recording which is, and which he knows or has reason to believe is, an illicit recording.
(2)   A person commits an offence who causes a recording of a performance made without sufficient consent to be—
   (a)   shown or played in public, or
   (b)   broadcast or included in a cable programme service,
thereby infringing any of the rights conferred by this Part, if he knows or has reason to believe that those rights are thereby infringed.
(3)   In subsections (1) and (2) "sufficient consent" means—
   (a)   in the case of a qualifying performance, the consent of the performer, and
   (b)   in the case of a non-qualifying performance subject to an exclusive recording contract—
      (i)   for the purposes of subsection (1)(a) (making of recording), the consent of the performer or the person having recording rights, and
      (ii)   for the purposes of subsection (1)(b), (c) and (d) and subsection (2) (dealing with or using recording), the consent of the person having recording rights.

The references in this subsection to the person having recording rights are to the person having those rights at the time the consent is given or, if there is more than one such person, to all of them.

(4)   No offence is committed under subsection (1) or (2) by the commission of an act which by virtue of any provision of Schedule 2 may be done without infringing the rights conferred by this Part.

(5)   A person guilty of an offence under subsection (1)(a), (b) or (d)(iii) is liable—

(a)   on summary conviction to imprisonment for a term not exceeding six months or a fine not exceeding the statutory maximum, or both;

(b)   on conviction on indictment to a fine or imprisonment for a term not exceeding two years, or both.

(6)   A person guilty of any other offence under this section is liable on summary conviction to a fine not exceeding level 5 on the standard scale or imprisonment for a term not exceeding six months, or both.

198A   Enforcement by local weights and measures authority

(1)   It is the duty of every local weights and measures authority to enforce within their area the provisions of section 198.

(2)   The following provisions of the Trade Descriptions Act 1968 apply in relation to the enforcement of that section by such an authority as in relation to the enforcement of that Act—

section 27 (power to make test purchases),

section 28 (power to enter premises and inspect and seize goods and documents),

section 29 (obstruction of authorised officers), and

section 33 (compensation for loss, &c. of goods seized).

. . .

199   Order for delivery up in criminal proceedings

(1)   The court before which proceedings are brought against a person for an offence under section 198 may, if satisfied that at the time of his arrest or charge he had in his possession, custody or control in the course of a business an illicit recording of a performance, order that it be delivered up to a person having performers' rights or recording rights in relation to the performance or to such other person as the court may direct.

. . .

201   False representation of authority to give consent

(1)   It is an offence for a person to represent falsely that he is authorised by any person to give consent for the purposes of this Part in relation to a performance, unless he believes on reasonable grounds that he is so authorised.

(2)   A person guilty of an offence under this section is liable on summary conviction to imprisonment for a term not exceeding six months or a fine not exceeding level 5 on the standard scale or both.

202   Offence by body corporate: liability of officers

(1)   Where an offence under this Part committed by a body corporate is proved to have been committed with the consent or connivance of a director, manager, secretary or other similar officer of the body, or a person purporting to act in any such capacity, he as well as the body corporate is guilty of the offence and liable to be proceeded against and punished accordingly.

(2)   In relation to a body corporate whose affairs are managed by its members "director" means a member of the body corporate.

. . .

205A

The provisions of Schedule 2A have effect with respect to the licensing of performers' property rights

Jurisdiction of Copyright Tribunal

205B   Jurisdiction of Copyright Tribunal

(1)   The Copyright Tribunal has jurisdiction under this Part to hear and determine proceedings under—

(a)   section 182D (amount of equitable remuneration for exploitation of commercial sound recording);

(b)   section 190 (application to give consent on behalf of owner of reproduction right);

(c)   section 191H (amount of equitable remuneration on transfer of rental right);

(d)   paragraph 3, 4 or 5 of Schedule 2A (reference of licensing scheme);

(e)   paragraph 6 or 7 of that Schedule (application with respect to licence under licensing scheme);

(f)   paragraph 10, 11 or 12 of that Schedule (reference or application with respect to licensing by licensing body);

(g)   paragraph 15 of that Schedule (application to settle royalty for certain lending);

(h)   paragraph 17 of that Schedule (application to settle terms of licence available as of right).

(2)   The provisions of Chapter VIII of Part I (general provisions relating to the Copyright Tribunal) apply in relation to the Tribunal when exercising any jurisdiction under this Part.

(3)   Provision shall be made by rules under section 150 prohibiting the Tribunal from entertaining a reference under paragraph 3, 4 or 5 of Schedule 2A (reference of licensing scheme) by a representative organisation unless the Tribunal is satisfied that the organisation is reasonably representative of the class of persons which it claims to represent.

Qualification for protection and extent

206   Qualifying countries, individuals and persons

(1)   In this Part—

"qualifying country" means—

(a)   the United Kingdom,

(b)   another member State of the European Economic Community, or

(c)   to the extent that an Order under section 208 so provides, a country designated under that section as enjoying reciprocal protection;

"qualifying individual" means a citizen or subject of, or an individual resident in, a qualifying country; and

"qualifying person" means a qualifying individual or a body corporate or other body having legal personality which—

(a)   is formed under the law of a part of the United Kingdom or another qualifying country, and

(b)   has in any qualifying country a place of business at which substantial business activity is carried on.

(2)   The reference in the definition of "qualifying individual" to a person's being a citizen or subject of a qualifying country shall be construed—

(a)   in relation to the United Kingdom, as a reference to his being a British Citizen, and

(b)   in relation to a colony of the United Kingdom, as a reference to his being a British Dependent Territories' citizen by connection with that colony.

(3)   In determining for the purpose of the definition of "qualifying person" whether substantial business activity is carried on at a place of business in any country, no account shall be taken of dealings in goods which are at all material times outside that country.

207   Countries to which this Part extends
This Part extends to England and Wales, Scotland and Northern Ireland.

208   Countries enjoying reciprocal protection
(1)   Her Majesty may by Order in Council designate as enjoying reciprocal protection under this Part—
   (a)   a Convention country, or
   (b)   a country as to which Her Majesty is satisfied that provision has been or will be made under its law giving adequate protection for British performances.
(2)   A "Convention country" means a country which is a party to a Convention relating to performers' rights to which the United Kingdom is also a party.
(3)   A "British performance" means a performance—
   (a)   given by an individual who is a British citizen or resident in the United Kingdom, or
   (b)   taking place in the United Kingdom.
(4)   If the law of that country provides adequate protection only for certain descriptions of performance, an Order under subsection (1)(b) designating that country shall contain provision limiting to a corresponding extent the protection afforded by this Part in relation to performances connected with that country.
(5)   The power conferred by subsection (1)(b) is exercisable in relation to any of the Channel Islands, the Isle of Man or any colony of the United Kingdom, as in relation to a foreign country.
(6)   A statutory instrument containing an Order in Council under this section shall be subject to annulment in pursuance of a resolution of either House of Parliament.

209   Territorial waters and the continental shelf
(1)   For the purposes of this Part the territorial waters of the United Kingdom shall be treated as part of the United Kingdom.
(2)   This Part applies to things done in the United Kingdom sector of the continental shelf on a structure or vessel which is present there for purposes directly connected with the exploration of the sea bed or subsoil or the exploitation of their natural resources as it applies to things done in the United Kingdom.
(3)   The United Kingdom sector of the continental shelf means the areas designated by order under section 1(7) of the Continental Shelf Act 1964.

210   British ships, aircraft and hovercraft
(1)   This Part applies to things done on a British ship, aircraft or hovercraft as it applies to things done in the United Kingdom.
(2)   In this section—
   "British ship" means a ship which is a British ship for the purposes of the Merchant Shipping Act 1995 otherwise than by virtue of registration in a country outside the United Kingdom; and
   "British aircraft" and "British hovercraft" mean an aircraft or hovercraft registered in the United Kingdom.

Interpretation

211   Expressions having same meaning as in copyright provisions
(1)   The following expressions have the same meaning in this Part as in Part I (copyright)—

broadcast,
business,
cable programme,
cable programme service,
country,
defendant (in Scotland),
delivery up (in Scotland),
EEA national
film,
literary work,
published, and
sound recording.

(2) The provisions of section 6(3) to (5), section 7(5) and 19(4) (supplementary provisions relating to broadcasting and cable programme services) apply for the purposes of this Part, and in relation to an infringement of the rights conferred by this Part, as they apply for the purposes of Part I and in relation to an infringement of copyright.

212 Index of defined expressions

The following Table shows provisions defining or otherwise explaining expressions used in this Part (other than provision defining or explaining an expression used only in the same section)—

broadcast (and related expressions)	section 211 (and section 6)
business	section 211(1) (and section 178)
cable programme, cable programme service (and related expressions)	section 211 (and section 7)
consent of performer (in relation to performer's property rights)	section 191A(2)
country	section 211(1) (and section 178)
defendant (in Scotland)	section 211(1) (and section 177)
delivery up (in Scotland)	section 211(1) (and section 177)
distribution right	section 182B(5)
EEA national	section 211(1) (and section 172A)
exclusive recording contract	section 185(1)
film	section 211(1) (and section 5B)
illicit recording	section 197
lending right	section 182C(7)
literary work	section 211(1) (and section 3(1))
performance	section 180(2)
performer's non-property rights	section 192A(1)
performer's property rights	section 191A(1)
published	section 211(1) (and section 175)
qualifying country	section 206(1)
qualifying individual	section 206(1) and (2)
qualifying performance	section 181
qualifying person	section 206(1) and (3)
recording (of a performance)	section 180(2)
recording rights (person having)	section 185(2) and (3)
rental right	section 182C(7)
reproduction right	section 182A(3)
right's owner (in relation to performer's property rights)	section 191A(3) and (4)
sound recording	section 211(1) (and section 5A).

PART III   DESIGN RIGHT

CHAPTER I   DESIGN RIGHT IN ORIGINAL DESIGNS

Introductory

213   Design right

(1)   Design right is a property right which subsists in accordance with this Part in an original design.

(2)   In this Part "design" means the design of any aspect of the shape or configuration (whether internal or external) of the whole or part of an article.

(3)   Design right does not subsist in—

  (a)   a method or principle of construction,

  (b)   features of shape or configuration of an article which—

      (i)   enable the article to be connected to, or placed in, around or against, another article so that either article may perform its function, or

      (ii)   are dependent upon the appearance of another article of which the article is intended by the designer to form an integral part, or

  (c)   surface decoration.

(4)   A design is not "original" for the purposes of this Part if it is commonplace in the design field in question at the time of its creation.

(5)   Design right subsists in a design only if the design qualifies for design right protection by reference to—

  (a)   the designer or the person by whom the design was commissioned or the designer employed (see sections 218 and 219), or

  (b)   the person by whom and country in which articles made to the design were first marketed (see section 220),

or in accordance with any Order under section 221 (power to make further provision with respect to qualification).

(5A)   Design right does not subsist in a design which consists of or contains a controlled representation within the meaning of the Olympic Symbol etc. (Protection) Act 1995.

(6)   Design right does not subsist unless and until the design has been recorded in a design document or an article has been made to the design.

(7)   Design right does not subsist in a design which was so recorded, or to which an article was made, before the commencement of this Part.

214   The designer

(1)   In this Part the "designer", in relation to a design, means the person who creates it.

(2)   In the case of a computer-generated design the person by whom the arrangements necessary for the creation of the design are undertaken shall be taken to be the designer.

215   Ownership of design right

(1)   The designer is the first owner of any design right in a design which is not created in pursuance of a commission or in the course of employment.

(2)   Where a design is created in pursuance of a commission, the person commissioning the design is the first owner of any design right in it.

(3)   Where, in a case not falling within subsection (2) a design is created by an employee in the course of his employment, his employer is the first owner of any design right in the design.

(4)   If a design qualifies for design right protection by virtue of section 220 (qualification by reference to first marketing of articles made to the design), the above rules do not apply and the person by whom the articles in question are marketed is the first owner of the design right.

216 Duration of design right

(1) Design right expires—

(a) fifteen years from the end of the calendar year in which the design was first recorded in a design document or an article was first made to the design, whichever first occurred, or

(b) if articles made to the design are made available for sale or hire within five years from the end of that calendar year, ten years from the end of the calendar year in which that first occurred.

(2) The reference in subsection (1) to articles being made available for sale or hire is to their being made so available anywhere in the world by or with the licence of the design right owner.

Qualification for design right protection

217 Qualifying individuals and qualifying persons

(1) In this Part—

"qualifying individual" means a citizen or subject of, or an individual habitually resident in, a qualifying country; and

"qualifying person" means a qualifying individual or a body corporate or other body having legal personality which—

(a) is formed under the law of a part of the United Kingdom or another qualifying country, and

(b) has in any qualifying country a place of business at which substantial business activity is carried on.

(2) References in this Part to a qualifying person include the Crown and the government of any other qualifying country.

(3) In this section "qualifying country" means—

(a) the United Kingdom,

(b) a country to which this Part extends by virtue of an Order under section 255,

(c) another member State of the European Economic Community, or

(d) to the extent that an Order under section 256 so provides, a country designated under that section as enjoying reciprocal protection.

(4) The reference in the definition of "qualifying individual" to a person's being a citizen or subject of a qualifying country shall be construed—

(a) in relation to the United Kingdom, as a reference to his being a British citizen, and

(b) in relation to a colony of the United Kingdom, as a reference to his being a British Dependent Territories' citizen by connection with that colony.

(5) In determining for the purpose of the definition of "qualifying person" whether substantial business activity is carried on at a place of business in any country, no account shall be taken of dealings in goods which are at all material times outside that country.

218 Qualification by reference to designer

(1) This section applies to a design which is not created in pursuance of a commission or in the course of employment.

(2) A design to which this section applies qualifies for design right protection if the designer is a qualifying individual or, in the case of a computer-generated design, a qualifying person.

(3) A joint design to which this section applies qualifies for design right protection if any of the designers is a qualifying individual or, as the case may be, a qualifying person.

(4) Where a joint design qualifies for design right protection under this section, only those designers who are qualifying individuals or qualifying persons are entitled to

design right under section 215(1) (first ownership of design right: entitlement of designer).

219   Qualification by reference to commissioner or employer

(1)   A design qualifies for design right protection if it is created in pursuance of a commission from, or in the course of employment with, a qualifying person.

(2)   In the case of a joint commission or joint employment a design qualifies for design right protection if any of the commissioners or employers is a qualifying person.

(3)   Where a design which is jointly commissioned or created in the course of joint employment qualifies for design right protection under this section, only those commissioners or employers who are qualifying persons are entitled to design right under section 215(2) or (3) (first ownership of design right: entitlement of commissioner or employer).

220   Qualification by reference to first marketing

(1)   A design which does not qualify for design right protection under section 218 or 219 (qualification by reference to designer, commissioner or employer) qualifies for design right protection if the first marketing of articles made to the design—

(a)   is by a qualifying person who is exclusively authorised to put such articles on the market in the United Kingdom, and

(b)   takes place in the United Kingdom, another country to which this Part extends by virtue of an Order under section 255, or another member State of the European Economic Community.

(2)   If the first marketing of articles made to the design is done jointly by two or more persons, the design qualifies for design right protection if any of those persons meets the requirements specified in subsection (1)(a).

(3)   In such a case only the persons who meet those requirements are entitled to design right under section 215(4) (first ownership of design right: entitlement of first marketer of articles made to the design).

(4)   In subsection (1)(a) "exclusively authorised" refers—

(a)   to authorisation by the person who would have been first owner of design right as designer, commissioner of the design or employer of the designer if he had been a qualifying person, or by a person lawfully claiming under such a person, and

(b)   to exclusivity capable of being enforced by legal proceedings in the United Kingdom.

221   Power to make further provision as to qualification

(1)   Her Majesty may, with a view to fulfilling an international obligation of the United Kingdom, by Order in Council provide that a design qualifies for design right protection if such requirements as are specified in the Order are met.

(2)   An Order may make different provision for different descriptions of design or article; and may make such consequential modifications of the operation of sections 215 (ownership of design right) and sections 218 to 220 (other means of qualification) as appear to Her Majesty to be appropriate.

(3)   A statutory instrument containing an Order in Council under this section shall be subject to annulment in pursuance of a resolution of either House of Parliament.

Dealings with design right

222   Assignment and licences

(1)   Design right is transmissible by assignment, by testamentary disposition or by operation of law, as personal or moveable property.

(2)   An assignment or other transmission of design right may be partial, that is, limited so as to apply—

(a)   to one or more, but not all, of the things the design right owner has the exclusive right to do;

(b)   to part, but not the whole, of the period for which the right is to subsist.

(3)   An assignment of design right is not effective unless it is in writing signed by or on behalf of the assignor.

(4)   A licence granted by the owner of design right is binding on every successor in title to his interest in the right, except a purchaser in good faith for valuable consideration and without notice (actual or constructive) of the licence or a person deriving title from such a purchaser; and references in this Part to doing anything with, or without, the licence of the design right owner shall be construed accordingly.

223   Prospective ownership of design right

(1)   Where by an agreement made in relation to future design right, and signed by or on behalf of the prospective owner of the design right, the prospective owner purports to assign the future design right (wholly or partially) to another person, then if, on the right coming into existence, the assignee or another person claiming under him would be entitled as against all other persons to require the right to be vested in him, the right shall vest in him by virtue of this section.

(2)   In this section—

"future design right" means design right which will or may come into existence in respect of a future design or class of designs or on the occurrence of a future event; and

"prospective owner" shall be construed accordingly, and includes a person who is prospectively entitled to design right by virtue of such an agreement as is mentioned in subsection (1).

(3)   A licence granted by a prospective owner of design right is binding on every successor in title to his interest (or prospective interest) in the right, except a purchaser in good faith for valuable consideration and without notice (actual or constructive) or the licence or a person deriving title from such a purchaser; and references in this Part to doing anything with, or without, the licence of the design right owner shall be construed accordingly.

224   Assignment of right in registered design presumed to carry with it design right

Where a design consisting of a design in which design right subsists is registered under the Registered Designs Act 1949 and the proprietor of the registered design is also the design right owner, an assignment of the right in the registered design shall be taken to be also an assignment of the design right, unless a contrary intention appears.

225   Exclusive licences

(1)   In this Part an "exclusive licence" means a licence in writing signed by or on behalf of the design right owner authorising the licensee to the exclusion of all other persons, including the person granting the licence, to exercise a right which would otherwise be exercisable exclusively by the design right owner.

(2)   The licensee under an exclusive licence has the same rights against any successor in title who is bound by the licence as he has against the person granting the licence.

CHAPTER II   RIGHTS OF DESIGN RIGHT OWNER AND REMEDIES

Infringement of design right

226   Primary infringement of design right

(1)   The owner of design right in a design has the exclusive right to reproduce the design for commercial purposes—

(a)   by making articles to that design, or

(b)   by making a design document recording the design for the purpose of enabling such articles to be made.

(2)   Reproduction of a design by making articles to the design means copying the design so as to produce articles exactly or substantially to that design, and references in this Part to making articles to a design shall be construed accordingly.

(3)   Design right is infringed by a person who without the licence of the design right owner does, or authorises another to do, anything which by virtue of this section is the exclusive right of the design right owner.

(4)   For the purposes of this section reproduction may be direct or indirect, and it is immaterial whether any intervening acts themselves infringe the design right.

(5)   This section has effect subject to the provisions of Chapter III (exceptions to rights of design right owner).

227   Secondary infringement: importing or dealing with infringing article

(1)   Design right is infringed by a person who, without the licence of the design right owner—

(a)   imports into the United Kingdom for commercial purposes, or

(b)   has in his possession for commercial purposes, or

(c)   sells, lets for hire, or offers or exposes for sale or hire, in the course of a business,

an article which is, and which he knows or has reason to believe is, an infringing article.

(2)   This section has effect subject to the provisions of Chapter III (exceptions to rights of design right owner).

228   Meaning of "infringing article"

(1)   In this Part "infringing article", in relation to a design, shall be construed in accordance with this section.

(2)   An article is an infringing article if its making to that design was an infringement of design right in the design.

(3)   An article is also an infringing article if—

(a)   it has been or is proposed to be imported into the United Kingdom, and

(b)   its making to that design in the United Kingdom would have been an infringement of design right in the design or a breach of an exclusive licence agreement relating to the design.

(4)   Where it is shown that an article is made to a design in which design right subsists or has subsisted at any time, it shall be presumed until the contrary is proved that the article was made at a time when design right subsisted.

(5)   Nothing in subsection (3) shall be construed as applying to an article which may lawfully be imported into the United Kingdom by virtue of any enforceable Community right within the meaning of section 2(1) of the European Communities Act 1972.

(6)   The expression "infringing article" does not include a design document, notwithstanding that its making was or would have been an infringement of design right.

Remedies for infringement

229   Rights and remedies of design right owner

(1)   An infringement of design right is actionable by the design right owner.

(2)   In an action for infringement of design right all such relief by way of damages, injunctions, accounts or otherwise is available to the plaintiff as is available in respect of the infringement of any other property right.

(3)   The court may in an action for infringement of design right, having regard to all the circumstances and in particular to—

(a)   the flagrancy of the infringement, and

(b)   any benefit accruing to the defendant by reason of the infringement,

award such additional damages as the justice of the case may require.

(4)   This section has effect subject to section 233 (innocent infringement).

230   Order for delivery up

(1)   Where a person—

(a)   has in his possession, custody or control for commercial purposes an infringing article, or

(b)   has in his possession, custody or control anything specifically designed or adapted for making articles to a particular design, knowing or having reason to believe that it has been or is to be used to make an infringing article,

the owner of the design right in the design in question may apply to the court for an order that the infringing article or other thing be delivered up to him or to such other person as the court may direct.

. . .

231   Order as to disposal of infringing articles &c.

(1)   An application may be made to the court for an order that an infringing article or other thing delivered up in pursuance of an order under section 230 shall be—

(a)   forfeited to the design right owner, or

(b)   destroyed or otherwise dealt with as the court may think fit,

or for a decision that no such order should be made.

(2)   In considering what order (if any) should be made, the court shall consider whether other remedies available in an action for infringement of design right would be adequate to compensate the design right owner and to protect his interests.

. . .

233   Innocent infringement

(1)   Where in an action for infringement of design right brought by virtue of section 226 (primary infringement) it is shown that at the time of the infringement the defendant did not know, and had no reason to believe, that design right subsisted in the design to which the action relates, the plaintiff is not entitled to damages against him, but without prejudice to any other remedy.

(2)   Where in an action for infringement of design right brought by virtue of section 227 (secondary infringement) a defendant shows that the infringing article was innocently acquired by him or a predecessor in title of his, the only remedy available against him in respect of the infringement is damages not exceeding a reasonable royalty in respect of the act complained of.

(3)   In subsection (2) "innocently acquired" means that the person acquiring the article did not know and had no reason to believe that it was an infringing article.

234   Rights and remedies of exclusive licensee

(1)   An exclusive licensee has, except against the design right owner, the same rights and remedies in respect of matters occurring after the grant of the licence as if the licence had been an assignment.

(2)   His rights and remedies are concurrent with those of the design right owner; and references in the relevant provisions of this Part to the design right owner shall be construed accordingly.

(3)   In an action brought by an exclusive licensee by virtue of this section a defendant may avail himself of any defence which would have been available to him if the action had been brought by the design right owner.

235   Exercise of concurrent rights

(1)   Where an action for infringement of design right brought by the design right owner or an exclusive licensee relates (wholly or partly) to an infringement in respect of which they have concurrent rights of action, the design right owner or, as the case may be, the exclusive licensee may not, without the leave of the

court, proceed with the action unless the other is either joined as a plaintiff or added as a defendant.

(2)   A design right owner or exclusive licensee who is added as a defendant in pursuance of subsection (1) is not liable for any costs in the action unless he takes part in the proceedings.

(3)   The above provisions do not affect the granting of interlocutory relief on the application of the design right owner or an exclusive licensee.

(4)   Where an action for infringement of design right is brought which relates (wholly or partly) to an infringement in respect of which the design right owner and an exclusive licensee have concurrent rights of action—

(a)   the court shall, in assessing damages, take into account—
        (i)   the terms of the licence, and
        (ii)   any pecuniary remedy already awarded or available to either of them in respect of the infringement;
(b)   no account of profits shall be directed if an award of damages has been made, or an account of profits has been directed, in favour of the other of them in respect of the infringement; and
(c)   the court shall if an account of profits is directed apportion the profits between them as the court considers just, subject to any agreement between them;

and these provisions apply whether or not the design right owner and the exclusive licensee are both parties to the action.

(5)   The design right owner shall notify any exclusive licensee having concurrent rights before applying for an order under section 230 (order for delivery up of infringing article, &c.); and the court may on the application of the licensee make such order under that section as it thinks fit having regard to the terms of the licence.

CHAPTER III   EXCEPTIONS TO RIGHTS OF DESIGN RIGHT OWNERS

Infringement of copyright

236   Infringement of copyright

Where copyright subsists in a work which consists of or includes a design in which design right subsists, it is not an infringement of design right in the design to do anything which is an infringement of the copyright in that work.

Availability of licences of right

237   Licences available in last five years of design right

(1)   Any person is entitled as of right to a licence to do in the last five years of the design right term anything which would otherwise infringe the design right.

(2)   The terms of the licence shall, in default of agreement, be settled by the comptroller.

(3)   The Secretary of State may if it appears to him necessary in order to—
(a)   comply with an international obligation of the United Kingdom, or
(b)   secure or maintain reciprocal protection for British designs in other countries,
by order exclude from the operation of subsection (1) designs of a description specified in the order or designs applied to articles of a description so specified.

(4)   An order shall be made by statutory instrument; and no order shall be made unless a draft of it has been laid before and approved by a resolution of each House of Parliament.

238   Powers exercisable for protection of the public interest

(1)   Where the matters specified in a report of the Monopolies and Mergers Commission as being those which in the Commission's opinion operate, may be expected to operate or have operated against the public interest include—

(a)   conditions in licences granted by a design right owner restricting the use of the design by the licensee or the right of the design right owner to grant other licences, or

(b)   a refusal of a design right owner to grant licences on reasonable terms,

the powers conferred by Part I of Schedule 8 to the Fair Trading Act 1973 (powers exercisable for purpose of remedying or preventing adverse effects specified in report of Commission) include power to cancel or modify those conditions and, instead or in addition, to provide that licences in respect of the design right shall be available as of right.

(2)   The references in sections 56(2) and 73(2) of that Act, and sections 10(2)(b) and 12(5) of the Competition Act 1980, to the powers specified in that Part of that Schedule shall be construed accordingly.

(3)   The terms of a licence available by virtue of this section shall, in default of agreement, be settled by the comptroller.

239   Undertaking to take licence of right in infringement proceedings

(1)   If in proceedings for infringement of design right in a design in respect of which a licence is available as of right under section 237 or 238 the defendant undertakes to take a licence on such terms as may be agreed or, in default of agreement, settled by the comptroller under that section—

(a)   no injunction shall be granted against him,

(b)   no order for delivery up shall be made under section 230, and

(c)   the amount recoverable against him by way of damages or on an account of profits shall not exceed double the amount which would have been payable by him as licensee if such a licence on those terms had been granted before the earliest infringement.

(2)   An undertaking may be given at any time before final order in the proceedings, without any admission of liability.

(3)   Nothing in this section affects the remedies available in respect of an infringement committed before licences of right were available.

Crown use of designs

240   Crown use of designs

(1)   A government department, or a person authorised in writing by a government department, may without the licence of the design right owner—

(a)   do anything for the purpose of supplying articles for the services of the Crown, or

(b)   dispose of articles no longer required for the services of the Crown;

and nothing done by virtue of this section infringes the design right.

(2)   References in this Part to "the services of the Crown" are to—

(a)   the defence of the realm,

(b)   foreign defence purposes, and

(c)   health service purposes.

. . .

243   Crown use: compensation for loss of profit

(1)   Where Crown use is made of a design, the government department concerned shall pay—

(a)   to the design right owner, or

(b)   if there is an exclusive licence in force in respect of the design, to the exclusive licensee,

compensation for any loss resulting from his not being awarded a contract to supply the articles made to the design.

. . .

General

245 Power to provide for further exceptions

(1) The Secretary of State may if it appears to him necessary in order to—

(a)   comply with an international obligation of the United Kingdom, or

(b)   secure or maintain reciprocal protection for British designs in other countries,

by order provide that acts of a description specified in the order do not infringe design right.

(2) An order may make different provision for different descriptions of design or article.

(3) An order shall be made by statutory instrument and no order shall be made unless a draft of it has been laid before and approved by a resolution of each House of Parliament.

CHAPTER IV JURISDICTION OF THE COMPTROLLER AND THE COURT

Jurisdiction of the comptroller

246 Jurisdiction to decide matters relating to design right

(1) A party to a dispute as to any of the following matters may refer the dispute to the comptroller for his decision—

(a)   the subsistence of design right,

(b)   the term of design right, or

(c)   the identity of the person in whom design right first vested;

and the comptroller's decision on the reference is binding on the parties to the dispute.

(2) No other court or tribunal shall decide any such matter except—

(a)   on a reference or appeal from the comptroller,

(b)   in infringement or other proceedings in which the issue arises incidentally, or

(c)   in proceedings brought with the agreement of the parties or the leave of the comptroller.

(3) The comptroller has jurisdiction to decide any incidental question of fact or law arising in the course of a reference under this section.

247 Application to settle terms of licence of right

(1) A person requiring a licence which is available as of right by virtue of—

(a)   section 237 (licences available in last few years of design right), or

(b)   an order under section 238 (licences made available in the public interest),

may apply to the comptroller to settle the terms of the licence.

(2) No application for the settlement of the terms of a licence available by virtue of section 237 may be made earlier than one year before the earliest date on which the licence may take effect under that section.

(3) The terms of a licence settled by the comptroller shall authorise the licensee to do—

(a)   in the case of licence available by virtue of section 237, everything which would be an infringement of the design right in the absence of a licence;

(b)   in the case of a licence available by virtue of section 238, everything in respect of which a licence is so available.

. . .

CHAPTER V MISCELLANEOUS AND GENERAL

Miscellaneous

253 Remedy for groundless threats of infringement proceedings

(1) Where a person threatens another person with proceedings for infringement of design right, a person aggrieved by the threats may bring an action against him claiming—

(a)   a declaration to the effect that the threats are unjustifiable;

(b)   an injunction against the continuance of the threats;

(c)   damages in respect of any loss which he has sustained by the threats.

(2)   If the plaintiff proves that the threats were made and that he is a person aggrieved by them, he is entitled to the relief claimed unless the defendant shows that the acts in respect of which proceedings were threatened did constitute, or if done would have constituted, an infringement of the design right concerned.

(3)   Proceedings may not be brought under this section in respect of a threat to bring proceedings for an infringement alleged to consist of making or importing anything.

(4)   Mere notification that a design is protected by design right does not constitute a threat of proceedings for the purposes of this section.

254   Licensee under licence of right not to claim connection with design right owner

(1)   A person who has a licence in respect of a design by virtue of section 237 or 238 (licences of right) shall not, without the consent of the design right owner

(a)   apply to goods which he is marketing, or proposes to market, in reliance on that licence a trade description indicating that he is the licensee of the design right owner, or

(b)   use any such trade description in an advertisement in relation to such goods.

(2)   A contravention of subsection (1) is actionable by the design right owner.

(3)   In this section "trade description", the reference to applying a trade description to goods and "advertisement" have the same meaning as in the Trade Descriptions Act 1968.

Extent of operation of this Part

255   Countries to which this Part extends

(1)   This Part extends to England and Wales, Scotland and Northern Ireland.

(2)   Her Majesty may by Order in Council direct that this Part shall extend, subject to such exceptions and modifications as may be specified in the Order, to—

(a)   any of the Channel Islands,

(b)   the Isle of Man, or

(c)   any colony.

(3)   That power includes power to extend, subject to such exceptions and modifications as may be specified in the Order, any Order in Council made under section 221 (further provision as to qualification for design right protection) or section 256 (countries enjoying reciprocal protection).

. . .

256   Countries enjoying reciprocal protection

(1)   Her Majesty may, if it appears to Her that the law of a country provides adequate protection for British design, by Order in Council designate that country as one enjoying reciprocal protection under this Part.

(2)   If the law of a country provides adequate protection only for certain classes of British designs, or only for designs applied to certain classes of article, any Order designating that country shall contain provision limiting, to a corresponding extent, the protection afforded by this Part in relation to designs connected with that country.

. . .

Interpretation

258   Construction of references to design right owner

(1)   Where different persons are (whether in consequence of a partial assignment or otherwise) entitled to different aspects of design right in a work, the design right owner for any purpose of this Part is the person who is entitled to the right in the respect relevant for that purpose.

(2)   Where design right (or any aspect of design right) is owned by more than one person jointly, references in this Part to the design right owner are to all the owners, so that, in particular, any requirement of the licence of the design right owner requires the licence of all of them.

259   Joint designs
(1)   In this Part a "joint design" means a design produced by the collaboration of two or more designers in which the contribution of each is not distinct from that of the other or others.

(2)   References in this Part to the designer of a design shall, except as otherwise provided, be construed in relation to a joint design as references to all the designers of the design.

260   Application of provisions to articles in kit form
(1)   The provisions of this Part apply in relation to a kit, that is, a complete or substantially complete set of components intended to be assembled into an article, as they apply in relation to the assembled article.

(2)   Subsection (1) does not affect the question whether design right subsists in any aspect of the design of the components of a kit as opposed to the design of the assembled article.

. . .

263   Minor definitions
(1)   In this Part—
"British design" means a design which qualifies for design right protection by reason of a connection with the United Kingdom of the designer or the person by whom the design is commissioned or the designer is employed;
"business" includes a trade or profession;
"commission" means a commission for money or money's worth;
"the comptroller" means the Comptroller-General of Patents, Designs and Trade Marks;
"computer-generated", in relation to a design, means that the design is generated by computer in circumstances such that there is no human designer,
"country" includes any territory;
"the Crown" includes the Crown in right of Her Majesty's Government in Northern Ireland;
"design document" means any record of a design, whether in the form of a drawing, a written description, a photograph, data stored in a computer or otherwise;
"employee", "employment" and "employer" refer to employment under a contract of service or of apprenticeship;
"government department" includes a Northern Ireland department.

(2)   References in this Part to "marketing", in relation to an article, are to its being sold or let for hire, or offered or exposed for sale or hire, in the course of a business, and related expressions shall be construed accordingly; but no account shall be taken for the purposes of this Part of marketing which is merely colourable and not intended to satisfy the reasonable requirements of the public.

(3)   References in this Part to an act being done in relation to an article for "commercial purposes" are to its being done with a view to the article in question being sold or hired in the course of a business.

264   Index of defined expressions
The following Table shows provisions defining or otherwise explaining expressions used in this Part (other than provisions defining or explaining an expression used only in the same section)—

. . .

PART VII   MISCELLANEOUS AND GENERAL

Devices designed to circumvent copy-protection

296   Devices designed to circumvent copy-protection

(1)   This section applies where copies of a copyright work are issued to the public, by or with the licence of the copyright owner, in an electronic form which is copy-protected.

(2)   The person issuing the copies to the public has the same rights against a person who, knowing or having reason to believe that it will be used to make infringing copies—

(a)   makes, imports, sells or lets for hire, offers or exposes for sale or hire, or advertises for sale or hire, any device or means specifically designed or adopted to circumvent the form of copy-protection employed, or

(b)   publishes information intended to enable or assist persons to circumvent that form of copy-protection,
as a copyright owner has in respect of an infringement of copyright.

(2A)   Where the copies being issued to the public as mentioned in subsection (1) are copies of a computer program, subsection (2) applies as if for the words "or advertises for sale or hire" there were substituted "advertises for sale or hire or possesses in the course of a business".

(3)   Further, he has the same rights under section 99 or 100 (delivery up or seizure of certain articles) in relation to any such device or means which a person has in his possession, custody or control with the intention that it should be used to make infringing copies of copyright works, as a copyright owner has in relation to an infringing copy.

(4)   References in this section to copy-protection include any device or means intended to prevent or restrict copying of a work or to impair the quality of copies made.

(5)   Expressions used in this section which are defined for the purposes of Part I of this Act (copyright) have the same meaning as in that Part.

(6)   The following provisions apply in relation to proceedings under this section as in relation to proceedings under Part I (copyright)—

(a)   sections 104 to 106 of this Act (presumptions as to certain matters relating to copyright), and

(b)   section 72 of the Supreme Court Act 1981, section 15 of the Law Reform (Miscellaneous Provisions) (Scotland) Act 1985 and section 94A of the Judicature (Northern Ireland) Act 1978 (withdrawal of privilege against self-incrimination in certain proceedings relating to intellectual property);

and section 114 of this Act applies, with the necessary modifications, in relation to the disposal of anything delivered up or seized by virtue of subsection (3) above.

Computer programs

296A   Avoidance of certain terms

(1)   Where a person has the use of a computer program under an agreement, any term or condition in the agreement shall be void in so far as it purports to prohibit or restrict—

(a)   the making of any back up copy of the program which it is necessary for him to have for the purposes of the agreed use;

(b)   where the conditions in section 50B(2) are met, the decompiling of the program; or

(c)   the use of any device or means to observe, study or test the functioning of the program in order to understand the ideas and principles which underlie any element of the program.

(2)   In this section, decompile, in relation to a computer program, has the same meaning as in section 50B.

296B   Avoidance of certain terms relating to databases

Where under an agreement a person has a right to use a database or part of a database, any term or condition in the agreement shall be void in so far as it purports to prohibit or restrict the performance of any act which would but for section 50D infringe the copyright in the database.

Fraudulent reception of transmissions

297   Offence of fraudulently receiving programmes

(1)   A person who dishonestly receives a programme included in a broadcasting or cable programme service provided from a place in the United Kingdom with intent to avoid payment of any charge applicable to the reception of the programme commits an offence and is liable on summary conviction to a fine not exceeding level 5 on the standard scale.

(2)   Where an offence under this section committed by a body corporate is proved to have been committed with the consent or connivance of a director, manager, secretary or other similar officer of the body, or a person purporting to act in any such capacity, he as well as the body corporate is guilty of the offence and liable to be proceeded against and punished accordingly.

In relation to a body corporate whose affairs are managed by its members "director" means a member of the body corporate.

297A   Unauthorised decoders

(1)   A person who makes, imports, sells or lets for hire, offers or exposes for sale or hire, or advertises for sale or hire, any unauthorised decoder shall be guilty of an offence and liable—

(a)   on summary conviction, to a fine not exceeding the statutory maximum;

(b)   on conviction on indictment, to imprisonment for a term not exceeding two years, or to a fine, or to both.

(2)   It is a defence to any prosecution for an offence under this section for the defendant to prove that he did not know, and had no reasonable ground for knowing, that the decoder was an unauthorised decoder.

(3)   In this section—

"apparatus" includes any device, component or electronic data;

"decoder" means any apparatus which is designed or adapted to enable (whether on its own or with any other apparatus) an encrypted transmission to be decoded;

"transmission" means any programme included in a broadcasting or cable programme service which is provided from a place in the United Kingdom; and

"unauthorised", in relation to a decoder, means a decoder which will enable encrypted transmissions to be viewed in decoded form without payment of the fee (however imposed) which the person making the transmission, or on whose behalf it is made, charges for viewing those transmissions, or viewing any service of which they form part.

298   Rights and remedies in respect of apparatus, &c. for unauthorised reception of transmissions

(1)   A person who—

(a)   makes charges for the reception of programmes included in a broadcasting or cable programme service provided from a place in the United Kingdom, or

(b)   sends encrypted transmissions of any other description from a place in the United Kingdom,

is entitled to the following rights and remedies.

(2)   He has the same rights and remedies against a person who—

(a)   makes, imports or sells or lets for hire offers or exposes for sale or hire, or advertises for sale or hire any apparatus or device designed or adapted to enable or assist persons to receive the programmes or other transmissions when they are not entitled to do so, or

(b)   publishes any information which is calculated to enable or assist persons to receive the programmes or other transmissions when they are not entitled to do so, as a copyright owner has in respect of an infringement of copyright.

(3)   Further, he has the same rights under section 99 or 100 (delivery up or seizure of certain articles) in relation to any such apparatus or device as a copyright owner has in relation to an infringing copy.

(4)   Section 72 of the Supreme Court Act 1981, section 15 of the Law Reform (Miscellaneous Provisions) (Scotland) Act 1985 and section 94A of the Judicature (Northern Ireland) Act 1978 (withdrawal of privilege against self-incrimination in certain proceedings relating to intellectual property) apply to proceedings under this section as to proceedings under Part I of this Act (copyright).

(5) In section 97(1) (innocent infringement of copyright) as it applies to proceedings for infringement of the rights conferred by this section, the reference to the defendant not knowing or having reason to believe that copyright subsisted in the work shall be construed as a reference to his not knowing or having reason to believe that his acts infringed the rights conferred by this section.

(6) Section 114 of this Act applies, with the necessary modifications, in relation to the disposal of anything delivered up or seized by virtue of subsection (3) above.

299 Supplementary provisions as to fraudulent reception

(1) Her Majesty may by Order in Council—

(a) provide that section 297 applies in relation to programmes included in services provided from a country or territory outside the United Kingdom, and

(b) provide that section 298 applies in relation to such programmes and to encrypted transmissions sent from such a country or territory.

(2) (repealed)

(3) A statutory instrument containing an Order in Council under subsection (1) shall be subject to annulment in pursuance of a resolution of either House of Parliament.

(4) Where sections 297, 297A and 298 apply in relation to a broadcasting service or cable programme service, they also apply to any service run for the person providing that service, or a person providing programmes for that service, which consists wholly or mainly in the sending by means of a telecommunications system of sounds or visual images, or both.

(5) In sections 297, 297A and 298, and this section, "programme", "broadcasting" and "cable programme service", and related expressions, have the same meaning as in Part I (copyright).

. . .

Provisions for the benefit of the Hospital for Sick Children

301 Provisions for the benefit of the Hospital for Sick Children

The provisions of Schedule 6 have effect for conferring on trustees for the benefit of the Hospital for Sick Children, Great Ormond Street, London, a right to a royalty in respect of the public performance, commercial publication, broadcasting or inclusion in a cable programme service of the play "Peter Pan" by Sir James Matthew Barrie, or of any adaptation of that work, notwithstanding that copyright in the work expired on 31 December 1987.

. . .

SCHEDULES

Section 170   SCHEDULE 1

COPYRIGHT: TRANSITIONAL PROVISIONS AND SAVINGS

Introductory

1.—(1) In this Schedule—

"the 1911 Act" means the Copyright Act 1911,

"the 1956 Act" means the Copyright Act 1956, and

"the new copyright provisions" means the provisions of this Act relating to copyright, that is, Part I (including this Schedule) and Schedules 3, 7 and 8 so far as they make amendments or repeals consequential on the provisions of Part I.

(2) References in this Schedule to "commencement", without more, are to the date on which the new copyright provisions come into force.

(3) References in this Schedule to "existing works" are to works made before commencement; and for this purpose a work of which the making extended over a period shall be taken to have been made when its making was completed.

. . .

General principles: continuity of the law

3.   The new copyright provisions apply in relation to things existing at commencement as they apply in relation to things coming into existence after commencement, subject to any express provision to the contrary.

4.—(1)   The provisions of this paragraph have effect for securing the continuity of the law so far as the new copyright provisions re-enact (with or without modification) earlier provisions.

(2)   A reference in an enactment, instrument or other document to copyright, or to a work or other subject-matter in which copyright subsists, which apart from this Act would be construed as referring to copyright under the 1956 Act shall be construed, so far as may be required for continuing its effect, as being, or as the case may require, including, a reference to copyright under this Act or to works in which copyright subsists under this Act.

(3)   Anything done (including subordinate legislation made), or having effect as done, under or for the purposes of a provision repealed by this Act has effect as if done under or for the purposes of the corresponding provision of the new copyright provisions.

(4)   References (expressed or implied) in this Act or any other enactment, instrument or document to any of the new copyright provisions shall, so far as the context permits, be construed as including, in relation to times, circumstances and purposes before commencement, a reference to corresponding earlier provisions.

(5)   A reference (express or implied) in an enactment, instrument or other document to a provision repealed by this Act shall be construed, so far as may be required for continuing its effect, as a reference to the corresponding provision of this Act.

(6)   The provisions of this paragraph have effect subject to any specific transitional provision or saving and to any express amendment made by this Act.

Subsistence of copyright

5.—(1)   Copyright subsists in an existing work after commencement only if copyright subsisted in it immediately before commencement.

(2)   Sub-paragraph (1) does not prevent an existing work qualifying for copyright protection after commencement—

(a)   under section 155 (qualification by virtue of first publication), or

(b)   by virtue of an Order under section 159 (application of Part I to countries to which it does not extend).

6.—(1)   Copyright shall not subsist by virtue of this Act in an artistic work made before 1 June 1957 which at the time when the work was made constituted a design capable of registration under the Registered Designs Act 1949 or under the enactments repealed by that Act, and was used, or intended to be used, as a model or pattern to be multiplied by an industrial process.

(2)   For this purpose a design shall be deemed to be used as a model or pattern to be multiplied by any industrial process—

(a)   when the design is reproduced or is intended to be reproduced on more than 50 single articles, unless all the articles in which the design is reproduced or is intended to be reproduced together form only a single set of articles as defined in section 44(1) of the Registered Designs Act 1949, or

(b)   when the design is to be applied to—

(i)   printed paper hangings,

(ii)   carpets, floor cloths or oil cloths, manufactured or sold in lengths or pieces,

(iii)   textile piece goods, or textile goods manufactured or sold in lengths or pieces, or

(iv)   lace, not made by hand.

7.—(1)   No copyright subsists in a film, as such, made before 1 June 1957.

(2)   Where a film made before that date was an original dramatic work within the meaning of the 1911 Act, the new copyright provisions have effect in relation to the film as if it was an original dramatic work within the meaning of Part I.

(3)   The new copyright provisions have effect in relation to photographs forming part of a film made before 1 June 1957 as they have effect in relation to photographs not forming part of a film.

8.—(1)   A film sound-track to which section 13(9) of the 1956 Act applied before commencement (film to be taken to include sounds in associated sound-track) shall be treated for the purposes of the new copyright provisions not as part of the film, but as a sound recording.

(2)   However—

(a)   copyright subsists in the sound recording only if copyright subsisted in the film immediately before commencement, and it continues to subsist until copyright in the film expires;

(b)   the author and first owner of copyright in the film shall be treated as having been author and first owner of the copyright in the sound recording; and

(c)   anything done before commencement under or in relation to the copyright in the film continues to have effect in relation to the sound recording as in relation to the film.

9.   No copyright subsists in—

(a)   a broadcast made before 1 June 1957, or

(b)   a cable programme included in a cable programme service before 1 January 1985;

and any such broadcast or cable programme shall be disregarded for the purposes of section 14(5) (duration of copyright in repeats).

Authorship of work

10.   The question who was the author of an existing work shall be determined in accordance with the new copyright provisions for the purposes of the rights conferred by Chapter IV or Part I (moral rights), and for all other purposes shall be determined in accordance with the law in force at the time the work was made.

First ownership of copyright

11.—(1)   The question who was first owner of copyright in an existing work shall be determined in accordance with the law in force at the time the work was made.

(2)   Where before commencement a person commissioned the making of a work in circumstances falling within—

(a)   section 4(3) of the 1956 Act or paragraph (a) of the proviso to section 5(1) of the 1911 Act (photographs, portraits and engravings), or

(b)   the proviso to section 12(4) of the 1956 Act (sound recordings),

those provisions apply to determine first ownership of copyright in any work made in pursuance of the commission after commencement.

Duration of copyright in existing works

12.—(1)   The following provisions have effect with respect to the duration of copyright in existing works.

The question which provision applies to a work shall be determined by reference to the facts immediately before commencement; and expressions used in this paragraph which were defined for the purposes of the 1956 Act have the same meaning as in that Act.

(2)   Copyright in the following descriptions of work continues to subsist until the date on which it would have expired under the 1956 Act—

(a)   literary, dramatic or musical works in relation to which the period of 50 years mentioned in the proviso to section 2(3) of the 1956 Act (duration of copyright in works made available to the public after the death of the author) has begun to run;

(b)   engravings in relation to which the period of 50 years mentioned in the proviso to section 3(4) of the 1956 Act (duration of copyright in works published after the death of the author) has begun to run;

(c)   published photographs and photographs taken before 1 June 1957;

...

Designs

19.—(1)   Section 51 (exclusion of copyright protection in relation to works recorded or embodied in design document or models) does not apply for ten years after commencement in relation to a design recorded or embodied in a design document or model before commencement.

(2)   During those ten years the following provisions of Part III (design right) apply to any relevant copyright as in relation to design right—

(a)   sections 237 to 239 (availability of licences of right), and

(b)   sections 247 and 248 (application to comptroller to settle terms of licence of right).

(3)   In section 237 as it applies by virtue of this paragraph, for the reference in subsection (1) to the last five years of the design right term there shall be substituted a reference to the last five years of the period of ten years referred to in sub-paragraph (1) above, or to so much of those last five years during which copyright subsists.

(4)   In section 239 as it applies by virtue of this paragraph, for the reference in subsection (1)(b) to section 230 there shall be substituted a reference to section 99.

(5)   Where a licence of right is available by virtue of this paragraph, a person to whom a licence was granted before commencement may apply to the comptroller for an order adjusting the terms of that licence.

(6)   The provisions of sections 249 and 250 (appeals and rules) apply in relation to proceedings brought under or by virtue of this paragraph as to proceedings under Part III.

(7)   A licence granted by virtue of this paragraph shall relate only to acts which would be permitted by section 51 if the design document or model had been made after commencement.

(8)   Section 100 (right to seize infringing copies, &c.) does not apply during the period of ten years referred to in sub-paragraph (1) in relation to anything to which it would not apply if the design in question had been first recorded or embodied in a design document or model after commencement.

(9)   Nothing in this paragrpah affects the operation of any rule of law preventing or restricting the enforcement of copyright in relation to a design.

20.—(1)   Where section 10 of the 1956 Act (effect of industrial application of design corresponding to artistic work) applied in relation to an artistic work at any time before commencement, section 52(2) of this Act applies with the substitution for the period of 25 years mentioned there of the relevant period of 15 years as defined in section 10(3) of the 1956 Act.

(2)   Except as provided in sub-paragraph (1), section 52 applies only where articles are marketed as mentioned in subsection (1)(b) after commencement.

...

Moral rights

22.—(1)   No act done before commencement is actionable by virtue of any provision of Chapter IV or Part I (moral rights).

(2)   Section 43 of the 1956 Act (false attribution of authorship) continues to apply in relation to acts done before commencement.

23.—(1)   The following provisions have effect with respect to the rights conferred by—

(a)   section 77 (right to be identified as author or director), and

(b)   section 80 (right to object to derogatory treatment of work).

(2)   The rights do not apply—

(a)   in relation to a literary, dramatic, musical and artistic work of which the author died before commencement; or

(b)   in relation to a film made before commencement.

(3)   The rights in relation to an existing literary, dramatic, musical or artistic work do not apply—

(a)   where copyright first vested in the author, to anything which by virtue of an assignment of copyright made or licence granted before commencement may be done without infringing copyright;

(b)   where copyright first vested in a person other than the author, to anything done by or with the licence of the copyright owner.

(4)   The rights do not apply to anything done in relation to a record made in pursuance of section 8 of the 1956 Act (statutory recording licence).

24.   The right conferred by section 85 (right to privacy of certain photographs and films) does not apply to photographs taken or films made before commencement.

. . .

Section 189   SCHEDULE 2

RIGHTS IN PERFORMANCES: PERMITTED ACTS

Introductory

1.—(1)   The provisions of this Schedule specify acts which may be done in relation to a performance or recording notwithstanding the rights conferred by Part II; they relate only to the question of infringement of those rights and do not affect any other right or obligation restricting the doing of any of the specified acts.

(2)   No inference shall be drawn from the description of any act which may by virtue of this Schedule be done without infringing the rights conferred by Part II as to the scope of those rights.

(3)   The provisions of this Schedule are to be construed independently of each other, so that the fact that an act does not fall within one provision does not mean that it is not covered by another provision.

Criticism, reviews and news reporting

2.—(1)   Fair dealing with a performance or recording—

(a)   for the purpose of criticism or review, of that or another performance or recording, or of a work, or

(b)   for the purpose of reporting current events,

does not infringe any of the rights conferred by Part II.

(2)   Expressions used in this paragraph have the same meaning as in section 30.

Incidental inclusion of performance or recording

3.—(1)   The rights conferred by Part II are not infringed by the incidental inclusion of a performance or recording in a sound recording, film, broadcast or cable programme.

(2)   Nor are those rights infringed by anything done in relation to copies of, or the playing, showing, broadcasting or inclusion in a cable programme service of, anything whose making was, by virtue of sub-paragraph (1), not an infringement of those rights.

(3)   A performance or recording so far as it consists of music, or words spoken or sung with music, shall not be regarded as incidentally included in a sound recording, broadcast or cable programme if it is deliberately included.

(4)   Expressions used in this paragraph have the same meaning as in section 31.

Things done for purposes of instruction or examination

4.—(1)   The rights conferred by Part II are not infringed by the copying of a recording of a performance in the course of instruction, or of preparation for instruction, in the making of films or film sound-tracks, provided the copying is done by a person giving or receiving instruction.

(2)   The rights conferred by Part II are not infringed—

(a)   by the copying of a recording of a performance for the purposes of setting or answering the questions in an examination, or

(b)   by anything done for the purposes of an examination by way of communicating the questions to the candidates.

(3)   Where a recording which would otherwise be an illicit recording is made in accordance with this paragraph but is subsequently dealt with, it shall be treated as an illicit recording for the purposes of that dealing, and if that dealing infringes any right conferred by Part II for all subsequent purposes.

For this purpose "dealt with" means sold or let for hire, or offered or exposed for sale or hire.

(4)   Expressions used in this paragraph have the same meaning as in section 32.

Playing or showing sound recording, film, broadcast or cable programme at educational establishment

5.—(1)   The playing or showing of a sound recording, film, broadcast or cable programme at an educational establishment for the purposes of instruction before an audience consisting of teachers and pupils at the establishment and other persons directly connected with the activities of the establishment is not a playing or showing of a performance in public for the purposes of infringement of the rights conferred by Part II.

(2)   A person is not for this purpose directly connected with the activities of the educational establishment simply because he is the parent of a pupil at the establishment.

(3)   Expressions used in this paragraph have the same meaning as in section 34 and any provision made under section 174(2) with respect to the application of that section also applies for the purposes of this paragraph.

Recording of broadcasts and cable programmes by educational establishments

6.—(1)   A recording of a broadcast or cable programme, or a copy of such a recording, may be made by or on behalf of an educational establishment for the educational purposes of that establishment without thereby infringing any of the rights conferred by Part II in relation to any performance or recording included in it.

(2)   Where a recording which would otherwise be an illicit recording is made in accordance with this paragraph but is subsequently dealt with, it shall be treated as an illicit recording for the purposes of that dealing, and if that dealing infringes any right conferred by Part II for all subsequent purposes.

For this purpose "dealt with" means sold or let for hire, or offered or exposed for sale or hire.

(3)   Expressions used in this paragraph have the same meaning as in section 35 and any provision made under section 174(2) with respect to the application of that section also applies for the purposes of this paragraph.

Lending of copies by educational establishments

6A.—(1)   The rights conferred by Part II are not infringed by the lending of copies of a recording of a performance by an educational establishment.

(2)   Expressions used in this paragraph have the same meaning as in section 36A; and any provision with respect to the application of that section made under section 174(2) (instruction given elsewhere than an educational establishment) applies also for the purposes of this pargraph.

Lending of copies by libraries or archives

6B.—(1)   The rights conferred by Part II are not infringed by the lending of copies of a recording of a performance by a prescribed library or archive (other than a public library) which is not conducted for profit.

(2)   Expressions used in this paragraph have the same meaning as in section 40A(2); and any provision under section 37 prescribing libraries or archives for the purposes of that section applies also for the purposes of this paragraph.

Copy of work required to be made as condition of export

7.—(1)   If an article of cultural or historical importance or interest cannot lawfully be exported from the United Kingdom unless a copy of it is made and deposited in an appropriate library or archive, it is not an infringement of any right conferred by Part II to make that copy.

(2)   Expressions used in this paragraph have the same meaning as in section 44.

Parliamentary and judicial proceedings

8.—(1)   The rights conferred by Part II are not infringed by anything done for the purposes of parliamentary or judicial proceedings or for the purpose of reporting such proceedings.

(2)   Expressions used in this paragraph have the same meaning as in section 45.

Royal Commissions and statutory inquiries

9.—(1)   The rights conferred by Part II are not infringed by anything done for the purposes of the proceedings of a Royal Commission or statutory inquiry or for the purpose of reporting any such proceedings held in public.

(2)   Expressions used in this paragraph have the same meaning as in section 46.

Public records

10.—(1)   Material which is comprised in public records within the meaning of the Public Records Act 1958, the Public Records (Scotland) Act 1937 or the Public Records Act (Northern Ireland) 1923 which are open to public inspection in pursuance of that Act, may be copied, and a copy may be supplied to any person, by or with the authority of any officer appointed under that Act, without infringing any right conferred by Part II.

(2)   Expressions used in this paragraph have the same meaning as in section 49.

Acts done under statutory authority

11.—(1)   Where the doing of a particular act is specifically authorised by an Act of Parliament, whenever passed, then, unless the Act provides otherwise, the doing of that act does not infringe the rights conferred by Part II.

(2)   Sub-paragraph (1) applies in relation to an enactment contained in Northern Ireland legislation as it applies to an Act of Parliament.

(3)   Nothing in this paragraph shall be construed as excluding any defence of statutory authority otherwise available under or by virtue of any enactment.

(4)   Expressions used in this paragraph have the same meaning as in section 50.

Transfer of copies of works in electronic form

12.—(1)   This paragraph applies where a recording of a performance in electronic form has been purchased on terms which, expressly or impliedly or by virtue of any rule of law, allow the purchaser to make further recordings in connection with his use of the recording.

(2)   If there are no express terms—

(a)   prohibiting the transfer of the recording by the purchaser, imposing obligations which continue after a transfer, prohibiting the assignment of any consent or terminating any consent on a transfer, or

(b)   providing for the terms on which a transferee may do the things which the purchaser was permitted to do,

anything which the purchaser was allowed to do may also be done by a transferee without infringement of the rights conferred by this Part, but any recording made by the purchaser which is not also transferred shall be treated as an illicit recording for all purposes after the transfer.

(3)   The same applies where the original purchased recording is no longer usable and what is transferred is a further copy used in its place.

(4)   The above provisions also apply on a subsequent transfer, with the substitution for references in sub-paragraph (2) to the purchaser of references to the subsequent transferor.

(5)   This paragraph does not apply in relation to a recording purchased before the commencement of Part II.

(6)   Expressions used in this paragraph have the same meaning as in section 56.

Use of recordings of spoken works in certain cases

13.—(1)   Where a recording of the reading or recitation of a literary work is made for the purpose—

(a)   of reporting current events, or

(b)   of broadcasting or including in a cable programme service the whole or part of the reading or recitation,

it is not an infringement of the rights conferred by Part II to use the recording (or to copy the recording and use the copy) for that purpose, provided the following conditions are met.

(2)   The conditions are that—

(a)   the recording is a direct recording of the reading or recitation and is not taken from a previous recording or from a broadcast or cable programme;

(b)   the making of the recording was not prohibited by or on behalf of the person giving the reading or recitation;

(c)   the use made of the recording is not of a kind prohibited by or on behalf of that person before the recording was made; and

(d)   the use is by or with the authority of a person who is lawfully in possession of the recording.

(3)   Expressions used in this paragraph have the same meaning as in section 58.

Recordings of folksongs

14.—(1)   A recording of a performance of a song may be made for the purpose of including it in an archive maintained by a designated body without infringing any of the rights conferred by Part II, provided the conditions in sub-paragraph (2) below are met.

(2)   The conditions are that—

(a)   the words are unpublished and of unknown authorship at the time the recording is made,

(b) the making of the recording does not infringe any copyright, and

(c) its making is not prohibited by any performer.

(3) Copies of a recording made in reliance on sub-paragraph (1) and included in an archive maintained by a designated body may, if the prescribed conditions are met, be made and supplied by the archivist without infringing any of the rights conferred by Part II.

(4) In this paragraph—

"designated body" means a body designated for the purposes of section 61, and

"the prescribed conditions" means the conditions prescribed for the purposes of subsection (3) of that section;

and other expressions used in this paragraph have the same meaning as in that section.

Lending of certain recordings

14A.—(1) The Secretary of State may by order provide that in such cases as may be specified in the order the lending to the public of copies of films or sound recordings shall be treated as licensed by the performer subject only to the payment of such reasonable royalty or other payment as may be agreed or determined in default of agreement by the Copyright Tribunal.

(2) No such order shall apply if, or to the extent that, there is a licensing scheme certified by the purposes of this paragraph under paragraph 16 of Schedule 2A providing for the grant of licences.

(3) An order may make different provision for different cases and may specify cases by reference to any factor relating to the work, the copies lent, the lender or the circumstances of the lending.

(4) An order shall be made by statutory instrument; and no order shall be made unless a draft of it has been laid before and approved by a resolution of each House of Parliament.

(5) Nothing in this section affects any liability under section 184(1)(b) (secondary infringement: possessing or dealing with illicit recording) in respect of the lending of illicit recordings.

(6) Expressions used in this paragraph have the same meaning as in section 66.

Playing of sound recordings for purposes of club, society, &c.

15.—(1) It is not an infringement of any right conferred by Part II to play a sound recording as part of the activities of, or for the benefit of, a club, society or other organisation if the following conditions are met.

(2) The conditions are—

(a) that the organisation is not established or conducted for profit and its main objects are charitable or are otherwise concerned with the advancement of religion, education or social welfare, and

(b) that the proceeds of any charge for admission to the place where the recording is to be heard are applied solely for the purposes of the organisation.

(3) Expressions used in this paragraph have the same meaning as in section 67.

Incidental recording for purposes of broadcast or cable programme

16.—(1) A person who proposes to broadcast a recording of a performance, or include a recording of a performance in a cable programme service, in circumstances not infringing the rights conferred by Part II shall be treated as having consent for the purposes of that Part for the making of a further recording for the purposes of the broadcast or cable programme.

(2) That consent is subject to the condition that the further recording—

(a) shall not be used for any other purpose, and

(b) shall be destroyed within 28 days of being first used for broadcasting the performance or including it in a cable programme service.

(3) A recording made in accordance with this paragraph shall be treated as an illicit recording—

(a) for the purposes of any use in breach of the condition mentioned in sub-paragraph (2)(a), and

(b) for all purposes after that condition or the condition mentioned in sub-paragraph (2)(b) is broken.

(4) Expressions used in this paragraph have the same meaning as in section 68.

. . .

Free public showing or playing of broadcast or cable programme

18.—(1) The showing or playing in public of a broadcast or cable programme to an audience who have not paid for admission to the place where the broadcast or programme is to be seen or heard does not infringe any right conferred by Part II in relation to a performance or recording included in—

(a) the broadcast or cable programme, or

(b) any sound recording or film which is played or shown in public by reception of the broadcast or cable programme.

(2) The audience shall be treated as having paid for admission to a place—

(a) if they have paid for admission to a place of which that place forms part; or

(b) if goods or services are supplied at that place (or a place of which it forms part)—

(i) at prices which are substantially attributable to the facilities afforded for seeing or hearing the broadcast or programme, or

(ii) at prices exceeding those usually charged there and which are partly attributable to those facilities.

(3) The following shall not be regarded as having paid for admission to a place—

(a) persons admitted as residents or inmates of the place;

(b) persons admitted as members of a club or society where the payment is only for membership of the club or society and the provision of facilities for seeing or hearing broadcasts or programmes is only incidental to the main purposes of the club or society.

(4) Where the making of the broadcast or inclusion of the programme in a cable programme service was an infringement of the rights conferred by Part II in relation to a performance or recording, the fact that it was heard or seen in public by the reception of the broadcast or programme shall be taken into account in assessing the damages for that infringement.

(5) Expressions used in this paragraph have the same meaning as in section 72.

Reception and re-transmission of broadcast in cable programme service

19.—(1) This paragraph applies where a broadcast made from a place in the United Kingdom is, by reception and immediate re-transmission, included in a cable programme service.

(2) The rights conferred by Part II in relation to a performance or recording included in the broadcast are not infringed if and to the extent that the broadcast is made for reception in the area in which the cable programme service is provided; but where the making of the broadcast was an infringement of those rights, the fact that the broadcast was re-transmitted as a programme in a cable programme service shall be taken into account in assessing the damages for that infringement.

(3) Where—

(a) the inclusion is in pursuance of a relevant requirement, but

(b) to any extent, the area in which the cable programme service is provided ("the cable area") falls outside the area for reception in which the broadcast is made ("the broadcast area").

the inclusion in the cable programme service (to the extent that it is provided for so much of the cable area as falls outside the broadcast area) of any performance or recording included in the broadcast shall, subject to sub-paragraph (4), be treated as licensed by the owner of the rights conferred by Part II in relation to the performance or recording, subject only to the payment to him by the person making the broadcast of such reasonable royalty or other payment in respect of the inclusion of the broadcast in the cable programme service as may be agreed or determined in default of agreement by the Copyright Tribunal.

(4)   Sub-paragraph (3) does not apply if, or to the extent that, the inclusion of the work in the cable programme service is (apart from that sub-paragraph) licensed by the owner of the rights conferred by Part II in relation to the performance or recording.

(5)   The Secretary of State may by order—

(a)   provide that in specified cases sub-paragraph (2) is to apply in relation to broadcasts of a specified description which are not made as mentioned in that sub-paragraph, or

(b)   exclude the application of that sub-paragraph in relation to broadcasts of a specified description made as mentioned in that sub-paragraph.

(6)   Where the Secretary of State exercises the power conferred by sub-paragraph (5)(b) in relation to broadcasts of any description, the order may also provide for sub-paragraph (3) to apply, subject to such modifications as may be specified in the order, in relation to broadcasts of that description.

(7)   An order under this paragraph may contain such transitional provision as appears to the Secretary of State to be appropriate.

(8)   An order under this paragraph shall be made by statutory instrument which shall be subject to annulment in pursuance of a resolution of either House of Parliament.

(9)   Expressions used in this paragraph have the same meaning as in section 73.

19A.—(1)An application to settle the royalty or other sum payable in pursuance of sub-paragraph (3) of paragraph 19 may be made to the Copyright Tribunal by the owner of the rights conferred by Part II or the person making the broadcast.

(2)   The Tribunal shall consider the matter and make such order as it may determine to be reasonable in the circumstances.

(3)   Either party may subsequently apply to the Tribunal to vary the order, and the Tribunal shall consider the matter and make such order confirming or varying the original order as it may determine to be reasonable in the circumstances.

(4)   An application under sub-paragrpah (3) shall not, except with the special leave of the Tribunal, be made within twelve months from the date of the original order or of the order on a previous application under that sub-paragraph.

(5)   An order under sub-paragraph (3) has effect from the date on which it is made or such later date as may be specified by the Tribunal.

Provision of sub-titled copies of broadcast or cable programme

20.—(1)   A designated body may, for the purpose of providing people who are deaf or hard of hearing, or physically or mentally handicapped in other ways, with copies which are sub-titled or otherwise modified for their special needs, make recordings or television broadcasts or cable programmes without infringing any right conferred by Part II in relation to a performance or recording included in the broadcast or cable programme.

(2)   n this paragraph "designated body" means a body designated for the purposes of section 74 and other expressions used in this paragraph have the same meaning as in that section.

Recording of broadcast or cable programme for archival purposes

21.—(1)   A recording of a broadcast or cable programme of a designated class, or a copy of such a recording, may be made for the purpose of being placed in an archive maintained by a designated body without thereby infringing any right conferred by Part II in relation to a performance or recording included in the broadcast or cable programme.

(2)   In this paragraph "designated class" and "designated body" means a class or body designated for the purposes of section 75 and other expressions used in this paragraph have the same meaning as in that section.

. . .

SCHEDULE 2A

LICENSING OF PERFORMERS' PROPERTY RIGHTS

Licensing schemes and licensing bodies

1.—(1)   In Part II a "licensing scheme" means a scheme setting out—
   (a)   the classes of case in which the operator of the scheme, or the person on whose behalf he acts, is willing to grant performers' property right licences, and
   (b)   the terms on which licences would be granted in those classes of case;
and for this purpose a "scheme" includes anything in the nature of a scheme, whether described as a scheme or as a tariff or by any other name.

(2)   In Part II a "licensing body" means a society or other organisation which has as its main object, or one of its main objects, the negotiating or granting, whether as owner or prospective owner of a performer's property rights or as agent for him, of performers' property right licences, and whose objects include the granting of licences covering the performances of more than one performer.

(3)   In this pargraph "performers' property right licences" means licences to do, or authorise the doing of, any of the things for which consent is required under section 182A, 182B or 182C.

(4)   References in this Part to licences or licensing schemes covering the performances of more than one performer do not include licences or schemes covering only—
   (a)   performances recorded in a single recording,
   (b)   performances recorded in more than one recording where—
      (i)   the performers giving the performances are the same, or
      (ii)   the recordings are made by, or by employees of or commissioned by, a single individual, firm, company or group of companies.
For purpose a group of companies means a holding company and its subsidiaries within the meaning of section 736 of the Companies Act 1985.

References and applications with respect to licensing schemes

2.   Paragraphs 3 to 8 (references and applications with respect to licensing schemes) apply to licensing schemes operated by licensing bodies in relation to a performer's property rights which cover the performances of more than one performer, so far as they relate to licences for—
   (a)   copying a recording of the whole or any substantial part of a qualifying performance, or
   (b)   renting or lending copies of a recording to the public;
and in those paragraphs "licensing scheme" means a licensing scheme of any of those descriptions.

Reference of proposed licensing scheme to tribunal

3.—(1)   The terms of a licensing scheme proposed to be operated by a licensing body may be referred to the Copyright Tribunal by an organisation claiming to be representative of persons claiming that they require licences in cases of a description to which the scheme would apply, either generally or in relation to any description of case.

(2)   The Tribunal shall first decide whether to entertain the reference, and may decline to do so on the ground that the reference is premature.

(3)   If the Tribunal decides to entertain the reference it shall consider the matter referred and make such order, either confirming or varying the proposed scheme, either generally or so far as it relates to cases of the description to which the reference relates, as the Tribunal may determine to be reasonable in the circumstances.

(4)   The order may be made so as to be in force indefinitely or for such period as the Tribunal may determine.

Reference of licensing scheme to tribunal

4.—(1)   If while a licensing scheme is in operation a dispute arises between the operator of the scheme and—

(a)   a person claiming that he requires a licence in a case of a description to which the scheme applies, or

(b)   an organisation claiming to be representative of such persons,

that person or organisation may refer the scheme to the Copyright Tribunal in so far as it relates to cases of that description.

(2)   A scheme which has been referred to the Tribunal under this paragraph shall remain in operation until proceedings on the reference are concluded.

(3)   The Tribunal shall consider the matter in dispute and make such order, either confirming or varying the scheme so far as it relates to cases of the description to which the reference relates, as the Tribunal may determine to be reasonable in the circumstances.

(4)   The order may be made so as to be in force indefinitely or for such period as the Tribunal may determine.

. . .

Application for grant of licence in connection with licensing scheme

6.—(1)   A person who claims, in a case covered by a licensing scheme, that the operator of the scheme has refused to grant him or procure the grant to him of a licence in accordance with the scheme, or has failed to do so within a reasonable time after being asked, may apply to the Copyright Tribunal.

(2)   A person who claims, in a case excluded from a licensing scheme, that the operator of the scheme either—

(a)   has refused to grant him a licence or procure the grant to him of a licence, or has failed to do so within a reasonable time of being asked, and that in the circumstances it is unreasonable that a licence should not be granted, or

(b)   proposes terms for a licence which are unreasonable,

may apply to the Copyright Tribunal.

(3)   A case shall be regarded as excluded from a licensing scheme for the purposes of sub-paragraph (2) if—

(a)   the scheme provides for the grant of licences subject to terms excepting matters from the licence and the case falls within such an exception, or

(b)   the case is so similar to those in which licences are granted under the scheme that it is unreasonable that it should not be dealt with in the same way.

(4)   If the Tribunal is satisfied that the claim is well-founded, it shall make an order declaring that, in respect of the matters specified in the order, the applicant is entitled to a licence on such terms as the Tribunal may determine to be applicable in accordance with the scheme or, as the case may be, to be reasonable in the circumstances.

(5)   The order may be made so as to be in force indefinitely or for such period as the Tribunal may determine.

. . .

Effect of order of tribunal as to licensing scheme

8.—(1)   A licensing scheme which has been confirmed or varied by the Copyright Tribunal—
   (a)   under paragraph 3 (reference of terms of proposed scheme), or
   (b)   under paragraph 4 or 5 (reference of existing scheme to Tribunal),
shall be in force or, as the case may be, remain in operation, so far as it relates to the description of case in respect of which the order was made, so long as the order remains in force.

   (2)   While the order is in force a person who in a case of a class to which the order applies—
   (a)   pays to the operator of the scheme any charges payable under the scheme in respect of a licence covering the case in question or, if the amount cannot be ascertained, gives an undertaking to the operator to pay them when ascertained, and
   (b)   complies with the other terms applicable to such a licence under the scheme,
shall be in the same position as regards infringement of performers' property rights as if he had at all material times been the holder of a licence granted by the rights owner in question in accordance with the scheme.

. . .

   (5)   Where the Tribunal has made an order under paragraph 6 (order as to entitlement to licence under licensing scheme) and the order remains in force, the person in whose favour the order is made shall if he—
   (a)   pays to the operator of the scheme any charges payable in accordance with the order or, if the amount cannot be ascertained, gives an undertaking to pay the charges when ascertained, and
   (b)   complies with the other terms specified in the order,
be in the same position as regards infringement of performers' property rights as if he had at all material times been the holder of a licence granted by the rights owner in question on the terms specified in the order.

References and applications with respect to licensing by licensing bodies

9.   Paragraphs 10 to 13 (references and applications with respect to licensing by licensing bodies) apply to licences relating to a performer's property rights which cover the performance of more than one performer granted by a licensing body otherwise than in pursuance of a licensing scheme, so far as the licences authorise—
   (a)   copying a recording of the whole or any substantial part of a qualifying performance, or
   (b)   renting or lending copies of a recording to the public;
and references in those paragraphs to a licence shall be construed accordingly.

Reference to tribunal of proposed licence

10.—(1)   The terms on which a licensing body proposes to grant a licence may be referred to the Copyright Tribunal by the prospective licensee.

. . .

   (3)   If the Tribunal decides to entertain the reference it shall consider the terms of the proposed licence and make such order, either confirming or varying the terms as it may determine to be reasonable in the circumstances.

. . .

Reference to tribunal of expiring licence

11.—(1)   A licensee under a licence which is due to expire, by effluxion of time or as a result of notice given by the licensing body, may apply to the Copyright Tribunal on the ground that it is unreasonable in the circumstances that the licence should cease to be in force.

. . .

(4)   If the Tribunal finds the application well-founded, it shall make an order declaring that the licensee shall continue to be entitled to the benefit of the licence on such terms as the Tribunal may determine to be reasonable in the circumstances.

. . .

Effect of order of tribunal as to licence

13.—(1)   Where the Copyright Tribunal has made an order under paragraph 10 or 11 and the order remains in force, the person entitled to the benefit of the order shall if he—

(a)   pays to the licensing body any charges payable in accordance with the order or, if the amount cannot be ascertained, gives an undertaking to pay the charges when ascertained, and

(b)   complies with the other terms specified in the order,

be in the same position as regards infringement of performers' property rights as if he had at all material times been the holder of a licence granted by the rights owner in question on the terms specified in the order.

(2)   The benefit of the order may be assigned—

(a)   in the case of an order under paragraph 10, if assignment is not prohibited under the terms of the Tribunal's order; and

(b)   in the case of an order under paragraph 11, if assignment was not prohibited under the terms of the original licence.

. . .

General considerations: unreasonable discrimination

14.—(1)   In determining what is reasonable on a reference or application under this Schedule relating to a licensing scheme or licence, the Copyright Tribunal shall have regard to—

(a)   the availability of other schemes, or the granting of other licences, to other persons in similar circumstances, and

(b)   the terms of those schemes or licences,

and shall exercise its powers so as to secure that there is no unreasonable discrimination between licensees, or prospective licensees, under the scheme or licence to which the reference or application relates and licensees under other schemes operated by, or other licences granted by, the same person.

(2)   This does not affect the Tribunal's general obligation in any case to have regard to all relevant circumstances.

Application to settle royalty or other sum payable for lending

15.—(1)   An application to settle the royalty or other sum payable in pursuance of paragraph 14A of Schedule 2 (lending of certain recordings) may be made to the Copyright Tribunal by the owner of a performer's property rights or the person claiming to be treated as licensed by him.

. . .

Certification of licensing schemes

16.—(1)   A person operating or proposing to operate a licensing scheme may apply to the Secretary of State to certify the scheme for the purposes of paragraph 14A of Schedule 2 (lending of certain recordings).

. . .

THE DESIGN RIGHT (SEMICONDUCTOR TOPOGRAPHIES)
REGULATIONS 1989
(SI 1989/1100)

1 Citation and commencement
These Regulations may be cited as the Design Right (Semiconductor Topographies) Regulations 1989 and shall come into force on 1 August 1989.

2 Interpretation
(1) In these Regulations—

"the Act" means the Copyright, Designs and Patents Act 1988;

"semiconductor product" means an article the purpose, or one of the purposes, of which is the performance of an electronic function and which consists of two or more layers, at least one of which is composed of semiconducting material and in or upon one or more of which is fixed a pattern appertaining to that or another function; and

"semiconductor topography" means a design within the meaning of section 213(2) of the Act which is a design of either of the following:

(a) the pattern fixed, or intended to be fixed, in or upon—

  (i) a layer of a semiconductor product, or

  (ii) a layer of material in the course of and for the purpose of the manufacture of a semiconductor product, or

(b) the arrangement of the patterns fixed, or intended to be fixed, in or upon the layers of a semiconductor product in relation to one another.

(2) Except where the context otherwise requires, these Regulations shall be construed as one with Part III of the Act (design right).

3 Application of Copyright, Designs and Patents Act 1988, Part III
In its application to a design which is a semiconductor topography, Part III of the Act shall have effect subject to regulations 4 to 9 below.

4 Qualification
(1) Section 213(5) of the Act has effect subject to paragraphs (2) to (4) below.

(2) Part III of the Act has effect as if for section 217 of the Act there was substituted the following:

"217.—(1) In this Part—

"qualifying individual" means a citizen or subject of, or an individual habitually resident in, a qualifying country; and

"qualifying person" means—

(a) a qualifying individual,

(b) a body corporate or other body having legal personality which has in any qualifying country or in Gibraltar a place of business at which substantial business activity is carried on, or

(c) a person who falls within one of the additional classes set out in Part I of the Schedule to the Design Right (Semiconductor Topographies) Regulations 1989.

(2) References in this Part to a qualifying person include the Crown and the government of any other qualifying country.

(3) the United Kingdom, or

(a) In this section "qualifying country" means—

(b) another member State of the European Economic Community.

(4) The reference in the definition of "qualifying individual" to a person's being a citizen or subject of a qualifying country shall be construed in relation to the United Kingdom as a reference to his being a British citizen.

(5)   In determining for the purpose of the definition of "qualifying person" whether substantial business activity is carried on at a place of business in any country, no account shall be taken of dealings in goods which are at all material times outside that country.".

(3)   Where a semiconductor topography is created in pursuance of a commission or in the course of employment and the designer of the topography is, by virtue of section 215 of the Act (as substituted by regulation 5 below), the first owner of design right in that topography, section 219 of the Act does not apply and section 218(2) to (4) of the Act shall apply to the topography as if it had not been created in pursuance of a commission or in the course of employment.

(4)   Section 220 of the Act has effect subject to regulation 7 below and as if for subsection (1) there was substituted the following:

"220.—(1)   A design which does not qualify for design right protection under section 218 or 219 (as modified by regulation 4(3) of the Design Right (Semiconductor Topographies) Regulations 1989) or under the said regulation 4(3) qualifies for design right protection if the first marketing of articles made to the design—

(a)   is by a qualifying person who is exclusively authorised to put such articles on the market in every member State of the European Economic Community, and

(b)   takes place within the territory of any member State.";

and subsection (4) of section 220 accordingly has effect as if the words "in the United Kingdom" were omitted.

5   Ownership of design right

Part III of the Act has effect as if for section 215 of the Act there was substituted the following:

"215.—(1)   The designer is the first owner of any design right in a design which is not created in pursuance of a commission or in the course of employment.

(2)   Where a design is created in pursuance of a commission, the person commissioning the design is the first owner of any design right in it subject to any agreement in writing to the contrary.

(3)   Where, in a case not falling within subsection (2) a design is created by an employee in the course of his employment, his employer is the first owner of any design right in the design subject to any agreement in writing to the contrary.

(4)   If a design qualifies for design right protection by virtue of section 220 (as modified by regulation 4(4) of the Design Right (Semiconductor Topographies) Regulations 1989), the above rules do not apply and, subject to regulation 7 of the said Regulations, the person by whom the articles in question are marketed is the first owner of the design right.".

6   Duration of design right

(1)   Part III of the Act has effect as if for section 216 of the Act there was substituted the following:

"216. The design right in a semiconductor topography expires—

(a)   ten years from the end of the calendar year in which the topography or articles made to the topography were first made available for sale or hire anywhere in the world by or with the licence of the design right owner, or

(b)   if neither the topography nor articles made to the topography are so made available within a period of fifteen years commencing with the earlier of the time when the topography was first recorded in a design document or the time when an article was first made to the topography, at the end of that period.".

(2)   Subsection (2) of section 263 of the Act has effect as if the words "or a semiconductor topography" were inserted after the words "in relation to an article".

(3)   The substitute provision set out in paragraph (1) above has effect subject to regulation 7 below.

7   Confidential information

In determining, for the purposes of section 215(4), 216 or 220 of the Act (as modified by these Regulations), whether there has been any marketing, or anything has been made available for sale or hire, no account shall be taken of any sale or hire, or any offer or exposure for sale or hire, which is subject to an obligation of confidence in respect of information about the semiconductor topography in question unless either—

(a)   the article or semiconductor topography sold or hired or offered or exposed for sale or hire has been sold or hired on a previous occasion (whether or not subject to an obligation of confidence), or

(b)   the obligation is imposed at the behest of the Crown, or of the government of any country outside the United Kingdom, for the protection of security in connection with the production of arms, munitions or war material.

8   Infringement

(1)   Section 226 of the Act has effect as if for subsection (1) there was substituted the following:

"226.—(1)   Subject to subsection (1A), the owner of design right in a design has the exclusive right to reproduce the design—

(a)   by making articles to that design, or

(b)   by making a design document recording the design for the purpose of enabling such articles to be made.

(1A)   Subsection (1) does not apply to—

(a)   the reproduction of a design privately for non-commercial aims; or

(b)   the reproduction of a design for the purpose of analysing or evaluating the design or analysing, evaluating or teaching the concepts, processes, systems or techniques embodied in it.".

(2)   Section 227 of the Act does not apply if the article in question has previously been sold or hired within—

(a)   the United Kingdom by or with the licence of the owner of design right in the semiconductor topography in question, or

(b)   the territory of any other member State of the European Economic Community or the territory of Gibraltar by or with the consent of the person for the time being entitled to import it into or sell or hire it within that territory.

(3)   Section 228(6) of the Act does not apply.

(4)   It is not an infringement of design right in a semiconductor topography to—

(a)   create another original semiconductor topography as a result of an analysis or evaluation of the first topography or of the concepts, processes, systems or techniques embodied in it, or

(b)   reproduce that other topography.

(5)   Anything which would be an infringement of the design right in a semiconductor topography if done in relation to the topography as a whole is an infringement of the design right in the topography if done in relation to a substantial part of the topography.

9   Licences of right

Section 237 of the Act does not apply.

10   Revocation and transitional provisions

(1)   The Semiconductor Products (Protection of Topography) Regulations 1987 are hereby revoked.

(2)　Sub-paragraph (1) of paragraph 19 of Schedule 1 to the Act shall not apply in respect of a semiconductor topography created between 7 November 1987 and 31 July 1989.

(3)　In its application to copyright in a semiconductor topography created before 7 November 1987, sub-paragraph (2) of the said paragraph 19 shall have effect as if the reference to sections 237 to 239 were a reference to sections 238 and 239; and sub-paragraph (3) of that paragraph accordingly shall not apply to such copyright.

SCHEDULE
ADDITIONAL CLASSES OF QUALIFYING PERSONS
PART I
DESCRIPTIONS OF ADDITIONAL CLASSES

1.　British Dependent Territory citizens.

2.　Citizens and subjects of any country specified in Part II below.

3.　Habitual residents of any country specified in Part II below, the Isle of Man, the Channel Islands or any colony.

4.　Firms and bodies corporate formed under the law of, or of any part of, the United Kingdom, Gibraltar, another member State of the European Economic Community or any country specified in Part II below with a place of business within any country so specified at which substantial business activity is carried on.

PART II
SPECIFIED COUNTRIES: CITIZENS, SUBJECTS, HABITUAL RESIDENTS, BODIES CORPORATE AND OTHER BODIES HAVING LEGAL PERSONALITY

Australia
Austria
Finland
French overseas territories (French Polynesia; French Southern and Antarctic Territories; Mayotte; New Caledonia and dependencies; Saint-Pierre and Miquelon; Wallis and Futuna Islands)
Iceland
Japan
Liechtenstein
Norway
Sweden
Switzerland
United States of America

THE COPYRIGHT (INDUSTRIAL PROCESS AND EXCLUDED ARTICLES) (NO. 2) ORDER 1989
(SI 1989/1070)

The Secretary of State, in exercise of the powers conferred upon him by section 52(4) of the Copyright, Designs and Patents Act 1988 ("the Act"), hereby makes the following Order:—

1.　This Order may be cited as the Copyright (Industrial Process and Excluded Articles) (No. 2) Order 1989 and shall come into force on 1 August 1989.

2.　An article is to be regarded for the purposes of section 52 of the Act (limitation of copyright protection for design derived from artistic work) as made by an industrial process if—

　　(a)　it is one of more than fifty articles which—

(i)   all fall to be treated for the purposes of Part I of the Act as copies of a particular artistic work, but

(ii)   do not all together constitute a single set of articles as defined in section 44(1) of the Registered Designs Act 1949; or

(b)   it consists of goods manufactured in lengths or pieces, not being hand-made goods.

3.—(1)   There are excluded from the operation of section 52 of the Act—

(a)   works of sculpture, other than casts or models used or intended to be used as models or patterns to be multiplied by any industrial process;

(b)   wall plaques, medals and medallions; and

(c)   printed matter primarily of a literary or artistic character, including book jackets, calendars, certificates, coupons, dress-making patterns, greetings cards, labels, leaflets, maps, plans, playing cards, postcards, stamps, trade advertisements, trade forms and cards, transfers and similar articles.

(2)   Nothing in article 2 of this Order shall be taken to limit the meaning of "industrial process" in paragraph (1)(a) of this article.

4.   The Copyright (Industrial Designs) Rules 1957 and the Copyright (Industrial Process and Excluded Articles) Order 1989 are hereby revoked.

<h1 style="text-align:center">TRADE MARKS ACT 1994</h1>
(1994, c. 26)

An Act to make new provision for registered trade marks, implementing Council Directive No. 89/104/EEC of 21st December 1988 to approximate the laws of the Member States relating to trade marks; to make provision in connection with Council Regulation (EC) No. 40/94 of 20th December 1993 on the Community trade mark; to give effect to the Madrid Protocol Relating to the International Registration of Marks of 27th June 1989, and to certain provisions of the Paris Convention for the Protection of Industrial Property of 20th March 1883, as revised and amended; and for connected purposes.   [21 July 1994]

. . .

<h2 style="text-align:center">PART I</h2>
<h2 style="text-align:center">REGISTERED TRADE MARKS</h2>

Introductory

1   Trade marks

(1)   In this Act a "trade mark" means any sign capable of being represented graphically which is capable of distinguishing goods or services of one undertaking from those of other undertakings.

A trade mark may, in particular, consist of words (including personal names), designs, letters, numerals or the shape of goods or their packaging.

(2)   References in this Act to a trade mark include, unless the context otherwise requires, references to a collective mark (see section 49) or certification mark (see section 50).

2   Registered trade marks

(1)   A registered trade mark is a property right obtained by the registration of the trade mark under this Act and the proprietor of a registered trade mark has the rights and remedies provided by this Act.

(2)   No proceedings lie to prevent or recover damages for the infringement of an unregistered trade mark as such; but nothing in this Act affects the law relating to passing off.

Grounds for refusal of registration

3 Absolute grounds for refusal of registration
(1) The following shall not be registered—
    (a) signs which do not satisfy the requirements of section 1(1),
    (b) trade marks which are devoid of any distinctive character,
    (c) trade marks which consist exclusively of signs or indications which may serve, in trade, to designate the kind, quality, quantity, intended purpose, value, geographical origin, the time of production of goods or of rendering of services, or other characteristics of goods or services,
    (d) trade marks which consist exclusively of signs or indications which have become customary in the current language or in the *bona fide* and established practices of the trade:
Provided that, a trade mark shall not be refused registration by virtue of paragraph (b), (c) or (d) above if, before the date of application for registration, it has in fact acquired a distinctive character as a result of the use made of it.
(2) A sign shall not be registered as a trade mark if it consists exclusively of—
    (a) the shape which results from the nature of the goods themselves,
    (b) the shape of goods which is necessary to obtain a technical result, or
    (c) the shape which gives substantial value to the goods.
(3) A trade mark shall not be registered if it is—
    (a) contrary to public policy or to accepted principles of morality, or
    (b) of such a nature as to deceive the public (for instance as to the nature, quality or geographical origin of the goods or service).
(4) A trade mark shall not be registered if or to the extent that its use is prohibited in the United Kingdom by any enactment or rule of law or by any provision of Community law.
(5) A trade mark shall not be registered in the cases specified, or referred to, in section 4 (specially protected emblems).
(6) A trade mark shall not be registered if or to the extent that the application is made in bad faith.

4 Specially protected emblems
(1) A trade mark which consists of or contains—
    (a) the Royal arms, or any of the principal armorial bearings of the Royal arms, or any insignia or device so nearly resembling the Royal arms or any such armorial bearing as to be likely to be mistaken for them or it,
    (b) a representation of the Royal crown or any of the Royal flags,
    (c) a representation of Her Majesty or any member of the Royal family, or any colourable imitation thereof, or
    (d) words, letters or devices likely to lead persons to think that the applicant either has or recently has had Royal patronage or authorisation,
shall not be registered unless it appears to the registrar that consent has been given by or on behalf of Her Majesty or, as the case may be, the relevant member of the Royal family.
(2) A trade mark which consists of or contains a representation of—
    (a) the national flag of the United Kingdom (commonly known as the Union Jack), or
    (b) the flag of England, Wales, Scotland, Northern Ireland or the Isle of Man,
shall not be registered if it appears to the registrar that the use of the trade mark would be misleading or grossly offensive.
Provision may be made by rules identifying the flags to which paragraph (b) applies.
(3) A trade mark shall not be registered in the cases specified in—
    section 57 (national emblems, &c. of Convention countries), or

section 58 (emblems, &c. of certain international organisations).

(4)   Provision may be made by rules prohibiting in such cases as may be prescribed the registration of a trade mark which consists of or contains—

(a)   arms to which a person is entitled by virtue of a grant of arms by the Crown, or

(b)   insignia so nearly resembling such arms as to be likely to be mistaken for them,

unless it appears to the registrar that consent has been given by or on behalf of that person.

Where such a mark is registered, nothing in this Act shall be construed as authorising its use in any way contrary to the laws of arms.

(5)   A trade mark which consists of or contains a controlled representation within the meaning of the Olympic Symbol etc. (Protection) Act 1995 shall not be registered unless it appears to the registrar—

(a)   that the application is made by the person for the time being appointed under section 1(2) of the Olympic Symbol etc. (Protection) Act 1995 (power of Secretary of State to appoint a person as the proprietor of the Olympics association right), or

(b)   that consent has been given by or on behalf of the person mentioned in paragraph (a) above.

5   Relative grounds for refusal of registration

(1)   A trade mark shall not be registered if it is identical with an earlier trade mark and the goods or services for which the trade mark is applied for are identical with the goods or services for which the earlier trade mark is protected.

(2)   A trade mark shall not be registered if because—

(a)   it is identical with an earlier trade mark and is to be registered for goods or services similar to those for which the earlier trade mark is protected, or

(b)   it is similar to an earlier trade mark and is to be registered for goods or services identical with or similar to those for which the earlier trade mark is protected,

there exists a likelihood of confusion on the part of the public, which includes the likelihood of association with the earlier trade mark.

(3)   A trade mark which—

(a)   is identical with or similar to an earlier trade mark, and

(b)   is to be registered for goods or services which are not similar to those for which the earlier trade mark is protected,

shall not be registered if, or to the extent that, the earlier trade mark has a reputation in the United Kingdom (or, in the case of a Community trade mark, in the European Community) and the use of the later mark without due cause would take unfair advantage of, or be detrimental to, the distinctive character or the repute of the earlier trade mark.

(4)   A trade mark shall not be registered if, or to the extent that, its use in the United Kingdom is liable to be prevented—

(a)   by virtue of any rule of law (in particular, the law of passing off) protecting an unregistered trade mark or other sign used in the course of trade, or

(b)   by virtue of an earlier right other than those referred to in subsections (1) to (3) or paragraph (a) above, in particular by virtue of the law of copyright, design right or registered designs.

A person thus entitled to prevent the use of a trade mark is referred to in this Act as the proprietor of an "earlier right" in relation to the trade mark.

(5)   Nothing in this section prevents the registration of a trade mark where the proprietor of the earlier trade mark or other earlier right consents to the registration.

6   Meaning of "earlier trade mark"

(1)   In this Act an "earlier trade mark" means—

(a)   a registered trade mark, international trade mark (UK) or Community trade mark which has a date of application for registration earlier than that of the trade mark in question, taking account (where appropriate) of the priorities claimed in respect of the trade marks,

(b)   a Community trade mark which has a valid claim to seniority from an earlier registered trade mark or international trade mark (UK), or

(c)   a trade mark which, at the date of application for registration of the trade mark in question or (where appropriate) of the priority claimed in respect of the application, was entitled to protection under the Paris Convention as a well known trade mark.

(2)   References in this Act to an earlier trade mark include a trade mark in respect of which an application for registration has been made and which, if registered, would be an earlier trade mark by virtue of subsection (1)(a) or (b), subject to its being so registered.

(3)   A trade mark within subsection (1)(a) or (b) whose registration expires shall continue to be taken into account in determining the registrability of a later mark for a period of one year after the expiry unless the registrar is satisfied that there was no *bona fide* use of the mark during the two years immediately preceding the expiry.

7   Raising of relative grounds in case of honest concurrent use

(1)   This section applies where on an application for the registration of a trade mark it appears to the registrar—

(a)   that there is an earlier trade mark in relation to which the conditions set out in section 5(1), (2) or (3) obtain, or

(b)   that there is an earlier right in relation to which the condition set out in section 5(4) is satisfied,

but the applicant shows to the satisfaction of the registrar that there has been honest concurrent use of the trade mark for which registration is sought.

(2)   In that case the registrar shall not refuse the application by reason of the earlier trade mark or other earlier right unless objection on that ground is raised in opposition proceedings by the proprietor of that earlier trade mark or other earlier right.

(3)   For the purposes of this section "honest concurrent use" means such use in the United Kingdom, by the applicant or with his consent, as would formerly have amounted to honest concurrent use for the purposes of section 12(2) of the Trade Marks Act 1938.

(4)   Nothing in this section affects—

(a)   the refusal of registration on the grounds mentioned in section 3 (absolute grounds for refusal), or

(b)   the making of an application for a declaration of invalidity under section 47(2) (application on relative grounds, where no consent to registration).

(5)   This section does not apply when there is an order in force under section 8 below.

. . .

Effects of registered trade mark

9   Rights conferred by registered trade mark

(1)   The proprietor of a registered trade mark has exclusive rights in the trade mark which are infringed by use of the trade mark in the United Kingdom without his consent.

The acts amounting to infringement, if done without the consent of the proprietor, are specified in section 10.

(2)   References in this Act to the infringement of a registered trade mark are to any such infringement of the rights of the proprietor.

(3)   The rights of the proprietor have effect from the date of registration (which in accordance with section 40(3) is the date of filing of the application for registration): Provided that—

(a)   no infringement proceedings may be begun before the date on which the trade mark is in fact registered; and

(b)   no offence under section 92 (unauthorised use of trade mark, &c. in relation to goods) is committed by anything done before the date of publication of the registration.

10   Infringement of registered trade mark

(1)   A person infringes a registered trade mark if he uses in the course of trade a sign which is identical with the trade mark in relation to goods or services which are identical with those for which it is registered.

(2)   A person infringes a registered trade mark if he uses in the course of trade a sign where because—

(a)   the sign is identical with the trade mark and is used in relation to goods or services similar to those for which the trade mark is registered, or

(b)   the sign is similar to the trade mark and is used in relation to goods or services identical with or similar to those for which the trade mark is registered,

there exists a likelihood of confusion on the part of the public, which includes the likelihood of association with the trade mark.

(3)   A person infringes a registered trade mark if he uses in the course of trade a sign which—

(a)   is identical with or similar to the trade mark, and

(b)   is used in relation to goods or services which are not similar to those for which the trade mark is registered,

where the trade mark has a reputation in the United Kingdom and the use of the sign, being without due cause, takes unfair advantage of, or is detrimental to, the distinctive character or the repute of the trade mark.

(4)   For the purposes of this section a person uses a sign if, in particular, he—

(a)   affixes it to goods or the packaging thereof,

(b)   offers or exposes goods for sale, puts them on the market or stocks them for those purposes under the, sign, or offers or supplies services under the sign;

(c)   imports or exports goods under the sign; or

(d)   uses the sign on business papers or in advertising.

(5)   A person who applies a registered trade mark to material intended to be used for labelling or packaging goods, as a business paper, or for advertising goods or services, shall be treated as a party to any use of the material which infringes the registered trade mark if when he applied the mark he knew or had reason to believe that the application of the mark was not duly authorised by the proprietor or a licensee.

(6)   Nothing in the preceding provisions of this section shall be construed as preventing the use of a registered trade mark by any person for the purpose of identifying goods or services as those of the proprietor or a licensee.

But any such use otherwise than in accordance with honest practices in industrial or commercial matters shall be treated as infringing the registered trade mark if the use without due cause takes unfair advantage of, or is detrimental to, the distinctive character or repute of the trade mark.

11   Limits on effect of registered trade mark

(1)   A registered trade mark is not infringed by the use of another registered trade mark in relation to goods or services for which the latter is registered (but see section 47(6) (effect of declaration of invalidity of registration)).

(2)   A registered trade mark is not infringed by—

(a)   the use by a person of his own name or address,

(b)   the use of indications concerning the kind, quality, quantity, intended purpose, value, geographical origin, the time of production of goods or of rendering of services, or other characteristics of goods or services, or

(c)   the use of the trade mark where it is necessary to indicate the intended purpose of a product or service (in particular, as accessories or spare parts), provided the use is in accordance with honest practices in industrial or commercial matters.

(3)   A registered trade mark is not infringed by the use in the course of trade in a particular locality of an earlier right which applies only in that locality.

For this purpose an "earlier right" means an unregistered trade mark or other sign continuously used in relation to goods or services by a person or a predecessor in title of his from a date prior to whichever is the earlier of—

(a)   the use of the first-mentioned trade mark in relation to those goods or services by the proprietor or a predecessor in title of his, or

(b)   the registration of the first-mentioned trade mark in respect of those goods or services in the name of the proprietor or a predecessor in title of his;

and an earlier right shall be regarded as applying in a locality if, or to the extent that, its use in that locality is protected by virtue of any rule of law (in particular, the law of passing off).

12   Exhaustion of rights conferred by registered trade mark

(1)   A registered trade mark is not infringed by the use of the trade mark in relation to goods which have been put on the market in the European Economic Area under that trade mark by the proprietor or with his consent.

(2)   Subsection (1) does not apply where there exist legitimate reasons for the proprietor to oppose further dealings in the goods (in particular, where the condition of the goods has been changed or impaired after they have been put on the market).

13   Registration subject to disclaimer or limitation

(1)   An applicant for registration of a trade mark, or the proprietor of a registered trade mark, may—

(a)   disclaim any right to the exclusive use of any specified element of the trade mark, or

(b)   agree that the rights conferred by the registration shall be subject to a specified territorial or other limitation;

and where the registration of a trade mark is subject to a disclaimer or limitation, the rights conferred by section 9 (rights conferred by registered trade mark) are restricted accordingly.

(2)   Provision shall be made by rules as to the publication and entry in the register of a disclaimer or limitation.

Infringement proceedings

14   Action for infringement

(1)   An infringement of a registered trade mark is actionable by the proprietor of the trade mark.

(2)   In an action for infringement all such relief by way of damages, injunctions, accounts or otherwise is available to him as is available in respect of the infringement of any other property right.

15   Order for erasure, &c. of offending sign

(1)   Where a person is found to have infringed a registered trade mark, the court may make an order requiring him—

(a)   to cause the offending sign to be erased, removed or obliterated from any infringing goods, material or articles in his possession, custody or control, or

(b)   if it is not reasonably practicable for the offending sign to be erased, removed or obliterated, to secure the destruction of the infringing goods, material or articles in question.

(2)   If an order under subsection (1) is not complied with, or it appears to the court likely that such an order would not be complied with, the court may order that the infringing goods, material or articles be delivered to such person as the court may direct for erasure, removal or obliteration of the sign, or for destruction, as the case may be.

16   Order for delivery up of infringing goods, material or articles

(1)   The proprietor of a registered trade mark may apply to the court for an order for the delivery up to him, or such other person as the court may direct, of any infringing goods, material or articles which a person has in his possession, custody or control in the course of a business.

(2)   An application shall not be made after the end of the period specified in section 18 (period after which remedy of delivery up not available); and no order shall be made unless the court also makes, or it appears to the court that there are grounds for making, an order under section 19 (order as to disposal of infringing goods, &c.).

(3)   A person to whom any infringing goods, material or articles are delivered up in pursuance of an order under this section shall, if an order under section 19 is not made, retain them pending the making of an order, or the decision not to make an order, under that section.

(4)   Nothing in this section affects any other power of the court.

17   Meaning of "infringing goods, material or articles"

(1)   In this Act the expressions "infringing goods", "infringing material" and "infringing articles" shall be construed as follows.

(2)   Goods are "infringing goods", in relation to a registered trade mark, if they or their packaging bear a sign identical or similar to that mark and—

(a)   the application of the sign to the goods or their packaging was an infringement of the registered trade mark, or

(b)   the goods are proposed to be imported into the United Kingdom and the application of the sign in the United Kingdom to them or their packaging would be an infringement of the registered trade mark, or

(c)   the sign has otherwise been used in relation to the goods in such a way as to infringe the registered trade mark.

(3)   Nothing in subsection (2) shall be construed as affecting the importation of goods which may lawfully be imported into the United Kingdom by virtue of an enforceable Community right.

(4)   Material is "infringing material", in relation to a registered trade mark if it bears a sign identical or similar to that mark and either—

(a)   it is used for labelling or packaging goods, as a business paper, or for advertising goods or services, in such a way as to infringe the registered trade mark, or

(b)   it is intended to be so used and such use would infringe the registered trade mark.

(5)   "Infringing articles", in relation to a registered trade mark, means articles—

(a)   which are specifically designed or adapted for making copies of a sign identical or similar to that mark, and

(b)   which a person has in his possession, custody or control, knowing or having reason to believe that they have been or are to be used to produce infringing goods or material.

18 Period after which remedy of delivery up not available

(1) An application for an order under section 16 (order for delivery up of infringing goods, material or articles) may not be made after the end of the period of six years from—

(a) in the case of infringing goods, the date on which the trade mark was applied to the goods or their packaging,

(b) in the case of infringing material, the date on which the trade mark was applied to the material, or

(c) in the case of infringing articles, the date on which they were made, except as mentioned in the following provisions.

(2) If during the whole or part of that period the proprietor of the registered trade mark—

(a) is under a disability, or

(b) is prevented by fraud or concealment from discovering the facts entitling him to apply for an order,

an application may be made at any time before the end of the period of six years from the date on which he ceased to be under a disability or, as the case may be, could with reasonable diligence have discovered those facts.

(3) In subsection (2) "disability"—

(a) in England and Wales, has the same meaning as in the Limitation Act 1980;

(b) in Scotland, means legal disability within the meaning of the Prescription and Limitation (Scotland) Act 1973;

(c) in Northern Ireland, has the same meaning as in the Limitation (Northern Ireland) Order 1989.

19 Order as to disposal of infringing goods, material or articles

(1) Where infringing goods, material or articles have been delivered up in pursuance of an order under section 16, an application may be made to the court—

(a) for an order that they be destroyed or forfeited to such person as the court may think fit, or

(b) for a decision that no such order should be made.

(2) In considering what order (if any) should be made, the court shall consider whether other remedies available in an action for infringement of the registered trade mark would be adequate to compensate the proprietor and any licensee and protect their interests.

(3) Provision shall be made by rules of court as to the service of notice on persons having an interest in the goods, material or articles, and any such person is entitled—

(a) to appear in proceedings for an order under this section, whether or not he was served with notice, and

(b) to appeal against any order made, whether or not he appeared;

and an order shall not take effect until the end of the period within which notice of an appeal may be given or, if before the end of that period notice of appeal is duly given, until the final determination or abandonment of the proceedings on the appeal.

(4) Where there is more than one person interested in the goods, material or articles, the court shall make such order as it thinks just.

(5) If the court decides that no order should be made under this section, the person in whose possession, custody or control the goods, material or articles were before being delivered up is entitled to their return.

(6) References in this section to a person having an interest in goods, material or articles include any person in whose favour an order could be made under this section or under section 114, 204 or 231 of the Copyright, Designs and Patents Act 1988 (which make similar provision in relation to infringement of copyright, rights in performances and design right).

20   Jurisdiction of sheriff court or county court in Northern Ireland

Proceedings for an order under section 16 (order for delivery up of infringing goods, material or articles) or section 19 (order as to disposal of infringing goods, &c.) may be brought—

    (a)   in the sheriff court in Scotland, or

    (b) . in a county court in Northern Ireland.

This does not affect the jurisdiction of the Court of Session or the High Court in Northern Ireland.

21   Remedy for groundless threats of infringement proceedings

    (1)   Where a person threatens another with proceedings for infringement of a registered trade mark other than—

    (a)   the application of the mark to goods or their packaging,

    (b)   the importation of goods to which, or to the packaging of which, the mark has been applied, or

    (c)   the supply of services under the mark,

any person aggrieved may bring proceedings for relief under this section.

    (2)   The relief which may be applied for is any of the following—

    (a)   a declaration that the threats are unjustifiable,

    (b)   an injunction against the continuance of the threats,

    (c)   damages in respect of any loss he has sustained by the threats;

and the plaintiff is entitled to such relief unless the defendant shows that the acts in respect of which proceedings were threatened constitute (or if done would constitute) an infringement of the registered trade mark concerned.

    (3)   If that is shown by the defendant, the plaintiff is nevertheless entitled to relief if he shows that the registration of the trade mark is invalid or liable to be revoked in a relevant respect.

    (4)   The mere notification that a trade mark is registered, or that an application for registration has been made, does not constitute a threat of proceedings for the purposes of this section.

Registered trade mark as object of property

22   Nature of registered trade mark

A registered trade mark is personal property (in Scotland, incorporeal moveable property).

23   Co-ownership of registered trade mark

    (1)   Where a registered trade mark is granted to two or more persons jointly, each of them is entitled, subject to any agreement to the contrary, to an equal undivided share in the registered trade mark.

    (2)   The following provisions apply where two or more persons are co-proprietors of a registered trade mark, by virtue of subsection (1) or otherwise.

    (3)   Subject to any agreement to the contrary, each co-proprietor is entitled, by himself or his agents, to do for his own benefit and without the consent of or the need to account to the other or others, any act which would otherwise amount to an infringement of the registered trade mark.

    (4)   One co-proprietor may not without the consent of the other or others—

    (a)   grant a licence to use the registered trade mark, or

    (b)   assign or charge his share in the registered trade mark (or, in Scotland, cause or permit security to be granted over it).

    (5)   Infringement proceedings may be brought by any co-proprietor, but he may not, without the leave of the court, proceed with the action unless the other, or each of the others, is either joined as a plaintiff or added as a defendant.

A co-proprietor who is thus added as a defendant shall not be made liable for any costs in the action unless he takes part in the proceedings.

Nothing in this subsection affects the granting of interlocutory relief on the application of a single co-proprietor.

(6)   Nothing in this section affects the mutual rights and obligations of trustees or personal representatives, or their rights and obligations as such.

24   Assignment, &c. of registered trade mark

(1)   A registered trade mark is transmissible by assignment, testamentary disposition or operation of law in the same way as other personal or moveable property.

It is so transmissible either in connection with the goodwill of a business or independently.

(2)   An assignment or other transmission of a registered trade mark may be partial, that is, limited so as to apply—

(a)   in relation to some but not all of the goods or services for which the trade mark is registered, or

b)   in relation to use of the trade mark in a particular manner or a particular locaⅼ ty.

(3)   An assignment of a registered trade mark, or an assent relating to a registered trade mark, is not effective unless it is in writing signed by or on behalf of the assignor or, as the case may be, a personal representative.

Except in Scotland, this requirement may be satisfied in a case where the assignor or personal representative is a body corporate by the affixing of its seal.

(4)   The above provisions apply to assignment by way of security as in relation to any other assignment.

(5)   A registered trade mark may be the subject of a charge (in Scotland, security) in the same way as other personal or moveable property.

(6)   Nothing in this Act shall be construed as affecting the assignment or other transmission of an unregistered trade mark as part of the goodwill of a business.

25   Registration of transactions affecting registered trade mark

(1)   On application being made to the registrar by—

(a)   a person claiming to be entitled to an interest in or under a registered trade mark by virtue of a registrable transaction, or

(b)   any other person claiming to be affected by such a transaction,

the prescribed particulars of the transaction shall be entered in the register.

(2)   The following are registrable transactions—

(a)   an assignment of a registered trade mark or any right in it;

(b)   the grant of a licence under a registered trade mark;

(c)   the granting of any security interest (whether fixed or floating) over a registered trade mark or any right in or under it;

(d)   the making by personal representatives of an assent in relation to a registered trade mark or any right in or under it;

(e)   an order of a court or other competent authority transferring a registered trade mark or any right in or under it.

(3)   Until an application has been made for registration of the prescribed particulars of a registrable transaction—

(a)   the transaction is ineffective as against a person acquiring a conflicting interest in or under the registered trade mark in ignorance of it, and

(b)   a person claiming to be a licensee by virtue of the transaction does not have the protection of section 30 or 31 (rights and remedies of licensee in relation to infringement).

(4)   Where a person becomes the proprietor or a licensee of a registered trade mark by virtue of a registrable transaction, then unless—

(a)   an application for registration of the prescribed particulars of the transaction is made before the end of the period of six months beginning with its date, or

(b)   the court is satisfied that it was not practicable for such an application to be made before the end of that period and that an application was made as soon as practicable thereafter,

he is not entitled to damages or an account of profits in respect of any infringement of the registered trade mark occurring after the date of the transaction and before the prescribed particulars of the transaction are registered.

(5)   Provision may be made by rules as to—

(a)   the amendment of registered particulars relating to a licence so as to reflect any alteration of the terms of the licence, and

(b)   the removal of such particulars from the register—

(i)   where it appears from the registered particulars that the licence was granted for a fixed period and that period has expired, or

(ii)   where no such period is indicated and, after such period as may be prescribed, the registrar h s notified the parties of his intention to remove the particulars from the register.

(6)   Provision may also be made by rules as to the amendment or removal from the register of particulars relating to a security interest on the application of, or with the consent of, the person entitled to the benefit of that interest.

26   Trusts and equities

(1)   No notice of any trust (express, implied or constructive) shall be entered in the register; and the registrar shall not be affected by any such notice.

(2)   Subject to the provisions of this Act, equities (in Scotland, rights) in respect of a registered trade mark may be enforced in like manner as in respect of other personal or moveable property.

27   Application for registration of trade mark as an object of property

(1)   The provisions of sections 22 to 26 (which relate to a registered trade mark as an object of property) apply, with the necessary modifications, in relation to an application for the registration of a trade mark as in relation to a registered trade mark.

(2)   In section 23 (co-ownership of registered trade mark) as it applies in relation to an application for registration the reference in subsection (1) to the granting of the registration shall be construed as a reference to the making of the application.

(3)   In section 25 (registration of transactions affecting registered trade marks) as it applies in relation to a transaction affecting an application for the registration of a trade mark, the references to the entry of particulars in the register, and to the making of an application to register particulars, shall be construed as references to the giving of notice to the registrar of those particulars.

Licensing

28   Licensing of registered trade mark

(1)   A licence to use a registered trade mark may be general or limited.

A limited licence may, in particular, apply—

(a)   in relation to some but not all of the goods or services for which the trade mark is registered, or

(b)   in relation to use of the trade mark in a particular manner or a particular locality.

(2)   A licence is not effective unless it is in writing signed by or on behalf of the grantor.

Except in Scotland, this requirement may be satisfied in a case where the grantor is a body corporate by the affixing of its seal.

(3)   Unless the licence provides otherwise, it is binding on a successor in title to the grantor's interest.

References in this Act to doing anything with, or without, the consent of the proprietor of a registered trade mark shall be construed accordingly.

(4)   Where the licence so provides, a sub-licence may be granted by the licensee; and references in this Act to a licence or licensee include a sub-licence or sub-licensee.

29   Exclusive licences

(1)   In this Act an "exclusive licence" means a licence (whether general or limited) authorising the licensee to the exclusion of all other persons, including the person granting the licence, to use a registered trade mark in the manner authorised by the licence.

The expression "exclusive licensee" shall be construed accordingly.

(2)   An exclusive licensee has the same rights against a successor in title who is bound by the licence as he has against the person granting the licence.

30   General provisions as to rights of licensees in case of infringement

(1)   This section has effect with respect to the rights of a licensee in relation to infringement of a registered trade mark.

The provisions of this section do not apply where or to the extent that, by virtue of section 31(1) below (exclusive licensee having rights and remedies of assignee), the licensee has a right to bring proceedings in his own name.

(2)   A licensee is entitled, unless his licence, or any licence through which his interest is derived, provides otherwise, to call on the proprietor of the registered trade mark to take infringement proceedings in respect of any matter which affects his interests.

(3)   If the proprietor—
    (a)   refuses to do so, or
    (b)   fails to do so within two months after being called upon,
the licensee may bring the proceedings in his own name as if he were the proprietor.

(4)   Where infringement proceedings are brought by a licensee by virtue of this section, the licensee may not, without the leave of the court, proceed with the action unless the proprietor is either joined as a plaintiff or added as a defendant.

This does not affect the granting of interlocutory relief on an application by a licensee alone.

(5)   A proprietor who is added as a defendant as mentioned in subsection (4) shall not be made liable for any costs in the action unless he takes part in the proceedings.

(6)   In infringement proceedings brought by the proprietor of a registered trade mark any loss suffered or likely to be suffered by licensees shall be taken into account; and the court may give such directions as it thinks fit as to the extent to which the plaintiff is to hold the proceeds of any pecuniary remedy on behalf of licensees.

(7)   The provisions of this section apply in relation to an exclusive licensee if or to the extent that he has, by virtue of section 31(1), the rights and remedies of an assignee as if he were the proprietor of the registered trade mark.

31   Exclusive licensee having rights and remedies of assignee

(1)   An exclusive licence may provide that the licensee shall have, to such extent as may be provided by the licence, the same rights and remedies in respect of matters occurring after the grant of the licence as if the licence had been an assignment.

Where or to the extent that such provision is made, the licensee is entitled, subject to the provisions of the licence and to the following provisions of this section, to bring infringement proceedings, against any person other than the proprietor, in his own name.

(2)   Any such rights and remedies of an exclusive licensee are concurrent with those of the proprietor of the registered trade mark; and references to the proprietor of a registered trade mark in the provisions of this Act relating to infringement shall be construed accordingly.

(3)   In an action brought by an exclusive licensee by virtue of this section a defendant may avail himself of any defence which would have been available to him if the action had been brought by the proprietor of the registered trade mark.

(4)   Where proceedings for infringement of a registered trade mark brought by the proprietor or an exclusive licensee relate wholly or partly to an infringement in respect of which they have concurrent rights of action, the proprietor or, as the case may be, the exclusive licensee may not, without the leave of the court, proceed with the action unless the other is either joined as a plaintiff or added as a defendant.

This does not affect the granting of interlocutory relief on an application by a proprietor or exclusive licensee alone.

(5)   A person who is added as a defendant as mentioned in subsection (4) shall not be made liable for any costs in the action unless he takes part in the proceedings.

(6)   Where an action for infringement of a registered trade mark is brought which relates wholly or partly to an infringement in respect of which the proprietor and an exclusive licensee have or had concurrent rights of action—

(a)   the court shall in assessing damages take into account—

(i)   the terms of the licence, and

(ii)   any pecuniary remedy already awarded or available to either of them in respect of the infringement;

(b)   no account of profits shall be directed if an award of damages has been made, or an account of profits has been directed, in favour of the other of them in respect of the infringement; and

(c)   the court shall if an account of profits is directed apportion the profits between them as the court considers just, subject to any agreement between them.

The provisions of this subsection apply whether or not the proprietor and the exclusive licensee are both parties to the action; and if they are not both parties the court may give such directions as it thinks fit as to the extent to which the party to the proceedings is to hold the proceeds of any pecuniary remedy on behalf of the other.

(7)   The proprietor of a registered trade mark shall notify any exclusive licensee who has a concurrent right of action before applying for an order under section 16 (order for delivery up); and the court may on the application of the licensee make such order under that section as it thinks fit having regard to the terms of the licence.

(8)   The provisions of subsections (4) to (7) above have effect subject to any agreement to the contrary between the exclusive licensee and the proprietor.

Application for registered trade mark

32   Application for registration

(1)   An application for registration of a trade mark shall be made to the registrar.

(2)   The application shall contain—

(a)   a request for registration of a trade mark,

(b)   the name and address of the applicant,

(c)   a statement of the goods or services in relation to which it is sought to register the trade mark, and

(d)   a representation of the trade mark.

(3)   The application shall state that the trade mark is being used, by the applicant or with his consent, in relation to those goods or services, or that he has a *bona fide* intention that it should be so used.

(4)   The application shall be subject to the payment of the application fee and such class fees as may be appropriate.

33   Date of filing

(1)   The date of filing of an application for registration of a trade mark is the date on which documents containing everything required by section 32(2) are furnished to the registrar by the applicant.

If the documents are furnished on different days, the date of filing is the last of those days.

(2)   References in this Act to the date of application for registration are to the date of filing of the application.

34   Classification of trade marks

(1)   Goods and services shall be classified for the purposes of the registration of trade marks according to a prescribed system of classification.

(2)   Any question arising as to the class within which any goods or services fall shall be determined by the registrar, whose decision shall be final.

Priority

35   Claim to priority of Convention application

(1)   A person who has duly filed an application for protection of a trade mark in a Convention country (a "Convention application"), or his successor in title, has a right to priority, for the purposes of registering the same trade mark under this Act for some or all of the same goods or services, for a period of six months from the date of filing of the first such application.

(2)   If the application for registration under this Act is made within that six-month period—

(a)   the relevant date for the purposes of establishing which rights take precedence shall be the date of filing of the first Convention application, and

(b)   the registrability of the trade mark shall not be affected by any use of the mark in the United Kingdom in the period between that date and the date of the application under this Act.

(3)   Any filing which in a Convention country is equivalent to a regular national filing, under its domestic legislation or an international agreement, shall be treated as giving rise to the right of priority.

A "regular national filing" means a filing which is adequate to establish the date on which the application was filed in that country, whatever may be the subsequent fate of the application.

(4)   A subsequent application concerning the same subject as the first Convention application, filed in the same Convention country, shall be considered the first Convention application (of which the filing date is the starting date of the period of priority), if at the time of the subsequent application—

(a)   the previous application has been withdrawn, abandoned or refused, without having been laid open to public inspection and without leaving any rights outstanding, and

(b)   it has not yet served as a basis for claiming a right of priority.

The previous application may not thereafter serve as a basis for claiming a right of priority.

. . .

(6)   A right to priority arising as a result of a Convention application may be assigned or otherwise transmitted, either with the application or independently.

The reference in subsection (1) to the applicant's "successor in title" shall be construed accordingly.

36 Claim to priority from other relevant overseas application

(1) Her Majesty may by Order in Council make provision for conferring on a person who has duly filed an application for protection of a trade mark in—

(a) any of the Channel Islands or a colony, or

(b) a country or territory in relation to which Her Majesty's Government in the United Kingdom have entered into a treaty, convention, arrangement or engagement for the reciprocal protection of trade marks,

a right to priority, for the purpose of registering the same trade mark under this Act for some or all of the same goods or services, for a specified period from the date of filing of that application.

. . .

Registration procedure

37 Examination of application

(1) The registrar shall examine whether an application for registration of a trade mark satisfies the requirements of this Act (including any requirements imposed by rules).

(2) For that purpose he shall carry out a search, to such extent as he considers necessary, of earlier trade marks.

(3) If it appears to the registrar that the requirements for registration are not met, he shall inform the applicant and give him an opportunity, within such period as the registrar may specify, to make representations or to amend the application.

(4) If the applicant fails to satisfy the registrar that those requirements are met, or to amend the application so as to meet them, or fails to respond before the end of the specified period, the registrar shall refuse to accept the application.

(5) If it appears to the registrar that the requirements for registration are met, he shall accept the application.

38 Publication, opposition proceedings and observations

(1) When an application for registration has been accepted, the registrar shall cause the application to be published in the prescribed manner.

(2) Any person may, within the prescribed time from the date of the publication of the application, give notice to the registrar of opposition to the registration.

The notice shall be given in writing in the prescribed manner, and shall include a statement of the grounds of opposition.

(3) Where an application has been published, any person may, at any time before the registration of the trade mark, make observations in writing to the registrar as to whether the trade mark should be registered; and the registrar shall inform the applicant of any such observations.

A person who makes observations does not thereby become a party to the proceedings on the application.

39 Withdrawal, restriction or amendment of application

(1) The applicant may at any time withdraw his application or restrict the goods or services covered by the application.

If the application has been published, the withdrawal or restriction shall also be published.

(2) In other respects, an application may be amended, at the request of the applicant, only by correcting—

(a) the name or address of the applicant,

(b) errors of wording or of copying, or

(c) obvious mistakes,

and then only where the correction does not substantially affect the identity of the trade mark or extend the goods or services covered by the application.

178 Trade Marks Act 1994

40 Registration
(1) Where an application has been accepted and—

(a) no notice of opposition is given within the period referred to in section 38(2), or

(b) all opposition proceedings are withdrawn or decided in favour of the applicant, the registrar shall register the trade mark, unless it appears to him having regard to matters coming to his notice since he accepted the application that it was accepted in error.

(2) A trade mark shall not be registered unless any fee prescribed for the registration is paid within the prescribed period.

If the fee is not paid within that period, the application shall be deemed to be withdrawn.

(3) A trade mark when registered shall be registered as of the date of filing of the application for registration; and that date shall be deemed for the purposes of this Act to be the date of registration.

(4) On the registration of a trade mark the registrar shall publish the registration in the prescribed manner and issue to the applicant a certificate of registration.

41 Registration: supplementary provisions
(1) Provision may be made by rules as to—

(a) the division of an application for the registration of a trade mark into several applications;

(b) the merging of separate applications or registrations;

(c) the registration of a series of trade marks.

(2) A series of trade marks means a number of trade marks which resemble each other as to their material particulars and differ only as to matters of a non-distinctive character not substantially affecting the identity of the trade mark.

...

Duration, renewal and alteration of registered trade mark

42 Duration of registration
(1) A trade mark shall be registered for a period of ten years from the date of registration.

(2) Registration may be renewed in accordance with section 43 for further periods of ten years.

43 Renewal of registration
(1) The registration of a trade mark may be renewed at the request of the proprietor, subject to payment of a renewal fee.

(2) Provision shall be made by rules for the registrar to inform the proprietor of a registered trade mark, before the expiry of the registration, of the date of expiry and the manner in which the registration may be renewed.

(3) A request for renewal must be made, and the renewal fee paid, before the expiry of the registration.

Failing this, the request may be made and the fee paid within such further period (of not less than six months) as may be prescribed, in which case an additional renewal fee must also be paid within that period.

(4) Renewal shall take effect from the expiry of the previous registration.

(5) If the registration is not renewed in accordance with the above provisions, the registrar shall remove the trade mark from the register.

Provision may be made by rules for the restoration of the registration of a trade mark which has been removed from the register, subject to such conditions (if any) as may be prescribed.

(6)   The renewal or restoration of the registration of a trade mark shall be published in the prescribed manner.

44   Alteration of registered trade mark

(1)   A registered trade mark shall not be altered in the register, during the period of registration or on renewal.

(2)   Nevertheless, the registrar may, at the request of the proprietor, allow the alteration of a registered trade mark where the mark includes the proprietor's name or address and the alteration is limited to alteration of that name or address and does not substantially affect the identity of the mark.

(3)   Provision shall be made by rules for the publication of any such alteration and the making of objections by any person claiming to be affected by it.

Surrender, revocation and invalidity

45   Surrender of registered trade mark

(1)   A registered trade mark may be surrendered by the proprietor in respect of some or all of the goods or services for which it is registered.

. . .

46   Revocation of registration

(1)   The registration of a trade mark may be revoked on any of the following grounds—

(a)   that within the period of five years following the date of completion of the registration procedure it has not been put to genuine use in the United Kingdom, by the proprietor or with his consent, in relation to the goods or services for which it is registered, and there are no proper reasons for non-use;

(b)   that such use has been suspended for an uninterrupted period of five years, and there are no proper reasons for non-use;

(c)   that, in consequence of acts or inactivity of the proprietor, it has become the common name in the trade for a product or service for which it is registered;

(d)   that in consequence of the use made of it by the proprietor or with his consent in relation to the goods or services for which it is registered, it is liable to mislead the public, particularly as to the nature, quality or geographical origin of those goods or services.

(2)   For the purposes of subsection (1) use of a trade mark includes use in a form differing in elements which do not alter the distinctive character of the mark in the form in which it was registered, and use in the United Kingdom includes affixing the trade mark to goods or to the packaging of goods in the United Kingdom solely for export purposes.

(3)   The registration of a trade mark shall not be revoked on the ground mentioned in subsection (1)(a) or (b) if such use as is referred to in that paragraph is commenced or resumed after the expiry of the five year period and before the application for revocation is made:

Provided that, any such commencement or resumption of use after the expiry of the five year period but within the period of three months before the making of the application shall be disregarded unless preparations for the commencement or resumption began before the proprietor became aware that the application might be made.

(4)   An application for revocation may be made by any person, and may be made either to the registrar or to the court, except that—

(a)   if proceedings concerning the trade mark in question are pending in the court, the application must be made to the court; and

(b)   if in any other case the application is made to the registrar, he may at any stage of the proceedings refer the application to the court.

(5)   Where grounds for revocation exist in respect of only some of the goods or services for which the trade mark is registered, revocation shall relate to those goods or services only.

(6)   Where the registration of a trade mark is revoked to any extent, the rights of the proprietor shall be deemed to have ceased to that extent as from—

    (a)   the date of the application for revocation, or

    (b)   if the registrar or court is satisfied that the grounds for revocation existed at an earlier date, that date.

47   Grounds for invalidity of registration

(1)   The registration of a trade mark may be declared invalid on the ground that the trade mark was registered in breach of section 3 or any of the provisions referred to in that section (absolute grounds for refusal of registration).

Where the trade mark was registered in breach of subsection (1)(b), (c) or (d) of that section, it shall not be declared invalid if, in consequence of the use which has been made of it, it has after registration acquired a distinctive character in relation to the goods or services for which it is registered.

(2)   The registration of a trade mark may be declared invalid on the ground—

    (a)   that there is an earlier trade mark in relation to which the conditions set out in section 5(1), (2) or (3) obtain, or

    (b)   that there is an earlier right in relation to which the condition set out in section 5(4) is satisfied,

unless the proprietor of that earlier trade mark or other earlier right has consented to the registration.

(3)   An application for a declaration of invalidity may be made by any person, and may be made either to the registrar or to the court, except that—

    (a)   if proceedings concerning the trade mark in question are pending in the court, the application must be made to the court; and

    (b)   if in any other case the application is made to the registrar, he may at any stage of the proceedings refer the application to the court.

(4)   In the case of bad faith in the registration of a trade mark, the registrar himself may apply to the court for a declaration of the invalidity of the registration.

(5)   Where the grounds of invalidity exist in respect of only some of the goods or services for which the trade mark is registered, the trade mark shall be declared invalid as regards those goods or services only.

(6)   Where the registration of a trade mark is declared invalid to any extent, the registration shall to that extent be deemed never to have been made:

Provided that this shall not affect transactions past and closed.

48   Effect of acquiescence

(1)   Where the proprietor of an earlier trade mark or other earlier right has acquiesced for a continuous period of five years in the use of a registered trade mark in the United Kingdom, being aware of that use, there shall cease to be any entitlement on the basis of that earlier trade mark or other right—

    (a)   to apply for a declaration that the registration of the later trade mark is invalid, or

    (b)   to oppose the use of the later trade mark in relation to the goods or services in relation to which it has been so used,

unless the registration of the later trade mark was applied for in bad faith.

(2)   Where subsection (1) applies, the proprietor of the later trade mark is not entitled to oppose the use of the earlier trade mark or, as the case may be, the exploitation of the earlier right, notwithstanding that the earlier trade mark or right may no longer be invoked against his later trade mark.

Collective marks

49 Collective marks

(1) A collective mark is a mark distinguishing the goods or services of members of the association which is the proprietor of the mark from those of other undertakings.

(2) The provisions of this Act apply to collective marks subject to the provisions of Schedule 1.

Certification marks

50 Certification marks

(1) A certification mark is a mark indicating that the goods or services in connection with which it is used are certified by the proprietor of the mark in respect of origin, material, mode of manufacture of goods or performance of services, quality, accuracy or other characteristics.

(2) The provisions of this Act apply to certification marks subject to the provisions of Schedule 2.

PART II
COMMUNITY TRADE MARKS AND INTERNATIONAL MATTERS

Community trade marks

51 Meaning of "Community trade mark"

In this Act—

"Community trade mark" has the meaning given by Article 1(1) of the Community Trade Mark Regulation; and

"the Community Trade Mark Regulation" means Council Regulation (EC) No. 40/94 of 20th December 1993 on the Community trade mark.

52 Power to make provision in connection with Community Trade Mark Regulation

(1) The Secretary of State may by regulations make such provision as he considers appropriate in connection with the operation of the Community Trade Mark Regulation.

(2) Provision may, in particular, be made with respect to—

(a) the making of applications for Community trade marks by way of the Patent Office;

(b) the procedures for determining *a posteriori* the invalidity, or liability to revocation, of the registration of a trade mark from which a Community trade mark claims seniority;

(c) the conversion of a Community trade mark, or an application for a Community trade mark, into an application for registration under this Act;

(d) the designation of courts in the United Kingdom having jurisdiction over proceedings arising out of the Community Trade Mark Regulation.

(3) Without prejudice to the generality of subsection (1), provision may be made by regulations under this section—

(a) applying in relation to a Community trade mark the provisions of—

(i) section 21 (remedy for groundless threats of infringement proceedings);

(ii) sections 89 to 91 (importation of infringing goods, material or articles); and

(iii) sections 92, 93, 95 and 96 (offences); and

(b) making in relation to the list of professional representatives maintained in pursuance of Article 89 of the Community Trade Mark Regulation, and persons on that list, provision corresponding to that made by, or capable of being made under, sections 84 to 88 in relation to the register of trade mark agents and registered trade mark agents.

. . .

The Madrid Protocol: international registration

53   The Madrid Protocol
In this Act—
    "the Madrid Protocol" means the Protocol relating to the Madrid Agreement concerning the International Registration of Marks, adopted at Madrid on 27th June 1989;
    "the International Bureau" has the meaning given by Article 2(1) of that Protocol; and
    "international trade mark (UK)" means a trade mark which is entitled to protection in the United Kingdom under that Protocol.

54   Power to make provision giving effect to Madrid Protocol
    (1)   The Secretary of State may by order make such provision as he thinks fit for giving effect in the United Kingdom to the provisions of the Madrid Protocol.
    (2)   Provision may, in particular, be made with respect to—
    (a)   the making of applications for international registrations by way of the Patent Office as office of origin;
    (b)   the procedures to be followed where the basic United Kingdom application or registration fails or ceases to be in force;
    (c)   the procedures to be followed where the Patent Office receives from the International Bureau a request for extension of protection to the United Kingdom;
    (d)   the effects of a successful request for extension of protection to the United Kingdom;
    (e)   the transformation of an application for an international registration, or an international registration, into a national application for registration;
    (f)   the communication of information to the International Bureau;
    (g)   the payment of fees and amounts prescribed in respect of applications for international registrations, extensions of protection and renewals.
    (3)   Without prejudice to the generality of subsection (1), provision may be made by regulations under this section applying in relation to an international trade mark (UK) the provisions of—
    (a)   section 21 (remedy for groundless threats of infringement proceedings);
    (b)   sections 89 to 91 (importation of infringing goods, material or articles); and
    (c)   sections 92, 93, 95 and 96 (offences).
. . .

The Paris Convention: supplementary provisions

55   The Paris Convention
    (1)   In this Act—
    (a)   "the Paris Convention" means the Paris Convention for the Protection of Industrial Property of March 20th 1883, as revised or amended from time to time, and
    (b)   a "Convention country" means a country, other than the United Kingdom, which is a party to that Convention.
    (2)   The Secretary of State may by order make such amendments of this Act, and rules made under this Act, as appear to him appropriate in consequence of any revision or amendment of the Paris Convention after the passing of this Act.
. . .

56   Protection of well-known trade marks: Article 6*bis*
    (1)   References in this Act to a trade mark which is entitled to protection under the Paris Convention as a well known trade mark are to a mark which is well-known in the United Kingdom as being the mark of a person who—
    (a)   is a national of a Convention country, or

(b)   is domiciled in, or has a real and effective industrial or commercial establishment in, a Convention country,
whether or not that person carries on business, or has any goodwill, in the United Kingdom.
References to the proprietor of such a mark shall be construed accordingly.

(2)   The proprietor of a trade mark which is entitled to protection under the Paris Convention as a well known trade mark is entitled to restrain by injunction the use in the United Kingdom of a trade mark which, or the essential part of which, is identical or similar to his mark, in relation to identical or similar goods or services, where the use is likely to cause confusion.

This right is subject to section 48 (effect of acquiescence by proprietor of earlier trade mark).

(3)   Nothing in subsection (2) affects the continuation of any *bona fide* use of a trade mark begun before the commencement of this section.

57   National emblems, &c. of Convention countries: Article 6*ter*

(1)   A trade mark which consists of or contains the flag of a Convention country shall not be registered without the authorisation of the competent authorities of that country, unless it appears to the registrar that use of the flag in the manner proposed is permitted without such authorisation.

(2)   A trade mark which consists of or contains the armorial bearings or any other state emblem of a Convention country which is protected under the Paris Convention shall not be registered without the authorisation of the competent authorities of that country.

(3)   A trade mark which consists of or contains an official sign or hallmark adopted by a Convention country and indicating control and warranty shall not, where the sign or hallmark is protected under the Paris Convention, be registered in relation to goods or services of the same, or a similar kind, as those in relation to which it indicates control and warranty, without the authorisation of the competent authorities of the country concerned.

(4)   The provisions of this section as to national flags and other state emblems, and official signs or hallmarks, apply equally to anything which from a heraldic point of view imitates any such flag or other emblem, or sign or hallmark.

(5)   Nothing in this section prevents the registration of a trade mark on the application of a national of a country who is authorised to make use of a state emblem, or official sign or hallmark, of that country, notwithstanding that it is similar to that of another country.

(6)   Where by virtue of this section the authorisation of the competent authorities of a Convention country is or would be required for the registration of a trade mark, those authorities are entitled to restrain by injunction any use of the mark in the United Kingdom without their authorisation.

58   Emblems, &c. of certain international organisations: Article 6*ter*

(1)   This section applies to—
   (a)   the armorial bearings, flags or other emblems, and
   (b)   the abbreviations and names,
of international intergovernmental organisations of which one or more Convention countries are members.

(2)   A trade mark which consists of or contains any such emblem, abbreviation or name which is protected under the Paris Convention shall not be registered without the authorisation of the international organisation concerned, unless it appears to the registrar that the use of the emblem, abbreviation or name in the manner proposed—
   (a)   is not such as to suggest to the public that a connection exists between the organisation and the trade mark, or

(b)   is not likely to mislead the public as to the existence of a connection between the user and the organisation.

(3)   The provisions of this section as to emblems of an international organisation apply equally to anything which from a heraldic point of view imitates any such emblem.

(4)   Where by virtue of this section the authorisation of an international organisation is or would be required for the registration of a trade mark, that organisation is entitled to restrain by injunction any use of the mark in the United Kingdom without its authorisation.

(5)   Nothing in this section affects the rights of a person whose *bona fide* use of the trade mark in question began before 4th January 1962 (when the relevant provisions of the Paris Convention entered into force in relation to the United Kingdom).

59   Notification under Article 6*ter* of the Convention

(1)   For the purposes of section 57 state emblems of a Convention country (other than the national flag), and official signs or hallmarks, shall be regarded as protected under the Paris Convention only if, or to the extent that—

(a)   the country in question has notified the United Kingdom in accordance with Article 6*ter*(3) of the Convention that it desires to protect that emblem, sign or hallmark,

(b)   the notification remains in force, and

(c)   the United Kingdom has not objected to it in accordance with Article 6*ter*(4) or any such objection has been withdrawn.

(2)   For the purposes of section 58 the emblems, abbreviations and names of an international organisation shall be regarded as protected under the Paris Convention only if, or to the extent that—

(a)   the organisation in question has notified the United Kingdom in accordance with Article 6*ter*(3) of the Convention that it desires to protect that emblem, abbreviation or name,

(b)   the notification remains in force, and

(c)   the United Kingdom has not objected to it in accordance with Article 6*ter*(4) or any such objection has been withdrawn.

(3)   Notification under Article 6*ter*(3) of the Paris Convention shall have effect only in relation to applications for registration made more than two months after the receipt of the notification.

(4)   The registrar shall keep and make available for public inspection by any person, at all reasonable hours and free of charge, a list of—

(a)   the state emblems and official signs or hallmarks, and

(b)   the emblems, abbreviations and names of international organisations,

which are for the time being protected under the Paris Convention by virtue of notification under Article 6*ter(3)*.

. . .

Miscellaneous

61   Stamp duty

Stamp duty shall not be chargeable on an instrument relating to a Community trade mark or an international trade mark (UK), or an application for any such mark, by reason only of the fact that such a mark has legal effect in the United Kingdom.

PART III
ADMINISTRATIVE AND OTHER SUPPLEMENTARY PROVISIONS

The registrar

62   The registrar

In this Act "the registrar" means the Comptroller-General of Patents, Designs and Trade Marks.

The register

63 The register

(1)   The registrar shall maintain a register of trade marks.

References in this Act to "the register" are to that register; and references to registration (in particular, in the expression "registered trade mark") are, unless the context otherwise requires, to registration in that register.

(2)   There shall be entered in the register in accordance with this Act—

    (a)   registered trade marks,

    (b)   such particulars as may be prescribed of registrable transactions affecting a registered trade mark, and

    (c)   such other matters relating to registered trade marks as may be prescribed.

(3)   The register shall be kept in such manner as may be prescribed, and provision shall in particular be made for—

    (a)   public inspection of the register, and

    (b)   the supply of certified or uncertified copies, or extracts, of entries in the register.

64 Rectification or correction of the register

(1)   Any person having a sufficient interest may apply for the rectification of an error or omission in the register:

Provided that an application for rectification may not be made in respect of a matter affecting the validity of the registration of a trade mark.

. . .

(3)   Except where the registrar or the court directs otherwise, the effect of rectification of the register is that the error or omission in question shall be deemed never to have been made.

. . .

70 Exclusion of liability in respect of official acts

(1)   The registrar shall not be taken to warrant the validity of the registration of a trade mark under this Act or under any treaty, convention, arrangement or engagement to which the United Kingdom is a party.

(2)   The registrar is not subject to any liability by reason of, or in connection with, any examination required or authorised by this Act, or any such treaty, convention, arrangement or engagement, or any report or other proceedings consequent on such examination.

(3)   No proceedings lie against an officer of the registrar in respect of any matter for which, by virtue of this section, the registrar is not liable.

. . .

Legal proceedings and appeals

72 Registration to be *prima facie* evidence of validity

In all legal proceedings relating to a registered trade mark (including proceedings for rectification of the register) the registration of a person as proprietor of a trade mark shall be prima facie evidence of the validity of the original registration and of any subsequent assignment or other transmission of it.

73 Certificate of validity of contested registration

(1)   If in proceedings before the court the validity of the registration of a trade mark is contested and it is found by the court that the trade mark is validly registered, the court may give a certificate to that effect.

(2)   If the court gives such a certificate and in subsequent proceedings—

    (a)   the validity of the registration is again questioned, and

  (b)   the proprietor obtains a final order or judgment in his favour,
he is entitled to his costs as between solicitor and client unless the court directs
otherwise.

This subsection does not extend to the costs of an appeal in any such proceedings.

74 Registrar's appearance in proceedings involving the register
  (1)   In proceedings before the court involving an application for—
  (a)   the revocation of the registration of a trade mark,
  (b)   a declaration of the invalidity of the registration of a trade mark, or
  (c)   the rectification of the register,
the registrar is entitled to appear and be heard, and shall appear if so directed by the
court.
  . . .

75 The court
In this Act, unless the context otherwise requires, "the court" means—
  (a)   in England and Wales and Northern Ireland, the High Court, and
  (b)   in Scotland, the Court of Session.

76 Appeals from the registrar
  (1)   An appeal lies from any decision of the registrar under this Act, except as
otherwise expressly provided by rules.

For this purpose "decision" includes any act of the registrar in exercise of a discretion
vested in him by or under this Act.
  (2)   Any such appeal may be brought either to an appointed person or to the court.
  (3)   Where an appeal is made to an appointed person, he may refer the appeal to the
court if—
  (a)   it appears to him that a point of general legal importance is involved,
  (b)   the registrar requests that it be so referred, or
  (c)   such a request is made by any party to the proceedings before the registrar in
which the decision appealed against was made.

Before doing so the appointed person shall give the appellant and any other party to
the appeal an opportunity to make representations as to whether the appeal should be
referred to the court.
  (4)   Where an appeal is made to an appointed person and he does not refer it to the
court, he shall hear and determine the appeal and his decision shall be final.
  (5)   The provisions of sections 68 and 69 (costs and security for costs; evidence)
apply in relation to proceedings before an appointed person as in relation to proceedings
before the registrar.

77 Persons appointed to hear and determine appeals
  (1)   For the purposes of section 76 an "appointed person" means a person
appointed by the Lord Chancellor to hear and decide appeals under this Act.
  . . .

81 The trade marks journal
Provision shall be made by rules for the publication by the registrar of a journal
containing particulars of any application for the registration of a trade mark (including
a representation of the mark) and such other information relating to trade marks as the
registrar thinks fit.

Trade mark agents

82 Recognition of agents
Except as otherwise provided by rules, any act required or authorised by this Act to be
done by or to a person in connection with the registration of a trade mark, or any

procedure relating to a registered trade mark, may be done by or to an agent authorised by that person orally or in writing.

83   The register of trade mark agents

(1)   The Secretary of State may make rules requiring the keeping of a register of persons who act as agent for others for the purpose of applying for or obtaining the registration of trade marks; and in this Act a "registered trade mark agent" means a person whose name is entered in the register kept under this section.

...

84   Unregistered persons not to be described as registered trade mark agents

(1)   An individual who is not a registered trade mark agent shall not—

(a)   carry on a business (otherwise than in partnership) under any name or other description which contains the words "registered trade mark agent" ; or

(b)   in the course of a business otherwise describe or hold himself out, or permit himself to be described or held out, as a registered trade mark agent.

(2)   A partnership shall not—

(a)   carry on a business under any name or other description which contains the words "registered trade mark agent"; or

(b)   in the course of a business otherwise describe or hold itself out, or permit itself to be described or held out, as a firm of registered trade mark agents,

unless all the partners are registered trade mark agents or the partnership satisfies such conditions as may be prescribed for the purposes of this section.

(3)   A body corporate shall not—

(a)   carry on a business (otherwise than in partnership) under any name or other description which contains the words "registered trade mark agent"; or

(b)   in the course of a business otherwise describe or hold itself out, or permit itself to be described or held out, as a registered trade mark agent,

unless all the directors of the body corporate are registered trade mark agents or the body satisfies such conditions as may be prescribed for the purposes of this section.

(4)   A person who contravenes this section commits an offence and is liable on summary conviction to a fine not exceeding level 5 on the standard scale; and proceedings for such an offence may be begun at any time within a year from the date of the offence.

...

86   Use of the term "trade mark attorney"

(1)   No offence is committed under the enactments restricting the use of certain expressions in reference to persons not qualified to act as solicitors by the use of the term "trade mark attorney" in reference to a registered trade mark agent.

(2)   The enactments referred to in subsection (1) are section 21 of the Solicitors Act 1974, section 31 of the Solicitors (Scotland) Act 1980 and Article 22 of the Solicitors (Northern Ireland) Order 1976.

87   Privilege for communications with registered trade mark agents

(1)   This section applies to communications as to any matter relating to the protection of any design or trade mark, or as to any matter involving passing off.

(2)   Any such communication—

(a)   between a person and his trade mark agent, or

(b)   for the purpose of obtaining, or in response to a request for, information which a person is seeking for the purpose of instructing his trade mark agent,

is privileged from, or in Scotland protected against, disclosure in legal proceedings in the same way as a communication between a person and his solicitor or, as the case may be, a communication for the purpose of obtaining, or in response to a request for, information which a person is seeking for the purpose of instructing his solicitor.

(3)   In subsection (2) "trade mark agent" means—
(a)   a registered trade mark agent, or
(b)   a partnership entitled to describe itself as a firm of registered trade mark agents, or
(c)   a body corporate entitled to describe itself as a registered trade mark agent.
...

Importation of infringing goods, material or articles

89   Infringing goods, material or articles may be treated as prohibited goods
(1)   The proprietor of a registered trade mark, or a licensee, may give notice in writing to the Commissioners of Customs and Excise—
(a)   that he is the proprietor or, as the case may be, a licensee of the registered trade mark
(b)   that, at a time and place specified in the notice, goods which are, in relation to that registered trade mark, infringing goods, material or articles are expected to arrive in the United Kingdom—
  (i)   from outside the European Economic Area, or
  (ii)   from within that Area but not having been entered for free circulation, and
(c)   that he requests the Commissioners to treat them as prohibited goods.
(2)   When a notice is in force under this section the importation of the goods to which the notice relates, otherwise than by a person for his private and domestic use, is prohibited; but a person is not by reason of the prohibition liable to any penalty other than forfeiture of the goods.
(3)   This section does not apply to goods entered, or expected to be entered, for free circulation, export, re-export or for a suspensive procedure in respect of which an application may be made under Article 3(1) of Council Regulation (EC) No. 3295/94 laying down measures to prohibit the release for free circulation, export, re-export or entry for a suspensive procedure of counterfeit and pirated goods.
...

91   Power of Commissioners of Customs and Excise to disclose information
Where information relating to infringing goods, material or articles has been obtained by the Commissioners of Customs and Excise for the purposes of, or in connection with, the exercise of their functions in relation to imported goods, the Commissioners may authorise the disclosure of that information for the purpose of facilitating the exercise by any person of any function in connection with the investigation or prosecution of an offence under section 92 below (unauthorised use of trade mark, &c. in relation to goods) or under the Trade Descriptions Act 1968.

Offences

92   Unauthorised use of trade mark, &c. in relation to goods
(1)   A person commits an offence who with a view to gain for himself or another, or with intent to cause loss to another, and without the consent of the proprietor—
(a)   applies to goods or their packaging a sign identical to, or likely to be mistaken for, a registered trade mark, or
(b)   sells or lets for hire, offers or exposes for sale or hire or distributes goods which bear, or the packaging of which bears, such a sign, or
(c)   has in his possession, custody or control in the course of a business any such goods with a view to the doing of anything, by himself or another, which would be an offence under paragraph (b).
(2)   A person commits an offence who with a view to gain for himself or another, or with intent to cause loss to another, and without the consent of the proprietor—

(a)   applies a sign identical to, or likely to be mistaken for, a registered trade mark to material intended to be used—
  (i)   for labelling or packaging goods,
  (ii)   as a business paper in relation to goods, or
  (iii)   for advertising goods, or
(b)   uses in the course of a business material bearing such a sign for labelling or packaging goods, as a business paper in relation to goods, or for advertising goods, or
(c)   has in his possession, custody or control in the course of a business any such material with a view to the doing of anything, by himself or another, which would be an offence under paragraph (b).

(3)   A person commits an offence who with a view to gain for himself or another, or with intent to cause loss to another, and without the consent of the proprietor—
(a)   makes an article specifically designed or adapted for making copies of a sign identical to, or likely to be mistaken for, a registered trade mark, or
(b)   has such an article in his possession, custody or control in the course of a business,
knowing or having reason to believe that it has been, or is to be, used to produce goods, or material for labelling or packaging goods, as a business paper in relation to goods, or for advertising goods.

(4)   A person does not commit an offence under this section unless—
(a)   the goods are goods in respect of which the trade mark is registered, or
(b)   the trade mark has a reputation in the United Kingdom and the use of the sign takes or would take unfair advantage of, or is or would be detrimental to, the distinctive character or the repute of the trade mark.

(5)   It is a defence for a person charged with an offence under this section to show that he believed on reasonable grounds that the use of the sign in the manner in which it was used, or was to be used, was not an infringement of the registered trade mark.

(6)   A person guilty of an offence under this section is liable—
(a)   on summary conviction to imprisonment for a term not exceeding six months or a fine not exceeding the statutory maximum, or both;
(b)   on conviction on indictment to a fine or imprisonment for a term not exceeding ten years, or both.

93   Enforcement function of local weights and measures authority

(1)   It is the duty of every local weights and measures authority to enforce within their area the provisions of section 92 (unauthorised use of trade mark, &c. in relation to goods).

(2)   The following provisions of the Trade Descriptions Act 1968 apply in relation to the enforcement of that section as in relation to the enforcement of that Act—
  section 27 (power to make test purchases),
  section 28 (power to enter premises and inspect and seize goods and documents),
  section 29 (obstruction of authorised officers), and
  section 33 (compensation for loss, &c. of goods seized).
. . .

94   Falsification of register, &c.

(1)   It is an offence for a person to make, or cause to be made, a false entry in the register of trade marks, knowing or having reason to believe that it is false.

(2)   It is an offence for a person—
(a)   to make or cause to be made anything falsely purporting to be a copy of an entry in the register, or
(b)   to produce or tender or cause to be produced or tendered in evidence any such thing,

knowing or having reason to believe that it is false.

(3)   A person guilty of an offence under this section is liable—

(a)   on conviction on indictment, to imprisonment for a term not exceeding two years or a fine, or both;

(b)   on summary conviction, to imprisonment for a term not exceeding six months or a fine not exceeding the statutory maximum, or both.

95   Falsely representing trade mark as registered

(1)   It is an offence for a person—

(a)   falsely to represent that a mark is a registered trade mark, or

(b)   to make a false representation as to the goods or services for which a trade mark is registered

knowing or having reason to believe that the representation is false.

(2)   For the purposes of this section, the use in the United Kingdom in relation to a trade mark—

(a)   of the word "registered", or

(b)   of any other word or symbol importing a reference (express or implied) to registration,

shall be deemed to be a representation as to registration under this Act unless it is shown that the reference is to registration elsewhere than in the United Kingdom and that the trade mark is in fact so registered for the goods or services in question.

(3)   A person guilty of an offence under this section is liable on summary conviction to a fine not exceeding level 3 on the standard scale.

. . .

Forfeiture of counterfeit goods, &c.

97   Forfeiture: England and Wales or Northern Ireland

(1)   In England and Wales or Northern Ireland where there has come into the possession of any person in connection with the investigation or prosecution of a relevant offence—

(a)   goods which, or the packaging of which, bears a sign identical to or likely to be mistaken for a registered trade mark,

(b)   material bearing such a sign and intended to be used for labelling or packaging goods, as a business paper in relation to goods, or for advertising goods, or

(c)   articles specifically designed or adapted for making copies of such a sign, that person may apply under this section for an order for the forfeiture of the goods, material or articles.

. . .

(6)   Subject to subsection (7), where any goods, material or articles are forfeited under this section they shall be destroyed in accordance with such directions as the court may give.

(7)   On making an order under this section the court may, if it considers it appropriate to do so, direct that the goods, material or articles to which the order relates shall (instead of being destroyed) be released, to such person as the court may specify, on condition that that person—

(a)   causes the offending sign to be erased, removed or obliterated, and

(b)   complies with any order to pay costs which has been made against him in the proceedings for the order for forfeiture.

(8)   For the purposes of this section a "relevant offence" means an offence under section 92 above (unauthorised use of trade mark, &c. in relation to goods) or under the Trade Descriptions Act 1968 or any offence involving dishonesty or deception.

98 Forfeiture: Scotland

(1)   In Scotland the court may make an order for the forfeiture of any—

(a)   goods which bear, or the packaging of which bears, a sign identical to or likely to be mistaken for a registered trade mark,

(b)   material bearing such a sign and intended to be used for labelling or packaging goods, as a business paper in relation to goods, or for advertising goods, or

(c)   articles specifically designed or adapted for making copies of such a sign.

. . .

(12)   Subject to subsection (13), goods, material or articles forfeited under this section shall be destroyed in accordance with such directions as the court may give.

(13)   On making an order under this section the court may if it considers it appropriate to do so, direct that the goods, material or articles to which the order relates shall (instead of being destroyed) be released, to such person as the court may specify, on condition that that person causes the offending sign to be erased, removed or obliterated.

(14)   For the purposes of this section—

"relevant offence" means an offence under section 92 (unauthorised use of trade mark, &c. in relation to goods) or under the Trade Descriptions Act 1968 or any offence involving dishonesty or deception,

"the court" means—

(a)   in relation to an order made on an application under subsection (2)(a), the sheriff, and

(b)   in relation to an order made under subsection (2)(b), the court which imposed the penalty.

PART IV
MISCELLANEOUS AND GENERAL PROVISIONS

Miscellaneous

99 Unauthorised use of Royal arms, &c.

(1)   A person shall not without the authority of Her Majesty use in connection with any business the Royal arms (or arms so closely resembling the Royal arms as to be calculated to deceive) in such manner as to be calculated to lead to the belief that he is duly authorised to use the Royal arms.

(2)   A person shall not without the authority of Her Majesty or of a member of the Royal family use in connection with any business any device, emblem or title in such a manner as to be calculated to lead to the belief that he is employed by, or supplies goods or services to, Her Majesty or that member of the Royal family.

(3)   A person who contravenes subsection (1) commits an offence and is liable on summary conviction to a fine not exceeding level 2 on the standard scale.

(4)   Contravention of subsection (1) or (2) may be restrained by injunction in proceedings brought by—

(a)   any person who is authorised to use the arms, device, emblem or title in question, or

(b)   any person authorised by the Lord Chamberlain to take such proceedings.

(5)   Nothing in this section affects any right of the proprietor of a trade mark containing any such arms, device, emblem or title to use that trade mark.

100 Burden of proving use of trade mark

If in any civil proceedings under this Act a question arises as to the use to which a registered trade mark has been put, it is for the proprietor to show what use has been made of it.

. . .

Interpretation

102   Adaptation of expressions for Scotland

In the application of this Act to Scotland—
"account of profits" means accounting and payment of profits;
"accounts" means count, reckoning and payment;
"assignment" means assignation;
"costs" means expenses;
"declaration" means declarator;
"defendant" means defender;
"delivery up" means delivery;
"injunction" means interdict;
"interlocutory relief" means interim remedy; and
"plaintiff" means pursuer.

103   Minor definitions

(1)   In this Act—
"business" includes a trade or profession;
"director", in relation to a body corporate whose affairs are managed by its members, means any member of the body;
"infringement proceedings", in relation to a registered trade mark, includes proceedings under section 16 (order for delivery up of infringing goods, &c.);
"publish" means make available to the public, and references to publication—
       (a)   in relation to an application for registration, are to publication under section 38(1), and
       (b)   in relation to registration, are to publication under section 40(4);
"statutory provisions" includes provisions of subordinate legislation within the meaning of the Interpretation Act 1978;
"trade" includes any business or profession.
(2)   References in this Act to use (or any particular description of use) of a trade mark, or of a sign identical with, similar to, or likely to be mistaken for a trade mark, include use (or that description of use) otherwise than by means of a graphic representation.
(3)   References in this Act to a Community instrument include references to any instrument amending or replacing that instrument.

104   Index of defined expressions

In this Act the expressions listed below are defined by or otherwise fall to be construed in accordance with the provisions indicated—

account of profits and accounts (in Scotland)	section 102
appointed person (for purposes of section 76)	section 77
assignment (in Scotland)	section 102
business	section 103(1)
certification mark	section 50(1)
collective mark	section 49(1)
commencement (of this Act)	section 109(2)
Community trade mark	section 51
Community Trade Mark Regulation	section 51
Convention country	section 55(1)(b)
costs (in Scotland)	section 102
the court	section 75
date of application	section 33(2)
date of filing	section 33(1)
date of registration	section 40(3)

defendant (in Scotland)	section 102
delivery up (in Scotland)	section 102
director	section 103(1)
earlier right	section 5(4)
earlier trade mark	section 6
exclusive licence and licensee	section 29(1)
infringement (of registered trade mark)	sections 9(1) and (2) and 10
infringement proceedings	section 103(1)
infringing articles	section 17
infringing goods	section 17
infringing material	section 17
injunction (in Scotland)	section 102
interlocutory relief (in Scotland)	section 102
the International Bureau	section 53
international trade mark (UK)	section 53
Madrid Protocol	section 53
Paris Convention	section 55(1)(a)
plaintiff (in Scotland)	section 102
prescribed	section 78(1)(b)
protected under the Paris Convention	
— well-known trade marks	section 56(1)
— state emblems and official signs or hallmarks	section 57(1)
— emblems, &c. of international organisations	section 58(2)
publish and references to publication	section 103(1)
register, registered (and related expressions)	section 63(1)
registered trade mark agent	section 83(1)
registrable transaction	section 25(2)
the registrar	section 62
rules	section 78
statutory provisions	section 103(1)
trade	section 103(1)
trade mark	
— generally	section 1(1)
— includes collective mark or certification mark	section 1(2)
United Kingdom (references include Isle of Man)	section 108(2)
use (of trade mark or sign)	section 103(2)
well-known trade mark (under Paris Convention)	section 56(1)

Other general provisions

105 Transitional provisions

The provisions of Schedule 3 have effect with respect to transitional matters, including the treatment of marks registered under the Trade Marks Act 1938, and applications for registration and other proceedings pending under that Act, on the commencement of this Act.

106 Consequential amendments and repeals

(1)   The enactments specified in Schedule 4 are amended in accordance with that Schedule, the amendments being consequential on the provisions of this Act.

(2)   The enactments specified in Schedule 5 are repealed to the extent specified.

107   Territorial waters and the continental shelf
(1)   For the purposes of this Act the territorial waters of the United Kingdom shall be treated as part of the United Kingdom.

(2)   This Act applies to things done in the United Kingdom sector of the continental shelf on a structure or vessel which is present there for purposes directly connected with the exploration of the sea bed or subsoil or the exploitation of their natural resources as it applies to things done in the United Kingdom.

(3)   The United Kingdom sector of the continental shelf means the areas designated by order under section 1(7) of the Continental Shelf Act 1964.

108   Extent
(1)   This Act extends to England and Wales, Scotland and Northern Ireland.

(2)   This Act also extends to the Isle of Man, subject to such exceptions and modifications as Her Majesty may specify by Order in Council; and subject to any such Order references in this Act to the United Kingdom shall be construed as including the Isle of Man.

. . .

110   Short title
This Act may be cited as the Trade Marks Act 1994.

Section 49   SCHEDULE 1   COLLECTIVE MARKS

General

1.   The provisions of this Act apply to collective marks subject to the following provisions.

Signs of which a collective mark may consist

2.   In relation to a collective mark the reference in section 1(1) (signs of which a trade mark may consist) to distinguishing goods or services of one undertaking from those of other undertakings shall be construed as a reference to distinguishing goods or services of members of the association which is the proprietor of the mark from those of other undertakings.

Indication of geographical origin

3.—(1)   Notwithstanding section 3(1)(c), a collective mark may be registered which consists of signs or indications which may serve, in trade, to designate the geographical origin of the goods or services.

(2)   However, the proprietor of such a mark is not entitled to prohibit the use of the signs or indications in accordance with honest practices in industrial or commercial matters (in particular, by a person who is entitled to use a geographical name).

Mark not to be misleading as to character or significance

4.—(1)   A collective mark shall not be registered if the public is liable to be misled as regards the character or significance of the mark, in particular if it is likely to be taken to be something other than a collective mark.

(2)   The registrar may accordingly require that a mark in respect of which application is made for registration include some indication that it is a collective mark. Notwithstanding section 39(2), an application may be amended so as to comply with any such requirement.

Regulations governing use of collective mark

5.—(1) An applicant for registration of a collective mark must file with the registrar regulations governing the use of the mark.

(2) The regulations must specify the persons authorised to use the mark, the conditions of membership of the association and, where they exist, the conditions of use of the mark, including any sanctions against misuse.

Further requirements with which the regulations have to comply may be imposed by rules.

Approval of regulations by registrar

6.—(1) A collective mark shall not be registered unless the regulations governing the use of the mark—

(a) comply with paragraph 5(2) and any further requirements imposed by rules, and

(b) are not contrary to public policy or to accepted principles of morality.

(2) Before the end of the prescribed period after the date of the application for registration of a collective mark, the applicant must file the regulations with the registrar and pay the prescribed fee.

If he does not do so, the application shall be deemed to be withdrawn.

7.—(1) The registrar shall consider whether the requirements mentioned in paragraph 6(1) are met.

(2) If it appears to the registrar that those requirements are not met, he shall inform the applicant and give him an opportunity, within such period as the registrar may specify, to make representations or to file amended regulations.

(3) If the applicant fails to satisfy the registrar that those requirements are met, or to file regulations amended so as to meet them, or fails to respond before the end of the specified period, the registrar shall refuse the application.

(4) If it appears to the registrar that those requirements, and the other requirements for registration, are met, he shall accept the application and shall proceed in accordance with section 38 (publication, opposition proceedings and observations).

8. The regulations shall be published and notice of opposition may be given, and observations may be made, relating to the matters mentioned in paragraph 6(1).

This is in addition to any other grounds on which the application may be opposed or observations made.

Regulations to be open to inspection

9. The regulations governing the use of a registered collective mark shall be open to public inspection in the same way as the register.

Amendment of regulations

10.—(1) An amendment of the regulations governing the use of a registered collective mark is not effective unless and until the amended regulations are filed with the registrar and accepted by him.

(2) Before accepting any amended regulations the registrar may in any case where it appears to him expedient to do so cause them to be published.

(3) If he does so, notice of opposition may be given, and observations may be made, relating to the matters mentioned in paragraph 6(1).

Infringement: rights of authorised users

11. The following provisions apply in relation to an authorised user of a registered collective mark as in relation to a licensee of a trade mark—

(a)   section 10(5) (definition of infringement: unauthorised application of mark to certain material);

(b)   section 19(2) (order as to disposal of infringing goods, material or articles: adequacy of other remedies);

(c)   section 89 (prohibition of importation of infringing goods, material or articles: request to Commissioners of Customs and Excise).

12.—(1)   The following provisions (which correspond to the provisions of section 30 (general provisions as to rights of licensees in case of infringement)) have effect as regards the rights of an authorised user in relation to infringement of a registered collective mark.

(2)   An authorised user is entitled, subject to any agreement to the contrary between him and the proprietor, to call on the proprietor to take infringement proceedings in respect of any matter which affects his interests.

(3)   If the proprietor—

(a)   refuses to do so, or

(b)   fails to do so within two months after being called upon,

the authorised user may bring the proceedings in his own name as if he were the proprietor.

(4)   Where infringement proceedings are brought by virtue of this paragraph, the authorised user may not, without the leave of the court, proceed with the action unless the proprietor is either joined as a plaintiff or added as a defendant.

This does not affect the granting of interlocutory relief on an application by an authorised user alone.

(5)   A proprietor who is added as a defendant as mentioned in sub-paragraph (4) shall not be made liable for any costs in the action unless he takes part in the proceedings.

(6)   In infringement proceedings brought by the proprietor of a registered collective mark any loss suffered or likely to be suffered by authorised users shall be taken into account; and the court may give such directions as it thinks fit as to the extent to which the plaintiff is to hold the proceeds of any pecuniary remedy on behalf of such users.

Grounds for revocation of registration

13.   Apart from the grounds of revocation provided for in section 46, the registration of a collective mark may be revoked on the ground—

(a)   that the manner in which the mark has been used by the proprietor has caused it to become liable to mislead the public in the manner referred to in paragraph 4(1), or

(b)   that the proprietor has failed to observe, or to secure the observance of, the regulations governing the use of the mark, or

(c)   that an amendment of the regulations has been made so that the regulations—

(i)   no longer comply with paragraph 5(2) and any further conditions imposed by rules, or

(ii)   are contrary to public policy or to accepted principles of morality.

Grounds for invalidity of registration

14.   Apart from the grounds of invalidity provided for in section 47, the registration of a collective mark may be declared invalid on the ground that the mark was registered in breach of the provisions of paragraph 4(1) or 6(1).

Section 50   SCHEDULE 2   CERTIFICATION MARKS

General

1.   The provisions of this Act apply to certification marks subject to the following provisions.

Signs of which a certification mark may consist

2.   In relation to a certification mark the reference in section 1(1) (signs of which a trade mark may consist) to distinguishing goods or services of one undertaking from those of other undertakings shall be construed as a reference to distinguishing goods or services which are certified from those which are not.

Indication of geographical origin

3.—(1)   Notwithstanding section 3(1)(c), a certification mark may be registered which consists of signs or indications which may serve, in trade, to designate the geographical origin of the goods or services.

(2)   However, the proprietor of such a mark is not entitled to prohibit the use of the signs or indications in accordance with honest practices in industrial or commercial matters (in particular, by a person who is entitled to use a geographical name).

Nature of proprietor's business

4.   A certification mark shall not be registered if the proprietor carries on a business involving the supply of goods or services of the kind certified.

Mark not to be misleading as to character or significance

5.—(1)   A certification mark shall not be registered if the public is liable to be misled as regards the character or significance of the mark, in particular if it is likely to be taken to be something other than a certification mark.

(2)   The registrar may accordingly require that a mark in respect of which application is made for registration include some indication that it is a certification mark.

Notwithstanding section 39(2), an application may be amended so as to comply with any such requirement.

Regulations governing use of certification mark

6.—(1)   An applicant for registration of a certification mark must file with the registrar regulations governing the use of the mark.

(2)   The regulations must indicate who is authorised to use the mark, the characteristics to be certified by the mark, how the certifying body is to test those characteristics and to supervise the use of the mark, the fees (if any) to be paid in connection with the operation of the mark and the procedures for resolving disputes.

Further requirements with which the regulations have to comply may be imposed by rules.

Approval of regulations, &c.

7.—(1)   A certification mark shall not be registered unless—

   (a)   the regulations governing the use of the mark—

      (i)   comply with paragraph 6(2) and any further requirements imposed by rules, and

      (ii)   are not contrary to public policy or to accepted principles of morality, and

   (b)   the applicant is competent to certify the goods or services for which the mark is to be registered.

(2)   Before the end of the prescribed period after the date of the application for registration of a certification mark, the applicant must file the regulations with the registrar and pay the prescribed fee.

If he does not do so, the application shall be deemed to be withdrawn.

8.—(1) The registrar shall consider whether the requirements mentioned in paragraph 7(1) are met.

(2) If it appears to the registrar that those requirements are not met, he shall inform the applicant and give him an opportunity, within such period as the registrar may specify, to make representations or to file amended regulations.

(3) If the applicant fails to satisfy the registrar that those requirements are met, or to file regulations amended so as to meet them, or fails to respond before the end of the specified period, the registrar shall refuse the application.

(4) If it appears to the registrar that those requirements, and the other requirements for registration, are met, he shall accept the application and shall proceed in accordance with section 38 (publication, opposition proceedings and observations).

9. The regulations shall be published and notice of opposition may be given, and observations may be made, relating to the matters mentioned in paragraph 7(1).

This is in addition to any other grounds on which the application may be opposed or observations made.

Regulations to be open to inspection

10. The regulations governing the use of a registered certification mark shall be open to public inspection in the same way as the register.

Amendment of regulations

11.—(1) An amendment of the regulations governing the use of a registered certification mark is not effective unless and until the amended regulations are filed with the registrar and accepted by him.

(2) Before accepting any amended regulations the registrar may in any case where it appears to him expedient to do so cause them to be published.

(3) If he does so, notice of opposition may be given, and observations may be made, relating to the matters mentioned in paragraph 7(1).

Consent to assignment of registered certification mark

12. The assignment or other transmission of a registered certification mark is not effective without the consent of the registrar.

Infringement: rights of authorised users

13. The following provisions apply in relation to an authorised user of a registered certification mark as in relation to a licensee of a trade mark—

(a) section 10(5) (definition of infringement: unauthorised application of mark to certain material);

(b) section 19(2) (order as to disposal of infringing goods, material or articles: adequacy of other remedies);

(c) section 89 (prohibition of importation of infringing goods, material or articles: request to Commissioners of Customs and Excise).

14. In infringement proceedings brought by the proprietor of a registered certification mark any loss suffered or likely to be suffered by authorised users shall be taken into account; and the court may give such directions as it thinks fit as to the extent to which the plaintiff is to hold the proceeds of any pecuniary remedy on behalf of such users.

Grounds for revocation of registration

15. Apart from the grounds of revocation provided for in section 46, the registration of a certification mark may be revoked on the ground—

(a)   that the proprietor has begun to carry on such a business as is mentioned in paragraph 4,

(b)   that the manner in which the mark has been used by the proprietor has caused it to become liable to mislead the public in the manner referred to in paragraph 5(1),

(c)   that the proprietor has failed to observe, or to secure the observance of, the regulations governing the use of the mark,

(d)   that an amendment of the regulations has been made so that the regulations—

(i)   no longer comply with paragraph 6(2) and any further conditions imposed by rules, or

(ii)   are contrary to public policy or to accepted principles of morality, or

(e)   that the proprietor is no longer competent to certify the goods or services for which the mark is registered.

Grounds for invalidity of registration

16.   Apart from the grounds of invalidity provided for in section 47, the registration of a certification mark may be declared invalid on the ground that the mark was registered in breach of the provisions of paragraph 4, 5(1) or 7(1).

Section 105   SCHEDULE 3   TRANSITIONAL PROVISIONS

Introductory

1.—(1)   In this Schedule—

"existing registered mark" means a trade mark, certification trade mark or service mark registered under the 1938 Act immediately before the commencement of this Act;

"the 1938 Act" means the Trade Marks Act 1938; and

"the old law" means that Act and any other enactment or rule of law applying to existing registered marks immediately before the commencement of this Act.

(2)   For the purposes of this Schedule—

(a)   an application shall be treated as pending on the commencement of this Act if it was made but not finally determined before commencement, and

(b)   the date on which it was made shall be taken to be the date of filing under the 1938 Act.

Existing registered marks

2.—(1)   Existing registered marks (whether registered in Part A or B of the register kept under the 1938 Act) shall be transferred on the commencement of this Act to the register kept under this Act and have effect, subject to the provisions of this Schedule, as if registered under this Act.

(2)   Existing registered marks registered as a series under section 21(2) of the 1938 Act shall be similarly registered in the new register.

Provision may be made by rules for putting such entries in the same form as is required for entries under this Act.

(3)   In any other case notes indicating that existing registered marks are associated with other marks shall cease to have effect on the commencement of this Act.

3.—(1)   A condition entered on the former register in relation to an existing registered mark immediately before the commencement of this Act shall cease to have effect on commencement.

Proceedings under section 33 of the 1938 Act (application to expunge or vary registration for breach of condition) which are pending on the commencement of this Act shall be dealt with under the old law and any necessary alteration made to the new register.

(2)   A disclaimer or limitation entered on the former register in relation to an existing registered mark immediately before the commencement of this Act shall be transferred to the new register and have effect as if entered on the register in pursuance of section 13 of this Act.

Effects of registration: infringement

4.—(1)   Sections 9 to 12 of this Act (effects of registration) apply in relation to an existing registered mark as from the commencement of this Act and section 14 of this Act (action for infringement) applies in relation to infringement of an existing registered mark committed after the commencement of this Act, subject to sub-paragraph (2) below.

The old law continues to apply in relation to infringements committed before commencement.

(2)   It is not an infringement of—
   (a)   an existing registered mark, or
   (b)   a registered trade mark of which the distinctive elements are the same or substantially the same as those of an existing registered mark and which is registered for the same goods or services,
to continue after commencement any use which did not amount to infringement of the existing registered mark under the old law.

Infringing goods, material or articles

5.   Section 16 of this Act (order for delivery up of infringing goods, material or articles) applies to infringing goods, material or articles whether made before or after the commencement of this Act.

Rights and remedies of licensee or authorised user

6.—(1)   Section 30 (general provisions as to rights of licensees in case of infringe-ment) of this Act applies to licences granted before the commencement of this Act, but only in relation to infringements committed after commencement.

(2)   Paragraph 14 of Schedule 2 of this Act (court to take into account loss suffered by authorised users, &c.) applies only in relation to infringements committed after commencement.

Co-ownership of registered mark

7.   The provisions of section 23 of this Act (co-ownership of registered mark) apply as from the commencement of this Act to an existing registered mark of which two or more persons were immediately before commencement registered as joint proprietors.

But so long as the relations between the joint proprietors remain such as are described in section 63 of the 1938 Act (joint ownership) there shall be taken to be an agreement to exclude the operation of subsections (1) and (3) of section 23 of this Act (ownership in undivided shares and right of co-proprietor to make separate use of the mark).

Assignment, &c. of registered mark

8.—(1)   Section 24 of this Act (assignment or other transmission of registered mark) applies to transactions and events occurring after the commencement of this Act in relation to an existing registered mark; and the old law continues to apply in relation to transactions and events occurring before commencement.
. . .

Licensing of registered mark

9.—(1)   Sections 28 and 29(2) of this Act (licensing of registered trade mark; rights of exclusive licensee against grantor's successor in title) apply only in relation to licences granted after the commencement of this Act; and the old law continues to apply in relation to licences granted before commencement.

. . .

Pending applications for registration

10.—(1)   An application for registration of a mark under the 1938 Act which is pending on the commencement of this Act shall be dealt with under the old law, subject as mentioned below, and if registered the mark shall be treated for the purposes of this Schedule as an existing registered mark.

. . .

(3)   Section 23 of the 1938 Act (provisions as to associated trade marks) shall be disregarded in dealing after the commencement of this Act with an application for registration.

Conversion of pending application

11.—(1)   In the case of a pending application for registration which has not been advertised under section 18 of the 1938 Act before the commencement of this Act, the applicant may give notice to the registrar claiming to have the registrability of the mark determined in accordance with the provisions of this Act.

. . .

Trade marks registered according to old classification

12.   The registrar may exercise the powers conferred by rules under section 65 of this Act (adaptation of entries to new classification) to secure that any existing registered marks which do not conform to the system of classification prescribed under section 34 of this Act are brought into conformity with that system.

This applies, in particular, to existing registered marks classified according to the pre-1938 classification set out in Schedule 3 to the Trade Marks Rules 1986.

Claim to priority from overseas application

13.   Section 35 of this Act (claim to priority of Convention application) applies to an application for registration under this Act made after the commencement of this Act notwithstanding that the Convention application was made before commencement.

14.—(1)   Where before the commencement of this Act a person has duly filed an application for protection of a trade mark in a relevant country within the meaning of section 39A of the 1938 Act which is not a Convention country (a "relevant overseas application"), he, or his successor in title, has a right to priority, for the purposes of registering the same trade mark under this Act for some or all of the same goods or services, for a period of six months from the date of filing of the relevant overseas application.

. . .

Duration and renewal of registration

15.—(1)   Section 42(1) of this Act (duration of original period of registration) applies in relation to the registration of a mark in pursuance of an application made after the commencement of this Act; and the old law applies in any other case.

(2)   Sections 42(2) and 43 of this Act (renewal) apply where the renewal falls due on or after the commencement of this Act; and the old law continues to apply in any other case.

(3)   In either case it is immaterial when the fee is paid.

Pending application for alteration of registered mark

16.   An application under section 35 of the 1938 Act (alteration of registered trade mark) which is pending on the commencement of this Act shall be dealt with under the old law and any necessary alteration made to the new register.

Revocation for non-use

17.—(1)   An application under section 26 of the 1938 Act (removal from register or imposition of limitation on ground of non-use) which is pending on the commencement of this Act shall be dealt with under the old law and any necessary alteration made to the new register.

(2)   An application under section 46(1)(a) or (b) of this Act (revocation for non-use) may be made in relation to an existing registered mark at any time after the commencement of this Act.

Provided that no such application for the revocation of the registration of an existing registered mark registered by virtue of section 27 of the 1938 Act (defensive registration of well-known trade marks) may be made until more than five years after the commencement of this Act.

Application for rectification, &c.

18.—(1)   An application under section 32 or 34 of the 1938 Act (rectification or correction of the register) which is pending on the commencement of this Act shall be dealt with under the old law and any necessary alteration made to the new register.

(2)   For the purposes of proceedings under section 47 of this Act (grounds for invalidity of registration) as it applies in relation to an existing registered mark, the provisions of this Act shall be deemed to have been in force at all material times.

Provided that no objection to the validity of the registration of an existing registered mark may be taken on the ground specified in subsection (3) of section 5 of this Act (relative grounds for refusal of registration: conflict with earlier mark registered for different goods or services).

Regulations as to use of certification mark

19.—(1)   Regulations governing the use of an existing registered certification mark deposited at the Patent Office in pursuance of section 37 of the 1938 Act shall be treated after the commencement of this Act as if filed under paragraph 6 of Schedule 2 to this Act.

(2)   Any request for amendment of the regulations which was pending on the commencement of this Act shall be dealt with under the old law.

Sheffield marks

20.—(1)   For the purposes of this Schedule the Sheffield register kept under Schedule 2 to the 1938 Act shall be treated as part of the register of trade marks kept under that Act.

(2)   Applications made to the Cutlers' Company in accordance with that Schedule which are pending on the commencement of this Act shall proceed after commencement as if they had been made to the registrar.

Certificate of validity of contested registration

21.   A certificate given before the commencement of this Act under section 47 of the 1938 Act (certificate of validity of contested registration) shall have effect as if given under section 73(1) of this Act.

Trade mark agents

22.—(1)   Rules in force immediately before the commencement of this Act under section 282 or 283 of the Copyright, Designs and Patents Act 1988 (register of trade mark agents; persons entitled to described themselves as registered) shall continue in force and have effect as if made under section 83 or 85 of this Act.

(2)   Rules in force immediately before the commencement of this Act under section 40 of the 1938 Act as to the persons whom the registrar may refuse to recognise as agents for the purposes of business under that Act shall continue in force and have effect as if made under section 88 of this Act.

(3)   Rules continued in force under this paragraph may be varied or revoked by further rules made under the relevant provisions of this Act.

Section 106(1)   SCHEDULE 4   CONSEQUENTIAL
                               AMENDMENTS

General adaptation of existing references

1.—(1)   References in statutory provisions passed or made before the commencement of this Act to trade marks or registered trade marks within the meaning of the Trade Marks Act 1938 shall, unless the context otherwise requires, be construed after the commencement of this Act as references to trade marks or registered trade marks within the meaning of this Act.
. . .

Restrictive Trade Practices Act 1976 (c.34)

7.   In Schedule 3 to the Restrictive Trade Practices Act 1976 (excepted agreements), for paragraph 4 (agreements relating to trade marks) substitute—
   "4.—(1)   This Act does not apply to an agreement authorising the use of a registered trade mark (other than a collective mark or certification mark) if no such restrictions as are described in section 6(1) or 11(2) above are accepted, and no such information provisions as are described in section 7(1) or 12(2) above are made, except in respect of—
      (a)   the descriptions of goods bearing the mark which are to be produced or supplied, or the processes of manufacture to be applied to such goods or to goods to which the mark is to be applied, or
      (b)   the kinds of services in relation to which the mark is to be used which are to be made available or supplied, or the form or manner in which such services are to be made available or supplied, or
      (c)   the descriptions of goods which are to be produced or supplied in connection with the supply of services in relation to which the mark is to be used, or the process of manufacture to be applied to such goods.
   (2)   This Act does not apply to an agreement authorising the use of a registered collective mark or certification mark if—
      (a)   the agreement is made in accordance with regulations approved by the registrar under Schedule 1 or 2 to the Trade Marks Act 1994, and
      (b)   no such restrictions as are described in section 6(1) or 11(2) above are accepted, and no such information provisions as are described in section 7(1) or 12(2) above are made, except as permitted by those regulations.".

Copyright, Designs and Patents Act 1988 (c.48)

8.—(1)   The Copyright, Designs and Patents Act 1988 is amended as follows.

(2)   In sections 114(6), 204(6) and 231(6) (persons regarded as having an interest in infringing copies, &c.), for "section 58C of the Trade Marks Act 1938" substitute "section 19 of the Trade Marks Act 1994".

(3)   In section 280(1) (privilege for communications with patent agents), for "trade mark or service mark" substitute "or trade mark".

. . .

Tribunals and Inquiries Act 1992 (c.53)

9.   In Part I of Schedule 1 to the Tribunals and Inquiries Act 1992 (tribunals under direct supervision of Council on Tribunals), for "Patents, designs, trade marks and service marks" substitute "Patents, designs and trade marks".

Section 106(2) SCHEDULE 5   REPEALS AND REVOCATIONS

Chapter or number	Short title	Extent of repeal or revocation
. . . 1938 c. 22.	Trade Marks Act 1938.	The whole Act.
. . . 1984 c. 19.	Trade Marks (Amendment) Act 1984.	The whole Act.
. . . 1988 c. 48.	Copyright, Designs and Patents Act 1988.	Sections 282 to 284. In section 286, the definition of "registered trade mark agent". Section 300.
. . .		

TRADE MARK RULES 1994
(SI 1994, No. 2583)

. . .

SCHEDULE 4   CLASSIFICATION OF GOODS AND SERVICES

Goods

Class 1   Chemicals used in industry, science and photography, as well as in agriculture horticulture and forestry; unprocessed artificial resins, unprocessed plastics; manures; fire extinguishing compositions; tempering and soldering preparations; chemical substances for preserving foodstuffs; tanning substances; adhesives used in industry.

Class 2   Paints, varnishes, lacquers; preservatives against rust and against deterioration of wood; colourants; mordants; raw natural resins; metals in foil and powder form for painters, decorators, printers and artists.

Class 3   Bleaching preparations and other substances for laundry use; cleaning, polishing, scouring and abrasive preparations; soaps; perfumery, essential oils, cosmetics, hair lotions; dentifrices.

Class 4   Industrial oils and greases; lubricants; dust absorbing, wetting and binding compositions; fuels (including motor spirit) and illuminants; candles, wicks.

Class 5   Pharmaceutical, veterinary and sanitary preparations; dietetic substances adapted for medical use, food for babies; plasters, materials for dressing; material for stopping teeth, dental wax; disinfectants; preparations for destroying vermin; fungicides, herbicides.

Class 6   Common metals and their alloys; metal building materials; transportable buildings of metal; materials of metal for railway tracks; non-electric cables and wires of common metal; ironmongery, small items of metal hardware; pipes and tubes of metal; safes; goods of common metal not included in other classes; ores.

Class 7   Machines and machine tools; motors and engines (except for land vehicles); machine coupling and transmission components (except for land vehicles); agricultural implements (other than hand operated); incubators for eggs.

Class 8   Hand tools and implements (hand operated); cutlery; side arms; razors.

Class 9   Scientific, nautical, surveying, electric, photographic, cinematographic, optical, weighing, measuring, signalling, checking (supervision), life-saving and teaching apparatus and instruments; apparatus for recording, transmission or reproduction of sound or images; magnetic data carriers, recording discs; automatic vending machines and mechanisms for coin-operated apparatus; cash registers, calculating machines, data processing equipment and computers; fire-extinguishing apparatus.

Class 10   Surgical, medical, dental and veterinary apparatus and instruments, artificial limbs, eyes and teeth; orthopaedic articles; suture materials.

Class 11   Apparatus for lighting, heating, steam generating, cooking, refrigerating, drying, ventilating, water supply and sanitary purposes.

Class 12   Vehicles; apparatus for locomotion by land, air or water.

Class 13   Firearms; ammunition and projectiles; explosives; fireworks.

Class 14   Precious metals and their alloys and goods in precious metals or coated therewith, not included in other classes; jewellery, precious stones; horological and chronometric instruments.

Class 15   Musical instruments.

Class 16   Paper, cardboard and goods made from these materials, not included in other classes; printed matter; bookbinding material; photographs; stationery; adhesives for stationery or household purposes; artists' materials; paint brushes; typewriters and office requisites (except furniture); instructional and teaching material (except apparatus); plastic materials for packaging (not included in other classes); playing cards; printers' type; printing blocks.

Class 17   Rubber, gutta-percha, gum, asbestos, mica and goods made from these materials and not included in other classes; plastics in extruded form for use in manufacture; packing, stopping and insulating materials; flexible pipes, not of metal.

Class 18   Leather and imitations of leather, and goods made of these materials and not included in other classes; animal skins, hides; trunks and travelling bags; umbrellas, parasols and walking sticks; whips, harness and saddlery.

Class 19   Building materials (non-metallic); non-metallic rigid pipes for buildings; asphalt, pitch and bitumen; non-metallic transportable buildings; monuments, not of metal.

Class 20   Furniture, mirrors, picture frames; goods (not included in other classes) of wood, cork, reed, cane, wicker, horn, bone, ivory, whalebone, shell, amber, mother-of-pearl, meerschaum and substitutes for all these materials, or of plastics.

Class 21   Household or kitchen utensils and containers (not of precious metal or coated therewith); combs and sponges; brushes (except paint brushes); brush-making materials; articles for cleaning purposes; steelwool; unworked or semi-worked glass (except glass used in building); glassware, porcelain and earthenware not included in other classes.

Class 22   Ropes, string, nets, tents, awnings, tarpau! r s, sails, sacks and bags (not included in other classes); padding and stuffing material₃ ₍except of rubber or plastics); raw fibrous textile materials.

Class 23   Yarns and threads, for textile use.

Class 24   Textiles and textile goods, not included in other classes; bed and table covers.

Class 25   Clothing, footwear, headgear.

Class 26   Lace and embroidery, ribbons and braid; buttons, hooks and eyes, pins and needles; artificial flowers.

Class 27   Carpets, rugs, mats and n. itting, linoleum and other materials for covering existing floors; wall hangings (non-textile).

Class 28   Games and playthings; gymnastic and sporting articles not included in other classes; decorations for Christmas trees.

Class 29   Meat, fish, poultry and game; meat extracts; preserved, dried and cooked fruits and vegetables; jellies, jams, fruit sauces; eggs, milk and milk products; edible oils and fats.

Class 30   Coffee, tea, cocoa, sugar, rice, tapioca, sago, artificial coffee; flour and preparations made from cereals, bread, pastry and confectionery, ices; honey, treacle; yeast, baking-powder; salt, mustard; vinegar, sauces (condiments); spices; ice.

Class 31   Agricultural, horticultural and forestry products and grains not included in other classes; live animals; fresh fruits and vegetables; seeds, natural plants and flowers; foodstuffs for animals, malt.

Class 32   Beers; mineral and aerated waters and other non-alcoholic drinks; fruit drinks and fruit juices; syrups and other preparations for making beverages.

Class 33   Alcoholic beverages (except beers).

Class 34   Tobacco; smokers' articles; matches.

Services

Class 35   Advertising; business management; business administration; office functions.

Class 36   Insurance; financial affairs; monetary affairs; real estate affairs.

Class 37   Building construction; repair; installation services.

Class 38   Telecommunications.

Class 39   Transport; packaging and storage of goods; travel arrangement.

Class 40   Treatment of materials.

Class 41   Education; providing of training; entertainment; sporting and cultural activities.

Class 42   Providing of food and drink; temporary accommodation; medical, hygienic and beauty care; veterinary and agricultural services; legal services; scientific and industrial research; computer programming; services that cannot be placed in other classes.

DURATION OF COPYRIGHT AND RIGHTS IN PERFORMANCES REGULATIONS 1995
(SI 1995/3297)

. . .

PART I
INTRODUCTORY PROVISIONS

1   Citation, commencement and extent
(1)   These Regulations may be cited as the Duration of Copyright and Rights in Performances Regulations 1995.
(2)   These Regulations come into force on 1st January 1996.
(3)   These Regulations extend to the whole of the United Kingdom.

2   Interpretation
In these Regulations—
"EEA Agreement" means the Agreement on the European Economic Area signed at Oporto on 2nd May 1992, as adjusted by the Protocol signed at Brussels on 17th March 1993; and
"EEA state" means a state which is a contracting party to the EEA Agreement.

3   Implementation of Directive, &c.
These Regulations make provision for the purpose of implementing—
       (a)   the main provisions of Council Directive No. 93/98/EEC of 29th October 1993 harmonizing the term of protection of copyright and certain related rights; and
       (b)   certain obligations of the United Kingdom created by or arising under the EEA Agreement so far as relevant to the implementation of that Directive.

4   Scheme of the regulations
The Copyright, Designs and Patents Act 1988 is amended in accordance with the provisions of Part II of these Regulations, subject to the savings and transitional provisions in Part III of these Regulations.
. . .

PART III
SAVINGS AND TRANSITIONAL PROVISIONS

Introductory

12   Introductory
(1)   References in this Part to "commencement", without more, are to the date on which these Regulations come into force.
(2)   In this Part—
"the 1988 Act" means the Copyright, Designs and Patents Act 1988;
"the 1988 provisions" means the provisions of that Act as they stood immediately before commencement (including the provisions of Schedule 1 to that Act continuing the effect of earlier enactments); and
"the new provisions" means the provisions of that Act as amended by these Regulations.
(3)   Expressions used in this Part which are defined for the purposes of Part I or II of the 1988 Act, in particular references to the copyright owner, have the same meaning as in that Part.

13   Films not protected as such
In relation to a film in which copyright does not or did not subsist as such but which is or was protected—

(a)   as an original dramatic work, or

(b)   by virtue of the protection of the photographs forming part of the film,

references in the new provisions, and in this Part, to copyright in a film are to any copyright in the film as an original dramatic work or, as the case may be, in photographs forming part of the film.

Copyright

14 Copyright: interpretation

(1)   In the provisions of this Part relating to copyright—

(a)   "existing", in relation to a work, means made before commencement; and

(b)   "existing copyright work" means a work in which copyright subsisted immediately before commencement.

(2)   For the purposes of those provisions a work of which the making extended over a period shall be taken to have been made when its making was completed.

(3)   References in those provisions to "moral rights" are to the rights conferred by Chapter IV of Part I of the 1988 Act.

15 Duration of copyright: general saving

(1)   Copyright in an existing copyright work shall continue to subsist until the date on which it would have expired under the 1988 provisions if that date is later than the date on which copyright would expire under the new provisions.

(2)   Where paragraph (1) has effect, section 57 of the 1988 Act (anonymous or pseudonymous works: acts permitted on assumptions as to expiry of copyright or death of author) applies as it applied immediately before commencement (that is, without the amendments made by Regulation 5(2)).

16 Duration of copyright: application of new provisions

The new provisions relating to duration of copyright apply—

(a)   to copyright works made after commencement;

(b)   to existing works which first qualify for copyright protection after commencement;

(c)   to existing copyright works, subject to Regulation 15 (general saving for any longer period applicable under 1988 provisions); and

(d)   to existing works in which copyright expired before 31st December 1995 but which were on 1st July 1995 protected in another EEA state under legislation relating to copyright or related rights.

17 Extended and revived copyright

In the following provisions of this Part—

"extended copyright" means any copyright which subsists by virtue of the new provisions after the date on which it would have expired under the 1988 provisions; and

"revived copyright" means any copyright which subsists by virtue of the new provisions after having expired under the 1988 provisions or any earlier enactment relating to copyright.

18 Ownership of extended copyright

(1)   The person who is the owner of the copyright in a work immediately before commencement is as from commencement the owner of any extended copyright in the work, subject as follows.

(2)   If he is entitled to copyright for a period less than the whole of the copyright period under the 1988 provisions, any extended copyright is part of the reversionary interest expectant on the termination of that period.

19   Ownership of revived copyright

(1)   The person who was the owner of the copyright in a work immediately before it expired (the "former copyright owner") is as from commencement the owner of any revived copyright in the work, subject as follows.

(2)   If the former copyright owner has died before commencement, or in the case of a legal person has ceased to exist before commencement, the revived copyright shall vest—

(a)   in the case of a film, in the principal director of the film or his personal representatives, and

(b)   in any other case, in the author of the work or his personal representatives.

(3)   Where revived copyright vests in personal representatives by virtue of paragraph (2), it shall be held by them for the benefit of the person who would have been entitled to it had it been vested in the principal director or author immediately before his death and had devolved as part of his estate.

20   Prospective ownership of extended or revived copyright

(1)   Where by an agreement made before commencement in relation to extended or revived copyright, and signed by or on behalf of the prospective owner of the copyright, the prospective owner purports to assign the extended or revived copyright (wholly or partially) to another person, then if, on commencement the assignee or another person claiming under him would be entitled as against all other persons to require the copyright to be vested in him, the copyright shall vest in the assignee or his successor in title by virtue of this paragraph.

(2)   A licence granted by a prospective owner of extended or revived copyright is binding on every successor in title to his interest (or prospective interest) in the right, except a purchaser in good faith for valuable consideration and without notice (actual or constructive) of the licence or a person deriving title from such a purchaser; and references in Part I of the 1988 Act to doing anything with, or without, the licence of the copyright owner shall be construed accordingly.

(3)   In paragraph (2) "prospective owner" includes a person who is prospectively entitled to extended or revived copyright by virtue of such an agreement as is mentioned in paragraph (1).

21   Extended copyright: existing licences, agreement, &c.

(1)   Any copyright licence, any term or condition of an agreement relating to the exploitation of a copyright work, or any waiver or assertion of moral rights, which—

(a)   subsists immediately before commencement in relation to an existing copyright work, and

(b)   is not to expire before the end of the copyright period under the 1988 provisions,

shall continue to have effect during the period of any extended copyright, subject to any agreement to the contrary.

(2)   Any copyright licence, or term or condition relating to the exploitation of a copyright work, imposed by order of the Copyright Tribunal which—

(a)   subsists immediately before commencement in relation to an existing copyright work, and

(b)   is not to expire before the end of the copyright period under the 1988 provisions,

shall continue to have effect during the period of any extended copyright, subject to any further order of the Tribunal.

22   Revived copyright: exercise of moral rights

(1)   The following provisions have effect with respect to the exercise of moral rights in relation to a work in which there is revived copyright.

(2)   Any waiver or assertion of moral rights which subsisted immediately before the expiry of copyright shall continue to have effect during the period of revived copyright.

(3)   Moral rights are exercisable after commencement by the author of a work or, as the case may be, the director of a film in which revived copyright subsists, as with any other copyright work.

(4)   Where the author or director died before commencement—

(a)   the rights conferred by—

section 77 (right to identification as author or director),

section 80 (right to object to derogatory treatment of work), or

section 85 (right to privacy of certain photographs and films),

are exercisable after commencement by his personal representatives, and

(b)   any infringement after commencement of the right conferred by section 84 (false attribution) is actionable by his personal representatives.

(5)   Any damages recovered by personal representatives by virtue of this Regulation in respect of an infringement after a person's death shall devolve as part of his estate as if the right of action had subsisted and been vested in him immediately before his death.

(6)   Nothing in these Regulations shall be construed as causing a moral right to be exercisable if, or to the extent that, the right was excluded by virtue of paragraph 23 or 24 of Schedule 1 on the commencement of the 1988 Act or would have been so excluded if copyright had not previously expired.

23 Revived copyright: saving for acts of exploitation when work in public domain, &c.

(1)   No act done before commencement shall be regarded as infringing revived copyright in a work.

(2)   It is not an infringement of revived copyright in a work—

(a)   to do anything after commencement in pursuance of arrangements made before 1st January 1995 at a time when copyright did not subsist in the work, or

(b)   to issue to the public after commencement copies of the work made before 1st July 1995 at a time when copyright did not subsist in the work.

(3)   It is not an infringement of revived copyright in a work to do anything after commencement in relation to a literary, dramatic, musical or artistic work or a film made before commencement, or made in pursuance of arrangements made before commencement, which contains a copy of that work or is an adaptation of that work if—

(a)   the copy or adaptation was made before 1st July 1995 at a time when copyright did not subsist in the work in which revived copyright subsists, or

(b)   the copy or adaptation was made in pursuance of arrangements made before 1st July 1995 at a time when copyright did not subsist in the work in which revived copyright subsists.

(4)   It is not an infringement of revived copyright in a work to do after commencement anything which is a restricted act in relation to the work if the act is done at a time when, or is done in pursuance of arrangements made at a time when, the name and address of a person entitled to authorise the act cannot by reasonable inquiry be ascertained.

(5)   In this Regulation "arrangements" means arrangements for the exploitation of the work in question.

(6)   It is not an infringement of any moral right to do anything which by virtue of this Regulation is not an infringement of copyright.

24 Revived copyright: use as of right subject to reasonable royalty

(1)   In the case of a work in which revived copyright subsists any acts restricted by the copyright shall be treated as licensed by the copyright owner, subject only to the payment of such reasonable royalty or other remuneration as may be agreed or determined in default of agreement by the Copyright Tribunal.

(2)   A person intending to avail himself of the right conferred by this Regulation must give reasonable notice of his intention to the copyright owner, stating when he intends to begin to do the acts.

(3)   If he does not give such notice, his acts shall not be treated as licensed.

(4)   If he does give such notice, his acts shall be treated as licensed and a reasonable royalty or other remuneration shall be payable in respect of them despite the fact that its amount is not agreed or determined until later.

(5)   This Regulation does not apply if or to the extent that a licence to do the acts could be granted by a licensing body (within the meaning of section 116(2) of the 1988 Act), whether or not under a licensing scheme.

(6)   No royalty or other remuneration is payable by virtue of this Regulation in respect of anything for which a royalty or other remuneration is payable under Schedule 6 to the 1988 Act.

25   Revived copyright: application to Copyright Tribunal

(1)   An application to settle the royalty or other remuneration payable in pursuance of Regulation 24 may be made to the Copyright Tribunal by the copyright owner or the person claiming to be treated as licensed by him.

(2)   The Tribunal shall consider the matter and make such order as it may determine to be reasonable in the circumstances.

(3)   Either party may subsequently apply to the Tribunal to vary the order, and the Tribunal shall consider the matter and make such order confirming or varying the original order as it may determine to be reasonable in the circumstances.

(4)   An application under paragraph (3) shall not, except with the special leave of the Tribunal, be made within twelve months from the date of the original order or of the order on a previous application under that paragraph.

(5)   An order under paragraph (3) has effect from the date on which it is made or such later date as may be specified by the Tribunal.

26   Film sound tracks: application of new provisions

(1)   The new provisions relating to the treatment of film sound tracks apply to existing sound tracks as from commencement.

(2)   The owner of any copyright in a film has as from commencement corresponding rights as copyright owner in any existing sound track treated as part of the film; but without prejudice to any rights of the owner of the copyright in the sound track as a sound recording.

(3)   Anything done before commencement under or in relation to the copyright in the sound recording continues to have effect and shall have effect, so far as concerns the sound track, in relation to the film as in relation to the sound recording.

(4)   It is not an infringement of the copyright in the film (or of any moral right in the film) to do anything after commencement in pursuance of arrangements for the exploitation of the sound recording made before commencement.

Rights in performances

27   Rights in performances: interpretation

(1)   In the provisions of this Part relating to rights in performances—

   (a)   "existing", in relation to a performance, means given before commencement; and

   (b)   "existing protected performance" means a performance in relation to which rights under Part II of the 1988 Act (rights in performances) subsisted immediately before commencement.

(2)   References in this Part to performers' rights are to the rights given by section 180(1)(a) of the 1988 Act and references to recording rights are to the rights given by section 180(1)(b) of that Act.

28 Duration of rights in performances: general saving
Any rights under Part II of the 1988 Act in an existing protected performance shall continue to subsist until the date on which they would have expired under the 1988 provisions if that date is later than the date on which the rights would expire under the new provisions.

29 Duration of rights in performances: application of new provisions
The new provisions relating to the duration of rights under Part II of the 1988 Act apply—
    (a)   to performances taking place after commencement;
    (b)   to existing performances which first qualify for protection under Part II of the 1988 Act after commencement;
    (c)   to existing protected performances, subject to Regulation 28 (general saving for any longer period applicable under 1988 provisions); and
    (d)   to existing performances—
        (i)   in which rights under Part II of the 1988 Act expired after the commencement of that Part and before 31st December 1995, or
        (ii)   which were protected by earlier enactments relating to the protection of performers and in which rights under that Part did not arise by reason only that the performance was given at a date such that the rights would have ceased to subsist before the commencement of that Part,
but which were on 1st July 1995 protected in another EEA state under legislation relating to copyright or related rights.

30 Extended and revived performance rights
In the following provisions of this Part—
    "extended performance rights" means rights under Part II of the 1988 Act which subsist by virtue of the new provisions after the date on which they would have expired under the 1988 provisions; and
    "revived performance rights" means rights under Part II of the 1988 Act which subsist by virtue of the new provisions—
    (a)   after having expired under the 1988 provisions, or
    (b)   in relation to a performance which was protected by earlier enactments relating to the protection of performers and in which rights under that Part did not arise by reason only that the performance was given at a date such that the rights would have ceased to subsist before the commencement of that Part.
References in the following provisions of this Part to "revived pre-1988 rights" are to revived performance rights within paragraph (b) of the above definition.

31 Entitlement to extended or revived performance rights
    (1)   Any extended performance rights are exercisable as from commencement by the person who was entitled to exercise those rights immediately before commencement, that is—
    (a)   in the case of performers' rights, the performer or (if he has died) the person entitled by virtue of section 192(2) of the 1988 Act to exercise those rights;
    (b)   in the case of recording rights, the person who was within the meaning of section 185 of the 1988 Act the person having those rights.
    (2)   Any revived performance rights are exercisable as from commencement—
    (a)   in the case of rights which expired after the commencement of the 1988 Act, by the person who was entitled to exercise those rights immediately before they expired;
    (b)   in the case of revived pre-1988 performers' rights, by the performer or his personal representatives;

(c)   in the case of revived pre-1988 recording rights, by the person who would have been the person having those rights immediately before the commencement of the 1988 Act or, if earlier, immediately before the death of the performer, applying the provisions of section 185 of that Act to the circumstances then obtaining.

(3)   Any remuneration or damages received by a person's personal representatives by virtue of a right conferred on them by paragraph (1) or (2) shall devolve as part of that person's estate as if the right had subsisted and been vested in him immediately before his death.

32   Extended performance rights: existing consents, agreement, &c.

Any consent, or any term or condition of an agreement, relating to the exploitation of an existing protected performance which—

(a)   subsists immediately before commencement, and

(b)   is not to expire before the end of the period for which rights under Part II of the 1988 Act subsist in relation to that performance,

shall continue to subsist during the period of any extended performance rights, subject to any agreement to the contrary.

33   Revived performance rights: saving for acts of exploitation when performance in public domain, &c.

(1)   No act done before commencement shall be regarded as infringing revived performance rights in a performance.

(2)   It is not an infringement of revived performance rights in a performance—

(a)   to do anything after commencement in pursuance of arrangements made before 1st January 1995 at a time when the performance was not protected, or

(b)   to issue to the public after commencement a recording of a performance made before 1st July 1995 at a time when the performance was not protected.

(3)   It is not an infringement of revived performance rights in a performance to do anything after commencement in relation to a sound recording or film made before commencement, or made in pursuance of arrangements made before commencement, which contains a recording of the performance if—

(a)   the recording of the performance was made before 1st July 1995 at a time when the performance was not protected, or

(b)   the recording of the performance was made in pursuance of arrangements made before 1st July 1995 at a time when the performance was not protected.

(4)   It is not an infringement of revived performance rights in a performance to do after commencement anything at a time when, or in pursuance of arrangements made at a time when, the name and address of a person entitled to authorise the act cannot by reasonable inquiry be ascertained.

(5)   In this Regulation "arrangements" means arrangements for the exploitation of the performance in question.

(6)   References in this Regulation to a performance being protected are—

(a)   in relation to the period after the commencement of the 1988 Act, to rights under Part II of that Act subsisting in relation to the performance, and

(b)   in relation to earlier periods, to the consent of the performer being required under earlier enactments relating to the protection of performers.

34   Revived performance rights: use as of right subject to reasonable remuneration

(1)   In the case of a performance in which revived performance rights subsist any acts which require the consent of any person under Part II of the 1988 Act (the "rights owner") shall be treated as having that consent, subject only to the payment of such

reasonable remuneration as may be agreed or determined in default of agreement by the Copyright Tribunal.

(2)   A person intending to avail himself of the right conferred by this Regulation must give reasonable notice of his intention to the rights owner, stating when he intends to begin to do the acts.

(3)   If he does not give such notice, his acts shall not be treated as having consent.

(4)   If he does give such notice, his acts shall be treated as having consent and reasonable remuneration shall be payable in respect of them despite the fact that its amount is not agreed or determined until later.

35   Revived performance rights: application to Copyright Tribunal

(1)   An application to settle the remuneration payable in pursuance of Regulation 34 may be made to the Copyright Tribunal by the rights owner or the person claiming to be treated as having his consent.

(2)   The Tribunal shall consider the matter and make such order as it may determine to be reasonable in the circumstances.

(3)   Either party may subsequently apply to the Tribunal to vary the order, and the Tribunal shall consider the matter and make such order confirming or varying the original order as it may determine to be reasonable in the circumstances.

(4)   An application under paragraph (3) shall not, except with the special leave of the Tribunal, be made within twelve months from the date of the original order or of the order on a previous application under that paragraph.

(5)   An order under paragraph (3) has effect from the date on which it is made or such later date as may be specified by the Tribunal.

36   Construction of references to EEA states

(1)   For the purpose of the new provisions relating to the term of copyright protection applicable to a work of which the country of origin is not an EEA state and of which the author is not a national of an EEA state—

(a)   a work first published before 1st July 1995 shall be treated as published in an EEA state if it was on that date regarded under the law of the United Kingdom or another EEA state as having been published in that state;

(b)   an unpublished film made before 1st July 1995 shall be treated as originating in an EEA state if it was on that date regarded under the law of the United Kingdom or another EEA state as a film whose maker had his headquarters in, or was domiciled or resident in, that state; and

(c)   the author of a work made before 1st July 1995 shall be treated as an EEA national if he was on the date regarded under the law of the United Kingdom or another EEA state as a national of that state.

The references above to the law of another EEA state are to the law of that state having effect for the purposes of rights corresponding to those provided for in Part I of the 1988 Act.

(2)   For the purposes of the new provisions relating to the term of protection applicable to a performance where the performer is not a national of an EEA state, the performer of a performance given before 1st July 1995 shall be treated as an EEA national if he was on that date regarded under the law of the United Kingdom or another EEA state as a national of that state.

The reference above to the law of another EEA state is to the law of that state having effect for the purposes of rights corresponding to those provided for in Part II of the 1988 Act.

(3)   In this Regulation "another EEA state" means an EEA state other than the United Kingdom.

THE COPYRIGHT AND RELATED RIGHTS REGULATIONS 1996
(SI 1996/2967)

...

PART I
INTRODUCTORY PROVISIONS

1 Citation, commencement and extent
(1) These Regulations may be cited as the Copyright and Related Rights Regulations 1996.

(2) These Regulations come into force on 1st December 1996.

(3) These Regulations extend to the whole of the United Kingdom.

2 Interpretation
In these Regulations—

"EEA Agreement" means the Agreement on the European Economic Area signed at Oporto on 2nd May 1992, as adjusted by the Protocol signed at Brussels on 17th March 1993; and

"EEA state" means a state which is a contracting party to the EEA Agreement.

3 Implementation of Directives, &c.
These Regulations make provision for the purpose of implementing—

(a) Council Directive No. 92/100/EEC of 19 November 1992 on rental right and lending right and on certain rights related to copyright in the field of intellectual property;

(b) Council Directive No. 93/83/EEC of 27 September 1993 on the coordination of certain rules concerning copyright and rights related to copyright applicable to satellite broadcasting and cable retransmission;

(c) the provisions of Council Directive No. 93/98/EEC of 29 October 1993 harmonizing the term of protection of copyright and certain related rights, so far as not implemented by the Duration of Copyright and Rights in Performances Regulations 1995; and

(d) certain obligations of the United Kingdom created by or arising under the EEA Agreement so far as relevant to the implementation of those Directives.

4 Scheme of the regulations
The Copyright, Designs, and Patents Act 1988 is amended in accordance with the provisions of Part II of these Regulations, subject to the savings and transitional provisions in Part III of these Regulations.

...

PART II
AMENDMENTS OF THE COPYRIGHT, DESIGNS AND PATENTS ACT 1988

Publication right

16 Publication right
(1) A person who after the expiry of copyright protection, publishes for the first time a previously unpublished work has, in accordance with the following provisions, a property right ("publication right") equivalent to copyright.

(2) For this purpose publication includes any communication to the public, in particular—

(a) the issue of copies to the public;

(b) making the work available by means of an electronic retrieval system;

(c) the rental or lending of copies of the work to the public;

(d) the performance, exhibition or showing of the work in public; or

(e)   broadcasting the work or including it in a cable programme service.
(3)   No account shall be taken for this purpose of any unauthorised act.
In relation to a time when there is no copyright in the work, an unauthorised act means an act done without the consent of the owner of the physical medium in which the work is embodied or on which it is recorded.
(4)   A work qualifies for publication right protection only if—
(a)   first publication is in the European Economic Area, and
(b)   the publisher of the work is at the time of first publication a national of an EEA state.
Where two or more persons jointly publish the work, it is sufficient for the purposes of paragraph (b) if any of them is a national of an EEA state.
(5)   No publication right arises from the publication of a work in which Crown copyright or Parliamentary copyright subsisted.
(6)   Publication right expires at the end of the period of 25 years from the end of the calendar year in which the work was first published.
(7)   In this regulation a "work" means a literary, dramatic, musical or artistic work or a film.
(8)   Expressions used in this regulation (other than "publication") have the same meaning as in Part I.

17   Application of copyright provisions to publication right
(1)   The substantive provisions of Part I relating to copyright (but not moral rights in copyright works), that is, the relevant provisions of—
Chapter II (rights of copyright owner),
Chapter III (acts permitted in relation to copyright works),
Chapter V (dealings with rights in copyright works),
Chapter VI (remedies for infringement), and
Chapter VII (copyright licensing).
apply in relation to publication right as in relation to copyright, subject to the following exceptions and modifications.
(2)   The following provisions do not apply—
(a)   in Chapter III (acts permitted in relation to copyright works), sections 57, 64, 66A and 67;
(b)   in Chapter VI (remedies for infringement), sections 104 to 106;
(c)   in Chapter VII (copyright licensing), section 116(4).
(3)   The following provisions have effect with the modifications indicated—
(a)   in section 107(4) and (5) (offences of making or dealing in infringing articles, &c.), the maximum punishment on summary conviction is imprisonment for a term not exceeding three months or a fine not exceeding level 5 on the standard scale, or both;
(b)   in sections 116(2), 117 and 124 for "works of more than one author" substitute "works of more than one publisher".
(4)   The other relevant provisions of Part I, that is—
in Chapter I, provisions defining expressions used generally in Part I,
Chapter VIII (the Copyright Tribunal),
in Chapter IX—
section 161 (territorial waters and the continental shelf), and
section 162 (British ships, aircraft and hovercraft), and
in Chapter X—
section 171(1) and (3) (savings for other rules of law, &c.), and
sections 172 to 179 (general interpretation provisions),
apply, with any necessary adaptations, for the purposes of supplementing the substantive provisions of that Part as applied by this regulation.

(5)   Except where the context otherwise requires, any other enactment relating to copyright (whether passed or made before or after these regulations) applies in relation to publication right as in relation to copyright.

In this paragraph "enactment" includes an enactment contained in subordinate legislation within the meaning of the Interpretation Act 1978.

...

19   Clarification of transitional provisions relating to pre-1989 photographs

Any question arising, in relation to photographs which were existing works within the meaning of Schedule 1, as to who is to be regarded as the author for the purposes of—

(a)   regulations 15 and 16 of the Duration of Copyright and Rights in Performances Regulations 1995 (duration of copyright: application of new provisions subject to general saving), or

(b)   regulation 19(2)(b) of those regulations (ownership of revived copyright),
is to be determined in accordance with section 9 as in force on the commencement of those regulations (and not, by virtue of paragraph 10 of Schedule 1, in accordance with the law in force at the time when the work was made).

...

PART III
TRANSITIONAL PROVISIONS AND SAVINGS

General provisions

25   Introductory

(1)   In this Part—

"commencement" means the commencement of these Regulations; and

"existing", in relation to a work or performance, means made or given before commencement.

(2)   For the purposes of this Part a work of which the making extended over a period shall be taken to have been made when its making was completed.

(3)   In this Part a "new right" means a right arising by virtue of these Regulations, in relation to a copyright work or a qualifying performance, to authorise or prohibit an act.

The expression does not include—

(a)   a right corresponding to a right which existed immediately before commencement, or

(b)   a right to remuneration arising by virtue of these Regulations.

(4)   Expressions used in this Part have the same meaning in relation to copyright as they have in Part I of the Copyright, Designs and Patents Act 1988, and in relation to performances as in Part II of that Act.

26   General rules

(1)   Subject to anything in regulations 28 to 36 (special transitional provisions and savings), these regulations apply to copyright works made, and to performances given, before or after commencement.

(2)   No act done before commencement shall be regarded as an infringement of any new right, or as giving rise to any right to remuneration arising by virtue of these Regulations.

27   Saving for certain existing agreements

(1)   Except as otherwise expressly provided, nothing in these Regulations affects an agreement made before 19th November 1992.

(2)   No act done in pursuance of any such agreement after commencement shall be regarded as an infringement of any new right.

28 Broadcasts

The provisions of—
   regulation 5 (place where broadcast treated as made) and
   regulation 6 (safeguards in relation to certain satellite broadcasts),
have effect in relation to broadcasts made after commencement.

29 Satellite broadcasting: international co-production agreements

(1)   This regulation applies to an agreement concluded before 1st January 1995—
   (a)   between two or more co-producers of a film, one of whom is a national of an EEA state, and
   (b)   the provisions of which grant to the parties exclusive rights to exploit all communication to the public of the film in separate geographical areas.

(2)   Where such an agreement giving such exclusive exploitation rights in relation to the United Kingdom does not expressly or by implication address satellite broadcasting from the United Kingdom, the person to whom those exclusive rights have been granted shall not make any such broadcast without the consent of any other party to the agreement whose language-related exploitation rights would be adversely affected by that broadcast.

30 New rights: exercise of rights in relation to performances

(1)   Any new right conferred by these Regulations in relation to a qualifying performance is exercisable as from commencement by the performer or (if he has died) by the person who immediately before commencement was entitled by virtue of section 192(2) to exercise the rights conferred on the performer by Part II in relation to that performance.

(2)   Any remuneration or damages received by a person's personal representatives by virtue of a right conferred on them by paragraph (1) shall devolve as part of that person's estate as if the right had subsisted and been vested in him immediately before his death.

31 New rights: effect of pre-commencement authorisation of copying

Where before commencement—
   (a)   the owner or prospective owner of copyright in a literary, dramatic, musical or artistic work has authorised a person to make a copy of the work, or
   (b)   the owner or prospective owner of performers' rights in a performance has authorised a person to make a copy of a recording of the performance,
any new right in relation to that copy shall vest on commencement in the person so authorised, subject to any agreement to the contrary.

32 New rights: effect of pre-commencement film production agreement

(1)   Sections 93A and 191F (presumption of transfer of rental right in case of production agreement) apply in relation to an agreement concluded before commencement.
   As section 93A so applies, the restriction in subsection (3) of that section shall be omitted (exclusion of presumption in relation to screenplay, dialogue or music specifically created for the film).

(2)   Sections 93B and 191G (right to equitable remuneration where rental right transferred) have effect accordingly, but subject to regulation 33 (right to equitable remuneration applicable to rental after 1st April 1997).

33 Right to equitable remuneration applicable to rental after 1st April 1997

No right to equitable remuneration under section 93B or 191G (right to equitable remuneration where rental right transferred) arises—
   (a)   in respect of any rental of a sound recording or film before 1st April 1997, or

(b)   in respect of any rental after that date of a sound recording or film made in pursuance of an agreement entered into before 1st July 1994, unless the author or performer (or a successor in title of his) has before 1st January 1997 notified the person by whom the remuneration would be payable that he intends to exercise that right.

34   Savings for existing stocks
(1)   Any new right in relation to a copyright work does not apply to a copy of the work acquired by a person before commencement for the purpose of renting or lending it to the public.
(2)   Any new right in relation to a qualifying performance does not apply to a copy of a recording of the performance acquired by a person before commencement for the purpose of renting or lending it to the public.

35   Lending of copies by libraries or archives
Until the making of regulations under section 37 of the Copyright, Designs and Patents Act 1988 for the purposes of section 40A(2) of that Act (lending of copies by libraries or archives), the reference in section 40A(2) (and in paragraph 6B of Schedule 2) to a prescribed library or archive shall be construed as a reference to any library or archive in the United Kingdom prescribed by paragraphs 2 to 6 of Part A of Schedule 1 to the Copyright (Librarians and Archivists) (Copying of Copyright Material) Regulations 1989.

36   Authorship of films
(1)   Regulation 18 (authorship of films) applies as from commencement in relation to films made on or after 1st July 1994.
(2)   It is not an infringement of any right which the principal director has by virtue of these Regulations to do anything after commencement in pursuance of arrangements for the exploitation of the film made before 19th November 1992.
This does not affect any right of his to equitable remuneration under section 93B.

PLANT VARIETIES ACT 1997
(1997, c. 66)

An Act to make provision about rights in relation to plant varieties; to make provision about the Plant Varieties and Seeds Tribunal; to extend the time limit for institution of proceedings for contravention of seeds regulations; and for connected purposes.   [27 November 1997]

PART I
PLANT VARIETIES

Preliminary

1   Plant breeders' rights
(1)   Rights, to be known as plant breeders' rights, may be granted in accordance with this Part of this Act.
(2)   Plant breeders' rights may subsist in varieties of all plant genera and species.
(3)   For the purposes of this Act, "variety" means a plant grouping within a single botanical taxon of the lowest known rank, which grouping, irrespective of whether the conditions for the grant of plant breeders' rights (which are laid down in section 4 below) are met, can be—
(a)   defined by the expression of the characteristics resulting from a given genotype or combination of genotypes,
(b)   distinguished from any other plant grouping by the expression of at least one of those characteristics, and
(c)   considered as a unit with regard to its suitability for being propagated unchanged.

2 The Plant Variety Rights Office

(1)   The office known as the Plant Variety Rights Office shall continue in being for the purposes of this Part of this Act under the immediate control of an officer appointed by the Ministers and known as the Controller of Plant Variety Rights ("the Controller").

(2)   Schedule 1 to this Act (which makes further provision about the Plant Variety Rights Office) shall have effect.

Grant of plant breeders' rights

3 Grant on application

(1)   Subject to this Part of this Act, plant breeders' rights shall be granted to an applicant by the Controller on being satisfied that the conditions laid down in section 4 below are met.

(2)   The Controller may by notice require an applicant for the grant of plant breeders' rights to provide him, within such time as may be specified in the notice, with such information, documents, plant or other material, facilities or test or trial results relevant to the carrying out of his function under subsection (1) above as may be so specified.

(3)   If an applicant fails to comply with a notice under subsection (2) above within the period specified in the notice, the Controller may refuse the application.

4 Conditions for the grant of rights

(1)   The conditions which must be met in relation to an application for the grant of plant breeders' rights are—

(a)   that the variety to which the application relates is a qualifying variety, and

(b)   that the person by whom the application is made is the person entitled to the grant of plant breeders' rights in respect of the variety to which it relates.

(2)   For the purposes of subsection (1) above, a variety is a qualifying variety if it is—

(a)   distinct,

(b)   uniform,

(c)   stable, and

(d)   new;

and Part I of Schedule 2 to this Act has effect for the purpose of determining whether these criteria are met.

(3)   Subject to subsections (4) and (5) below, the person entitled to the grant of plant breeders' rights in respect of a variety is the person who breeds it, or discovers and develops it, or his successor in title.

(4)   If a person breeds a variety, or discovers and develops it, in the course of his employment, then, subject to agreement to the contrary, his employer, or his employer's successor in title, is the person entitled to the grant of plant breeders' rights in respect of it.

(5)   Part II of Schedule 2 to this Act shall have effect as respects priorities between two or more persons who have independently bred, or discovered and developed, a variety.

(6)   In this section and Schedule 2 to this Act, references to the discovery of a variety are to the discovery of a variety, whether growing in the wild or occurring as a genetic variant, whether artificially induced or not.

5 Rights in relation to application period

(1)   If an application for plant breeders' rights is granted, the holder of the rights shall be entitled to reasonable compensation for anything done during the application period which, if done after the grant of the rights, would constitute an infringement of them.

(2)   In subsection (1) above, "application period", in relation to a grant of plant breeders' rights, means the period—
(a)   beginning with the day on which details of the application for the grant of the rights are published in the gazette, and
(b)   ending with the grant of the rights.

Scope of plant breeders' rights

6   Protected variety

(1)   Plant breeders' rights shall have effect to entitle the holder to prevent anyone doing any of the following acts as respects the propagating material of the protected variety without his authority, namely—
(a)   production or reproduction (multiplication),
(b)   conditioning for the purpose of propagation,
(c)   offering for sale,
(d)   selling or other marketing,
(e)   exporting,
(f)   importing,
(g)   stocking for any of the purposes mentioned in paragraphs (a) to (f) above, and
(h)   any other act prescribed for the purposes of this provision.
(2)   The holder of plant breeders' rights may give authority for the purposes of subsection (1) above with or without conditions or limitations.
(3)   The rights conferred on the holder of plant breeders' rights by subsections (1) and (2) above shall also apply as respects harvested material obtained through the unauthorised use of propagating material of the protected variety, unless he has had a reasonable opportunity before the harvested material is obtained to exercise his rights in relation to the unauthorised use of the propagating material.
(4)   In the case of a variety of a prescribed description, the rights conferred on the holder of plant breeders' rights by subsections (1) and (2) above shall also apply as respects any product which—
(a)   is made directly from harvested material in relation to which subsection (3) above applies, and
(b)   is of a prescribed description,
unless subsection (5) below applies.
(5)   This subsection applies if, before the product was made, any act mentioned in subsection (1) above was done as respects the harvested material from which the product was made and either—
(a)   the act was done with the authority of the holder of the plant breeders' rights, or
(b)   the holder of those rights had a reasonable opportunity to exercise them in relation to the doing of the act.
(6)   In this section—
(a)   "prescribed" means prescribed by regulations made by the Ministers, and
(b)   references to harvested material include entire plants and parts of plants.

7   Dependent varieties

(1)   The holder of plant breeders' rights shall have, in relation to any variety which is dependent on the protected variety, the same rights as he has under section 6 above in relation to the protected variety.
(2)   For the purposes of this section, one variety is dependent on another if—
(a)   its nature is such that repeated production of the variety is not possible without repeated use of the other variety, or
(b)   it is essentially derived from the other variety and the other variety is not itself essentially derived from a third variety.

(3)   For the purposes of subsection (2) above, a variety shall be deemed to be essentially derived from another variety ("the initial variety") if—

(a)   it is predominantly derived from—

(i)   the initial variety, or

(ii)   a variety that is itself predominantly derived from the initial variety,

while retaining the expression of the essential characteristics resulting from the genotype or combination or genotypes of the initial variety,

(b)   it is clearly distinguishable from the initial variety by one or more characteristics which are capable of a precise description, and

(c)   except for the differences which result from the act of derivation, it conforms to the initial variety in the expression of the essential characteristics that result from the genotype or combination of genotypes of the initial variety.

(4)   For the purposes of subsection (3) above, derivation may, for example, be by—

(a)   the selection of—

(i)   a natural or induced mutant,

(ii)   a somaclonal variant, or

(iii) a variant individual from plants of the initial variety,

(b)   backcrossing, or

(c)   transformation by genetic engineering.

(5)   Subsection (1) above shall not apply where the existence of the dependent variety was common knowledge immediately before the coming into force of this Act.

Exceptions

8   General exceptions

Plant breeders' rights shall not extend to any act done—

(a)   for private and non-commercial purposes,

(b)   for experimental purposes, or

(c)   for the purpose of breeding another variety.

9   Farm saved seed

(1)   Subject to subsection (2) below, plant breeders' rights shall not extend to the use by a farmer for propagating purposes in the field, on his own holding, of the product of the harvest which he has obtained by planting on his own holding propagating material of—

(a)   the protected variety, or

(b)   a variety which is essentially derived from the protected variety.

(2)   Subsection (1) above only applies if the material is of a variety which is of a species or group specified for the purposes of this subsection by order made by the Ministers.

(3)   If a farmer's use of material is excepted from plant breeders' rights by subsection (1) above, he shall, at the time of the use, become liable to pay the holder of the rights equitable remuneration, which shall be sensibly lower than the amount charged for the production of propagating material of the same variety in the same area with the holder's authority.

(4)   Subsection (3) above shall not apply to a farmer who is considered to be a small farmer for the purposes of Article 14(3) third indent of the Council Regulation.

(5)   Subsection (3) above shall not apply if—

(a)   before the day on which this Part of this Act comes into force, the farmer has, in relation to the variety concerned, engaged in use of the kind to which subsection (1) above applies, and

(b)   no remuneration was payable in respect of that use.

(6)   The Ministers may by order provide that, on such date after 30 June 2001 as may be specified in the order, subsection (5) above shall cease to have effect in relation to a variety so specified, or varieties of a species or group so specified.

(7)   The Ministers may by regulations—
    (a)   make provision enabling—
        (i)   holders of plant breeders' rights to require farmers or seed processors, and
        (ii)   farmers or seed processors to require holders of plant breeders' rights,
to supply such information as may be specified in the regulations, being information the supply of which the Ministers consider necessary for the purposes of this section,
    (b)   make provision restricting the circumstances in which the product of a harvest of a variety which is subject to plant breeders' rights may be moved, for the purpose of being processed for planting, from the holding on which it was obtained, and
    (c)   make provision for the purpose of enabling the Ministers to monitor the operation of any provision of this section or regulations under this section.
(8)   Regulations under subsection (7)(a) above may include provision imposing obligations of confidence in relation to information supplied by virtue of the regulations.
(9)   Subsections (3) and (4) of section 7 above shall apply for the purposes of subsection (1)(b) above as they apply for the purposes of subsection (2) of that section.
(10)   For the purposes of subsection (3) above, remuneration shall be taken to be sensibly lower if it would be taken to be sensibly lower within the meaning of Article 14(3) fourth indent of the Council Regulation.
(11)   In this section, references to a farmer's own holding are to any land which he actually exploits for plant growing, whether as his property or otherwise managed under his own responsibility and on his own account.
(12)   The Ministers may by order amend this section as they think fit for the purpose of securing that it corresponds with the provisions for the time being of the law relating to Community plant variety rights about farm saved seed.

10   Exhaustion of rights

(1)   Plant breeders' rights shall not extend to any act concerning material of a variety if the material—
    (a)   has been sold or otherwise marketed in the United Kingdom by, or with the consent of, the holder of the rights, or
    (b)   is derived from material which has been so sold or otherwise marketed.
(2)   Subsection (1) above shall not apply where the act involves—
    (a)   further propagation of the variety, or
    (b)   the export of material which enables propagation of the variety to a non-qualifying country, otherwise than for the purposes of final consumption.
(3)   For the purposes of subsection (2)(b) above, a non-qualifying country is one which does not provide for the protection of varieties of the genus or species to which the variety belongs.
(4)   In this section, "material", in relation to a variety, means—
    (a)   any kind of propagating material of the variety,
    (b)   harvested material of the variety, including entire plants and parts of plants, and
    (c)   any product made directly from material falling within paragraph (b) above.

Duration and transmission of plant breeders' rights

11   Duration

(1)   A grant of plant breeders' rights shall have effect—
    (a)   in the case of potatoes, trees and vines, for 30 years from the date of the grant, and
    (b)   in other cases, for 25 years from that date.
(2)   The Ministers may by regulations provide that, in relation to varieties of a species or group specified in the regulations, subsection (1) above shall have effect with the substitution in paragraph (a) or (b), as the case may be, of such longer period, not exceeding—

(a)   in the case of paragraph (a), 35 years, and
(b)   in the case of paragraph (b), 30 years,
as may be so specified.
(3)   The period for which a grant of plant breeders' rights has effect shall not be affected by the fact it becomes impossible to invoke the rights—
(a)   because of Article 92(2) of the Council Regulation (effect of subsequent grant of Community plant variety right), or
(b)   because of suspension under section 23 below.

12   Transmission

Plant breeders' rights shall be assignable like other kinds of proprietary rights, but in any case rights under section 6 above and rights under section 7 above may not be assigned separately.

Remedies for infringement

13   Remedies for infringement

(1)   Plant breeders' rights shall be actionable at the suit of the holder of the rights.
(2)   In any proceedings for the infringement of plant breeders' rights, all such relief by way of damages, injunction, interdict, account or otherwise shall be available as is available in any corresponding proceedings in respect of infringements of other proprietary rights.

14   Presumptions in proceedings relating to harvested material

(1)   This section applies to any proceedings for the infringement of plant breeders' rights as respects harvested material.
(2)   If, in any proceedings to which this section applies, the holder of the plant breeders' rights proves, in relation to any of the material to which the proceedings relate—
(a)   that it has been the subject of an information notice given to the defendant by or on behalf of the holder, and
(b)   that the defendant has not, within the prescribed time after the service of the notice, supplied the holder with the information about it requested in the notice,
then, as regards the material in relation to which the holder proves that to be the case, the presumptions mentioned in subsection (3) below shall apply, unless the contrary is proved or the defendant shows that he had a reasonable excuse for not supplying the information.
(3)   The presumptions are—
(a)   that the material was obtained through unauthorised use of propagating material, and
(b)   that the holder did not have a reasonable opportunity before the material was obtained to exercise his rights in relation to the unauthorised use of the propagating material.
(4)   The reference in subsection (2) above to an information notice is to a notice which—
(a)   is in the prescribed form,
(b)   specifies the material to which it relates,
(c)   contains, in relation to that material, a request for the supply of the prescribed, but no other, information, and
(d)   contains such other particulars as may be prescribed.
(5)   In this section, "prescribed" means prescribed by regulations made by the Ministers.

15   Presumptions in proceedings relating to products made from harvested material

(1)   This section applies to any proceedings for the infringement of plant breeders' rights as respects any product made directly from harvested material.

(2)   If, in any proceedings to which this section applies, the holder of the plant breeders' rights proves, in relation to any product to which the proceedings relate—

(a)   that it has been the subject of an information notice given to the defendant by or on behalf of the holder, and

(b)   that the defenant has not, within the prescribed time after the service of the notice, supplied the holder with the information about it requested in the notice,

then, as regards the product in relation to which the holder proves that to be the case, the presumptions mentioned in subsection (3) below shall apply, unless the contrary is proved or the defendant shows that he had a reasonable excuse for not supplying the information.

(3)   The presumptions are—

(a)   that the harvested material from which the product was made was obtained through unauthorised use of propagating material,

(b)   that the holder did not have a reasonable opportunity before the harvested material was obtained to exercise his rights in relation to the unauthorised use of the propagating material, and

(c)   that no relevant act was done, before the product was made, as respects the harvested material from which it was made.

(4)   An act is relevant for the purposes of subsection (3)(c) above if it is mentioned in section 6(1) above and is—

(a)   done with the authority of the holder, or

(b)   one in relation to the doing of which he has a reasonable opportunity to exercise his rights.

(5)   The reference in subsection (2) above to an information notice is to a notice which—

(a)   is in the prescribed form,

(b)   specifies the product to which it relates,

(c)   contains, in relation to that product, a request for the supply of the prescribed, but no other, information, and

(d)   contains such other particulars as may be prescribed.

(6)   In this section, "prescribed" means prescribed by regulations made by the Ministers.

Duties of holders of plant breeders' rights

16   Maintenance of protected variety

(1)   The holder of any plant breeders' rights shall ensure that, throughout the period for which the grant of the rights has effect, he is in a position to produce to the Controller propagating material which is capable of producing the protected variety.

(2)   The holder of any plant breeders' rights shall give to the Controller, within such time as he may specify, all such information and facilities as he may request for the purpose of satisfying himself that the holder is fulfilling his duty under subsection (1) above.

(3)   The facilities to be given under subsection (2) above include facilities for the inspection by or on behalf of the Controller of the measures taken for the preservation of the protected variety.

17   Compulsory licences

(1)   Subject to subsections (2) and (3) below, if the Controller is satisfied on application that the holder of any plant breeders' rights—

(a)   has unreasonably refused to grant a licence to the applicant, or

(b)   has imposed or put forward unreasonable terms in granting, or offering to grant, a licence to the applicant,

he may grant to the applicant in the form of a licence under this section any such rights as might have been granted by the holder.

(2)   The Controller shall not grant an application for a licence under this section unless he is satisfied—

(a)   that it is necessary to do so for the purpose of securing that the variety to which the application relates—

(i)   is available to the public at reasonable prices,

(ii)   is widely distributed, or

(iii) is maintained in quality,

(b)   that the applicant is financially and otherwise in a position to exploit in a competent and businesslike manner the rights to be conferred on him, and

(c)   that the applicant intends so to exploit those rights.

(3)   A licence under this section shall not be an exclusive licence.

(4)   A licence under this section shall be on such terms as the Controller thinks fit and, in particular, may include—

(a)   terms as to the remuneration payable to the holder of the plant breeders' rights, and

(b)   terms obliging the holder of the plant breeders' rights to make propagating material available to the holder of the licence.

(5)   In deciding on what terms to grant an application for a licence under this section, the Controller shall have regard to the desirability of securing—

(a)   that the variety to which the application relates—

(i)   is available to the public at reasonable prices,

(ii)   is widely distributed, and

(iii) is maintained in quality, and

(b)   that there is reasonable remuneration for the holder of the plant breeders' rights to which the application relates.

(6)   An application for a licence under this section may be granted whether or not the holder of the plant breeders' rights to which the application relates has granted licences to the applicant or any other person.

(7)   If and so far as any agreement purports to bind any person not to apply for a licence under this section, it shall be void.

(8)   If—

(a)   a licence under this section is granted as respects a variety of a species or group in relation to which a period is specified for the purposes of this provision by regulations made by the Ministers, and

(b)   the grant takes place before a period of that length has passed since the date of grant of the plant breeders' rights to which the licence relates,

the licence shall not have effect until a period of that length has passed since that date.

(9)   The Controller may, at any time, on the application of any person, extend, limit or in any other respect vary a licence under this section, or revoke it.

Naming of protected varieties

18   Selection and registration of names

(1)   The Ministers may by regulations—

(a)   make provision for the selection of names for varieties which are the subject of applications for the grant of plant breeders' rights,

(b)   make provision about change of name in relation to varieties in respect of which plant breeders' rights have been granted, and

(c)   make provision for the keeping of a register of the names of varieties in respect of which plant breeders' rights have been granted.

(2)   Regulations under subsection (1) above may, in particular—

(a)   make provision enabling the Controller to require an applicant for the grant of plant breeders' rights to select a name for the variety to which the application relates,

(b)   make provision enabling the Controller to require the holder of plant breeders' rights to select a different name for the protected variety,

(c)   prescribe classes of variety for the purposes of the regulations,

(d)   prescribe grounds on which the registration of a proposed name may be refused,

(e)   prescribe the circumstances in which representations may be made regarding any decision as to the name to be registered in respect of any variety,

(f)   make provision enabling the Controller—

(i)   to refuse an application for the grant of plant breeders' rights, or

(ii)   to terminate the period for which a grant of plant breeders' rights has effect,

if the applicant or holder fails to comply with a requirement imposed under the regulations,

(g)   make provision for the publication or service of notices of decisions which the Controller proposes to take, and

(h)   prescribe the times at which, and the circumstances in which, the register may be inspected by members of the public.

(3)   The Controller shall publish notice of all entries made in the register, including alterations, corrections and erasures—

(a)   in the gazette, and

(b)   in such other manner as appears to the Controller to be convenient for the publication of these to all concerned.

(4)   For the purposes of subsection (1) above, the variety in respect of which plant breeders' rights are granted is the protected variety.

19   Duty to use registered name

(1)   Where a name is registered under section 18 above in respect of a variety, a person may not use any other name in selling, offering for sale or otherwise marketing propagating material of the variety.

(2)   Subsection (1) above shall have effect in relation to any variety from the date on which plant breeders' rights in respect of that variety are granted, and shall continue to apply after the period for which the grant of those rights has effect.

(3)   Subsection (1) above shall not preclude the use of any trade mark or trade name (whether registered under the Trade Marks Act 1994 or not) if—

(a)   that mark or name and the registered name are juxtaposed, and

(b)   the registered name is easily recognisable.

(4)   A person who contravenes subsection (1) above shall be liable on summary conviction to a fine not exceeding level 3 on the standard scale.

(5)   In any proceedings for an offence under subsection (4) above, it shall be a defence to prove that the accused took all reasonable precautions against committing the offence and had not at the time of the offence any reason to suspect that he was committing an offence.

20   Improper use of registered name

(1)   If any person uses the registered name of a protected variety in offering for sale, selling or otherwise marketing material of a different variety within the same class, the use of the name shall be a wrong actionable in proceedings by the holder of the rights.

(2)   Subsection (1) above shall also apply to the use of a name so nearly resembling the registered name as to be likely to deceive or cause confusion.

(3)   In any proceedings under this section, it shall be a defence to a claim for damages to prove that the defendant took all reasonable precautions against committing the wrong and had not, when using the name, any reason to suspect that it was wrongful.

(4)   In this section—

"class" means a class prescribed for the purposes of regulations under section 18(1) above,

"registered name", in relation to a protected variety, means the name registered in respect of it under section 18 above.

Termination and suspension of plant breeders' rights

21 Nullity

(1)   The Controller shall declare the grant of plant breeders' rights null and void if it is established—

(a)   that when the rights were granted the protected variety did not meet the criterion specified in paragraph (a) or (d) of section 4(2) above,

(b)   where the grant of the rights was essentially based upon information and documents furnished by the applicant, that when the rights were granted the protected variety did not meet the criterion specified in paragraph (b) or (c) of that provision, or

(c)   that the person to whom the rights were granted was not the person entitled to the grant of the rights and the rights have not subsequently been transferred to him, or his successor in title.

(2)   If, because of paragraph 6 of Schedule 2 to this Act, priority is established for an application for the grant of plant breeders' rights after such rights have been granted in pursuance of an application against which priority is established, subsection (1)(c) above shall only apply to the grant if the Controller decides that the application for which priority is established should be granted.

(3)   Where the grant of plant breeders' rights is declared null and void under this section, it shall be deemed never to have had effect.

22 Cancellation

(1)   The Controller may terminate the period for which a grant of plant breeders' rights has effect if—

(a)   he is satisfied that the protected variety no longer meets the criterion specified in paragraph (b) or (c) of section 4(2) above,

(b)   it appears to him that the holder of the rights is no longer in a position to provide him with the propagating material mentioned in section 16(1) above,

(c)   he is satisfied that the holder of the rights has failed to comply with a request under section 16(2) above, or

(d)   on application by the holder of the rights, he is satisfied that the rights may properly be surrendered.

(2)   Before determining an application under subsection (1)(d) above, the Controller shall—

(a)   give notice of the application in the manner prescribed by regulations made by the Ministers, and

(b)   follow the procedure so prescribed for hearing any person on whom the right to object is conferred by such regulations.

(3)   If the Controller is satisfied, not only that the protected variety no longer meets the criterion specified in paragraph (b) or (c) of section 4(2) above, but also that it ceased to do so at some earlier date, he may make the termination retrospective to that date.

23 Suspension

(1)   The Controller may suspend the exercise of any plant breeders' rights if, on application by the holder of a licence under section 17 above, he is satisfied that the holder of the rights is in breach of any obligation imposed on him by the licence.

(2)   The Controller shall terminate a suspension under subsection (1) above if, on application by the holder of the plant breeders' rights concerned, he is satisfied that the holder is no longer in breach of the obligation whose breach led to the suspension.

(3)   Subsection (1) above is without prejudice to the remedies available to the holder of a licence under section 17 above by the taking of proceedings in any court.

. . .

26   Appeals to the Tribunal

(1)   An appeal shall lie to the Tribunal against the following decision of the Controller—

(a)   a decision to allow or refuse an application for the grant of plant breeders' rights,

(b)   any decision preliminary to the determination of such an application as to the conditions laid down in section 4 above,

(c)   a decision to allow or refuse an application under section 17(1) or (9) above,

(d)   any decision under section 21 or 22(1)(a), (b) or (c) above,

(e)   a decision to refuse an application under section 22(1)(d) above, and

(f)   a decision to allow or refuse an application under section 23(1) or (2) above.

. . .

False information and representations as to rights

31   False information

(1)   If any information to which this section applies is false in a material particular and the person giving the information knows that it is false or gives it recklessly, he shall be guilty of an offence and liable on summary conviction to a fine not exceeding level 3 on the standard scale.

(2)   The information to which this section applies is—

(a)   information given in an application to the Controller for a decision against which an appeal lies to the Tribunal,

(b)   information given by or on behalf of the applicant in connection with such an application, and

(c)   information given in pursuance of a request under section 16(2) above.

32   False representations as to rights

(1)   If, in relation to any variety, a person falsely represents that he is entitled to exercise plant breeders' rights, or any rights derived from such rights, and he knows that the representation is false, or makes it recklessly, he shall be guilty of an offence and liable on summary conviction to a fine not exceeding level 3 on the standard scale.

(2)   It is immaterial for the purposes of subsection (1) above whether or not the variety to which the representation relates is the subject of plant breeders' rights.

Miscellaneous

33   Exclusion from Restrictive Trade Practices Act 1976

The Restrictive Trade Practices Act 1976 shall not apply—

(a)   to any licence granted by the holder of plant breeders' rights or by any other person authorised to grant a licence in respect of such rights,

(b)   to any assignment of plant breeders' rights or of the title to apply for the grant of such rights, or

(c)   to any agreement for such a licence or assignment,

being a licence, assignment or agreement under which no such restrictions as are described in section 6(1) of that Act are accepted, except in respect of goods which are plants or parts of plants of a variety to which the plant breeders' rights relate, or a variety to which those rights will relate if they are granted.

34 Disclosure of information obtained under section 14 or 15
(1)   If the holder of plant breeders' rights obtains information pursuant to a notice given for the purposes of section 14 or 15 above, he shall owe an obligation of confidence in respect of the information to the person who supplied it.

(2)   Subsection (1) above shall not have effect to restrict disclosure of information—

(a)   for the purposes of, or in connection with, establishing whether plant breeders' rights have been infringed, or

(b)   for the purposes of, or in connection with, any proceedings for the infringement of plant breeders' rights.

. . .

General

. . .

38 Interpretation of Part I
(1)   In this Part of this Act—

"the Council Regulation" means Council Regulation (EC) No 2100/94 of 27 July 1994 on Community plant variety rights, and references to particular provisions of the Council Regulation shall be construed as references to those provisions, or provisions of any Community instrument replacing them, as amended from time to time;

"gazette" means the gazette published under section 34 of the Plant Varieties and Seeds Act 1964;

"name" includes any designation;

"protected variety", in relation to any plant breeders' rights, means the variety which was the basis of the application for the grant of the rights;

"variety" has the meaning given by section 1(3) above.

(2)   In this Part of this Act references to an applicant for the grant of plant breeders' rights, or to the holder of plant breeders' rights, include, where the context allows, references to his predecessors in title or his successors in title.

(3)   For the purposes of this Part of this Act, the existence of a variety shall be taken to be a matter of common knowledge if—

(a)   it is, or has been, the subject of a plant variety right under any jurisdiction,

(b)   it is, or has been, entered in an official register of plant varieties under any jurisdiction, or

(c)   it is the subject of an application which subsequently leads to its falling within paragraph (a) or (b) above.

(4)   Otherwise, common knowledge may be established for those purposes by reference, for example, to—

(a)   plant varieties already in cultivation or exploited for commercial purposes,

(b)   plant varieties included in a recognised commercial or botanical reference collection, or

(c)   plant varieties of which there are precise descriptions in any publication.

. . .

40 Application of Part I to existing rights
(1)   Subject to the following provisions of this section, this Part of this Act applies in relation to existing rights as it applies in relation to plant breeders' rights granted under this Part of this Act.

(2)   Section 5 above shall not apply in relation to existing rights.

(3)   Section 11 above shall only apply to existing rights if the effect is to extend the period for which the rights are exercisable.

(4)   In this section, "existing rights" means plant breeders' rights granted under Part I of the Plant Varieties and Seeds Act 1964 which are exercisable on the coming into force of this Part of this Act.

. . .

Section 4   SCHEDULE 2
              CONDITIONS FOR THE GRANT OF PLANT BREEDERS' RIGHTS
                                         PART I
                            CRITERIA FOR GRANT OF RIGHTS

Distinctness

1.   The variety shall be deemed to be distinct if it is clearly distinguishable by one or
more characteristics which are capable of a precise description from any other variety
whose existence is a matter of common knowledge at the time of the application.

Uniformity

2.   The variety shall be deemed to be uniform if, subject to the variation that may be
expected from the particular features of its propagation, it is sufficiently uniform in those
characteristics which are included in the examination for distinctness.

Stability

3.   The variety shall be deemed to be stable if those characteristics which are
included in the examination for distinctness, as well as any others used for the variety
description, remain unchanged after repeated propagation or, in the case of a particular
cycle of propagation, at the end of each such cycle.

Novelty

4.—(1)   The variety shall be deemed to be new if sub-paragraphs (2) and (3) below
apply.
    (2)   This sub-paragraph applies if no sale or other disposal of propagating or
harvested material of the variety for the purposes of exploiting the variety has, with the
consent of the applicant, taken place in the United Kingdom earlier than one year before
the date of the application.
    (3)   This sub-paragraph applies if no sale or other disposal of propagating or
harvested material of the variety for the purposes of exploiting the variety has, with the
consent of the applicant, taken place elsewhere than in the United Kingdom earlier than
4 years, or, in the case of trees or vines, 6 years, before the date of the application.
    (4)   For the purposes of sub-paragraphs (2) and (3) above, there shall be disregarded
any sale or other disposal to which sub-paragraph (5), (6), (8) or (9) below applies.
    (5)   This sub-paragraph applies to any sale or other disposal of a stock of material of
the variety to a person who at the time of the sale or other disposal is, or who
subsequently becomes, the person entitled to the grant of plant breeders' rights in
respect of the variety.
    (6)   This sub-paragraph applies to—
    (a)   any sale or other disposal of propagating material of the variety to a person as
part of qualifying arrangements, and
    (b)   any sale or other disposal to the applicant, by a person who uses propagating
material of the variety under any such arrangements, or the material produced directly
or indirectly from the use.
    (7)   For the purposes of sub-paragraph (6) above, qualifying arrangements are
arrangements under which—
    (a)   a person uses propagating material of the variety under the applicant's control
for the purpose of increasing the applicant's stock, or of carrying out tests or trials, and
    (b)   the whole of the material produced, directly or indirectly, from the material
becomes or remains the property of the applicant.
    (8)   This sub-paragraph applies to any sale or other disposal of material of the
variety, other than propagating material, produced in the course of—

(a)   the breeding of the variety,

(b)   increasing the applicant's stock of material of the variety, or

(c)   carrying out tests or trials of the variety,

which does not involve identifying the variety from which the material is produced.

(9)   This sub-paragraph applies to any disposal of material of the variety, otherwise than by way of sale, at an exhibition or for the purposes of display at an exhibition.

(10)   For the purposes of sub-paragraphs (2) and (3) above, any sale or other disposal of propagating or harvested material of a variety for the purposes of exploiting the variety shall, if the variety is related to another variety, be treated as being also a sale or other disposal of propagating or harvested material of the other variety for the purposes of exploiting that variety.

(11)   For the purposes of sub-paragraph (10) above, a variety is related to another if its nature is such that repeated production of the variety is not possible without repeated use of the other variety.

PART II
PRIORITIES BETWEEN APPLICANTS FOR RIGHTS

5.—(1)   If a variety is bred, or discovered and developed, by two or more persons independently, the first of those persons, and any successors in title of theirs, to apply for the grant of plant breeders' rights in respect of it shall be the person entitled to the grant.

(2)   As between persons making applications for the grant of plant breeders' rights in respect of the same variety on the same date, the one who was first in a position to make an application for the grant of plant breeders' rights in respect of the variety, or who would have been first in that position if this Part of this Act had always been in force, shall be the person entitled to the grant.

6.—(1)   If the following conditions are met, an application for the grant of plant breeders' rights shall be treated for the purposes of paragraphs 1, 4 and 5 above as made, not on the date on which it is in fact made, but on the earlier date mentioned in sub-paragraph (7) below.

(2)   The first condition is that, in the 12 months immediately preceding the application under this Part of this Act, the applicant has duly made a parallel application under the law of—

(a)   the European Community,

(b)   any other intergovernmental organisation, or any State, which is, and was at the time of the application, a member of the Union as defined by Article 1(xi) of the Convention, or

(c)   any country or territory which is, and was at the time of the application, designated for the purposes of this provision by order made by the Ministers.

(3)   The second condition is that the applicant has not duly made such a parallel application earlier than 12 months before the application under this Part of this Act.

(4)   The third condition is that the application under this Part of this Act includes a claim to priority under this paragraph by reference to the parallel application.

(5)   The fourth condition is that the application by reference to which priority is claimed has not been withdrawn or refused when the application under this Part of this Act is made.

(6)   The fifth condition is that, within 3 months from the date of the application under this Part of this Act, the applicant submits to the Controller a copy of the documents constituting the parallel application, certified as a true copy by the authority to whom it is made.

(7)   The earlier date referred to in sub-paragraph (1) above is the date of the parallel application mentioned in sub-paragraph (2) above.

(8)   If more than one parallel application has been duly made as mentioned in sub-paragraph (2) above, the references in sub-paragraphs (4) to (7) above to the parallel application shall be construed as references to the earlier, or earliest, of the applications.

(9)   In this paragraph—

(a)   "the Convention' means the International Convention for the Protection of New Varieties of Plants done on 2 December 1961 and revised at Geneva on 10 November 1972, 23 October 1978 and 19 March 1991, and

(b)   references to a parallel application, in relation to an application for the grant of plant breeders' rights, are to an application for the grant of plant variety rights in respect of the variety to which the application under this Part of this Act relates.

7.—(1)   Any priority which an application for the grant of plant breeders' rights enjoys by virtue of paragraph 6 above shall be forfeited if the applicant does not, before the end of the relevant period, satisfy all the requirements which are to be satisfied by an applicant before plant breeders' rights can be granted to him.

(2)   For the purposes of sub-paragraph (1) above, the relevant period is the period of 2 years beginning with the day after the last day on which the applicant could have claimed priority under paragraph 6 above for his application.

(3)   Where—

(a)   an application for the grant of plant breeders' rights enjoys priority by virtue of paragraph 6 above, and

(b)   the application by reference to which it enjoys priority is withdrawn or refused before the applicant has satisfied all the requirements which are to be satisfied by an application before plant breeders' rights can be granted to him, sub-paragraph (1) above shall have effect with the substitution for "the relevant period" of "such period as the Controller may specify".

. . .

THE COPYRIGHT AND RIGHTS IN DATABASES REGULATIONS 1997
(SI 1997/3032)

PART I
INTRODUCTORY PROVISIONS

1   Citation, commencement and extent

(1)   These Regulations may be cited as the Copyright and Rights in Databases Regulations 1997.

(2)   These Regulations come into force on 1 January 1998.

(3)   These Regulations extend to the whole of the United Kingdom.

2   Implementation of Directive

(1)   These Regulations make provision for the purposes of implementing—

(a)   Council Directive No. 96/9/EC of 11 March 1996 on the legal protection of databases, and

(b)   certain obligations of the United Kingdom created by or arising under the EEA Agreement so far as relating to the implementation of that Directive.

(2)   In this Regulation "the EEA Agreement" means the Agreement on the European Economic Area signed at Oporto on 2 May 1992, as adjusted by the Protocol signed at Brussels on 17 March 1993.

3   Interpretation

In these Regulations "the 1998 Act" means the Copyright, Designs and Patents Act 1988.

4   Scheme of the Regulations

(1)   The 1988 Act is amended in accordance with the provisions of Part II of these Regulations, subject to the savings and transitional provisions in Part IV of these Regulations.

(2)   Part III of these Regulations has effect subject to those savings and transitional provisions.

...

PART III
DATABASE RIGHT

12   Interpretation

(1)   In this Part—

"database" has the meaning given by section 3A(1) of the 1988 Act (as inserted by Regulation 6);

"extraction", in relation to any contents of a database, means the permanent or temporary transfer of those contents to another medium by any means or in any form;

"insubstantial", in relation to part of the contents of a database, shall be construed subject to Regulation 16(2);

"investment" includes any investment, whether of financial, human or technical resources;

"jointly", in relation to the making of a database, shall be construed in accordance with Regulation 14(6);

"lawful user", in relation to a database, means any person who (whether under a licence to do any of the acts restricted by any database right in the database or otherwise) has a right to use the database;

"maker", in relation to a database, shall be construed in accordance with Regulation 14;

"re-utilisation", in relation to any contents of a database, means making those contents available to the public by any means;

"substantial", in relation to any investment, extraction or re-utilisation, means substantial in terms of quantity or quality or a combination of both.

(2)   The making of a copy of a database available for use, on terms that it will or may be returned, otherwise than for direct or indirect economic or commercial advantage, through an establishment which is accessible to the public shall not be taken for the purposes of this Part to constitute extraction or re-utilisation of the contents of the database.

(3)   Where the making of a copy of a database available through an establishment which is accessible to the public gives rise to a payment the amount of which does not go beyond what is necessary to cover the costs of the establishment, there is no direct or indirect economic or commercial advantage for the purposes of paragraph (2).

(4)   Paragraph (2) does not apply to the making of a copy of a database available for on-the-spot reference use.

(5)   Where a copy of a database has been sold within the EEA by, or with the consent of, the owner of the database right in the database, the further sale within the EEA of that copy shall not be taken for the purposes of this Part to constitute extraction or re-utilisation of the contents of the database.

13   Database right

(1)   A property right ("database right") subsists, in accordance with this Part, in a database if there has been a substantial investment in obtaining, verifying or presenting the contents of the database.

(2)   For the purposes of paragraph (1) it is immaterial whether or not the database or any of its contents is a copyright work, within the meaning of Part I of the 1988 Act.

(3)   This Regulation has effect subject to Regulation 18.

14   The maker of a database

(1)   Subject to paragraphs (2) to (4), the person who takes the initiative in obtaining, verifying or presenting the contents of a database and assumes the risk of investing in that obtaining, verification or presentation shall be regarded as the maker of, and as having made, the database.

(2)   Where a database is made by an employee in the course of his employment, his employer shall be regarded as the maker of the database, subject to any agreement to the contrary.

(3)   Subject to paragraph (4), where a database is made by Her Majesty or by an officer or servant of the Crown in the course of his duties, Her Majesty shall be regarded as the maker of the database.

(4)   Where a database is made by or under the direction or control of the House of Commons or the House of Lords—

(a)   the House by whom, or under whose direction or control, the database is made shall be regarded as the maker of the database, and

(b)   if the database is made by or under the direction or control of both Houses, the two Houses shall be regarded as the joint makers of the database.

(5)   For the purposes of this Part a database is made jointly if two or more persons acting together in collaboration take the initiative in obtaining, verifying or presenting the contents of the database and assume the risk of investing in that obtaining, verification or presentation.

(6)   References in this Part to the maker of a database shall, except as otherwise provided, be construed, in relation to a database which is made jointly, as references to all the makers of the database.

15   First ownership of database right

The maker of a database is the first owner of database right in it.

16   Acts infringing database right

(1)   Subject to the provisions of this Part, a person infringes database right in a database if, without the consent of the owner of the right, he extracts or re-utilises all or a substantial part of the contents of the database.

(2)   For the purposes of this Part, the repeated and systematic extraction or re-utilisation of insubstantial parts of the contents of a database may amount to the extraction or re-utilisation of a substantial part of those contents.

17   Term of protection

(1)   Database right in a database expires at the end of the period of fifteen years from the end of the calendar year in which the making of the database was completed.

(2)   Where a database is made available to the public before the end of the period referred to in paragraph (1), database right in the database shall expire fifteen years from the end of the calendar year in which the database was first made available to the public.

(3)   Any substantial change to the contents of a database, including a substantial change resulting from the accumulation of successive additions, deletions or alterations, which would result in the database being considered to be a substantial new investment shall qualify the database resulting from that investment for its own term of protection.

(4)   This Regulation has effect subject to Regulation 30.

18   Qualification for database right

(1)   Database right does not subsist in a database unless, at the material time, its maker, or if it was made jointly, one or more of its makers, was—

(a)   an individual who was a national of an EEA state or habitually resident within the EEA,

(b)   a body which was incorporated under the law of an EEA state and which, at that time, satisfied one of the conditions in paragraph (2), or

(c)   a partnership or other unincorporated body which was formed under the law of an EEA state and which, at that time, satisfied the condition in paragraph (2)(a).

(2)   The conditions mentioned in paragraphs (1)(b) and (c) are—

(a)   that the body has its central administration or principal place of business within the EEA, or

(b)   that the body has its registered office within the EEA and the body's operations are linked on an ongoing basis with the economy of an EEA state.

(3)   Paragraph (1) does not apply in any case falling within Regulation 14(4).

(4)   In this Regulation—

(a)   "EEA" and "EEA state" have the meaning given by section 172A of the 1988 Act;

(b)   "the material time" means the time when the database was made, or if the making extended over period, a substantial part of that period.

19   Avoidance of certain terms affecting lawful users

(1)   A lawful user of a database which has been made available to the public in any manner shall be entitled to extract or re-utilise insubstantial parts of the contents of the database for any purpose.

(2)   Where under an agreement a person has a right to use a database, or part of a database, which has been made available to the public in any manner, any term or condition in the agreement shall be void in so far as it purports to prevent that person from extracting or re-utilising insubstantial parts of the contents of the database, or of that part of the database, for any purpose.

20   Exceptions to database right

(1)   Database right in a database which has been made available to the public in any manner is not infringed by fair dealing with a substantial part of its contents if—

(a)   that part is extracted from the database by a person who is apart from this paragraph a lawful user of the database,

(b)   it is extracted for the purpose of illustration for teaching or research and not for any commercial purpose, and

(c)   the source is indicated.

(2)   The provisions of Schedule 1 specify other acts which may be done in relation to a database notwithstanding the existence of database right.

21   Acts permitted on assumption as to expiry of database right

(1)   Database right in a database is not infringed by the extraction or re-utilisation of a substantial part of the contents of the database at a time when, or in pursuance of arrangements made at a time when—

(a)   it is not possible by reasonable inquiry to ascertain the identity of the maker, and

(b)   it is reasonable to assume that database right has expired.

(2)   In the case of a database alleged to have been made jointly, paragraph (1) applies in relation to each person alleged to be one of the makers.

22   Presumptions relevant to database right

(1)   The following presumptions apply in proceedings brought by virtue of this Part of these Regulations with respect to a database.

(2)   Where a name purporting to be that of the maker appeared on copies of the database as published, or on the database when it was made, the person whose name appeared shall be presumed, until the contrary is proved—

   (a)   to be the maker of the database, and
   (b)   to have made it in circumstances not falling within Regulation 14(2) to (4).
  (3)   Where copies of the database as published bear a label or a mark stating—
   (a)   that a named person was the maker of the database, or
   (b)   that the database was first published in a specified year,
the label or mark shall be admissible as evidence of the facts stated and shall be presumed to be correct until the contrary is proved.

  (4)   In the case of a database alleged to have been made jointly, paragraphs (2) and (3), so far as is applicable, apply in relation to each person alleged to be one of the makers.

23   Application of copyright provisions to database right
The following provisions of the 1988 Act—
   sections 90 to 93 (dealing with rights in copyright works);
   sections 96 to 98 (rights and remedies of copyright owner);
   sections 101 and 102 (rights and remedies of exclusive licensee);
apply in relation to database right and databases in which that right subsists as they apply in relation to copyright and copyright works.

24   Licensing of database right
The provisions of Schedule 2 have effect with respect to the licensing of database right.

25   Database right: jurisdiction of Copyright Tribunal
  (1)   The Copyright Tribunal has jurisdiction under this Part to hear and determine proceedings under the following provisions of Schedule 2—
   (a)   paragraph 3, 4 or 5 (reference of licensing scheme);
   (b)   paragraph 6 or 7 (application with respect to licence under licensing scheme);
   (c)   paragraph 10, 11 or 12 (reference or application with respect to licence by licensing body).
  (2)   The provisions of Chapter VIII of Part I of the 1988 Act (general provisions relating to the Copyright Tribunal) apply in relation to the Tribunal when exercising any jurisdiction under this Part.
  (3)   Provision shall be made by rules under section 150 of the 1988 Act prohibiting the Tribunal from entertaining a reference under paragraph 3, 4 or 5 of Schedule 2 (reference of licensing scheme) by a representative organisation unless the Tribunal is satisfied that the organisation is reasonably representative of the class of persons which it claims to represent.

PART IV
SAVINGS AND TRANSITIONAL PROVISIONS

26   Introductory
  (1)   In this Part "commencement" means the commencement of these Regulations.
  (2)   Expressions used in this Part which are defined for the purposes of Part I of the 1988 Act have the same meaning as in that Part.

27   General rule
Subject to Regulations 28 and 29, these Regulations apply to databases made before or after commencement.

28   General savings
  (1)   Nothing in these Regulations affects any agreement made before commencement.
  (2)   No act done—
   (a)   before commencement, or

(b)   after commencement, in pursuance of an agreement made before commencement, shall be regarded as an infringement of database right in a database.

29   Saving for copyright in certain existing databases

(1)   Where a database—

(a)   was created on or before 27 March 1996, and

(b)   is a copyright work immediately before commencement,

copyright shall continue to subsist in the database for the remainder of its copyright
term.

(2)   In this Regulation "copyright term" means the period of the duration of
copyright under section 12 of the 1988 Act (duration of copyright in literary, dramatic,
musical or artistic works).

30   Database right: term applicable to certain existing databases

Where—

(a)   the making of a database was completed on or after 1 January 1983, and

(b)   on commencement, database right begins to subsist in the database,

database right shall subsist in the database for the period of fifteen years beginning with
1 January 1998.

Regulation 20(2)   SCHEDULE 1
EXCEPTIONS TO DATABASE RIGHT FOR PUBLIC ADMINISTRATION

Parliamentary and judicial proceedings

1.   Database right in a database is not infringed by anything done for the purposes of
parliamentary or judicial proceedings or for the purposes of reporting such proceedings.

Royal Commissions and statutory inquiries

2.—(1)   Database right in a database is not infringed by anything done for—

(a)   the purposes of the proceedings of a Royal Commission or statutory inquiry,
or

(b)   the purpose of reporting any such proceedings held in public.

(2)   Database right in a database is not infringed by the issue to the public of copies
of the report of a Royal Commission or statutory inquiry containing the contents of the
database.

(3)   In this paragraph "Royal Commission" and "statutory inquiry" have the same
meaning as in section 46 of the 1988 Act.

Material open to public inspection or on official register

3.—(1)   Where the contents of a database are open to public inspection pursuant to
a statutory requirement, or are on a statutory register, database right in the database is
not infringed by the extraction of all or a substantial part of the contents containing
factual information of any description, by or with the authority of the appropriate
person, for a purpose which does not involve re-utilisation of all or a substantial part of
the contents.

(2)   Where the contents of a database are open to public inspection pursuant to a
statutory requirement, database right in the database is not infringed by the extraction
or re-utilisation of all or a substantial part of the contents, by or with the authority of the
appropriate person, for the purpose of enabling the contents to be inspected at a more
convenient time or place or otherwise facilitating the exercise of any right for the
purpose of which the requirement is imposed.

(3)   Where the contents of a database which is open to public inspection pursuant to
a statutory requirement, or which is on a statutory register, contain information about
matters of general scientific, technical, commercial or economic interest, database right

in the database is not infringed by the extraction or re-utilisation of all or a substantial part of the contents, by or with the authority of the appropriate person, for the purpose of disseminating that information

(4) In this paragraph—

"appropriate person" means the person required to make the contents of the database open to public inspection or, as the case may be, the person maintaining the register;

"statutory register" means a register maintained in pursuance of a statutory requirement; and

"statutory requirement" means a requirement imposed by provision made by or under an enactment.

Material communicated to the Crown in the course of public business

4.—(1) This paragraph applies where the contents of a database have in the course of public business been communicated to the Crown for any purpose, by or with the licence of the owner of the database right and a document or other material thing recording or embodying the contents of the datbase is owned by or in the custody or control of the Crown.

(2) The Crown may, for the purpose for which the contents of the database were communicated to it, or any related purpose which could reasonably have been anticipated by the owner of the database right in the database, extract or re-utilise all or a substantial part of the contents without infringing database right in the database.

(3) The Crown may not re-utilise the contents of a database by virtue of this paragraph if the contents have previously been published otherwise than by virtue of this paragraph.

(4) In sub-paragraph (1) "public business" includes any activity carried on by the Crown.

(5) This paragraph has effect subject to any agreement to the contrary between the Crown and the owner of the database right in the database.

Public records

5. The contents of a database which are comprised in public records within the meaning of the Public Records Act 1958, the Public Records (Scotland) Act 1937 or the Public Records Act (Northern Ireland) 1923 which are open to public inspection in pursuance of that Act, may be re-utilised by or with the authority of any officer appointed under that Act, without infringement of database right in the database.

Acts done under statutory authority

6.—(1) Where the doing of a particular act is specifically authorised by an Act of Parliament, whenever passed, then, unless the Act provides otherwise, the doing of that act does not infringe database right in a database.

(2) Sub-paragraph (1) applies in relation to an enactment contained in Northern Ireland legislation as it applies in relation to an Act of Parliament.

(3) Nothing in this paragraph shall be construed as excluding any defence of statutory authority otherwise available under or by virtue of any enactment.

Regulation 24   SCHEDULE 2
LICENSING OF DATABASE RIGHT

Licensing scheme and licensing bodies

1.—(1) In this Schedule a "licensing scheme" means a scheme setting out—

(a) the classes of case in which the operator of the scheme, or the person on whose behalf he acts, is willing to grant database right licences, and

(b)   the term on which licences would be granted in those classes of case;
and for this purpose a "scheme" includes anything in the nature of a scheme, whether described as a scheme or as a tariff or by any other name.

(2)   In this Schedule a "licensing body" means a society or other organisation which has as its main object, or one of its main objects, the negotiating or granting, whether as owner or prospective owner of a database right or as agent for him, of database right licences, and whose objects include the granting of licences covering the databases of more than one maker.

(3)   In this paragraph "database right licences" means licences to do, or authorise the doing of, any of the things for which consent is required under Regulation 16.

2.   Paragraphs 3 to 8 apply to licensing schemes which are operated by licensing bodies and cover databases of more than one maker so far as they relate to licences for extracting or re-utilising all or a substantial part of the contents of a database; and references in those paragraphs to a licensing scheme shall be construed accordingly.

Reference of proposed licensing scheme to tribunal

3.—(1)   The terms of a licensing scheme proposed to be operated by a licensing body may be referred to the Copyright Tribunal by an organisation claiming to be representative of persons claiming that they require licences in cases of a description to which the scheme would apply, either generally or in relation to any description of case.

(2)   The Tribunal shall first decide whether to entertain the reference, and may decline to do so on the ground that the reference is premature.

(3)   If the Tribunal decides to entertain the reference it shall consider the matter referred and make such order, either confirming or varying the proposed scheme, either generally or so far as it relates to cases of the description to which the reference relates, as the Tribunal may determine to be reasonable in the circumstances.

(4)   The order may be made so as to be in force indefinitely or for such period as the Tribunal may determine.

Reference of licensing scheme to tribunal

4.—(1)   If while a licensing scheme is in operation a dispute arises between the operator of the scheme and—

(a)   a person claiming that he requires a licence in a case of a description to which the scheme applies, or

(b)   an organisation claiming to be representative of such persons,
that person or organisation may refer the scheme to the Copyright Tribunal in so far as it relates to cases of that description.

(2)   A scheme which has been referred to the Tribunal under this paragraph shall remain in operation until proceedings on the reference are concluded.

(3)   The Tribunal shall consider the matter in dispute and make such order, either confirming or varying the scheme so far as it relates to cases of the description to which the reference relates, as the Tribunal may determine to be reasonable in the circumstances.

(4)   The order may be made so as to be in force indefinitely or for such period as the Tribunal may determine.

. . .

Application for grant of licence in connection with licensing scheme

6.—(1)   A person who claims, in a case covered by a licensing scheme, that the operator of the scheme has refused to grant him or procure the grant to him of a licence in accordance with the scheme, or has failed to do so within a reasonable time after being asked, may apply to the Copyright Tribunal.

. (2)   A person who claims, in a case excluded from a licensing scheme, that the operator of the scheme either—

(a)   has refused to grant him a licence or procure the grant to him of a licence, or has failed to do so within a reasonable time of being asked, and that in the circumstances it is unreasonable that a licence should not be granted, or

(b)   proposes terms for a licence which are unreasonable,

may apply to the Copyright Tribunal.

(3)   A case shall be regarded as excluded from a licensing scheme for the purposes of sub-paragraph (2) if—

(a)   the scheme provides for the grant of licences subject to terms excepting matters from the licence and the case falls within such an exception, or

(b)   the case is so similar to those in which licences are granted under the scheme that it is unreasonable that it shoud not be dealt with in the same way.

(4)   If the Tribunal is satisfied that the claim is well-founded, it shall make an order declaring that, in respect of the matters specified in the order, the applicant is entitled to a licence on such terms as the Tribunal may determine to be applicable in accordance with the scheme or, as the case may be, to be reasonable in the circumstances.

(5)   The order may be made so as to be in force indefinitely or for such period as the Tribunal may determine.

. . .

Effect of order of tribunal as to licensing scheme

8.—(1)   A licensing scheme which has been confirmed or varied by the Copyright Tribunal—

(a)   under paragraph 3 (reference of terms of proposed scheme), or

(b)   under paragraph 4 or 5 (reference of existing scheme to Tribunal),

shall be in force or, as the case may be, remain in operation, so far as it relates to the description of case in respect of which the order was made, so long as the order remains in force.

(2)   While the order is in force a person who in a case of a class to which the order applies—

(a)   pays to the operator of the scheme any charges payable under the scheme in respect of a licence covering the case in question or, if the amount cannot be ascertained, gives an undertaking to the operator to pay them when ascertained, and

(b)   complies with the other terms applicable to such a licence under the scheme,

shall be in the same position as regards infringement of database right as if he had at all material times been the holder of a licence granted by the owner of the database right in question in accordance with the scheme.

. . .

(4)   Where the Tribunal has made an order under paragraph 6 (order as to entitlement to licence under licensing scheme) and the order remains in force, the person in whose favour the order is made shall if he—

(a)   pays to the operator of the scheme any charges payable in accordance with the order or, if the amount cannot be ascertained, gives an undertaking to pay the charges when ascertained, and

(b)   complies with the other terms specified in the order,

be in the same position as regards infringement of database right as if he had at all material times been the holder of a licence granted by the owner of the database right in question on the terms specified in the order.

References and applications with respect to licences by licensing bodies

9.   Paragraphs 10 to 13 (references and applications with respect to licensing by licensing bodies) apply to licences relating to database right which cover databases of

more than one maker granted by a licensing body otherwise than in pursuance of a licensing scheme, so far as the licences authorise extracting or re-utilising all or a substantial part of the contents of a database; and references in those paragraphs to a licence shall be construed accordingly.

Reference to tribunal of proposed licence

10.—(1)   The terms on which a licensing body proposes to grant a licence may be referred to the Copyright Tribunal by the prospective licensee.

(2)   The Tribunal shall first decide whether to entertain the reference, and may decline to do so on the ground that the reference is premature.

(3)   If the Tribunal decides to entertain the reference it shall consider the terms of the proposed licence and make such order, either confirming or varying the terms, as it may determine to be reasonable in the circumstances.

(4)   The order may be made so as to be in force indefinitely or for such period as the Tribunal may determine.

. . .

Effect of order of tribunal as to licence

13.—(1)   Where the Copyright Tribunal has made an order under paragraph 10 or 11 and the order remains in force, the person entitled to the benefit of the order shall if he—

(a)   pays to the licensing body any charges payable in accordance with the order or, if the amount cannot be ascertained, gives an undertaking to pay the charges when ascertained, and

(b)   complies with the other terms specified in the order,

be in the same position as regards infringement of database right as if he had at all material times been the holder of a licence granted by the owner of the database right in question on the terms specified in the order.

(2)   The benefit of the order may be assigned—

(a)   in the case of an order under paragraph 10, if assignment is not prohibited under the terms of the Tribunal's order; and

(b)   in the case of an order under paragraph 11, if assignment was not prohibited under the terms of the original licence.

. . .

General considerations: unreasonable discrimination

14.   In determining what is reasonable on a reference or application under this Schedule relating to a licensing scheme or licence, the Copyright Tribunal shall have regard to—

(a)   the availability of other schemes, or the granting of other licences, to other persons in similar circumstances, and

(b)   the terms of those schemes or licences,

and shall exercise its powers so as to secure that there is no unreasonable discrimination between licensees, or prospective licensees, under the scheme or licence to which the reference or application relates and licensees under other schemes operated by, or other licences granted by, the same person.

. . .

PART II   EC LEGISLATION

TREATY ESTABLISHING THE EUROPEAN COMMUNITY (1957)
(as amended by the Treaty on European Union)

[THE HIGH CONTRACTING PARTIES]
DETERMINED to lay the foundations of an ever closer union among the peoples of Europe,

RESOLVED to ensure the economic and social progress of their countries by common action to eliminate the barriers which divide Europe,

AFFIRMING as the essential objective of their efforts the constant improvement of the living and working conditions of their peoples,

RECOGNIZING that the removal of existing obstacles calls for concerted action in order to guarantee steady expansion, balanced trade and fair competition,

ANXIOUS to strengthen the unity of their economies and to ensure their harmonious development by reducing the differences existing between the various regions and the backwardness of the less favoured regions,

DESIRING to contribute, by means of a common commercial policy, to the progressive abolition of restrictions on international trade,

INTENDING to confirm the solidarity which binds Europe and the overseas countries and desiring to ensure the development of their prosperity, in accordance with the principles of the Charter of the United Nations,

RESOLVED by thus pooling their resources to preserve and strengthen peace and liberty, and calling upon the other peoples of Europe who share their ideal to join in their efforts,

HAVE DECIDED to create a European Community . . .

PART ONE   PRINCIPLES

. . .

Article 2
The Community shall have as its task, by establishing a common market and an economic and monetary union and by implementing the common policies or activities referred to in Articles 3 and 3a, to promote throughout the Community a harmonious and balanced development of economic activities, sustainable and non-inflationary growth respecting the environment, a high degree of convergence of economic performance, a high level of employment and of social protection, the raising of the standard of living and quality of life, and economic and social cohesion and solidarity among Member States.

Article 3
For the purposes set out in Article 2, the activities of the Community shall include, as provided in this Treaty and in accordance with the timetable set out therein

(a)   the elimination, as between Member States, of customs duties and of quantitative restrictions on the import and export of goods, and of all other measures having equivalent effect;

(b)   a common commercial policy;

(c)   an internal market characterised by the abolition, as between Member States, of obstacles to the free movement of persons, services and capital;

(d)   measures concerning the entry and movement of persons in the internal market as provided for in Article 100c;

(e)   a common policy in the sphere of agriculture and fisheries;

(f)   a common policy in the sphere of transport;

(g)   a system ensuring that competition in the internal market is not distorted;

(h)   the approximation of the laws of Member States to the extent required for the functioning of the common market;

(i)   a policy in the social sphere comprising a European Social Fund;

(j)   the strengthening of economic and social cohesion;

(k)   a policy in the sphere of the environment;

(l)   the strengthening of the competitiveness of Community Industry;

(m)   the promotion of research and technological development;

(n)   encouragement for the establishment and development of trans-European networks;

(o)   a contribution to the attainment of a high level of health protection;

(p)   a contribution to education and training of quality and to the flowering of the cultures of the Member States;

(q)   a policy in the sphere of development cooperation;

(r)   the association of the overseas countries and territories in order to increase trade and promote jointly economic and social development;

(s)   a contribution to the strengthening of consumer protection;

(t)   measures in the spheres of energy, civil protection and tourism.

Article 3a

1.   For the purposes set out in Article 2, the activities of the Member States and the Community shall include, as provided in this Treaty and in accordance with the timetable set out therein, the adoption of an economic policy which is based on the close coordination of Member States' economic policies, on the internal market and on the definition of common objectives, and conducted in accordance with the principle of an open market economy with free competition.

. . .

Article 3b

The Community shall act within the limits of the powers conferred upon it by this Treaty and of the objectives assigned to it therein.

In areas which do not fail within its exclusive competence, the Community shall take action, in accordance with the principle of subsidiarity, only if and in so far as the objectives of the proposed action cannot be sufficiently achieved by the Member States and can therefore, by reason of the scale or effects of the proposed action, be better achieved by the Community.

Any action by the Community shall not go beyond what is necessary to achieve the objectives of this Treaty.

. . .

PART THREE   COMMUNITY POLICIES

Elimination of Quantitative Restrictions Between Member States

. . .

Article 30

Quantitative restrictions on imports and all measures having equivalent effect shall, without prejudice to the following provisions, be prohibited between Member States.

. . .

Article 34

1.   Quantitative restrictions on exports, and all measures having equivalent effect, shall be prohibited between Member States.

2.   Member States shall, by the end of the first stage at the latest, abolish all quantitative restrictions on exports and any measures having equivalent effect which are in existence when this Treaty enters into force.

. . .

Article 36

The provisions of Articles 30 to 34 shall not preclude prohibitions or restrictions on imports, exports or goods in transit justified on grounds of public morality, public policy or public security; the protection of health and life of humans, animals or plants; the protection of national treasures possessing artistic, historic or archaeological value; or the protection of industrial and commercial property. Such prohibitions or restrictions shall not, however, constitute a means of arbitrary discrimination or a disguised restriction on trade between Member States.

. . .

Rules on Competition

Article 85

1.   The following shall be prohibited as incompatible with the common market: all agreements between undertakings, decisions by associations of undertakings and concerted practices which may affect trade between Member States and which have as their object or effect the prevention, restriction or distortion of competition within the common market, and in particular those which:

(a)   directly or indirectly fix purchase or selling prices or any other trading conditions;

(b)   limit or control production, markets, technical development, or investment;

(c)   share markets or sources of supply;

(d)   apply dissimilar conditions to equivalent transactions with other trading parties, thereby placing them at a competitive disadvantage;

(e)   make the conclusion of contracts subject to acceptance by the other parties of supplementary obligations which, by their nature or according to commercial usage, have no connection with the subject of such contracts.

2.   Any agreements or decisions prohibited pursuant to this Article shall be automatically void.

3.   The provisions of paragraph 1 may, however, be declared inapplicable in the case of:

— any agreement or category of agreements between undertakings;

— any decision or category of decisions by associations of undertakings;

— any concerted practice or category of concerted practices;

which contributes to improving the production or distribution of goods or to promoting technical or economic progress, while allowing consumers a fair share of the resulting benefit, and which does not:

(a)   impose on the undertakings concerned restrictions which are not indispensable to the attainment of these objectives:

(b)   afford such undertakings the possibility of eliminating competition in respect of a substantial part of the products in question.

Article 86

Any abuse by one or more undertakings of a dominant position within the common market or in a substantial part of it shall be prohibited as incompatible with the common market in so far as it may affect trade between Member States.

Such abuse may, in particular, consist in:

(a)   directly or indirectly imposing unfair purchase or selling prices or other unfair trading conditions;

(b)   limiting production, markets or technical development to the prejudice of consumers;

(c)   applying dissimilar conditions to equivalent transactions with other trading parties, thereby placing them at a competitive disadvantage;

(d)   making the conclusion of contracts subject to acceptance by the other parties of supplementary obligations which, by their nature or according to commercial usage, have no connection with the subject of such contracts.

...

PART FIVE   INSTITUTIONS OF THE COMMUNITY

The Court of Justice

...

Article 169
If the Commission considers that a Member State has failed to fulfil an obligation under this Treaty, it shall deliver a reasoned opinion on the matter after giving the State concerned the opportunity to submit its observations.

If the State concerned does not comply with the opinion within the period laid down by the Commission, the latter may bring the matter before the Court of Justice.

...

Article 173
The Court of Justice shall review the legality of acts adopted jointly by the European Parliament and the Council, of acts of the Council, of the Commission and of the ECB, other than recommendations and opinions, and of acts of the European Parliament intended to produce legal effects *vis-à-vis* third parties.

It shall for this purpose have jurisdiction in actions brought by a Member State, the Council or the Commission on grounds of lack of competence, infringement of an, essential procedural requirement, infringement of this Treaty or of any rule of law relating to its application, or misuse of powers.

...

Any natural or legal person may, under the same conditions, institute proceedings against a decision addressed to that person or against a decision which, although in the form of a regulation or a decision addressed to another person, is of direct and individual concern to the former.

The proceedings provided for in this Article shall be instituted within two months of the publication of the measure, or of its notification to the plaintiff, or, in the absence thereof, of the day on which it came to the knowledge of the latter, as the case may be.

...

Article 175
Should the European Parliament, the Council or the Commission, in infringement of this Treaty, fail to act, the Member States and the other institutions of the Community may bring an action before the Court of Justice to have the infringement established.

The action shall be admissible only if the institution concerned has first been called upon to act. If, within two months of being so called upon, the institution concerned has not defined its position, the action may be brought within a further period of two months.

Any natural or legal person may, under the conditions laid down in the preceding paragraphs, complain to the Court of Justice that an institution of the Community has failed to address to that person any act other than a recommendation or an opinion.

...

Article 177
The Court of Justice shall have jurisdiction to give preliminary rulings concerning:
    (a)   the interpretation of this Treaty;
    (b)   the validity and interpretation of acts of the institutions of the Community...;

(c)   the interpretation of the statutes of bodies established by an act of the Council, where those statutes so provide.

Where such a question is raised before any court or tribunal of a Member State, that court or tribunal may, if it considers that a decision on the question is necessary to enable it to give judgment, request the Court of Justice to give a ruling thereon.

Where any such question is raised in a case pending before a court or tribunal of a Member State, against whose decisions there is no judicial remedy under national law, that court or tribunal shall bring the matter before the Court of Justice.

. . .

PART SIX   GENERAL AND FINAL PROVISIONS

. . .

Article 222
This Treaty shall in no way prejudice the rules in Member States governing the system of property ownership.

. . .

COUNCIL REGULATION No 17/62
of 6 February 1962
First Regulation implementing Articles 85 and 86 of the Treaty

THE COUNCIL OF THE EUROPEAN ECONOMIC COMMUNITY,

Having regard to the Treaty establishing the European Economic Community, and in particular Article 87 thereof;

Having regard to the proposal from the Commission;

Having regard to the Opinion of the Economic and Social Committee;

Having regard to the Opinion of the European Parliament;

Whereas, in order to establish a system ensuring that competition shall not be distorted in the common market, it is necessary to provide for balanced application of Articles 85 and 86 in a uniform manner in the Member States;

Whereas in establishing the rules for applying Article 85(3) account must be taken of the need to ensure effective supervision and to simplify administration to the greatest possible extent;

Whereas it is accordingly necessary to make it obligatory, as a general principle, for undertakings which seek application of Article 85(3) to notify to the Commission their agreements, decisions and concerted practices;

Whereas, on the one hand, such agreements, decisions and concerted practices are probably very numerous and cannot therefore all be examined at the same time and, on the other hand, some of them have special features which may make them less prejudicial to the development of the common market;

Whereas there is consequently a need to make more flexible arrangements for the time being in respect of certain categories of agreement, decision and concerted practice without prejudging their validity under Article 85;

Whereas it may be in the interest of undertakings to know whether any agreements, decisions or practices to which they are party, or propose to become party, may lead to action on the part of the Commission pursuant to Article 85(1) or Article 86;

Whereas, in order to secure uniform application of Articles 85 and 86 in the common market, rules must be made under which the Commission, acting in close and constant liaison with the competent authorities of the Member States, may take the requisite measures for applying those Articles;

Whereas for this purpose the Commission must have the co-operation of the competent authorities of the Member States and be empowered, throughout the common market, to require such information to be supplied and to undertake such investigations as are necessary to bring to light any agreement, decision or concerted practice prohibited by Article 85(1) or any abuse of a dominant position prohibited by Article 86:

Whereas, in order to carry out its duty of ensuring that the provisions of the Treaty are applied, the Commission must be empowered to address to undertakings or associations of undertakings recommendations and decisions for the purpose of bringing to an end infringements of Articles 85 and 86;

Whereas compliance with Articles 85 and 86 and the fulfilment of obligations imposed on undertakings and associations of undertakings under this Regulation must be enforceable by means of fines and periodic penalty payments;

Whereas undertakings concerned must be accorded the right to be heard by the Commission, third parties whose interests may be affected by a decision must be given the opportunity of submitting their comments beforehand, and it must be ensured that wide publicity is given to decisions taken;

Whereas all decisions taken by the Commission under this Regulation are subject to review by the Court of Justice under the conditions specified in the Treaty; whereas it is moreover desirable to confer upon the Court of Justice, pursuant to Article 172, unlimited jurisdiction in respect of decisions under which the Commission imposes fines or periodic penalty payments;

Whereas this Regulation may enter into force without prejudice to any other provisions that may hereafter be adopted pursuant to Article 87,

HAS ADOPTED THIS REGULATION:

Article 1   Basic provision
Without prejudice to Articles 6, 7 and 23 of this Regulation, agreements, decisions and concerted practices of the kind described in Article 85(1) of the Treaty and the abuse of a dominant position in the market, within the meaning of Article 86 of the Treaty, shall be prohibited, no prior decision to that effect being required.

Article 2   Negative clearance
Upon application by the undertakings or associations of undertakings concerned, the Commission may certify that, on the basis of the facts in its possession, there are no grounds under Article 85(1) or Article 86 of the Treaty for action on its part in respect of an agreement, decision or practice.

Article 3   Termination of infringements
1.   Where the Commission, upon application or upon its own initiative, finds that there is infringement of Article 85 or Article 86 of the Treaty, it may by decision require the undertakings or associations of undertakings concerned to bring such infringement to an end.

2.   Those entitled to make application are:
   (a)   Member States;
   (b)   natural or legal persons who claim a legitimate interest.

3.   Without prejudice to the other provisions of this Regulation, the Commission may, before taking a decision under paragraph 1, address to the undertakings or associations of undertakings concerned recommendations for termination of the infringement.

Article 4   Notification of new agreements, decisions and practices
1.   Agreements, decisions and concerted practices of the kind described in Article 85(1) of the Treaty which come into existence after the entry into force of this Regulation and in respect of which the parties seek application of Article 85(3) must be notified to the Commission. Until they have been notified, no decision in application of Article 85(3) may be taken.

2.   Paragraph 1 shall not apply to agreements, decisions or concerted practices where:

(1)   the only parties thereto are undertakings from one Member State and the agreements, decisions or practices do not relate either to imports or to exports between Member States;

(2)   not more than two undertakings are party thereto, and the agreements only:

(a)   restrict the freedom of one party to the contract in determining the prices or conditions of business upon which the goods which he has obtained from the other party to the contract may be resold; or

(b)   impose restrictions on the exercise of the rights of the assignee or user of industrial property rights — in particular patents, utility models, designs or trade marks — or of the person entitled under a contract to the assignment, or grant, of the right to use a method of manufacture or knowledge relating to the use and to the application of industrial processes;

(3)   they have as their sole object:

(a)   the development or uniform application of standards or types; or

(b)   joint research and development;

(c)   specialisation in the manufacture of products, including agreements necessary for the achievement thereof;

— where the products which are the object of specialisation do not, in a substantial part of the common market, represent more than 15% of the volume of business done in identical products or those considered by the consumers to be similar by reason of their characteristics, price and use, and

— where the total annual turnover of the participating undertakings does not exceed 200 million units of accounts.

These agreements, decisions and concerted practices may be notified to the Commission.

Article 5   Notification of existing agreements, decisions and practices

1.   Agreements, decisions and concerted practices of the kind described in Article 85(1) of the Treaty which are in existence at the date of entry into force of this Regulation and in respect of which the parties seek application of Article 85(3) shall be notified to the Commission before 1 November 1962. However, notwithstanding the foregoing provisions, any agreements, decisions and concerted practices to which not more than two undertakings are party shall be notified before 1 February 1963.

2.   Paragraph 1 shall not apply to agreements, decisions or concerned practices falling within Article 4(2); these may be notified to the Commission.

Article 6   Decisions pursuant to Article 85(3)

1.   Whenever the Commission takes a decision pursuant to Article 85(3) of the Treaty, it shall specify therein the date from which the decision shall take effect. Such date shall not be earlier than the date of notification.

2.   The second sentence of paragraph 1 shall not apply to agreements, decisions or concerted practices falling within Article 4(2) and Article 5(2), nor to those falling within Article 5(1) which have been notified within the time limit specified in Article 5(1).

Article 7   Special provisions for existing agreements, decisions and practices

1.   Where agreements, decisions and concerted practices in existence at the date of entry into force of this Regulation and notified within the limits specified in Article 5(1) do not satisfy the requirements of Article 85(3) of the Treaty and the undertakings or associations of undertakings concerned cease to give effect to them or modify them in such manner that they no longer fall within the prohibition contained in Article 85(1) or that they satisfy the requirements of Article 85(3), the prohibition contained in Article

85(1) shall apply only for a period fixed by the Commission. A decision by the Commission pursuant to the foregoing sentence shall not apply as against undertakings and associations of undertakings which did not expressly consent to the notification.

2.   Paragraph 1 shall apply to agreements, decisions and concerted practices falling within Article 4(2) which are in existence at the date of entry into force of this Regulation if they are notified before 1 January 1967.

Article 8   Duration and revocation of decisions under Article 85(3)

1.   A decision in application of Article 85(3) of the Treaty shall be issued for a specified period and conditions and obligations may be attached thereto.

2.   A decision may on application be renewed if the requirements of Article 85(3) of the Treaty continue to be satisfied.

3.   The Commission may revoke or amend its decision or prohibit specified acts by the parties:

(a)   where there has been a change in any of the facts which were basic to the making of the decision;

(b)   where the parties commit a breach of any obligation attached to the decision;

(c)   where the decision is based on incorrect information or was induced by deceit;

(d)   where the parties abuse the exemption from the provision of Article 85(1) of the Treaty granted to them by the decision.

In cases to which subparagraphs (b), (c) or (d) apply, the decision may be revoked with retroactive effect.

Article 9   Powers

1.   Subject to review of its decision by the Court of Justice, the Commission shall have sole power to declare Article 85(1) inapplicable pursuant to Article 85(3) of the Treaty.

2.   The Commission shall have power to apply Article 85(1) and Article 86 of the Treaty; this power may be exercised notwithstanding that the time limits specified in Article 5(1) and in Article 7(2) relating to notification have not expired.

3.   As long as the Commission has not initiated any procedure under Articles 2, 3 or 6, the authorities of the Member States shall remain competent to apply Article 85(1) and Article 86 in accordance with Article 88 of the Treaty; they shall remain competent in this respect notwithstanding that the time limits specified in Article 5(1) and in Article 7(2) relating notification have not expired.

Article 10   Liaison with the authorities of the Member States

1.   The Commission shall forthwith transmit to the competent authorities of the Member States a copy of the applications and notifications together with copies of the most important documents lodged with the Commission for the purpose of establishing the existence of infringements of Articles 85 or 86 of the Treaty or of obtaining negative clearance or a decision in application of Article 85(3).

2.   The Commission shall carry out the procedure set out in paragraph 1 in close and constant liaison with the competent authorities of the Member States; such authorities shall have the right to express their views upon that procedure.

3.   An Advisory Committee on Restrictive Practices and Monopolies shall be consulted prior to the taking of any decision following upon a procedure under paragraph 1, and of any decision concerning the renewal, amendment or revocation of a decision pursuant to Article 85(3) of the Treaty.

4.   The Advisory Committee shall be composed of officials competent in the matter of restrictive practices and monopolies. Each Member State shall appoint an official to represent it who, if prevented from attending, may be replaced by another official.

5.   The consultation shall take place at a joint meeting convened by the Commission; such meeting shall be held not earlier than fourteen days after dispatch of the

notice convening it. The notice shall, in respect of each case to be examined, be accompanied by a summary of the case together with an indication of the most important documents, and a preliminary draft decision.

6.   The Advisory Committee may deliver an opinion notwithstanding that some of its members or their alternates are not present. A report of the outcome of the consultative proceedings shall be annexed to the draft decision. It shall not be made public.

Article 11   Request for information

1.   In carrying out the duties assigned to it by Article 89 and by provisions adopted under Article 87 of the Treaty, the Commission may obtain all necessary information from the Governments and competent authorities of the Member States and from undertakings and associations of undertakings.

2.   When sending a request for information to an undertaking or association of undertakings, the Commission shall at the same time forward a copy of the request to the competent authority of the Member State in whose territory the seat of the undertaking or association of undertakings is situated.

3.   In its request the Commission shall state the legal basis and the purpose of the request and also the penalties provided for in Article 15(1)(b) for supplying incorrect information.

4.   The owners of the undertakings or their representatives and, in the case of legal persons, companies or firms, or of associations having no legal personality, the persons authorised to represent them by law or by their constitution shall supply the information requested.

5.   Where an undertaking or association of undertakings does not supply the information requested within the time limit fixed by the Commission, or supplies incomplete information, the Commission shall by decision require the information to be supplied. The decision shall specify what information is required, fix an appropriate time limit within which it is to be supplied and indicate the penalties provided for in Article 15(1)(b) and Article 16(1)(c) and the right to have the decision reviewed by the Court of Justice.

6.   The Commission shall at the same time forward a copy of its decision to the competent authority of the Member State in whose territory the seat of the undertaking or association of undertakings is situated.

Article 12   Inquiry into sectors of the economy

1.   If in any sector of the economy the trend of trade between Member States, price movements, in flexibility of prices or other circumstances suggest that in the economic sector concerned competition is being restricted or distorted within the common market, the Commission may decide to conduct a general inquiry into that economic sector and in the course thereof may request undertakings in the sector concerned to supply the information necessary for giving effect to the principles formulated in Articles 85 and 86 of the Treaty and for carrying out the duties entrusted to the Commission.

2.   The Commission may in particular request every undertaking or association of undertakings in the economic sector concerned to communicate to it all agreements, decisions and concerted practices which are exempt from notification by virtue of Article 4(2) and Article 5(2).

3.   When making inquiries pursuant to paragraph 2, the Commission shall also request undertakings or groups of undertakings whose size suggests that they occupy a dominant position within the common market or a substantial part thereof to supply to the Commission such particulars of the structure of the undertakings and of their behaviour as are requisite to an appraisal of their position in the light of Article 86 of the Treaty.

4.   Article 10(3) to (6) and Articles 11, 13 and 14 shall apply correspondingly.

Article 13   Investigations by the authorities of the Member States
    1.   At the request of the Commission, the competent authorities of the Member States shall undertake the investigations which the Commission considers to be necessary under Article 14(1), or which it has ordered by decision pursuant to Article 14(3). The officials of the competent authorities of the Member States responsible for conducting those investigations shall exercise their powers upon production of an authorisation in writing issued by the competent authority of the Member State in whose territory the investigation is to be made. Such authorisation shall specify the subject matter and purpose of the investigation.
    2.   If so requested by the Commission or by the competent authority of the Member State in whose territory the investigation is to be made, the officials of the Commission may assist the officials of such authorities in carrying out their duties.

Article 14   Investigating powers of the Commission
    1.   In carrying out the duties assigned to it by Article 89 and by provisions adopted under Article 87 of the Treaty, the Commission may undertake all necessary investigations into undertakings and associations of undertakings. To this end the officials authorised by the Commission are empowered:
    (a)   to examine the books and other business records;
    (b)   to take copies of or extracts from the books and business records;
    (c)   to ask for oral explanations on the spot;
    (d)   to enter any premises; land and means of transport of undertakings.
    2.   The officials of the Commission authorised for the purpose of these investigations shall exercise their powers upon production of an authorisation in writing specifying the subject matter and purpose of the investigation and the penalties provided for in Article 15(1)(c) in cases where production of the required books or other business records is incomplete. In good time before the investigation, the Commission shall inform the competent authority of the Member State in whose territory the same is to be made of the investigation and of the identity of the authorised officials.
    3.   Undertakings and associations of undertakings shall submit to investigations ordered by decision of the Commission. The decision shall specify the subject matter and purpose of the investigation, appoint the date on which it is to begin and indicate the penalties provided for in Article 15(1)(c) and Article 16(1)(d) and the right to have the decision reviewed by the Court of Justice.
    4.   The Commission shall take decisions referred to in paragraph 3 after consultation with the competent authority of the Member State in whose territory the investigation is to be made.
    5.   Officials of the competent authority of the Member State in whose territory the investigation is to be made may, at the request of such authority or of the Commission, assist the officials of the Commission in carrying out their duties.
    6.   Where an undertaking opposes an investigation ordered pursuant to this Article, the Member State concerned shall afford the necessary assistance to the officials authorised by the Commission to enable them to make their investigation. Member States shall, after consultation with the Commission, take the necessary measures to this end before 1 October 1962.

Article 15   Fines
    1.   The Commission may by decision impose on undertakings or associations of undertakings fines of from 100 to 5,000 units of account where, intentionally or negligently:
    (a)   they supply incorrect or misleading information in an application pursuant to Article 2 or in a notification pursuant to Articles 4 or 5; or
    (b)   they supply incorrect information in response to a request made pursuant to Article 11(3) or (5) or to Article 12, or do not supply information within the time limit fixed by a decision taken under Article 11(5); or

(c)   they produce the required books or other business records in incomplete form during investigations under Article 13 or 14, or refuse to submit to an investigation ordered by decision issued in implementation of Article 14(3).

2.   The Commission may by decision impose on undertakings or associations of undertakings fines of from 1,000 to 1,000,000 units of account, or a sum in excess thereof but not exceeding 10% of the turnover in the preceding business year of each of the undertakings participating in the infringement where, either intentionally or negligently:

(a)   they infringe Article 85(1) or Article 86 of the Treaty; or

(b)   they commit a breach of any obligation imposed pursuant to Article 8(1).

In fixing the amount of the fine, regard shall be had both to the gravity and to the duration of the infringement.

3.   Article 10(3) to (6) shall apply.

4.   Decisions taken pursuant to paragraphs 1 and 2 shall not be of a criminal law nature.

5.   The fines provided for in paragraph 2(a) shall not be imposed in respect of acts taking place:

(a)   after notification to the Commission and before its decision in application of Article 85(3) of the Treaty, provided they fall within the limits of the activity described in the notification;

(b)   before notification and in the course of agreements, decisions or concerned practices in existence at the date of entry into force of this Regulation, provided that notification was effected within the time limits specified in Article 5(1) and Article 7(2).

6.   Paragraph 5 shall not have effect where the Commission has informed the undertakings concerned that after preliminary examination it is of opinion that Article 85(1) of the Treaty applies and that application of Article 85(3) is not justified.

Article 16   Periodic penalty payments

1.   The Commission may by decision impose on undertakings or associations of undertakings periodic penalty payments of from 50 to 1,000 units of account per day, calculated from the date appointed by the decision, in order to compel them:

(a)   to put an end to an infringement of Article 85 or 86 of the Treaty, in accordance with a decision taken pursuant to Article 3 of this Regulation;

(b)   to refrain from any act prohibited under Article 8(3);

(c)   to supply complete and correct information which it has requested by decision taken pursuant to Article 11(5);

(d)   to submit to an investigation which it has ordered by decision taken pursuant to Article 14(3).

2.   Where the undertakings or associations of undertakings have satisfied the obligation which it was the purpose of the periodic penalty payment to enforce, the Commission may fix the total amount of the periodic penalty payment at a lower figure than that which would arise under the original decision.

3.   Article 10(3) to (6) shall apply.

Article 17   Review by the Court of Justice

The Court of Justice shall have unlimited jurisdiction within the meaning of Article 172 of the Treaty to review decisions whereby the Commission has fixed a fine or periodic penalty payment; it may cancel, reduce or increase the fine or periodic penalty payment imposed.

Article 18   Unit of account

For the purposes of applying Articles 15 to 17 the unit of account shall be that adopted in drawing up the budget of the Community in accordance with Articles 207 and 209 of the Treaty.

Article 19   Hearing of the parties and of third persons

1.   Before taking decisions as provided for in Articles 2, 3, 6, 7, 8, 15 and 16, the Commission shall give the undertakings or associations of undertakings concerned the opportunity of being heard on the matters to which the Commission has taken objection.

2.   If the Commission or the competent authorities of the Member States consider it necessary, they may also hear other natural or legal persons. applications to be heard on the part of such persons shall where they show a sufficient interest, be granted.

3.   Where the Commission intends to give negative clearance pursuant to Article 2 or take a decision in application of Article 85(3) of the Treaty, it shall publish a summary of the relevant application or notification and invite all interested third parties to submit their observations within a time limit which it shall fix being not less than one month. Publication shall have regard to the legitimate interest of undertakings in the protection of their business secrets.

Article 20   Professional secrecy

1.   Information acquired as a result of the application of Articles 11, 12, 13 and 14 shall be used only for the purpose of the relevant request or investigation.

2.   Without prejudice to the provisions of Articles 19 and 21, the Commission and the competent authorities of the Member States, their officials and other servants shall not disclose information acquired by them as a result of the application of this Regulation and of the kind covered by the obligation of professional secrecy.

3.   The provisions of paragraphs 1 and 2 shall not prevent publication of general information or surveys which do not contain information relating to particular undertakings or associations of undertakings.

Article 21   Publication of decisions

1.   The Commission shall publish the decisions which it takes pursuant to Articles 2, 3, 6, 7 and 8.

2.   The publication shall state the names of the parties and the main content of the decision; it shall have regard to the legitimate interest of undertakings in the protection of their business secrets.

Article 22   Special provisions

1.   The Commission shall submit to the Council proposals for making certain categories of agreement, decision and concerted practice falling within Article 4(2) or Article 5(2) compulsorily notifiable under Article 4 or 5.

2.   Within one year from the date of entry into force of this Regulation, the Council shall examine, on a proposal from the Commission, what special provisions might be made for exempting from the provisions of this Regulation agreements, decisions and concerted practices falling within Article 4(2) or Article 5(2).

Article 23   Transitional provisions applicable to decisions of authorities of the Member States

1.   Agreements, decisions and concerted practices of the kind described in Article 85(1) of the Treaty to which, before the entry into force of this Regulation, the competent authority of a Member State has declared Article 85(1) to be inapplicable pursuant to Article 85(3) shall not be subject to compulsory notification under Article 5. The decision of the competent authority of the Member State shall be deemed to be a decision within the meaning of Article 6; it shall cease to be valid upon expiration of the period fixed by such authority but in any event not more than three years after the entry into force of this Regulation. Article 8(3) shall apply.

2.   Applications for renewal of decisions of the kind described in paragraph 1 shall be decided upon by the Commission in accordance with Article 8(2).

Article 24   Implementing provisions

The Commission shall have power to adopt implementing provisions concerning the form, content and other details of applications pursuant to Articles 2 and 3 and of notifications pursuant to Articles 4 and 5, and concerning hearings pursuant to Article 19(1) and (2).

Article 25

1.   As regards agreements, decisions and concerted practices to which Article 85 of the Treaty applies by virtue of accession, the date of accession shall be substituted for the date of entry into force of this regulation in every place where reference is made in this regulation to this latter date.

2.   Agreements, decisions and concerted practices existing at the date of accession to which Article 85 of the Treaty applies by virtue of accession shall be notified pursuant to Article 5(1) or Article 7(1) and (2) within six months from the date of accession.

3.   Fines under Article 15(2)(a) shall not be imposed in respect of any act prior to notification of the agreements, decisions and practices to which paragraph (2) applies and which have been notified within the period therein specified.

4.   New Member States shall take the measures referred to in Article 14(6) within six months from the date of accession after consulting the Commission.

5.   The provisions of paragraphs (1) to (4) above still apply in the same way in the case of accession of the Hellenic Republic, the Kingdom of Spain and of the Portuguese Republic.

This Regulation shall be binding in its entirety and directly applicable in all Member States.

COMMISSION REGULATION (EEC) No 418/85
of 19 December 1984
on the application of Article 85(3) of the Treaty to categories of research and development agreements

THE COMMISSION OF THE EUROPEAN COMMUNITIES,

Having regard to the Treaty establishing the European Economic Community,

Having regard to Council Regulation (EEC) No. 2821/71 of 20 December 1971 on the application of Article 85(3) of the Treaty to categories of agreements, decisions and concerted practices, as last amended by the Act of Accession of Greece, and in particular Article 1 thereof,

Having published a draft of this Regulation,

Having consulted the Advisory Committee on Restrictive Practices and Dominant Positions,

Whereas:

(1)   Regulation (EEC) No 2821/71 empowers the Commission to apply Article 85(3) of the Treaty by Regulation to certain categories of agreements, decisions and concerted practices falling within the scope of Article 85(1) which have as their object the research and development of products or processes up to the stage of industrial application, and exploitation of the results, including provisions regarding industrial property rights and confidential technical knowledge.

(2)   As stated in the Commission's 1968 notice concerning agreements, decisions and concerted practices in the field of cooperation between enterprises, agreements on the joint execution of research work or the joint development of the results of the research, up to but not including the stage of industrial application, generally do not fall within the scope of Article 85(1) of the Treaty. In certain circumstances, however, such as where the parties agree not to carry out other research and development in the same field, thereby forgoing the opportunity of gaining competitive advantages over the other

parties, such agreements may fall within Article 85(1) and should therefore not be excluded from this Regulation.

(3) Agreements providing for both joint research and development and joint exploitation of the results may fall within Article 85(1) because the parties jointly determine how the products developed are manufactured or the processes developed are applied or how related intellectual property rights or know-how are exploited.

(4) Cooperation in research and development and in the exploitation of the results generally promotes technical and economic progress by increasing the dissemination of technical knowledge between the parties and avoiding duplication of research and development work, by stimulating new advances through the exchange of complement-ary technical knowledge, and by rationalising the manufacture of the products or application of the processes arising out of the research and development. These aims can be achieved only where the research and development programme and its objectives are clearly defined and each of the parties is given the opportunity of exploiting any of the results of the programme that interest it; where universities or research institutes participate and are not interested in the industrial exploitation of the results, however, it may be agreed that they may use the said results solely for the purpose of further research.

(5) Consumers can generally be expected to benefit from the increased volume and effectiveness of research and development through the introduction of new or improved products or services or the reduction of prices brought about by new or improved processes.

(6) This Regulation must specify the restrictions of competition which may be included in the exempted agreements. The purpose of the permitted restrictions is to concentrate the research activities of the parties in order to improve their chances of success, and to facilitate the introduction of new products and services onto the market. These restrictions are generally necessary to secure the desired benefits for the parties and consumers.

(7) The joint exploitation of results can be considered as the natural consequence of joint research and development. It can take different forms ranging from manufacture to the exploitation of intellectual property rights or know-how that substantially contributes to technical or economic progress. In order to attain the benefits and objectives described above and to justify the restrictions of competition which are exempted, the joint exploitation must relate to products or processes for which the use of the results of the research and development is decisive. Joint exploitation is not therefore justified where it relates to improvements which were not made within the framework of a joint research and development programme but under an agreement having some other principal objective, such as the licensing of intellectual property rights, joint manufacture or specialisation, and merely containing ancillary provisions on joint research and development.

(8) The exemption granted under the Regulation must be limited to agreements which do not afford the undertakings the possibility of eliminating competition in respect of a substantial part of the products in question. In order to guarantee that several independent poles of research can exist in the common market in any economic sector, it is necessary to exclude from the block exemption agreements between competitors whose combined share of the market for products capable of being improved or replaced by the results of the research and development exceeds a certain level at the time the agreement is entered into.

(9) In order to guarantee the maintenance of effective competition during joint exploitation of the results, it is necessary to provide that the block exemption will cease to apply if the parties' combined shares of the market for the products arising out of the joint research and development become too great. However, it should be provided that

the exemption will continue to apply, irrespective of the parties' market shares, for a certain period after the commencement of joint exploitation, so as to await stabilisation of their market shares, particularly after the introduction of an entirely new product, and to guarantee a minimum period of return on the generally substantial investments involved.

(10)   Agreements between undertakings which do not fulfil the market share conditions laid down in the Regulation may, in appropriate cases, be granted an exemption by individual decision, which will in particular take account of world competition and the particular circumstances prevailing in the manufacture of high technology products.

(11)   It is desirable to list in the Regulation a number of obligations that are commonly found in research and development agreements but that are normally not restrictive of competition and to provide that, in the event that, because of the particular economic or legal circumstances, they should fall within Article 85(1), they also would be covered by the exemption. This list is not exhaustive.

(12)   The Regulation must specify what provisions may not be included in agreements if these are to benefit from the block exemption by virtue of the fact that such provisions are restrictions falling within Article 85(1) for which there can be no general presumption that they will lead to the positive effects required by Article 85(3).

(13)   Agreements which are not automatically covered by the exemption because they include provisions that are not expressly exempted by the Regulation and are not expressly excluded from exemption are none the less capable of benefiting from the general presumption of compatibility with Article 85(3) on which the block exemption is based. It will be possible for the Commission rapidly to establish whether this is the case for a particular agreement. Such an agreement should therefore be deemed to be covered by the exemption provided for in this Regulation where it is notified to the Commission and the Commission does not oppose the application of the exemption within a specified period of time.

(14)   Agreements covered by this Regulation may also take advantage of provisions contained in other block exemption Regulations of the Commission, and in particular Regulation (EEC) No 417/85 on specialisation agreements, Regulation (EEC) No 1983/83 on exclusive distribution agreements, Regulation (EEC) No 1984/83, on exclusive purchasing agreements and Regulation (EEC) No 2349/84 on patent licensing agreements, if they fulfil the conditions set out in these Regulations. The provisions of the aforementioned Regulations are, however, not applicable in so far as this Regulation contains specific rules.

(15)   If individual agreements exempted by this Regulation nevertheless have effects which are incompatible with Article 85(3), the Commission may withdraw the benefit of the block exemption.

(16)   The Regulation should apply with retroactive effect to agreements in existence when the Regulation comes into force where such agreements already fulfil its conditions or are modified to do so. The benefit of these provisions may not be claimed in actions pending at the date of entry into force of this Regulation, nor may it be relied on as grounds for claims for damages against third parties.

(17)   Since research and development cooperation agreements are often of a long-term nature, especially where the cooperation extends to the exploitation of the results, it is appropriate to fix the period of validity of the Regulation at 13 years. If the circumstances on the basis of which the Regulation was adopted should change significantly within this period, the Commission will make the necessary amendments.

(18)   Agreements which are automatically exempted pursuant to this Regulation need not be notified. Undertakings may nevertheless in a particular case request a decision pursuant to Council Regulation No 17, as last amended by the Act of Accession of Greece,

HAS ADOPTED THIS REGULATION:

Article 1
1. Pursuant to Article 85(3) of the Treaty and subject to the provisions of this Regulation, it is hereby declared that Article 85(1) of the Treaty shall not apply to agreements entered into between undertakings for the purpose of:

(a) joint research and development of products or processes and joint exploitation of the results of that research and development;

(b) joint exploitation of the results of research and development of products or processes jointly carried out pursuant to a prior agreement between the same undertakings; or

(c) joint research and development of products or processes excluding joint exploitation of the results, in so far as such agreements fall within the scope of Article 85(1).

2. For the purposes of this Regulation:

(a) *research and development of products or processes* means the acquisition of technical knowledge and the carrying out of theoretical analysis, systematic study or experimentation, including experimental production, technical testing of products or processes, the establishment of the necessary facilities and the obtaining of intellectual property rights for the results;

(b) *contract processes* means processes arising out of the research and development;

(c) *contract products* means products or services arising out of the research and development or manufactured or provided applying the contract processes;

(d) *exploitation of the results* means the manufacture of the contract products or the application of the contract processes or the assignment or licensing of intellectual property rights or the communication of know-how required for such manufacture or application;

(e) *technical knowledge* means technical knowledge which is either protected by an intellectual property right or is secret (know-how).

3. Research and development of the exploitation of the results are carried out *jointly* where:

(a) the work involved is:

— carried out by a joint team, organisation or undertaking,

— jointly entrusted to a third party, or

— allocated between the parties by way of specialisation in research, development or production;

(b) the parties collaborate in any way in the assignment or the licensing of intellectual property rights or the communication of know-how, within the meaning of paragraph 2(d), to third parties.

Article 2
The exemption provided for in Article 1 shall apply on condition that:

(a) the joint research and development work is carried out within the framework of a programme defining the objectives of the work and the field in which it is to be carried out;

(b) all the parties have access to the results of the work;

(c) where the agreement provides only for joint research and development, each party is free to exploit the results of the joint research and development and any pre-existing technical knowledge necessary therefor independently;

(d) the joint exploitation relates only to results which are protected by intellectual property rights or constitute know-how which substantially contributes to technical or economic progress and that the results are decisive for the manufacture of the contract products or the application of the contract processes;

(e) (deleted)

(f)   undertakings charged with manufacture by way of specialisation in production are required to fulfil orders for supplies from all the parties.

Article 3

1.   Where the parties are not competing manufacturers of products capable of being improved or replaced by the contract products, the exemption provided for in Article 1 shall apply for the duration of the research and development programme and, where the results are jointly exploited, for five years from the time the contract products are first put on the market within the common market.

2.   Where two or more of the parties are competing manufacturers within the meaning of paragrpah 1, the exemption provided for in Article 1 shall apply for the period specified in paragraph 1 only if, at the time the agreement is entered into, the parties' combined production of the products capable of being improved or replaced by the contract products does not exceed 20% of the market for such products in the common market or a substantial part thereof.

3.   After the end of the period referred to in paragraph 1, the exemption provided for in Article 1 shall continue to apply as long as the production of the contract products together with the parties' combined production of other products which are considered by users to be equivalent in view of their characteristics, price and intended use does not exceed 20% of the total market for such products in the common market or a substantial part thereof. Where contract products are components used by the parties of the manufacture of other products, reference shall be made to the markets for such of those latter products for which the components represent a significant part.

3a.   Where one of the parties, a joint undertaking, a third undertaking or more than one joint undertaking or third undertaking are entrusted with the distribution of the products which are the subject of the agreement under Article 4(1)(fa), (fb), or (fc), the exemption provided for in Article 1 shall apply only if the parties production of the products referred to in paragraphs 2 and 3 does not exceed 10% of the market for all such products in the common market or a substantial part thereof.

4.   The exemption provided for in Article 1 shall continue to apply where the market shares referred to in paragraphs 3 and 4 are exceeded during any period of two consecutive financial years by not more than one-tenth.

5.   Where the limits laid down in paragraph 5 are also exceeded, the exemption provided for in Article 1 shall continue to apply for a period of six months following the end of the financial year during which they were exceeded.

Article 4

1.   The exemption provided for in Article 1 shall also apply to the following restrictions of competition imposed on the parties:

(a)   an obligation not to carry out independently research and development in the field to which the programme relates or in a closely connected field during the execution of the programme;

(b)   an obligation not to enter into agreements which third parties on research and development in the field to which the programme relates or in a closely connected field during the execution of the programme;

(c)   an obligation to procure the contract products exclusively from parties, joint organisations or undertakings or third parties, jointly charged with their manufacture;

(d)   an obligation not to manufacture the contract products or apply the contract processes in territories reserved for other parties;

(e)   an obligation to restrict the manufacture of the contract products or application of the contract processes to one or more technical fields of application, except where two or more of the parties are competitors within the meaning of Article 3 at the time the agreement is entered into;

(f)   an obligation not to pursue, for a period of five years from the time the contract products are first put on the market within the common market, an active policy of putting the products on the market in territories reserved for other parties, and in particular not to engage in advertising specifically aimed at such territories or to establish any branch or maintain any distribution depot there for the distribution of the products, provided that users and intermediaries can obtain the contract products from other suppliers and the parties do not render it difficult for intermediaries and users to thus obtain the products;

(fa)   an obligation to grant one of the parties the exclusive right to distribute the contract products, provided that that party does not distribute products manufactured by a third producer which compete with the contract products;

(fb)   an obligation to grant the exclusive right to distribute the contract products to a joint undertaking of a third undertaking provided that the joint undertaking or third undertaking does not manufacture or distribute products which compete with the contract products;

(fc)   an obligation to grant the exclusive right to distribute the contract products in the whole or a defined area of the common market to joint undertakings or third undertakings which do not manufacture or distribute products which compete with the contract products, provided that users and intermediaries are also able to obtain the contract products from other suppliers and neither the parties nor the joint undertakings or third undertakings entrusted with the exclusive distribution of the contract products render it difficult for users and intermediaries to thus obtain the contract products.

(g)   an obligation on the parties to communicate to each other any experience they may gain in exploiting the results and to grant each other non-exclusive licences for inventions relating to improvements or new applications.

2.   The exemption provided for in Article 1 shall also apply where in a particular agreement the parties undertake obligations of the types referred to in paragraph 1 but with a more limited scope than is permitted by that paragraph.

Article 5

1.   Article 1 shall apply notwithstanding that any of the following obligations, in particular, are imposed on the parties during the currency of the agreement:

(a)   an obligation to communicate patented or non-patented technical knowledge necessary for the carrying out of the research and development programme for the exploitation of its results;

(b)   an obligation not to use any know-how received from another party for purposes other than carrying out the research and development programme and the exploitation of its results;

(c)   an obligation to obtain and maintain in force intellectual property rights for the contract products of processes;

(d)   an obligation to preserve the confidentiality of any know-how received or jointly developed under the research and development programme; this obligation may be imposed even after the expiry of the agreement;

(e)   an obligation:

(i)   to inform other parties of infringements of their intellectual property rights,

(ii)   to take legal action against infringers, and

(iii)   to assist in any such legal action or share with the other parties in the cost thereof;

(f)   an obligation to pay royalties or render services to other parties to compensate for unequal contributions to the joint research and development or unequal exploitation of its results;

(g)   an obligation to share royalties received from third parties with other parties;

(h)   an obligation to supply other parties with minimum quantities of contract products and to observe minimum standards of quality.

2.   In the event that, because of particular circumstances, the obligations referred to in paragraph 1 fall within the scope of Article 85(1), they also shall be covered by the exemption. The exemption provided for in this paragraph shall also apply where in a particular agreement the parties undertake obligations of the types referred to in paragraph 1 but with a more limited scope than is permitted by the paragraph.

Article 6

The exemption provided for in Article 12 shall not apply where the parties, by agreement, decision or concerted practice:

(a)   are restricted in their freedom to carry out research and development independently or in cooperation with third parties in a field unconnected with that to which the programme relates or, after its completion, in the field to which the programme relates or in a connected field;

(b)   are prohibited after completion of the research and development programme from challenging the validity of intellectual property rights which the parties hold in the common market and which are relevant to the programme or, after the expiry of the agreement, from challenging the validity of intellectual property rights which the parties hold in the common market and which protect the results of the research and development;

(c)   are restricted as to the quantity of the contract products they may manufacture or sell or as to the number of operations employing the contract process they may carry out;

(d)   are restricted in their determination of prices, components of prices or discounts when selling the contract products to third parties;

(e)   are restricted as to the customers they may serve, without prejudice to Article 4(1)(e);

(f)   are prohibited from putting the contract products on the market or pursuing an active sales policy for them in territories within the common market that are reserved for other parties after the end of the period referred to in Article 4(1)(f);

(g)   are required not to grant licences to third parties to manufacture the contract products or to apply the contract processes even though the exploitation by the parties themselves of the results of the joint research and development is not provided for or does not take place.

(h)   are required:

— to refuse without any objectively justified reason to meet demand from users or dealers established in their respective territories who would market the contract products in other territories within the common market, or

— to make it difficult for users or dealers to obtain the contract products from other dealers within the common market, and in particular to exercise intellectual property rights or take measures so as to prevent users or dealers from obtaining, or from putting on the market within the common market, products which have been lawfully put on the market within the common market by another party or with its consent.

Article 7

1.   The exemption provided for in this Regulation shall also apply to agreements of the kinds described in Article 1 which fulfil the conditions laid down in Articles 2 and 3 and which contain obligations restrictive of competition which are not covered by Articles 4 and 5 and do not fall within the scope of Article 6, on condition that the agreements in question are notified to the Commission in accordance with the provisions of Commission Regulation No 27, and that the Commission does not oppose such exemption within a period of six months.

2.   The period of six months shall run from the date on which the notification is received by the Commission. Where, however, the notification is made by registered post, the period shall run from the date shown on the postmark of the place of posting.

3.   Paragraph 1 shall apply only if:

(a)   express reference is made to this Article in the notification or in a communication accompanying it, and

(b)   the information furnished with the notification is complete and in accordance with the facts.

4.   The benefit of paragraph 1 may be claimed for agreements notified before the entry into force of this Regulation by submitting a communication to the Commission referring expressly to this Article and to the notification. Paragraphs 2 and 3(b) shall apply *mutatis mutandis*.

5.   The Commission may oppose the exemption. It shall oppose exemption if it receives a request to do so from a Member State within three months of the forwarding to the Member State of the notification referred to in paragraph 1 or of the communication referred to in paragraph 4. This request must be justified on the basis of considerations relating to the competition rules of the Treaty.

6.   The Commission may withdraw the opposition to the exemption at any time. However, where the opposition was raised at the request of a Member State and this request is maintained, it may be withdrawn only after consultation of the Advisory Committee on Restrictive Practices and Dominant Positions.

7.   If the opposition is withdrawn because the undertakings concerned have shown that the conditions of Article 85(3) are fulfilled, the exemption shall apply from the date of notification.

8.   If the opposition is withdrawn because the undertakings concerned have amended the agreement so that the conditions of Article 85(3) are fulfilled, the exemption shall apply from the date on which the amendments take effect.

9.   If the Commission opposes exemption and the opposition is not withdrawn, the effects of the notification shall be governed by the provisions of Regulation No 17.

Article 8

1.   Information acquired pursuant to Article 7 shall be used only for the purposes of this Regulation.

2.   The Commission and the authorities of the Member States, their officials and other servants shall not disclose information acquired by them pursuant to this Regulation of a kind that is covered by the obligation of professional secrecy.

3.   Paragraphs 1 and 2 shall not prevent publication of general information or surveys which do not contain information relating to particular undertakings or associations of undertakings.

Article 9

1.   The provisions of this Regulation shall also apply to rights and obligations which the parties create for undertakings connected with them. The market shares held and the actions and measures taken by connected undertakings shall be treated as those of the parties themselves.

2.   Connected undertakings for the purposes of this Regulation are:

(a)   undertakings in which a party to the agreement, directly or indirectly;

— owns more than half the capital or business assets,

— has the power to exercise more than half the voting rights,

— has the power to appoint more than half the members of the supervisory board, board of directors or bodies legally representing the undertakings, or

— has the right to manage the affairs;

(b)   undertakings which directly have in or over a party to the agreement the rights or powers listed in (a);

(c)   undertakings in or over which an undertaking referred to in (b) directly or indirectly has the rights or powers listed in (a);

3.   Undertakings in which the parties to the agreement or undertakings connected with them jointly have, directly or indirectly, the rights or powers set out in paragraph 2(a) shall be considered to be connected with each of the parties to the agreement.

Article 10

The Commission may withdraw the benefit of this Regulation, pursuant to Article 7 of Regulation (EEC) No 2821/71, where it finds in a particular case that an agreement exempted by this Regulation nevertheless has certain effects which are incompatible with the conditions laid down in Article 85(3) of the Treaty, and in particular where:

(a)   the existence of the agreement substantially restricts the scope for third parties to carry out research and development in the relevant field because of the limited research capacity available elsewhere;

(b)   because of the particular structure of supply, the existence of the agreement substantially restricts the access of third parties to the market for the contract products;

(c)   without any objectively valid reason, the parties do not exploit the results of the joint research and development;

(d)   the contract products are not subject in the whole or a substantial part of the common market to effective competition from identical products or products considered by users as equivalent in view of their characteristics, price and intended use.

Article 11

1.   In the case of agreements notified to the Commission before 1 March 1985, the exemption provided for in Article 1 shall have retroactive effect from the time at which the conditions for application of this Regulation were fulfilled or, where the agreement does not fall within Article 4(2)(3)(b) of Regulation No 17, not earlier than the date of notification.

2.   In the case of agreements existing on 13 March 1962 and notified to the Commission before 1 February 1963, the exemption shall have retroactive effect from the time at which the conditions for application of this Regulation were fulfilled.

3.   Where agreements which were in existence on 13 March 1962 and which were notified to the Commission before 1 February 1963, or which are covered by Article 4(2)(3)(b) of Regulation No 17 and were notified to the Commission before 1 January 1967, are amended before 1 September 1985 so as to fulfil the conditions for application of this Regulation, such amendment being communicated to the Commission before 1 October 1985, the prohibition laid down in Article 85(1) of the Treaty shall not apply in respect of the period prior to the amendment. The communication of amendments shall take effect from the date of their receipt by the Commission. Where the communication is sent by registered post, it shall take effect from the date shown on the postmark of the place of posting.

4.   In the case of agreements to which Article 85 of the Treaty applies as a result of the accession of the United Kingdom, Ireland and Denmark, paragraphs 1 to 3 shall apply except that the relevant dates shall be 1 January 1973 instead of 13 March 1962 and 1 July 1973 instead of 1 February 1963 and 1 January 1967.

5.   In the case of agreements to which Article 85 of the Treaty applies as a result of the accession of Greece, paragraphs 1 to 3 shall apply except that the relevant dates shall be 1 January 1981 instead of 13 March 1962 and 1 July 1981 instead of 1 February 1963 and 1 January 1967.

6.   As regards agreements to which Article 83 of the Treaty applies as a result of the accession of the Kingdom of Spain and of the Portuguese Republic, paragraphs 1 to 3 shall apply except that the relevant dates should be 1 January 1986 instead of 13 March 1962 and 1 July 1986 instead of 1 February 1963, 1 January 1967, 1 March 1985 and 1 September 1985. The amendment made to the agreements in accordance with the provisions of paragraph 3 need not be notified to the Commission.

Article 12
This Regulation shall apply *mutatis mutandis* to decisions of associations of undertakings.

Article 13
This Regulation shall enter into force on 1 March 1985.
It shall apply until 31 December 1997.

This Regulation shall be binding in its entirety and directly applicable in all Member States.

COMMISSION REGULATION (EEC) No 4087/88
of 30 November 1988
on the application of Article 85(3) of the Treaty to categories of franchise agreements

THE COMMISSION OF THE EUROPEAN COMMUNITIES,
  Having regard to the Treaty establishing the European Economic Community,
  Having regard to Council Regulation No 19/65/EEC of 2 March 1965 on the application of Article 85(3) of the Treaty to certain categories of agreements and concerted practices, as last amended by the Act of Accession of Spain and Portugal, and in particular Article 1 thereof,
  Having published a draft of this Regulation,
  Having consulted the Advisory Committee on Restrictive Practices and Dominant Positions,
  Whereas:
  (1)   Regulation No 19/65/EEC empowers the Commission to apply Article 85(3) of the Treaty of Regulation to certain categories of bilateral exclusive agreements falling within the scope of Article 85(1) which either have as their object the exlcusive distribution or exclusive purchase of goods, or include restrictions imposed in relation to the assignment or use of industrial property rights.
  (2)   Franchise agreements consist essentially of licences of industrial or intellectual property rights relating to trade marks or signs and know-how, which can be combined with restrictions relating to supply or purchase of goods.
  (3)   Several types of franchise can be distinguished according to their object: industrial franchise concerns the manufacturing of goods, distribution franchise concerns the sale of goods, and service franchise concerns the supply of services.
  (4)   It is possible on the basis of the experience of the Commission to define categories of franchise agreements which fall under Article 85(1) but can normally by regarded as satisfying the conditions laid down in Article 85(3). This is the case for franchise agreements whereby one of the parties supplies goods or provides services to end users. On the other hand, industrial franchise agreements should not be covered by this Regulation. Such agreements, which usually govern relationships between producers, present different characteristics than the other types of franchise. They consist of manufacturing licences based on patents and/or technical know-how, combined with trade-mark licences. Some of them may benefit from other block exemptions if they fulfil the necessary conditions.
  (5)   This Regulation covers franchise agreements between two undertakings, the franchisor and the franchisee, for the retailing of goods or the provision of service to end users, or a combination of these activities, such as the processing or adaptation of goods to fit specific needs of their customers. It also covers cases where the relationship between franchisor and franchisees is made through a third undertaking, the master franchisee. It does not cover wholesale franchise agreements because of the lack of experience of the Commission in that field.

(6)   Franchise agreements as defined in this Regulation can fall under Article 85(1). They may in particular affect intra-Community trade where they are concluded between undertakings from different Member States or where they form the basis of a network which extends beyond the boundaries of a single Member State.

(7)   Franchise agreements as defined in this Regulation normally improve the distribution of goods and/or the provision of services as they give franchisors the possibility of establishing a uniform network with limited investments, which may assist the entry of new competitors on the market, particularly in the case of small and medium-sized undertakings, thus increasing interbrand competition. They also allow independent traders to set up outlets more rapidly and with higher chance of success than if they had to do so without the franchisor's experience and assistance. They have therefore the possibility of competing more efficiently with large distribution undertakings.

(8)   As a rule, franchise agreements also allow consumers and other end users a fair share of the resulting benefit, as they combine the advantage of a uniform network with the existence of traders personally interested in the efficient operation of their business. The homogeneity of the network and the constant cooperation between the franchisor and the franchisees ensure a constant quality of the products and services. The favourable effect and franchising on interbrand competition and the fact that consumers are free to deal with any franchisee in the network guarantees that a reasonable part of the resulting benefits will be passed on to the consumers.

(9)   This Regulation must define the obligations restrictive or competition which may be included in franchise agreements. This is the case in particular for the granting of an exclusive territory to the franchisees combined with the prohibition on actively seeking customers outside that territory, which allows them to concentrate their efforts on their allotted territory. The same applies to the granting of an exclusive territory to a master franchisee combined with the obligation not to conclude franchise agreements with third parties outside that territory. Where the franchisees sell or use in the process of providing services, goods manufactured by the franchisor or according to its instructions and or bearing its trade mark, an obligation on the franchisees not to sell, or use in the process of the provision of services, competing goods, makes it possible to establish a coherent network which is identified with the franchised goods. However, this obligation should only be accepted with respect to the goods which form the essential subject-matter of the franchise. It should notably not relate to accessories or spare parts for these goods.

(10)   The obligations referred to above thus do not impose restrictions which are not necessary for the attainment of the abovementioned objectives. In particular, the limited territorial protection granted to the franchisees is indispensable to protect their investment.

(11)   It is desirable to list in the Regulation a number of obligations that are commonly found in franchise agreements and are normally not restrictive of competition and to provide that if, because of the particular economic or legal circumstances, they fall under Article 85(1), they are also covered by the exemption. This list, which is not exhaustive, includes in particular clauses which are essential either to preserve the common identity and reputation of the network or to prevent the know-how made available and the assistance given by the franchisor from benefiting competitors.

(12)   The Regulation must specify the conditions which must be satisfied for the exemption to apply. To guarantee that competition is not eliminated for a substantial part of the goods which are the subject of the franchise, it is necessary that parallel imports remain possible. Therefore, cross deliveries between franchisees should always be possible. Furthermore, where a franchise network is combined with another distribution system, franchisees should be free to obtain supplies from authorised

distributors. To better inform consumers, thereby helping to ensure that they receive a fair share of the resulting benefits, it must be provided that the franchisee shall be obliged to indicate its status as an independent undertaking, by any appropriate means which does not jeopardise the common identity of the franchised network. Furthermore, where the franchisees have to honour guarantees for the franchisor's goods, this obligation should also apply to goods supplied by the franchisor, other franchisees or other agreed dealers.

(13) The Regulation must also specify restrictions which may not be included in franchise agreements if these are to benefit from the exemption granted by the Regulation, by virtue of the fact that such provisions are restrictions falling under Article 85(1) for which there is no general presumption that they will lead to the positive effects required by Article 85(3). This applies in particular to market sharing between competing manufacturers, to clauses unduly limiting the franchisee's choice of suppliers or customers, and to cases where the franchisee is restricted in determining its prices. However, the franchisor should be free to recommend prices to the franchisees, where it is not prohibited by national laws and to the extent that it does not lead to concerted practices for the effective application of these prices.

(14) Agreements which are not automatically covered by the exemption because they contain provisions that are not expressly exempted by the Regulation and not expressly excluded from exemption may nonetheless generally be presumed to be eligible for application of Article 85(3). It will be possible for the Commission rapidly to establish whether this is the case for a particular agreement. Such agreements should therefore be deemed to be covered by the exemption provided for in this Regulation where they are notified to the Commission and the Commission does not oppose the application of the exemption within a specified period of time.

(15) If individual agreements exempted by this Regulation nevertheless have effects which are incompatible with Article 85(3), in particular as interpreted by the administrative practice of the Commission and the case law of the Court of Justice, the Commission may withdraw the benefit of the block exemption. This applies in particular where competition is significantly restricted because of the structure of the relevant market.

(16) Agreements which are automatically exempted pursuant to this Regulation need not be notified. Undertakings may nevertheless in a particular case request a decision pursuant to Council Regulation No 17 as last amended by the Act of Accession of Spain and Portugal.

(17) Agreements may benefit from the provisions either of this Regulation or of another Regulation, according to their particular nature and provided that they fulfil the necessary conditions of application. They may not benefit from a combination of the provisions of this Regulation with those of another block exemption Regulation,

HAS ADOPTED THIS REGULATION:

Article 1

1. Pursuant to Article 85(3) of the Treaty and subject to the provisions of this Regulation, it is hereby declared that Article 85(1) of the Treaty shall not apply to franchise agreements to which two undertakings are party, which include one or more of the restrictions listed in Article 2.

2. The exemption provided for in paragraph 1 shall also apply to master franchise agreements to which two undertakings are party. Where applicable, the provisions of this Regulation concerning the relationship between franchisor and franchisee shall apply *mutatis mutandis* to the relationship between franchisor and master franchisee and between master franchisee and franchisee.

3. For the purposes of this Regulation:

(a) 'franchise' means a package of industrial or intellectual property rights relating to trade marks, trade names, shop signs, utility models, designs, copyrights, know-how or patents, to be exploited for the resale of goods or the provision of services to end users;

(b) 'franchise agreement' means an agreement whereby one undertaking, the franchisor, grants the other, the franchisee, in exchange for direct or indirect financial consideration, the right to exploit a franchise for the purposes of marketing specified types of goods and/or services; it includes at least obligations relating to:

— the use of a common name or shop sign and a uniform presentation of contract premises and/or means of transport,

— the communication by the franchisor to the franchisee of know-how,

— the continuing provision by the franchisor to the franchisee of commercial or technical assistance during the life of the agreement;

(c) 'master franchise agreement' means an agreement whereby one undertaking, the franchisor, grants the other, the master franchisee, in exchange of direct or indirect financial consideration, the right to exploit a franchise for the purposes of concluding franchise agreements with third parties, the franchisees;

(d) 'franchisor's goods' means goods produced by the franchisor or according to its instructions, and/or bearing the franchisor's name or trade mark;

(e) 'contract premises' means the premises used for the exploitation of the franchise or, when the franchise is exploited outside those premises, the base from which the franchisee operates the means of transport used for the exploitation of the franchise (contract means of transport);

(f) 'know-how' means a package of non-patented practical information, resulting from experience and testing by the franchisor, which is secret, substantial and identified;

(g) 'secret' means that the know-how, as a body or in the precise configuration and assembly of its components, is not generally known or easily accessible; it is not limited in the narrow sense that each individual component of the know-how should be totally unknown or unobtainable outside the franchisor's business;

(h) 'substantial' means that the know-how includes information which is of importance for the sale of goods or the provision of services to end users, and in particular for the presentation of goods for sale, the processing of goods in connection which the provision of services, methods of dealing with customers, and administration and financial management; the know-how must be useful for the franchisee by being capable, at the date of conclusion of the agreement, of improving the competitive position of the franchisee, in particular by improving the franchisee's performance or helping it to enter a new market;

(i) 'identified' means that the know-how must be described in a sufficiently comprehensive manner so as to make it possible to verify that it fulfils the criteria of secrecy and substantiality; the description of the know-how can either be set out in the franchise agreement or in a separate document or recorded in any other appropriate form.

Article 2

The exemption provided for in Article 1 shall apply to the following restrictions of competition:

(a) an obligation on the franchisor, in a defined area of the common market, the contract territory, not to:

— grant the right to exploit all or part of the franchise to third parties,

— itself exploit the franchise, or itself market the goods or services which are the subject-matter of the franchise under a similar formula.

— itself supply the franchisor's goods to third parties;

(b) an obligation on the master franchisee not to conclude franchise agreement with third parties outside its contract territory;

(c)   an obligation on the franchisee to exploit the franchise only from the contract premises;

(d)   an obligation on the franchisee to refrain, outside the contract territory, from seeking customers for the goods or the services which are the subject-matter of the franchise;

(e)   an obligation on the franchisee not to manufacture, sell or use in the course of the provision of services, goods competing with the franchisor's goods which are the subject-matter of the franchise; where the subject-matter of the franchise is the sale or use in the course of the provision of services both certain types of goods and spare parts or accessories therefor, that obligation may not be imposed in respect of these spare parts or accessories.

Article 3

1.   Article 1 shall apply notwithstanding the presence of any of the following obligations on the franchisee, in so far as they are necessary to protect the franchisor's industrial or intellectual property rights or to maintain the common identity and reputation of the franchised network:

(a)   to sell, or use in the course of the provision of services, exclusively goods matching minimum objective quality specifications laid down by the franchisor;

(b)   to sell, or use in the course of the provision of services, goods which are manufactured only by the franchisor or by third parties designed by it, where it is impracticable, owing to the nature of the goods which are the subject-matter of the franchise, to apply objective quality specifications;

(c)   not to engage, directly or indirectly, in any similar business in a territory where it would compete with a member of the franchised network, including the franchisor; the franchisee may be held to this obligation after termination of the agreement, for a reasonable period which may not exceed one year, in the territory where it has exploited the franchise;

(d)   not to acquire financial interests in the capital of a competing undertaking, which would give the franchisee the power to influence the economic conduct of such undertaking;

(e)   to sell the goods which are the subject-matter of the franchise only to end users, to other franchisees and to resellers within other channels of distribution supplied by the manufacturer of these goods or with its consent;

(f)   to use its best endeavours to sell the goods or provide the services that are the subject-matter of the franchise; to offer for sale a minimum range of goods, achieve a minimum turnover, plan its orders in advance, keep minimum stocks and provide customer and warranty services;

(g)   to pay to the franchisor a specified proportion of its revenue for advertising and itself carry out advertising for the nature of which it shall obtain the franchisor's approval.

2.   Article 1 shall apply notwithstanding the presence of any of the following obligations on the franchisee:

(a)   not to disclose to third parties the know-how provided by the franchisor; the franchisee may be held to this obligation after termination of the agreement;

(b)   to communicate to the franchisor any experience gained in exploiting the franchise and to grant it, and other franchisees, a non-exclusive licence for the know-how resulting from that experience;

(c)   to inform the franchisor of infringements of licensed industrial or intellectual property rights, to take legal action against infringers or to assist the franchisor in any legal actions against infringers;

(d)   not to use know-how licensed by the franchisor for purposes other than the exploitation of the franchise; the franchisee may be held to this obligation after termination of the agreement;

(e)   to attend or have its staff attend training courses arranged by the franchisor;

(f)   to apply the commercial methods devised by the franchisor, including any subsequent modification thereof, and use the licensed industrial or intellectual property rights;

(g)   to comply with the franchisor's standards for the equipment and presentation of the contract premises and/or means of transport;

(h)   to allow the franchisor to carry out checks of the contract premises and/or means of transport, including the goods sold and the services provided, and the inventory and accounts of the franchisee;

(i)   not without the franchisor's consent to change the location of the contract premises;

(j)   not without the franchisor's consent to assign the rights and obligations under the franchise agreement.

3.   In the event that, because of particular circumstances, obligations referred to in paragraph 2 fall within the scope of Article 85(1), they shall also be exempted even if they are not accompanied by any of the obligations exempted by Article 1.

Article 4
The exemption provided for in Article 1 shall apply on condition that:

(a)   the franchisee is free to obtain the goods that are the subject-matter of the franchise from other franchisees; where such goods are also distributed through another network of authorised distributors, the franchisee must be free to obtain the goods from the latter;

(b)   where the franchisor obliges the franchisee to honour guarantees for the franchisor's goods, that obligation shall apply in respect of such goods supplied by any member of the franchised network or other distributors which give a similar guarantee, in the common market;

(c)   the franchisee is obliged to indicate its status as an independent undertaking; this indication shall however not interfere with the common identity of the franchised network resulting in particular from the common name or shop sign and uniform appearance of the contract premises and/or means of transport.

Article 5
The exemption granted by Article 1 shall not apply where:

(a)   undertakings producing goods or providing services which are identical or are considered by users as equivalent in view of their characteristics, price and intended use, enter into franchise agreements in respect of such goods or services;

(b)   without prejudice to Article 2(e) and Article 3(1)(b), the franchisee is prevented from obtaining supplies of goods of a quality equivalent to those offered by the franchisor;

(c)   without prejudice to Article 2(e), the franchisee is obliged to sell, or use in the process of providing services, goods manufactured by the franchisor or third parties designated by the franchisor and the franchisor refuses, for reasons other than protecting the franchisor's industrial or intellectual property rights, or maintaining the common identity and reputation of the franchised network, to designate as authorised manufacturers third parties proposed by the franchisee;

(d)   the franchisee is prevented from continuing to use the licensed know-how after termination of the agreement where the know-how has become generally known or easily accessible, other than by breach of an obligation by the franchisee;

(e)   the franchisee is restricted by the franchisor, directly or indirectly, in the determination of sale prices for the goods or services which are the subject-matter of the franchise, without prejudice to the possibility for the franchisor of recommending sale prices;

(f)   the franchisor prohibits the franchisee from challenging the validity of the industrial or intellectual property rights which form part of the franchise, without prejudice to the possibility for the franchisor of terminating the agreement in such a case;

(g)   franchisees are obliged not to supply within the common market the goods or services which are the subject-matter of the franchise to end users because of their place of residence.

Article 6

1.   The exemption provided for in Article 1 shall also apply to franchise agreements which fulfil the conditions laid down in Article 4 and include obligations restrictive of competition which are not covered by Articles 2 and 3(3) and do not fall within the scope of Article 5, on condition that the agreements in question are notified to the Commission in accordance with the provisions of Commission Regulation No 27 and that the Commission does not oppose such exemption within a period of six months.

2.   The period of six months shall run from the date on which the notification is received by the Commission. Where, however, the notification is made by registered post, the period shall run from the date shown on the postmark of the place of posting.

3.   Paragraph 1 shall apply only if:

(a)   express reference is made to this Article in the notification or in a communication accompanying it; and

(b)   the information furnished with the notification is complete and in accordance with the facts.

4.   The benefit of paragraph 1 can be claimed for agreements notified before the entry into force of this Regulation by submitting a communication to the Commission referring expressly to this Article and to the notification. Paragraphs 2 and 3(b) shall apply *mutatis mutandis*.

5.   The Commission may oppose exemption. It shall oppose exemption if it receives a request to do so from a Member State within three months of the forwarding to the Member State of the notification referred to in paragraph 1 of the communication referred to in paragraph 4. This request must be justified on the basis of considerations relating to the competition rules of the Treaty.

6.   The Commission may withdraw its opposition to the exemption at any time. However, where that opposition was raised at the request of a Member State, it may be withdrawn only after consultation of the advisory Committee on Restrictive Practices and Dominant Positions.

7.   If the opposition is withdrawn because the undertakings concerned have shown that the conditions of Article 85(3) are fulfilled, the exemption shall apply from the date of the notification.

8.   If the opposition is withdrawn because the undertakings concerned have amended the agreement so that the conditions of Article 85(3) are fulfilled, the exemption shall apply from the date on which the amendments take effect.

9.   If the Commission opposes exemption and its opposition is not withdrawn, the effects of the notification shall be governed by the provisions of Regulation No 17.

Article 7

1.   Information acquired pursuant to Article 6 shall be used only for the purposes of this Regulation.

2.   The Commission and the authorities of the Member States, their officials and other servants shall not disclose information acquired by them pursuant to this Regulation of a kind that is covered by the obligation of professional secrecy.

3.   Paragraphs 1 and 2 shall not prevent publication of general information or surveys which do not contain information relating to particular undertakings or associations of undertakings.

Article 8
The Commission may withdraw the benefit of this Regulation, pursuant to Article 7 of Regulation No 19/65/EEC, where it finds in a particular case that an agreement exempted by this Regulation nevertheless has certain effects which are incompatible with the conditions laid down in Article 85(3) of the EEC Treaty, and in particular where territorial protection is awarded to the franchisee and:

(a)   access to the relevant market or competition therein is significantly restricted by the cumulative effect of parallel networks of similar agreements established by competing manufacturers or distributors;

(b)   the goods or services which are the subject-matter of the franchise do not face, in a substantial part of the common market, effective competition from goods or services which are identical or considered by users as equivalent in view of their characteristics, price and intended use;

(c)   the parties, or one of them, prevent end users, because of their place of residence, from obtaining, directly or through intermediaries, the goods or services which are the subject-matter of the franchise within the common market, or use differences in specifications concerning those goods or services in different Member States, to isolate markets;

(d)   franchisees engage in concerted practices relating to the sale prices of the goods or services which are the subject-matter of the franchise;

(e)   the franchisor uses its right to check the contract premises and means of transport, or refuses its agreement to requests by the franchisee to move the contract premises or assign its right and obligations under the franchise agreement, for reasons other than protecting the franchisor's industrial or intellectual property rights, maintaining the common identity and reputation of the franchised network or verifying that the franchisee abides by its obligations under the agreement.

Article 9
This Regulation shall enter into force on 1 February 1989.
  It shall remain in force until 31 December 1999.

This Regulation shall be binding in its entirety and directly applicable in all Member States.

FIRST COUNCIL DIRECTIVE
of 21 December 1988
to approximate the laws of the Member States relating to trade marks
(89/104/EEC)

THE COUNCIL OF THE EUROPEAN COMMUNITIES,
  Having regard to the Treaty establishing the European Economic Community, and in particular Article 100a thereof,
  Having regard to the proposal from the Commission,
  In cooperation with the European Parliament,
  Having regard to the opinion of the Economic and Social Committee,
  Whereas the trade mark laws at present applicable in the Member States contain disparities which may impede the free movement of goods and freedom to provide services and may distort competition within the common market; whereas it is therefore necessary, in view of the establishment and functioning of the internal market, to approximate the laws of Member States;
  Whereas it is important not to disregard the solutions and advantages which the Community trade mark system may afford to undertakings wishing to acquire trade marks;
  Whereas it does not appear to be necessary at present to undertake full-scale approximation of the trade mark laws of the Member States and it will be sufficient if

approximation is limited to those national provisions of law which most directly affect the functioning of the internal market;

Whereas the Directive does not deprive the Member States of the right to continue to protect trade marks acquired through use but takes them into account only in regard to the relationship between them and trade marks acquired by registration;

Whereas Member States also remain free to fix the provisions of procedure concerning the registration, the revocation and the invalidity of trade marks acquired by registration; whereas they can, for example, determine the form of trade mark registration and invalidity procedures, decide whether earlier rights should be invoked either in the registration procedure or in the invalidity procedure or in both and, if they allow earlier rights to be invoked in the registration procedure, have an opposition procedure or an *ex officio* examination procedure or both; whereas Member States remain free to determine the effects of revocation or invalidity of trade marks;

Whereas this Directive does not exclude the application to trade marks of provisions of law of the Member States other than trade mark law, such as the provisions relating to unfair competition, civil liablity or consumer protection;

Whereas attainment of the objectives at which this approximation of laws is aiming requires that the conditions for obtaining and continuing to hold a registered trade mark are, in general, identical in all Member States; whereas, to this end, it is necessary to list examples of signs which may constitute a trade mark, provided that such signs are capable of distinguishing the goods or services of one undertaking from those of other undertakings; whereas the grounds for refusal or invalidity concerning the trade mark itself, for example, the absence of any distinctive character, or concerning conflicts between the trade mark and earlier rights, are to be listed in an exhaustive manner, even if some of these grounds are listed as an option for the Member States which will therefore be able to maintain or introduce those grounds in their legislation; whereas Member States will be able to maintain or introduce into their legislation grounds of refusal or invalidity linked to conditions for obtaining and continuing to hold a trade mark for which there is no provision of approximation, concerning, for example, the eligibility for the grant of a trade mark, the renewal of the trade mark or rules on fees, or related to the non-compliance with procedural rules;

Whereas in order to reduce the total number of trade marks registered and protected in the Community and, consequently, the number of conflicts which arise between them, it is essential to require that registered trade marks must actually be used or, if not used, be subject to revocation; whereas it is necessary to provide that a trade mark cannot be invalidated on the basis of the existence of a non-used earlier trade mark, while the Member States remain free to apply the same principle in respect of the registration of a trade mark or to provide that a trade mark may not be successfully invoked in infringement proceedings if it is established as a result of a plea that the trade mark could be revoked; whereas in all these cases it is up to the Member States to establish the applicable rules of procedure;

Whereas it is fundamental, in order to facilitate the free circulation of goods and services, to ensure that henceforth registered trade marks enjoy the same protection under the legal system of all the Member States; whereas this should however not prevent the Member States from granting at their option extensive protection to those trade marks which have a reputation;

Whereas the protection afforded by the registered trade mark, the function of which is in particular to guarantee the trade mark as an indication of origin, is absolute in the case of identity between the mark and the sign and goods or services; whereas the protection applies also in case of similarity between the mark and the sign and the goods or services; whereas it is indispensable to give an interpretation of the concept of similarity in relation to the likelihood of confusion; whereas the likelihood of confusion, the appreciation of which depends on numerous elements and, in particular, on the recognition of the trade mark on the market, of the association which can be made with the used or registered sign, of the degree of similarity between the trade mark and the sign and between the goods or services identified, constitutes the specific condition for such protection; whereas the way in which likelihood of confusion may be established, and in particular the onus of proof, are a matter for national procedural rules which are not prejudiced by the Directive;

Whereas it is important, for reasons of legal certainty and without inequitably prejudicing the interests of a proprietor of an earlier trade mark, to provide that the latter may no longer request a declaration of invalidity nor may he oppose the use of a trade mark subsequent to his own of which he has knowingly tolerated the use for a substantial length of time, unless the application for the subsequent trade mark was made in bad faith;

Whereas all Member States of the Community are bound by the Paris Convention for the Protection of Industrial Property; whereas it is necessary that the provisions of this Directive are entirely consistent with those of the Paris Convention; whereas the obligations of the Member States resulting from this Convention are not affected by this Directive; whereas, where appropriate, the second subparagraph of Article 234 of the Treaty is applicable,

HAS ADOPTED THIS DIRECTIVE:

Article 1   Scope

This Directive shall apply to every trade mark in respect of goods or services which is the subject of registration or of an application in a Member State for registration as an individual trade mark, a collective mark or a guarantee or certification mark, or which is the subject of a registration or an application for registration in the Benelux Trade Mark Office or of an international registration having effect in a Member State.

Article 2   Signs of which a trade mark may consist

A trade mark may consist of any sign capable of being represented graphically, particularly words, including personal names, designs, letters, numerals, the shape of goods or of their packaging, provided that such signs are capable of distinguishing the goods or services of one undertaking from those of other undertakings.

Article 3   Grounds for refusal or invalidity

1.   The following shall not be registered or if registered shall be liable to be declared invalid:

    (a)   signs which cannot constitute a trade mark;

    (b)   trade marks which are devoid of any distinctive character;

    (c)   trade marks which consist exclusively of signs or indications which may serve, in trade, to designate the kind, quality, quantity, intended purpose, value, geographical origin, or the time of production of the goods or of rendering of the service, or other characteristics of the goods or service;

    (d)   trade marks which consist exclusively of signs or indications which have become customary in the current language or in the *bona fide* and established practices of the trade;

    (e)   signs which consist exclusively of:

— the shape which results from the nature of the goods themselves, or

— the shape of goods which is necessary to obtain a technical result, or

— the shape which gives substantial value to the goods;

    (f)   trade marks which are contrary to public policy or to accepted principles of morality;

    (g)   trade marks which are of such a nature as to deceive the public, for instance as to the nature, quality or geographical origin of the goods or service;

(h)   trade marks which have not been authorised by the competent authorities and are to be refused or invalidated pursuant to Article 6ter of the Paris Convention for the Protection of Industrial Property, hereinafter referred to as the "Paris Convention".

2.   Any Member State may provide that a trade mark shall not be registered or, if registered, shall be liable to be declared invalid where and to the extent that:

(a)   the use of that trade mark may be prohibited pursuant to provisions of law other than trade mark law of the Member State concerned or of the Community;

(b)   the trade mark covers a sign of high symbolic value, in particular a religious symbol;

(c)   the trade mark includes badges, emblems and escutcheons other than those covered by Article 6 *ter* of the Paris Convention and which are of public interest, unless the consent of the appropriate authorities to its registration has been given in conformity with the legislation of the Member State;

(d)   the application for registration of the trade mark was made in bad faith by the applicant.

3.   A trade mark shall not be refused registration or be declared invalid in accordance with paragraph 1(b), (c) or (d) if, before the date of application for registration and following the use which has been made of it, it has acquired a distinctive character. Any Member State may in addition provide that this provision shall also apply where the distinctive character was acquired after the date of application for registration or after the date of registration.

4.   Any Member State may provide that, by derogation from the preceding paragraphs, the grounds of refusal of registration or invalidity in force in that State prior to the date on which the provisions necessary to comply with this Directive enter into force, shall apply to trade marks for which application has been made prior to that date.

Article 4   Further grounds for refusal or invalidity concerning conflicts with earlier rights

1.   A trade mark shall not be registered or, if registered, shall be liable to be declared invalid:

(a)   if it is identical with an earlier trade mark, and the goods or services for which the trade mark is applied for or is registered are identical with the goods or services for which the earlier trade mark is protected;

(b)   if because of its identity with, or similarity to, the earlier trade mark and the identity or similarity of the goods or services covered by the trade marks, there exists a likelihood of confusion on the part of the public, which includes the likelihood of association with the earlier trade mark.

2.   'Earlier trade marks' within the meaning of paragraph 1 means:

(a)   trade marks of the following kinds with a date of application for registration which is earlier than the date of application for registration of the trade mark, taking account, where appropriate, of the priorities claimed in respect of those trade marks:

(i)   Community trade marks;

(ii)   trade marks registered in the Member State or, in the case of Belgium, Luxembourg or the Netherlands, at the Benelux Trade Mark Office;

(iii)   trade marks registered under international arrangements which have effect in the Member State;

(b)   Community trade marks which validly claim seniority, in accordance with the Regulation on the Community trade mark, from a trade mark referred to in (a)(ii) and (iii), even when the latter trade mark has been surrendered or allowed to lapse;

(c)   applications for the trade marks referred to in (a) and (b), subject to their registration;

(d)   trade marks which, on the date of application for registration of the trade mark, or, where appropriate, of the priority claimed in respect of the application for registration of the trade mark, are well known in a Member State, in the sense in which the words 'well known' are used in Article 6 *bis* of the Paris Convention;

3.   A trade mark shall furthermore not be registered or, if registered, shall be liable to be declared invalid if it is identical with, or similar to, an earlier Community trade mark within the meaning of paragraph 2 and is to be, or has been, registered for goods or services which are not similar to those for which the earlier Community trade mark has a reputation in the Community and where the use of the later trade mark without due cause would take unfair advantage of, or be detrimental to, the distinctive character or the repute of the earlier Community trade mark.

4.   Any Member State may furthermore provide that a trade mark shall not be registered or, if registered, shall be liable to be declared invalid where, and to the extent that:

(a)   the trade mark is identical with, or similar to, an earlier national trade mark within the meaning of paragraph 2 and is to be, or has been, registered for goods or services which are not similar to those for which the earlier trade mark is registerd, where the earlier trade mark has a reputation in the Member State concerned and where the use of the later trade mark without due cause would take unfair advantage of, or be detrimental to, the distinctive character or the repute of the earlier trade mark;

(b)   rights to a non-registered trade mark or to another sign used in the course of trade were acquired prior to the date of application for registration of the subsequent trade mark, or the date of the priority claimed for the application for registration of the subsequent trade mark and that non-registered trade mark or other sign confers on its proprietor the right to prohibit the use of a subsequent trade mark;

(c)   the use of the trade mark may be prohibited by virtue of an earlier right other than the rights referred to in paragraphs 2 and 4(b) and in particular:

(i)   a right to a name;
(ii)   a right of personal portrayal;
(iii)   a copyright;
(iv)   an industrial property right;

(d)   the trade mark is identical with, or similar to, an earlier collective trade mark conferring a right which expired within a period of a maximum of three years preceding application;

(e)   the trade mark is identical with, or similar to, an earlier guarantee or certification mark conferring a right which expired within a period preceding application the length of which is fixed by the Member State;

(f)   the trade mark is identical with, or similar to, an earlier trade mark which was registered for identical or similar goods or services and conferred on them a right which has expired for failure to renew within a period of a maximum of two years preceding application, unless the proprietor of the earlier trade mark gave his agreement for the registration of the later mark or did not use his trade mark;

(g)   the trade mark is liable to be confused with a mark which was in use abroad on the filing date of the application and which is still in use there, provided that at the date of the application the applicant was acting in bad faith.

5.   The Member States may permit that in appropriate circumstances registration need not be refused or the trade mark need not be declared invalid where the proprietor of the earlier trade mark or other earlier right consents to the registration of the later trade mark.

6.   Any Member State may provide that, by derogation from paragraphs 1 to 5, the grounds for refusal of registration or invalidity in force in that State prior to the date on which the provisions necessary to comply with this Directive enter into force, shall apply to trade marks for which application has been made prior to that date.

Article 5   Rights conferred by a trade mark

1.   The registered trade mark shall confer on the proprietor exclusive rights therein. The proprietor shall be entitled to prevent all third parties not having his consent from using in the course of trade:

(a)   any sign which is identical with the trade mark in relation to goods or services which are identical with those for which the trade mark is registered;

(b)   any sign where, because of its identity with, or similarity to, the trade mark and the identity or similarity of the goods or services covered by the trade mark and the sign, there exists a likelihood of confusion on the part of the public, which includes the likelihood of association between the sign and the trade mark.

2.   Any Member State may also provide that the proprietor shall be entitled to prevent all third parties not having his consent from using in the course of trade any sign which is identical with, or similar to, the trade mark in relation to goods or services which are not similar to those for which the trade mark is registered, where the latter has a reputation in the Member State and where use of that sign without due cause takes unfair advantage of, or is detrimental to, the distinctive character or the repute of the trade mark.

3.   The following, *inter alia*, may be prohibited under paragraphs 1 and 2:

(a)   affixing the sign to the goods or to the packaging thereof;

(b)   offering the goods, or putting them on the market or stocking them for these purposes under that sign, or offering or supplying services thereunder;

(c)   importing or exporting the goods under the sign;

(d)   using the sign on business papers and in advertising.

4.   Where, under the law of the Member State, the use of a sign under the conditions referred to in 1(b) or 2 could not be prohibited before the date on which the provisions necessary to comply with this Directive entered into force in the Member State concerned, the rights conferred by the trade mark may not be relied on to prevent the continued use of the sign.

5.   Paragraphs 1 to 4 shall not affect provisions in any Member State relating to the protection against the use of a sign other than for the purposes of distinguishing goods or services, where use of that sign without due cause takes unfair advantage of, or is detrimental to, the distinctive character or the repute of the trade mark.

Article 6   Limitation of the effects of trade mark

1.   The trade mark shall not entitle the proprietor to prohibit a third party from using, in the course of trade,

(a)   his own name or address;

(b)   indications concerning the kind, quality, quantity, intended purpose, value, geographical origin, the time of production of goods or of rendering of the service, or other characteristics of goods or services;

(c)   the trade mark where it is necessary to indicate the intended purpose of a product or service, in particular as accessories or spare parts;

provided he uses them in accordance with honest practices in industrial or commercial matters.

2.   The trade mark shall not entitle the proprietor to prohibit a third party from using, in the course of trade, an earlier right which only applies in a particular locality if that right is recognised by the laws of the Member State in question and within the limits of the territory in which it is recognised.

Article 7   Exhaustion of the rights conferred by a trade mark

1.   The trade mark shall not entitle the proprietor to prohibit its use in relation to goods which have been put on the market in the Community under that trade mark by the proprietor or with his consent.

2.   Paragraph 1 shall not apply where there exist legitimate reasons for the proprietor to oppose further commercialisation of the goods, especially where the condition of the goods is changed or impaired after they have been put on the market.

Article 8   Licensing

1.   A trade mark may be licensed for some or all of the goods or services for which it is registered and for the whole or part of the Member State concerned. A license may be exclusive or non-exclusive.

2.   The proprietor of a trade mark may invoke the rights conferred by that trade mark against a licensee who contravenes any provision in his licensing contract with regard to its duration, the form covered by the registration in which the trade mark may be used, the scope of the goods or services for which the licence is granted, the territory in which the trade mark may be affixed, or the quality of the goods manufactured or of the services provided by the licensee.

Article 9   Limitation in consequence of acquiescence

1.   Where, in a Member State, the proprietor of an earlier trade mark as referred to in Article 4(2) has acquiesced, for a period of five successive years, in the use of a later trade mark registered in that Member State while being aware of such use, he shall no longer be entitled on the basis of the earlier trade mark either to apply for a declaration that the later trade mark is invalid or to oppose the use of the later trade mark in respect of the goods or services for which the later trade mark has been used, unless registration of the later trade mark was applied for in bad faith.

2.   Any Member State may provide that paragraph 1 shall apply *mutatis mutandis* to the proprietor of an earlier trade mark referred to in Article 4(4)(a) or an other earlier right referred to in Article 4(4)(b) or (c).

3.   In the cases referred to in paragraph 1 and 2, the proprietor of a later registered trade mark shall not be entitled to oppose the use of the earlier right, even though that right may no longer be invoked against the later trade mark.

Article 10   Use of trade marks

1.   If, within a period of five years following the date of the completion of the registration procedure, the proprietor has not put the trade mark to genuine use in the Member State in connection with the goods or services in respect of which it is registered, or if such use has been suspended during an uninterrupted period of five years, the trade mark shall be subject to the sanctions provided for in this Directive, unless there are proper reasons for non-use.

2.   The following shall also constitute use within the meaning of paragraph 1:

   (a)   use of the trade mark in a form differing in elements which do not alter the distinctive character of the mark in the form in which it was registered;

   (b)   affixing of the trade mark to goods or to the packaging thereof in the Member State concerned solely for export purposes.

3.   Use of the trade mark with the consent of the proprietor or by any person who has authority to use a collective mark or a guarantee or certification mark shall be deemed to constitute use by the proprietor.

4.   In relation to trade marks registered before the date on which the provisions necessary to comply with this Directive enter into force in the Member State concerned:

   (a)   where a provision in force prior to that date attaches sanctions to non-use of a trade mark during an uninterrupted period, the relevant period of five years mentioned in paragraph 1 shall be deemed to have begun to run at the same time as any period of non-use which is already running at that date;

   (b)   where there is no use provision in force prior to that date, the periods of five years mentioned in paragraph 1 shall be deemed to run from that date at the earliest.

Article 11   Sanctions for non use of a trade mark in legal or administrative proceedings

1.   A trade mark may not be declared invalid on the ground that there is an earlier conflicting trade mark if the latter does not fulfil the requirements of use set out in Article 10(1), (2) and (3) or in Article 10(4), as the case may be.

2.   Any Member State may provide that registration of a trade mark may not be refused on the ground that there is an earlier conflicting trade mark if the latter does not fulfil the requirements of use set out in Article 10(1), (2) and (3) or in Article 10(4), as the case may be.

3.   Without prejudice to the application of Article 12, where a counter-claim for revocation is made, any Member State may provide that a trade mark may not be successfully invoked in infringement proceedings if it is established as a result of a plea that the trade mark could be revoked pursuant to Article 12(1).

4.   If the earlier trade mark has been used in relation to part only of the goods or services for which it is registered, it shall, for purposes of applying paragraphs 1, 2 and 3, be deemed to be registered in respect only of that part of the goods or services.

Article 12   Grounds for revocation

1.   A trade mark shall be liable to revocation if, within a continuous period of five years, it has not been put to genuine use in the Member State in connection with the goods or services in respect of which it is registered, and there are no proper reasons for non-use; however, no person may claim that the proprietor's rights in a trade mark should be revoked where, during the interval between expiry of the five-year period and filing of the application for revocation, genuine use of the trade mark has been started or resumed; the commencement or resumption of use within a period of three months preceding the filing of the application for revocation which began at the earliest on expiry of the continuous period of five years of non-use, shall, however, be disregarded where preparations for the commencement or resumption occur only after the proprietor becomes aware that the application for revocation may be filed.

2.   A trade mark shall also be liable to revocation if, after the date on which it was registered,

(a)   in consequence of acts or inactivity of the proprietor, it has become the common name in the trade for a product or service in respect of which it is registered;

(b)   in consequence of the use made of it by the proprietor of the trade mark or with his consent in respect of the goods or services for which it is registered, it is liable to mislead the public, particularly as to the nature, quality or geographical origin of those goods or services.

Article 13   Grounds for refusal or revocation or invalidity relating to only some of the goods of services

Where grounds for refusal of registration or for revocation or invalidity of a trade mark exist in respect of only some of the goods or services for which that trade mark has been applied for or registered, refusal of registration or revocation or invalidity shall cover those goods or services only.

Article 14   Establishment *a posteriori* of invalidity or revocation of a trade mark

Where the seniority of an earlier trade mark which has been surrendered or allowed to lapse, is claimed for a Community trade mark, the invalidity or revocation of the earlier trade mark may be established *a posteriori*.

Article 15   Special provisions in respect of collective marks, guarantee marks and certification marks

1.   Without prejudice to Article 4, Member States whose laws authorise the registration of collective marks or of guarantee or certification marks may provide that

such marks shall not be registered, or shall be revoked or declared invalid, on grounds additional to those specified in Articles 3 and 12 where the function of those marks so requires.

2.   By way of derogation from Article 3(1)(c), Member States may provide that signs or indications which may serve, in trade, to designate the geographical origin of the goods or services may constitute collective, guarantee or certification marks. Such a mark does not entitle the proprietor to prohibit a third party from using in the course of trade such signs or indications, provided he uses them in accordance with honest practices in industrial or commercial matters; in particular, such a mark may not be invoked against a third party who is entitled to use a geographical name.

Article 16   National provisions to be adopted pursuant to this Directive

1.   The Member States shall bring into force the laws, regulations and administrative provisions necessary to comply with this Directive not later than 31 December 1992. They shall immediately inform the Commission thereof.

2.   Acting on a proposal from the Commission, the Council, acting by qualified majority, may defer the date referred to in paragraph 1 until 31 December 1992 at the latest.

3.   Member States shall communicate to the Commission the text of the main provisions of national law which they adopt in the field governed by the Directive.

Article 17   Addressees

This Directive is addressed to the Member States.

COUNCIL DIRECTIVE
of 14 May 1991
on the legal protection of computer programs
(91/250/EEC)

THE COUNCIL OF THE EUROPEAN COMMUNITIES,

Having regard to the Treaty establishing the European Economic Community and in particular Article 100a thereof,

Having regard to the proposal from the Commission,

In cooperation with the European Parliament,

Having regard to the opinion of the Economic and Social Committee,

Whereas computer programs are at present not clearly protected in all Member States by existing legislation and such protection, where it exists, has different attributes;

Whereas the development of computer programs requires the investment of considerable human, technical and financial resources while computer programs can be copied at a fraction of the cost needed to develop them independently;

Whereas computer programs are playing an increasingly important role in a broad range of industries and computer program technology can accordingly be considered as being of fundamental importance for the Community's industrial development;

Whereas certain differences in the legal protection of computer programs offered by the laws of the Member States have direct and negative effects on the functioning of the common market as regards computer programs and such differences could well become greater as Member States introduce new legislation on this subject;

Whereas existing differences having such effects need to be removed and new ones prevented from arising, while differences not adversely affecting the functioning of the common market to a substantial degree need not be removed or prevented from arising;

Whereas the Community's legal framework on the protection of computer programs can accordingly in the first instance be limited to establishing that Member States should accord protection to computer programs under copyright law as literary works and, further, to establishing who and what should be protected, the exclusive rights on which protected persons should be able to rely in order to authorise or prohibit certain acts and for how long the protection should apply;

Whereas, for the purpose of this Directive, the term "computer program' shall include programs in any form, including those which are incorporated into hardware; whereas this term also includes preparatory design work leading to the development of a computer program provided that the nature of the preparatory work is such that a computer program can result from it at the later stage;

Whereas, in respect of the criteria to be applied in determining whether or not a computer program is an original work, no tests as to the qualitative or aesthetic merits of the program should be applied;

Whereas the Community is fully committed to the promotion of international standardisation;

Whereas the function of a computer program is to communicate and work together with other components of a computer system and with users and, for this purpose, a logical and, where appropriate, physical interconnection and interaction is required to permit all elements of software and hardware to work with other software and hardware and with users in all the ways in which they are intended to function;

Whereas the parts of the program which provide for such interconnection and interaction between elements of software and hardware are generally known as 'interfaces';

Whereas this functional interconnection and interaction is generally known as "interoperability'; whereas such interoperability can be defined as the ability to exchange information and mutually to use the information which has been exchanged;

Whereas, for the avoidance of doubt, it has to be made clear that only the expression of a computer program is protected and that ideas and principles which underlie any element of a program, including those which underlie its interfaces, are not protected by copyright under this Directive;

Whereas, in accordance with this principle of copyright, to the extent that logic, algorithms and programming languages comprise ideas and principles, those ideas and principles are not protected under this Directive;

Whereas, in accordance with the legislation and jurisprudence of the Member States and the international copyright conventions, the expression of those ideas and principles is to be protected by copyright;

Whereas, for the purposes of this Directive, the term "rental' means the making available for use, for a limited period of time and for profit-making purposes, of a computer program or a copy thereof; whereas this term does not include public lending, which, accordingly, remains outside the scope of this Directive;

Whereas the exclusive rights of the author to prevent the unauthorised reproduction of his work have to be subject to a limited exception in the case of a computer program to allow the reproduction technically necessary for the use of that program by the lawful acquirer;

Whereas this means that the acts of loading and running necessary for the use of a copy of a program which has been lawfully acquired, and the act of correction of its errors, may not be prohibited by contract; whereas, in the absence of specific contractual provisions, including when a copy of the program has been sold, any other act necessary for the use of the copy of a program may be performed in accordance with its intended purpose by a lawful acquirer of that copy;

Whereas a person having a right to use a computer program should not be prevented from performing acts necessary to observe, study or test the functioning of the program, provided that these acts do not infringe the copyright in the program;

Whereas the unauthorised reproduction, translation, adoption or transformation of the form of the code in which a copy of a computer program has been made available constitutes an infringement of the exclusive rights of the author;

Whereas, nevertheless, circumstances may exist when such a reproduction of the code and translation of its form within the meaning of Article 4(a) and (b) are indispensable to obtain the necessary information to achieve the interoperability of an independently created program with other programs;

Whereas it has therefore to be considered that in these limited circumstances only, performance of the acts of reproduction and translation by or on behalf of a person having a right to use a copy of the program is legitimate and compatible with fair practice and must therefore be deemed not to require the authorisation of the rightholder;

Whereas an objective of this exception is to make it possible to connect all components of a computer system, including those of different manufacturers, so that they can work together;

Whereas such an exception to the author's exclusive rights may not be used in a way which prejudices the legitimate interests of the rightholder or which conflicts with a normal exploitation of the program;

Whereas, in order to remain in accordance with the provisions of the Berne Convention for the Protection of Literary and Artistic Works, the term of protection should be the life of the author and fifty years from the first of January of the year following the year of his death or, in the case of an anonymous or pseudonymous work, 50 years from the first of January of the year following the year in which the work is first published;

Whereas protection of computer programs under copyright laws should be without prejudice to the application, in appropriate cases, of other forms of protection; whereas, however, any contractual provisions contrary to Article 6 or to the exceptions provided for in Article 5(2) and (3) should be null and void;

Whereas the provisions of this Directive are without prejudice to the application of the competition rules under Articles 85 and 86 of the Treaty if a dominant supplier refuses to make information available which is necessary for interoperability as defined in this Directive;

Whereas the provisions of this Directive should be without prejudice to specific requirements of Community law already enacted in respect of the publication of interfaces in the telecommunications sector or Council Decisions relating to standardisation in the field of information technology and telecommunication;

Whereas this Directive does not affect derogations provided for under national legislation in accordance with the Berne Convention on points not covered by this Directive,

HAS ADOPTED THIS DIRECTIVE:

Article 1 Object of protection

1. In accordance with the provisions of this Directive, Member States shall protect computer programs, by copyright, as literary works within the meaning of the Berne Convention for the Protection of Literary and Artistic Works. For the purposes of this Directive, the term 'computer programs' shall include their preparatory design material.

2. Protection in accordance with this Directive shall apply to the expression in any form of a computer program. Ideas and principles which underlie any element of a computer program, including those which underlie its interfaces, are not protected by copyright under this Directive.

3. A computer program shall be protected if it is original in the sense that it is the author's own intellectual creation. No other criteria shall be applied to determine its eligibility for protection.

Article 2 Authorship of computer programs

1. The author of a computer program shall be the natural person or group of natural persons who has created the program or, where the legislation of the Member State permits, the legal person designated as the rightholder by that legislation. Where collective works are recognised by the legislation of a Member State, the person

considered by the legislation of the Member State to have created the work shall be deemed to be its author.

2.   In respect of a computer program created by a group of natural persons jointly, the exclusive rights shall be owned jointly.

3.   Where a computer program is created by an employee in the execution of his duties or following the instructions given by his employer, the employer exclusively shall be entitled to exercise all economic rights in the program so created, unless otherwise provided by contract.

Article 3   Beneficiaries of protection

Protection shall be granted to all natural or legal persons eligible under national copyright legislation as applied to literary works.

Article 4   Restricted acts

Subject to the provisions of Articles 5 and 6, the exclusive rights of the rightholder within the meaning of Article 2, shall include the rights to do or to authorise:

(a)   the permanent or temporary reproduction of a computer program by any means and in any form, in part or in whole. Insofar as loading, displaying, running, transmission or storage of the computer program necessitate such reproduction, such acts shall be subject to authorisation by the rightholder;

(b)   the translation, adaptation, arrangement and any other alteration of a computer program and the reproduction of the results thereof, without prejudice to the rights of the person who alters the program;

(c)   any form of distribution to the public, including the rental, of the original computer program or of copies thereof. The first sale in the Community of a copy of a program by the rightholder or with his consent shall exhaust the distribution right within the Community of that copy, with the exception of the right to control further rental of the program or a copy thereof.

Article 5   Exceptions to the restricted acts

1.   In the absence of specific contractual provisions, the acts referred to in Article 4(a) and (b) shall not require authorisation by the rightholder where they are necessary for the use of the computer program by the lawful acquirer in accordance with its intended purpose, including for error correction.

2.   The making of a back-up copy by a person having a right to use the computer program may not be prevented by contract insofar as it is necessary for that use.

3.   The person having a right to use a copy of a computer program shall be entitled, without the authorisation of the rightholder, to observe, study or test the functioning of the program in order to determine the ideas and principles which underlie any element of the program if he does so while performing any of the acts of loading, displaying, running, transmitting or storing the program which he is entitled to do.

Article 6   Decompilation

1.   The authorisation of the rightholder shall not be required where reproduction of the code and translation of its form within the meaning of Article 4(a) and (b) are indispensable to obtain the information necessary to achieve the interoperability of an independently created computer program with other programs, provided that the following conditions are met:

(a)   these acts are performed by the licensee or by another person having a right to use a copy of a program, or on their behalf by a person authorised to do so;

(b)   the information necessary to achieve interoperability has not previously been readily available to the persons referred to in subparagraph (a); and

(c)   these acts are confined to the parts of the original program which are necessary to achieve interoperability.

2. The provisions of paragraph 1 shall not permit the information obtained through its application:

(a) to be used for goals other than to achieve the interoperability of the independently created computer program;

(b) to be given to others, except when necessary for the interoperability of the independently created computer program; or

(c) to be used for the development, production or marketing of a computer program substantially similar in its expression, or for any other act which infringes copyright.

3. In accordance with the provisions of the Berne Convention for the protection of Literary and Artistic Works, the provisions of this Article may not be interpreted in such a way as to allow its application to be used in a manner which unreasonably prejudices the right holder's legitimate interests or conflicts with a normal exploitation of the computer program.

Article 7 Special measures of protection

1. Without prejudice to the provisions of Articles 4, 5 and 6, Member States shall provide, in accordance with their national legislation, appropriate remedies against a person committing any of the acts listed in subparagraphs (a), (b) and (c) below:

(a) any act of putting into circulation a copy of a computer program knowing, or having reason to believe, that it is an infringing copy;

(b) the possession, for commercial purposes, of a copy of a computer program knowing, or having reason to believe, that it is an infringing copy;

(c) any act of putting into circulation, or the possession for commercial purposes of, any means the sole intended purpose of which is to facilitate the unauthorised removal or circumvention of any technical device which may have been applied to protect a computer program.

2. Any infringing copy of a computer program shall be liable to seizure in accordance with the legislation of the Member State concerned.

3. Member States may provide for the seizure of any means referred to in paragraph 1(c).

Article 8 (Repealed)

Article 9 Continued application of other legal provisions

1. The provisions of this Directive shall be without prejudice to any other legal provisions such as those concerning patent rights, trade-marks, unfair competition, trade secrets, protection of semi-conductor products or the law of contract. Any contractual provisions contrary to Article 6 or to the exceptions provided for in Article 5(2) and (3) shall be null and void.

2. The provisions of this Directive shall apply also to programs created before 1 January 1993 without prejudice to any acts concluded and rights acquired before that date.

Article 10 Final provisions

1. Member States shall bring into force the laws, regulations and administrative provisions necessary to comply with this Directive before 1 January 1993.

When Member States adopt these measures, the latter shall contain a reference to this Directive or shall be accompanied by such reference on the occasion of their official publication. The methods of making such a reference shall be laid down by the Member States.

2. Member States shall communicate to the Commission the provisions of national law which they adopt in the field governed by this Directive.

Article 11

This Directive is addressed to the Member States.

COUNCIL DIRECTIVE 92/100/EEC
of 19 November 1992
on rental right and lending right and on certain rights related to copyright in the field of intellectual property

THE COUNCIL OF THE EUROPEAN COMMUNITIES,

Having regard to the Treaty establishing the European Economic Community, and in particular Articles 57(2), 66 and 100a thereof,

Having regard to the proposal from the Commission,

In cooperation with the European Parliament,

Having regard to the opinion of the Economic and Social Committee,

Whereas differences exist in the legal protection provided by the laws and practices of the Member States for copyright works and subject matter of related rights protection as regards rental and lending; whereas such differences are sources of barriers to trade and distortions of competition which impede the achievement and proper functioning of the internal market;

Whereas such differences in legal protection could well become greater as Member States adopt new and different legislation or as national case-law interpreting such legislation develops differently;

Whereas such differences should therefore be eliminated in accordance with the objective of introducing an area without internal frontiers as set out in Article 8a of the Treaty so as to institute, pursuant to Article 3(f) of the Treaty, a system ensuring that competition in the common market is not distorted;

Whereas rental and lending of copyright works and the subject matter of related rights protection is playing an increasingly important role in particular for authors, performers and producers of phonograms and films; whereas piracy is becoming an increasing threat;

Whereas the adequate protection of copyright works and subject matter of related rights protection by rental and lending rights as well as the protection of the subject matter of related rights protection by the fixation right, reproduction right, distribution right, right to broadcast and communication to the public can accordingly be considered as being of fundamental importance for the Community's economic and cultural development;

Whereas copyright and related rights protection must adapt to new economic developments such as new forms of exploitation;

Whereas the creative and artistic work of authors and performers necessitates an adequate income as a basis for further creative and artistic work, and the investments required particularly for the production of phonograms and films are especially high and risky; whereas the possibility for securing that income and recouping that investment can only effectively be guaranteed through adequate legal protection of the rightholders concerned;

Whereas these creative, artistic and entrepreneurial activities are, to a large extent, activities of self-employed persons; whereas the pursuit of such activities must be made easier by providing a harmonised legal protection within the Community;

Whereas, to the extent that the activities principally constitute services, their provision must equally be facilitated by the establishment in the Community of a harmonised legal framework;

Whereas the legislation of the Member States should be approximated in such a way so as not to conflict with the international conventions on which many Member States' copyright and related rights laws are based;

Whereas the Community's legal framework on the rental right and lending right and on certain rights related to copyright can be limited to establishing that Member States provide rights with respect to rental and lending for certain groups of rightholders and further to establishing the rights of fixation, reproduction, distribution, broadcasting and communication to the public for certain groups of rightholders in the field of related rights protection;

Whereas it is necessary to define the concepts of rental and lending for the purposes of this Directive;

Whereas it is desirable, with a view to clarity, to exclude from rental and lending within the meaning of this Directive certain forms of making available, as for instance making available phonograms or films (cinematographic or audiovisual works or moving images, whether or not accompanied by sound) for the purpose of public performance or broadcasting, making available for the purpose of exhibition, or making available for on-the-spot reference use; whereas lending within the meaning of this Directive does not include making available between establishments which are accessible to the public;

Whereas, where lending by an establishment accessible to the public gives rise to a payment the amount of which does not go beyond what is necessary to cover the operating costs of the establishment, there is no direct or indirect economic or commercial advantage within the meaning of this Directive;

Whereas it is necessary to introduce arrangements ensuring that an unwaivable equitable remuneration is obtained by authors and performers who must retain the possibility to entrust the administration of this right to collecting societies representing them;

Whereas the equitable remuneration may be paid on the basis of one or several payments at any time on or after the conclusion of the contract;

Whereas the equitable remuneration must take account of the importance of the contribution of the authors and performers concerned to the phonogram or film;

Whereas it is also necessary to protect the rights at least of authors as regards public lending by providing for specific arrangements; whereas, however, any measures based on Article 5 of this Directive have to comply with Community law, in particular with Article 7 of the Treaty;

Whereas the provisions of Chapter II do not prevent Member States from extending the presumption set out in Article 2(5) to the exclusive rights included in that chapter; whereas furthermore the provisions of Chapter II do not prevent Member States from providing for a rebuttable presumption of the authorisation of exploitation in respect of the exclusive rights of performers provided for in those articles, in so far as such presumption is compatible with the International Convention for the Protection of Performers, Producers of Phonograms and Broadcasting Organisations (hereinafter referred to as the Rome Convention);

Whereas Member States may provide for more far-reaching protection for owners of rights related to copyright than that required by Article 8 of this Directive;

Whereas the harmonised rental and lending rights and the harmonised protection in the field of rights related to copyright should not be exercised in a way which constitutes a disguised restriction on trade between Member States or in a way which is contrary to the rule of media exploitation chronology, as recognised in the Judgment handed down in Société Cinéthèque v FNCF

HAS ADOPTED THIS DIRECTIVE:

CHAPTER I
RENTAL AND LENDING RIGHT

Article 1 Object of harmonisation

1. In accordance with the provisions of this Chapter, Member States shall provide, subject to Article 5, a right to authorise or prohibit the rental and lending of originals and copies of copyright works, and other subject matter as set out in Article 2(1).

2.   For the purposes of this Directive, 'rental' means making available for use, for a limited period of time and for direct or indirect economic or commercial advantage.

3.   For the purposes of this Directive, 'lending' means making available for use, for a limited period of time and not for direct or indirect economic or commercial advantage, when it is made through establishments which are accessible to the public.

4.   The rights referred to in paragraph 1 shall not be exhausted by any sale or other act of distribution of originals and copies of copyright works and other subject matter as set out in Article 2(1).

Article 2   Rightholders and subject matter of rental and lending right

1.   The exclusive right to authorise or prohibit rental and lending shall belong:
— to the author in respect of the original and copies of his work,
— to the performer in respect of fixations of his performance,
— to the phonogram producer in respect of his phonograms, and
— to the producer of the first fixation of a film in respect of the original and copies of his film. For the purposes of this Directive, the term 'film' shall designate a cinematographic or audiovisual work or moving images, whether or not accompanied by sound.

2.   For the purposes of this Directive the principal director of a cinematographic or audiovisual work shall be considered as its author or one of its authors. Member States may provide for others to be considered as its co-authors.

3.   This Directive does not cover rental and lending rights in relation to buildings and to works of applied art.

4.   The rights referred to in paragraph 1 may be transferred, assigned or subject to the granting of contractual licences.

5.   Without prejudice to paragraph 7, when a contract concerning film production is concluded, individually or collectively, by performers with a film producer, the performer covered by this contract shall be presumed, subject to contractual clauses to the contrary, to have transferred his rental right, subject to Article 4.

6.   Member States may provide for a similar presumption as set out in paragraph 5 with respect to authors.

7.   Member States may provide that the signing of a contract concluded between a performer and a film producer concerning the production of a film has the effect of authorising rental, provided that such contract provides for an equitable remuneration within the meaning of Article 4. Member States may also provide that this paragraph shall apply *mutatis mutandis* to the rights included in Chapter II.

Article 3   Rental of computer programs

This Directive shall be without prejudice to Article 4(c) of Council Directive 91/250/EEC of 14 May 1991 on the legal protection of computer programs.

Article 4   Unwaivable right to equitable remuneration

1.   Where an author or performer has transferred or assigned his rental right concerning a phonogram or an original or copy of a film to a phonogram or film producer, that author or performer shall retain the right to obtain an equitable remuneration for the rental.

2.   The right to obtain an equitable remuneration for rental cannot be waived by authors or performers.

3.   The administration of this right to obtain an equitable remuneration may be entrusted to collecting societies representing authors or performers.

4.   Member States may regulate whether and to what extent administration by collecting societies of the right to obtain an equitable remuneration may be imposed, as well as the question from whom this remuneration may be claimed or collected.

Article 5   Derogation from the exclusive public lending right

1.   Member States may derogate from the exclusive right provided for in Article 1 in respect of public lending, provided that at least authors obtain a remuneration for such lending. Member States shall be free to determine this remuneration taking account of their cultural promotion objectives.

2.   When Member States do not apply the exclusive lending right provided for in Article 1 as regards phonograms, films and computer programs, they shall introduce, at least for authors, a remuneration.

3.   Member States may exempt certain categories of establishments from the payment of the remuneration referred to in paragraphs 1 and 2.

4.   The Commission, in cooperation with the Member States, shall draw up before 1 July 1997 a report on public lending in the Community. It shall forward this report to the European Parliament and to the Council.

CHAPTER II
RIGHTS RELATED TO COPYRIGHT

Article 6   Fixation right

1.   Member States shall provide for performers the exclusive right to authorise or prohibit the fixation of their performances.

2.   Member States shall provide for broadcasting organisations the exclusive right to authorise or prohibit the fixation of their broadcasts, whether these broadcasts are transmitted by wire or over the air, including by cable or satellite.

3.   A cable distributor shall not have the right provided for in paragraph 2 where it merely retransmits by cable the broadcasts of broadcasting organisations.

Article 7   Reproduction right

1.   Member States shall provide the exclusive right to authorise or prohibit the direct or indirect reproduction:
— for performers, of fixations of their performances,
— for phonogram producers, of their phonograms,
— for producers of the first fixations of films, in respect of the original and copies of their films, and
— for broadcasting organisations, of fixations of their broadcasts, as set out in Article 6(2).

2.   The reproduction right referred to in paragraph 1 may be transferred, assigned or subject to the granting of contractual licences.

Article 8   Broadcasting and communication to the public

1.   Member States shall provide for performers the exclusive right to authorise or prohibit the broadcasting by wireless means and the communication to the public of their performances, except where the performance is itself already a broadcast performance or is made from a fixation.

2.   Member States shall provide a right in order to ensure that a single equitable remuneration is paid by the user, if a phonogram published for commercial purposes, or a reproduction of such phonogram, is used for broadcasting by wireless means or for any communication to the public, and to ensure that this remuneration is shared between the relevant performers and phonogram producers. Member States may, in the absence of agreement between the performers and phonogram producers, lay down the conditions as to the sharing of this remuneration between them.

3.   Member States shall provide for broadcasting organisations the exclusive right to authorise or prohibit the rebroadcasting of their broadcasts by wireless means, as well as the communication to the public of their broadcasts if such communication is made in places accessible to the public against payment of an entrance fee.

Article 9   Distribution right
1.   Member States shall provide
— for performers, in respect of fixations of their performances,
— for phonogram producers, in respect of their phonograms,
— for producers of the first fixations of films, in respect of the original and copies of their films,
— for broadcasting organisations, in respect of fixations of their broadcast as set out in Article 6(2),
the exclusive right to make available these objects, including copies thereof, to the public by sale or otherwise, hereafter referred to as the 'distribution right'.
2.   The distribution right shall not be exhausted within the Community in respect of an object as referred to in paragraph 1, except where the first sale in the Community of that object is made by the rightholder or with his consent.
3.   The distribution right shall be without prejudice to the specific provisions of Chapter I, in particular Article 1(4).
4.   The distribution right may be transferred, assigned or subject to the granting of contractual licences.

Article 10   Limitations to rights
1.   Member States may provide for limitations to the rights referred to in Chapter II in respect of:
(a)   private use;
(b)   use of short excerpts in connection with the reporting of current events;
(c)   ephemeral fixation by a broadcasting organisation by means of its own facilities and for its own broadcasts;
(d)   use solely for the purposes of teaching or scientific research.
2.   Irrespective of paragraph 1, any Member State may provide for the same kinds of limitations with regard to the protection of performers, producers of phonograms, broadcasting organisations and of producers of the first fixations of films, as it provides for in connection with the protection of copyright in literary and artistic works. However, compulsory licences may be provided for ony to the extent to which they are compatible with the Rome Convention.
3.   Paragraph 1(a) shall be without prejudice to any existing or future legislation on remuneration for reproduction for private use.

CHAPTER III
DURATION

Article 11   (Repealed)

Article 12   (Repealed)

CHAPTER IV
COMMON PROVISIONS

Article 13   Application in time
1.   This Directive shall apply in respect of all copyright works, performances, phonograms, broadcasts and first fixations of films referred to in this Directive which are, on 1 July 1994, still protected by the legislation of the Member States in the field of copyright and related rights or meet the criteria for protection under the provisions of this Directive on that date.
2.   This Directive shall apply without prejudice to any acts of exploitation performed before 1 July 1994.
3.   Member States may provide that the rightholders are deemed to have given their authorisation to the rental or lending of an object referred to in Article 2(1) which is proven to have been made available to third parties for this purpose or to have been

acquired before 1 July 1994. However, in particular where such an object is a digital recording, Member States may provide that rightholders shall have a right to obtain an adequate remuneration for the rental or lending of the object.

4.   Member States need not apply the provisions of Article 2(2) to cinematographic or audiovisual works created before 1 July 1994.

5.   Member States may determine the date as from which the Article 2(2) shall apply, provided that that date is no later than 1 July 1997.

6.   This Directive shall, without prejudice to paragraph 3 and subject to paragraphs 8 and 9, not affect any contracts concluded before the date of its adoption.

7.   Member States may provide, subject to the provisions of paragraphs 8 and 9, that when rightholders who acquire new rights under the national provisions adopted in implementation of this Directive have, before 1 July 1994, given their consent for exploitation, they shall be presumed to have transferred the new exclusive rights.

8.   Member States may determine the date as from which the unwaivable right to an equitable remuneration referred to in Article 4 exists, provided that that date is no later than 1 July 1997.

9.   For contracts concluded before 1 July 1994, the unwaivable right to an equitable remuneration provided for in Article 4 shall apply only where authors or performers or those representing them have submitted a request to that effect before 1 January 1997. In the absence of agreement between rightholders concerning the level of remuneration, Member States may fix the level of equitable remuneration.

Article 14   Relation between copyright and related rights
Protection of copyright-related rights under this Directive shall leave intact and shall in no way affect the protection of copyright.

Article 15   Final provisions
1.   Member States shall bring into force the laws, regulations and administrative provisions necessary to comply with this Directive not later than 1 July 1994. They shall forthwith inform the Commission thereof.

When Member States adopt these measures, they shall contain a reference to this Directive or shall be accompanied by such reference at the time of their official publication. The methods of making such a reference shall be laid down by the Member States.

2.   Member States shall communicate to the Commission the main provisions of domestic law which they adopt in the field covered by this Directive.

Article 16
This Directive is addressed to the Member States.

COUNCIL DIRECTIVE 93/83/EEC
of 27 September 1993
on the coordination of certain rules concerning copyright and rights related to copyright applicable to satellite broadcasting and cable retransmission

THE COUNCIL OF THE EUROPEAN COMMUNITIES,

Having regard to the Treaty establishing the European Economic Community, and in particular Articles 57(2) and 66 thereof,

Having regard to the proposal from the Commission,

In cooperation with the European Parliament,

Having regard to the opinion of the Economic and Social Committee,

(1)   Whereas the objectives of the Community as laid down in the Treaty include establishing an ever closer union among the peoples of Europe, fostering closer relations between the States belonging to the Community and ensuring the economic and social progress of the Community countries by common action to eliminate the barriers which divide Europe;

(2)   Whereas, to that end, the Treaty provides for the establishment of a common market and an area without internal frontiers; whereas measures to achieve this include the abolition of obstacles to the free movement of services and the institution of a system ensuring that competition in the common market is not distorted; whereas, to that end, the Council may adopt directives for the coordination of the provisions laid down by law, regulation or administrative action in Member States concerning the taking up and pursuit of activities as self-employed persons;

(3)   Whereas broadcasts transmitted across frontiers within the Community, in particular by satellite and cable, are one of the most important ways of pursuing these Community objectives, which are at the same time political, economic, social, cultural and legal;

(4)   Whereas the Council has already adopted Directive 89/552/EEC of 3 October 1989 on the coordination of certain provisions laid down by law, regulation or administrative action in Member States concerning the pursuit of television broadcasting activities which makes provision for the promotion of the distribution and production of European television programmes and for advertising and sponsorship, the protection of minors and the right of reply;

(5)   Whereas, however, the achievement of these objectives in respect of cross-border satellite broadcasting and the cable retransmission of programmes from other Member States is currently still obstructed by a series of differences between national rules of copyright and some degree of legal uncertainty; whereas this means that holders of rights are exposed to the threat of seeing their works exploited without payment of remuneration or that the individual holders of exclusive rights in various Member States block the exploitation of their rights; whereas the legal uncertainty in particular constitutes a direct obstacle in the free circulation of programmes within the Community;

(6)   Whereas a distinction is currently drawn for copyright purposes between communication to the public by direct satellite and communication to the public by communications satellite; whereas, since individual reception is possible and affordable nowadays with both types of satellite, there is no longer any justification for this differing legal treatment;

(7)   Whereas the free broadcasting of programmes is further impeded by the current legal uncertainty over whether broadcasting by a satellite whose signals can be received directly affects the rights in the country of transmission only or in all countries of reception together; whereas, since communications satellites and direct satellites are treated alike for copyright purposes, this legal uncertainty now affects almost all programmes broadcast in the Community by satellite;

(8)   Whereas, furthermore, legal certainty, which is a prerequisite for the free movement of broadcasts within the Community, is missing where programmes transmitted across frontiers are fed into and retransmitted through cable networks;

(9)   Whereas the development of the acquisition of rights on a contractual basis by authorisation is already making a vigorous contribution to the creation of the desired European audiovisual area; whereas the continuation of such contractual agreements should be ensured and their smooth application in practice should be promoted wherever possible;

(10)   Whereas at present cable operators in particular cannot be sure that they have actually acquired all the programme rights covered by such an agreement;

(11)   Whereas, lastly, parties in different Member States are not all similarly bound by obligations which prevent them from refusing without valid reasons to negotiate on the acquisition of the rights necessary for cable distribution or allowing such negotiations to fail;

(12)   Whereas the legal framework for the creation of a single audiovisual area laid down in Directive 89/552/EEC must, therefore, be supplemented with reference to copyright;

(13)   Whereas, therefore, an end should be put to the differences of treatment of the transmission of programmes by communications satellite which exist in the Member States, so that the vital distinction throughout the Community becomes whether works and other protected subject matter are communicated to the public; whereas this will also ensure equal treatment of the suppliers of cross-border broadcasts, regardless of whether they use a direct broadcasting satellite or a communications satellite;

(14)   Whereas the legal uncertainty regarding the rights to be acquired which impedes cross-border satellite broadcasting should be overcome by defining the notion of communication to the public by satellite at a Community level; whereas this definition should at the same time specify where the act of communication takes place; whereas such a definition is necessary to avoid the cumulative application of several national laws to one single act of broadcasting; whereas communication to the public by satellite occurs only when, and in the Member State where, the programme-carrying signals are introduced under the control and responsibility of the broadcasting organisation into an uninterrupted chain of communication leading to the satellite and down towards the earth; whereas normal technical procedures relating to the pro-gramme-carrying signals should not be considered as interruptions to the chain of broadcasting;

(15)   Whereas the acquisition on a contractual basis of exclusive broadcasting rights should comply with any legislation on copyright and rights related to copyright in the Member State in which communication to the public by satellite occurs;

(16)   Whereas the principle of contractual freedom on which the Directive is based will make it possible to continue limiting the exploitation of these rights, especially as far as certain technical means of transmission or certain language versions are concerned;

(17)   Whereas, in arriving at the amount of the payment to be made for the rights acquired, the parties should take account of all aspects of the broadcast, such as the actual audience, the potential audience and the language version;

(18)   Whereas the application of the country-of-origin principle contained in this Directive could pose a problem with regard to existing contracts; whereas this Directive should provide for a period of five years for existing contracts to be adapted, where necessary, in the light of the Directive; whereas the said country-of-origin principle should not, therefore, apply to existing contracts which expire before 1 January 2000; whereas if by that date parties still have an interest in the contract, the same parties should be entitled to renegotiate the conditions of the contract;

(19)   Whereas existing international co-production agreements must be interpreted in the light of the economic purpose and scope envisaged by the parties upon signature; whereas in the past international co-production agreements have often not expressly and specifically addressed communication to the public by satellite within the meaning of this Directive a particular form of exploitation; whereas the underlying philosophy of many existing international co-production agreements is that the rights in the co-production are exercised separately and independently by each co-producer, by dividing the exploitation rights between them along territorial lines; whereas, as a general rule, in the situation where a communication to the public by satellite authorised by one co-producer would prejudice the value of the exploitation rights of another co-producer, the interpretation of such an existing agreement would normally suggest that the latter co-producer would have to give his consent to the authorisation, by the former co-producer, of the communication to the public by satellite; whereas the language exclusivity of the latter co-producer will be prejudiced where the language version or versions of the communication to the public, including where the version is dubbed or subtitled, coincide(s) with the language or the languages widely understood in the territory allotted by the agreement to the latter co-producer; whereas the notion of exclusivity should be understood in a wider sense where the communication to the public by satellite concerns a work which consists merely of images and contains no

dialogue or subtitles; whereas a clear rule is necessary in cases where the international co-production agreement does not expressly regulate the division of rights in the specific case of communication to the public by satellite within the meaning of this Directive;

(20)   Whereas communications to the public by satellite from non-member countries will under certain conditions be deemed to occur within a Member State of the Community;

(21)   Whereas it is necessary to ensure that protection for authors, performers, producers of phonograms and broadcasting organisations is accorded in all Member States and that this protection is not subject to a statutory licence system; whereas only in this way is it possible to ensure that any difference in the level of protection within the common market will not create distortions of competition;

(22)   Whereas the advent of new technologies is likely to have an impact on both the quality and the quantity of the exploitation of works and other subject matter;

(23)   Whereas in the light of these developments the level of protection granted pursuant to this Directive to all rightholders in the areas covered by this Directive should remain under consideration;

(24)   Whereas the harmonisation of legislation envisaged in this Directive entails the harmonisation of the provisions ensuring a high level of protection of authors, performers, phonogram producers and broadcasting organisations; whereas this harmonisation should not allow a broadcasting organisation to take advantage of differences in levels of protection by relocating activities, to the detriment of audiovisual productions;

(25)   Whereas the protection provided for rights related to copyright should be aligned on that contained in Council Directive 92/100/EEC of 19 November 1992 on rental right and lending right and on certain rights related to copyright in the field of intellectual property for the purposes of communication to the public by satellite; whereas, in particular, this will ensure that performers and phonogram producers are guaranteed an appropriate remuneration for the communication to the public by satellite of their performances or phonograms;

(26)   Whereas the provisions of Article 4 do not prevent Member States from extending the presumption set out in Article 2(5) of Directive 92/100/EEC to the exclusive rights referred to in Article 4; whereas, furthermore, the provisions of Article 4 do not prevent Member States from providing for a rebuttable presumption of the authorisation of exploitation in respect of the exclusive rights of performers referred to in that Article, in so far as such presumption is compatible with the International Convention for the Protection of Performers, Producers of Phonograms and Broadcasting Organisations;

(27)   Whereas the cable retransmission of programmes from other Member States in an act subject to copyright and, as the case may be, rights related to copyright; whereas the cable operator must, therefore, obtain the authorisation from every holder of rights in each part of the programme retransmitted; whereas, pursuant to this Directive, the authorisations should be granted contractually unless a temporary exception is provided for in the case of existing legal licence schemes;

(28)   Whereas, in order to ensure that the smooth operation of contractual arrangements is not called into question by the intervention of outsiders holding rights in individual parts of the programme, provision should be made, through the obligation to have recourse to a collecting society, for the exclusive collective exercise of the authorisation right to the extent that this is required by the special features of cable retransmission; whereas the authorisation right as such remains intact and only the exercise of this right is regulated to some extent, so that the right to authorise a cable retransmission can still be assigned; whereas this Directive does not affect the exercise of moral rights;

(29)   Whereas the exemption provided for in Article 10 should not limit the choice of holders of rights to transfer their rights to a collecting society and thereby have a direct share in the remuneration paid by the cable distributor for cable retransmission;

(30)   Whereas contractual arrangements regarding the authorisation of cable retransmission should be promoted by additional measures; whereas a party seeking the conclusion of a general contract should, for its part, be obliged to submit collective proposals for an agreement; whereas, furthermore, any party shall be entitled, at any moment, to call upon the assistance of impartial mediators whose task is to assist negotiations and who may submit proposals; whereas any such proposals and any opposition thereto should be served on the parties concerned in accordance with the applicable rules concerning the service of legal documents, in particular as set out in existing international conventions; whereas, finally, it is necessary to ensure that the negotiations are not blocked without valid justification or that individual holders are not prevented without valid justification from taking part in the negotiations; whereas none of these measures for the promotion of the acquisition of rights calls into question the contractual nature of the acquisition of cable retransmission rights;

(31)   Whereas for a transitional period Member States should be allowed to retain existing bodies with jurisdiction in their territory over cases where the right to retransmit a programme by cable to the public has been unreasonably refused or offered on unreasonable terms by a broadcasting organisation; whereas it is understood that the right of parties concerned to be heard by the body should be guaranteed and that the existence of the body should not prevent the parties concerned from having normal access to the courts;

(32)   Whereas, however, Community rules are not needed to deal with all of those matters, the effects of which perhaps with some commercially insignificant expectations, are felt only inside the borders of a single Member State;

(33)   Whereas minimum rules should be laid down in order to establish and guarantee free and uninterrupted cross-border broadcasting by satellite and simultaneous, unaltered cable retransmission of programmes broadcast from other Member States, on an essentially contractual basis;

(34)   Whereas this Directive should not prejudice further harmonisation in the field of copyright and rights related to copyright and the collective administration of such rights; whereas the possibility for Member States to regulate the activities of collecting societies should not prejudice the freedom of contractual negotiation of the rights provided for in this Directive, on the understanding that such negotiation takes place within the framework of general or specific national rules with regard to competition law or the prevention of abuse of monopolies;

(35)   Whereas it should, therefore, be for the Member States to supplement the general provisions needed to achieve the objectives of this Directive by taking legislative and administrative measures in their domestic law, provided that these do not run counter to the objectives of this Directive and are compatible with Community law;

(36)   Whereas this Directive does not affect the applicability of the competition rules in Articles 85 and 86 of the Treaty,

HAS ADOPTED THIS DIRECTIVE:

CHAPTER I
DEFINITIONS

Article 1   Definitions
1.   For the purpose of this Directive, 'satellite' means any satellite operating on frequency bands which, under telecommunications law, are reserved for the broadcast of signals for reception by the public or which are reserved for closed, point-to-point

communication. In the latter case, however, the circumstances in which individual reception of the signals takes place must be comparable to those which apply in the first case.

2. (a)   For the purpose of this Directive, 'communication to the public by satellite' means the act of introducing, under the control and responsibility of the broadcasting organisation, the programme-carrying signals intended for reception by the public into an uninterrupted chain of communication leading to the satellite and down towards the earth.

(b)   The act of communication to the public by satellite occurs solely in the Member State where, under the control and responsibility of the broadcasting organisation, the programme-carrying signals are introduced into an uninterrupted chain of communication leading to the satellite and down towards the earth.

(c)   If the programme-carrying signals are encrypted, then there is communication to the public by satellite on condition that the means for decrypting the broadcast are provided to the public by the broadcasting organisation or with its consent.

(d)   Where an act of communication to the public by satellite occurs in a non-Community State which does not provide the level of protection provided for under Chapter II,

(i)   if the programme-carrying signals are transmitted to the satellite from an uplink situation situated in a Member State, that act of communication to the public by satellite shall be deemed to have occurred in that Member State and the rights provided for under Chapter II shall be exercisable against the person operating the uplink station; or

(ii)   if there is no use of an uplink station situated in a Member State but a broadcasting organisation established in a Member State has commissioned the act of communication to the public by satellite, that act shall be deemed to have occurred in the Member State in which the broadcasting organisation has its principal establishment in the Community and the rights provided for under Chapter II shall be exercisable against the broadcasting organisation.

3.   For the purposes of this Directive, 'cable retransmission' means the simultaneous, unaltered and unabridged retransmission by a cable or microwave system for reception by the public of an initial transmission from another Member State, by wire or over the air, including that by satellite, of television or radio programmes intended for reception by the public.

4.   For the purposes of this Directive 'collecting society' means any organisation which manages or administers copyright or rights related to copyright as its sole purpose or as one of its main purposes.

5.   For the purposes of this Directive, the principal director of a cinematographic or audiovisual work shall be considered as its author or one of its authors. Member States may provide for others to be considered as its co-authors.

CHAPTER II
BROADCASTING OF PROGRAMMES BY SATELLITE

Article 2   Broadcasting right
Member States shall provide an exclusive right for the author to authorise the communication to the public by satellite of copyright works, subject to the provisions set out in this chapter.

Article 3   Acquisition of broadcasting rights
1.   Member States shall ensure that the authorisation referred to in Article 2 may be acquired only by agreement.

2.   A Member State may provide that a collective agreement between a collecting society and a broadcasting organisation concerning a given category of works may be

extended to rightholders of the same category who are not represented by the collecting society, provided that:

— the communication to the public by satellite simulcasts a terrestrial broadcast by the same broadcaster, and

— the unrepresented rightholder shall, at any time, have the possibility of excluding the extension of the collective agreement to his works and of exercising his rights either individually or collectively.

3. Paragraph 2 shall not apply to cinematographic works, including works created by a process analogous to cinematography.

4. Where the law of a Member State provides for the extension of a collective agreement in accordance with the provisions of paragraph 2, that Member States shall inform the Commission which broadcasting organisations are entitled to avail themselves of that law. The Commission shall publish this information in the *Official Journal of the European Communities* (C series).

Article 4   Rights of performers, phonogram producers and broadcasting organisations

1. For the purposes of communication to the public by satellite, the rights of performers, phonogram producers and broadcasting organisations shall be protected in accordance with the provisions of Articles 6, 7, 8 and 10 of Directive 92/100/EEC.

2. For the purposes of paragraph 1, 'broadcasting by wireless means' in Directive 92/100/EEC shall be understood as including communication to the public by satellite.

3. With regard to the exercise of the rights referred to in paragraph 1, Articles 2(7) and 12 of Directive 92/100/EC shall apply.

Article 5   Relation between copyright and related rights

Protection of copyright-related rights under this Directive shall leave intact and shall in no way affect the protection of copyright.

Article 6   Minimum protection

1. Member States may provide for more far-reaching protection for holders of rights related to copyright than that required by Article 8 of Directive 92/100/EEC.

2. In applying paragraph 1 Member States shall observe the definitions contained in Article 1(1) and (2).

Article 7   Transitional provisions

1. With regard to the application in time of the rights referred to in Article 4(1) of this Directive, Article 13(1), (2), (6) and (7) of Directive 92/100/EEC shall apply. Article 13(4) and (5) of Directive 92/100/EEC shall apply *mutatis mutandis*.

2. Agreements concerning the exploitation of works and other protected subject matter which are in force on the date mentioned in Article 14(1) shall be subject to the provisions of Articles 1(2), 2 and 3 as from 1 January 2000 if they expire after that date.

3. When an international co-production agreement concluded before the date mentioned in Article 14(1) between a co-producer from a Member State and one or more co-producers from other Member States or third countries expressly provides for a system of division of exploitation rights between the co-producers by geographical areas for all means of communication to the public, without distinguishing the arrangement applicable to communication to the public by satellite from the provisions applicable to the other means of communication, and where communication to the public by satellite of the co-production would prejudice the exclusivity, in particular the language exclusivity, of one of the co-producers or his assignees in a given territory, the authorisation by one of the co-producers or his assignees for a communication to the public by satellite shall require the prior consent of the holder of that exclusivity, whether co-producer or assignee.

CHAPTER III
CABLE RETRANSMISSION

Article 8   Cable retransmission right

1.   Member States shall ensure that when programmes from other Member States are retransmitted by cable in their territory the applicable copyright and related rights are observed and that such retransmission takes place on the basis of individual or collective contractual agreements between copyright owners, holders or related rights and cable operators.

2.   Notwithstanding paragraph 1, Member States may retain until 31 December 1997 such statutory licence systems which are in operation or expressly provided for by national law on 31 July 1991.

Article 9   Exercise of the cable retransmission right

1.   Member States shall ensure that the right of copyright owners and holders or related rights to grant or refuse authorisation to a cable operator for a cable retransmission may be exercised only through a collecting society.

2.   Where a rightholder has not transferred the management of his rights to a collecting society, the collecting society which manages rights of the same category shall be deemed to be mandated to manage his rights. Where more than one collecting society manages rights of that category, the rightholder shall be free to choose which of those collecting societies is deemed to be mandated to manage his rights. A rightholder referred to in this paragraph shall have the same rights and obligations resulting from the agreement between the cable operator and the collecting society which is deemed to be mandated to manage his rights as the rightholders who have mandated that collecting society and he shall be able to claim those rights within a period, to be fixed by the Member State concerned, which shall not be shorter than three years from the date of the cable retransmission which includes his work or other protected subject matter.

3.   A Member State may provide that, when a rightholder authorises the initial transmission within its territory of a work or other protected subject matter, he shall be deemed to have agreed not to exercise his cable retransmission rights on an individual basis but to exercise them in accordance with the provisions of this Directive.

Article 10   Exercise of the cable retransmission right by broadcasting organisations

Member States shall ensure that Article 9 does not apply to the rights exercised by a broadcasting organisation in respect of its own transmission, irrespective of whether the rights concerned are its own or have been transferred to it by other copyright owners and/or holders of related rights.

Article 11   Mediators

1.   Where no agreement is concluded regarding authorisation of the cable retransmission of a broadcast. Member States shall ensure that either party may call upon the assistance of one or more mediators.

2.   The task of the mediators shall be to provide assistance with negotiation. They may also submit proposals to the parties.

3.   It shall be assumed that all the parties accept a proposal as referred to in paragraph 2 if none of them expresses its opposition within a period of three months. Notice of the proposal and of any opposition thereto shall be served on the parties concerned in accordance with the applicable rules concerning the service of legal documents.

4.   The mediators shall be so selected that their independence and impartiality are beyond reasonable doubt.

Article 12   Prevention of the abuse of negotiating positions
   1.   Member States shall ensure by means of civil or administrative law, as appropriate, that the parties enter and conduct negotiations regarding authorisation for cable retransmission in good faith and do not prevent or hinder negotiation without valid justification.
   2.   A Member State which, on the date mentioned in Article 14(1), has a body with jurisdiction in its territory over cases where the right to retransmit a programme by cable to the public in the Member State has been unreasonably refused or offered on unreasonable terms by a broadcasting organisation may retain that body.
   3.   Paragraph 2 shall apply for a transitional period of eight years from the date mentioned in Article 14(1).

CHAPTER IV
GENERAL PROVISIONS

Article 13   Collective administration of rights
This Directive shall be without prejudice to the regulation of the activities of collecting societies by the Member States.

Article 14   Final provisions
   1.   Member States shall bring into force the laws, regulations and administrative provisions necessary to comply with this Directive before 1 January 1995. They shall immediately inform the Commission thereof.
   When Member States adopt these measures, the latter shall contain a reference to this Directive or shall be accompanied by such reference at the time of their official publication. The methods of making such a reference shall be laid down by the Member States.
   2.   Member States shall communicate to the Commission the provisions of national law which they adopt in the field covered by this Directive.
   3.   Not later than 1 January 2000, the Commission shall submit to the European Parliament, the Council and the Economic and Social Committee a report on the application of this Directive and, if necessary, make further proposals to adapt it to developments in the audio and audiovisual sector.

Article 15
This Directive is addressed to the Member States.

COUNCIL DIRECTIVE 93/98/EEC
of 29 October 1993
harmonising the term of protection of copyright and certain related rights

THE COUNCIL OF THE EUROPEAN COMMUNITIES,
   Having regard to the Treaty establishing the European Economic Community, and in particular Articles 57(2), 66 and 100a thereof,
   Having regard to the proposal from the Commission,
   In cooperation with the European Parliament,
   Having regard to the opinion of the Economic and Social Committee,
   (1)   Whereas the Berne Convention for the protection of literary and artistic works and the International Convention for the protection of performers, producers of phonograms and broadcasting organisations (Rome Convention) lay down only minimum terms of protection of the rights they refer to, leaving the Contracting States free to grant longer terms; whereas certain Member States have exercised this entitlement; whereas in addition certain Member States have not become party to the Rome Convention;

(2)   Whereas there are consequently differences between the national laws governing the terms of protection of copyright and related rights, which are liable to impede the free movement of goods and freedom to provide services, and to distort competition in the common market; whereas therefore with a view to the smooth operation of the internal market, the laws of the Member States should be harmonised so as to make terms of protection identical throughout the Community;

(3)   Whereas harmonisation must cover not ony the terms of protection as such, but also certain implementing arrangements such as the date from which each term of protection is calculated;

(4)   Whereas the provisions of this Directive do not affect the application by the Member States of the provisions of Article 14a(2)(b), (c) and (d) and (3) of the Berne Convention;

(5)   Whereas the minimum term of protection laid down by the Berne Convention, namely the life of the author and 50 years after his death, was intended to provide protection for the author and the first two generations of his descendants; whereas the average lifespan in the Community has grown longer, to the point where this term is no longer sufficient to cover two generations;

(6)   Whereas certain Member States have granted a term longer than 50 years after the death of the author in order to offset the effects of the world wars on the exploitation of authors' works;

(7)   Whereas for the protection of related rights certain Member States have introduced a term of 50 years after lawful publication or lawful communication to the public;

(8)   Whereas under the Community position adopted for the Uruguay Round negotiations under the General Agreement on Tariffs and Trade (GATT) the term of protection for producers of phonograms should be 50 years after first publication;

(9)   Whereas due regard for established rights is one of the general principles of law protected by the Community legal order; whereas, therefore, a harmonisation of the terms of protection of copyright and related rights cannot have the effect of reducing the protection currently enjoyed by rightholders in the Community; whereas in order to keep the effects of transitional measures to a minimum and to allow the internal market to operate in practice, the harmonisation of the term of protection should take place on a long term basis;

(10)   Whereas in its communication of 17 January 1991 'Follow-up to the Green Paper — Working programme of the Commission in the field of copyright and neighbouring rights' the Commission stresses the need to harmonise copyright and neighbouring rights at a high level of protection since these rights are fundamental to intellectual creation and stresses that their protection ensures the maintenance and development of creativity in the interest of authors, cultural industries, consumers and society as a whole;

(11)   Whereas in order to establish a high level of protection which at the same time meets the requirements of the internal market and the need to establish a legal environment conducive to the harmonious development of literary and artistic creation in the Community, the term of protection for copyright should be harmonised at 70 years after the death of the author or 70 years after the work is lawfully made available to the public, and for related rights at 50 years after the event which sets the term running;

(12)   Whereas collections are protected according to Article 2(5) of the Berne Convention when, by reason of the selection and arrangement of their content, they constitute intellectual creations; whereas those works are protected as such, without prejudice to the copyright in each of the works forming part of such collections, whereas in consequence specific terms of protection may apply to works included in collections;

(13)   Whereas in all cases where one or more physical persons are identified as authors the term of protection should be calculated after their death; whereas the

question of authorship in the whole or a part of a work is a question of fact which the national courts may have to decide;

(14)   Whereas terms of protection should be calculated from the first day of January of the year following the relevant event, as they are in the Berne and Rome Conventions;

(15)   Whereas Article 1 of Council Directive 91/250/EEC of 14 May 1991 on the legal protection of computer programs provides that Member States are to protect computer programs, by copyright, as literary works within the meaning of the Berne Convention; whereas this Directive harmonises the term of protection of literary works in the Community; whereas Article 8 of Directive 91/250/EEC, which merely makes provisional arrangements governing the term of protection of computer programs, should accordingly be repealed;

(16)   Whereas Articles 11 and 12 of Council Directive 92/100/EEC of 19 November 1992 on rental right and lending right and on certain rights related to copyright in the field of intellectual property make provision for minimum terms of protection only, subject to any further harmonisation; whereas this Directive provides such further harmonisation; whereas these Articles should accordingly be repealed;

(17)   Whereas the protection of photographs in the Member States is the subject of varying regimes; whereas in order to achieve a sufficient harmonisation of the term of protection of photographic works, in particular of those which, due to their artistic or professional character, are of importance within the internal market, it is necessary to define the level of originality required in this Directive; whereas a photographic work within the meaning of the Berne Convention is to be considered original if it is the author's own intellectual creation reflecting his personality, no other criteria such as merit or purpose being taken into account; whereas the protection of other photographs should be left to national law;

(18)   Whereas, in order to avoid differences in the term of protection as regards related rights it is necessary to provide the same starting point for the calculation of the term throughout the Community; whereas the performance, fixation, transmission, lawful publication, and lawful communication to the public, that is to say the means of making a subject of a related right perceptible in all appropriate ways to persons in general, should be taken into account for the calculation of the term of protection regardless of the country where this performance, fixation, transmission, lawful publication, or lawful communication to the public takes place;

(19)   Whereas the rights of broadcasting organisations in their broadcasts, whether these broadcasts are transmitted by wire or over the air, including by cable or satellite, should not be perpetual; whereas it is therefore necessary to have the term of protection running from the first transmission of a particular broadcast only; whereas this provision is understood to avoid a new term running in cases where a broadcast is identical to a previous one;

(20)   Whereas the Member States should remain free to maintain or introduce other rights related to copyright in particular in relation to the protection of critical and scientific publications; whereas, in order to ensure transparency at Community level, it is however necessary for Member States which introduce new related rights to notify the Commission;

(21)   Whereas it is useful to make clear that the harmonisation brought about by this Directive does not apply to moral rights;

(22)   Whereas, for works whose country of origin within the meaning of the Berne Convention is a third country and whose author is not a Community national, comparison of terms of protection should be applied, provided that the term accorded in the Community does not exceed the term laid down in this Directive;

(23)   Whereas where a rightholder who is not a Community national qualifies for protection under an international agreement the term of protection of related rights

should be the same as that laid down in this Directive, except that it should not exceed that fixed in the country of which the right-holder is a national;

(24)   Wheras comparison of terms should not result in Member States being brought into conflict with their international obligations;

(25)   Whereas, for the smooth functioning of the internal market this Directive should be applied as from 1 July 1995;

(26)   Whereas Member States should remain free to adopt provisions on the interpretation, adaptation and further execution of contracts on the exploitation of protected works and other subject matter which were concluded before the extension of the term of protection resulting from this Directive;

(27)   Whereas respect of acquired rights and legitimate expectations is part of the Community legal order; whereas Member States may provide in particular that in certain circumstances the copyright and related rights which are revived pursuant to this Directive may not give rise to payments by persons who undertook in good faith the exploitation of the works at the time when such works lay within the public domain,

HAS ADOPTED THIS DIRECTIVE:

Article 1   Duration of authors' rights

1.   The rights of an author of a literary or artistic work within the meaning of Article 2 of the Berne Convention shall run for the life of the author and for 70 years after his death, irrespective of the date when the work is lawfully made available to the public.

2.   In the case of a work of joint authorship the term referred to in paragraph 1 shall be calculated from the death of the last surviving author.

3.   In the case of anonymous or pseudonymous works, the term of protection shall run for seventy years after the work is lawfully made available to the public. However, when the pseudonym adopted by the author leaves no doubt as to his identity, or if the author discloses his identity during the period referred to in the first sentence, the term of protection applicable shall be that laid down in paragraph 1.

4.   Where a Member State provides for particular provisions on copyright in respect of collective works or for a legal person to be designated as the rightholder, the term of protection shall be calculated according to the provisions of paragraph 3, except if the natural persons who have created the work as such are identified as such in the versions of the work which are made available to the public. This paragraph is without prejudice to the rights of identified authors whose identifiable contributions are included in such works, to which contributions paragraph 1 or 2 shall apply.

5.   Where a work is published in volumes, parts, instalments, issues or episodes and the term of protection runs from the time when the work was lawfully made available to the public, the term of protection shall run for each such item separately.

6.   In the case of works for which the term of protection is not calculated from the death of the author or authors and which have not been lawfully made available to the public within seventy years from their creation, the protection shall terminate.

Article 2   Cinematographic or audiovisual works

1.   The principal director of a cinematographic or audiovisual work shall be considered as its author or one of its authors. Member States shall be free to designate other co-authors.

2.   The term of protection of cinematographic or audiovisual works shall expire 70 years after the death of the last of the following persons to survive, whether or not these persons are designated as co-authors: the principal director, the author of the screenplay, the author of the dialogue and the composer of music specifically created for use in the cinematographic or audiovisual work.

Article 3   Duration of related rights

1.   The rights of performers shall expire 50 years after the date of the performance. However, if a fixation of the performance is lawfully published or lawfully com-

municated to the public within this period, the rights shall expire 50 years from the date of the first such publication or the first such communication to the public, whichever is the earlier.

2.   The rights of producers of phonograms shall expire 50 years after the fixation is made. However, if the phonogram is lawfully published or lawfully communicated to the public during this period, the rights shall expire 50 years from the date of the first such publication or the first such communication to the public, whichever is the earlier.

3.   The rights of producers of the first fixation of a film shall expire 50 years after the fixation is made. However, if the film is lawfully published or lawfully communicated to the public during this period, the rights shall expire 50 years from the date of the first such publication or the first such communication to the public, whichever is the earlier. The term 'film' shall designate a cinematographic or audiovisual work or moving images, whether or not accompanied by sound.

4.   The rights of broadcasting organisations shall expire 50 years after the first transmission of a broadcast, whether this broadcast is transmitted by wire or over the air, including by cable or satellite.

Article 4   Protection of previously unpublished works

Any person who, after the expiry of copyright protection, for the first time lawfully publishes or lawfully communicates to the public a previously unpublished work, shall benefit from a protection equivalent to the economic rights of the author. The term of protection of such rights shall be 25 years from the time when the work was first lawfully published or lawfully communicated to the public.

Article 5   Critical and scientific publications

Member States may protect critical and scientific publications of works which have come into the public domain. The maximum term of protection of such rights shall be 30 years from the time when the publication was first lawfully published.

Article 6   Protection of photographs

Photographs which are original in the sense that they are the author's own intellectual creation shall be protected in accordance with Article 1. No other criteria shall be applied to determine their eligibility for protection. Member States may provide for the protection of other photographs.

Article 7   Protection *vis-à-vis* third countries

1   Where the country of origin of a work, within the meaning of the Berne Convention, is a third country, and the author of the work is not a Community national, the term of protection granted by the Member States shall expire on the date of expiry of the protection granted in the country of origin of the work, but may not exceed the term laid down in Article 1.

2.   The terms of protection laid down in Article 3 shall also apply in the case of rightholders who are not Community nationals, provided Member States grant them protection. However, without prejudice to the international obligations of the Member States, the term of protection granted by Member States shall expire no later than the date of expiry of the protection granted in the country of which the rightholder is a national and may not exceed the term laid down in Article 3.

3.   Member States which, at the date of adoption of this Directive, in particular pursuant to their international obligations, granted a longer term of protection than that which would result from the provisions, referred to in paragraphs 1 and 2 may maintain this protection until the conclusion of international agreements on the term of protection by copyright or related rights.

Article 8   Calculation of terms
The terms laid down in this Directive are calculated from the first day of January of the year following the event which gives rise to them.

Article 9   Moral rights
This Directive shall be without prejudice to the provisions of the Member States regulating moral rights.

Article 10   Application in time
1.   Where a term of protection, which is longer than the corresponding term provided for by this Directive, is already running in a Member State on the date referred to in Article 13(1), this Directive shall not have the effect of shortening that term of protection in that Member State.

2.   The terms of protection provided for in this Directive shall apply to all works and subject matter which are protected in at least one Member State, on the date referred to in Article 13(1), pursuant to national provisions on copyright or related rights or which meet the criteria for protection under Directive 92/100/EEC.

3.   This Directive shall be without prejudice to any acts of exploitation performed before the date referred to in Article 13(1). Member States shall adopt the necessary provisions to protect in particular acquired rights of third parties.

4.   Member States need not apply the provisions of Article 2(1) to cinematographic or audiovisual works created before 1 July 1994.

5.   Member States may determine the date as from which Article 2(1) shall apply, provided that date is no later than 1 July 1997.

...

Article 12   Notification procedure
Member States shall immediately notify the Commission of any governmental plan to grant new related rights, including the basic reasons for their introduction and the term of protection envisaged.

Article 13   General provisions
1.   Member States shall bring into force the laws, regulations and administrative provisions necessary to comply with Articles 1 to 11 of this Directive before 1 July 1995.

When Member States adopt these provisions, they shall contain a reference to this Directive or shall be accompanied by such reference at the time of their official publication. The methods of making such a reference shall be laid down by the Member States.

Member States shall communicate to the Commission the texts of the provisions of national law which they adopt in the field governed by this Directive.

2.   Member States shall apply Article 12 from the date of notification of this Directive.

Article 14
This Directive is addressed to the Member States.

COUNCIL REGULATION (EC) No. 40/94
of 20 December 1993
on the Community trade mark

THE COUNCIL OF THE EUROPEAN UNION,

Having regard to the Treaty establishing the European Community, and in particular Article 235 thereof,

Having regard to the proposal from the Commission,

Having regard to the opinion of the European Parliament,

Having regard to the opinion of the Economic and Social Committee,

Whereas it is desirable to promote throughout the Community a harmonious development of economic activities and a continuous and balanced expansion by completing an internal market which functions properly and offers conditions which are similar to those obtaining in a national market; whereas in order to create a market of this kind and make it increasingly a single market, not only must barriers to free movement of goods and services be removed and arrangements be instituted which ensure that competition is not distorted, but, in addition, legal conditions must be created which enable undertakings to adapt their activities to the scale of the Community, whether in manufacturing and distributing goods or in providing services; whereas for those purposes, trade marks enabling the products and services of undertakings to be distinguished by identical means throughout the entire Community, regardless of frontiers, should feature amongst the legal instruments which undertakings have at their disposal;

Whereas action by the Community would appear to be necessary for the purpose of attaining the Community's said objectives; whereas such action involves the creation of Community arrangements for trade marks whereby undertakings can by means of one procedural system obtain Community trade marks to which uniform protection is given and which produce their effects throughout the entire area of the Community; whereas the principle of the unitary character of the Community trade mark thus stated will apply unless otherwise provided for in this Regulation;

Whereas the barrier of territoriality of the rights conferred on proprietors of trade marks by the laws of the Member States cannot be removed by approximation of laws; whereas in order to open up unrestricted economic activity in the whole of the common market for the benefit of undertakings, trade marks need to be created which are governed by a uniform Community law directly applicable in all Member States;

Whereas since the Treaty has not provided the specific powers to establish such a legal instrument, Article 235 of the Treaty should be applied;

Whereas the Community law relating to trade marks nevertheless does not replace the laws of the Member States on trade marks; whereas it would not in fact appear to be justified to require undertakings to apply for registration of their trade marks as Community trade marks; whereas national trade marks continue to be necessary for those undertakings which do not want protection of their trade marks at Community level;

Whereas the rights in a Community trade mark may not be obtained otherwise than by registration, and registration is to be refused in particular if the trade mark is not distinctive, if it is unlawful or if it conflicts with earlier rights;

Whereas the protection afforded by a Community trade mark, the function of which is in particular to guarantee the trade mark as an indication of origin, is absolute in the case of identity between the mark and the sign and the goods or services; whereas the protection applies also in cases of similarity between the mark and the sign and the goods or services; whereas an interpretation should be given of the concept of similarity in relation to the likelihood of confusion; whereas the likelihood of confusion, the appreciation of which depends on numerous elements and, in particular, on the recognition of the trade mark on the market, the association which can be made with the used or registered sign, the degree of similarity between the trade mark and the sign and between the goods or services identified, constitutes the specific condition for such protection;

Whereas it follows from the principle of free flow of goods that the proprietor of a Community trade mark must not be entitled to prohibit its use by a third party in relation to goods which have been put into circulation in the Community, under the trade mark, by him or with his consent, save where there exist legitimate reasons for the proprietor to oppose further commercialisation of the goods;

Whereas there is no justification for protecting Community trade marks or, as against them, any trade mark which has been registered before them, except where the trade marks are actually used;

Whereas a Community trade mark is to be regarded as an object of property which exists separately from the undertakings whose goods or services are designated by it; whereas accordingly, it must be capable of being transferred, subject to the overriding need to prevent the public being misled as a result of the transfer. It must also be capable of being charged as security in favour of a third party and of being the subject-matter of licences;

Whereas administrative measures are necessary at Community level for implementing in relation to every trade mark the trade mark law created by this Regulation; whereas it is therefore essential, while retaining the Community's existing institutional structure and balance of powers, to establish an Office for Harmonisation in the Internal Market (trade marks and designs) which is independent in relation to technical matters and has legal, administrative and financial autonomy; whereas to this end it is necessary and appropriate that it should be a body of the Community having legal personality and exercising the implementing powers which are conferred on it by this Regulation, and that it should operate within the framework of Community law without detracting from the competencies exercised by the Community institutions;

Whereas it is necessary to ensure that parties who are affected by decisions made by the Office are protected by the law in a manner which is suited to the special character of trade mark law; whereas to that end provision is made for an appeal to lie from decisions of the examiners and of the various divisions of the Office; whereas if the department whose decision is contested does not rectify its decision it is to remit the appeal to a Board of Appeal of the Office, which is to decide on it; whereas decisions of the Boards of Appeal are, in turn, amenable to actions before the Court of Justice of the European Communities, which has jurisdiction to annul or to alter the contested decision;

Whereas under Council Decision 88/591/ECSC, EEC, Euratom of 24 October 1988 establishing a Court of First Instance of the European Communities, as amended by Decision 93/350/Euratom, ECSC, EEC of 8 June 1993, that Court shall exercise at the first instance the jurisdiction conferred on the Court of Justice by the Treaties establishing the Communities — with particular regard to appeals lodged under the second subparagraph of Article 173 of the EC Treaty — and by the acts adopted in implementation thereof, save as otherwise provided in an act setting up a body governed by Community law; whereas the jurisdiction which this Regulation confers on the Court of Justice to cancel and reform decisions of the appeal courts shall accordingly be exercised at the first instance by the Court in accordance with the above Decision;

Whereas in order to strengthen the protection of Community trade marks the Member States should designate, having regard to their own national system, as limited a number as possible of national courts of first and second instance having jurisdiction in matters of infringement and validity of Community trade marks;

Whereas decisions regarding the validity and infringement of Community trade marks must have effect and cover the entire area of the Community, as this is the only way of preventing inconsistent decisions on the part of the courts and the Office and of ensuring that the unitary character of Community trade marks is not undermined; whereas the rules contained in the Brussels Convention of Jurisdiction and the Enforcement of Judgments in Civil and Commercial Matters will apply to all actions at law relating to Community trade marks, save where this Regulation derogates from those rules;

Whereas contradictory judgments should be avoided in actions which involve the same acts and the same parties and which are brought on the basis of a Community trade mark and parallel national trade marks; whereas for this purpose, when the actions are brought in the same Member State, the way in which this is to be achieved is a matter for national procedural rules, which are not prejudiced by this Regulation, whilst when the actions are brought in different Member States, provisions modelled on the rules on *lis pendens* and related actions of the abovementioned Brussels Convention appear appropriate;

Whereas in order to guarantee the full autonomy and independence of the Office, it is considered necessary to grant it an autonomous budget whose revenue comes principally from fees paid by the users of the system; whereas however, the Community budgetary procedure remains applicable as far as any subsidies chargeable to general budget of the European Communities are concerned; whereas moreover, the auditing of accounts should be undertaken by the Court of Auditors;

Whereas implementing measures are required for the Regulation's application, particularly as regards the adoption and amendment of fees regulations and an Implementing Regulation; whereas such measures should be adopted by the Commission, assisted by a Committee composed of representatives of the Member States, in accordance with the procedural rules laid down in Article 2, procedure III(b), of Council Decisions 87/373/EEC of 13 July 1987 laying down the procedures for the exercise of implementing powers conferred on the Commission,

HAS ADOPTED THIS REGULATION:

TITLE I
GENERAL PROVISIONS

Article 1 Community trade mark

1.   A trade mark for goods or services which is registered in accordance with the conditions contained in this Regulation and in the manner herein provided is hereinafter referred to as a "Community trade mark".

2.   A Community trade mark shall have a unitary character. It shall have equal effect throughout the Community: it shall not be registered, transferred or surrendered or be the subject of a decision revoking the rights of the proprietor or declaring it invalid, nor shall its use be prohibited, save in respect of the whole Community. This principle shall apply unless otherwise provided in this Regulation.

Article 2 Office

An Office for Harmonisation in the Internal Market (trade marks and designs), hereinafter referred to as "the Office", is hereby established.

. . .

TITLE II
THE LAW RELATING TO TRADE MARKS

SECTION 1
DEFINITION OF A COMMUNITY TRADE MARK
OBTAINING A COMMUNITY TRADE MARK

Article 4 Signs of which a Community trade mark may consist

A Community trade mark may consist of any signs capable of being represented graphically, particularly words, including personal names, designs, letters, numerals, the shape of goods or of their packaging, provided that such signs are capable of distinguishing the goods or services of one undertaking from those of other undertakings.

Article 5 Persons who can be proprietors of Community trade marks

1.   The following natural or legal persons, including authorities established under public law, may be proprietors of Community trade marks:

    (a)   nationals of the Member States; or

(b)   nationals of other States which are parties to the Paris Convention for the protection of industrial property, hereinafter referred to as "the Paris Convention"; or

(c)   nationals of States which are not parties to the Paris Convention who are domiciled or have their seat or who have real and effective industrial or commercial establishments within the territory of the Community or of a State which is party to the Paris Convention; or

(d)   nationals, other than those referred to under subparagraph (c), of any State which is not party to the Paris Convention and which, according to published findings, accords to nationals of all the Member States the same protection for trade marks as it accords to its own nationals and, if nationals of the Member States are required to prove registration in the country of origin, recognises the registration of Community trade marks as such proof.

. . .

Article 6   Means whereby a Community trade mark is obtained
A Community trade mark shall be obtained by registration.

Article 7   Absolute grounds for refusal
1.   The following shall not be registered:
   (a)   signs which do not conform to the requirements of Article 4;
   (b)   trade marks which are devoid of any distinctive character;
   (c)   trade marks which consist exclusively of signs or indications which may serve, in trade, to designate the kind, quality, quantity, intended purpose, value, geographical origin or the time of production of the goods or of rendering of the service, or other characteristics of the goods or service;
   (d)   trade marks which consist exclusively of signs or indications which have become customary in the current language or in the bona fide and established practices of the trade;
   (e)   signs which consist exclusively of:
      (i)   the shape which results from the nature of the goods themselves; or
      (ii)   the shape of goods which is necessary to obtain a technical result; or
      (iii)   the shape which gives substantial value to the goods;
   (f)   trade marks which are contrary to public policy or to accepted principles of morality;
   (g)   trade marks which are of such a nature as to deceive the public, for instance as to the nature, quality or geographical origin of the goods or service;
   (h)   trade marks which have not been authorised by the competent authorities and are to be refused pursuant to Article 6ter of the Paris Convention;
   (i)   trade marks which include badges, emblems or escutcheons other than those covered by Article 6ter of the Paris Convention and which are of particular public interest, unless the consent of the appropriate authorities to their registration has been given.
2.   Paragraph 1 shall apply notwithstanding that the grounds of non-registrability obtain in only part of the Community.
3.   Paragraph 1(b), (c) and (d) shall not apply if the trade mark has become distinctive in relation to the goods or services for which registration is requested in consequence of the use which has been made of it.

Article 8   Relative grounds for refusal
1.   Upon opposition by the proprietor of an earlier trade mark, the trade mark applied for shall not be registered:
   (a)   if it is identical with the earlier trade mark and the goods or services for which registration is applied for are identical with the goods or services for which the earlier trade mark is protected;

(b)   if because of its identity with or similarity to the earlier trade mark and the identity or similarity of the goods or services covered by the trade marks there exists a likelihood of confusion on the part of the public in the territory in which the earlier trade mark is protected; the likelihood of confusion includes the likelihood of association with the earlier trade mark.

2.   For the purposes of paragraph 1, "Earlier trade marks" means:

(a)   trade marks of the following kinds with a date of application for registration which is earlier than the date of application for registration of the Community trade mark, taking account, where appropriate, of the priorities claimed in respect of those trade marks:

(i)   Community trade marks;

(ii)   trade marks registered in a Member State, or, in the case of Belgium, the Netherlands or Luxembourg, at the Benelux Trade Mark Office;

(iii)   trade marks registered under international arrangements which have effect in a Member State;

(b)   applications for the trade marks referred to in subparagraph (a), subject to their registration;

(c)   trade marks which, on the date of application for registration of the Community trade mark, or, where appropriate, of the priority claimed in respect of the application for registration of the Community trade mark, are well known in a Member State, in the sense in which the words "well known" are used in Article 6bis of the Paris Convention.

. . .

4.   Upon opposition by the proprietor of a non-registered trade mark or of another sign used in the course of trade of more than mere local significance, the trade mark applied for shall not be registered where and to the extent that, pursuant to the law of the Member State governing that sign,

(a)   rights to that sign were acquired prior to the date of application for registration of the Community trade mark, or the date of the priority claimed for the application for registration of the Community trade mark;

(b)   that sign confers on its proprietor the right to prohibit the use of a subsequent trade mark.

5.   Furthermore, upon opposition by the proprietor of an earlier trade mark within the meaning of paragraph 2, the trade mark applied for shall not be registered where it is identical with or similar to the earlier trade mark and is to be registered for goods or services which are not similar to those for which the earlier trade mark is registered, where in the case of an earlier Community trade mark the trade mark has a reputation in the Community and, in the case of an earlier national trade mark, the trade mark has a reputation in the Member State concerned and where the use without due cause of the trade mark applied for would take unfair advantage of, or be detrimental to, the distinctive character or the repute of the earlier trade mark.

SECTION 2
EFFECTS OF COMMUNITY TRADE MARKS

Article 9   Rights conferred by a Community trade mark

1.   A Community trade mark shall confer on the proprietor exclusive rights therein. The proprietor shall be entitled to prevent all third parties not having his consent from using in the course of trade:

(a)   any sign which is identical with the Community trade mark in relation to goods or services which are identical with those for which the Community trade mark is registered;

(b)   any sign where, because of its identity with or similarity to the Community trade mark and the identity or similarity of the goods or services covered by the

Community trade mark and the sign, there exists a likelihood of confusion on the part of the public; the likelihood of confusion includes the likelihood of association between the sign and the trade mark;

(c)   any sign which is identical with or similar to the Community trade mark in relation to goods or services which are not similar to those for which the Community trade mark is registered, where the latter has a reputation in the Community and where use of that sign without due cause takes unfair advantage of, or is detrimental to, the distinctive character or the repute of the Community trade mark.

2.   The following, inter alia, may be prohibited under paragraph 1:

(a)   affixing the sign to the goods or to the packaging thereof;

(b)   offering the goods, putting them on the market or stocking them for these purposes under that sign, or offering or supplying services thereunder;

(c)   importing or exporting the goods under that sign;

(d)   using the sign on business papers and in advertising.

3.   The rights conferred by a Community trade mark shall prevail against third parties from the date of publication of registration of the trade mark. Reasonable compensation may, however, be claimed in respect of matters arising after the date of publication of a Community trade mark application, which matters would, after publication of the registration of the trade mark, be prohibited by virtue of that publication. The court seised of the case may not decide upon the merits of the case until the registration has been published.

...

Article 12   Limitation of the effects of a Community trade mark

A Community trade mark shall not entitle the proprietor to prohibit a third party from using in the course of trade:

(a)   his own name or address;

(b)   indications concerning the kind, quality, quantity, intended purpose, value, geographical origin, the time of production of the goods or of rendering of the service, or other characteristics of the goods or service;

(c)   the trade mark where it is necessary to indicate the intended purpose of a product or service, in particular as accessories or spare parts,

provided he uses them in accordance with honest practices in industrial or commercial matters.

Article 13   Exhaustion of the rights conferred by a Community trade mark

1.   A Community trade mark shall not entitle the proprietor to prohibit its use in relation to goods which have been put on the market in the Community under that trade mark by the proprietor or with his consent.

2.   Paragraph 1 shall not apply where there exist legitimate reasons for the proprietor to oppose further commercialisation of the goods, especially where the condition of the goods is changed or impaired after they have been put on the market.

Article 14   Complementary application of national law relating to infringement

1.   The effects of Community trade marks shall be governed solely by the provisions of this Regulation. In other respects, infringement of a Community trade mark shall be governed by the national law relating to infringement of a national trade mark in accordance with the provisions of Title X.

2.   This Regulation shall not prevent actions concerning a Community trade mark being brought under the law of Member States relating in particular to civil liability and unfair competition.

3.   The rules of procedure to be applied shall be determined in accordance with the provisions of Title X.

SECTION 3
USE OF COMMUNITY TRADE MARKS

Article 15   Use of Community trade marks
1. If, within a period of five years following registration, the proprietor has not put the Community trade mark to genuine use in the Community in connection with the goods or services in respect of which it is registered, or if such use has been suspended during an uninterrupted period of five years, the Community trade mark shall be subject to the sanctions provided for in this Regulation, unless there are proper reasons for non-use.
2. The following shall also constitute use within the meaning of paragraph 1:
    (a)   use of the Community trade mark in a form differing in elements which do not alter the distinctive character of the mark in the form in which it was registered;
    (b)   affixing of the Community trade mark to goods or to the packaging thereof in the Community solely for export purposes.
3. Use of the Community trade mark with the consent of the proprietor shall be deemed to constitute use by the proprietor.

SECTION 4
COMMUNITY TRADE MARKS AS OBJECTS OF PROPERTY

Article 16   Dealing with Community trade marks as national trade marks
1. Unless Articles 17 to 24 provide otherwise, a Community trade mark as an object of property shall be dealt with in its entirety, and for the whole area of the Community, as a national trade mark registered in the Member State in which, according to the Register of Community trade marks,
    (a)   the proprietor has his seat or his domicile on the relevant date; or
    (b)   where subparagraph (a) does not apply, the proprietor has an establishment on the relevant date.
2. In cases which are not provided for by paragraph 1, the Member State referred to in that paragraph shall be the Member State in which the seat of the Office is situated.
3. If two or more persons are mentioned in the Register of Community trade marks as joint proprietors, paragraph 1 shall apply to the joint proprietor first mentioned; failing this, it shall apply to the subsequent joint proprietors in the order in which they are mentioned. Where paragraph 1 does not apply to any of the joint proprietors, paragraph 2 shall apply.

Article 17   Transfer
1. A Community trade mark may be transferred, separately from any transfer of the undertaking, in respect of some or all of the goods or services for which it is registered.
2. A transfer of the whole of the undertaking shall include the transfer of the Community trade mark except where, in accordance with the law governing the transfer, there is agreement to the contrary or circumstances clearly dictate otherwise. This provision shall apply to the contractual obligation to transfer the undertaking.
3. Without prejudice to paragraph 2, an assignment of the Community trade mark shall be made in writing and shall require the signature of the parties to the contract, except when it is a result of a judgment; otherwise it shall be void.
4. Where it is clear from the transfer documents that because of the transfer the Community trade mark is likely to mislead the public concerning the nature, quality or geographical origin of the goods or services in respect of which it is registered, the Office shall not register the transfer unless the successor agrees to limit registration of the Community trade mark to goods or services in respect of which it is not likely to mislead.
5. On request of one of the parties a transfer shall be entered in the Register and published.

6.　As long as the transfer has not been entered in the Register, the successor in title may not invoke the rights arising from the registration of the Community trade mark.
. . .

Article 22　Licensing

1.　A Community trade mark may be licensed for some or all of the goods or services for which it is registered and for the whole or part of the Community. A licence may be exclusive or non-exclusive.

2.　The proprietor of a Community trade mark may invoke the rights conferred by that trade mark against a licensee who contravenes any provision in his licensing contract with regard to its duration, thè form covered by the registration in which the trade mark may be used, the scope of the goods or services for which the licence is granted, the territory in which the trade mark may be affixed, or the quality of the goods manufactured or of the services provided by the licensee.

3.　Without prejudice to the provisions of the licensing contract, the licensee may bring proceedings for infringement of a Community trade mark only if its proprietor consents thereto. However, the holder of an exclusive licence may bring such proceedings if the proprietor of the trade mark, after formal notice, does not himself bring infringement proceedings within an appropriate period.

4.　A licensee shall, for the purpose of obtaining compensation for damage suffered by him, be entitled to intervene in infringement proceedings brought by the proprietor of the Community trade mark.

5.　On request of one of the parties the grant or transfer of a licence in respect of a Community trade mark shall be entered in the Register and published.
. . .

Article 24　The application for a Community trade mark as an object of property

Articles 16 to 23 shall apply to applications for Community trade marks.

TITLE III
APPLICATION FOR COMMUNITY TRADE MARKS

SECTION 1
FILING OF APPLICATIONS AND THE CONDITIONS
WHICH GOVERN THEM

Article 25　Filing of applications

1.　An application for a Community trade mark shall be filed, at the choice of the applicant,

　　(a)　at the Office; or

　　(b)　at the central industrial property office of a Member State or at the Benelux Trade Mark Office. An application filed in this way shall have the same effect as if it had been filed on the same date at the Office.
. . .

Article 27　Date of filing

The date of filing of a Community trade mark application shall be the date on which documents containing the information specified in Article 26(1) are filed with the Office by the applicant or, if the application has been filed with the central office of a Member State or with the Benelux Trade Mark Office, with that office, subject to payment of the application fee wthin a period of one month of filing the abovementioned documents.
. . .

SECTION 2
PRIORITY

Article 29   Right of priority
1.   A person who has duly filed an application for a trade mark in or for any State party to the Paris Convention, or to the Agreement establishing the World Trade Organisation, or his successors in title, shall enjoy, for the purpose of filing a Community trade mark application for the same trade mark in respect of goods or services which are identical with or contained within those for which the application has been filed, a right of priority during a period of six months from the date of filing of the first application.
...

Article 31   Effect of priority right
The right of priority shall have the effect that the date of priority shall count as the date of filing of the Community trade mark application for the purposes of establishing which rights take precedence.
...

SECTION 4
CLAIMING THE SENIORITY OF A NATIONAL TRADE MARK

Article 34   Claiming the seniority of a national trade mark
1.   The proprietor of an earlier trade mark registered in a Member State, including a trade mark registered in the Benelux countries, or registered under international arrangements having effect in a Member State, who applies for an identical trade mark for registration as a Community trade mark for goods or services which are identical with or contained within those for which the earlier trade mark has been registered, may claim for the Community trade mark the seniority of the earlier trade mark in respect of the Member State in or for which it is registered.
2.   Seniority shall have the sole effect under this Regulation that, where the proprietor of the Community trade mark surrenders the earlier trade mark or allows it to lapse, he shall be deemed to continue to have the same rights as he would have had if the earlier trade mark had continued to be registered.
3.   The seniority claimed for the Community trade mark shall lapse if the earlier trade mark the seniority of which is claimed is declared to have been revoked or to be invalid or if it is surrendered prior to the registration of the Community trade mark.

Article 35   Claiming seniority after registration of the Community trade mark
1.   The proprietor of a Community trade mark who is the proprietor of an earlier identical trade mark registered in a Member State, including a trade mark registered in the Benelux countries, or of a trade mark registered under international arrangements having effect in a Member State, for identical goods or services, may claim the seniority of the earlier trade mark in respect of the Member State in or for which it is registered.
2.   Article 34(2) and (3) shall apply.

TITLE IV
REGISTRATION PROCEDURE

SECTION 1
EXAMINATION OF APPLICATIONS

Article 36   Examination of the conditions of filing
1.   The Office shall examine whether:
(a)   the Community trade mark application satisfies the requirements for the accordance of a date of filing in accordance with Article 27;

(b)   the Community trade mark application complies with the conditions laid down in the Implementing Regulation;

(c)   where appropriate, the class fees have been paid within the prescribed period.

. . .

Article 37   Examination of the conditions relating to the entitlement of the proprietor

1.   Where, pursuant to Article 5, the applicant may not be the proprietor of a Community trade mark, the application shall be refused.

. . .

Article 38   Examination as to absolute grounds for refusal

1.   Where, under Article 7, a trade mark is ineligible for registration in respect of some or all of the goods or services covered by the Community trade mark application, the application shall be refused as regards those goods or services.

. . .

SECTION 2
SEARCH

Article 39   Search

1.   Once the Office has accorded a date of filing to a Community trade mark application and has established that the applicant satisfies the conditions referred to in Article 5, it shall draw up a Community search report citing those earlier Community trade marks or Community trade mark applications discovered which may be invoked under Article 8 against the registration of the Community trade mark applied for.

2.   As soon as a Community trade mark application has been accorded a date of filing, the Office shall transmit a copy thereof to the central industrial property office of each Member State which has informed the Office of its decision to operate a search in its own register of trade marks in respect of Community trade mark applications.

3.   Each of the central industrial property offices referred to in paragraph 2 shall communicate to the Office within three months as from the date on which it received the Community trade mark application a search report which shall either cite those earlier national trade marks or trade mark applications discovered which may be invoked under Article 8 against the registration of the Community trade mark applied for, or state that the search has revealed no such rights.

. . .

SECTION 3
PUBLICATION OF THE APPLICATION

Article 40   Publication of the application

1.   If the conditions which the application for a Community trade mark must satisfy have been fulfilled and if the period referred to in Article 39(6) has expired, the application shall be published to the extent that it has not been refused pursuant to Articles 37 and 38.

2.   Where, after publication, the application is refused under Articles 37 and 38, the decision that it has been refused shall be published upon becoming final.

SECTION 4
OBSERVATIONS BY THIRD PARTIES AND OPPOSITION

Article 41   Observations by third parties

1.   Following the publication of the Community trade mark application, any natural or legal person and any group or body representing manufacturers, producers, suppliers of services, traders or consumers may submit to the Office written observations, explaining on which grounds under Article 7, in particular, the trade mark shall not be registered *ex officio*. They shall not be parties to the proceedings before the Office.

...

Article 42   Opposition
1.   Within a period of three months following the publication of a Community trade mark application, notice of opposition to registration of the trade mark may be given on the grounds that it may not be registered under Article 8:

(a)   by the proprietors of earlier trade marks referred to in Article 8(2) as well as licensees authorised by the proprietors of those trade marks, in respect of Article 8(1) and (5);

(b)   by the proprietors of trade marks referred to in Article 8(3);

(c)   by the proprietors of earlier marks or signs referred to in Article 8(4) and by persons authorised under the relevant national law to exercise these rights.

...

SECTION 6
REGISTRATION

Article 45   Registration
Where an application meets the requirements of this Regulation and where no notice of opposition has been given within the period referred to in Article 42(1) or where opposition has been rejected by a definitive decision, the trade mark shall be registered as a Community trade mark, provided that the registration fee has been paid within the period prescribed. If the fee is not paid within this period the application shall be deemed to be withdrawn.

TITLE V
DURATION, RENEWAL AND ALTERATION OF COMMUNITY
TRADE MARKS

Article 46   Duration of registration
Community trade marks shall be registered for a period of ten years from the date of filing of the application. Registration may be renewed in accordance with Article 47 for further periods of ten years.

Article 47   Renewal
1.   Registration of the Community trade mark shall be renewed at the request of the proprietor of the trade mark or any person expressly authorised by him, provided that the fees have been paid.

...

TITLE VI
SURRENDER, REVOCATION AND INVALIDITY

...

SECTION 2
GROUNDS FOR REVOCATION

Article 50   Grounds for revocation
1.   The rights of the proprietor of the Community trade mark shall be declared to be revoked on application to the Office or on the basis of a counterclaim in infringement proceedings:

(a)   if, within a continuous period of five years, the trade mark has not been put to genuine use in the Community in connection with the goods or services in respect of which it is registered, and there are no proper reasons for non-use; however, no person may claim that the proprietor's rights in a Community trade mark should be revoked where, during the interval between expiry of the five-year period and filing of the application or counterclaim, genuine use of the trade mark has been started or resumed; the commencement or resumption of use within a period of three months preceding the filing of the application or counterclaim which began at the earliest on expiry of the continuous period of five years of non-use shall, however, be disregarded where preparations for the commencement or resumption occur only after the proprietor becomes aware that the application or counterclaim may be filed;

(b)   if, in consequence of acts or inactivity of the proprietor, the trade mark has become the common name in the trade for a product or service in respect of which it is registered;

(c)   if, in consequence of the use made of it by the proprietor of the trade mark or with his consent in respect of the goods or services for which it is registered, the trade mark is liable to mislead the public, particularly as to the nature, quality or geographical origin of those goods or services;

(d)   if the proprietor of the trade mark no longer satisfies the conditions laid down by Article 5.

2.   Where the grounds for revocation of rights exist in respect of only some of the goods or services for which the Community trade mark is registered, the rights of the proprietor shall be declared to be revoked in respect of those goods or services only.

SECTION 3
GROUNDS FOR INVALIDITY

Article 51   Absolute grounds for invalidity

1.   A Community trade mark shall be declared invalid on application to the Office or on the basis of a counterclaim in infringement proceedings,

(a)   where the Community trade mark has been registered in breach of the provisions of Article 5 or of Article 7;

(b)   where the applicant was acting in bad faith when he filed the application for the trade mark.

2.   Where the Community trade mark has been registered in breach of the provisions of Article 7(1)(b), (c) or (d), it may nevertheless not be declared invalid if, in consequence of the use which has been made of it, it has after registration acquired a distinctive character in relation to the goods or services for which it is registered.

3.   Where the ground for invalidity exists in respect of only some of the goods or services for which the Community trade mark is registered, the trade mark shall be declared invalid as regards those goods or services only.

Article 52   Relative grounds for invalidity

1.   A Community trade mark shall be declared invalid on application to the Office or on the basis of a counterclaim in infringement proceedings:

(a)   where there is an earlier trade mark as referred to in Article 8(2) and the conditions set out in paragraph 1 or paragraph 5 of that Article are fulfilled;

(b)   where there is a trade mark as referred to in Article 8(3) and the conditions set out in that paragraph are fulfilled;

(c)   where there is an earlier right as referred to in Article 8(4) and the conditions set out in that paragraph are fulfilled.

2.   A Community trade mark shall also be declared invalid on application to the Office or on the basis of a counterclaim in infringement proceedings where the use of such trade mark may be prohibited pursuant to the national law governing the protection of any other earlier right and in particular:

(a)   a right to a name;

(b)   a right of personal portrayal;

(c)   a copyright;

(d)   an industrial property right.

...

5.   Article 51(3) shall apply.

Article 53   Limitation in consequence of acquiescence

1.   Where the proprietor of a Community trade mark has acquiesced, for a period of five successive years, in the use of a later Community trade mark in the Community while being aware of such use, he shall no longer be entitled on the basis of the earlier trade mark either to apply for a declaration that the later trade mark is invalid or to oppose the use of the later trade mark in respect of the goods or services for which the later trade mark has been used, unless registration of the later Community trade mark was applied for in bad faith.

2.   Where the proprietor of an earlier national trade mark as referred to in Article 8(2) or of another earlier sign referred to in Article 8(4) has acquiesced, for a period of five successive years, in the use of a later Community trade mark in the Member State in which the earlier trade mark or the other earlier sign is protected while being aware of such use, he shall no longer be entitled on the basis of the earlier trade mark or of the other earlier sign either to apply for a declaration that the later trade mark is invalid or to oppose the use of the later trade mark in respect of the goods or services for which the later trade mark has been used, unless registration of the later Community trade mark was applied for in bad faith.

3.   In the cases referred to in paragraphs 1 and 2, the proprietor of a later Community trade mark shall not be entitled to oppose the use of the earlier right, even though that right may no longer be invoked against the later Community trade mark.

SECTION 4
CONSEQUENCES OF REVOCATION AND INVALIDITY

Article 54   Consequences of revocation and invalidity

1.   The Community trade mark shall be deemed not to have had, as from the date of the application for revocation or of the counterclaim, the effects specified in this Regulation, to the extent that the rights of the proprietor have been revoked. An earlier date, on which one of the grounds for revocation occurred, may be fixed in the decision at the request of one of the parties.

2.   The Community trade mark shall be deemed not to have had, as from the outset, the effects specified in this Regulation, to the extent that the trade mark has been declared invalid.

...

TITLE VIII
COMMUNITY COLLECTIVE MARKS

Article 64   Community collective marks

1.   A Community collective mark shall be a Community trade mark which is described as such when the mark is applied for and is capable of distinguishing the goods or services of the members of the association which is the proprietor of the mark from those of other undertakings. Associations of manufacturers, producers, suppliers of services, or traders which, under the terms of the law governing them, have the capacity in their own name to have rights and obligations of all kinds, to make contracts or accomplish other legal acts and to sue and be sued, as well as legal persons governed by public law, may apply for Community collective marks.

2.   In derogation from Article 7(1)(c), signs or indications which may serve, in trade, to designate the geographical origin of the goods or services may constitute Community collective marks within the meaning of paragraph 1. A collective mark shall not entitle the proprietor to prohibit a third party from using in the course of trade such signs or indications, provided he uses them in accordance with honest practices in industrial or

commercial matters; in particular, such a mark may not be invoked against a third party who is entitled to use a geographical name.

3.   The provisions of this Regulation shall apply to Community collective marks, unless Articles 65 to 72 provide otherwise.

Article 65   Regulations governing use of the mark

1.   An applicant for a Community collective mark must submit regulations governing its use within the period prescribed.

2.   The regulations governing use shall specify the persons authorised to use the mark, the conditions of membership of the association and, where they exist, the conditions of use of the mark including sanctions. The regulations governing use of a mark referred to in Article 64(2) must authorise any person whose goods or services originate in the geographical area concerned to become a member of the association which is the proprietor of the mark.

Article 66   Refusal of the application

1.   In addition to the grounds for refusal of a Community trade mark application provided for in Articles 36 and 38, an application for a Community collective mark shall be refused where the provisions of Article 64 or 65 are not satisfied, or where the regulations governing use are contrary to public policy or to accepted principles of morality.

2.   An application for a Community collective mark shall also be refused if the public is liable to be misled as regards the character or the significance of the mark, in particular if it is likely to be taken to be something other than a collective mark.

...

Article 68   Use of marks

Use of a Community collective mark by any person who has authority to use it shall satisfy the requirements of this Regulation, provided that the other conditions which this Regulation imposes with regard to the use of Community trade marks are fulfilled.

...

Article 70   Persons who are entitled to bring an action for infringement

1.   The provisions of Article 22(3) and (4) concerning the rights of licensees shall apply to every person who has authority to use a Community collective mark.

2.   The proprietor of a Community collective mark shall be entitled to claim compensation on behalf of persons who have authority to use the mark where they have sustained damage in consequence of unauthorised use of the mark.

Article 71   Grounds for revocation

Apart from the grounds for revocation provided for in Article 50, the rights of the proprietor of a Community collective mark shall be revoked on application to the Office or on the basis of a counterclaim in infringement proceedings, if:

    (a)   the proprietor does not take reasonable steps to prevent the mark being used in a manner incompatible with the conditions of use, where these exist, laid down in the regulations governing use, amendments to which have, where appropriate, been mentioned in the Register;

    (b)   the manner in which the mark has been used by the proprietor has caused it to become liable to mislead the public in the manner referred to in Article 66(2);

    (c)   an amendment to the regulations governing use of the mark has been mentioned in the Register in breach of the provisions of Article 69(2), unless the proprietor of the mark, by further amending the regulations governing use, complies with the requirements of those provisions.

Article 72   Grounds for invalidity

Apart from the grounds for invalidity provided for in Articles 51 and 52, a Community collective mark which is registered in breach of the provisions of Article 66 shall be declared invalid on application to the Office or on the basis of a counterclaim n infringement proceedings, unless the proprietor of the mark, by amending the regulations governing use, complies with the requirements of those provisions.

...

COUNCIL REGULATION (EC) No. 2100/94
on 27 July 1994
on Community plant variety rights

THE COUNCIL OF THE EUROPEAN UNION,

Having regard to the Treaty establishing the European Community, and in particular Article 235 thereof,

Having regard to the proposal from the Commission,

Having regard to the opinion of the European Parliament,

Having regard to the opinion of the Economic and Social Committee,

Whereas plant varieties pose specific problems as regards the industrial property regime which may be applicable;

Whereas industrial property regimes for plant varieties have not been harmonised at Community level and therefore continue to be regulated by the legislation of the Member States, the content of which is not uniform;

Whereas in such circumstances it is appropriate to create a Community regime which, although co-existing with national regimes, allows for the grant of industrial property rights valid throughout the Community;

Whereas it is appropriate that the implementation and application of this Community regime should not be carried out by the authorities of the Member States but by a Community Office with legal personality, the 'Community Plan Variety Office';

Whereas the system must also have regard to developments in plant breeding techniques including biotechnology; whereas in order to stimulate the breeding and development of new varieties, there should be improved protection compared with the present situation for all plant breeders without, however, unjustifiably impairing access to protection generally or in the case of certain breeding techniques;

Whereas varieties of all botanical genera and species should be protectable;

Whereas protectable varieties must comply with internationally recognised requirements, i.e., distinctness, uniformity, stability and novelty, and also be designated by a prescribed variety denomination;

Whereas it is important to provide for a definition of a plant variety, in order to ensure the proper functioning of the system;

Whereas this definition is not intended to alter definitions which may have been established in the field of intellectual property rights, especially the patent field, nor to interfere with or exclude from application laws governing the protectability of products, including plants and plant material, or processes under such other industrial property rights;

Whereas it is however highly desirable to have a common definition in both fields; whereas therefore appropriate efforts at international level should be supported to reach such a common definition;

Whereas for the grant of Community plant variety rights an assessment of important characteristics relating to the variety is necessary; whereas, however, these characteristics need not necessarily relate to their economic importance;

Whereas the system must also clarify to whom the right to Community plant variety protection pertains; whereas in some cases it would be to several persons in common, not just to one; whereas the formal entitlement to make applications must be regulated;

Whereas the system must also define the term 'holder' used in this Regulation; whereas that term 'holder' without further specification is used in this Regulation including in its Article 29(5), it is intended to be within the meaning of Article 13(1) thereof;

Whereas, since the effect of a Community plant variety right should be uniform throughout the Community, commercial transactions subject to the holder's agreement must be precisely delimited; whereas the scope of protection should be extended, compared with most national systems, to certain material of the variety to take account of trade via countries outside the Community without protection; whereas, however, the introduction of the principle of exhaustion of rights must ensure that the protection is not excessive;

Whereas in order to stimulate plant breeding, the system basically confirms the internationally accepted rule of free access to protected varieties for the development therefrom, and exploitation, of new varieties;

Whereas in certain cases where the new variety, although distinct, is essentially derived from the initial variety, a certain form of dependency from the holder of the latter one should be created;

Whereas, the exercise of Community plant variety rights must be subjected to restrictions laid down in provisions adopted in the public interest;

Whereas this includes safeguarding agricultural production; whereas that purpose requires an authorisation for farmers to use the product of the harvest for propagation under certain conditions;

Whereas it must be ensured that the conditions are laid down at Community level;

Whereas compulsory licensing should also be provided for under certain circumstances in the public interest, which may include the need to supply the market with material offering specified features, or to maintain the incentive for continued breeding of improved varieties;

Whereas the use of prescribed variety denominations should be made obligatory;

Whereas the Community plant variety right should in principle have a life of at least 25 years and in the case of vine and tree species, at least 30 years; whereas other grounds for termination must be specified;

Whereas a Community plant variety right is an object of the holder's property and its role in relation to the non-harmonised legal provisions of the Member States, particularly of civil law, must therefore be clarified; whereas this applies also to the settlement of infringements and the enforcement of entitlement to Community plant variety rights;

Whereas, it is necessary to ensure that the full application of the principles of the Community plant variety rights system is not impaired by the effects of other systems; whereas for this purpose certain rules, in conformity with Member States' existing international commitments, are required concerning the relationship to other industrial property rights;

Whereas it is indispensable to examine whether and to what extent the conditions for the protection accorded in other industrial property systems, such as patents, should be adapted or otherwise modified for consistency with the Community plant variety rights system; whereas this, where necessary, should be laid down in balanced rules by additional Community law;

Whereas the duties and powers of the Community Plant Variety Office, including its Boards of Appeal, relating to the grant, termination or verification of

Community plant variety rights and publications are as far as possible to be modelled on rules developed for other systems, as are also the Office's structure and Rules of Procedure, the collaboration with the Commission and Member States particularly through an Administrative Council, the involvement of Examination Offices in technical examination and moreover the necessary budgetary measures;

Whereas the Office should be advised and supervised by the aforementioned Administrative Council, composed of representatives of Member States and the Commission;

Whereas the Treaty does not provide, for the adoption of this Regulation, powers other than those of Article 235;

Whereas this Regulation takes into account existing international conventions such as the International Convention for the Protection of New Varieties of Plants (UPOV Convention), the Convention of the Grant of European Patents (European Patent Convention) or the Agreement on trade-related aspects of intellectual property rights, including trade in counterfeit goods; whereas it consequently implements the ban on patenting plant varieties only to the extent that the European Patent Convention so requires, i.e., to plant varieties as such;

Whereas this Regulation should be re-examined for amendment as necessary in the light of future developments in the aforementioned Conventions,

HAS ADOPTED THIS REGULATION:

PART ONE
GENERAL PROVISIONS

Article 1 Community plant variety rights
A system of Community plant variety rights is hereby established as the sole and exclusive form of Community industrial property rights for plant varieties.

Article 2 Uniform effect of Community plant variety rights
Community plant variety rights shall have uniform effect within the territory of the Community and may not be granted, transferred or terminated in respect of the abovementioned territory otherwise than on a uniform basis.

Article 3 National property rights for plant varieties
This Regulation shall be without prejudice to the right of the Member States to grant national property rights for plant varieties, subject to the provisions of Article 92(1).

Article 4 Community Office
For the purpose of the implementation of this Regulation a Community Plant Variety Office, hereinafter referred to as 'the Office', is hereby established.

PART TWO
SUBSTANTIVE LAW

CHAPTER I
CONDITIONS GOVERNING THE GRANT OF COMMUNITY PLANT VARIETY RIGHTS

Article 5 Object of Community plant variety rights
1. Varieties of all botanical genera and species, including, *inter alia*, hybrids between genera or species, may form the object of Community plant variety rights.

2. For the purpose of this Regulation, 'variety' shall be taken to mean a plant grouping within a single botanical taxon of the lowest known rank, which grouping, irrespective of whether the conditions for the grant of a plant variety right are fully met, can be:

— defined by the expression of the characteristics that result from a given genotype or combination of genotypes,

— distinguished from any other plant grouping by the expression of at least one of the said characteristics, and

— considered as a unit with regard to its suitability for being propagated unchanged.

3.   A plant grouping consists of entire plants or parts of plants as far as such parts are capable of producing entire plants, both referred to hereinafter as 'variety constituents'.

4.   The expression of the characteristics referred to in paragraph 2, first indent, may be either invariable or variable between variety constituents of the same kind provided that also the level of variation results from the genotype or combination of genotypes.

Article 6   Protectable varieties

Community plant variety rights shall be granted for varieties that are:
    (a)   distinct;
    (b)   uniform;
    (c)   stable; and
    (d)   new.

Moreover, the variety must be designated by a denomination in accordance with the provisions of Article 63.

Article 7   Distinctness

1.   A variety shall be deemed to be distinct if it is clearly distinguishable by reference to the expression of the characteristics that results from a particular genotype or combination of genotypes, from any other variety whose existence is a matter of common knowledge on the date of application determined pursuant to Article 51.

2.   The existence of another variety shall in particular be deemed to be a matter of common knowledge if on the date of application determined pursuant to Article 51:

    (a)   it was the object of a plant variety right or entered in an official register of plant varieties, in the Community or any State, or in any intergovernmental organisation with relevant competence;

    (b)   an application for the granting of a plant variety right in its respect or for its entering in such an official register was filed, provided the application has led to the granting or entering in the meantime.

The implementing rules pursuant to Article 114 may specify further cases as examples which shall be deemed to be a matter of common knowledge.

Article 8   Uniformity

A variety shall be deemed to be uniform if, subject to the variation that may be expected from the particular features of its propagation, it is sufficiently uniform in the expression of those characteristics which are included in the examination for distinctness, as well as any other used for the variety description.

Article 9   Stability

A variety shall be deemed to be stable if the expression of the characteristics which are included in the examination for distinctness as well as any others used for the variety description, remain unchanged after repeated propagation or, in the case of a particular cycle of propagation, at the end of each such cycle.

Article 10   Novelty

1.   A variety shall be deemed to be new if, at the date of application determined pursuant to Article 51, variety constituents or harvested material of the variety have not

been sold or otherwise disposed of to others, by or with the consent of the breeder within the meaning of Article 11, for purposes of exploitation of the variety:

(a) earlier than one year before the abovementioned date, within the territory of the Community;

(b) earlier than four years or, in the case of trees or of vines, earlier than six years before the said date, outside the territory of the Community.

2. The disposal of variety constituents to an official body for statutory purposes, or to others on the basis of a contractual or other legal relationship solely for production, reproduction, multiplication, conditioning or storage, shall not be deemed to be a disposal to others within the meaning of paragraph 1, provided that the breeder preserves the exclusive right of disposal of these and other variety constituents, and no further disposal is made. However, such disposal of variety constituents shall be deemed to be a disposal in terms of paragraph 1 if these constituents are repeatedly used in the production of a hybrid variety and if there is disposal of variety constituents or harvested material of the hybrid variety.

Likewise, the disposal of variety constituents by one company or firm within the meaning of the second paragraph of Article 58 of the Treaty to another of such companies or firms shall not be deemed to be a disposal to others, if one of them belongs entirely to the other or if both belong entirely to a third such company or firm, provided no further disposal is made. This provision shall not apply in respect of cooperative societies.

3. The disposal of variety constituents or harvested material of the variety, which have been produced from plants grown for the purposes specified in Article 15(b) and (c) and which are not used for further reproduction or multiplication, shall not be deemed to be exploitation of the variety, unless reference is made to the variety for purposes of that disposal.

Likewise, no account shall be taken of any disposal to others, if it either was due to, or in consequence of the fact that the breeder had displayed the variety at an official or officially recognised exhibition within the meaning of the Convention on International Exhibitions, or at an exhibition in a Member State which was officially recognised as equivalent by that Member State.

CHAPTER II
PERSONS ENTITLED

Article 11   Entitlement to Community plant variety rights

1. The person who bred, or discovered and developed the variety, or his successor in title, both — the person and his successor — referred to hereinafter as 'the breeder', shall be entitled to the Community plant variety right.

2. If two or more persons bred, or discovered and developed the variety jointly, entitlement shall be vested jointly in them or their respective successors in title. This provision shall also apply to two or more persons in cases where one or more of them discovered the variety and the other or the others developed it.

3. Entitlement shall also be invested jointly in the breeder and any other person or persons, if the breeder and the other person or persons have agreed to joint entitlement by written declaration.

4. If the breeder is an employee, the entitlement to the Community plant variety right shall be determined in accordance with the national law applicable to the employment relationship in the context of which the variety was bred, or discovered and developed.

5. Where entitlement to a Community plant variety right is vested jointly in two or more persons pursuant to paragraphs 2 to 4, one or more of them may empower the other by written declaration to such effect to claim entitlement thereto.

Article 12   Entitlement to file an application for a Community plant variety right

1.   An application for a Community plant variety right may be filed by any natural or legal person, or any body ranking as a legal person under the law applicable to that body, provided they are:

(a)   nationals of one of the Member States or nationals of a member of the Union for the Protection of New Varieties of Plants within the meaning of Article 1(xi) of the Act of 1991 of the International Convention for the Protection of New Varieties of Plants, or are domiciled or have their seat or an establishment in such a State;

(b)   nationals of any other State who do not meet the requirements laid down in (a) in respect of domicile, seat or establishment, in so far as the Commission, after obtaining the opinion of the Administrative Council referred to in Article 36, has so decided. Such a decision may be made dependent on the other State affording protection for varieties of the same botanical taxon to nationals of all the Member States, which corresponds to the protection afforded pursuant to this Regulation; the Commission shall establish whether this condition is met.

2.   An application may be filed jointly by two or more such persons.

CHAPTER III
EFFECTS OF COMMUNITY PLANT VARIETY RIGHTS

Article 13   Rights of the holder of a Community plant variety right and prohibited acts

1.   A Community plant variety right shall have the effect that the holder or holders of the Community plant variety right, hereinafter referred to as 'the holder', shall be entitled to effect the acts set out in paragraph 2.

2.   Without prejudice to the provisions of Articles 15 and 16, the following acts in respect of variety constituents, or harvested material of the protected variety, both referred to hereinafter as 'material', shall require the authorisation of the holder:

(a)   production or reproduction (multiplication);
(b)   conditioning for the purpose of propagation;
(c)   offering for sale;
(d)   selling or other marketing;
(e)   exporting from the Community;
(f)   importing to the Community;
(g)   stocking for any of the purposes mentioned in (a) to (f).

The holder may make his authorisation subject to conditions and limitations.

3.   The provisions of paragraph 2 shall apply in respect of harvested material only if this was obtained through the unauthorised use of variety constituents of the protected variety, and unless the holder has had reasonable opportunity to exercise his right in relation to the said variety constituents.

4.   In the implementing rules pursuant to Article 114, it may be provided that in specific cases the provisions of paragraph 2 of this Article shall also apply in respect of products obtained directly from material of the protected variety. They may apply only if such products were obtained through the unauthorised use of material of the protected variety, and unless the holder has had reasonable opportunity to exercise his right in relation to the said material. To the extent that the provisions of paragraph 2 apply to products directly obtained, they shall also be considered to be 'material'.

5.   The provisions of paragraphs 1 to 4 shall also apply in relation to:

(a)   varieties which are essentially derived from the variety in respect of which the Community plant variety right has been granted, where this variety is not itself an essentially derived variety;

(b)   varieties which are not distinct in accordance with the provisions of Article 7 from the protected variety; and

(c)   varieties whose production requires the repeated use of the protected variety.

6.   For the purposes of paragraph 5(a), a variety shall be deemed to be essentially derived from another variety, referred to hereinafter as 'the initial variety' when:

(a)   it is predominantly derived from the initial variety, or from a variety that is itself predominantly derived from the initial variety;

(b)   it is distinct in accordance with the provisions of Article 7 from the initial variety; and

(c)   except for the differences which result from the act of derivation, it conforms essentially to the initial variety in the expression of the characteristics that results from the genotype or combination of genotypes of the initial variety.

7.   The implementing rules pursuant to Article 114 may specify possible acts of derivation which come at least under the provisions of paragraph 6.

8.   Without prejudice to Article 14 and 29, the exercise of the rights conferred by Community plant variety rights may not violate any provisions adopted on the grounds of public morality, public policy or public security, the protection of health and life of humans, animals or plants, the protection of the environment, the protection of industrial or commercial property, or the safeguarding of competition, of trade or of agricultural production.

Article 14   Derogation from Community plant variety right

1.   Notwithstanding Article 13(2), and for the purposes of safeguarding agricultural production, farmers are authorised to use for propagating purposes in the field, on their own holding the product of the harvest which they have obtained by planting, on their own holding, propagating material of a variety other than a hybrid of synthetic variety, which is covered by a Community plant variety right.

2.   The provisions of paragraph 1 shall only apply to agricultural plant species of:

(a)   Fodder plants:
Cicer arietinum L. — Chickpea milkvetch
Lupinus luteus L. — Yellow lupin
Medicago sativa L. — Lucerne
Pisum sativum L. (partim) — Field pea
Trifolium alexandrinum L. — Berseem/Egyptian clover
Trifolium resupinatum L. —Persian clover
Vicia faba — Field bean
Vicia sativa L. Common vetch
and in the case of Portugal, Lolium multiflorum lam — Italian rye-grass

(b)   Cereals:
Avena sativa — Oats
Hordeum vulgare L. — Barley
Oryza sativa L. — Rice
Phalaris canariensis L. — Canary grass
Secale cereale L. — Rye
X Triticosecale Wittm. — Triticale
Triticium aestivum L. emend. Fiori et Paol. — Wheat
Triticum durum Desf. — Durum wheat
Triticum spelta L. — Spelt wheat

(c)   Potatoes:
Solanum tuberosum — Potatoes

(d)   Oil and fibre plants:
Brassica napus L. (partim) — Swede rape
Brassica rapa L. (partim) — Turnip rape

Linum usitatissimum — linseed with the exclusion of flax.

3.   Conditions to give effect to the derogation provided for in paragraph 1 and to safeguard the legitimate interests of the breeder and of the farmer, shall be established, before the entry into force of this Regulation, in implementing rules pursuant to Article 114, on the basis of the following criteria:

— there shall be no quantitative restriction of the level of the farmer's holding to the extent necessary for the requirements of the holding,

— the product of the harvest may be processed for planting, either by the farmer himself or through services supplied to him, without prejudice to certain restrictions which Member States may establish regarding the organisation of the processing of the said product of the harvest, in particular in order to ensure identity of the product entered for processing with that resulting from processing,

— small farmers shall not be required to pay any remuneration to the holder, small farmers shall be considered to be:

— in the case of those of the plant species referred to in paragraph 2 of this Article to which Council Regulation (EEC) No 1765/92 of 30 June 1992 establishing a support system for producers of certain arable crops applies, farmers who do not grow plants on an area bigger than the area which would be needed to produce 92 tonnes of cereals; for the calculation of the area, Article 8(2) of the aforesaid Regulation shall apply,

— in the case of other plant species referred to in paragraph 2 of this Article, farmers who meet comparable appropriate criteria,

— other farmers shall be required to pay an equitable remuneration to the holder, which shall be sensibly lower than the amount charged for the licensed production of propagating material of the same variety in the same area; the actual level of this equitable remuneration may be subject to variation over time, taking into account the extent to which use will be made of the derogation provided for in paragraph 1 in respect of the variety concerned,

— monitoring compliance with the provisions of this Article or the provisions adopted pursuant to this Article shall be a matter of exclusive responsibility of holders; in organising that monitoring, they may not provide for assistance from official bodies,

— relevant information shall be provided to the holders on their request, by farmers and by suppliers of processing services; relevant information may equally be provided by official bodies involved in the monitoring of agricultural production, if such information has been obtained through ordinary performance of their tasks, without additional burden or costs. These provisions are without prejudice, in respect of personal data, to Community and national legislation on the protection of individuals with regard to the processing and free movement of personal data.

Article 15   Limitation of the effects of Community plant variety rights
The Community plant variety rights shall not extend to:

(a)   acts done privately and for non-commercial purposes;

(b)   acts done for experimental purposes;

(c)   acts done for the purpose of breeding, or discovering and developing other varieties;

(d)   acts referred to in Article 13(2) to (4), in respect of such other varieties, except where the provisions of Article 13(5) apply, or where the other variety or the material of this variety comes under the protection of a property right which does not contain a comparable provision; and

(e)   acts whose prohibition would violate the provisions laid down in Articles 13(8), 14 or 29.

Article 16   Exhaustion of Community plant variety rights

The Community plant variety right shall not extend to acts concerning any material of the protected variety, or of a variety covered by the provisions of Article 13(5), which has been disposed of to others by the holder or with his consent, in any part of the Community, or any material derived from the said material, unless such acts:

(a)   involve further propagation of the variety in question, except where such propagation was intended when the material was disposed of; or

(b)   involve an export of variety constituents into a third country which does not protect varieties of the plant genus or species to which the variety belongs, except where the exported materials is for final consumption purposes.

Article 17   Use of variety denominations

1.   Any person who, within the territory of the Community, offers or disposes of to others for commercial purposes variety constituents of a protected variety, or a variety covered by the provisions of Article 13(5), must use the variety denomination designated pursuant to Article 63; where it is used in writing, the variety denomination shall be readily distinguishable and clearly legible. If a trade mark, trade name or similar indication is associated with the designated denomination, this denomination must be easily recognisable as such.

2.   Any person effecting such acts in respect of any other material of the variety, must inform of that denomination in accordance with other provisions in law or if a request is made by an authority, by the purchaser or by any other person having a legitimate interest.

3.   Paragraphs 1 and 2 shall apply even after the termination of the Community plant variety right.

Article 18   Limitation of the use of variety denominations

1.   The holder may not use any right granted in respect of a designation that is identical with the variety denomination to hamper the free use of that denomination in connection with the variety, even after the termination of the Community plant variety right.

2.   A third party may use a right granted in respect of a designation that is identical with the variety denomination to hamper the free use of that denomination only if that right was granted before the variety denomination was designated pursuant to Article 63.

3.   Where a variety is protected by a Community plant variety right or, in a Member State or in a Member of the International Union for the Protection of New Varieties of Plants by a national property right, neither its designated denomination or any designation which might be confused with it can be used, within the territory of the Community, in connection with another variety of the same botanical species or a species regarded as related pursuant to the publication made in accordance with Article 63(5), or for material of such variety.

CHAPTER IV
DURATION AND TERMINATION OF COMMUNITY PLANT
VARIETY RIGHTS

Article 19   Duration of Community plant variety rights

1.   The term of the Community plant variety right shall run until the end of the 25th calendar year or, in the case of varieties of vine and tree species, until the end of the 30th calendar year, following the year of grant.

2.   The Council, acting by qualified majority on proposal from the Commission, may, in respect of specific genera or species, provide for an extension of these terms up to a further five years.

3.   A Community plant variety right shall lapse before the expiry of the terms laid down in paragraph 1 or pursuant to paragraph 2, if the holder surrenders it by sending a written declaration to such effect to the Office, and with effect from the day following the day on which the declaration is received by the Office.

Article 20   Nullity of Community plant variety rights

1.   The Office shall declare the Community plant variety right null and void if it is established:

(a)   that the conditions laid down in Articles 7 or 10 were not complied with at the time of the Community plant variety right; or

(b)   that where the grant of the Community plant variety right has been essentially based upon information and documents furnished by the applicant, the conditions laid down in Articles 8 and 9 were not complied with at the time of the grant of the right; or

(c)   that the right has been granted to a person who is not entitled to it, unless it is transferred to the person who is so entitled.

2.   Where the Community plant variety right is declared null and void, it shall be deemed not to have had, as from the outset, the effects specified in this Regulation.

Article 21   Cancellation of Community plant variety rights

1.   The Office shall cancel the Community plant variety right with effect in futurum if it is established that the conditions laid down in Article 8 or 9 are no longer complied with. If it is established that these conditions were already no longer complied with from a point in time prior to cancellation, cancellation may be made effective as from that juncture.

2.   The Office may cancel a Community plant variety right with effect in futurum if the holder, after being requested to do so, and within a time limit specified by the Office:

(a)   has not fulfilled an obligation pursuant to Article 64(3); or

(b)   in the case referred to in Article 66, does not propose another suitable variety denomination; or

(c)   fails to pay such fees as may be payable to keep the Community plant variety right in force; or

(d)   either as the initial holder or as a successor in title as a result of a transfer pursuant to Article 23, no longer satisfies the conditions laid down in Articles 12 and 82.

CHAPTER V
COMMUNITY PLANT VARIETY RIGHTS AS OBJECTS OF PROPERTY

Article 22   Assimilation with national laws

1.   Save where otherwise provided in Articles 23 to 29, a Community plant variety right as an object of property shall be regarded in all respects, and for the entire territory of the Community, as a corresponding property right in the Member State in which:

(a)   according to the entry in the Register of Community Plant Variety Rights, the holder was domiciled or had his seat or an establishment on the relevant date; or

(b)   if the conditions laid down in subparagraph (a) are not fulfilled, the first-mentioned procedural representative of the holder, as indicated in the said Register, was domiciled or had his seat or an establishment on the date of registration.

2.   Where the conditions laid down in paragraph 1 are not fulfilled, the Member State referred to in paragraph 1 shall be the Member State in which the seat of the Office is located.

3.   Where domiciles, seats or establishments in two or more Member States are entered in respect of the holder or the procedural representatives in the Register referred to in paragraph 1, the first-mentioned domicile or seat shall apply for the purposes of paragraph 1.

4.   Where two or more persons are entered in the Register referred to in paragraph 1 as joint holders, the relevant holder for the purposes of applying paragraph 1(a) shall be

the first joint holder taken in order of entry in the Register who fulfils the conditions. Where none of the joint holders fulfils the conditions laid down in paragraph 1(a), paragraph 2 shall be applicable.

Article 23   Transfer

1.   A Community plant variety right may be the object of a transfer to one or more successors in title.

2.   Transfer of a Community plant variety right by assignment can be made only to successors who comply with the conditions laid down in Article 12 and 82. It shall be made in writing and shall require the signature of the parties to the contract, except when it is a result of a judgment or of any other acts terminating court proceedings. Otherwise it shall be void.

3.   Save as otherwise provided in Article 100, a transfer shall have no bearing on the rights acquired by third parties before the date of transfer.

4.   A transfer shall not take effect for the Office and may not be cited *vis-à-vis* third parties unless documentary evidence thereof as provided for in the implementing rules is provided and until it has been entered in the Register of Community Plant Variety Rights. A transfer that has not yet been entered in the Register may, however, be cited *vis-à-vis* third parties who have acquired rights after the date of transfer but who knew of the transfer at the date on which they acquired those rights.

. . .

Article 26   The application for a Community plant variety right as an object of property

Articles 22 to 25 shall apply to applications for Community plant variety rights. Concerning such applications, the references made in those Articles to the Register of Community Plant Variety Rights shall be regarded as references to the Register of Application for Community Plant Variety Rights.

Article 27   Contractual exploitation rights

1.   Community plant variety rights may form in full or in part the subject of contractually granted exploitation rights. Exploitation rights may be exclusive or non-exclusive.

2.   The holder may invoke the rights conferred by the Community plant variety right against a person enjoying the right of exploitation who contravenes any of the conditions or limitations attached to his exploitation right pursuant to paragraph 1.

Article 28   Joint holdership

Articles 22 to 27 shall apply *mutatis mutandis* in the event of joint holdership of a Community plant variety right in proportion to the respective share held, where such shares have been determined.

Article 29   Compulsory exploitation right

1.   Compulsory exploitation rights shall be granted to one or more persons by the Office, on application by that person or those persons, but only on grounds of public interest and after consulting the Administrative Council referred to in Article 36.

2.   On application by a Member State, by the Commission or by an organisation set up at Community level and registered by the Commission, a compulsory exploitation right may be granted, either to a category of persons satisfying specific requirements, or to anyone in one or more Member States or throughout the Community. It may be granted only on grounds of public interest and with the approval of the Administrative Council.

3.   The Office shall, when granting the compulsory exploitation right, stipulate the type of acts covered and specify the reasonable conditions pertaining thereto as well as the specific requirements referred to in paragraph 2. The reasonable conditions shall

take into account the interests of any holder of plant variety rights who would be affected by the grant of the compulsory exploitation right. The reasonable conditions may include a possible time limitation, the payment of an appropriate royalty as equitable remuneration to the holder, and may impose certain obligations on the holder, the fulfilment of which are necessary to make use of the compulsory exploitation right.

4.   On the expiry of each one-year period after the grant of the compulsory exploitation right and within the aforementioned possible time limitation, any of the parties to proceedings may request that the decision on the grant of the compulsory exploitation right be cancelled or amended. The sole grounds for such a request shall be that the circumstances determining the decision taken have in the meantime undergone change.

5.   On application, the compulsory exploitation right shall be granted to the holder in respect of an essentially derived variety if the criteria set out in paragraph 1 are met. The reasonable conditions referred to in paragraph 3 shall include the payment of an appropriate royalty as equitable remuneration to the holder of the initial variety.

6.   The implementing rules pursuant to Article 114 may specify certain cases as examples of public interest referred to in paragraph 1 and moreover lay down details for the implementation of the provisions of the above paragraphs.

7.   Compulsory exploitation rights may not be granted by Member States in respect of a Community plant variety right.

. . .

PART FOUR
PROCEEDINGS BEFORE THE OFFICE
CHAPTER I
APPLICATIONS

Article 49   Filing of applications
1.   An application for a Community plant variety right shall be filed at the choice of the applicant:
(a)   at the Office directly; or
(b)   at one of the sub-offices or national agencies, established or entrusted, pursuant to Article 30(4), subject to the applicant forwarding an information on this filing to the Office directly within two weeks after filing.
. . .

Article 50   Conditions governing applications
1.   The application for a Community plant variety right must contain at least the following:
(a)   a request for the grant of a Community plant variety right;
(b)   identification of the botanical taxon;
(c)   information identifying the applicant or, where appropriate, the joint applicants;
(d)   the name of the breeder and an assurance that, to the best of the applicants knowledge, no further persons have been involved in the breeding, or discovery and development, of the variety; if the applicant is not the breeder, or not the only breeder, he shall provide the relevant documentary evidence as to how the entitlement to the Community plant variety right came into his possession;
(e)   a provisional designation for the variety;
(f)   a technical description of the variety;
(g)   the geographic origin of the variety;
(h)   the credentials of any procedural representatives;
(i)   details of any previous commercialisation of the variety;
(j)   details of any other application made in respect of the variety.
. . .

3.   An application shall propose a variety denomination which may accompany the application.

Article 51   Date of application
The date of application for a Community plant variety right shall be the date on which a valid application was received by the Office pursuant to Article 49(1)(a) or by a sub-office or national agency pursuant to Article 49(1)(b), provided it complies with Article 50(1) and subject to payment of the fees due pursuant to Article 83 within a time limit specified by the Office.

Article 52   The right of priority
1.   The right of priority of an application shall be determined by the date of receipt of the application. Where applications have the same date of application, the priorities thereof shall be determined according to the order in which they were received, if this can be established. Otherwise they shall have the same priority.

2.   If the applicant or his predecessor in title has already applied for a property right for the variety in a Member State or in a Member of the International Union for the Protection of New Varieties of Plants, and the date of application is within 12 months of the filing of the earlier application, the applicant shall enjoy a right of priority for the earlier application as regards the application for the Community plant variety right, provided the earlier application still exists on the date of application.

3.   The right of priority shall have the effect that the date on which the earlier application was filed shall count as the date of application for the Community plant variety right for the purposes of Articles 7, 10 and 11.

4.   Paragraphs 2 and 3 shall also apply in respect of earlier applications that were filed in another Member State, provided the conditions set out in Article 12(1)(b), second sentence, is met regarding this State on the date of application for the Community plant variety right.

5.   Any claim for a right of priority earlier than that provided for in paragraph 2 shall lapse if the applicant does not submit to the Office within three months of the date of application copies of the earlier application that have been certified by the authorities responsible for such application. If the earlier application has not been made in one of the official languages of the European Communities, the Office may require, in addition, a translation of the earlier application in one of these languages.

CHAPTER II
EXAMINATION

Article 53   Formal examination of application
1.   The Office shall examine whether:
    (a)   the application has effectively been filed pursuant to Article 49;
    (b)   the application complies with the conditions laid down in Article 50 and the conditions laid down in the implementing rules pursuant to that Article;
    (c)   where appropriate, a claim for priority complies with the provision laid down in Article 52(2), (4) and (5); and
    (d)   the fees due pursuant to Article 83 have been paid within a time limit specified by the Office.

2.   If the application, although complying with the conditions referred to in Article 51, does not comply with other conditions laid down in Article 50, the Office shall give the applicant an opportunity to correct any deficiencies that may have been identified.

3.   If the application does not comply with the conditions referred to in Article 51, the Office shall inform the applicant thereof, or, where this is not possible, publish the information pursuant to Article 89.

Article 54   Substantive examination
1.   The Office shall examine whether the variety may be the object of a Community plant variety right pursuant to Article 5, whether the variety is new pursuant to Article 10, whether the applicant is entitled to file an application pursuant to Article 12 and whether the conditions laid down in Article 82 are complied with. The Office shall also examine whether the proposed variety denomination is suitable pursuant to Article 63. For such purposes, it may avail itself of the services of other bodies.
2.   The first applicant shall be deemed to be entitled to the Community plant variety right pursuant to Article 11. This shall not apply if, before a decision on the application is taken, the Office is aware, or it is shown by a final judgment delivered with regard to a claim for entitlement pursuant to Article 98(4), that entitlement is not or is not solely vested in the first applicant. Where the identity of the sole or other person entitled has been determined, the person or persons may enter the proceedings as applicant or applicants.

Article 55   Technical examination
1.   Where the Office has not discovered any impediment to the grant of a Community plant variety right on the basis of the examination pursuant to Articles 53 and 54, it shall arrange for the technical examination relating to compliance with the conditions laid down in Articles 7, 8 and 9 to be carried out by the competent office or offices in at least one of the Member States entrusted with responsibility for the technical examination of varieties of the species concerned by the Administrative Council, hereafter referred to as the 'Examination Office or Offices'.
. . .

Article 59   Objections to grant of right
1.   Any person may lodge with the Office a written objection to the grant of a Community plant variety right.
2.   Objectors shall be party to the proceedings for grant of the Community plant variety right in addition to the applicant. Without prejudice to Article 88, objectors shall have access to the documents, including the results of the technical examination and the variety description as referred to in Article 57(2).
3.   Objections may be based only on the contention that:
    (a)   the conditions laid down in Articles 7 to 11 are not complied with;
    (b)   there is an impediment under Article 63(3) or (4) to a proposed variety denomination.
4.   Objections may be lodged:
    (a)   at any time after the application and prior to a decision pursuant to Articles 61 or 62, in the case of paragraph 3(a) hereof;
    (b)   within three months of the publication of the proposed variety denomination pursuant to Article 89, in the case of objections under paragraph 3(b) hereof.
5.   The decisions on objections may be taken together with the decisions pursuant to Articles 61, 62 or 63.

Article 60   Priority of a new application in the case of objections
Where an objection on the grounds that the conditions laid down in Article 11 are not met leads to the withdrawal or refusal of the application for a Community plant variety right and if the objector files an application for a Community plant variety right within one month following the withdrawal or within one month of the date on which the refusal becomes final in respect of the same variety, he may require that the date of the withdrawn or refused application be deemed to be the date of his application.

CHAPTER III
DECISIONS

Article 61   Refusal

1.   The Office shall refuse applications for a Community plant variety right if and as soon as it establishes that the applicant:

(a) ` has not remedied any deficiencies within the meaning of Article 53 which he was given as opportunity to correct within the time limit notified to him;

(b)   has not complied with a rule or request pursuant to Article 55(4) or (5) within the time limit laid down, unless the Office has consented to non-submission; or

(c)   has not proposed a variety denomination which is suitable pursuant to Article 63.

2.   The Office shall also refuse applications for a Community plant variety right if:

(a)   it establishes that the conditions it is required to verify pursuant to Article 54 have not been fulfilled; or

(b)   it reaches the opinion on the basis of the examination reports pursuant to Article 57, that the conditions laid down in Articles 7, 8 and 9 have not been fulfilled.

Article 62   Grant

If the Office is of the opinion that the findings of the examination are sufficient to decide on the application and there are no impediments pursuant to Articles 59 and 61, it shall grant the Community plant variety right. The decision shall include an official description of the variety.

Article 63   Variety denomination

1.   Where a Community plant variety right is granted, the Office shall approve, for the variety in question, the variety denomination proposed by the applicant pursuant to Article 50(3), if it considers, on the basis of the examination made pursuant to the second sentence of Article 54(1), that this denomination is suitable.

2.   A variety denomination is suitable, if there is no impediment pursuant to paragraphs 3 or 4 of this Article.

3.   There is an impediment for the designation of a variety denomination where:

(a)   its use in the territory of the Community is precluded by the prior right of a third party;

(b)   it may commonly cause its users difficulties as regards recognition of reproduction;

(c)   it is identical or may be confused with a variety denomination under which another variety of the same or of a closely related species is entered in an official register of plant varieties or under which material or another variety has been marketed in a Member State or in a Member of the International Unit for the Protection of New Varieties of Plants, unless the other variety no longer remains in existence and its denomination has acquired no special significance;

(d)   it is identical or may be confused with other designations which are commonly used for the marketing of goods or which have to be kept free under other legislation;

(e)   it is liable to give offence in one of the Member States or is contrary to public policy;

(f)   it is liable to mislead or to cause confusion concerning the characteristics, the value or the identity of the variety or the identity of the breeder or any other party to proceedings.

4.   There is another impediment where, in the case of a variety which has already been entered:

(a)   in one of the Member States; or

(b)   in a Member of the International Union for the Protection of New Varieties of Plants; or

(c)   in another State for which it has been established in a Community act that varieties are evaluated there under rules which are equivalent to those laid down in the Directives on common catalogues;
in an official register of plant varieties or material thereof and has been marketed there for commercial purposes, and the proposed variety denomination differs from that which has been registered or used there, unless the latter one is the object of an impediment pursuant to paragraph 3.

5.   The Office shall publish the species which it considers 'closely related' within the meaning of paragraph 3(c).

CHAPTER IV
THE MAINTENANCE OF COMMUNITY PLANT VARIETY RIGHTS

Article 64   Technical verification

1.   The Office shall verify the continuing existence unaltered of the protected varieties.
. . .

Article 66   Amendment of the variety denomination

1.   The Office shall amend a variety denomination designated pursuant to Article 63 if it establishes that the denomination does not satisfy, or no longer satisfies, the conditions laid down in Article 63 and in the event of a prior conflicting right of a third party, if the holder agrees to the amendment or the holder or any other person required to use the variety denomination has been prohibited, by a final judgment, for this reason from using the variety denomination.
. . .

PART FIVE
IMPACT ON OTHER LAWS

Article 92   Cumulative protection prohibited

1.   Any variety which is the subject matter of a Community plant variety right shall not be the subject of a national plant variety right or any patent for that variety. Any rights granted contrary to the first sentence shall be ineffective.

2.   Where the holder has been granted another right as referred to in paragraph 1 for the same variety prior to grant of the Community plant variety right, he shall be unable to invoke the rights conferred by such protection for the variety for as long as the Community plant variety right remains effective.

Article 93   Application of national law

Claims under Community plant variety rights shall be subject to limitations imposed by the law of the Member States only as expressly referred to in this Regulation.

PART SIX
CIVIL LAW CLAIMS, INFRINGEMENTS, JURSIDICTION

Article 94   Infringement

1.   Whosoever:
(a)   effects one of the acts set out in Article 13(2) without being entitled to do so, in respect of a variety for which a Community plant variety right has been granted; or
(b)   omits the correct usage of a variety denomination as referred to in Article 17(1) or omits the relevant information as referred to in Article 17(2); or
(c)   contrary to Article 18(3) uses the variety denomination of a variety for which a Community plant variety right has been granted or a designation that may be confused with it;
may be sued by the holder to enjoin such infringement or to pay reasonable compensation or both.

2.   Whosoever acts intentionally or negligently shall moreover be liable to compensate the holder for any further damage resulting from the act in question. In cases of slight negligence, such claims may be reduced according to the degree of such slight negligence, but not however to the extent that they are less than the advantage derived therefrom by the person who committed the infringement.

Article 95   Acts prior to grant of Community plant variety rights
The holder may require reasonable compensation from any person who has, in the time between publication of the application for a Community plant variety right and grant thereof, effected an act that he would be prohibited from performing subsequent thereto.

Article 96   Prescription
Claims pursuant to Articles 94 and 95 shall be time barred after three years from the time at which the Community plant variety right has finally been granted and the holder has knowledge of the act and of the identity of the party liable or, in the absence of such knowledge, after 30 years from the termination of the act concerned.

Article 97   Supplementary application of national law regarding infringement
1.   Where the party liable pursuant to Article 94 has, by virtue of the infringement, made any gain at the expense of the holder or of a person entitled to exploitation rights, the courts competent pursuant to Articles 101 or 102 shall apply their national law, including their private international law, as regards restitution.

2.   Paragraph 1 shall also apply as regards other claims that may arise in respect of the performance or omission of acts pursuant to Article 95 in the time between publication of the application for grant of a Community plant variety right and the disposal of the request.

3.   In all other respects the effects of Community plant variety rights shall be determined solely in accordance with this Regulation.

Article 98   Claiming entitlement to a Community plant variety right
1.   If a Community plant variety right has been granted to a person who is not entitled to it under Article 11, the person entitled to it may, without prejudice to any other remedy which may be open to him under the laws of the Member States, claim to have the Community plant variety right transferred to him.

2.   Where a person is entitled to only part of a Community plant variety right, that person may, in accordance with paragraph 1, claim to be made a joint holder.

3.   Claims pursuant to paragraphs 1 and 2 may be invoked only within a period of up to five years of publication of the grant of the Community plant variety right. This provision shall not apply if the holder knew, at the time it was granted to or acquired by him, that he was not entitled to such rights or that entitlement thereto was not vested solely in him.

4.   The person entitled shall be eligible *mutatis mutandis* to pursue claims pursuant to paragraphs 1 and 2 in respect of an application for grant of a Community plant variety right filed by a person who was not entitled to it or whom the entitlement was not vested solely.

Article 99   Obtaining identification of a variety
The holder of an initial variety and the breeder of a variety essentially derived from the initial variety shall be entitled to obtain an acknowledgement of the identification of the varieties concerned as initial and essentially derived.

Article 100   Consequences of a change in holdership of a Community plant variety right
1.   In the event of a complete change in the holdership of a Community plant variety right in consequence of a final judgment delivered pursuant to Articles 101 or 102 for

the purposes of claiming entitlement under Article 98(1), any exploitation or other rights shall lapse with the entry of the person entitled in the Register of Community Plant Variety Rights.

2.   Where the holder or a person enjoying the right of exploitation has effected one of the acts set out in Article 13(2) or has made effective and genuine arrangements to do so prior to the commencement of the proceedings pursuant to Articles 101 or 102, he may continue or perform such acts provided he requests a non-exclusive exploitation right from the new holder entered in the Register of Community Plant Variety Rights. Such requests must be made within the time limit laid down in the implementing rules. The exploitation right may be granted by the Office in the absence of an agreement between the parties. Article 29(3) to (7) shall apply *mutatis mutandis*.

3.   Paragraph 2 shall not apply where the holder or persons enjoying the right of exploitation acted in bad faith when they effected the acts or began to make the arrangements.

. . .

Article 104   Entitlement to bring an action for infringement
1.   Actions for infringement may be brought by the holder. Persons enjoying exploitation rights may bring such actions unless that has been expressly excluded by agreement with the holder in the case of an exclusive exploitation right or by the Office pursuant to Articles 2 or 100(2).

2.   Any person enjoying exploitation rights shall, for the purpose of obtaining compensation for damage suffered by him, be entitled to intervene in an infringement action brought by the holder.

Article 105   Obligation of national courts or other bodies
A national court or other body hearing an action relating to a Community plant variety right shall treat the Community plant variety right as valid.

Article 106   Stay of proceedings
1.   Where an action relates to claims pursuant to Article 98(4) and the decision depends upon the protectability of the variety pursuant to Article 6, this decision may not be given before the Office has decided on the application for a Community plant variety right.

2.   Where an action relates to a Community plant variety right that has been granted and in respect of which proceedings for revocation or cancellation pursuant to Articles 20 or 21 have been initiated, the proceedings may be stayed in so far as the decision depends upon the validity of the Community plant variety right.

Article 107   Penalties for infringement of Community plant variety rights
Member States shall take all appropriate measures to ensure that the same provisions are made applicable to penalise infringements of Community plant variety rights as apply in the matter of infringements of corresponding national rights.

. . .

PART EIGHT
TRANSITIONAL AND FINAL PROVISIONS

Article 116   Derogations
1.   Notwithstanding Article 10(1)(a) and without prejudice to the provisions of Article 10(2) and (3), a variety shall be deemed to be new also in cases where variety constituents or harvested material thereof have not been sold or otherwise disposed of to others, by or with the consent of the breeder, within the territory of the Community for purposes of exploitation of the variety, earlier than four years, in the case of trees or of vines earlier than six years, before the entry into force of this Regulation, if the date of application is within one year of that date.

2. The provision of paragraph 1 shall apply to such varieties also in cases where a national plant variety right was granted in one or more Member States before the entry into force of this Regulation.

3. Notwithstanding Articles 55 and 56, the technical examination of these varieties shall be carried out to the extent possible by the Office on the basis of the available findings resulting from any proceedings for the grant of a national plant variety right, in agreement with the authority before which these proceedings were held.

4. In the case of a Community plant variety right granted pursuant to paragraphs 1 or 2:

— Article 13(5)(a) shall not apply in relation to essentially derived varieties, the existence of which was a matter of common knowledge in the Community before the date of entry into force of this Regulation.

— Article 14(3), fourth indent shall not apply to farmers who continue to use an established variety in accordance with the authorisation of Article 14(1) if, before the entry into force of this Regulation, they have already used the variety for the purposes described in Article 14(1) without payment of a remuneration; this provision shall apply until 30 June of the seventh year following that of the entry into force of this Regulation. Before that date the Commission shall submit a report on the situation of the established varieties dealing with each variety individually. That period may be extended, in the implementing provisions adopted pursuant to Article 114, in so far as the Commission's report justifies it.

— without prejudice to the rights conferred by national protection, the provisions of Article 16 shall apply *mutatis mutandis* to acts concerning material disposed of to others by the breeder or with his consent prior to the date of entry into force of this Regulation, and effected by person who, prior to that date, have already effected such acts or have made effective and genuine arrangements to do so.

If such earlier acts have involved further propagation which was intended within the meaning of Article 16(a), the authorisation of the holder shall be required for any further propagation after the expiry of the second year, in the case of varieties of vine and tree species after the expiry of the fourth year, following the date of entry into force of this Regulation.

— Notwithstanding Article 19, the duration of the Community plant variety right shall be reduced by the longest period:

— during which variety constituents or harvested material thereof have been sold or otherwise disposed of to others, by or with the consent of the breeder, within the territory of the Community for purposes of exploitation of the variety, as established in the findings resulting from the procedure for the grant of the Community plant variety right, in the case of paragraph 1,

— during which any national plant variety right or rights have been effective, in the case of paragraph 2,

but not more than by five years.

Article 117   Transitional provisions

The Office shall be set up in good time to assume fully the tasks incumbent upon it pursuant to this Regulation as from 27 April 1995.

Article 118   Entry into force

1. This Regulation shall enter into force on the day of its publication in the *Official Journal of the European Communities*.

2. Articles 1, 2, 3, 5 to 29 and 49 to 106 shall apply from 27 April 1995.

This Regulation shall be binding in its entirety and directly applicable in all Member States.

COMMISSION REGULATION (EC) No. 240/96
of 31 January 1996
on the application of Article 85(3) of the Treaty to certain categories of technology transfer agreements

THE COMMISSION OF THE EUROPEAN COMMUNITIES,

Having regard to the Treaty establishing the European Community,

Having regard to Council Regulation No. 19/65/EEC of 2 March 1965 on the application of Article 85(3) of the Treaty to certain categories of agreements and concerted practices, as last amended by the Act of Accession of Austria, Finland and Sweden, and in particular Article 1 thereof,

Having published a draft of this Regulation,

After consulting the Advisory Committee on Restrictive Practices and Dominant Positions,

Whereas:

(1) Regulation No. 19/65/EEC empowers the Commission to apply Article 85(3) of the Treaty by regulation to certain categories of agreements and concerted practices falling within the scope of Article 85(1) which include restrictions imposed in relation to the acquisition or use of industrial property rights — in particular of patents, utility models, designs or trademarks — or to the rights arising out of contracts for assignment of, or the right to use, a method of manufacture of knowledge relating to use or to the application of industrial processes.

(2) The Commission has made use of this power by adopting Regulation (EEC) No. 2349/84 of 23 July 1984 on the application of Article 85(3) of the Treaty to certain categories of patent licensing agreements, as last amended by Regulation (EC) No. 2131/95, and Regulation (EEC) No. 556/89 of 30 November 1988 on the application of Article 85(3) of the Treaty to certain categories of know-how licensing agreements, as last amended by the Act of Accession of Austria, Finland and Sweden.

(3) These two block exemptions ought to be combined into a single regulation covering technology transfer agreements, and the rules governing patent licensing agreements and agreements for the licensing of know-how ought to be harmonised and simplified as far as possible, in order to encourage the dissemination of technical knowledge in the Community and to promote the manufacture of technically more sophisticated products. In those circumstances Regulation (EEC) No. 556/89 should be repealed.

(4) This Regulation should apply to the licensing of Member States' own patents, Community patents and European patents ("pure" patent licensing agreements). It should also apply to agreements for the licensing of non-patented technical information such as descriptions of manufacturing processes, recipes, formulae, designs or drawings, commonly termed "know-how" ("pure" know-how licensing agreements), and to combined patent and know-how licensing agreements ("mixed" agreements), which are playing an increasingly important role in the transfer of technology. For the purposes of this Regulation, a number of terms are defined in Article 10.

(5) Patent or know-how licensing agreements are agreements whereby one undertaking which holds a patent or know-how ("the licensor") permits another undertaking ("the licensee") to exploit the patent thereby licensed, or communicates the know-how to it, in particular for purposes of manufacture, use or putting on the market. In the light of experience acquired so far, it is possible to define a category of licensing agreements covering all or part of the common market which are capable of falling within the scope of Article 85(1) but which can normally be regarded as satisfying the conditions laid down in Article 85(3), where patents are necessary for the achievement of the objects of the licensed technology by a mixed agreement or where know-how — whether it is ancillary to patents or independent of them — is secret, substantial and identified in any

appropriate form. These criteria are intended only to ensure that the licensing of the know-how or the grant of the patent licence justifies a block exemption of obligations restricting competition. This is without prejudice to the right of the parties to include in the contract provisions regarding other obligations, such as the obligation to pay royalties, even if the block exemption no longer applies.

(6) It is appropriate to extend the scope of this Regulation to pure or mixed agreements containing the licensing of intellectual property rights other than patents (in particular, trademarks, design rights and copyright, especially software protection), when such additional licensing contributes to the achievement of the objects of the licensed technology and contains only ancillary provisions.

(7) Where such pure or mixed licensing agreements contain not only obligations relating to territories within the common market but also obligations relating to non-member countries, the presence of the latter does not prevent this Regulation from applying to the obligations relating to territories within the common market. Where licensing agreements for non-member countries or for territories which extend beyond the frontiers of the Community have effects within the common market which may fall within the scope of Article 85(1), such agreements should be covered by this Regulation to the same extent as would agreements for territories within the common market.

(8) The objective being to facilitate the dissemination of technology and the improvement of manufacturing processes, this Regulation should apply only where the licensee himself manufactures the licensed products or has them manufactured for his account, or where the licensed product is a service, provides the service himself or has the service provided for his account, irrespective of whether or not the licensee is also entitled to use confidential information provided by the licensor for the promotion and sale of the licensed product. The scope of this Regulation should therefore exclude agreements solely for the purpose of sale. Also to be excluded from the scope of this Regulation are agreements relating to marketing know-how communicated in the context of franchising arrangements and certain licensing agreements entered into in connection with arrangements such as joint ventures or patent pools and other arrangements in which a licence is granted in exchange for other licences not related to improvements to or new applications of the licensed technology. Such agreements pose different problems which cannot at present be dealt with in a single regulation (Article 5).

(9) Given the similarity between sale and exclusive licensing, and the danger that the requirements of this Regulation might be evaded by presenting as assignments what are in fact exclusive licenses restrictive of competition, this Regulation should apply to agreements concerning the assignment and acquisition of patents or know-how where the risk associated with exploitation remains with the assignor. It should also apply to licensing agreements in which the licensor is not the holder of the patent or know-how but is authorised by the holder to grant the licence (as in the case of sublicences) and to licensing agreements in which the parties' rights or obligations are assumed by connected undertakings (Article 6).

(10) Exclusive licensing agreements, i.e. agreements in which the licensor under-takes not to exploit the licensed technology in the licensed territory himself or to grant further licences there, may not be in themselves incompatible with Article 85(1) where they are concerned with the introduction and protection of a new technology in the licensed territory, by reason of the scale of the research which has been undertaken, of the increase in the level of competition, in particular inter-brand competition, and of the competitiveness of the undertakings concerned resulting from the dissemination of innovation within the Community. In so far as agreements of this kind fall, in other circumstances, within the scope of Article 85(1), it is appropriate to include them in Article 1 in order that they may also benefit from the exemption.

(11) The exemption of export bans on the licensor and on the licensees does not prejudice any developments in the case law of the Court of Justice in relation to such

agreements, notably with respect to Articles 30 to 36 and Article 85(1). This is also the case, in particular, regarding the prohibition on the licensee from selling the licensed product in territories granted to other licensees (passive competition).

(12)   The obligations listed in Article 1 generally contribute to improving the production of goods and to promoting technical progress. They make the holders of patents or know-how more willing to grant licences and licensees more inclined to undertake the investment required to manufacture, use and put on the market a new product or to use a new process. Such obligations may be permitted under this Regulation in respect of territories where the licensed product is protected by patents as long as these remain in force.

(13)   Since the point at which the know-how ceases to be secret can be difficult to determine, it is appropriate, in respect of territories where the licensed technology comprises know-how only, to limit such obligations to a fixed number of years. Moreover, in order to provide sufficient periods of protection, it is appropriate to take as the starting-point for such periods the date on which the product is first put on the market in the Community by a licensee.

(14)   Exemption under Article 85(3) of longer periods of territorial protection for know-how agreements, in particular in order to protect expensive and risky investment or where the parties were not competitors at the date of the grant of the licence, can be granted only by individual decision. On the other hand, parties are free to extend the term of their agreements in order to exploit any subsequent improvement and to provide for the payment of additional royalties. However, in such cases, further periods of territorial protection may be allowed only starting from the date of licensing of the secret improvements in the Community, and by individual decision. Where the research for improvements results in innovations which are distinct from the licensed technology the parties may conclude a new agreement benefitting from an exemption under this Regulation.

(15)   Provision should also be made for exemption of an obligation on the licensee not to put the product on the market in the territories of other licensees, the permitted period for such an obligation (this obligation would ban not just active competition but passive competition too) should, however, be limited to a few years from the date on which the licensed product is first put on the market in the Community by a licensee, irrespective of whether the licensed technology comprises know-how, patents or both in the territories concerned.

(16)   The exemption of territorial protection should apply for the whole duration of the periods thus permitted, as long as the patents remain in force or the know-how remains secret and substantial. The parties to a mixed patent and know-how licensing agreement must be able to take advantage in a particular territory of the period of protection conferred by a patent or by the know-how, whichever is the longer.

(17)   The obligations listed in Article 1 also generally fulfil the other conditions for the application of Article 85(3). Consumers will, as a rule, be allowed a fair share of the benefit resulting from the improvement in the supply of goods on the market. To safeguard this effect, however, it is right to exclude from the application of Article 1 cases where the parties agree to refuse to meet demand from users or resellers within their respective territories who would resell for export, or to take other steps to impede parallel imports. The obligations referred to above thus only impose restrictions which are indispensable to the attainment of their objectives.

(18)   It is desirable to list in this Regulation a number of obligations that are commonly found in licensing agreements but are normally not restrictive of competition, and to provide that in the event that because of the particular economic or legal circumstances they should fall within Article 85(1), they too will be covered by the exemption. This list, in Article 2, is not exhaustive.

(19)   This Regulation must also specify what restrictions or provisions may not be included in licensing agreements if these are to benefit from the block exemption. The

restrictions listed in Article 3 may fall under the prohibition of Article 85(1), but in their case there can be no general presumption that, although they relate to the transfer of technology, they will lead to the positive effects required by Article 85(3), as would be necessary for the granting of a block exemption. Such restrictions can be declared exempt only by an individual decision, taking account of the market position of the undertakings concerned and the degree of concentration on the relevant market.

(20)   The obligations on the licensee to cease using the licensed technology after the termination of the agreement (Article 2(1)(3)) and to make improvements available to the licensor (Article 2(1)(4)) do not generally restrict competition. The post-term use ban may be regarded as a normal feature of licensing, as otherwise the licensor would be forced to transfer his know-how or patents in perpetuity. Undertakings by the licensee to grant back to the licensor a licence for improvements to the licensed know-how and/or patents are generally not restrictive of competition if the licensee is entitled by the contract to share in future experience and inventions made by the licensor. On the other hand, a restrictive effect on competition arises where the agreement obliges the licensee to assign to the licensor rights to improvements of the originally licensed techology that he himself has brought about (Article 3(6)).

(21)   The list of clauses which do not prevent exemption also includes an obligation on the licensee to keep paying royalties until the end of the agreement independently of whether or not the licensed know-how has entered into the public domain through the action of third parties or of the licensee himself (Article 2(1)(7)). Moreover, the parties must be free, in order to facilitate payment, to spread the royalty payments for the use of the licensed technology over a period extending beyond the duration of the licensed patents, in particular by setting lower royalty rates. As a rule, parties do not need to be protected against the foreseeable financial consequences of an agreement freely entered into, and they should therefore be free to choose the appropriate means of financing the technology transfer and sharing between them the risks of such use. However, the setting of rates of royalty so as to achieve one of the restrictions listed in Article 3 renders the agreement ineligible for the block exemption.

(22)   An obligation on the licensee to restrict his exploitation of the licensed technology to one or more technical fields of application ("fields of use") or to one or more product markets is not caught by Article 85(1) either, since the licensor is entitled to transfer the technology only for a limited purpose (Article 2(1)(8)).

(23)   Clauses whereby the parties allocate customers within the same technological field of use or the same product market, either by an actual prohibition on supplying certain classes of customer or through an obligation with an equivalent effect, would also render the agreement ineligible for the block exemption where the parties are competitors for the contract products (Article 3(4)). Such restrictions between undertakings which are not competitors remain subject to the opposition procedure. Article 3 does not apply to cases where the patent or know-how licence is granted in order to provide a single customer with a second source of supply. In such a case, a prohibition on the second licensee from supplying persons other than the customer concerned is an essential condition for the grant of a second licence, since the purpose of the transaction is not to create an independent supplier in the market. The same applies to limitations on the quantities the licensee may supply to the customer concerned (Article 2(1)(13)).

(24)   Besides the clauses already mentioned, the list of restrictions which render the block exemption inapplicable also includes restrictions regarding the selling prices of the licensed product or the quantities to be manufactured or sold, since they seriously limit the extent to which the licensee can exploit the licensed technology and since quantity restrictions particularly may have the same effect as export bans (Article 3(1) and (5)). This does not apply where a licence is granted for use of the technology in specific production facilities and where both a specific technology is communicated for the

setting-up, operation and maintenance of these facilities and the licensee is allowed to increase the capacity of the facilities or to set up further facilities for its own use on normal commercial terms. On the other hand, the licensee may lawfully be prevented from using the transferred technology to set up facilities for third parties, since the purpose of the agreement is not to permit the licensee to give other producers access to the licensor's technology while it remains secret or protected by patent (Article 2(1)(12)).

(25) Agreements which are not automatically covered by the exemption because they contain provisions that are not expressly exempted by this Regulation and not expressly excluded from exemption, including those listed in Article 4(2), may, in certain circumstances, nonetheless be presumed to be eligible for application of the block exemption. It will be possible for the Commission rapidly to establish whether this is the case on the basis of the information undertakings are obliged to provide under Commission Regulation (EC) No. 3385/94. The Commission may waive the requirement to supply specific information required in form A/B but which it does not deem necessary. The Commission will generally be content with communication of the text of the agreement and with an estimate, based on directly available data, of the market structure and of the licensee's market share. Such agreements should therefore be deemed to be covered by the exemption provided for in this Regulation where they are notified to the Commission and the Commission does not oppose the application of the exemption within a specified period of time.

(26) Where agreements exempted under this Regulation nevertheless have effects incompatible with Article 85(3), the Commission may withdraw the block exemption, in particular where the licensed products are not faced with real competition in the licensed territory (Article 7). This could also be the case where the licensee has a strong position on the market. In assessing the competition the Commission will pay special attention to cases where the licensee has more than 40% of the whole market for the licensed products and of all the products or services which customers consider interchangeable or substitutable on account of their characteristics, prices and intended use.

(27) Agreements which come within the terms of Articles 1 and 2 and which have neither the object nor the effect of restricting competition in any other way need no longer be notified. Nevertheless, undertakings will still have the right to apply in individual cases for negative clearance or for exemption under Article 85(3) in accordance with Council Regulation No. 17; as last amended by the Act of Accession of Austria, Finland and Sweden. They can in particular notify agreements obliging the licensor not to grant other licences in the territory, where the licensee's market share exceeds or is likely to exceed 40%,

HAS ADOPTED THIS REGULATION:

Article 1

1. Pursuant to Article 85(3) of the Treaty and subject to the conditions set out below, it is hereby declared that Article 85(1) of the Treaty shall not apply to pure patent licensing or know-how licensing agreements and to mixed patent and know-how licensing agreements, including those agreements containing ancillary provisions relating to intellectual property rights other than patents, to which only two undertakings are party and which include one or more of the following obligations:

(1) an obligation on the licensor not to license other undertakings to exploit the licensed technology in the licensed territory;

(2) an obligation on the licensor not to exploit the licensed technology in the licensed territory himself;

(3) an obligation on the licensee not to exploit the licensed technology in the territory of the licensor within the common market;

(4)   an obligation on the licensee not to manufacture or use the licensed product, or use the licensed process, in territories within the common market which are licensed to other licensees;

(5)   an obligation on the licensee not to pursue an active policy of putting the licensed product on the market in the territories within the common market which are licensed to other licensees, and in particular not to engage in advertising specifically aimed at those territories or to establish any branch or maintain a distribution depot there;

(6)   an obligation on the licensee not to put the licensed product on the market in the territories licensed to other licensees within the common market in response to unsolicited orders;

(7)   an obligation on the licensee to use only the licensor's trademark or get up to distinguish the licensed product during the term of the agreement, provided that the licensee is not prevented from identifying himself as the manufacturer of the licensed products;

(8)   an obligation on the licensee to limit his production of the licensed product to the quantities he requires in manufacturing his own products and to sell the licensed product only as an integral part of or a replacement part for his own products or otherwise in connection with the sale of his own products, provided that such quantities are freely determined by the licensee.

2.   Where the agreement is a pure patent licensing agreement, the exemption of the obligations referred to in paragraph 1 is granted only to the extent that and for as long as the licensed product is protected by parallel patents, in the territories respectively of the licensee (points (1), (2), (7) and (8)), the licensor (point (3)) and other licensees (points (4) and (5)). The exemption of the obligation referred to in point (6) of paragraph 1 is granted for a period not exceeding five years from the date when the licensed product is first put on the market within the common market by one of the licensees, to the extent that and for as long as, in these territories, this product is protected by parallel patents.

3.   Where the agreement is a pure know-how licensing agreement, the period for which the exemption of the obligations referred to in points (1) to (5) of paragraph 1 is granted may not exceed ten years from the date when the licensed product is first put on the market within the common market by one of the licensees.

The exemption of the obligation referred to in point (6) of paragraph 1 is granted for a period not exceeding five years from the date when the licensed product is first put on the market within the common market by one of the licensees.

The obligations referred to in points (7) and (8) of paragraph 1 are exempted during the lifetime of the agreement for as long as the know-how remains secret and substantial.

However, the exemption in paragraph 1 shall apply only where the parties have identified in any appropriate form the initial know-how and any subsequent improvements to it which become available to one party and are communicated to the other party pursuant to the terms of the agreement and to the purpose thereof, and only for as long as the know-how remains secret and substantial.

4.   Where the agreement is a mixed patent and know-how licensing agreement, the exemption of the obligations referred to in points (1) to (5) of paragraph 1 shall apply in Member States in which the licensed technology is protected by necessary patents for as long as the licensed product is protected in those Member States by such patents if the duration of such protection exceeds the periods specified in paragraph 3.

The duration of the exemption provided in point (6) of paragraph 1 may not exceed the five-year period provided for in paragraphs 2 and 3.

However, such agreements qualify for the exemption referred to in paragraph 1 only for as long as the patents remain in force or to the extent that the know-how is identified and for as long as it remains secret and substantial whichever period is the longer.

5.   The exemption provided for in paragraph 1 shall also apply where in a particular agreement the parties undertake obligations of the types referred to in that paragraph but with a more limited scope than is permitted by that paragraph.

Article 2

1.   Article 1 shall apply notwithtanding the presence in particular of any of the following clauses, which are generally not restrictive of competition:

(1)   an obligation on the licensee not to divulge the know-how communicated by the licensor; the licensee may be held to this obligation after the agreement has expired;

(2)   an obligation on the licensee not to grant sublicences or assign the licence;

(3)   an obligation on the licensee not to exploit the licensed know-how or patents after termination of the agreement in so far and as long as the know-how is still secret or the patents are still in force;

(4)   an obligation on the licensee to grant to the licensor a licence in respect of his own improvements to or his new applications of the licensed technology, provided:

— that, in the case of severable improvements, such a licence is not exclusive, so that the licensee is free to use his own improvements or to license them to third parties, in so far as that does not involve disclosure of the know-how communicated by the licensor that is still secret,

— and that the licensor undertakes to grant an exclusive or non-exclusive licence of his own improvements to the licensee;

(5)   an obligation on the licensee to observe minimum quality specifications, including technical specifications, for the licensed product or to procure goods or services from the licensor or from an undertaking designated by the licensor, in so far as these quality specifications, products or services are necessary for:

(a)   a technically proper exploitation of the licensed technology; or

(b)   ensuring that the product of the licensee conforms to the minimum quality specifications that are applicable to the licensor and other licensees;

and to allow the licensor to carry out related checks;

(6)   obligations:

(a)   to inform the licensor of misappropriation of the know-how or of infringements of the licensed patents; or

(b)   to take or to assist the licensor in taking legal action against such misappropriation or infringements;

(7)   an obligation on the licensee to continue paying the royalties:

(a)   until the end of the agreement in the amounts, for the periods and according to the methods freely determined by the parties, in the event of the know-how becoming publicly known other than by action of the licensor, without prejudice to the payment of any additional damages in the event of the know-how becoming publicly known by the action of the licensee in breach of the agreement;

(b)   over a period going beyond the duration of the licensed patents, in order to facilitate payment;

(8)   an obligation on the licensee to restrict his exploitation of the licensed technology to one or more technical fields of application covered by the licensed technology or to one or more product markets;

(9)   an obligation on the licensee to pay a minimum royalty or to produce a minimum quantity of the licensed product or to carry out a minimum number of operations exploiting the licensed technology;

(10)   an obligation on the licensor to grant the licensee any more favourable terms that the licensor may grant to another undertaking after the agreement is entered into;

(11)   an obligation on the licensee to mark the licensed product with an indication of the licensor's name or of the licensed patent;

(12) an obligation on the licensee not to use the licensor's technology to construct facilities for third parties; this is without prejudice to the right of the licensee to increase the capacity of his facilities or to set up additional facilities for his own use on normal commercial terms, including the payment of additional royalties;

(13) an obligation on the licensee to supply only a limited quantity of the licensed product to a particular customer, where the licence was granted so that the customer might have a second source of supply inside the licensed territory; this provision shall also apply where the customer is the licensee, and the licence which was granted in order to provide a second source of supply provides that the customer is himself to manufacture the licensed products or to have them manufactured by a subcontractor;

(14) a reservation by the licensor of the right to exercise the rights conferred by a patent to oppose the exploitation of the technology by the licensee outside the licensed territory;

(15) a reservation by the licensor of the right to terminate the agreement if the licensee contests the secret or substantial nature of the licensed know-how or challenges the validity of licensed patents within the common market belonging to the licensor or undertakings connected with him;

(16) a reservation by the licensor of the right to terminate the licence agreement of a patent if the licensee raises the claim that such a patent is not necessary;

(17) an obligation on the licensee to use his best endeavours to manufacture and market the licensed product;

(18) a reservation by the licensor of the right to terminate the exclusivity granted to the licensee and to stop licensing improvements to him when the licensee enters into competition within the common market with the licensor, with undertakings connected with the licensor or with other undertakings in respect of research and development, production, use or distribution of competing products, and to require the licensee to prove that the licensed know-how is not being used for the production of products and the provision of services other than those licensed.

2. In the event that, because of particular circumstances, the clauses referred to in paragraph 1 fall within the scope of Article 85(1), they shall also be exempted even if they are not accompanied by any of the obligations exempted by Article 1.

3. The exemption in paragraph 2 shall also apply where an agreement contains clauses of the types referred to in paragraph 1 but with a more limited scope than is permitted by that paragraph.

Article 3

Article 1 and Article 2(2) shall not apply where:

(1) one party is restricted in the determination of prices, components of prices or discounts for the licensed products;

(2) one party is restricted from competing within the common market with the other party, with undertakings connected with the other party or with other undertakings in respect of research and development, production, use or distribution of competing products without prejudice to the provisions of Article 2(1)(17) and (18);

(3) one or both of the parties are required without any objectively justified reason:

(a) to refuse to meet orders from users or resellers in their respective territories who would market products in other territories within the common market;

(b) to make it difficult for users or resellers to obtain the products from other resellers within the common market, and in particular to exercise intellectual property rights or take measures so as to prevent users or resellers from obtaining outside, or from putting on the market in the licensed territory products which have been lawfully put on the market within the common market by the licensor or with his consent; or do so as a result of a concerted practice between them;

(4)   the parties were already competing manufacturers before the grant of the licence and one of them is restricted, within the same technical field of use or within the same product market, as to the customers he may serve, in particular by being prohibited from supplying certain classes of user, employing certain forms of distribution or, with the aim of sharing customers, using certain types of packaging for the products, save as provided in Article 1(1)(7) and Article 2(1)(13);

(5)   the quantity of the licensed product one party may manufacture or sell or the number of operations exploiting the licensed technology he may carry out are subject to limitations, save as provided in Article 1(8) and Article 2(1)(13);

(6)   the licensee is obliged to assign in whole or in part to the licensor rights to improvements to or new applications of the licensed technology;

(7)   the licensor is required, albeit in separate agreements or through automatic prolongation of the initial duration of the agreement by the inclusion of any new improvements, for a period exceeding that referred to in Article 1(2) and (3) not to license other undertakings to exploit the licensed technology in the licensed territory, or a party is required for a period exceeding that referred to in Article 1(2) and (3) or Article 1(4) not to exploit the licensed technology in the territory of the other party or of other licencees.

Article 4
1.   The exemption provided for in Articles 1 and 2 shall also apply to agreements containing obligations restrictive of competition which are not covered by those Articles and do not fall within the scope of Article 3, on condition that the agreements in question are notified to the Commission in accordance with the provisions of Articles 1, 2 and 3 of Regulation (EC) No. 3385/94 and that the Commission does not oppose such exemption within a period of four months.

2.   Paragraph 1 shall apply, in particular, where:

(a)   the licensee is obliged at the time the agreement is entered into to accept quality specifications or further licences or to procure goods or services which are not necessary for a technically satisfactory exploitation of the licensed technology or for ensuring that the production of the licensee conforms to the quality standards that are respected by the licensor and other licensees;

(b)   the licensee is prohibited from contesting the secrecy or the substantiality of the licensed know-how or from challenging the validity of patents licensed within the common market belonging to the licensor or undertakings connected with him.

3.   The period of four months referred to in paragraph 1 shall run from the date on which the notification takes effect in accordance with Article 4 of Regulation (EC) No. 3385/94.

4.   The benefit of paragraphs 1 and 2 may be claimed for agreements notified before the entry into force of this Regulation by submitting a communication to the Commission referring expressly to this Article and to the notification. Paragraph 3 shall apply *mutatis mutandis*.

5.   The Commission may oppose the exemption within a period of four months. It shall oppose exemption if it receives a request to do so from a Member State within two months of the transmission to the Member State of the notification referred to in paragraph 1 or of the communication referred to in paragraph 4. This request must be justified on the basis of considerations relating to the competition rules of the Treaty.

6.   The Commission may withdraw the opposition to the exemption at any time. However, where the opposition was raised at the request of a Member State and this request is maintained, it may be withdrawn only after consultation of the Advisory Committee on Restrictive Practices and Dominant Positions.

7.   If the opposition is withdrawn because the undertakings concerned have shown that the conditions of Article 85(3) are satisfied, the exemption shall apply from the date of notification

8. If the opposition is withdrawn because the undertakings concerned have amended the agreement so that the conditions of Article 85(3) are satisfied, the exemption shall apply from the date on which the amendments take effect.

9. If the Commission opposes exemption and the opposition is not withdrawn, the effects of the notification shall be governed by the provisions of Regulation No. 17.

Article 5

1. This Regulation shall not apply to:

(1) agreements between members of a patent or know-how pool which relate to the pooled technologies;

(2) licensing agreements between competing undertakings which hold interests in a joint venture, or between one of them and the joint venture, if the licensing agreements relate to the activities of the joint venture;

(3) agreements under which one party grants the other a patent and/or know-how licence and in exchange the other party, albeit in separate agreements or through connected undertakings, grants the first party a patent, trademark or know-how licence or exclusive sales rights, where the parties are competitors in relation to the products covered by those agreements;

(4) licensing agreements containing provisions relating to intellectual property rights other than patents which are not ancillary;

(5) agreements entered into solely for the purpose of sale.

2. This Regulation shall nevertheless apply:

(1) to agreements to which paragraph 1(2) applies, under which a parent undertaking grants the joint venture a patent or know-how licence, provided that the licensed products and the other goods and services of the participating undertakings which are considered by users to be interchangeable or substitutable in view of their characteristics, price and intended use represent:

— in case of a licence limited to production, not more than 20%, and

— in case of a licence covering production and distribution, not more than 10%;

of the market for the licensed products and all interchangeable or substitutable goods and services;

(2) to agreements to which paragraph 1(1) applies and to reciprocal licences within the meaning of paragraph 1(3), provided the parties are not subject to any territorial restriction within the common market with regard to the manufacture, use or putting on the market of the licensed products or to the use of the licensed or pooled technologies.

3. This Regulation shall continue to apply where, for two consecutive financial years, the market shares in paragraph 2(1) are not exceeded by more than one-tenth; where that limit is exceeded, this Regulation shall continue to apply for a period of six months from the end of the year in which the limit was exceeded.

Article 6

This Regulation shall also apply to:

(1) agreements where the licensor is not the holder of the know-how or the patentee, but is authorised by the holder or the patentee to grant a licence;

(2) assignments of know-how, patents or both where the risk associated with exploitation remains with the assignor, in particular where the sum payable in consideration of the assignment is dependent on the turnover obtained by the assignee in respect of products made using the know-how or the patents, the quantity of such products manufactured or the number of operations carried out employing the know-how or the patents;

(3) licensing agreements in which the rights or obligations of the licensor or the licensee are assumed by undertakings connected with them.

Article 7

The Commission may withdraw the benefit of this Regulation, pursuant to Article 7 of Regulation No. 19/65/EEC, where it finds in a particular case that an agreement exempted by this Regulation nevertheless has certain effects which are incompatible with the conditions laid down in Article 85(3) of the Treaty, and in particular where:

(1)   the effect of the agreement is to prevent the licensed products from being exposed to effective competition in the licensed territory from identical goods or services considered by users as interchangeable or substitutable in view of their characteristics, price and intended use, which may in particular occur where the licensee's market share exceeds 40%;

(2)   without prejudice to Article 1(1)(6), the licensee refuses, without any objectively justified reason, to meet unsolicited orders from users or resellers in the territory of other licensees;

(3)   the parties:

(a)   without any objectively justified reason, refuse to meet orders from users or resellers in their respective territories who would market the products in other territories within the common market; or

(b)   make it difficult for users or resellers to obtain the products from other resellers within the common market, and in particular where they exercise intellectual property rights or take measures so as to prevent resellers or users from obtaining outside, or from putting on the market in the licensed territory products which have been lawfully put on the market within the common market by the licensor or with his consent;

(4)   the parties were competing manufacturers at the date of the grant of the licence and obligations on the licensee to produce a minimum quantity or to use his best endeavours as referred to in Article 2(1), (9) and (17) respectively have the effect of preventing the licensee from using competing technologies.

Article 8

1.   For purposes of this Regulation:

(a)   patent applications;

(b)   utility models;

(c)   applications for registration of utility models;

(d)   topographies of semiconductor products;

(e)   *certificats d'utilité* and *certificats d'addition* under French law;

(f)   applications for *certificats d'utilité* and *certificats d'addition* under French law;

(g)   supplementary protection certificates for medicinal products or other products for which such supplementary protection certificates may be obtained;

(h)   plant breeder's certificates,

shall be deemed to be patents.

2.   This Regulation shall also apply to agreements relating to the exploitation of an invention if an application within the meaning of paragraph 1 is made in respect of the invention for a licensed territory after the date when the agreements were entered into but within the time-limits set by the national law or the international convention to be applied.

3.   This Regulation shall furthermore apply to pure patent or know-how licensing agreements or to mixed agreements whose initial duration is automatically prolonged by the inclusion of any new improvements, whether patented or not, communicated by the licensor, provided that the licensee has the right to refuse such improvements or each party has the right to terminate the agreement at the expiry of the initial term of an agreement and at least every three years thereafter.

Article 9

1.   Information acquired pursuant to Article 4 shall be used only for the purposes of this Regulation.

2.   The Commission and the authorities of the Member States, their officials and other servants shall not disclose information acquired by them pursuant to this Regulation of the kind covered by the obligation of professional secrecy.

3.   The provisions of paragraphs 1 and 2 shall not prevent publication of general information or surveys which do not contain information relating to particular undertakings or associations of undertakings.

Article 10
For purposes of this Regulation:

(1)   "know-how" means a body of technical information that is secret, substantial and identified in any appropriate form;

(2)   "secret" means that the know-how package as a body or in the precise configuration and assembly of its components is not generally known or easily accessible, so that part of its value consists in the lead which the licensee gains when it is communicated to him; it is not limited to the narrow sense that each individual component of the know-how should be totally unknown or unobtainable outside the licensor's business;

(3)   "substantial" means that the know-how includes information which must be useful, i.e. can reasonably be expected at the date of conclusion of the agreement to be capable of improving the competitive position of the licensee, for example by helping him to enter a new market or giving him an advantage in competition with other manufacturers or providers of services who do not have access to the licensed secret know-how or other comparable secret know-how;

(4)   "identified" means that the know-how is described or recorded in such a manner as to make it possible to verify that it satisfies the criteria of secrecy and substantiality and to ensure that the licensee is not unduly restricted in his exploitation of his own technology, to be identified the know-how can either be set out in the licence agreement or in a separate document or recorded in any other appropriate form at the latest when the know-how is transferred or shortly thereafter, provided that the separate document or other record can be made available if the need arises;

(5)   "necessary patents" are patents where a licence under the patent is necessary for the putting into effect of the licensed technology in so far as, in the absence of such a licence, the realisation of the licensed technology would not be possible or would be possible only to a lesser extent or in more difficult or costly conditions. Such patents must therefore be of technical, legal or economic interest to the licensee;

(6)   "licensing agreement" means pure patent licensing agreements and pure know-how licensing agreements as well as mixed patent and know-how licensing agreements;

(7)   "licensed technology" means the initial manufacturing know-how or the necessary product and process patents, or both, existing at the time the first licensing agreement is concluded, and improvements subsequently made to the know-how or patents, irrespective of whether and to what extent they are exploited by the parties or by other licensees;

(8)   "the licensed products" are goods or services the production or provision of which requires the use of the licensed technology;

(9)   "the licensee's market share" means the proportion which the licensed products and other goods or services provided by the licensee, which are considered by users to be interchangeable or substitutable for the licensed products in view of their characteristics, price and intended use, represent the entire market for the licensed products and all other interchangeable or substitutable goods and services in the common market or a substantial part of it;

(10) "exploitation" refers to any use of the licensed technology in particular in the production, active or passive sales in a territory even if not coupled with manufacture in that territory, or leasing of the licensed products;

(11)   "the licensed territory" is the territory covering all or at least part of the common market where the licensee is entitled to exploit the licensed technology;

(12)   "territory of the licensor" means territories in which the licensor has not granted any licences for patents and/or know-how covered by the licensing agreement;

(13)   "parallel patents" means patents which, in spite of the divergences which remain in the absence of any unification of national rules concerning industrial property, protect the same invention in various Member States;

(14)   "connected undertakings" means:

(a)   undertakings in which a party to the agreement, directly or indirectly:

— owns more than half the capital or business assets, or

— has the power to exercise more than half the voting rights, or

— has the power to appoint more than half the members of the supervisory board, board of directors or bodies legally representing the undertaking, or

— has the right to manage the affairs of the undertaking;

(b)   undertakings which, directly or indirectly, have in or over a party to the agreement the rights or powers listed in (a);

(c)   undertakings in which an undertaking referred to in (b), directly or indirectly, has the rights or powers listed in (a);

(d)   undertakings in which the parties to the agreement or undertakings connected with them jointly have the rights or powers listed in (a): such jointly controlled undertakings are considered to be connected with each of the parties to the agreement;

(15)   "ancillary provisions" are provisions relating to the exploitation of intellectual property rights other than patents, which contain no obligations restrictive of competition other than those also attached to the licensed know-how or patents and exempted under this Regulation;

(16)   "obligation" means both contractual obligation and a concerted practice;

(17)   "competing manufactures" or manufactures of "competing products" means manufacturers who sell products which, in view of their characteristics, price and intended use, are considered by users to be interchangeable or substitutable for the licensed products.

Article 11

1.   Regulation (EEC) No. 556/89 is hereby repealed with effect from 1 April 1996.

2.   Regulation (EEC) No. 2349/84 shall continue to apply until 31 March 1996.

3.   The prohibition in Article 85(1) of the Treaty shall not apply to agreements in force on 31 March 1996 which fulfil the exemption requirements laid down by Regulation (EEC) No. 2349/84 or (EEC) No. 556/89.

Article 12

1.   The Commission shall undertake regular assessments of the application of this Regulation, and in particular of the opposition procedure provided for in Article 4.

2.   The Commission shall draw up a report on the operation of this Regulation before the end of the fourth year following its entry into force and shall, on that basis, assess whether any adaptation of the Regulation is desirable.

Article 13

This Regulation shall enter into force on 1 April 1996.

It shall apply until 31 March 2006.

Article 11(2) of this Regulation shall, however, enter into force on 1 January 1996.

This Regulation shall be binding in its entirety and directly applicable in all Member States.

DIRECTIVE 96/9/EC OF THE EUROPEAN PARLIAMENT AND OF THE COUNCIL
of 11 March 1996
on the legal protection of databases

THE EUROPEAN PARLIAMENT AND THE COUNCIL OF THE EUROPEAN UNION,

Having regard to the Treaty establishing the European Community, and in particular Article 57(2), 66 and 100a thereof,

Having regard to the proposal from the Commission,

Having regard to the opinion of the Economic and Social Committee,

Acting in accordance with the procedure laid down in Article 189b of the Treaty,

(1)   Whereas databases are at present not sufficiently protected in all Member States by existing legislation; whereas such protection, where it exists, has different attributes;

(2)   Whereas such differences in the legal protection of databases offered by the legislation of the Member States have direct negative effects on the functioning of the internal market as regards databases and in particular on the freedom of natural and legal persons to provide on-line database goods and services on the basis of harmonised legal arrangements throughout the Community; whereas such differences could well become more pronounced as Member States introduce new legislation in this field, which is now taking on an increasingly international dimension;

(3)   Whereas existing differences distorting the functioning of the internal market need to be removed and new ones prevented from arising, while differences not adversely affecting the functioning of the internal market or the development of an information market within the Community need not be removed or prevented from arising;

(4)   Whereas copyright protection for databases exists in varying forms in the Member States according to legislation or case-law, and whereas, if differences in legislation in the scope and conditions of protection remain between the Member States, such unharmonised intellectual property rights can have the effect of preventing the free movement of goods or services within the Community;

(5)   Whereas copyright remains an appropriate form of exclusive right for authors who have created databases;

(6)   Whereas, nevertheless, in the absence of a harmonised system of unfair-competition legislation or of case-law, other measures are required in addition to prevent the unauthorised extraction and/or re-utilisation of the contents of a database;

(7)   Whereas the making of databases requires the investment of considerable human, technical and financial resources while such databases can be copied or accessed at a fraction of the cost needed to design them independently;

(8)   Whereas the unauthorised extraction and/or re-utilisation of the contents of a database constitute acts which can have serious economic and technical consequences;

(9)   Whereas databases are a vital tool in the development of an information market within the Community; whereas this tool will also be of use in many other fields;

(10)   Whereas the exponential growth, in the Community and worldwide, in the amount of information generated and processed annually in all sectors of commerce and industry calls for investment in all the Member States in advanced information processing systems;

(11)   Whereas there is at present a very great imbalance in the level of investment in the database sector both as between the Member States and between the Community and the world's largest database-producing third countries;

(12)   Whereas such an investment in modern information storage and processing systems will not take place within the Community unless a stable and uniform legal protection regime is introduced for the protection of the rights of makers of databases;

(13)   Whereas this Directive protects collections, sometimes called "compilations", of works, data or other materials which are arranged, stored and accessed by means which include electronic, electromagnetic or electro-optical processes or analogous processes;

(14)   Whereas protection under this Directive should be extended to cover non-electronic databases;

(15)   Whereas the criteria used to determine whether a database should be protected by copyright should be defined to the fact that the selection or the arrangement of the contents of the database is the author's own intellectual creation; whereas such protection should cover the structure of the database;

(16)   Whereas no criterion other than originality in the sense of the author's intellectual creation should be applied to determine the eligibility of the database for copyright protection, and in particular no aesthetic or qualitative criteria should be applied;

(17)   Whereas the term "database" should be understood to include literary, artistic, musical or other collections of works or collections of other material such as texts, sound, images, numbers, facts, and data; whereas it should cover collections of independent works, data or other materials which are systematically or methodically arranged and can be individually accessed; whereas this means that a recording or an audiovisual, cinematographic, literary or musical work as such does not fall within the scope of this Directive;

(18)   Whereas this Directive is without prejudice to the freedom of authors to decide whether, or in what manner, they will allow their works to be included in a database, in particular whether or not the authorisation given is exclusive; whereas the protection of databases by the *sui generis* right is without prejudice to existing rights over their contents, and whereas in particular where an author or the holder of a related right permits some of his works or subject matter to be included in a database pursuant to a non-exclusive agreement, a third party may make use of those works or subject matter subject to the required consent of the author or of the holder of the related right without the *sui generis* right of the maker of the database being invoked to prevent him doing so, on condition that those works or subject matter are neither extracted from the database nor re-utilised on the basis thereof;

(19)   Whereas, as a rule, the compilation of several recordings of musical perform-ances on a CD does not come within the scope of this Directive, both because, as a compilation, it does not meet the conditions for copyright protection and because it does not represent a substantial enough investment to be eligible under the *sui generis* right;

(20)   Whereas protection under this Directive may also apply to the materials necessary for the operation or consultation of certain databases such as thesaurus and indexation systems;

(21)   Whereas the protection provided for in this Directive relates to databases in which works, data or other materials have been arranged systematically or methodically; whereas it is not necessary for those materials to have been physically stored in an organised manner;

(22)   Whereas electronic databases within the meaning of this Directive may also include devices such as CD-ROM and CD-i;

(23)   Whereas the term "database" should not be taken to extend to computer programs used in the making or operation of a database, which are protected by Council Directive 91/250/EEC of 14 May 1991 on the legal protection of computer programs;

(24)   Whereas the rental and lending of databases in the field of copyright and related rights are governed exclusively by Council Directive 92/100/EEC of 19 November 1992 on rental right and lending right and on certain rights related to copyright in the field of intellectual property;

(25)   Whereas the term of copyright is already governed by Council Directive 93/98/EEC of 29 October 1993 harmonising the term of protection of copyright and certain related rights;

(26)   Whereas works protected by copyright and subject matter protected by related rights, which are incorporated into a database, remain nevertheless protected by the respective exclusive rights and may not be incorporated into, or extracted from, the database without the permission of the right-holder or his successors in title;

(27)   Whereas copyright in such works and related rights in subject matter thus incorporated into a database are in no way affected by the existence of a separate right in the selection or arrangement of these works and subject matter in a database;

(28)   Whereas the moral rights of the natural person who created the database belong to the author and should be exercised according to the legislation of the Member States and the provisions of the Berne Convention for the Protection of Literary and Artistic Works; whereas such moral rights remain outside the scope of this Directive;

(29)   Whereas the arrangements applicable to databases created by employees are left to the discretion of the Member States; whereas, therefore nothing in this Directive prevents Member States from stipulating in their legislation that where a database is created by an employee in the execution of his duties or following the instructions given by his employer, the employer exclusively shall be entitled to exercise all economic rights in the database so created, unless otherwise provided by contract;

(30)   Whereas the author's exclusive rights should include the right to determine the way in which his work is exploited and by whom, and in particular to control the distribution of his work to unauthorised persons;

(31)   Whereas the copyright protection of databases includes making databases available by means other than the distribution of copies;

(32)   Whereas Member States are required to ensure that their national provisions are at least materially equivalent in the case of such acts subject to restrictions as are provided for by this Directive;

(33)   Whereas the question of exhaustion of the right of distribution does not arise in the case of on-line databases, which come within the field of provision of services; whereas this also applies with regard to a material copy of such a database made by the user of such a service with the consent of the rightholder; whereas, unlike CD-ROM or CD-i, where the intellectual property is incorporated in a material medium, namely an item of goods, every on-line service is in fact an act which will have to be subject to authorisation where the copyright so provides;

(34)   Whereas, nevertheless, once the rightholder has chosen to make available a copy of the database to a user, whether by an on-line service or by other means of distribution, that lawful user must be able to access and use the database for the purposes and in the way set out in the agreement with the rightholder, even if such access and use necessitate performance of otherwise restricted acts;

(35)   Whereas a list should be drawn up of exceptions to restricted acts, taking into account the fact that copyright as covered by this Directive applies only to the selection or arrangements of the contents of a database; whereas Member States should be given the option of providing for such exceptions in certain cases; whereas, however, this option should be exercised in accordance with the Berne Convention and to the extent that the exceptions relate to the structure of the database; whereas a distinction should be drawn between exceptions for private use and exceptions for reproduction for private purposes, which concerns provisions under national legislation of some Member States on levies on blank media or recording equipment;

(36)   Whereas the term "scientific research" within the meaning of this Directive covers both the natural sciences and the human sciences;

(37)   Whereas Article 10(1) of the Berne Convention is not affected by this Directive;

(38) Whereas the increasing use of digital recording technology exposes the database maker to the risk that the contents of his database may be copied and rearranged electronically, without his authorisation, to produce a database of identical content which, however, does not infringe any copyright in the arrangement of his database;

(39) Whereas, in addition to aiming to protect the copyright in the original selection or arrangement of the contents of a database, this Directive seeks to safeguard the position of makers of databases against misappropriation of the results of the financial and professional investment made in obtaining and collection the contents by protecting the whole or substantial parts of a database against certain acts by a user or competitor;

(40) Whereas the object of this *sui generis* right is to ensure protection of any investment in obtaining, verifying or presenting the contents of a database for the limited duration of the right; whereas such investment may consist in the deployment of financial resources and/or the expending of time, effort and energy;

(41) Whereas the objective of the *sui generis* right is to give the maker of a database the option of preventing the unauthorised extraction and/or re-utilisation of all or a substantial part of the contents of that database; whereas the maker of a database is the person who takes the initiative and the risk of investing; whereas this excludes subcontractors in particular from the definition of maker;

(42) Whereas the special right to prevent unauthorised extraction and/or re-utilisation relates to acts by the user which go beyond his legitimate rights and thereby harm the investment; whereas the right to prohibit extraction and/or re-utilisation of all or a substantial part of the contents relates not only to the manufacture of a parasitical competing product but also to any user who, through his acts, causes significant detriment, evaluated qualitatively or quantitatively, to the investment;

(43) Whereas, in the case of on-line transmission, the right to prohibit re-utilisation is not exhausted either as regards the database or as regards a material copy of the database or of part thereof made by the addressee of the transmission with the consent of the rightholder;

(44) Whereas, when on-screen display of the contents of a database necessitates the permanent or temporary transfer of all or a substantial part of such contents to another medium, that act should be subject to authorisation by the rightholder;

(45) Whereas the right to prevent unauthorised extraction and/or re-utilisation does not in any way constitute an extension of copyright protection to mere facts or data;

(46) Whereas the existence of a right to prevent the unauthorised extraction and/or re-utilisation of the whole or a substantial part of works, data or materials from a database should not give rise to the creation of a new right in the works, data or materials themselves;

(47) Whereas, in the interests of competition between suppliers of information products and services, protection by the *sui generis* right must not be afforded in such a way as to facilitate abuses of a dominant position, in particular, as regards the creation and distribution of new products and services which have an intellectual, documentary, technical, economic or commercial added value; whereas, therefore, the provisions of this Directive are without prejudice to the application of Community or national competition rules;

(48) Whereas the objective of this Directive, which is to afford an appropriate and uniform level of protection of databases as a means to secure the remuneration of the maker of the database, is different from the aim of Directive 95/46/EC of the European Parliament and of the Council of 24 October 1995 on the protection of individuals with regard to the processing of personal data and on the free movement of such data, which is to guarantee free circulation of personal data on the basis of harmonised rules designed to protect fundamental rights, notably the right to privacy which is recognised in Article 8 of the European Convention for the Protection of Human Rights and

Fundamental Freedoms; whereas the provisions of this Directive are without prejudice to data protection legislation;

(49)   Whereas, notwithstanding the right to prevent extraction and/or re-utilisation of all or a substantial part of a database, it should be laid down that the maker of a database or rightholder may not prevent a lawful user of the database from extracting and re-utilising insubstantial parts; whereas, however, that user may not unreasonably prejudice either the legitimate interests of the holder of the *sui generis* right or the holder of copyright or a related right in respect of the works or subject matter contained in the database;

(50)   Whereas the Member States should be given the option of providing for exceptions to the right to prevent the unauthorised extraction and/or re-utilisation of a substantial part of the contents of a database in the case of extraction for private purposes, for the purposes of illustration for teaching or scientific research, or where extraction and/or re-utilisation are/is carried out in the interests of public security or for the purposes of an administrative or judicial procedure; whereas such operations must not prejudice the exclusive rights of the maker to exploit the database and their purpose must not be commercial;

(51)   Whereas the Member States, where they avail themselves of the option to permit a lawful user of a database to extract a substantial part of the contents for the purposes of illustration for teaching or scientific research, may limit that permission to certain categories of teaching or scientific research institution;

(52)   Whereas those Member States which have specific rules providing for a right comparable to the *sui generis* right provided for in this Directive should be permitted to retain, as far as the new right is concerned, the expectations traditionally specified by such rules;

(53)   Whereas the burden of proof regarding the date of completion of the making of a database lies with the maker of the database;

(54)   Whereas the burden of proof that the criteria exist for concluding that a substantial modification of the contents of a database is to be regarded as a substantial new investment lies with the maker of the database resulting from such investment;

(55)   Whereas a substantial new investment involving a new term of protection may include a substantial verification of the contents of the database;

(56)   Whereas the right to prevent unauthorised extraction and/or re-utilisation in respect of a database should apply to databases whose makers are nationals or habitual residents of third countries or to those produced by legal persons not established in a Member State, within the meaning of the Treaty, only if such third countries offer comparable protection to databases produced by nationals of a Member State or persons who have their habitual residence in the territory of the Community;

(57)   Whereas, in addition to remedies provided under the legislation of the Member States for infringements of copyright or other rights, Member States should provide for appropriate remedies against unauthorised extraction and/or re-utilisation of the contents of a database;

(58)   Whereas, in addition to the protection given under this Directive to the structure of the database by copyright, and to its contents against unauthorised extraction and/or re-utilisation under the *sui generis* right, other legal provisions in the Member States relevant to the supply of database goods and services continue to apply;

(59)   Whereas this Directive is without prejudice to the application to databases composed of audiovisual works of any rules recognised by a Member State's legislation concerning the broadcasting of audiovisual programmes;

(60)   Whereas some Member States currently protect under copyright arrangements databases which do not meet the criteria for eligibility for copyright protection laid down in this Directive; whereas, even if the databases concerned are eligible for protection under the right laid down in this Directive to prevent unauthorised extraction and/or

re-utilisation of their contents, the term of protection under that right is considerably shorter than that which they enjoy under the national arrangements currently in force; whereas harmonisation of the criteria for determining whether a database is to be protected by copyright may not have the effect of reducing the term of protection currently enjoyed by the rightholders concerned; whereas a derogation should be laid down to that effect; whereas the effects of such derogation must be confined to the territories of the Member States concerned,

HAVE ADOPTED THIS DIRECTIVE:

CHAPTER I
SCOPE

Article 1   Scope
1.   This Directive concerns the legal protection of databases in any form.
2.   For the purposes of this Directive, "database" shall mean a collection of independent works, data or other materials arranged in a systematic or methodical way and individually accessible by electronic or other means.
3.   Protection under this Directive shall not apply to computer programs used in the making or operation of databases accessible by electronic means.

Article 2   Limitations on the scope
This Directive shall apply without prejudice to Community provisions relating to:
   (a)   the legal protection of computer programs;
   (b)   rental right, lending right and certain rights related to copyright in the field of intellectual property;
   (c)   the term of protection of copyright and certain related rights.

CHAPTER II
COPYRIGHT

Article 3   Object of protection
1.   In accordance with this Directive, databases which, by reason of the selection or arrangement of their contents, constitute the author's own intellectual creation shall be protected as such by copyright. No other criteria shall be applied to determine their eligibility for that protection.
2.   The copyright protection of databases provided for by this Directive shall not extend to their contents and shall be without prejudice to any rights subsisting in those contents themselves.

Article 4   Database authorship
1.   The author of a database shall be the natural person or group of natural persons who created the base or, where the legislation of the Member States so permits, the legal person designated as the rightholder by the legislation.
2.   Where collective works are recognised by the legislation of a Member State, the economic rights shall be owned by the person holding the copyright.
3.   In respect of a database created by a group of natural persons jointly, the exclusive rights shall be owned jointly.

Article 5   Restricted acts
In respect of the expression of the database which is protectable by copyright, the author of a database shall have the exclusive right to carry out or to authorise:
   (a)   temporary or permanent reproduction by any means and in any form, in whole or in part;
   (b)   translation, adaptation, arrangement and any other alteration;

(c)   any form of distribution to the public of the database or of copies thereof. The first sale in the Community of a copy of the database by the rightholder or with his consent shall exhaust the right to control resale of that copy within the Community;

(d)   any communication, display or performance to the public;

(e)   any reproduction, distribution, communication, display or performance to the public of the results of the acts referred to in (b).

Article 6   Exceptions to restricted acts

1.   The performance by the lawful user of a database or of a copy thereof of any of the acts listed in Article 5 which is necessary for the purposes of access to the contents of the databases and normal use of the contents by the lawful user shall not require the authorisation of the author of the database. Where the lawful user is authorised to use only part of the database, this provision shall apply only to that part.

2.   Member States shall have the option of providing for limitations on the rights set out in Article 5 in the following cases:

(a)   in the case of reproduction for private purposes of a non-electronic database;

(b)   where there is use for the sole purpose of illustration for teaching or scientific research, as long as the source is indicated and to the extent justified by the non-commercial purpose to be achieved;

(c)   where there is use for the purposes of public security or for the purposes of an administrative or judicial procedure;

(d)   where other exceptions to copyright which are traditionally authorised under national law are involved, without prejudice to points (a), (b) and (c).

3.   In accordance with the Berne Convention for the protection of Literary and Artistic Works, this Article may not be interpreted in such a way as to allow its application to be used in a manner which unreasonably prejudices the rightholder's legitimate interests or conflicts with normal exploitation of the database.

CHAPTER III
SUI GENERIS RIGHT

Article 7   Object of protection

1.   Member States shall provide for a right for the maker of a database which shows that there has been qualitatively and/or quantitatively a substantial investment in either the obtaining, verification or presentation of the contents to prevent extraction and/or re-utilisation of the whole or of a substantial part, evaluated qualitatively and/or quantitatively, of the contents of that database.

2.   For the purposes of this Chapter:

(a)   "extraction" shall mean the permanent or temporaray transfer of all or a substantial part of the contents of a database to another medium by any means or in any form;

(b)   "re-utilisation" shall mean any form of making available to the public all or a substantial part of the contents of a database by the distribution of copies, by renting, by on-line or other forms of transmission. The first sale of a copy of a database within the Community be the rightholder or with his consent shall exhaust the right to control resale of that copy within the Community;

Public lending is not an act of extraction or re-utilisation.

3.   The right referred to in paragraph 1 may be transferred, assigned or granted under contractual licence.

4.   The right provided for in paragraph 1 shall apply irrespective of the eligibility of that database for protection by copyright or by other rights. Moreover, it shall apply irrespective of eligibility of the contents of that database for protection by copyright or by other rights. Protection of databases under the right provided for in paragraph 1 shall be without prejudice to rights existing in respect of their contents.

5.   The repeated and systematic extraction and/or re-utilisation of insubstantial parts of the contents of the database implying acts which conflict with a normal exploitation of that database or which unreasonably prejudice the legitimate interests of the maker of the database shall not be permitted.

Article 8   Rights and obligations of lawful users
1.   The maker of a database which is made available to the public in whatever manner may not prevent a lawful user of the database from extracting and/or re-utilising insubstantial parts of its contents, evaluated qualitatively and/or quantitatively, for any purposes whatsoever. Where the lawful user is authorised to extract and/or re-utilise only part of the database, this paragraph shall apply only to that part.

2.   A lawful user of a database which is made available to the public in whatever manner may not perform acts which conflict with normal exploitation of the database or unreasonably prejudice the legitimate interests of the maker of the database.

3.   A lawful user of a database which is made available to the public in any manner may not cause prejudice to the holder of a copyright or related right in respect of the works or subject matter contained in the database.

Article 9   Exception to the *sui generis* right
Member States may stipulate that lawful users of a database which is made available to the public in whatever manner may, without the authorisation of its maker, extract or re-utilise a substantial part of its contents:

(a)   in the case of extraction for private purposes of the contents of a non-electronic database;

(b)   in the case of extraction for the purposes of illustration for teaching or scientific research, as long as the source is indicated and to the extent justified by the non-commercial purpose to be achieved;

(c)   in the case of extraction and/or re-utilisation for the purposes of public security or an administrative or judicial procedure.

Article 10   Term of protection
1.   The right provided for in Article 7 shall run from the date of completion of the making of the database. It shall expire fifteen years from the first of January of the year following the date of completion.

2.   In the case of a database which is made available to the public in whatever manner before expiry of the period provided for in paragraph 1, the term of protection by that right shall expire fifteen years from the first of January of the year following the date when the database was first made available to the public.

3.   Any substantial change, evaluated qualitatively or quantitatively, to the contents of a database, including any substantial change resulting from the accumulation of successive additions, deletions or alterations, which would result in the database being considered to be a substantial new investment, evaluated qualitatively or quantitatively, shall qualify the database resulting from that investment for its own term of protection.

Article 11   Beneficiaries of protection under the *sui generis* right
1.   The right provided for in Article 7 shall apply to database whose makers or rightholders are nationals of a Member State or who have their habitual residence in the territory of the Community.

2.   Paragraph 1 shall also apply to companies and firms formed in accordance with the law of a Member State and having their registered office, central administration or principal place of business within the Community; however, where such a company or firm has only its registered office in the territory of the Community, its operations must be genuinely linked on an ongoing basis with the economy of a Member State.

3.   Agreements extending the right provided for in Article 7 to databases made in third countries and falling outside the provisions of paragraphs 1 and 2 shall be

concluded by the Council acting on a proposal from the Commission. The term of any protection extended to databases by virtue of that procedure shall not exceed that available pursuant to Article 10.

CHAPTER IV
COMMON PROVISIONS

Article 12   Remedies
Member States shall provide appropriate remedies in respect of infringements of the rights provided for in this Directive.

Article 13   Continued application of other legal provisions
This Directive shall be without prejudice to provisions concerning in particular copyright, rights related to copyright or any other rights or obligations subsisting in the data, works or other materials incorporated into a database, patent rights, trade marks, design rights, the protection of national treasures, laws on restrictive practices and unfair competition, trade secrets, security, confidentiality, data protection and privacy, access to public documents, and the law of contract.

Article 14   Application over time
1.   Protection pursuant to this Directive as regards copyright shall also be available in respect of databases created prior to the date referred to in Article 16(1) which on that date fulfil the requirements laid down in this Directive as regards copyright protection of databases.

2.   Notwithstanding paragraph 1, where a database protected under copyright arrangements in a Member State on the date of publication of this Directive does not fulfil the eligibility criteria for copyright protection laid down in Article 3(1), this Directive shall not result in any curtailing in that Member State of the remaining term of protection afforded under those arrangements.

3.   Protection pursuant to the provisions of this Directive as regards the right provided for in Article 7 shall also be available in respect of databases the making of which was completed not more than fifteen years prior to the date referred to in Article 16(1) and which on that date fulfil the requirements laid down in Article 7.

4.   The protection provided for in paragraphs 1 and 3 shall be without prejudice to any acts concluded and rights acquired before the date referred to in those paragraphs.

5.   In the case of a database the making of which was completed not more than fifteen years prior to the date referred to in Article 16(1), the term of protection by the right provided for in Article 7 shall expire fifteen years from the first of January following that date.

Article 15   Binding nature of certain provisions
Any contractual provision contrary to Articles 6(1) and 8 shall be null and void.

Article 16   Final provisions
1.   Member States shall bring into force the laws, regulations and administrative provisions necessary to comply with this Directive before 1 January 1998.

When Member States adopt these provisions, they shall contain a reference to this Directive or shall be accompanied by such reference on the occasion of their official publication. The methods of making such reference shall be laid down by Member States.

2.   Member States shall communicate to the Commission the text of the provisions of domestic law which they adopt in the field governed by this Directive.

3.   Not later than at the end of the third year after the date referred to in paragraph 1, and every three years thereafter, the Commission shall submit to the European Parliament, the Council and the Economic and Social Committee a report on the application of this Directive, in which, *inter alia*, on the basis of specific information

supplied by the Member States, it shall examine in particular the application of the *sui generis* right, including Articles 8 and 9, and shall verify especially whether the application of this right has led to abuse of a dominant position or other interference with free competition which would justify appropriate measures being taken, including the establishment of non-voluntary licensing arrangements. Where necessary, it shall submit proposals for adjustment of this Directive in line with developments in the area of databases.

Article 17
This Directive is addressed to the Member States.

DIRECTIVE 98/44/EC OF THE EUROPEAN PARLIAMENT AND OF THE COUNCIL
of 6 July 1998
on the legal protection of biotechnological inventions

THE EUROPEAN PARLIAMENT AND THE COUNCIL OF THE EUROPEAN UNION,

Having regard to the Treaty establishing the European Community, and in particular Article 100a thereof,

Having regard to the proposal from the Commission,

Having regard to the opinion of the Economic and Social Committee,

Acting in accordance with the procedure laid down in Article 189b of the Treaty,

(1) Whereas biotechnology and genetic engineering are playing an increasingly important role in a broad range of industries and the protection of biotechnological inventions will certainly be of fundamental importance for the Community's industrial development;

(2) Whereas, in particular in the field of genetic engineering, research and development require a considerable amount of high-risk investment and therefore only adequate legal protection can make them profitable;

(3) Whereas effective and harmonised protection throughout the Member States is essential in order to maintain and encourage investment in the field of biotechnology;

(4) Whereas following the European Parliament's rejection of the joint text, approved by the Conciliation Committee, for a European Parliament and Council Directive on the legal protection of biotechnological inventions, the European Parliament and the Council have determined that the legal protection of biotechnological inventions requires clarification;

(5) Whereas differences exist in the legal protection of biotechnological inventions offered by the laws and practices of the different Member States; whereas such differences could create barriers to trade and hence impede the proper functioning of the internal market;

(6) Whereas such differences could well become greater as Member States adopt new and different legislation and administrative practices, or whereas national case-law interpreting such legislation develops differently;

(7) Whereas uncoordinated development of national laws on the legal protection of biotechnological inventions in the Community could lead to further disincentives to trade, to the detriment of the industrial development of such inventions and of the smooth operation of the internal market;

(8) Whereas legal protection of biotechnological inventions does not necessitate the creation of a separate body of law in place of the rules of national patent law; whereas the rules of national patent law remain the essential basis for the legal protection of biotechnological inventions given that they must be adapted or added to in certain specific respects in order to take adequate account of technological developments involving biological material which also fulfil the requirements for patentability;

(9)   Whereas in certain cases, such as the exclusion from patentability of plant and animal varieties and of essentially biological processes for the production of plants and animals, certain concepts in national laws based upon internal patent and plant variety conventions have created uncertainty regarding the protection of biotechnological and certain microbiological inventions; whereas harmonisation is necessary to clarify the said uncertainty;

(10)   Whereas regard should be had to the potential of the development of biotechnology for the environment and in particular the utility of this technology for the development of methods of cultivation which are less polluting and more economical in their use of ground; whereas the patent system should be used to encourage research into, and the application of, such processes;

(11)   Whereas the development of biotechnology is important to developing countries, both in the field of health and combating major epidemics and endemic diseases and in that of combating hunger in the world; whereas the patent system should likewise be used to encourage research in these fields; whereas international procedures for the dissemination of such technology in the Third World and to the benefit of the population groups concerned should be promoted;

(12)   Whereas the Agreement on Trade-Related Aspects of Intellectual Property Rights (TRIPs) signed by the European Community and the Member States, has entered into force and provides that patent protection must be guaranteed for products and processes in all areas of technology;

(13)   Whereas the Community's legal framework for the protection of biotechnological inventions can be limited to laying down certain principles as they apply to the patentability of biological material as such, such principles being intended in particular to determine the difference between inventions and discoveries with regard to the patentability of certain elements of human origin, to the scope of protection conferred by a patent on a biotechnological invention, to the right to use a deposit mechanism in addition to written descriptions and lastly to the option of obtaining non-exclusive compulsory licences in respect of interdependence between plant varieties and inventions, and conversely;

(14)   Whereas a patent for invention does not authorise the holder to implement that invention, but merely entitles him to prohibit third parties from exploiting it for industrial and commercial purposes; whereas, consequently, substantive patent law cannot serve to replace or render superfluous national, European or international law which may impose restrictions or prohibitions or which concerns the monitoring of research and of the use or commercialisation of its results, notaby from the point of view of the requirements of public health, safety, environmental protection, animal welfare, the preservation of genetic diversity and compliance with certain ethical standards;

(15)   Whereas no prohibition or exclusion exists in national or European patent law (Munich Convention) which precludes a priori the patentability of biological matter;

(16)   Whereas patent law must be applied so as to respect the fundamental principles safeguarding the dignity and integrity of the person; whereas it is important to assert the principle that the human body, at any stage in its formation or development, including germ cells, and the simple discovery of one of its elements or one of its products, including the sequence or partial sequence of a human gene, cannot be patented; whereas these principles are in line with the criteria of patentability proper to patent law, whereby a mere discovery cannot be patented;

(17)   Whereas significant progress in the treatment of diseases has already been made thanks to the existence of medicinal products derived from elements isolated from the human body and/or otherwise produced, such medicinal products resulting from technical processes aimed at obtaining elements similar in structure to those existing naturally in the human body and whereas, consequently, research aimed at obtaining and isolating such elements valuable to medicinal production should be encouraged by means of the patent system;

(18)   Whereas, since the patent system provides insufficient incentive for encouraging research into the production of biotechnological medicines which are needed to combat rare or "orphan" diseases, the Community and the Member States have a duty to respond adequately to this problem;

(19)   Whereas account has been taken of Opinion No. 8 of the Group of Advisers on the Ethical Implications of Biotechnology to the European Commission;

(20)   Whereas, therefore, it should be made clear that an invention based on an element isolated from the human body or otherwise produced by means of a technical process, which is susceptible of industrial application, is not excluded from patentability, even where the structure of that element is identical to that of a natural element, given that the rights conferred by the patent do not extend to the human body and its elements in their natural environment;

(21)   Whereas such an element isolated from the human body or otherwise produced is not excluded from patentability since it is, for example, the result of technical processes used to identify, purify and classify it and to reproduce it outside the human body, techniques which human beings alone are capable of putting into practice and which nature is incapable of accomplishing by itself;

(22)   Whereas the discussion on the patentability of sequences or partial sequences of genes is controversial; whereas, according to this Directive, the granting of a patent for inventions which concern such sequences or partial sequences should be subject to the same criteria of patentability as in all other areas of technology: novelty, inventive step and industrial application; whereas the industrial application of a sequence or partial sequence must be disclosed in the patent application as filed;

(23)   Whereas a mere DNA sequence without indication of a function does not contain any technical information and is therefore not a patentable invention;

(24)   Whereas, in order to comply with the industrial application criterion it is necessary in cases where a sequence or partial sequqence of a gene is used to produce a protein or part of a protein, to specify which protein or part of a protein is produced or what function it performs;

(25)   Whereas, for the purposes of interpreting rights conferred by a patent, when sequences overlap only in parts which are not essential to the invention, each sequence will be considered as an independent sequence in patent law terms;

(26)   Whereas if an invention is based on biological material of human origin or if it uses such material, where a patent application is filed, the person from whose body the material is taken must have had an opportunity of expressing free and informed consent thereto, in accordance with national law;

(27)   Whereas if an invention is based on biological material of plant or animal origin or if it uses such material, the patent application should, where appropriate, include information on the geographical origin of such material, if known; whereas this is without prejudice to the processing of patent applications or the validity of rights arising from granted patents;

(28)   Whereas this Directive does not in any way affect the basis of current patent law, according to which a patent may be granted for any new application of a patented product;

(29)   Whereas this Directive is without prejudice to the exclusion of plant and animal varieties from patentability; whereas on the other hand inventions which concern plants or animals are patentable provided that the application of the invention is not technically confined to a single plant or animal variety;

(30)   Whereas the concept "plant variety" is defined by the legislation protecting new varieties, pursuant to which a variety is defined by its whole genome and therefore possesses individuality and is clearly distinguishable from other varieties;

(31)   Whereas a plant grouping which is charcterised by a particular gene (and not its whole genome) is not covered by the protection of new varieties and is therefore not excluded from patentability even if it comprises new varieties of plants;

(32)   Whereas, however, if an invention consists only in genetically modifying a particular plant variety, and if a new plant variety is bred, it will still be excluded from patentability even if the genetic modification is the result not of an essentially biological process but of a biotechnological process;

(33)   Whereas it is necessary to define for the purposes of this Directive when a process for the breeding of plants and animals is essentially biological;

(34)   Whereas this Directive shall be without prejudice to concepts of invention and discovery, as developed by national, European or international patent law;

(35)   Whereas this Directive shall be without prejudice to the provisions of national patent law whereby processes for treatment of the human or animal body by surgery or therapy and diagnostic methods practised on the human or animal body are excluded from patentability;

(36)   Whereas the TRIPs Agreement provides for the possibility that members of the World Trade Organisation may exclude from patentability inventions, the prevention within their territory of the commercial exploitation of which is necessary to protect *ordre public* or morality, including to protect human, animal or plant life or health or to avoid serious prejudice to the environment, provided that such exclusion is not made merely because the exploitation is prohibited by their law;

(37)   Whereas the principle whereby inventions must be excluded from patentability where their commercial exploitation offends against *ordre public* or morality must also be stressed in this Directive;

(38)   Whereas the operative part of this Directive should also include an illustrative list of inventions excluded from patentability so as to provide national courts and patent offices with a general guide to interpreting the reference to *ordre public* and morality; whereas this list obviously cannot presume to be exhaustive; whereas processes, the use of which offend against human dignity, such as processes to produce chimeras from germ cells or totipotent cells of humans and animals, are obviously also excluded from patentability;

(39)   Whereas *ordre public* and morality correspond in particular to ethical or moral principles recognised in a Member State, respect for which is particularly important in the field of biotechnology in view of the potential scope of inventions in this field and their inherent relationship to living matter; whereas such ethical or moral principles supplement the standard legal examinations under patent law regardless of the technical field of the invention;

(40)   Whereas there is a consensus within the Community that interventions in the human germ line and the cloning of human beings offends against *ordre public* and morality; whereas it is therefore important to exclude unequivocally from patentability processes for modifying the germ line genetic identity of human beings and processes for cloning human beings;

(41)   Whereas a process for cloning human beings may be defined as any process, including techniques of embryo splitting, designed to create a human being with the same nuclear genetic information as another living or deceased human being;

(42)   Whereas, moreover, uses of human embryos for industrial or commercial purposes must also be excluded from patentability; whereas in any case such exclusion does not affect inventions for therapeutic or diagnostic purposes which are applied to the human embryo and are useful to it;

(43)   Whereas pursuant to Article F(2) of the Treaty on European Union, the Union is to respect fundamental rights, as guaranteed by the European Convention for the Protection of Human Rights and Fundamental Freedoms signed in Rome on 4 November 1950 and as they result from the constitutional traditions common to the Member States, as general principles of Community law;

(44)   Whereas the Commission's European Group on Ethics in Science and New Technologies evaluates all ethical aspects of biotechnology; whereas it should be pointed

out in this connection that that Group may be consulted only where biotechnology is to be evaluated at the level of basic ethical principles, including where it is consulted on patent law;

(45) Whereas processes for modifying the genetic identity of animals which are likely to cause them suffering without any substantial medical benefit in terms of research, prevention, diagnosis or therapy to man or animal, and also animals resulting from such processes, must be excluded from patentability;

(46) Whereas, in view of the fact that the function of a patent is to reward the inventor for his creative efforts by granting an exclusive but time-bound right, and thereby encourage inventive activities, the holder of the patent should be entitled to prohibit the use of patented self-reproducing material in situations analogous to those where it would be permitted to prohibit the use of patented, non-self-reproducing products, that is to say the production of the patented product itself;

(47) Whereas it is necessary to provide for a first derogation from the rights of the holder of the patent when the propagating material incorporating the protected invention is sold to a farmer for farming purposes by the holder of the patent or with his consent; whereas that initial derogation must authorise the farmer to use the product of his harvest for further multiplication or propagation on his own farm; whereas the extent and the conditions of that derogation must be limited in accordance with the extent and conditions set out in Council Regulation (EC) No. 2100/94 of 27 July 1994 on Community plant variety rights;

(48) Whereas only the fee envisaged under Community law relating to plant variety rights as a condition for applying the derogation from Community plant variety rights can be required of the farmer;

(49) Whereas, however, the holder of the patent may defend his rights against a farmer abusing the derogation or against a breeder who has developed a plant variety incorporating the protected invention if the latter fails to adhere to his commitments;

(50) Whereas a second derogation from the rights of the holder of the patent must authorise the farmer to use protected livestock for agricultural purposes;

(51) Whereas the extent and the conditions of that second derogation must be determined by national laws, regulations and practices, since there is no Community legislation on animal variety rights;

(52) Whereas, in the field of exploitation of new plant characteristics resulting from genetic engineering, guaranteed access must, on payment of a fee, be granted in the form of a compulsory licence where, in relation to the genus or species concerned, the plant variety represents significant technical progress of considerable economic interest compared to the invention claimed in the patent;

(53) Whereas, in the field of the use of new plant characteristics resulting from new plant varieties in genetic engineering, guaranteed access must, on payment of a fee, be granted in the form of a compulsory licence where the invention represents significant technical progress of considerable economic interest;

(54) Whereas Article 34 of the TRIPs Agreement contains detailed provisions on the burden of proof which is binding on all Member States; whereas, therefore, a provision in this Directive is not necessary;

(55) Whereas following Decision 93/626/EEC the Community is party to the Convention on Biological Diversity of 5 June 1992; whereas, in this regard, Member States must give particular weight to Article 3 and Article 8(j), the second sentence of Article 16(2) and Article 16(5) of the Convention when bringing into force the laws, regulations and administrative provisions necessary to comply with this Directive;

(56) Whereas the Third Conference of the Parties to the Biodiversity Convention, which took place in November 1996, noted in Decision III/17 that "further work is required to help develop a common appreciation of the relationship between intellectual property rights and the relevant provisions of the TRIPs Agreement and the Convention

on Biological Diversity, in particular on issues relating to technology transfer and conservation and sustainable use of biological diversity and the fair and equitable sharing of benefits arising out of the use of genetic resources, including the protection of knowledge, innovations and practices of indigenous and local communities embodying traditional lifestyles relevant for the conservation and sustainable use of biological diversity'',

HAVE ADOPTED THIS DIRECTIVE:

CHAPTER 1
PATENTABILITY

Article 1

1. Member States shall protect biotechnological inventions under national patent law. They shall, if necessary, adjust their national patent law to take account of the provisions of this Directive.

2. This Directive shall be without prejudice to the obligations of the Member States pursuant to international agreements, and in particular the TRIPs Agreement and the Convention on Biological Diversity.

Article 2

1. For the purposes of this Directive,

  (a) "biological material" means any material containing genetic information and capable of reproducing itself or being reproduced in a biological system;

  (b) "microbiological process" means any process involving or performed upon or resulting in microbiological material.

2. A process for the production of plants or animals is essentially biological if it consists entirely of natural phenomena such as crossing or selection.

3. The concept of "plant variety" is defined by Article 5 of Regulation (EC) No. 2100/94.

Article 3

1. For the purposes of this Directive, inventions which are new, which involve an inventive step and which are susceptible of industrial application shall be patentable even if they concern a product consisting of or containing biological material or a process by means of which biological material is produced, processed or used.

2. Biological material which is isolated from its natural environment or produced by means of a technical process may be the subject of an invention even if it previously occurred in nature.

Article 4

1. The following shall not be patentable:

  (a) plant and animal varieties;

  (b) essentially biological processes for the production of plants or animals.

2. Inventions which concern plants or animals shall be patentable if the technical feasibility of the invention is not confined to a particular plant or animal variety.

3. Paragraph 1(b) shall be without prejudice to the patentability of inventions which concern a microbiological or other technical process or a product obtained by means of such a process.

Article 5

1. The human body, at the various stages of its formation and development, and the simple discovery of one of its elements, including the sequence or partial sequence of a gene, cannot constitute patentable inventions.

2. An element isolated from the human body or otherwise produced by means of a technical process, including the sequence or partial sequence of a gene, may constitute a patentable invention, even if the structure of that element is identical to that of a natural element.

3.   The industrial application of a sequence or a partial sequence of a gene must be disclosed in the patent application.

Article 6

1.   Inventions shall be considered unpatentable where their commercial exploitation would be contrary to *ordre public* or morality; however, exploitation shall not be deemed to be so contrary merely because it is prohibited by law or regulation.

2.   On the basis of paragraph 1, the following, in particular, shall be considered unpatentable:
   (a)   processes for cloning human beings;
   (b)   processes for modifying the germ line genetic identity of human beings;
   (c)   uses of human embryos for industrial or commercial purposes;
   (d)   processes for modifying the genetic identity of animals which are likely to cause them suffering without any substantial medical benefit to man or animal, and also animals resulting from such processes.

Article 7

The Comission's European Group on Ethics in Science and New Technologies evaluates all ethical aspects of biotechnology.

<h2 style="text-align:center">CHAPTER II
SCOPE OF PROTECTION</h2>

Article 8

1.   The protection conferred by a patent on a biological material possessing specific characteristics as a result of the invention shall extend to any biological material derived from that biological material through propagation or multiplication in an identical or divergent form and possessing those same characteristics.

2.   The protection conferred by a patent on a process that enables a biological material to be produced possessing specific characteristics as a result of the invention shall extend to biological material directly obtained through that process and to any other biological material derived from the directly obtained biological material through propagation or multiplication in an identical or divergent form and possessing those same characteristics.

Article 9

The protection conferred by a patent on a product containing or consisting of genetic information shall extend to all material, save as provided in Article 5(1), in which the product is incorporated and in which the genetic information is contained and performs its function.

Article 10

The protection referred to in Articles 8 and 9 shall not extend to biological material obtained from the propagation or multiplication of biological material placed on the market in the territory of a Member State by the holder of the patent or with his consent, where the multiplication or propagation necessarily results from the application for which the biological material was marketed, provided that the material obtained is not subsequently used for other propagation or multiplication.

Article 11

1.   By way of derogation from Articles 8 and 9, the sale or other form of commercialisation of plant propagating material to a farmer by the holder of the patent or with his consent for agricultural use implies authorisation for the farmer to use the product of his harvest for propagation or multipliction by him on his own farm, the extent and conditions of this derogation corresponding to those under Article 14 of Regulation (EC) No. 2100/94.

2.   By way of derogation from Articles 8 and 9, the sale or any other form of commercialisation of breeding stock or other animal reproductive material to a farmer by the holder of the patent or with his consent implies authorisation for the farmer to use the protected livestock for an agricultural purpose. This includes making the animal or other animal reproductive material available for the purposes of pursuing his agricultural activity but not sale within the framework or for the purpose of a commercial reproductin activity.

3.   The extent and the conditions of the derogation provided for in paragraph 2 shall be determined by national laws, regulations and practices.

CHAPTER III
COMPULSORY CROSS-LICENSING

Article 12

1.   Where a breeder cannot acquire or exploit a plant variety right without infringing a prior patent, he may apply for a compulsory licence for non-exclusive use of the invention protected by the patent inasmuch as the licence is necessary for the exploitation of the plant variety to be protected, subject to payment of an appropriate royalty. Member States shall provide that, where such a licence is granted, the holder of the patent will be entitled to a cross-licence on reasonable terms to use the protected variety.

2.   Where the holder of a patent concerning a biotechnological invention cannot exploit it without infringing a prior plant variety right, he may apply for a compulsory licence for non-exclusive use of the plant variety protected by that right, subject to payment of an appropriate royalty. Member States shall provide that, where such a licence is granted, the holder of the variety right will be entitled to a cross-licence on reasonable terms to use the protected invention.

3.   Applicants for the licences referred to in paragraphs 1 and 2 must demonstrate that:

(a)   they have applied unsuccessfully to the holder of the patent or of the plant variety right to obtain a contractual licence;

(b)   the plant variety or the invention constitutes significant technical progress of considerable economic interest compared with the invention claimed in the patent or the protected plant variety.

4.   Each Member State shall designate the authority or authorities responsible for granting the licence. Where a licence for a plant variety can be granted only by the Community Plant Variety Office, Article 29 of Regulation (EC) No. 2100/94 shall apply.

CHAPTER IV
DEPOSIT, ACCESS AND RE-DEPOSIT OF A BIOLOGICAL MATERIAL

Article 13

1.   Where an invention involves the use of or concerns biological material which is not available to the public and which cannot be described in a patent application in such a manner as to enable the invention to be reproduced by a person skilled in the art, the description shall be considered inadequate for the purposes of patent law unless:

(a)   the biological material has been deposited no later than the date on which the patent application was filed with a recognised depositary institution. At least the international depositary authorities which acquired this status by virtue of Article 7 of the Budapest Treaty of 28 April 1977 on the international recognition of the deposit of micro-organisms for the purposes of patent procedure, hereinafter referred to as the "Budapest Treaty", shall be recognised;

(b)   the application as filed contains such relevant informtion as is available to the applicant on the characteristics of the biological material deposited;

(c)   the patent application states the name of the depository institution and the accession number.

2.   Access to the deposited biological material shall be provided through the supply of a sample:

(a)   up to the first publication of the patent application, only to those persons who are authorised under national patent law;

(b)   between the first publication of the application and the granting of the patent, to anyone requesting it or, if the applicant so requests, only to an independent expert;

(c)   after the patent has been granted, and notwithstanding revocation or cancellation of the patent, to anyone requesting it.

3.   The sample shall be supplied only if the person requesting it undertakes, for the term during which the patent is in force:

(a)   not to make it or any material derived from it available to third parties; and

(b)   not to use it or any material derived from it except for experimental purposes, unless the applicant for or proprietor of the patent, as applicable, expressly waives such an undertaking.

4.   At the applicant's request, where an application is refused or withdrawn, access to the deposited material shall be limited to an independent expert for 20 years from the date on which the patent application was filed. In that case, paragraph 3 shall apply.

5.   The applicant's requests referred to in point (b) of paragraph 2 and in paragraph 4 may only be made up to the date on which the technical preparations for publishing the patent application are deemed to have been completed.

Article 14

1.   If the biological material deposited in accordance with Article 13 ceases to be available from the recognised depositary institution, a new deposit of the material shall be permitted on the same terms as those laid down in the Budapest Treaty.

2.   Any new deposit shall be accompanied by a statement signed by the depositor certifying that the newly deposited biological material is the same as that originally deposited.

CHAPTER V
FINAL PROVISIONS

Article 15

1.   Member States shall bring into force the laws, regulations and administrative provisions necessary to comply with this Directive not later than 30 July 2000. They shall forthwith inform the Commission thereof.

When Member States adopt these measures, they shall contain a reference to this Directive or shall be accompanied by such reference on the occasion of their official publication. The methods of making such reference shall be laid down by Member States.

2.   Member States shall communicate to the Commission the text of the provisions of national law which they adopt in the field covered by this Directive.

Article 16

The Commission shall send the European Parliament and the Council:

(a)   every five years as from the date specified in Article 15(1) a report on any problems encountered with regard to the relationship between this Directive and international agreements on the protection of human rights to which the Member States have acceded;

(b)   within two years of entry into force of this Directive, a report assessing the implications for basic genetic engineering research of failure to publish, or late publication of, papers on subjects which could be patentable;

(c) annually as from the date specified in Article 15(1), a report on the development and implications of patent law in the field of biotechnology and genetic engineering.

Article 17

This Directive shall enter into force on the day of its publication in the *Official Journal of the European Communities*.

Article 18

This Directive is addressed to the Member States.

PART III INTERNATIONAL AGREEMENTS

PARIS CONVENTION FOR THE PROTECTION OF INDUSTRIAL PROPERTY
of March 20, 1883,

as revised at BRUSSELS on December 14, 1900, at WASHINGTON on June 2, 1911, at THE HAGUE on November 6, 1925, at LONDON on June 2, 1934, at LISBON on October 31, 1958, and at STOCKHOLM on July 14, 1967, and as amended on September 28, 1979

Article 1 Establishment of the Union; Scope of Industrial Property

(1) The countries to which this Convention applies constitute a Union for the protection of industrial property.

(2) The protection of industrial property has as its object patents, utility models, industrial designs, trademarks, service marks, trade names, indications of source or appellations of origin, and the repression of unfair competition.

(3) Industrial property shall be understood in the broadest sense and shall apply not only to industry and commerce proper, but likewise to agricultural and extractive industries and to all manufactured or natural products, for example, wines, grain, tobacco leaf, fruit, cattle, minerals, mineral waters, beer, flowers, and flour.

(4) Patents shall include the various kinds of industrial patents recognised by the laws of the countries of the Union, such as patents of importation, patents of improvement, patents and certificates of addition, etc.

Article 2 National Treatment for Nationals of Countries of the Union

(1) Nationals of any country of the Union shall, as regards the protection of industrial property, enjoy in all the other countries of the Union the advantages that their respective laws now grant, or may hereafter grant, to nationals; all without prejudice to the rights specially provided for by this Convention. Consequently, they shall have the same protection as the latter, and the same legal remedy against any infringement of their rights, provided that the conditions and formalities imposed upon nationals are complied with.

(2) However, no requirement as to domicile or establishment in the country where protection is claimed may be imposed upon nationals of countries of the Union for the enjoyment of any industrial property rights.

(3) The provisions of the laws of each of the countries of the Union relating to judicial and administrative procedure and to jurisdiction, and to the designation of an address for service or the appointment of an agent, which may be required by the laws on industrial property are expressly reserved.

Article 3 Same Treatment for Certain Categories of Persons as for Nationals of Countries of the Union

Nationals of countries outside the Union who are domiciled or who have real and effective industrial or commercial establishments in the territory of one of the countries of the Union shall be treated in the same manner as nationals of the countries of the Union.

Article 4 A to I. Patents, Utility Models, Industrial Designs, Marks, Inventors' Certificates: Right of Priority. — G. Patents: Division of the Application

A.—(1) Any person who has duly filed an application for a patent, or for the registration of a utility model, or of an industrial design, or of a trademark, in one of the countries of the Union, or his successor in title, shall enjoy, for the purpose of filing in the other countries, a right of priority during the periods hereinafter fixed.

(2) Any filing that is equivalent to a regular national filing under the domestic legislation of any country of the Union or under bilateral or multilateral treaties

concluded between countries of the Union shall be recognised as giving rise to the right of priority.

(3)   By a regular national filing is meant any filing that is adequate to establish the date on which the application was filed in the country concerned, whatever may be the subsequent fate of the application.

B.—Consequently, any subsequent filing in any of the other countries of the Union before the expiration of the periods referred to above shall not be invalidated by reason of any acts accomplished in the interval, in particular, another filing, the publication or exploitation of the invention, the putting on sale of copies of the design, or the use of the mark, and such acts cannot give rise to any third-party right or any right of personal possession. Rights acquired by third parties before the date of the first application that serves as the basis for the right of priority are reserved in accordance with the domestic legislation of each country of the Union.

C.—(1)   The periods of priority referred to above shall be twelve months for patents and utility models, and six months for industrial designs and trademarks.

(2)   These periods shall start from the date of filing of the first application; the day of filing shall not be included in the period.

(3)   If the last day of the period is an official holiday, or a day when the Office is not open for the filing of applications in the country where protection is claimed, the period shall be extended until the first following working day.

(4)   A subsequent application concerning the same subject as a previous first application within the meaning of paragraph (2), above, filed in the same country of the Union, shall be considered as the first application, of which the filing date shall be the starting point of the period of priority, if, at the time of filing the subsequent application, the said previous application has been withdrawn, abandoned, or refused, without having been laid open to public inspection and without leaving any rights outstanding, and if it has not yet served as a basis for claiming a right of priority. The previous application may not thereafter serve as a basis for claiming a right of priority.

D.—(1)   Any person desiring to take advantage of the priority of a previous filing shall be required to make a declaration indicating the date of such filing and the country in which it was made. Each country shall determine the latest date on which such declaration must be made.

(2)   These particulars shall be mentioned in the publications issued by the competent authority, and in particular in the patents and the specifications relating thereto.

(3)   The countries of the Union may require any person making a declaration of priority to produce a copy of the application (description, drawings, etc.) previously filed. The copy, certified as correct by the authority which received such application, shall not require any authentication, and may in any case be filed, without fee, at any time within three months of the filing of the subsequent application. They may require it to be accompanied by a certificate from the same authority showing the date of filing, and by a translation.

(4)   No other formalities may be required for the declaration of priority at the time of filing the application. Each country of the Union shall determine the consequences of failure to comply with the formalities prescribed by this Article, but such consequences shall in no case go beyond the loss of the right of priority.

(5)   Subsequently, further proof may be required.

Any person who avails himself of the priority of a previous application shall be required to specify the number of that application; this number shall be published as provided for by paragraph (2), above.

E.—(1)   Where an industrial design is filed in a country by virtue of a right of priority based on the filing of a utility model, the period of priority shall be the same as that fixed for industrial designs.

(2)   Furthermore, it is permissible to file a utility model in a country by virtue of a right of priority based on the filing of a patent application, and vice versa.

F.—(1)   No country of the Union may refuse a priority or a patent application on the ground that the applicant claims multiple priorities, even if they originate in different countries, or on the ground that an application claiming one or more priorities contains one or more elements that were not included in the application or applications whose priority is claimed, provided that, in both cases, there is unity of invention within the meaning of the law of the country.

With respect to the elements not included in the application or applications whose priority is claimed, the filing of the subsequent application shall give rise to a right of priority under ordinary conditions.

G.—(1)   If the examination reveals that an application for a patent contains more than one invention, the applicant may divide the application into a certain number of divisional applications and preserve as the date of each the date of the initial application and the benefit of the right of priority, if any.

(2)   The applicant may also, on his own initiative, divide a patent application and preserve as the date of each divisional application the date of the initial application and the benefit of the right of priority, if any. Each country of the Union shall have the right to determine the conditions under which such division shall be authorised.

H.—Priority may not be refused on the ground that certain elements of the invention for which priority is claimed do not appear among the claims formulated in the application in the country of origin, provided that the application documents as a whole specifically disclose such elements.

I.—(1)   Applications for inventors' certificates filed in a country in which applicants have the right to apply at their own option either for a patent or for an inventor's certificate shall give rise to the right of priority provided for by this Article, under the same conditions and with the same effects as applications for patents.

(2)   In a country in which applicants have the right to apply at their own option either for a patent or for an inventor's certificate, an applicant for an inventor's certificate shall, in accordance with the provisions of this Article relating to patent applications, enjoy a right of priority based on an application for a patent, a utility model, or an inventor's certificate.

Article 4bis   Patents: Independence of Patents Obtained for the Same Invention in Different Countries

(1)   Patents applied for in the various countries of the Union by nationals of countries of the Union shall be independent of patents obtained for the same invention in other countries, whether members of the Union or not.

(2)   The foregoing provision is to be understood in an unrestricted sense, in particular, in the sense that patents applied for during the period of priority are independent, both as regards the grounds for nullity and forfeiture, and as regards their normal duration.

(3)   The provision shall apply to all patents existing at the time when it comes into effect.

(4)   Similarly, it shall apply, in the case of the accession of new countries, to patents in existence on either side at the time of accession.

(5)   Patents obtained with the benefit of priority shall, in the various countries of the Union, have a duration equal to that which they would have, had they been applied for or granted without the benefit of priority.

Article 4ter   Patents: Mention of the Inventor in the Patent
The inventor shall have the right to be mentioned as such in the patent.

Article 4^{quater} Patents: Patentability in Case of Restrictions of Sale by Law

The grant of a patent shall not be refused and a patent shall not be invalidated on the ground that the sale of the patented product or of a product obtained by means of a patented process is subject to restrictions or limitations resulting from the domestic law.

Article 5 A. Patents: Importation of Articles; Failure to Work or Insufficient Working; Compulsory Licences. — B. Industrial Designs: Failure to Work; Importation of Articles. — C. Marks: Failure to Use; Different Forms; Use by Co-proprietors. — D. Patents, Utility Models, Marks, Industrial Designs: Marking

A.—(1) Importation by the patentee into the country where the patent has been granted of articles manufactured in any of the countries of the Union shall not entail forfeiture of the patent.

(2) Each country of the Union shall have the right to take legislative measures providing for the grant of compulsory licences to prevent the abuses which might result from the exercise of the exclusive rights conferred by the patent, for example, failure to work.

(3) Forfeiture of the patent shall not be provided for except in cases where the grant of compulsory licenses would not have been sufficient to prevent the said abuses. No proceedings for the forfeiture or revocation of a patent may be instituted before the expiration of two years from the grant of the first compulsory license.

(4) A compulsory license may not be applied for on the ground of failure to work or insufficient working before the expiration of a period of four years from the date of filing of the patent application or three years from the date of the grant of the patent, whichever period expires last; it shall be refused if the patentee justifies his inaction by legitimate reasons. Such a compulsory license shall be non-exclusive and shall not be transferable, even in the form of the grant of a sub-license, except with that part of the enterprise or goodwill which exploits such license.

(5) The foregoing provisions shall be applicable, *mutatis mutandis*, to utility models.

B.—The protection of industrial designs shall not, under any circumstance, be subject to any forfeiture, either by reason of failure to work or by reason of the importation of articles corresponding to those which are protected.

C.—(1) If, in any country, use of the registered mark is compulsory, the registration may be cancelled only after a reasonable period, and then only if the person concerned does not justify his inaction.

(2) Use of a trademark by the proprietor in a form differing in elements which do not alter the distinctive character of the mark in the form in which it was registered in one of the countries of the Union shall not entail invalidation of the registration and shall not diminish the protection granted to the mark.

(3) Concurrent use of the same mark on identical or similar goods by industrial or commercial establishments considered as co-proprietors of the mark according to the provisions of the domestic law of the country where protection is claimed shall not prevent registration or diminish in any way the protection granted to the said mark in any country of the Union, provided that such use does not result in misleading the public and is not contrary to the public interest.

D.—No indication or mention of the patent, of the utility model, of the registration of the trademark, or of the deposit of the industrial design, shall be required upon the goods as a condition of recognition of the right to protection.

Article 5bis All Industrial Property Rights: Period of Grace for the Payment of Fees for the Maintenance of Rights; Patents: Restoration

(1) A period of grace of not less than six months shall be allowed for the payment of the fees prescribed for the maintenance of industrial property rights, subject, if the domestic legislation so provides, to the payment of a surcharge.

(2)   The countries of the Union shall have the right to provide for the restoration of patents which have lapsed by reason of non-payment of fees.

Article 5ter   Patents: Patented Devices Forming Part of Vessels, Aircraft or Land Vehicles

In any country of the Union the following shall not be considered as infringements of the rights of a patentee:

1.   the use on board vessels of other countries of the Union of devices forming the subject of his patent in the body of the vessel, in the machinery, tackle, gear and other accessories, when such vessels temporarily or accidentally enter the waters of the said country, provided that such devices are used there exclusively for the needs of the vessel;

2.   the use of devices forming the subject of the patent in the construction or operation of aircraft or land vehicles of other countries of the Union, or of accessories of such aircraft or land vehicles, when those aircraft or land vehicles temporarily or accidentally enter the said country.

Article 5quater   Patents: Importation of Products Manufactured by a Process Patented in the Importing Country

When a product is imported into a country of the Union where there exists a patent protecting a process of manufacture of the said product, the patentee shall have all the rights, with regard to the imported product, that are accorded to him by the legislation of the country of importation, on the basis of the process patent, with respect to products manufactured in that country.

Article 5quinquies   Industrial Designs

Industrial designs shall be protected in all the countries of the Union.

Article 6   Marks: Conditions of Registration; Independence of Protection of Same Mark in Different Countries

(1)   The conditions for the filing and registration of trademarks shall be determined in each country of the Union by its domestic legislation.

(2)   However, an application for the registration of a mark filed by a national of a country of the Union in any country of the Union may not be refused, nor may a registration be invalidated, on the ground that filing, registration, or renewal, has not been effected in the country of origin.

(3)   A mark duly registered in a country of the Union shall be regarded as independent of marks registered in the other countries of the Union, including the country of origin.

Article 6bis   Marks: Well-Known Marks

(1)   The countries of the Union undertake, ex officio if their legislation so permits, or at the request of an interested party, to refuse or to cancel the registration, and to prohibit the use, of a trademark which constitutes a reproduction, an imitation, or a translation, liable to create confusion, of a mark considered by the competent authority of the country of registration or use to be well known in that country as being already the mark of a person entitled to the benefits of this Convention and used for identical or similar goods. These provisions shall also apply when the essential part of the mark constitutes a reproduction of any such well-known mark or an imitation liable to create confusion therewith.

(2)   A period of at least five years from the date of registration shall be allowed for requesting the cancellation of such a mark. The countries of the Union may provide for a period within which the prohibition of use must be requested.

(3)   No time limit shall be fixed for requesting the cancellation or the prohibition of the use of marks registered or used in bad faith.

Article 6ter Marks: Prohibitions concerning State Emblems, Official Hallmarks, and Emblems of Intergovernmental Organisations

(1)(a) The countries of the Union agree to refuse or to invalidate the registration, and to prohibit by appropriate measures the use, without authorisation by the competent authorities, either as trademarks or as elements of trademarks, of armorial bearings, flags, and other State emblems, of the countries of the Union, official signs and hallmarks indicating control and warranty adopted by them, and any imitation from a heraldic point of view.

(b) The provisions of subparagraph (a), above, shall apply equally to armorial bearings, flags, other emblems, abbreviations, and names, of international intergovernmental organisations of which one or more countries of the Union are members, with the exception of armorial bearings, flags, other emblems, abbreviations, and names, that are already the subject of international agreements in force, intended to ensure their protection.

(c) No country of the Union shall be required to apply the provisions of subparagraph (b), above, to the prejudice of the owners of rights acquired in good faith before the entry into force, in that country, of this Convention. The countries of the Union shall not be required to apply the said provisions when the use or registration referred to in subparagraph (a), above, is not of such a nature as to suggest to the public that a connection exists between the organisation concerned and the armorial bearings, flags, emblems, abbreviations, and names, or if such use or registration is probably not of such a nature as to mislead the public as to the existence of a connection between the user and the organisation.

(2) Prohibition of the use of official signs and hallmarks indicating control and warranty shall apply solely in cases where the marks in which they are incorporated are intended to be used on goods of the same or a similar kind.

(3)(a) For the application of these provisions, the countries of the Union agree to communicate reciprocally, through the intermediary of the International Bureau, the list of State emblems, and official signs and hallmarks indicating control and warranty, which they desire, or may hereafter desire, to place wholly or within certain limits under the protection of this Article, and all subsequent modifications of such list. Each country of the Union shall in due course make available to the public the lists so communicated.

Nevertheless such communication is not obligatory in respect of flags of States.

(b) The provisions of subparagraph (b) of paragraph (1) of this Article shall apply only to such armorial bearings, flags, other emblems, abbreviations, and names, of international intergovernmental organisations as the latter have communicated to the countries of the Union through the intermediary of the International Bureau.

(4) Any country of the Union may, within a period of twelve months from the receipt of the notification, transmit its objections, if any, through the intermediary of the International Bureau, to the country or international intergovernmental organisation concerned.

(5) In the case of State flags, the measures prescribed by paragraph (1), above, shall apply solely to marks registered after 6 November 1925.

(6) In the case of State emblems other than flags, and of official signs and hallmarks of the countries of the Union, and in the case of armorial bearings, flags, other emblems, abbreviations, and names, of international intergovernmental organisations, these provisions shall apply only to marks registered more than two months after receipt of the communication provided for in paragraph (3), above.

(7) In cases of bad faith, the countries shall have the right to cancel even those marks incorporating State emblems, signs, and hallmarks, which were registered before 6 November 1925.

(8) Nationals of any country who are authorised to make use of the State emblems, signs, and hallmarks, of their country may use them even if they are similar to those of another country.

(9)   The countries of the Union undertake to prohibit the unauthorised use in trade of the State armorial bearings of the other countries of the Union, when the use is of such a nature as to be misleading as to the origin of the goods.

(10)   The above provisions shall not prevent the countries from exercising the right given in paragraph (3) of Article 6^{quinquies}, Section B, to refuse or to invalidate the registration of marks incorporating, without authorisation, armorial bearings, flags, other State emblems, or official signs and hallmarks adopted by a country of the Union, as well as the distinctive signs of international intergovernmental organisations referred to in paragraph (1), above.

Article 6^{quater} Marks: Assignment of Marks

(1)   When, in accordance with the law of a country of the Union, the assignment of a mark is valid only if it takes place at the same time as the transfer of the business or goodwill to which the mark belongs, it shall suffice for the recognition of such validity that the portion of the business or goodwill located in that country be transferred to the assignee, together with the exclusive right to manufacture in the said country, or to sell therein, the goods bearing the mark assigned.

(2)   The foregoing provision does not impose upon the countries of the Union any obligation to regard as valid the assignment of any mark the use of which by the assignee would, in fact, be of such a nature as to mislead the public, particularly as regards the origin, nature, or essential qualities, of the goods to which the mark is applied.

Article 6^{quinquies} Marks: Protection of Marks Registered in One Country of the Union in the Other Countries of the Union

A.—(1) Every trademark duly registered in the country of origin shall be accepted for filing and protected as is in the other countries of the Union, subject to the reservations indicated in this Article. Such countries may, before proceeding to final registration, require the production of a certificate of registration in the country of origin, issued by the competent authority. No authentication shall be required for this certificate.

(2)   Shall be considered the country of origin the country of the Union where the applicant has a real and effective industrial or commercial establishment, or, if he has no such establishment within the Union, the country of the Union where he has his domicile, or, if he has no domicile within the Union but is a national of a country of the Union, the country of which he is a national.

B.—Trademarks covered by this Article may be neither denied registration nor invalidated except in the following cases:

1.   when they are of such a nature as to infringe rights acquired by third parties in the country where protection is claimed;

2.   when they are devoid of any distinctive character, or consist exclusively of signs or indications which may serve, in trade, to designate the kind, quality, quantity, intended purpose, value, place of origin, of the goods, or the time of production, or have become customary in the current language or in the bona fide and established practices of the trade of the country where protection is claimed;

3.   when they are contrary to morality or public order and, in particular, of such a nature as to deceive the public. It is understood that a mark may not be considered contrary to public order for the sole reason that it does not conform to a provision of the legislation on marks, except if such provision itself relates to public order.

This provision is subject, however, to the application of Article 10bis.

C.—(1)   In determining whether a mark is eligible for protection, all the factual circumstances must be taken into consideration, particularly the length of time the mark has been in use.

(2)   No trademark shall be refused in the other countries of the Union for the sole reason that it differs from the mark protected in the country of origin only in respect of

elements that do not alter its distinctive character and do not affect its identity in the form in which it has been registered in the said country of origin.

D.—No person may benefit from the provisions of this Article if the mark for which he claims protection is not registered in the country of origin.

E.—However, in no case shall the renewal of the registration of the mark in the country of origin involve an obligation to renew the registration in the other countries of the Union in which the mark has been registered.

F.—The benefit of priority shall remain unaffected for applications for the registration of marks filed within the period fixed by Article 4, even if registration in the country of origin is effected after the expiration of such period.

Article 6^{sexies} Marks: Service Marks
The countries of the Union undertake to protect service marks. They shall not be required to provide for the registration of such marks.

Article 6^{septies} Marks: Registration in the Name of the Agent or Representative of the Proprietor Without the Latter's Authorisation
(1)   If the agent or representative of the person who is the proprietor of a mark in one of the countries of the Union applies, without such proprietor's authorisation, for the registration of the mark in his own name, in one or more countries of the Union, the proprietor shall be entitled to oppose the registration applied for or demand its cancellation or, if the law of the country so allows, the assignment in his favour of the said registration, unless such agent or representative justifies his action.

(2)   The proprietor of the mark shall, subject to the provisions of paragraph (1), above, be entitled to oppose the use of his mark by his agent or representative if he has not authorised such use.

(3)   Domestic legislation may provide an equitable time limit within which the proprietor of a mark must exercise the rights provided for in this Article.

Article 7   Marks: Nature of the Goods to which the Mark is Applied
The nature of the goods to which a trademark is to be applied shall in no case form an obstacle to the registration of the mark.

Article 7bis Marks: Collective Marks
(1)   The countries of the Union undertake to accept for filing and to protect collective marks belonging to associations the existence of which is not contrary to the law of the country of origin, even if such associations do not possess an industrial or commercial establishment.

(2)   Each country shall be the judge of the particular conditions under which a collective mark shall be protected and may refuse protection if the mark is contrary to the public interest.

(3)   Nevertheless, the protection of these marks shall not be refused to any association the existence of which is not contrary to the law of the country of origin, on the ground that such association is not established in the country where protection is sought or is not constituted according to the law of the latter country.

Article 8   Trade Names
A trade name shall be protected in all the countries of the Union without the obligation of filing or registration, whether or not it forms part of a trademark.

Article 9   Marks, Trade Names: Seizure, on Importation, etc., of Goods Unlawfully Bearing a Mark or Trade Name
(1)   All goods unlawfully bearing a trademark or trade name shall be seized on importation into those countries of the Union where such mark or trade name is entitled to legal protection.

(2)   Seizure shall likewise be effected in the country where the unlawful affixation occurred or in the country into which the goods were imported.

(3)   Seizure shall take place at the request of the public prosecutor, or any other competent authority, or any interested party, whether a natural person or a legal entity, in conformity with the domestic legislation of each country.

(4)   The authorities shall not be bound to effect seizure of goods in transit.

(5)   If the legislation of a country does not permit seizure on importation, seizure shall be replaced by prohibition of importation or by seizure inside the country.

(6)   If the legislation of a country permits neither seizure on importation nor prohibition of importation nor seizure inside the country, then, until such time as the legislation is modified accordingly, these measures shall be replaced by the actions and remedies available in such cases to nationals under the law of such country.

Article 10   False Indications: Seizure, on Importation, etc., of Goods Bearing False Indications as to their Source or the Identity of the Producer

(1)   The provisions of the preceding Article shall apply in cases of direct or indirect use of a false indication of the source of the goods or the identity of the producer, manufacturer, or merchant.

(2)   Any producer, manufacturer, or merchant, whether a natural person or a legal entity, engaged in the production or manufacture of or trade in such goods and established either in the locality falsely indicated as the source, or in the region where such locality is situated, or in the country falsely indicated, or in the country where the false indication of source is used, shall in any case be deemed an interested party.

Article 10bis   Unfair Competition

(1)   The countries of the Union are bound to assure to nationals of such countries effective protection against unfair competition.

(2)   Any act of competition contrary to honest practices in industrial or commercial matters constitutes an act of unfair competition.

(3)   The following in particular shall be prohibited:

    1.   all acts of such a nature as to create confusion by any means whatever with the establishment, the goods, or the industrial or commercial activities, of a competitor;

    2.   false allegations in the course of trade of such a nature as to discredit the establishment, the goods, or the industrial or commercial activities, of a competitor;

    3.   indications or allegations the use of which in the course of trade is liable to mislead the public as to the nature, the manufacturing process, the characteristics, the suitability for their purpose, or the quantity, of the goods.

Article 10ter   Marks, Trade Names, False Indications, Unfair Competition: Remedies, Right to Sue

(1)   The countries of the Union undertake to assure to nationals of the other countries of the Union appropriate legal remedies effectively to repress all the acts referred to in Articles 9, 10, and 10bis.

(2)   They undertake, further, to provide measures to permit federations and associations representing interested industrialists, producers, or merchants, provided that the existence of such federations and associations is not contrary to the laws of their countries, to take action in the courts or before the administrative authorities, with a view to the repression of the acts referred to in Articles 9, 10, and 10bis, in so far as the law of the country in which protection is claimed allows such action by federations and associations of that country.

Article 11 Inventions, Utility Models, Industrial Designs, Marks: Temporary Protection at Certain International Exhibitions

(1)   The countries of the Union shall, in conformity with their domestic legislation, grant temporary protection to patentable inventions, utility models, industrial designs, and trademarks, in respect of goods exhibited at official or officially recognised international exhibitions held in the territory of any of them.

(2)   Such temporary protection shall not extend the periods provided by Article 4. If, later, the right of priority is invoked, the authorities of any country may provide that the period shall start from the date of introduction of the goods into the exhibition.

(3)   Each country may require, as proof of the identity of the article exhibited and of the date of its introduction, such documentary evidence as it considers necessary.

Article 12 Special National Industrial Property Services

(1)   Each country of the Union undertakes to establish a special industrial property service and a central office for the communication to the public of patents, utility models, industrial designs, and trademarks.

(2)   This service shall publish an official periodical journal. It shall publish regularly:

(a)   the names of the proprietors of patents granted, with a brief designation of the inventions patented;

(b)   the reproductions of registered trademarks.

. . .

Article 19 Special Agreements

It is understood that the countries of the Union reserve the right to make separately between themselves special agreements for the protection of industrial property, in so far as these agreements do not contravene the provisions of this Convention.

. . .

BERNE CONVENTION FOR THE PROTECTION OF LITERARY AND ARTISTIC WORKS
of September 9, 1886,
completed at PARIS on May 4, 1896, revised at BERLIN on November 13, 1908, completed at BERNE on March 20, 1914, revised at ROME on June 2, 1928, at BRUSSELS on June 26, 1948, at STOCKHOLM on July 14, 1967, and at PARIS on July 24, 1971, and amended on September 28, 1979

The countries of the Union, being equally animated by the desire to protect, in as effective and uniform a manner as possible, the rights of authors in their literary and artistic works,

Recognising the importance of the work of the Revision Conference held at Stockholm in 1967,

Have resolved to revise the Act adopted by the Stockholm Conference, while maintaining without change Articles 1 to 20 and 22 to 26 of that Act.

Consequently, the undersigned Plenipotentiaries, having presented their full powers, recognised as in good and due form, have agreed as follows:

Article 1   Establishment of a Union

The countries to which this Convention applies constitute a Union for the protection of the rights of authors in their literary and artistic works.

Article 2　Protected Works: 1. "Literary and artistic works"; 2. Possible requirement of fixation; 3. Derivative works; 4. Official texts; 5. Collections; 6. Obligation to protect; beneficiaries of protection; 7. Works of applied art and industrial designs; 8. News

(1)　The expression "literary and artistic works" shall include every production in the literary, scientific and artistic domain, whatever may be the mode or form of its expression, such as books, pamphlets and other writings; lectures, addresses, sermons and other works of the same nature; dramatic or dramatico- musical works; choreographic works and entertainments in dumb show; musical compositions with or without words; cinematographic works to which are assimilated works expressed by a process analogous to cinematography; works of drawing, painting, architecture, sculpture, engraving and lithography; photographic works to which are assimilated works expressed by a process analogous to photography; works of applied art; illustrations, maps, plans, sketches and three-dimensional works relative to geography, topography, architecture or science.

(2)　It shall, however, be a matter for legislation in the countries of the Union to prescribe that works in general or any specified categories of works shall not be protected unless they have been fixed in some material form.

(3)　Translations, adaptations, arrangements of music and other alterations of a literary or artistic work shall be protected as original works without prejudice to the copyright in the original work.

(4)　It shall be a matter for legislation in the countries of the Union to determine the protection to be granted to official texts of a legislative, administrative and legal nature, and to official translations of such texts.

(5)　Collections of literary or artistic works such as encyclopaedias and anthologies which, by reason of the selection and arrangement of their contents, constitute intellectual creations shall be protected as such, without prejudice to the copyright in each of the works forming part of such collections.

(6)　The works mentioned in this Article shall enjoy protection in all countries of the Union. This protection shall operate for the benefit of the author and his successors in title.

(7)　Subject to the provisions of Article 7(4) of this Convention, it shall be a matter for legislation in the countries of the Union to determine the extent of the application of their laws to works of applied art and industrial designs and models, as well as the conditions under which such works, designs and models shall be protected. Works protected in the country of origin solely as designs and models shall be entitled in another country of the Union only to such special protection as if granted in that country to designs and models; however, if no such special protection is granted in that country, such works shall be protected as artistic works.

(8)　The protection of this Convention shall not apply to news of the day or to miscellaneous facts having the character of mere items of press information.

Article 2bis　Possible Limitation of Protection of Certain Works: 1. Certain speeches; 2. Certain uses of lectures and addresses; 3. Right to make collections of such works

(1)　It shall be a matter for legislation in the countries of the Union to exclude, wholly or in part, from the protection provided by the preceding Article political speeches and speeches delivered in the course of legal proceedings.

(2)　It shall also be a matter for legislation in the countries of the Union to determine the conditions under which lectures, addresses and other works of the same nature which are delivered in public may be reproduced by the press, broadcast, communicated to the public by wire and made the subject of public communication as envisaged in Article 11bis(1) of this Convention, when such use is justified by the informatory purpose.

(3)   Nevertheless, the author shall enjoy the exclusive right of making a collection of his works mentioned in the preceding paragraphs.

Article 3   Criteria of Eligibility for Protection: 1. Nationality of author; place of publication of work; 2. Residence of author; 3. "Published" works; 4. "Simultaneously published" works

(1)   The protection of this Convention shall apply to:

(a)   authors who are nationals of one of the countries of the Union, for their works, whether published or not;

(b)   authors who are not nationals of one of the countries of the Union, for their works first published in one of those countries, or simultaneously in a country outside the Union and in a country of the Union.

(2)   Authors who are not nationals of one of the countries of the Union but who have their habitual residence in one of them shall, for the purposes of this Convention, be assimilated to nationals of that country.

(3)   The expression "published works" means works published with the consent of their authors, whatever may be the means of manufacture of the copies, provided that the availability of such copies has been such as to satisfy the reasonable requirements of the public, having regard to the nature of the work. The performance of a dramatic, dramatico-musical, cinematographic or musical work, the public recitation of a literary work, the communication by wire or the broadcasting of literary or artistic works, the exhibition of a work of art and the construction of a work of architecture shall not constitute publication.

(4)   A work shall be considered as having been published simultaneously in several countries if it has been published in two or more countries within thirty days of its first publication.

Article 4   Criteria of eligibility for protection of cinematographic works, works of architecture and certain artistic works

The protection of this Convention shall apply, even if the conditions of Article 3 are not fulfilled, to:

(a)   authors of cinematographic works the maker of which has his headquarters or habitual residence in one of the countries of the Union;

(b)   authors of works of architecture erected in a country of the Union or of other artistic works incorporated in a building or other structure located in a country of the Union.

Article 5   Rights Guaranteed: 1. and 2. Outside the country of origin; 3. In the country of origin; 4. "Country of origin"

(1)   Authors shall enjoy, in respect of works for which they are protected under this Convention, in countries of the Union other than the country of origin, the rights which their respective laws do now or may hereafter grant to their nationals, as well as the rights specially granted by this Convention.

(2)   The enjoyment and the exercise of these rights shall not be subject to any formality; such enjoyment and such exercise shall be independent of the existence of protection in the country of origin of the work. Consequently, apart from the provisions of this Convention, the extent of protection, as well as the means of redress afforded to the author to protect his rights, shall be governed exclusively by the laws of the country where protection is claimed.

(3)   Protection in the country of origin is governed by domestic law. However, when the author is not a national of the country of origin of the work for which he is protected under this Convention, he shall enjoy in that country the same rights as national authors.

(4)   The country of origin shall be considered to be:

(a)   in the case of works first published in a country of the Union, that country; in the case of works published simultaneously in several countries of the Union which grant different terms of protection, the country whose legislation grants the shortest term of protection;

(b)   in the case of works published simultaneously in a country outside the Union and in a country of the Union, the latter country;

(c)   in the case of unpublished works or of works first published in a country outside the Union, without simultaneous publication in a country of the Union, the country of the Union of which the author is a national, provided that:

(i)   When these are cinematographic works the maker of which has his headquarters or his habitual residence in a country of the Union, the country of origin shall be that country, and

(ii)   when these are works of architecture created in a country of the Union or other artistic works incorporated in a building or other structure located in a country of the Union, the country of origin shall be that country.

Article 6   Possible Restrictions of Protection in Respect of Certain Works of Nationals of Certain Countries Outside the Union: 1. In the country of the first publication and in other countries; 2. No retroactivity; 3. Notice

(1)   Where any country outside the Union fails to protect in an adequate manner the works of authors who are nationals of one of the countries of the Union, the latter country may restrict the protection given to the works of authors who are, at the date of the first publication thereof, nationals of the other country and are not habitually resident in one of the countries of the Union. If the country of first publication avails itself of this right, the other countries of the Union shall not be required to grant to works thus subjected to special treatment a wider protection than that granted to them in the country of first publication.

(2)   No restrictions introduced by virtue of the preceding paragraph shall affect the rights which an author may have acquired in respect of a work published in a country of the Union before such restrictions were put into force.

(3)   The countries of the Union which restrict the grant of copyright in accordance with this Article shall give notice thereof to the Director General of the World Intellectual Property Organisation (hereinafter designated as "the Director General") by a written declaration specifying the countries in regard to which protection is restricted, and the restrictions to which rights of authors who are nationals of those countries are subjected. The Director General shall immediately communicate this declaration to all the countries of the Union.

Article 6bis   Moral Rights: 1. To claim authorship; to object to certain modifications and other derogatory actions; 2. After the author's death; 3. Means of redress

(1)   Independently of the author's economic rights, and even after the transfer of the said rights, the author shall have the right to claim authorship of the work and to object to any distortion, mutilation or other modification of, or other derogatory action in relation to, the said work, which would be prejudicial to his honour or reputation.

(2)   The rights granted to the author in accordance with the preceding paragraph shall, after his death, be maintained, at least until the expiry of the economic rights, and shall be exercisable by the persons or institutions authorised by the legislation of the country where protection is claimed. However, those countries whose legislation, at the moment of their ratification of or accession to this Act, does not provide for the protection after the death of the author of all the rights set out in the preceding paragraph may provide that some of these rights may, after his death, cease to be maintained.

(3)   The means of redress for safeguarding the rights granted by this Article shall be governed by the legislation of the country where protection is claimed.

Article 7   Term of Protection: 1. Generally; 2. For cinematographic works; 3. For anonymous and pseudonymous works; 4. For photographic works and works of applied art; 5. Starting date of computation; 6. Longer terms; 7. Shorter terms; 8. Applicable law; "comparison" of terms

(1)   The term of protection granted by this Convention shall be the life of the author and fifty years after his death.

(2)   However, in the case of cinematographic works, the countries of the Union may provide that the term of protection shall expire fifty years after the work has been made available to the public with the consent of the author, or, failing such an event within fifty years from the making of such a work, fifty years after the making.

(3)   In the case of anonymous or pseudonymous works, the term of protection granted by this Convention shall expire fifty years after the work has been lawfully made available to the public. However, when the pseudonym adopted by the author leaves no doubt as to his identity, the term of protection shall be that provided in paragraph (1). If the author of an anonymous or pseudonymous work discloses his identity during the above-mentioned period, the term of protection applicable shall be that provided in paragraph (1). The countries of the Union shall not be required to protect anonymous or pseudonymous works in respect of which it is reasonable to presume that their author has been dead for fifty years.

(4)   It shall be a matter for legislation in the countries of the Union to determine the term of protection of photographic works and that of works of applied art in so far as they are protected as artistic works; however, this term shall last at least until the end of a period of twenty-five years from the making of such a work.

(5)   The term of protection subsequent to the death of the author and the terms provided by paragraphs (2), (3) and (4) shall run from the date of death or of the event referred to in those paragraphs, but such terms shall always be deemed to begin on the first of January of the year following the death or such event.

(6)   The countries of the Union may grant a term of protection in excess of those provided by the preceding paragraphs.

(7)   Those countries of the Union bound by the Rome Act of this Convention which grant, in their national legislation in force at the time of signature of the present act, shorter terms of protection than those provided for in the preceding paragraphs shall have the right to maintain such terms when ratifying or acceding to the present Act.

(8)   In any case, the term shall be governed by the legislation of the country where protection is claimed; however, unless the legislation of that country otherwise provides, the term shall not exceed the term fixed in the country of origin of the work.

Article 7bis   Term of Protection for Works of Joint Authorship

The provisions of the preceding Article shall also apply in the case of a work of joint authorship, provided that the terms measured from the death of the author shall be calculated from the death of the last surviving author.

Article 8   Right of Translation

Authors of literary and artistic works protected by this Convention shall enjoy the exclusive right of making and of authorising the translation of their works throughout the term of protection of their rights in the original works.

Article 9   Right of Reproduction: 1. Generally; 2. Possible exceptions; 3. Sound and visual recordings

(1)   Authors of literary and artistic works protected by this Convention shall have the exclusive right of authorising the reproduction of these works, in any manner or form.

(2)   It shall be a matter for legislation in the countries of the Union to permit the reproduction of such works in certain special cases, provided that such reproduction does not conflict with a normal exploitation of the work and does not unreasonably prejudice the legitimate interests of the author.

(3)   Any sound or visual recording shall be considered as a reproduction for the purposes of this Convention.

Article 10   Certain Free Uses of Works: 1. Quotations; 2. Illustrations for teaching; 3. Indication of source and author

(1)   It shall be permissible to make quotations from a work which has already been lawfully made available to the public, provided that their making is compatible with fair practice, and their extent does not exceed that justified by the purpose, including quotations from newspaper articles and periodicals in the form of press summaries.

(2)   It shall be a matter for legislation in the countries of the Union, and for special agreements existing or to be concluded between them, to permit the utilisation, to the extent justified by the purpose, of literary or artistic works by way of illustration in publications, broadcasts or sound or visual recordings for teaching, provided such utilisation is compatible with fair practice.

(3)   Where use is made of works in accordance with the preceding paragraphs of this Article, mention shall be made of the source, and of the name of the author if it appears thereon.

Article 10bis   Further Possible Free Uses of Works: 1. Of certain articles and broadcast works; 2. Of works seen or heard in connection with current events

(1)   It shall be a matter for legislation in the countries of the Union to permit the reproduction by the press, the broadcasting or the communication to the public by wire of articles published in newspapers or periodicals on current economic, political or religious topics, and of broadcast works of the same character, in cases in which the reproduction, broadcasting or such communication thereof is not expressly reserved. Nevertheless, the source must always be clearly indicated; the legal consequences of a breach of this obligation shall be determined by the legislation of the country where protection is claimed.

(2)   It shall also be a matter for legislation in the countries of the Union to determine the conditions under which, for the purpose of reporting current events by means of photography, cinematography, broadcasting or communication to the public by wire, literary or artistic works seen or heard in the course of the event may, to the extent justified by the informatory purpose, be reproduced and made available to the public.

Article 11   Certain Rights in Dramatic and Musical Works: 1. Right of public performance and of communication to the public of a performance; 2. In respect of translations

(1)   Author of dramatic, dramatico-musical and musical works shall enjoy the exclusive right of authorising:

   (i)   the public performance of their works, including such public performance by any means or process;

   (ii)   any communication to the public of the performance of their works.

(2)   Authors of dramatic or dramatico-musical works shall enjoy, during the full term of their rights in the original works, the same rights with respect to translations thereof.

Article 11bis   Broadcasting and Related Rights: 1. Broadcasting and other wireless communications, public communications of broadcast by wire or rebroadcast, public communication of broadcast by loudspeaker or analogous instruments; 2. Compulsory licences; 3. Recording; ephemeral recordings

(1)   Authors of literary and artistic works shall enjoy the exclusive right of authorising:

(i) the broadcasting of their works or the communication thereof to the public by any other means of wireless diffusion of signs, sounds or images;

(ii) any communication to the public by wire or by rebroadcasting of the broadcast of the work, when this communication is made by an organisation other than the original one;

(iii) the public communication by loudspeaker or any other analogous instrument transmitting, by signs, sounds or images, the broadcast of the work.

(2) It shall be a matter for legislation in the countries of the Union to determine the conditions under which the rights mentioned in the preceding paragraph may be exercised, but these conditions shall apply only in the countries where they have been prescribed. They shall not in any circumstances be prejudicial to the moral rights of the author, nor to his right to obtain equitable remuneration which, in the absence of agreement, shall be fixed by component authority.

(3) In the absence of any contrary stipulation, permission granted in accordance with paragraph (1) of this Article shall not imply permission to record, by means of instruments recording sounds or images, the work broadcast. It shall, however, be a matter for legislation in the countries of the Union to determine the regulations for ephemeral recordings made by a broadcasting organisation by means of its own facilities and used for its own broadcasts. The preservation of these recordings in official archives may, on the ground of their exceptional documentary character, be authorised by such legislation.

Article 11ter Certain Rights in Literary Works: 1. Right of public recitation and of communication to the public of a recitation; 2. In respect of translations

(1) Authors of literary works shall enjoy the exclusive right of authorising:

(i) the public recitation of their works, including such public recitation by any means or process;

(ii) any communication to the public of the recitation of their works.

(2) Authors of literary works shall enjoy, during the full term of their rights in the original works, the same rights with respect to translations thereof.

Article 12 Right of Adaptation, Arrangement and Other Alteration

Authors of literary or artistic works shall enjoy the exclusive right of authorising adaptations, arrangements and other alterations of their works.

Article 13 Possible Limitation of the Right of Recording of Musical Works and Any Words Pertaining Thereto: 1. Compulsory licences; 2. Transitory measures; 3. Seizure on importation of copies made without the author's permission

(1) Each country of the Union may impose for itself reservations and conditions on the exclusive right granted to the author of a musical work and to the author of any words, the recording of which together with the musical work has already been authorised by the latter, to authorise the sound recording of that musical work, together with such words, if any; but all such reservations and conditions shall apply only in the countries which have imposed them and shall not, in any circumstances, be prejudicial to the rights of these authors to obtain equitable remuneration which, in the absence of agreement, shall be fixed by competent authority.

(2) Recordings of musical works made in a country of the Union in accordance with Article 13(3) of the Conventions signed at Rome on 2 June 1928, and at Brussels on 26 June 1948, may be reproduced in that country without the permission of the author of the musical work until a date two years after that country becomes bound by this Act.

(3) Recordings made in accordance with paragraphs (1) and (2) of this Article and imported without permission from the parties concerned into a country where they are treated as infringing recordings shall be liable to seizure.

Article 14   Cinematographic and Related Rights: 1. Cinematographic adaptation and reproduction; distribution; public performance and public communication by wire of works thus adapted or reproduced; 2. Adaptation of cinematographic productions; 3. No compulsory licences

(1)   Authors of literary or artistic works shall have the exclusive right of authorising:

(i)   the cinematographic adaptation and reproduction of these works, and the distribution of the works thus adapted or reproduced;

(ii)   the public performance and communication to the public by wire of the works thus adapted or reproduced.

(2)   The adaptation into any other artistic form of a cinematographic production derived from literary or artistic works shall, without prejudice to the authorisation of the author of the cinematographic production, remain subject to the authorisation of the authors of the original works.

(3)   The provisions of Article 13(1) shall not apply.

Article 14bis Special Provisions Concerning Cinematographic Works: 1. Assimilation to "original" works; 2. Ownership; limitation of certain rights of certain contributors; 3. Certain other contributors

(1)   Without prejudice to the copyright in any work which may have been adapted or reproduced, a cinematographic work shall be protected as an original work. The owner of copyright in a cinematographic work shall enjoy the same rights as the author of an original work, including the rights referred to in the preceding Article.

(2)(a)   Ownership of copyright in a cinematographic work shall be a matter for legislation in the country where protection is claimed.

(b)   However, in the countries of the Union which, by legislation, include among the owners of copyright in a cinematographic work authors who have brought contributions to the making of the work, such authors, if they have undertaken to bring such contributions, may not, in the absence of any contrary or special stipulation, object to the reproduction, distribution, public performance, communication to the public by wire, broadcasting or any other communication to the public, or to the subtitling or dubbing of texts, of the work.

(c)   The question whether or not the form of the undertaking referred to above should, for the application of the preceding subparagraph (b), be in a written agreement or a written act of the same effect shall be a matter for the legislation of the country where the maker of the cinematographic work has his headquarters or habitual residence. However, it shall be a matter for the legislation of the country of the Union where protection is claimed to provide that the said undertaking shall be in a written agreement or a written act of the same effect. The countries whose legislation so provides shall notify the Director General by means of a written declaration, which will be immediately communicated by him to all the other countries of the Union.

(d)   By "contrary or special stipulation" is meant any restrictive condition which is relevant to the aforesaid undertaking.

(3)   Unless the national legislation provides to the contrary, the provisions of paragraph (2)(b) above shall not be applicable to authors of scenarios, dialogues and musical works created for the making of the cinematographic work, or to the principal director thereof. However, those countries of the Union whose legislation does not contain rules providing for the application of the said paragraph (2)(b) to such director shall notify the Director General by means of a written declaration, which will be immediately communicated by him to all the other countries of the Union.

Article 14ter "Droit de suite" in Works of Art and Manuscripts: 1. Right to an interest in resales; 2. Applicable law; 3. Procedure

(1)   The author, or after his death the persons or institutions authorised by national legislation, shall, with respect to original works of art and original manuscripts of writers

and composers, enjoy the inalienable right to an interest in any sale of the work subsequent to the first transfer by the author of the work.

(2) The protection provided by the preceding paragraph may be claimed in a country of the Union only if legislation in the country to which the author belongs so permits, and to the extent permitted by the country where this protection is claimed.

(3) The procedure for collection and the amounts shall be matters for determination by national legislation.

Article 15 Right to Enforce Protected Rights: 1. Where author's name is indicated or where pseudonym leaves no doubt as to author's identity; 2. In the case of cinematographic works; 3. In the case of anonymous and pseudonymous works; 4. In the case of certain unpublished works of unknown authorship

(1) In order that the author of a literary or artistic work protected by this Convention shall, in the absence of proof to the contrary, be regarded as such, and consequently be entitled to institute infringement proceedings in the countries of the Union, it shall be sufficient for his name to appear on the work in the usual manner. This paragraph shall be applicable even if this name is a pseudonym, where the pseudonym adopted by the author leaves no doubt as to his identity.

(2) The person or body corporate whose name appears on a cinematographic work in the usual manner shall, in the absence of proof to the contrary, be presumed to be the maker of the said work.

(3) In the case of anonymous and pseudonymous works, other than those referred to in paragraph (1) above, the publisher whose name appears on the work shall, in the absence of proof to the contrary, be deemed to represent the author, and in this capacity he shall be entitled to protect and enforce the author's rights. The provisions of this paragraph shall cease to apply when the author reveals his identity and establishes his claim to authorship of the work.

(4)(a) In a case of unpublished works where the identity of the author is unknown, but where there is every ground to presume that he is a national of a country of the Union, it shall be a matter for legislation in that country to designate the competent authority which shall represent the author and shall be entitled to protect and enforce his rights in the countries of the Union.

(b) Countries of the Union which make such designation under the terms of this provision shall notify the Director General by means of a written declaration giving full information concerning the authority thus designated. The Director General shall at once communicate this declaration to all other countries of the Union.

Article 16 Infringing Copies: 1. Seizure; 2. Seizure on importation; 3. Applicable law

(1) Infringing copies of a work shall be liable to seizure in any country of the Union where the work enjoys legal protection.

(2) The provisions of the preceding paragraph shall also apply to reproductions coming from a country where the work is not protected, or has ceased to be protected.

(3) The seizure shall take place in accordance with the legislation of each country.

Article 17 Possibility of Control of Circulation, Presentation and Exhibition of Works

The provisions of this Convention cannot in any way affect the right of the Government of each country of the Union to permit, to control, or to prohibit, by legislation or regulation, the circulation, presentation, or exhibition of any work or production in regard to which the competent authority may find it necessary to exercise that right.

Article 18   Works Existing on Convention's Entry Into Force: 1. Protectable where protection not yet expired in country of origin; 2. Non-protectable where protection already expired in country where it is claimed; 3. Application of these principles; 4. Special cases

(1)   This Convention shall apply to all works which, at the moment of its coming into force, have not yet fallen into the public domain in the country of origin through the expiry of the term of protection.

(2)   If, however, through the expiry of the term of protection which was previously granted, a work has fallen into the public domain of the country where protection is claimed, that work shall not be protected anew.

(3)   The application of this principle shall be subject to any provisions contained in special conventions to that effect existing or to be concluded between countries of the Union. In the absence of such provisions, the respective countries shall determine, each in so far as it is concerned, the conditions of application of this principle.

(4)   The preceding provisions shall also apply in the case of new accessions to the Union and to cases in which protection is extended by the application of Article 7 or by the abandonment of reservations.

Article 19   Protection Greater than Resulting from Convention
The provisions of this Convention shall not preclude the making of a claim to the benefit of any greater protection which may be granted by legislation in a country of the Union.

Article 20   Special Agreements Among Countries of the Union
The Governments of the countries of the Union reserve the right to enter into special agreements among themselves, in so far as such agreements grant to authors more extensive rights than those granted by the Convention, or contain other provisions not contrary to this Convention. The provisions of existing agreements which satisfy these conditions shall remain applicable.

Article 21   Special Provisions Regarding Developing Countries: 1. Reference to Appendix; 2. Appendix part of Act
(1)   Special provisions regarding developing countries are included in the Appendix.
. . .

MADRID AGREEMENT CONCERNING THE INTERNATIONAL REGISTRATION OF MARKS
of April 14, 1891, as revised at Brussels on December 14, 1900, at Washington on June 2, 1911, at The Hague on November 6, 1925, at London on June 2, 1934, at Nice on June 15, 1957, and at Stockholm on July 14, 1967, and as amended on September 28, 1979

Article 1   Establishment of a Special Union. Filing of Marks at International Bureau. Definition of Country of Origin
(1)   The countries to which this Agreement applies constitute a Special Union for the international registration of marks.

(2)   Nationals of any of the contracting countries may, in all the other countries party to this Agreement, secure protection for their marks applicable to goods or services, registered in the country of origin, by filing the said marks at the International Bureau of Intellectual Property (hereinafter designated as "the International Bureau") referred to in the Convention establishing the World Intellectual Property Organisation (hereinafter designated as "the Organisation"), through the intermediary of the Office of the said country of origin.

(3)   Shall be considered the country of origin the country of the Special Union where the applicant has a real and effective industrial or commercial establishment; if he has no such establishment in a country of the Special Union, the country of the Special Union where he has his domicile; if he has no domicile within the Special Union but is a national of a country of the Special Union, the country of which he is a national.

Article 2   Reference to Article 3 of Paris Convention (Same Treatment for Certain Categories of Persons as for Nationals of Countries of the Union)
Nationals of countries not having acceded to this Agreement who, within the territory of the Special Union constituted by the said Agreement, satisfy the conditions specified in Article 3 of the Paris Convention for the Protection of Industrial Property shall be treated in the same manner as nationals of the contracting countries.

Article 3   Contents of Application for International Registration
(1)   Every application for international registration must be presented on the form prescribed by the Regulations; the Office of the country of origin of the mark shall certify that the particulars appearing in such application correspond to the particulars in the national register, and shall mention the dates and numbers of the filing and registration of the mark in the country of origin and also the date of the application for international registration.

(2)   The applicant must indicate the goods or services in respect of which protection of the mark is claimed and also, if possible, the corresponding class or classes according to the classification established by the Nice Agreement concerning the International Classification of Goods and Services for the Purposes of the Registration of Marks. If the applicant does not give such indication, the International Bureau shall classify the goods or services in the appropriate classes of the said classification. The indication of classes given by the applicant shall be subject to control by the International Buearu, which shall exercise the said control in association with the national Office. In the event of disagreement between the national Office and the International Bureau, the opinion of the latter shall prevail.

(3)   If the applicant claims colour as a distinctive feature of his mark, he shall be required:
   1.   to state the fact, and to file with his application a notice specifying the colour or the combination of colours claimed;
   2.   to append to his application copies in colour of the said mark, which shall be attached to the notification given by the International Bureau. The number of such copies shall be fixed by the Regulations.

(4)   The International Bureau shall register immediately the marks filed in accordance with Article 1. The registration shall bear the date of the application for international registration in the country of origin, provided that the application has been received by the International Bureau within a period of two months from the date. If the application has not been received within that period, the International Bureau shall record it as at the date on which it received the said application. The International Bureau shall notify such registration without delay to the Offices concerned. Registered marks shall be published in a periodical journal issued by the International Bureau, on the basis of the particulars contained in the application for registration. In the case of marks comprising a figurative element or a special form of writing, the Regulations shall determine whether a printing block must be supplied by the applicant.

(5)   With a view to the publicity to be given in the contracting countries to registered marks, each Office shall receive from the International Bureau a number of copies of the said publication free of charge and a number of copies at a reduced price, in proportion to the number of units mentioned in Article 16(4)(a) of the Paris Convention for the Protection of Industrial Property, under the conditions fixed by the Regulations. Such publicity shall be deemed in all the contracting countries to be sufficient, and no other publicity may be required of the applicant.

Article 3bis   "Territorial Limitation"

(1)   Any contracting country may, at any time, notify the Director General of the Organisation (hereinafter designated as "the Director General") in writing that the protection resulting from the international registration shall extend to that country only at the express request of the proprietor of the mark.

(2)   Such notification shall not take effect until six months after the date of the communication thereof by the Director General to the other contracting countries.

Article 3ter   Request for "Territorial Extension"

(1)   Any request for extension of the protection resulting from the international registration to a country which has availed itself of the right provided for in Article 3bis must be specially mentioned in the application referred to in Article 3(1).

(2)   Any request for territorial extension made subsequently to the international registration must be presented through the intermediary of the Office of the country of origin on a form prescribed by the Regulations. It shall be immediately registered by the International Bureau, which shall notify it without delay to the Office or Offices concerned. It shall be published in the periodical journal issued by the International Bureau. Such territorial extension shall be effective from the date on which it has been recorded in the International Register; it shall cease to be valid on the expiration of the international registration of the mark to which it relates.

Article 4   Effects of International Registration

(1)   From the date of the registration so effected at the International Bureau in accordance with the provisions of Articles 3 and 3ter, the protection of the mark in each of the contracting countries concerned shall be the same as if the mark had been filed therein direct. The indication of classes of goods or services provided for in Article 3 shall not bind the contracting countries with regard to the determination of the scope of the protection of the mark.

(2)   Every mark which has been the subject of an international registration shall enjoy the right of priority provided for by Article 4 of the Paris Convention for the Protection of Industrial Property, without requiring compliance with the formalities prescribed in Section D of that Article.

Article 4bis   Substitution of International Registration for Earlier National Registrations

(1)   When a mark already filed in one or more of the contracting countries is later registered by the International Bureau in the name of the same proprietor or his successor in title, the international registration shall be deemed to have replaced the earlier national registrations, without prejudice to any rights acquired by reason of such earlier registrations.

(2)   The national Office shall, upon request, be required to take note in its registers of the international registration.

Article 5   Refusal by National Offices

(1)   In countries where the legislation so authorises, Offices notified by the International Bureau of the registration of a mark or of a request for extension of protection made in accordance with Article 3ter shall have the right to declare that protection cannot be granted to such mark in their territory. Any such refusal can be based only on the grounds which would apply, under the Paris Convention for the Protection of Industrial Property, in the case of a mark filed for national registration. However, protection may not be refused, even partially, by reason only that national legislation would not permit registration except in a limited number of classes or for a limited number of goods or services.

(2)   Offices wishing to exercise such right must give notice of their refusal to the International Bureau, together with a statement of all grounds, within the period

prescribed by their domestic law and, at the latest, before the expiration of one year from the date of the international registration of the mark or of the request for extension of protection made in accordance with Article 3ter.

(3) The International Bureau shall, without delay, transmit to the Office of the country of origin and to the proprietor of the mark, or to his agent if an agent has been mentioned to the Bureau by the said Office, one of the copies of the declaration of refusal so notified. The interested party shall have the same remedies as if the mark had been filed by him direct in the country where protection is refused.

(4) The grounds for refusing a mark shall be communicated by the International Bureau to any interested party who may so request.

(5) Offices which, within the aforesaid maximum period of one year, have not communicated to the International Bureau any provisional or final decision of refusal with regard to the registration of a mark or a request for extension of protection shall lose the benefit of the right provided for in paragraph (1) of this Article with respect to the mark in question.

(6) Invalidation of an international mark may not be pronounced by the competent authorities without the proprietor of the mark having, in good time, been afforded the opportunity of defending his rights. Invalidation shall be notified to the International Bureau.

Article 5bis Documentary Evidence of Legitimacy of Use of Certain Elements of Mark

Documentary evidence of the legitimacy of the use of certain elements incorporated in a mark, such as armorial bearings, escutcheons, portraits, honorary distinctions, titles, trade names, names of persons other than the name of the applicant, or other like inscriptions, which might be required by the Offices of the contracting countries shall be exempt from any legalisation or certification other than that of the Office of the country of origin.

Article 5ter Copies of Entries in International Register. Searches for Anticipation. Extracts from International Register

(1) The International Bureau shall issue to any person applying therefor, subject to a fee fixed by the Regulations, a copy of the entries in the Register relating to a specific mark.

(2) The International Bureau may also, upon payment, undertake searches for anticipation among international marks.

(3) Extracts from the International Register requested with a view to their production in one of the contracting countries shall be exempt from all legalisation.

Article 6 Period of Validity of International Registration. Independence of International Registration. Termination of Protection in Country of Origin

(1) Registration of a mark at the International Bureau is effected for twenty years, with the possibility of renewal under the conditions specified in Article 7.

(2) Upon expiration of a period of five year from the date of the international registration, such registration shall become independent of the national mark registered earlier in the country of origin, subject to the following provisions.

(3) The protection resulting from the international registration, whether or not it has been the subject of a transfer, may no longer be invoked, in whole or in part, if, within five years from the date of the international registration, the national mark, registered earlier in the country of origin in accordance with Article 1, no longer enjoys, in whole or in part, legal protection in that country. This provision shall also apply when legal protection has later ceased as the result of an action begun before the expiration of the period of five years.

(4) In the case of voluntary or ex officio cancellation, the Office of the country of origin shall request the cancellation of the mark at the International Bureau, and the

latter shall effect the cancellation. In the case of judicial action, the said Office shall send to the International Bureau, ex officio or at the request of the plaintiff, a copy of the complaint or any other documentary evidence that an action has begun, and also of the final decision of the court; the Bureau shall enter notice thereof in the International Register.

Article 7   Renewal of International Registration

(1)   Any registration may be renewed for a period of twenty years from the expiration of the preceding period, by payment only of the basic fee and, where necessary, of the supplementary and complementary fees provided for in Article 8(2).

(2)   Renewal may not include any change in relation to the previous registration in its latest form.

(3)   The first renewal effected under the provisions of the Nice Act of 15 June 1957, or of this Act, shall include an indication of the classes of the International Classification to which the registration relates.

(4)   Six months before the expiration of the term of protection, the International Buearu shall, by sending an unofficial notice, remind the proprietor of the mark and his agent of the exact date of expiration.

(5)   Subject to the payment of a surcharge fixed by the Regulations, a period of grace of six months shall be granted for renewal of the international registration.

Article 8   National Fee. International Fee. Division of Excess Receipts, Supplementary Fees, and Complementary Fees

(1)   The Office of the country of origin may fix, at its own discretion, and collect, for its own benefit, a national fee which it may require from the proprietor of the mark in respect of which international registration or renewal is applied for.

(2)   Registration of a mark at the International Bureau shall be subject to the advance payment of an international fee which shall include:

   (a)   a basic fee;

   (b)   a supplementary fee for each class of the International Classification, beyond three, into which the goods or services to which the mark is applied will fall;

   (c)   a complementary fee for any request for extension of protection under Article 3ter.

(3)   However, the supplementary fee specified in paragraph (2)(b) may, without prejudice to the date of registration, be paid within a period fixed by the Regulations if the number of classes of goods or services has been fixed or disputed by the International Bureau. If, upon expiration of the said period, the supplementary fee has not been paid or the list of goods or services has not been reduced to the required extent by the applicant, the application for international registration shall be deemed to have been abandoned.

(4)   The annual returns from the various receipts from international registration, with the exception of those provided for under (b) and (c) of paragraph (2), shall be divided equally among the countries party to this Act by the International Bureau, after deduction of the expenses and charges necessitated by the implementation of the said Act. If, at the time this Act enters into force, a country has not yet ratified or acceded to the said Act, it shall be entitled, until the date on which its ratification or accession becomes effective, to a share of the excess receipts calculated on the basis of that earlier Act which is applicable to it.

(5)   The amounts derived from the supplementary fees provided for in paragraph (2)(b) shall be divided at the expiration of each year among the countries party to this Act or to the Nice Act of 15 June 1957, in proportion to the number of marks for which protection has been applied for in each of them during that year, this number being multiplied, in the case of countries which make a preliminary examination, by a coefficient which shall be determined by the Regulations. If, at the time this Act enters

into force, a country has not yet ratified or acceded to the said Act, it shall be entitled, until the date on which its ratification or accession becomes effective, to a share of the amounts calculated on the basis of the Nice Act.

(6) The amounts derived from the complementary fees provided for in paragraph (2)(c) shall be divided according to the requirements of paragraph (5) among the countries availing themselves of the right provided for in Article 3bis. If, at the time this Act enters into force, a country has not yet ratified or acceded to the said Act, it shall be entitled, until the date on which its ratification or accession becomes effective, to a share of the amounts calculated on the basis of the Nice Act.

Article 8bis Renunciation in Respect of One or More Countries

The person in whose name the international registration stands may at any time renounce protection in one or more of the contracting countries by means of a declaration filed with the Office of his own country, for communication to the International Bureau, which shall notify accordingly the countries in respect of which renunciation has been made. Renunciation shall not be subject to any fee.

Article 9 Changes in National Registers also Affecting International Registration. Reduction of List of Goods and Services Mentioned in International Registration. Additions to the List. Substitutions in that List.

(1) The Office of the country of the person in whose name the international registration stands shall likewise notify the International Bureau of all annulments, cancellations, renunciations, transfers, and other changes made in the entry of the mark in the national register, if such changes also affect the international registration.

(2) The Bureau shall record those changes in the International Register, shall notify them in turn to the Offices of the contracting countries, and shall publish them in its journal.

(3) A similar procedure shall be followed when the person in whose name the international registration stands requests a reduction of the list of goods or services to which the registration applies.

(4) Such transactions may be subject to a fee, which shall be fixed by the Regulations.

(5) The subsequent addition of new goods or services to the said list can be obtained only by filing a new application as prescribed in Article 3.

(6) The substitution of one of the goods or services for another shall be treated as an addition.

Article 9bis Transfer of International Mark Entailing Change in Country of Proprietor

(1) When a mark registered in the International Register is transferred to a person established in a contracting country other than the country of the person in whose name the international registration stands, the transfer shall be notified to the International Bureau by the Office of the latter country. The International Bureau shall record the transfer, shall notify the other Offices thereof, and shall publish it in its journal. If the transfer has been effected before the expiration of a period of five years from the international registration, the International Bureau shall seek the consent of the Office of the country of the new proprietor, and shall publish, if possible, the date and registration number of the mark in the country of the new proprietor.

(2) No transfer of a mark registered in the International Register for the benefit of a person who is not entitled to file an international mark shall be recorded.

(3) When it has not been possible to record a transfer in the International Register, either because the country of the new proprietor has refused its consent or because the said transfer has been made for the benefit of a person who is not entitled to apply for international registration, the Office of the country of the former proprietor shall have the right to demand that the International Bureau cancel the mark in its Register.

Article 9ter   Assignment of International Mark for Part Only of Registered Goods or Services or for Certain Contracting Countries. Reference to Article 6quater of Paris Convention (Assignment of Mark)

(1)   If the assignment of an international mark for part only of the registered goods or services is notified to the International Bureau, the Bureau shall record it in its Register. Each of the contracting countries shall have the right to refuse to recognise the validity of such assignment if the goods or services included in the part so assigned are similar to those in respect of which the mark remains registered for the benefit of the assignor.

(2)   The International Bureau shall likewise record the assignment of an international mark in respect of one or several of the contracting countries only.

(3)   If, in the above cases, a change occurs in the country of the proprietor, the Office of the country to which the new proprietor belongs shall, if the international mark has been transferred before the expiration of a period of five years from the international registration, give its consent as required by Article 9bis.

(4)   The provisions of the foregoing paragraphs shall apply subject to Article 6quater of the Paris Convention for the Protection of Industrial Property.

Article 9quater   Common Office for Several Contracting Countries. Request by Several Contracting Countries to be Treated as a Single Country

(1)   If several countries of the Special Union agree to effect the unification of their domestic legislations on marks, they may notify the Director General:

(a)   that a common Office shall be substituted for the national Office of each of them, and

(b)   that the whole of their respective territories shall be deemed to be a single country for the purpose of the application of all or part of the provisions preceding this Article.

(2)   Such notification shall not take effect until six months after the date of the communication thereof by the Director General to the other contracting countries.

. . .

PROTOCOL RELATING TO THE MADRID AGREEMENT CONCERNING THE INTERNATIONAL REGISTRATION OF MARKS
adopted at Madrid on 27 June 1989

Article 1   Membership in the Madrid Union

The States party to this Protocol (hereinafter referred to as "the Contracting States"), even where they are not party to the Madrid Agreement Concerning the International Registration of Marks as revised at Stockholm in 1967 and as amended in 1979 (hereinafter referred to as "the Madrid (Stockholm) Agreement"), and the organisations referred to in Article 14(1)(b) which are party to this Protocol (hereinafter referred to as "the Contracting Organisations") shall be members of the same Union of which countries party to the Madrid (Stockholm) Agreement are members. Any reference in this Protocol to "Contracting Parties" shall be construed as a reference to both Contracting States and Contracting Organisations.

Article 2   Securing Protection through International Registration

(1)   Where an application for the registration of a mark has been filed with the Office of a Contracting Party, or where a mark has been registered in the register of the Office of a Contracting Party, the person in whose name that application (hereinafter referred to as "the basic application") or that registration (hereinafter referred to as "the basic registration") stands may, subject to the provisions of this Protocol, secure protection for his mark in the territory of the Contracting Parties, by obtaining the registration of that mark in the register of the International Bureau of the World Intellectual Property

Organisation (hereinafter referred to as "the international registration", "the International Register", "the International Bureau" and "the Organisation", respectively), provided that,

(i) where the basic application has been filed with the Office of a Contracting State or where the basic registration has been made by such an Office, the person in whose name that application or registration stands is a national of that Contracting State, or is domiciled, or has a real and effective industrial or commercial establishment, in the said Contracting State,

(ii) where the basic application has been filed with the Office of a Contracting Organisation or where the basic registration has been made by such an Office, the person in whose name that application or registration stands is a national or a State member of that Contracting Organisation, or is domiciled, or has a real and effective industrial or commercial establishment, in the territory of the said Contracting Organisation.

(2) The application for international registration (hereinafter referred to as "the international application") shall be filed with the International Bureau through the intermediary of the Office with which the basic application was filed or by which the basic registration was made (hereinafter referred to as "the Office of origin"), as the case may be.

(3) Any reference in this Protocol to an "Office" or an "Office of a Contracting Party" shall be construed as a reference to the office that is in charge, on behalf of a Contracting Party, of the registration of marks, and any reference in this Protocol to "marks" shall be construed as a reference to trademarks and service marks.

(4) For the purposes of this Protocol, "territory of a Contracting Party" means, where the Contracting Party is a State, the territory of that State and, where the Contracting Party is an intergovernmental organisation, the territory in which the constituting treaty of that intergovernmental organisation applies.

Article 3 International Application

(1) Every international application under this Protocol shall be presented on the form prescribed by the Regulations. The Office of origin shall certify that the particulars appearing in the international application correspond to the particulars appearing, at the times of the certification, in the basic application or basic registration, as the case may be. Furthermore, the said Office shall indicate,

(i) in the case of a basic application, the date and number of that application,

(ii) in the case of a basic registration, the date and number of that registration as well as the date and number of the application from which the basic registration resulted.

The Office of origin shall also indicate the date of the international application.

(2) The applicant must indicate the goods and services in respect of which protection of the mark is claimed and also, if possible, the corresponding class or classes according to the classification established by the Nice Agreement Concerning the International Classification of Goods and Services for the Purposes of the Registration of Marks. If the applicant does not give such indication, the International Bureau shall classify the goods and services in the appropriate classes of the said classification. The indication of classes given by the applicant shall be subject to control by the International Bureau, which shall exercise the said control in association with the Office of origin. In the event of disagreement between the said Office and the International Bureau, the opinion of the latter shall prevail.

(3) If the applicant claims colour as a distinctive feature of his mark, he shall be required

(i) to state the fact, and to file with his international application a notice specifying the colour or the combination of colours claimed;

(ii)   to append to his international application copies in colour of the said mark, which shall be attached to the notifications given by the International Bureau; the number of such copies shall be fixed by the Regulations.

(4)   The International Bureau shall register immediately the marks filed in accordance with Article 2. The international registration shall bear the date on which the international application was received in the Office of origin, provided that the international application has been received by the International Bureau within a period of two months from that date. If the international application has not been received within that period, the international registration shall bear the date on which the said international application was received by the International Bureau. The International Bureau shall notify the international registration without delay to the Offices concerned. Marks registered in the International Register shall be published in a periodical gazette issued by the International Bureau, on the basis of the particulars contained in the international application.

(5)   With a view to the publicity to be given to marks registered in the International Register, each Office shall receive from the International Bureau a number of copies of the said gazette free of charge and a number of copies at a reduced price, under the conditions fixed by the Assembly referred to in Article 10 (hereinafter referred to as "the Assembly"). Such publicity shall be deemed to be sufficient for the purposes of all the Contracting Parties, and no other publicity may be required of the holder of the international registration.

Article 3bis Territorial Effect

The protection resulting from the international registration shall extend to any Contracting Party only at the request of the person who files the international application or who is the holder of the international registration. However, no such request can be made with respect to the Contracting Party whose Office is the Office of origin.

Article 3ter Request for "Territorial Extension"

(1)   Any request for extension of the protection resulting from the international registration to any Contracting Party shall be specially mentioned in the international application.

(2)   A request for territorial extension may also be made subsequently to the international registration. Any such request shall be presented on the form prescribed by the Regulations. It shall be immediately recorded by the International Bureau, which shall notify such recordal without delay to the Office or Offices concerned. Such recordal shall be published in the periodical gazette of the International Bureau. Such territorial extension shall be effective from the date on which it has been recorded in the International Register; it shall cease to be valid on the expiry of the international registration to which it relates.

Article 4   Effects of International Registration

(1)(a)   From the date of the registration or recordal effected in accordance with the provisions of Articles 3 and 3ter, the protection of the mark in each of the Contracting Parties concerned shall be the same as if the mark had been deposited direct with the Office of that Contracting Party. If no refusal has been notified to the International Bureau in accordance with Article 5(1) and (2) or if a refusal notified in accordance with the said Article has been withdrawn subsequently, the protection of the mark in the Contracting Party concerned shall, as from the said date, be the same as if the mark had been registered by the Office of that Contracting Party.

(b)   The indication of classes of goods and services provided for in Article 3 shall not bind the Contracting Parties with regard to the determination of the scope of the protection of the mark.

(2)   Every international registration shall enjoy the right of priority provided for by Article 4 of the Paris Convention for the Protection of Industrial Property, without it being necessary to comply with the formalities prescribed in Section D of that Article.

Article 4bis Replacement of a National or Regional Registration by an International Registration

(1)   Where a mark that is the subject of a national or regional registration in the Office of a Contracting Party is also the subject of an international registration and both registrations stand in the name of the same person, the international registration is deemed to replace the national or regional registration, without prejudice to any rights acquired by virtue of the latter, provided that

(i)   the protection resulting from the international registration extends to the said Contracting Party under Article 3*ter*(1) or (2),

(ii)   all the goods and services listed in the national or regional registration are also listed in the international registration in respect of the said Contracting Party,

(iii)   such extension takes effect after the date of the national or regional registration.

(2)   The Office referred to in paragraph (1) shall, upon request, be required to take note in its register of the international registration.

Article 5   Refusal and Invalidation of Effects of International Registration in Respect of Certain Contracting Parties

(1)   Where the applicable legislation so authorises, any Office of a Contracting Party which has been notified by the International Bureau of an extension to the Contracting Party, under Article 3*ter*(1) or (2), of the protection resulting from the international registration shall have the right to declare in a notification of refusal that protection cannot be granted in the said Contracting Party to the mark which is the subject of such extension. Any such refusal can be based only on the grounds which would apply, under the Paris Convention for the Protection of Industrial Property, in the case of a mark deposited direct with the Office which notifies the refusal. However, protection may not be refused, even partially, by reason only that the applicable legislation would permit registration only in a limited number of classes or for a limited number of goods or services.

(2)(a)   Any Office wishing to exercise such right shall notify its refusal to the International Bureau, together with a statement of all grounds, within the period prescribed by the law applicable to that Office and at the latest, subject to subparagraphs (b) and (c), before the expiry of one year from the date on which the notification of the extension referred to in paragraph (1) has been sent to that Office by the International Bureau.

(b)   Notwithstanding subparagraph (a), any Contracting Party may declare that, for international restrictions made under this Protocol, the time limit of one year referred to in subparagraph (a) is replaced by 18 months.

(c)   Such declaration may also specify that, when a refusal of protection may result from an opposition to the granting of protection, such refusal may be notified by the Office of the said Contracting Party to the International Bureau after the expiry of the 18-month time limit. Such an Office may, with respect to any given international registration, notify a refusal of protection after the expiry of the 18-month time limit, but only if

(i)   it has, before the expiry of the 18-month time limit, informed the International Bureau of the possibility that oppositions may be filed after the expiry of the 18-month time limit, and

(ii)   the notification of the refusal based on an opposition is made within a time limit of not more than seven months from the date on which the opposition period begins; if the opposition period expires before this time limit of seven months, the notification must be made within a time limit of one month from the expiry of the opposition period.

(d)   Any declaration under subparagraphs (b) or (c) may be made in the instruments referred to in Article 14(2), and the effective date of the declaration shall be the same as the date of entry into force of this Protocol with respect to the State or intergovernmental organisation having made the declaration. Any such declaration may also be made later, in which case the declaration shall have effect three months after its receipt by the Director General of the Organisation (hereinafter referred to as "the Director General"), or at any later date indicated in the declaration, in respect of any international registration whose date is the same as or is later than the effective date of the declaration.

(e)   Upon the expiry of a period of ten years from the entry into force of this Protocol, the Assembly shall examine the operation of the system established by subparagraphs (a) to (d). Thereafter, the provisions of the said subparagraphs may be modified by a unanimous decision of the Assembly.

(3)   The International Bureau shall, without delay, transmit one of the copies of the notification of refusal to the holder of the international registration. The said holder shall have the same remedies as if the mark had been deposited by him direct with the Office which has notified its refusal. Where the International Bureau has received information under paragraph (2)(c)(i), it shall, without delay, transmit the said information to the holder of the international registration.

(4)   The grounds for refusing a mark shall be communicated by the International Bureau to any interested party who may so request.

(5)   Any Office which has not notified, with respect to a given international registration, any provisional or final refusal to the International Bureau in accordance with paragraphs (1) and (2) shall, with respect to that international registration, lose the benefit of the right provided for in paragraph (1).

(6)   Invalidation, by the competent authorities of a Contracting Party, of the effects, in the territory of that Contracting Party, of an international registration may not be pronounced without the holder of such international registration having, in good time, been afforded the opportunity of defending his rights. Invalidation shall be notified to the International Bureau.

Article 5bis Documentary Evidence of Legitimacy of Use of Certain Elements of the Mark

Documentary evidence of the legitimacy of the use of certain elements incorporated in a mark, such as armorial bearings, escutcheons, portraits, honorary distinctions, titles, trade names, names of persons other than the name of the applicant, or other like inscriptions, which might be required by the Offices of the Contracting Parties shall be exempt from any legislation as well as from any certification other than that of the Office of origin.

Article 5ter Copies of Entries in International Register; Searches for Anticipations; Extracts from International Register

(1)   The International Bureau shall issue to any person applying therefor, upon the payment of a fee fixed by the Regulations, a copy of the entries in the International Register concerning a specific mark.

(2)   The International Bureau may also, upon payment, undertake searches for anticipations among marks that are the subject of international registrations.

(3)   Extracts from the International Register requested with a view to their production in one of the Contracting Parties shall be exempt from any legislation.

Article 6   Period of Validity of International Registration; Dependence and Independence of International Registration

(1)   Registration of a mark at the International Bureau is effected for ten years, with the possibility of renewal under the conditions specified in Article 7.

(2)   Upon expiry of a period of five years from the date of the international registration, such registration shall become independent of the basic application or the registration resulting therefrom, or of the basic registration, as the case may be, subject to the following provisions.

(3)   The protection resulting from the international registration, whether or not it has been the subject of a transfer, may no longer be invoked if, before the expiry of five years from the date of the international registration, the basic application or the registration resulting therefrom, or the basic registration, as the case may be, has been withdrawn, has lapsed, has been renounced or has been the subject of a final decision of rejection, revocation, cancellation or invalidation, in respect of all or some of the goods and services listed in the international registration. The same applies if

(i)   an appeal against a decision refusing the effects of the basic application,

(ii)   an action requesting the withdrawal of the basic application or the revocation, cancellation or invalidation of the registration resulting from the basic application or of the basic registration, or

(iii)   an opposition to the basic application

results, after the expiry of the five-year period, in a final decision of rejection, revocation, cancellation or invalidation, or ordering the withdrawal, of the basic application, or the registration resulting therefrom, or the basic registration, as the case may be, provided that such appeal, action or opposition had begun before the expiry of the said period. The same also applies if the basic application is withdrawn, or the registration resulting from the basic application or the basic registration is renounced, after the expiry of the five-year period, provided that, at the time of the withdrawal or renunciation, the said application or registration was the subject of a proceeding referred to in item (i), (ii) or (iii) and that such proceeding had begun before the expiry of the said period.

(4)   The Office of origin shall, as prescribed in the Regulations, notify the International Bureau of the facts and decisions relevant under paragraph (3), and the International Bureau shall, as prescribed in the Regulations, notify the interested parties and effect any publication accordingly. The Office of origin shall, where applicable, request the International Bureau to cancel, to the extent applicable, the international registration, and the International Bureau shall proceed accordingly.

Article 7   Renewal of International Registration

(1)   Any international registration may be renewed for a period of ten years from the expiry of the preceding period, by the mere payment of the basic fee and, subject to Article 8(7), of the supplementary and complementary fees provided for in Article 8(2).

(2)   Renewal may not bring about any change in the international registration in its latest form.

(3)   Six months before the expiry of the term of protection, the International Bureau shall, by sending an unofficial notice, remind the holder of the international registration and his representative, if any, of the exact date of expiry.

(4)   Subject to the payment of a surcharge fixed by the Regulations, a period of grace of six months shall be allowed for renewal of the international registration.

Article 8   Fees for International Application and Registration

(1)   The Office of origin may fix, at its own discretion, and collect, for its own benefit, a fee which it may require from the applicant for international registration or

from the holder of the international registration in connection with the filing of the international application or the renewal of the international registration.

(2)   Registration of a mark at the international Bureau shall be subject to the advance payment of an international fee which shall, subject to the provisions of paragraph (7)(a), include

(i)   a basic fee;

(ii)   a supplementary fee for each class of the International Classification, beyond three, into which the goods or services to which the mark is applied will fall;

(iii)   a complementary fee for any request for extension of protection under Article 3*ter*.

(3)   However, the supplementary fee specified in paragraph (2)(ii) may, without prejudice to the date of the international registration, be paid within the period fixed by the Regulations if the number of classes of goods or services has been fixed or disputed by the International Bureau. If, upon expiry of the said period, the supplementary fee has not been paid or the list of goods or services has not been reduced to the required extent by the applicant, the international application shall be deemed to have been abandoned.

(4)   The annual product of the various receipts from international registration, with the exception of the receipts derived from the fees mentioned in paragraph (2)(ii) and (iii), shall be divided equally among the Contracting Parties by the International Bureau, after deduction of the expenses and charges necessitated by the implementation of this Protocol.

(5)   The amounts derived from the supplementary fees provided for in paragraph (2)(ii) shall be divided, at the expiry of each year, among the interested Contracting Parties in proportion to the number of marks for which protection has been applied for in each of them during that year, this number being multiplied, in the case of Contracting Parties which make an examination, by a coefficient which shall be determined by the Regulations.

(6)   The amounts derived from the complementary fees provided for in paragraph 2(iii) shall be divided according to the same rules as those provided for in paragraph (5).

(7)(a)   Any Contracting Party may declare that, in connection with each international registration in which it is mentioned under Article 3*ter*, and in connection with the renewal of any such international registration, it wants to receive, instead of a share in the revenue produced by the supplementary and complementary fees, a fee (hereinafter referred to as "the individual fee") whose amount shall be indicated in the declaration, and can be changed in further declarations, but may not be higher than the equivalent of the amount which the said Contracting Party's Office would be entitled to receive from an applicant for a ten-year renewal of that registration, of the mark in the register of the said Office, the said amount being diminished by the savings resulting from the international procedure. Where such an individual fee is payable,

(i)   no supplementary fees referred to in paragraph (2)(ii) shall be payable if only Contracting Parties which have made a declaration under this subparagraph are mentioned under Article 3*ter*, and

(ii)   no complementary fee referred to in paragraph (2)(iii) shall be payable in respect of any Contracting Party which has made a declaration under this subparagraph.

(b)   Any declaration under subparagraph (a) may be made in the instruments referred to in Article 14(2), and the effective date of the declaration shall be the same as the date of entry into force of this Protocol with respect to the State or intergovernmental organisation having made the declaration. Any such declaration may also be made later, in which case the declaration shall have effect three months after its receipt by the Director General, or at any later date indicated in the declaration, in respect of any international registration whose date is the same as or is later than the effective date of the declaration.

Article 9   Recordal of Change in the Ownership of an International Registration
At the request of the person in whose name the international registration stands, or at the request of an interested Office made *ex officio* or at the request of an interested person, the International Bureau shall record in the International Register any change in the ownership of that registration, in respect of all or some of the Contracting Parties in whose territories the said registration has effect and in respect of all or some of the goods and services listed in the registration, provided that the new holder is a person who, under Article 2(1), is entitled to file international applications.

Article 9bis   Recordal of Certain Matters concerning an International Registration
The International Bureau shall record in the International Register
    (i)   any change in the name or address of the holder of the international registration,
    (ii)   the appointment of a representative of the holder of the international registration and any other relevant fact concerning such representative,
    (iii)   any limitation, in respect of all or some of the Contracting Parties, of the goods and services listed in the international registration,
    (iv)   any renunciation, cancellation or invalidation of the international registration in respect of all or some of the Contracting Parties,
    (v)   any other relevant fact, identified in the Regulations, concerning the rights in a mark that is the subject of an international registration.

Article 9ter   Fees for Certain Recordals
Any recordal under Article 9 or under Article 9*bis* may be subject to the payment of a fee.

Article 9^{quater}   Common Office of Several Contracting States
(1)   If several Contracting States agree to effect the unification of their domestic legislations on marks, they may notify the Director General
    (i)   that a common Office shall be substituted for the national Office of each of them, and
    (ii)   that the whole of their respective territories shall be deemed to be a single State for the purposes of the application of all or part of the provisions preceding this Article as well as the provisions of Articles 9*quinquies* and 9*sexies*.
(2)   Such notification shall not take effect until three months after the date of the communication thereof by the Director General to the other Contracting Parties.

Article 9^{quinquies}   Transformation of an International Registration into National or Regional Applications
Where, in the event that the international registration is cancelled at the request of the Office of origin under Article 6(4), in respect of all or some of the goods and services listed in the said registration, the person who was the holder of the international registration files an application for the registration of the same mark with the Office of any of the Contracting Parties in the territory of which the international registration had effect, that application shall be treated as if it had been filed on the date of the international registration according to Article 3(4) or on the date of recordal of the territorial extension according to Article 3*ter*(2) and, if the international registration enjoyed priority, shall enjoy the same priority, provided that
    (i)   such application is filed within three months from the date on which the international registration was cancelled,
    (ii)   the goods and services listed in the application are in fact covered by the list of goods and services contained in the international registration in respect of the Contracting Party concerned, and
    (iii)   such application complies with all the requirements of the applicable law, including the requirements concerning fees.

Article 9^{sexies}   Safeguard of the Madrid (Stockholm) Agreement

(1)   Where, with regard to a given international application or a given international registration, the Office of origin is the Office of a State that is party to both this Protocol and the Madrid (Stockholm) Agreement, the provisions of this Protocol shall have no effect in the territory of any other State that is also party to both this Protocol and the Madrid (Stockholm) Agreement.

(2)   The Assembly may, by a three-fourths majority, repeal paragraph (1), or restrict the scope of paragraph (1), after the expiry of a period of ten years from the entry into force of this Protocol, but not before the expiry of a period of five years from the date on which the majority of the countries party to the Madrid (Stockholm) Agreement have become party to this Protocol. In the vote of the Assembly, only those States which are party to both the said Agreement and this Protocol shall have the right to participate.

. . .

UNIVERSAL COPYRIGHT CONVENTION
AS REVISED AT PARIS ON 24 JULY 1971

The Contracting States.

Moved by the desire to ensure in all countries copyright protection of literary, scientific and artistic works,

Convinced that a system of copyright protection appropriate to all nations of the world and expressed in a universal convention, additional to, and without impairing international systems already in force, will ensure respect for the rights of the individual and encourage the development of literature, the sciences and the arts,

Persuaded that such a universal copyright system will facilitate a wider dissemination of works of the human mind and increase international understanding,

Have resolved to revise the Universal Copyright Convention as signed at Geneva on 6 September 1952 (hereinafter called "the 1952 Convention"), and consequently,

Have agreed as follows:

Article I

Each Contracting State undertakes to provide for the adequate and effective protection of the rights of authors and other copyright proprietors in literary, scientific and artistic works, including writings, musical, dramatic and cinematographic works, and paintings, engravings and sculpture.

Article II

1.   Published works of nationals of any Contracting State and works first published in that State shall enjoy in each other Contracting State the same protection as that other State accords to works of its nationals first published in its own territory, as well as the protection specially granted by this Convention.

2.   Unpublished works of nationals of each Contracting State shall enjoy in each other Contracting State the same protection as that other State accords to unpublished works of its own nationals, as well as the protection specially granted by this Convention.

3.   For the purpose of this Convention any Contracting State may, by domestic legislation, assimilate to its own nationals any person domiciled in that State.

Article III

1.   Any Contracting State which, under its domestic law, requires as a condition of copyright, compliance with formalities such as deposit, registration, notice, notarial certificates, payment of fees or manufacture or publication in that Contracting State, shall regard these requirements as satisfied with respect to all works protected in accordance with this Convention and first published outside its territory and the author

of which is not one of its nationals, if from the time of the first publication all the copies of the work published with the authority of the author or other copyright proprietor bear the symbol © accompanied by the name of the copyright proprietor and the year of first publication placed in such manner and location as to give reasonable notice of claim of copyright.

2.   The provisions of paragraph 1 shall not preclude any Contracting State from requiring formalities or other conditions for the acquisition and enjoyment of copyright in respect of works first published in its territory or works of its nationals wherever published.

3.   The provisions of paragraph 1 shall not preclude any Contracting State from providing that a person seeking judicial relief must, in bringing the action, comply with procedural requirements, such as that the complainant must appear through domestic counsel or that the complainant must deposit with the court or an administrative office, or both, a copy of the work involved in the litigation; provided that failure to comply with such requirements shall not affect the validity of the copyright, nor shall any such requirement be imposed upon a national of another Contracting State if such requirement is not imposed on nationals of the State in which protection is claimed.

4.   In each Contracting State there shall be legal means of protecting without formalities the unpublished works of nationals of other Contracting States.

5.   If a Contracting State grants protection for more than one term of copyright and the first term is for a period longer than one of the minimum periods prescribed in Article IV, such State shall not be required to comply with the provisions of paragraph 1 of this Article in respect of the second or any subsequent term of copyright.

Article IV

1.   The duration of protection of a work shall be governed, in accordance with the provisions of Article II and this Article, by the law of the Contracting State in which protection is claimed.

2.(a)   The term of protection for works protected under this Convention shall not be less than the life of the author and twenty-five years after his death. However, any Contracting State which, on the effective date of this Convention in that State, has limited this term for certain classes of works to a period computed from the first publication of the work, shall be entitled to maintain these exceptions and to extend them to other classes of works. For all these classes the term of protection shall not be less than twenty-five years from the date of first publication.

(b)   Any Contracting State which, upon the effective date of this Convention in that State, does not compute the term of protection upon the basis of the life of the author, shall be entitled to compute the term of protection from the date of the first publication of the work or from its registration prior to publication, as the case may be, provided the term of protection shall not be less than twenty-five years from the date of first publication or from its registration prior to publication, as the case may be.

(c)   If the legislation of a Contracting State grants to or more successive terms of protection, the duration of the first term shall not be less than one of the minimum periods specified in sub-paragraphs (a) and (b).

3.   The provisions of paragraph 2 shall not apply to photographic works or to works of applied art; provided, however, that the term of protection in those Contracting States which protect photographic works, or works of applied art in so far as they are protected as artistic works, shall not be less than ten years for each of said classes of works.

4.(a)   No Contracting State shall be obliged to grant protection to a work for a period longer than that fixed for the class of works to which the work in question belongs, in the case of unpublished works by the law of the Contracting State of which the author is a national, and in the case of published works by the law of the Contracting State in which the work has been first published.

(b)   For the purposes of the application of sub-paragraph (a), if the law of any Contracting State grants two or more successive terms of protection, the period of protection of that State shall be considered to be the aggregate of those terms. However, if a specified work is not protected by such State during the second or any subsequent term for any reason, the other Contracting States shall not be obliged to protect it during the second or any subsequent term.

5.   For the purposes of the application of paragraph 4, the work of a national of a Contracting State, first published in a non-Contracting State, shall be treated as though first published in the Contracting State of which the author is a national.

6.   For the purpose of the application of paragraph 4, in case of simultaneous publication in two or more Contracting States, the work shall be treated as though first published in the State which affords the shortest term; any work published in two or more Contracting States within thirty days of its first publication shall be considered as having been published simultaneously in said Contracting States.

Article IVbis

1.   The rights referred to in Article I shall include the basic rights ensuring the author's economic interests, including the exclusive right to authorise reproduction by any means, public performance and broadcasting. The provisions of this Article shall extend to works protected under this Convention either in their original form or in any form recognisably derived from the original.

2.   However, any Contracting State may, by its domestic legislation, make exceptions that do not conflict with the spirit and provisions of this Convention, to the rights mentioned in paragraph 1 of this Article. Any State whose legislation so provides, shall nevertheless accord a reasonable degree of effective protection to each of the rights to which exception has been made.

Article V

1.   The rights referred to in Article I shall include the exclusive right of the author to make, publish and authorise the making and publication of translations of works protected under this Convention.

2.   However, any Contracting State may, by its domestic legislation, restrict the right of translation of writings, but only subject to the following provisions:

(a)   If, after the expiration of a period of seven years from the date of the first publication of a writing, a translation of such writing has not been published in a language in general use in the Contracting State, by the owner of the right of translation or with his authorisation, any national of such Contracting State may obtain a non-exclusive licence from the competent authority thereof to translate the work into that language and publish the work so translated.

(b)   Such national shall in accordance with the procedure of the State concerned, establish either that he has requested, and been denied, authorisation by the proprietor of the right to make and publish the translation, or that, after due diligence on his part, he was unable to find the owner of the right. A licence may also be granted on the same conditions if all previous editions of a translation in a language in general use in the Contracting State are out of print.

(c)   If the owner of the right of translation cannot be found, then the applicant for a licence shall send copies of his application to the publisher whose name appears on the work and, if the nationality of the owner of the right of translation is known, to the diplomatic or consular representative of the State of which such owner is a national, or to the organisation which may have been designated by the government of that State. The licence shall not be granted before the expiration of a period of two months from the date of the dispatch of the copies of the application.

(d)   Due provision shall be made by domestic legislation to ensure to the owner of the right of translation a compensation which is just and conforms to international standards, to ensure payment and transmittal of such compensation, and to ensure a correct translation of the work.

(e)   The original title and the name of the author of the work shall be printed on all copies of the published translation. The licence shall be valid only for publication of the translation in the territory of the Contracting State where it has been applied for. Copies so published may be imported and sold in another Contracting State if a language in general use in such other State is the same language as that into which the work has been so translated, and if the domestic law in such other State makes provision for such licences and does not prohibit such importation and sale. Where the foregoing conditions do not exist, the importation and sale of such copies in a Contracting State shall be governed by its domestic law and its agreements. The licence shall not be transferred by the licensee.

(f)   The licence shall not be granted when the author has withdrawn from circulation all copies of the work.

Article V^{bis}

1.   Any Contracting State regarded as a developing country in conformity with the established practice of the General Assembly of the United Nations may, by a notification deposited with the Director-General of the United Nations Educational, Scientific and Cultural Organisation (hereinafter called "the Director-General") at the time of its ratification, acceptance or accession or thereafter, avail itself of any or all of the exceptions provided for in Article Vter and V$quater$.

2.   Any such notification shall be effective for ten years from the date of coming into force of this Convention, or for such part of that ten-year period as remains at the date of deposit of the notification, and may be renewed in whole or in part for further periods of ten years each if, not more than fifteen or less than three months before the expiration of the relevant ten-year period, the Contracting State deposits a further notification with the Director-General. Initial notifications may also be made during these further periods of ten years in accordance with the provisions of this Article.

3.   Notwithstanding the provisions of paragraph 2, a Contracting State that has ceased to be regarded as a developing country as referred to in paragraph 1 shall no longer be entitled to renew its notification made under the provisions of paragraph 1 or 2, and whether or not it formally withdraws the notification such State shall be precluded from availing itself of the exceptions provided for in Articles Vter and V$quater$ at the end of the current ten-year period, or at the end of three years after it has ceased to be regarded as a developing country, whichever period expires later.

4.   Any copies of a work already made under the exceptions provided for in Articles Vter and V$quater$ may continue to be distributed after the expiration of the period for which notifications under this Article were effective until their stock is exhausted.

5.   Any Contracting State that has deposited a notification in accordance with Article XIII with respect to the application of this Convention to a particular country or territory, the situation of which can be regarded as analogous to that of the States referred to in paragraph 1 of this Article, may also deposit notifications and renew them in accordance with the provisions of this Article with respect to any such country or territory. During the effective period of such notifications, the provisions of Articles Vter and V$quater$ may be applied with respect to such country or territory. The sending of copies from the country or territory to the Contracting State shall be considered as export within the meaning of Articles Vter and V$quater$.

Article V^{ter}

1.(a)   Any Contracting State to which Article Vbis (1) applies may substitute for the period of seven years provided for in Article V(2) a period of three years or any longer period prescribed by its legislation. However, in the case of a translation into a language not in general use in one or more developed countries that are party to the Convention or only the 1952 Convention, the period shall be one year instead of three.

(b) A Contracting State to which Article Vbis(1) applies may, with the unanimous agreement of the developed countries party to this Convention or only the 1952 Convention and in which the same language is in general use, substitute, in the case of translation into that language, for the period of three years provided for in sub-paragraph (a) another period as determined by such agreement but not shorter than one year. However, this sub-paragraph shall not apply where the language in question is English, French or Spanish. Notification of any such agreement shall be made to the Director-General.

(c) The licence may only be granted if the applicant, in accordance with the procedure of the State concerned, establishes either that he has requested, and been denied, authorisation by the owner of the right of translation, or that, after the due diligence on his part, he was unable to find the owner of the right. At the same time as he makes his request he shall inform either the International Copyright Information Centre established by the United Nations Educational, Scientific and Cultural Organisation or any national or regional information centre which may have been designated in a notification to that effect deposited with the Director-General by the government of the State in which the publisher is believed to have his principal place of business.

(d) If the owner of the right of translation cannot be found, the applicant for a licence shall send, by registered airmail, copies of his application to the publisher whose name appears on the work and to any national or regional information centre as mentioned in sub-paragraph (c). If no such centre is notified he shall also send a copy to the International Copyright Information Centre established by the United Nations Educational, Scientific and Cultural Organisation.

2.(a) Licences obtainable after three years shall not be granted under this Article until a further period of six months has elapsed and licences obtainable after one year until a further period of nine months has elapsed. The further period shall begin either from the date of the request for permission to translate mentioned in paragraph 1(c) or, if the identity or address of the owner of the right of translation is not known, from the date of dispatch of the copies of the application for a licence mentioned in paragraph 1(d).

(b) Licences shall not be granted if a translation has been published by the owner of the right of translation or with his authorisation during the said period of six or nine months.

3. Any licence under this Article shall be granted only for the purpose of teaching, scholarship or research.

4.(a) Any licence granted under this Article shall not extend to the export of copies and shall be valid only for publication in the territory of the Contracting State where it has been applied for.

(b) Any copy published in accordance with a licence granted under this Article shall bear a notice in the appropriate language stating that the copy is available for distribution only in the Contracting State granting the licence. If the writing bears the notice specified in Article III(1) the copies shall bear the same notice.

(c) The prohibition of export provided for in sub-paragraph (a) shall not apply where a governmental or other public entity of a State which has granted a licence under this Article to translate a work into a language other than English, French or Spanish sends copies of a translation prepared under such licence to another country if:

(i)   the recipients are individuals who are nationals of the Contracting State granting the licence, or organisations grouping such individuals;

(ii) the copies are to be used only for the purpose of teaching, scholarship or research;

(iii)   the sending of the copies and their subsequent distribution to recipients is without the object of commercial purpose; and

(iv)   the country to which the copies have been sent has agreed with the Contracting State to allow the receipt, distribution or both and the Director-General has been notified of such agreement by any one of the governments which have concluded it.

5.   Due provision shall be made at the national level to ensure:

(a)   that the licence provides for just compensation that is consistent with standards of royalties normally operating in the case of licences freely negotiated between persons in the two countries concerned; and

(b)   payment and transmittal of the compensation; however, should national currency regulations intervene, the competent authority shall make all efforts, by the use of international machinery, to ensure transmittal in internationally convertible currency or its equivalent.

6.   Any licence granted by a Contracting State under this Article shall terminate if a translation of the work in the same language with substantially the same content as the edition in respect of which the licence was granted is published in the said State by the owner of the right of translation or with his authorisation, at a price reasonably related to that normally charged in the same State for comparable works. Any copies already made before the licence is terminated may continue to be distributed until their stock is exhausted.

7.   For works which are composed mainly of illustrations a licence to translate the text and to reproduce the illustrations may be granted only if the conditions of Article V*quater* are also fulfilled.

8.(a)   A licence to translate a work protected under this Convention, published in printed or analogous forms of reproduction, may also be granted to a broadcasting organisation having its headquarters in a Contracting State to which Article V*bis*(1) applies, upon an application made in that State by the said organisation under the following conditions:

(i)   the translation is made from a copy made and acquired in accordance with the laws of the Contracting State;

(ii)   the translation is for use only in broadcasts intended exclusively for teaching or for the dissemination of the results of specialised technical or scientific research to experts in a particular profession;

(iii)   the translation is used exclusively for the purposes set out in condition (ii), through broadcasts lawfully made which are intended for recipients on the territory of the Contracting State, including broadcasts made through the medium of sound or visual recordings lawfully and exclusively made for the purpose of such broadcasts;

(iv)   sound or visual recordings of the translation may be exchanged only between broadcasting organisations having their headquarters in the Contracting State granting the licence; and

(v)   all uses made of the translation are without any commercial purpose.

(b)   Provided all of the criteria and conditions set out in sub-paragraph (a) are met, a licence may also be granted to a broadcasting organisation to translate any text incorporated in an audio-visual fixation which was itself prepared and published for the sole purpose of being used in connection with systematic instructional activities.

(c)   Subject to sub-paragraphs (a) and (b), the other provisions of this Article shall apply to the grant and exercise of the licence.

9.   Subject to the provisions of this Article, any licence granted under this Article shall be governed by the provisions of Article V, and shall continue to be governed by the provisions of Article V and of this Article, even after the seven-year period provided for in Article V(2) has expired. However, after the said period has expired, the licensee shall

be free to request that the said licence be replaced by a new licence governed exclusively by the provisions of Article V.

Article V^quater

1. Any Contracting State to which Article V*bis*(1) applies may adopt the following provisions:

(a)   If, after the expiration of (i) the relevant period specified in sub-paragraph (c) commencing from the date of first publication of a particular edition of a literary, scientific or artistic work referred to in paragraph 3, or (ii) any longer period determined by national legislation of the State, copies of such edition have not been distributed in that State to the general public or in connection with systematic instructional activities at a price reasonably related to that normally charged in the State for comparable works, by the owner of the right of reproduction or with his authorisation, any national of such State may obtain a non-exclusive licence from the competent authority to publish such edition at that or a lower price for use in connection with systematic instructional activities. The licence may only be granted if such national, in accordance with the procedure of the State concerned, establishes either that he has requested, and been denied, authorisation by the proprietor of the right to publish such work, or that, after due diligence on his part, he was unable to find the owner of the right. At the same time as he makes his request he shall inform either the International Copyright Information Centre established by the United Nations Educational, Scientific and Cultural Organisation or any national or regional information centre referred to in sub-paragraph (d).

(b)   A licence may also be granted on the same conditions if, for a period of six months, no authorised copies of the edition in question have been on sale in the State concerned to the general public or in connection with systematic instructional activities at a price reasonably related to that normally charged in the State for comparable works.

(c)   The period referred to in subparagraph (a) shall be five years except that:

(i)   for works of the natural and physical sciences, including mathematics, and of technology, the period shall be three years;

(ii)   for works of fiction, poetry, drama and music, and for art books, the period shall be seven years.

(d)   If the owner of the right of reproduction cannot be found, the applicant for a licence shall send, by registered air mail, copies of his application to the publisher whose name appears on the work and to any national or regional information centre identified as such in a notification deposited with the Director-General by the State in which the publisher is believed to have his principal place of business. In the absence of any such notification, he shall also send a copy to the International Copyright Information Centre established by the United Nations Educational, Scientific and Cultural Organisation. The licence shall not be granted before the expiration of a period of three months from the date of dispatch of the copies of the application.

(e)   Licences obtainable after three years shall not be granted under this Article:

(i)   until a period of six months has elapsed from the date of the request for permission referred to in sub-paragraph (a) or, if the identity or address of the owner of the right of reproduction is unknown, from the date of the dispatch of the copies of the application for a licence referred to in sub-paragraph (d);

(ii)   if any such distribution of copies of the edition as is mentioned in sub-paragraph (a) has taken place during that period.

(f)   The name of the author and the title of the particular edition of the work shall be printed on all copies of the published reproduction. The licence shall not extend to the export of copies and shall be valid only for publication in the territory of the Contracting State where it has been applied for. The licence shall not be transferable by the licensee.

(g)   Due provision shall be made by domestic legislation to ensure an accurate reproduction of the particular edition in question.

(h)   A licence to reproduce and publish a translation of a work shall not be granted under this Article in the following cases:

(i)   where the translation was not published by the owner of the right of translation or with his authorisation;

(ii)   where the translation is not in a language in general use in the State with power to grant the licence.

2.   The exceptions provided for in paragraph 1 are subject to the following additional provisions:

(a)   Any copy published in accordance with a licence granted under this Article shall bear a notice in the appropriate language stating that the copy is available for distribution only in the Contracting State to which the said licence applies. If the edition bears the notice specified in Article III(1), the copies shall bear the same notice.

(b)   Due provision shall be made at the national level to ensure:

(i)   that the licence provides for just compensation that is consistent with standards of royalties normally operating in the case of licences freely negotiated between persons in the two countries concerned; and

(ii)   payment and transmittal of the compensation; however, should national currency regulations intervene, the competent authority shall make all efforts, by the use of international machinery, to ensure transmittal in internationally convertible currency or its equivalent.

(c)   Whenever copies of an edition of a work are distributed in the Contracting State to the general public or in connection with systematic instructional activities, by the owner of the right of reproduction or with his authorisation, at a price reasonably related to that normally charged in the State for comparable works, any licence granted under this Article shall terminate if such edition is in the same language and is substantially the same in content as the edition published under the licence. Any copies already made before the licence is terminated may continue to be distributed until their stock is exhausted.

(d)   No licence shall be granted when the author has withdrawn from circulation all copies of the edition in question.

3.(a)   Subject to sub-paragraph (b), the literary, scientific or artistic works to which this Article applies shall be limited to works published in printed or analogous forms of reproduction.

(b)   The provisions of this Article shall also apply to reproduction in audio-visual form of lawfully made audio-visual fixations including any protected works incorporated therein and to the translation of any incorporated text into a language in general use in the State with power to grant the licence; always provided that the audio-visual fixations in question were prepared and published for the sole purpose of being used in connection with systematic instructional activities.

Article VI

"Publication", as used in this Convention, means the reproduction in tangible form and the general distribution to the public of copies of a work from which it can be read or otherwise visually perceived.

Article VII

This Convention shall not apply to works or rights in works which, at the effective date of this Convention in a Contracting State where protection is claimed, are permanently in the public domain in the said Contracting State.

...

LISBON AGREEMENT FOR THE PROTECTION OF APPELLATIONS OF ORIGIN AND THEIR INTERNATIONAL REGISTRATION
of 31 October 1958, as revised at Stockholm on 14 July 1967, and as amended on 28 September 1979

Article 1 Establishment of a Special Union; Protection of Appellations of Origin Registered at the International Bureau

(1) The countries to which this Agreement applies constitute a Special Union within the framework of the Union for the Protection of Industrial Property.

(2) They undertake to protect on their territories, in accordance with the terms of this Agreement, the appellations of origin of products of the other countries of the Special Union, recognised and protected as such in the country of origin and registered at the International Bureau of Intellectual Property (hereinafter designated as "the International Bureau" or "the Bureau") referred to in the Convention establishing the World Intellectual Property Organisation (hereinafter designated as "the Organisation").

Article 2 Definition of Notions of Appellation of Origin and Country of Origin

(1) In this Agreement, "appellation of origin" means the geographical name of a country, region, or locality, which serves to designate a product originating therein, the quality and characteristics of which are due exclusively or essentially to the geographical environment, including natural and human factors.

(2) The country of origin is the country whose name, or the country in which is situated the region or locality whose name, constitutes the appellation of origin which has given the product its reputation.

Article 3 Content of Protection

Protection shall be ensured against any usurpation or imitation, even if the true origin of the product is indicated or if the appellation is used in translated form or accompanied by terms such as "kind", "type", "make", "imitation", or the like.

Article 4 Protection by virtue of Other Texts

The provisions of this Agreement shall in no way exclude the protection already granted to appellations of origin in each of the countries of the Special Union by virtue of other international instruments, such as the Paris Convention of 20 March 1883, for the Protection of Industrial Property and its subsequent revisions, and the Madrid Agreement of 14 April 1891, for the Repression of False or Deceptive Indications of Source on Goods and its subsequent revisions, or by virtue of national legislation or court decisions.

Article 5 International Registration; Refusal and Opposition to Refusal; Notifications; Use Tolerated for a Fixed Period

(1) The registration of appellations of origin shall be effected at the International Bureau, at the request of the Offices of the countries of the Special Union, in the name of any natural persons or legal entities, public or private, having, according to their national legislation, a right to use such appellations.

(2) The International Bureau shall, without delay, notify the Offices of the various countries of the Special Union of such registrations, and shall publish them in a periodical.

(3) The Office of any country may declare that it cannot ensure the protection of an appellation of origin whose registration has been notified to it, but only in so far as its declaration is notified to the International Bureau, together with an indication of the grounds therefor, within a period of one year from the receipt of the notification of registration, and provided that such declaration is not detrimental, in the country

concerned, to the other forms of protection of the appellation which the owner thereof may be entitled to claim under Article 4, above.

(4)   Such declaration may not be opposed by the Offices of the countries of the Union after the expiration of the period of one year provided for in the foregoing paragraph.

(5)   The International Bureau shall, as soon as possible, notify the Office of the country of origin of any declaration made under the terms of paragraph (3) by the Office of another country. The interested party, when informed by his national Office of the declaration made by another country, may resort, in that other country, to all the judicial and administrative remedies open to the nationals of that country.

(6)   If an appellation which has been granted protection in a given country pursuant to notification of its international registration has already been used by third parties in that country from a date prior to such notification, the competent Office of the said country shall have the right to grant to such third parties a period not exceeding two years to terminate such use, on condition that it advise the International Bureau accordingly during the three months following the expiration of the period of one year provided for in paragraph (3), above.

Article 6   Generic Appellations
An appellation which has been granted protection in one of the countries of the Special Union pursuant to the procedure under Article 5 cannot, in that country, be deemed to have become generic, as long as it is protected as an appellation of origin in the country of origin.

Article 7   Period of Validity of Registration; Fee
(1)   Registration effected at the International Bureau in conformity with Article 5 shall ensure, without renewal, protection for the whole of the period referred to in the foregoing Article.

(2)   A single fee shall be paid for the registration of each appellation of origin.

Article 8   Legal Proceedings
Legal action required for ensuring the protection of appellations of origin may be taken in each of the countries of the Special Union under the provisions of the national legislation:
   1.   at the instance of the competent Office or at the request of the public prosecutor;
   2.   by any interested party, whether a natural person or a legal entity, whether public or private.
...

Article 16   Application of the Original Act of 1958
(1)(a)   This Act shall, as regards the relations between the countries of the Special Union by which it has been ratified or acceded to, replace the original Act of 31 October 1958.

(b)   However, any country of the Special Union which has ratified or acceded to this Act shall be bound by the original Act of 31 October 1958, as regards its relations with countries of the Special Union which have not ratified or acceded to this Act.

(2)   Countries outside the Special Union which become party to this Act shall apply it to international registrations of appellations of origin effected at the International Bureau at the request of the Office of any country of the Special Union not party to this Act, provided that such registrations satisfy, with respect to the said countries, the requirements of this Act. With regard to international registrations effected at the International Bureau at the request of the Offices of the said countries outside the Special Union which become party to this Act, such countries recognise that the aforesaid country of the Special Union may demand compliance with the requirements of the original Act of 31 October 1958.
...

INTERNATIONAL CONVENTION FOR THE PROTECTION OF PERFORMERS, PRODUCERS OF PHONOGRAMS AND BROADCASTING ORGANISATIONS (ROME CONVENTION)
Done at Rome, on 26 October 1961

The Contracting States, moved by the desire to protect the rights of performers, producers of phonograms, and broadcasting organisations,
    Have agreed as follows:

Article 1
Protection granted under this Convention shall leave intact and shall in no way affect the protection of copyright in literary and artistic works. Consequently, no provision of this Convention may be interpreted as prejudicing such protection.

Article 2
    1.   For the purposes of this Convention, national treatment shall mean the treatment accorded by the domestic law of the Contracting State in which protection is claimed:
        (a)   to performers who are its nationals, as regards performances taking place, broadcast, or first fixed, on its territory;
        (b)   to producers of phonograms who are its nationals, as regards phonograms first fixed or first published on its territory;
        (c)   to broadcasting organisations which have their headquarters on its territory, as regards broadcasts transmitted from transmitters situated on its territory.
    2.   National treatment shall be subject to the protection specifically guaranteed, and the limitations specifically provided for, in this Convention.

Article 3
For the purposes of this Convention:
        (a)   "performers" means actors, singers, musicians, dancers, and other persons who act, sing, deliver, declaim, play in, or otherwise perform literary or artistic works;
        (b)   "phonogram" means any exclusively aural fixation of sounds of a performance or of other sounds;
        (c)   "producer of phonograms" means the person who, or the legal entity which, first fixes the sounds of a performance or other sounds;
        (d)   "publication" means the offering of copies of a phonogram to the public in reasonable quantity;
        (e)   "reproduction" means the making of a copy or copies of a fixation;
        (f)   "broadcasting" means the transmission by wireless means for public reception of sounds or of images and sounds;
        (g)   "rebroadcasting" means the simultaneous broadcasting by one broadcasting organisation of the broadcast of another broadcasting organisation.

Article 4
Each Contracting State shall grant national treatment to performers if any of the following conditions is met:
        (a)   the performance takes place in another Contracting State;
        (b)   the performance is incorporated in a phonogram which is protected under Article 5 of the Convention;
        (c)   the performance, not being fixed on a phonogram, is carried by a broadcast which is protected by Article 6 of this Convention.

Article 5
    1.   Each Contracting State shall grant national treatment to producers of phonograms if any of the following conditions is met:

(a)   the producer of the phonogram is a national of another Contracting State (criterion of nationality);

(b)   the first fixation of the sound was made in another Contracting State (criterion of fixation);

(c)   the phonogram was first published in another Contracting State (criterion of publication).

2.   If a phonogram was first published in a non-contracting State but if it was also published, within thirty days of its first publication, in a Contracting State (simultaneous publication), it shall be considered as first published in the Contracting State.

3.   By means of a notification deposited with the Secretary-General of the United Nations, any Contracting State may declare that it will not apply the criterion of publication or, alternatively, the criterion of fixation. Such notification may be deposited at the time of ratification, acceptance or accession, or at any time thereafter; in the last case, it shall become effective six months after it has been deposited.

Article 6

1.   Each Contracting State shall grant national treatment to broadcasting organisations if either of the following conditions is met:

(a)   the headquarters of the broadcasting organisation is situated in another Contracting State;

(b)   the broadcast was transmitted from a transmitter situated in another Contracting State.

2.   By means of a notification deposited with the Secretary-General of the United Nations, any Contracting State may declare that it will protect broadcasts only if the headquarters of the broadcasting organisation is situated in another Contracting State and the broadcast was transmitted from a transmitter situated in the same Contracting State. Such notification may be deposited at the time of ratification, acceptance or accession, or at any time thereafter; in the last case, it shall become effective six months after it has been deposited.

Article 7

1.   The protection provided for performers by this Convention shall include the possibility of preventing:

(a)   the broadcasting and the communication to the public, without their consent, of their performance, except where the performance used in the broadcasting or the public communication is itself already a broadcast performance or is made from a fixation;

(b)   the fixation, without their consent, of their unfixed performance;

(c)   the reproduction, without their consent, of a fixation of their performance:

(i)   if the original fixation itself was made without their consent;

(ii)   if the reproduction is made for purposes different from those for which the performers gave their consent;

(iii) if the original fixation was made in accordance with the provisions of Article 15, and the reproduction is made for purposes different from those referred to in those provisions.

2.(1) If broadcasting was consented to by the performers, it shall be a matter for the domestic law of the Contracting State where protection is claimed to regulate the protection against rebroadcasting, fixation for broadcasting purposes, and the reproduction of such fixation for broadcasting purposes.

(2)   The terms and conditions governing the use by broadcasting organisations of fixations made for broadcasting purposes shall be determined in accordance with the domestic law of the Contracting State where protection is claimed.

(3)   However, the domestic law referred to in sub-paragraphs (1) and (2) of this paragraph shall not operate to deprive performers of the ability to control, by contract, their relations with broadcasting organisations.

Article 8
Any Contracting State may, by its domestic laws and regulations, specify the manner in which performers will be represented in connexion with the exercise of their rights if several of them participate in the same performance.

Article 9
Any Contracting State may, by its domestic laws and regulations, extend the protection provided for in this Convention to artists who do not perform literary or artistic works.

Article 10
Producers of phonograms shall enjoy the right to authorise or prohibit the direct or indirect reproduction of their phonograms.

Article 11
If, as a condition of protecting the rights of producers of phonograms, or of performers, or both, in relation to phonograms, a Contracting State, under its domestic law, requires compliance with formalities, these shall be considered as fulfilled if all the copies in commerce of the published phonogram or their containers bear a notice consisting of the symbol Ⓟ, accompanied by the year date of the first publication, placed in such a manner as to give reasonable notice of claim of protection; and if the copies or their containers do not identify the producer or the licensee of the producer (by carrying his name, trade mark or other appropriate designation), the notice shall also include the name of the owner of the rights of the producer; and, furthermore, if the copies or their containers do not identify the principal performers, the notice shall also include the name of the person who, in the country in which the fixation was effected, owns the rights of such performers.

Article 12
If a phonogram published for commercial purposes, or a reproduction of such phonogram, is used directly for broadcasting or for any communication to the public, a single equitable remuneration shall be paid by the user to the performers, or to the producers of the phonograms, or to both. Domestic law may, in the absence of agreement between these parties, lay down the conditions as to the sharing of this remuneration.

Article 13
Broadcasting organisations shall enjoy the right to authorise or prohibit:
    (a)   the rebroadcasting of their broadcasts;
    (b)   the fixation of their broadcasts;
    (c)   the reproduction:
        (i)   of fixations, made without their consent, of their broadcasts;
        (ii)   of fixations, made in accordance with the provisions of Article 15, of their broadcasts, if the reproduction is made for purposes different from those referred to in those provisions;
    (d)   the communication to the public of their television broadcasts if such communication is made in places accessible to the public against payment of an entrance fee; it shall be a matter for the domestic law of the State where protection of this right is claimed to determine the conditions under which it may be exercised.

Article 14
The term of protection to be granted under this Convention shall last at least until the end of a period of twenty years computed from the end of the year in which:
    (a)   the fixation was made — for phonograms and for performances incorporated therein;

(b)   the performance took place — for performances not incorporated in phonograms;

(c)   the broadcast took place — for broadcasts.

Article 15

1.   Any Contracting State may, in its domestic laws and regulations, provide for exceptions to the protection guaranteed by this Convention as regards:

(a)   private use;

(b)   use of short excerpts in connexion with the reporting of current events;

(c)   ephemeral fixation by a broadcasting organisation by means of its own facilities and for its own broadcasts;

(d)   use solely for the purposes of teaching or scientific research.

2.   Irrespective of paragraph 1 of this Article, any Contracting State may, in its domestic laws and regulations, provide for the same kinds of limitations with regard to the protection of performers, producers of phonograms and broadcasting organisations, as it provides for, in its domestic laws and regulations, in connexion with the protection of copyright in literary and artistic works. However, compulsory licences may be provided for only to the extent to which they are compatible with this Convention.

Article 16

1.   Any State, upon becoming party to this Convention, shall be bound by all the obligations and shall enjoy all the benefits thereof. However, a State may at any time, in a notification deposited with the Secretary-General of the United Nations, declare that:

(a)   as regards Article 12:

(i)   it will not apply the provisions of that Article;

(ii)   it will not apply the provisions of that Article in respect of certain uses;

(iii)   as regard phonograms the producer of which is not a national of another Contracting State, it will not apply that Article;

(iv)   as regards phonograms the producer of which is a national of another Contracting State, it will limit the protection provided for by that Article to the extent to which, and to the term for which, the latter State grants protection to phonograms first fixed by a national of the State making the declaration; however, the fact that the Contracting State of which the producer is a national does not grant the protection to the same beneficiary or beneficiaries as the State making the declaration shall not be considered as a difference in the extent of the protection;

(b)   as regards Article 13, it will not apply item (d) of that Article; if a Contracting State makes such a declaration, the other Contracting States shall not be obliged to grant the right referred to in Article 13, item (d), to broadcasting organisations whose headquarters are in that State.

2.   If the notification referred to in paragraph 1 of this Article is made after the date of the deposit of the instrument of ratification, acceptance or accession, the declaration will become effective six months after it has been deposited.

Article 17

Any State which, on October 26, 1961, grants protection to producers of phonograms solely on the basis of the criterion of fixation may, by a notification deposited with the Secretary-General of the United Nations at the time of ratification, acceptance or accession, declare that it will apply, for the purposes of Article 5, the criterion of fixation alone and, for the purposes of paragraph 1 (a)(iii) and (iv) of Article 16, the criterion of fixation instead of the criterion of nationality.

Article 18

Any State which has deposited a notification under paragraph 3 of Article 5, paragraph 2 of Article 6, paragraph 1 of Article 16 or Article 17, may, by a further notification deposited with the Secretary-General of the United Nations, reduce its scope or withdraw it.

Article 19
Notwithstanding anything in this Convention, once a performer has consented to the incorporation of his performance in a visual or audio-visual fixation, Article 7 shall have no further application.

Article 20
   1.   This Convention shall not prejudice rights acquired in any Contracting State before the date of coming into force of this Convention for that State.
   2.   No Contracting State shall be bound to apply the provisions of this Convention to performances or broadcasts which took place, or to phonograms which were fixed, before the date of coming into force of this Convention for that State.

Article 21
The protection provided for in this Convention shall not prejudice any protection otherwise secured to performers, producers of phonograms and broadcasting organisations.

Article 22
Contracting States reserve the right to enter into special agreements among themselves in so far as such agreements grant to performers, producers of phonograms or broadcasting organisations more extensive rights than those granted by this Convention or contain other provisions not contrary to this Convention.
. . .

Article 31
Without prejudice to the provisions of paragraph 3 of Article 5, paragraph 2 of Article 6, paragraph 1 of Article 16 and Article 17, no reservation may be made to this Convention.
. . .

INTERNATIONAL CONVENTION FOR THE PROTECTION OF NEW VARIETIES OF PLANTS (UPOV CONVENTION)
on 2 December 1961,
as revised at Geneva on 10 November 1972, on 23 October 1978, and on 19 March 1991

CHAPTER I   DEFINITIONS

Article 1   Definitions
For the purpose of this Act:
   (i)   "this Convention" means the present (1991) Act of the International Covention for the Protection of New Varieties of Plants;
   (ii)   "Act of 1961/1972" means the International Convention for the Protection of New Varieties of Plants of 2 December 1961, as amended by the Additional Act of 10 November 1972;
   (iii)   "Act of 1978" means the Act of 23 October 1978, of the International Convention for the Protection of New Varieties of Plants;
   (iv)   "breeder" means
— the person who bred, or discovered and developed, a variety,
— the person who is the complo|er of the aforementioned person or who has commissioned the latter's work, where the laws of the relevant Contracting Party so provide, or
— the successor in title of the first or second aforementioned person, as the case may be;
   (v)   "breeder's right" means the right of the breeder provided for in this Convention;

(vi)   "variety" means a plant grouping within a single botanical taxon of the lowest known rank, which grouping, irrespective of whether the conditions for the grant of a breeder's right are fully met, can be
— defined by the expression of the characteristics resulting from a given genotype or combination of genotypes,
— distinguished from any other plant grouping by the expression of at least one of the said characteristics and
— considered as a unit with regard to its suitability for being propagated unchanged;

(vii)   "Contracting Party" means a State or an intergovernmental organisation party to this Convention;

(viii)   "territory," in relation to a Contracting Party, means, where the Contracting Party is a State, the territory of that State and, where the Contracting Party is an intergovernmental organisation, the territory in which the constituting treaty of that intergovernmental organisation applies;

(ix)   "authority" means the authority referred to in Article 30(1)(ii);

(x)   "Union" means the Union for the Protection of New Varieties of Plants founded by the Act of 1961 and further mentioned in the Act of 1972, the Act of 1978 and in this Convention;

(xi)   "member of the Union" means a State party to the Act of 1961/1972 or the Act of 1978, or a Contracting Party.

CHAPTER II   GENERAL OBLIGATIONS OF THE CONTRACTING PARTIES

Article 2   Basic Obligation of the Contracting Parties
Each Contracting Party shall grant and protect breeders' rights.

Article 3   Genera and Species to be Protected
(1)   [*States already members of the Union*] Each Contracting Party which is bound by the Act of 1961/1972 or the Act of 1978 shall apply the provisions of this Convention,

(i)   at the date on which it becomes bound by this Convention, to all plant genera and species to which it applies, on the said date, the provisions of the Act of 1961/1972 or the Act of 1978 and,

(ii)   at the latest by the expiration of a period of five years after the said date, to all plant genera and species.

(2)   [*New members of the Union*] Each Contracting Party which is not bound by the Act of 1961/1972 or the Act of 1978 shall apply the provisions of this Convention,

(i)   at the date on which it becomes bound by the Convention, to at least 15 plant genera or species and,

(ii)   at the latest by the expiration of a period of 10 years from the said date, to all plant genera and species.

Article 4   National Treatment
(1)   [*Treatment*] Without prejudice to the rights specified in this Convention, nationals of a Contracting Party as well as natural persons resident and legal entities having their registered offices within the territory of a Contracting Party shall, insofar as the grant and protection of breeders' rights are concerned, enjoy within the territory of each other Contracting Party the same treatment as is accorded or may hereafter be accorded by the laws of each such other Contracting Party to its own nationals, provided that the said nationals, natural persons or legal entities comply with the conditions and formalities imposed on the nationals of the said other Contracting Party.

(2)   [*"Nationals"*] For the purposes of the preceding paragraph, "nationals" means, where the Contracting Party is a State, the nationals of that State and, where the contracting Party is an intergovernmental organisation, the nationals of the States which are members of that organisation.

CHAPTER III CONDITIONS FOR THE GRANT OF THE BREEDER'S RIGHT

Article 5 Conditions of Protection

(1) [*Criteria to be satisfied*] The breeder's right shall be granted where the variety is

(i) new,
(ii) distinct,
(iii) uniform and
(iv) stable.

(2) [*Other conditions*] The grant of the breeder's right shall not be subject to any further or different conditions, provided that the variety is designated by a denomination in accordance with the provisions of Article 20, that the applicant complies with the formalities provided for by the law of the Contracting Party with whose authority the application has been filed and that he pays the required fees.

Article 6 Novelty

(1) [*Criteria*] The variety shall be deemed to be new if, at the date of filing of the application for a breeder's right, propagating or harvested material of the variety has not been sold or otherwise disposed of to others, by or with the consent of the breeder, for purposes of exploitation of the variety

(i) in the territory of the Contracting Party in which the application has been filed earlier than one year before that date and

(ii) in a territory other than that of the Contracting Party in which the application has been filed earlier than four years or, in the case of trees or of vines, earlier than six years before the said date.

(2) [*Varieties of recent creation*] Where a Contracting Party applies this Convention to a plant genus or species to which it did not previously apply this Convention or an earlier Act, it may consider a variety of recent creation existing at the date of such extension of protection to satisfy the condition of novelty defined in paragraph (1) even where the sale or disposal to others described in that paragraph took place earlier than the time limits defined in that paragraph.

(3) [*"Territory" in certain cases*] For the purposes of paragraph (1), all the Contracting Parties which are member States of one and the same intergovernmental organisation may act jointly, where the regulations of that organisation so require, to assimilate acts done on the territories of the States members of that organisation to acts done on their own territories and, should they do so, shall notify the Secretary-General accordingly.

Article 7 Distinctness

The variety shall be deemed to be distinct if it is clearly distinguishable from any other variety whose existence is a matter of common knowledge at the time of the filing of the application. In particular, the filing of an application for the granting of a breeder's right or for the entering of another variety in an official register of varieties, in any country, shall be deemed to render that other variety a matter of common knowledge from the date of the application, provided that the application leads to the granting of a breeder's right or to the entering of the said other variety in the official register of varieties, as the case may be.

Article 8 Uniformity

The variety shall be deemed to be uniform if, subject to the variation that may be expected from the particular features of its propagation, it is sufficiently uniform in its relevant characteristics.

Article 9   Stability
The variety shall be deemed to be stable if its relevant characteristics remain unchanged after repeated propagation or, in the case of a particular cycle of propagation, at the end of each such cycle.

CHAPTER IV   APPLICATION FOR THE GRANT OF THE BREEDER'S RIGHT

Article 10   Filing of applications
(1)   [*Place of first application*] The breeder may choose the Contracting Party with whose authority he wishes to file his first application for a breeder's right.

(2)   [*Time of subsequent applications*] The breeder may apply to the authorities of other Contracting Parties for the grant of breeders' rights without waiting for the grant to him of a breeder's right by the authority of the Contracting Party with which the first application was filed.

(3)   [*Independence of protection*] No Contracting Party shall refuse to grant a breeder's right or limit its duration on the ground that protection for the same variety has not been applied for, has been refused or has expired in any other State or intergovernmental organisation.

Article 11   Right of Priority
(1)   [*The right; its period*] Any breeder who has duly filed an application for the protection of a variety in one of the Contracting Parties (the "first application") shall, for the purpose of filing an application for the grant of a breeder's right for the same variety with the authority of any other Contracting Party (the "subsequent application"), enjoy a right of priority for a period of 12 months. This period shall be computed from the date of filing of the first application. The day of filing shall not be included in the latter period.

. . .

(4)   [*Events occurring during the period*] Events occurring within the period provided for in paragraph (1), such as the filing of another application or the publication or use of the variety that is the subject of the first application, shall not constitute a ground for rejecting the subsequent application. Such events shall also not give rise to any third-party right.

Article 12   Examination of the application
Any decision to grant a breeder's right shall require an examination for compliance with the conditions under Articles 5 to 9. In the course of the examination, the authority may grow the variety or carry out other necessary tests, cause the growing of the variety or the carrying out of other necessary tests, or take into account the results of growing tests or other trials which have already been carried out. For the purposes of examination, the authority may require the breeder to furnish all the necessary information, documents or material.

Article 13   Provisional protection
Each Contracting Party shall provide measures designed to safeguard the interest of the breeder during the period between the filing or the publication of the application for the grant of a breeder's right and the grant of that right. Such measures shall have the effect that the holder of a breeder's right shall at least be entitled to equitable remuneration from any person who, during the said period, has carried out acts which, once the right is granted, require the breeder's authorisation as provided in Article 14. A Contracting Party may provide that the said measures shall only take effect in relation to persons whom the breeder has notified of the filing of the application.

CHAPTER V   THE RIGHTS OF THE BREEDER

Article 14   Scope of the breeder's right

(1)   *[Act in respect of the propagating material]*

(a)   Subject to Articles 15 and 16, the following acts in respect of the propagating material of the protected variety shall require the authorisation of the breeder:

(i)   production or reproduction (multiplication),

(ii)   conditioning for the purpose of propagation,

(iii)   offering for sale,

(iv)   selling or other marketing,

(v)   exporting,

(vi)   importing,

(vii)   stocking for any of the purposes mentioned in (i) to (iv), above.

(b)   The breeder may make his authorisation subject to conditions and limitations.

(2)   *[Acts in respect of the harvested material]* Subject to Articles 15 and 16, the acts referred to in items (i) to (vii) of paragraph (1)(a) in respect of harvested material, including entire plants and parts of plants, obtained through the unauthorised use of propagating material of the protected variety shall require the authorisation of the breeder, unless the breeder has had reasonable opportunity to exercise his right in relation to the said propagating material.

(3)   *[Acts in respect of certain products]* Each Contracting Party may provide that, subject to Articles 15 and 16, the acts referred to in items (i) to (vii) of paragraph (1)(a) in respect of products made directly from harvested material of the protected variety falling within the provisions of paragraph (2) through the unauthorised use of the said harvested material shall require the authorisation of the breeder, unless the breeder has had reasonable opportunity to exercise his right in relation to the said harvested material.

(4)   *[Possible additional acts]* Each Contracting Party may provide that, subject to Articles 15 and 16, acts other than those referred to in items (i) to (vii) of paragraph (1)(a) shall also require the authorisation of the breeder.

(5)   *[Essentially derived and certain other varieties]*

(a)   The provisions of paragraphs (1) to (4) shall also apply in relation to

(i)   varieties which are essentially derived from the protected variety, where the protected variety is not itself an essentially derived variety,

(ii)   varieties which are not clearly distinguishable in accordance with Article 7 from the protected variety and

(iii)   varieties whose production requires the repeated use of the protected variety.

(b)   For the purposes of subparagraph (a)(i), a variety shall be deemed to be essentially derived from another variety ("the initial variety") when

(i)   it is predominantly derived from the initial variety, or from a variety that is itself predominantly derived from the initial variety, while retaining the expression of the essential characteristics that result from the genotype or combination of genotypes of the initial variety,

(ii)   it is clearly distinguishable from the initial variety and

(iii)   except for the differences which result from the act of derivation, it conforms to the initial variety in the expression of the essential characteristics that result from the genotype or combination of genotypes of the initial variety.

(c)   Essentially derived varieties may be obtained for example by the selection of a natural or induced mutant, or of a somaclonal variant, the selection of a variant individual from plants of the initial variety, backcrossing, or transformation by genetic engineering.

Article 15   Exceptions to the breeder's right

(1)   [*Compulsory exceptions*] The breeder's right shall not extend to

    (i)   acts done privately and for non-commercial purposes,

    (ii)   acts done for experimental purposes and

    (iii)   acts done for the purpose of breeding other varieties, and, except where the provisions of Article 14(5) apply, acts referred to in Article 14(1) to (4) in respect of such other varieties.

(2)   [*Optional exception*] Notwithstanding Article 14, each Contracting Party may, within reasonable limits and subject to the safeguarding of the legitimate interests of the breeder, restrict the breeder's right in relation to any variety in order to permit farmers to use for propagating purposes, on their own holdings, the product of the harvest which they have obtained by planting, on their own holdings, the protected variety or a variety covered by Article 14(5)(a)(i) or (ii).

Article 16   Exhaustion of the breeder's right

(1)   [*Exhaustion of right*] The breeder's right shall not extend to acts concerning any material of the protected variety, or of a variety covered by the provisions of Article 14(5), which has been sold or otherwise marketed by the breeder or with his consent in the territory of the Contracting Party concerned, or any material derived from the said material, unless such acts

    (i)   involve further propagation of the variety in question or

    (ii)   involve an export of material of the variety, which enables the propagation of the variety, into a country which does not protect varieties of the plant genus or species to which the variety belongs, except where the exported material is for final consumption purposes.

(2)   [*Meaning of "material"*] For the purposes of paragraph (1), "material" means, in relation to a variety,

    (i)   propagating material of any kind,

    (ii)   harvested material, including entire plants and parts of plants, and

    (iii)   any product made directly from the harvested material.

(3)   [*"Territory" in certain cases*] For the purposes of paragraph (1), all the Contracting Parties which are member States of one and the same intergovernmental organisation may act jointly, where the regulations of that organisation so require, to assimilate acts done on the territories of the States members of that organisation to acts done on their own territories and, should they do so, shall notify the Secretary-General accordingly.

Article 17   Restrictions on the exercise of the breeder's right

(1)   [*Public interest*] Except where expressly provided in this Convention, no Contracting Party may restrict the free exercise of a breeder's right for reasons other than of public interest.

(2)   [*Equitable remuneration*] When any such restriction has the effect of authorising a third party to perform any act for which the breeder's authorisation is required, the Contracting Party concerned shall take all measures necessary to ensure that the breeder receives equitable remuneration.

Article 18   Measures regulating commerce

The breeder's right shall be independent of any measure taken by a Contracting Party to regulate within its territory the production, certification and marketing of material of varieties or the importing or exporting of such material. In any case, such measures shall not affect the application of the provisions of this Convention.

Article 19   Duration of the breeder's right

(1)   [*Period of protection*] The breeder's right shall be granted for a fixed period.

(2) [*Minimum period*] The said period shall not be shorter than 20 years from the date of the grant of the breeder's right. For trees and vines, the said period shall not be shorter than 25 years from the said date.

CHAPTER VI VARIETY DENOMINATION

Article 20 Variety denomination

(1) [*Designation of varieties by denominations; use of the denomination*]

(a) The variety shall be designated by a denomination which will be its generic designation.

(b) Each Contracting Party shall ensure that, subject to paragraph (4), no rights in the designation registered as the denomination of the variety shall hamper the free use of the denomination in connection with the variety, even after the expiration of the breeder's right.

(2) [*Charaterics of the denomination*] The denomination must enable the variety to be identified. It may not consist solely of figures except where this is an established practice for designating varieties. It must not be liable to mislead or to cause confusion concerning the characteristics, value or identity of the variety or the identity of the breeder. In particular, it must be different from every denomination which designates, in the territory of any Contracting Party, an existing variety of the same plant species or of a closely related species.

(3) [*Registration of the denomination*] The denomination of the variety shall be submitted by the breeder to the authority. If it is found that the denomination does not satisfy the requirements of paragraph (2), the authority shall refuse to register it and shall require the breeder to propose another denomination within a prescribed period. The denomination shall be registered by the authority at the same time as the breeder's right is granted.

(4) [*Prior rights of third persons*] Prior rights of third persons shall not be affected. If, by reason of a prior right, the use of the denomination of a variety is forbidden to a person who, in accordance with the provisions of paragraph (7), is obliged to use it, the authority shall require the breeder to submit another denomination for the variety.

(5) [*Same denomination in all Contracting Parties*] A variety must be submitted to all Contracting Parties under the same denomination. The authority of each Contracting Party shall register the denomination so submitted, unless it considers the denomination unsuitable within its territory. In the latter case, it shall require the breeder to submit another denomination.

(6) [*Information among the authorities of Contracting Parties*] The authority of a Contracting Party shall ensure that the authorities of all the other Contracting Parties are informed of matters concerning variety denominations, in particular the submission, registration and cancellation of denominations. Any authority may address its observations, if any, on the registration of a denomination to the authority which communicated that denomination.

(7) [*Obligation to use the denomination*] Any person who, within the territory of one of the Contracting Parties, offers for sale or markets propagating material of a variety protected within the said territory shall be obliged to use the denomination of that variety, even after the expiration of the breeder's right in that variety, except where, in accordance with the provisions of paragraph (4), prior rights prevent such use.

(8) [*Indications used in association with denominations*] When a variety is offered for sale or marketed, it shall be permitted to associate a trademark, trade name or other similar indication with a registered variety denomination. If such an indication is so associated, the denomination must nevertheless be easily recognisable.

CHAPTER VII   NULLITY AND CANCELLATION OF THE BREEDER'S RIGHT

Article 21   Nullity of the breeder's right
(1)   [*Reasons of nullity*] Each Contracting Party shall declare a breeder's right granted by it null and void when it is established
    (i)   that the conditions laid down in Articles 6 or 7 were not complied with at the time of the grant of the breeder's right,
    (ii)   that, where the grant of the breeder's right has been essentially based upon information and documents furnished by the breeder, the conditions laid down in Articles 8 or 9 were not complied with at the time of the grant of the breeder's right, or
    (iii)   that the breeder's right has been granted to a person who is not entitled to it, unless it is transferred to the person who is so entitled.
(2)   [*Exclusion of other reasons*] No breeder's right shall be declared null and void for reasons other than those referred to in paragraph (1).

Article 22   Cancellation of the breeder's right
(1)   [*Reasons for cancellation*]
    (a)   Each Contracting Party may cancel a breeder's right granted by it if it is established that the conditions laid down in Articles 8 or 9 are no longer fulfilled.
    (b)   Furthermore, each Contracting Party may cancel a breeder's right granted by it if, after being requested to do so and within a prescribed period,
    (i)   the breeder does not provide the authority with the information, documents or material deemed necessary for verifying the maintainance of the variety,
    (ii)   the breeder fails to pay such fees as may be payable to keep his right in force, or
    (iii)   the breeder does not propose, where the denomination of the variety is cancelled after the grant of the right, another suitable denomination.
(2)   [*Exclusion of other reasons*] No breeder's right shall be cancelled for reasons other than those referred to in paragraph (1).
. . .

CONVENTION FOR THE PROTECTION OF PRODUCERS OF PHONOGRAMS AGAINST UNAUTHORISED DUPLICATION OF THEIR PHONOGRAMS (GENEVA CONVENTION)
29 October 1971

The Contracting States,
    Concerned at the widespread and increasing unauthorised duplication of phonograms and the damage this is occasioning to the interests of authors, performers and producers of phonograms;
    Convinced that the protection of producers of phonograms against such acts will also benefit the performers whose performances, and the authors whose works, are recorded on the said phonograms;
    Recognising the value of the work undertaken in this field by the United Nations Educational, Scientific and Cultural Organisation and the World Intellectual Property Organisation;
    Anxious not to impair in any way international agreements already in force and in particular in no way to prejudice wider acceptance of the Rome Convention of October 26, 1961, which affords protection to performers and to broadcasting organisations as well as to producers of phonograms;
    Have agreed as follows:

Article 1
For the purposes of this Convention:
    (a) "phonogram" means any exclusively aural fixation of sounds of a performance or of other sounds;
    (b) "producer of phonograms" means the person who, or the legal entity which, first fixes the sounds of a performance or other sounds;
    (c) "duplicate" means an article which contains sounds taken directly or indirectly from a phonogram and which embodies all or a substantial part of the sounds fixed in that phonogram;
    (d) "distribution to the public" means any act by which duplicates of a phonogram are offered, directly or indirectly, to the general public or any section thereof.

Article 2
Each Contracting State shall protect producers of phonograms who are nationals of other Contracting States against the making of duplicates without the consent of the producer and against the importation of such duplicates, provided that any such making or importation is for the purpose of distribution to the public, and against the distribution of such duplicates to the public.

Article 3
The means by which this Convention is implemented shall be a matter for the domestic law of each Contracting State and shall include one or more of the following: protection by means of the grant of a copyright or other specific right; protection by means of the law relating to unfair competition; protection by means of penal sanctions.

Article 4
The duration of the protection given shall be a matter for the domestic law of each Contracting State. However, if the domestic law prescribes a specific duration for the protection, that duration shall not be less than twenty years from the end either of the year in which the sounds embodied in the phonogram were first fixed or of the year in which the phonogram was first published.

Article 5
If, as a condition of protecting the producers of phonograms, a Contracting State, under its domestic law, requires compliance with formalities, these shall be considered as fulfilled if all the authorised duplicates of the phonogram distributed to the public or their containers bear a notice consisting of the symbol ℗, accompanied by the year date of the first publication, placed in such manner as to give reasonable notice of claim of protection; and, if the duplicates or their containers do not identify the producer, his successor in title or the exclusive licensee (by carrying his name, trademark or other appropriate designation), the notice shall also include the name of the producer, his successor in title or the exclusive licensee.

Article 6
Any Contracting State which affords protection by means of copyright or other specific right, or protection by means of penal sanctions, may in its domestic law provide, with regard to the protection of producers of phonograms, the same kinds of limitations as are permitted with respect to the protection of authors of literary and artistic works. However, no compulsory licenses may be permitted unless all of the following conditions are met:
    (a) the duplication is for use solely for the purpose of teaching or scientific research;
    (b) the license shall be valid for duplication only within the territory of the Contracting State whose competent authority has granted the license and shall not extend to the export of duplicates;

(c)   the duplication made under the license gives rise to an equitable remuneration fixed by the said authority taking into account, *inter alia*, the number of duplicates which will be made.

Article 7

(1)   This Convention shall in no way be interpreted to limit or prejudice the protection otherwise secured to authors, to performers, to producers of phonograms or to broadcasting organisations under any domestic law or international agreement.

(2)   It shall be a matter for the domestic law of each Contracting State to determine the extent, if any, to which performers whose performances are fixed in a phonogram are entitled to enjoy protection and the conditions for enjoying any such protection.

(3)   No Contracting State shall be required to apply the provisions of this Convention to any phonogram fixed before this Convention entered into force with respect to that State.

(4)   Any Contracting State which, on October 29, 1971, affords protection to producers of phonograms solely on the basis of the place of first fixation may, by a notification deposited with the Director General of the World Intellectual Property Organisation, declare that it will apply this criterion instead of the criterion of the nationality of the producer.

Article 8

(1)   The International Bureau of the World Intellectual Property Organisation shall assemble and publish information concerning the protection of phonograms. Each Contracting State shall promptly communicate to the International Bureau all new laws and official texts on this subject.

(2)   The International Bureau shall, on request, furnish information to any Contracting State on matters concerning this Convention, and shall conduct studies and provide services designed to facilitate the protection provided for therein.

(3)   The International Bureau shall exercise the functions enumerated in paragraphs (1) and (2) above in cooperation, for matters within their respective competence, with the United Nations Educational, Scientific and Cultural Organisation and the International Labour Organisation.

. . .

Article 10

No reservations to this Convention are permitted.

. . .

CONVENTION ON THE GRANT OF EUROPEAN PATENTS (EUROPEAN PATENT CONVENTION)
Munich, 5 October 1973
[The United Kingdom Instrument of Ratification was deposited on 3 March 1977, and the Convention entered into force on 7 October 1977]

PREAMBLE

The Contracting States,

Desiring to strengthen co-operation between the States of Europe in respect of the protection of inventions,

Desiring that such protection may be obtained in those States by a single procedure for the grant of patents, and by the establishment of certain standard rules governing patents so granted,

Desiring, for this purpose, to conclude a Convention which establishes a European Patent Organisation and which constitutes a special agreement within the meaning of Article 19 of the Convention for the Protection of Industrial Property, signed in Paris on 20 March 1883 and last revised on 14 July 1967, and a regional patent treaty within the meaning of Article 45, paragraph 1, of the Patent Co-operation Treaty of 19 June 1970,

Have agreed on the following provisions:

PART I   GENERAL AND INSTITUTIONAL PROVISIONS
Chapter I   General provisions

Article 1   European law for the grant of patents
A system of law, common to the Contracting States, for the grant of patents for invention is hereby established.

Article 2   European patent
(1)   Patents granted by virtue of this Convention shall be called European patents.
(2)   The European patent shall, in each of the Contracting States for which it is granted, have the effect of and be subject to the same conditions as a national patent granted by that State, unless otherwise provided in this Convention.

Article 3   Territorial effect
The grant of a European patent may be requested for one or more of the Contracting States.
...

PART II   SUBSTANTIVE PATENT LAW
Chapter I   Patentability

Article 52   Patentable inventions
(1)   European patents shall be granted for any inventions which are susceptible of industrial application, which are new and which involve an inventive step.
(2)
The following in particular shall not be regarded as inventions within the meaning of paragraph 1:
    (a)   discoveries, scientific theories and mathematical methods;
    (b)   aesthetic creations;
    (c)   schemes, rules and methods for performing mental acts, playing games or doing business, and programs for computers;
    (d)   presentations of information.
(3)   The provisions of paragraph 2 shall exclude patentability of the subject-matter or activities referred to in that provision only to the extent to which a European patent application or European patent relates to such subject-matter or activities as such.
(4)   Methods for treatment of the human or animal body by surgery or therapy and diagnostic methods practised on the human or animal body shall not be regarded as inventions which are susceptible of industrial application within the meaning of paragraph 1. This provision shall not apply to products, in particualr substances or compositions, for use in any of these methods.

Article 53   Exceptions to patentability
European patents shall not be granted in respect of:
    (a)   inventions the publication or exploitation of which would be contrary to "order public" or morality, provided that the exploitation shall not be deemed to be so contrary merely because it is prohibited by law or regulation in some or all of the Contracting States;
    (b)   plant or animal varieties or essentially biological processes for the production of plants or animals; this provision does not apply to microbiological processes or the products thereof.

Article 54   Novelty

(1)   An invention shall be considered to be new if it does not form part of the state of the art.

(2)   The state of the art shall be held to comprise everything made available to the public by means of a written or oral description, by use, or in any other way, before the date of filing of the European patent application.

(3)   Additionally, the content of European patent applications as filed, of which the dates of filing are prior to the date referred to in paragraph 2 and which were published under Article 93 on or after that date, shall be considered as comprised in the state of the art.

(4)   Paragraph 3 shall be applied only in so far as a Contracting State designated in respect of the later application, was also designated in respect of the earlier application as published.

(5)   The provisions of paragraphs 1 to 4 shall not exclude the patentability of any substance or composition, comprised in the state of the art, for use in a method referred to in Article 52, paragraph 4, provided that its use for any method referred to in that paragraph is not comprised in the state of the art.

Article 55   Non-prejudicial disclosures

(1)   For the application of Article 54 a disclosure of the invention shall not be taken into consideration if it occurred no earlier than six months preceding the filing of the European patent application and if it was due to, or in consequence of:

(a)   an evident abuse in relation to the applicant or his legal predecessor, or

(b)   the fact that the applicant or his legal predecessor has displayed the invention at an official, or officially recognised, international exhibition falling within the terms of the Convention on international exhibitions signed at Paris on 22 November 1928 and last revised on 30 November 1972.

(2)   In the case of paragraph 1(b), paragraph 1 shall apply only if the applicant states, when filing the European patent application, that the invention has been so displayed and files a supporting certificate within the period and under the conditions laid down in the Implementing Regulations.

Article 56   Inventive step

An invention shall be considered as involving an inventive step if, having regard to the state of the art, it is not obvious to a person skilled in the art. If the state of the art also includes documents within the meaning of Article 54, paragraph 3, these documents are not to be considered in deciding whether there has been an inventive step.

Article 57   Industrial application

An invention shall be considered as susceptible of industrial application if it can be made or used in any kind of industry, including agriculture.

**Chapter II   Persons entitled to apply for and obtain European patents —
Mention of the inventor**

Article 58   Entitlement to file a European patent application

A European patent application may be filed by any natural or legal person, or any body equivalent to a legal person by virtue of the law governing it.

Article 59   Multiple applicants

A European patent application may also be filed either by joint applicants or by two or more applicants designating different Contracting States.

Article 60   Right to a European patent

(1)   The right to a European patent shall belong to the inventor or his successor in title. If the inventor is an employee the right to the European patent shall be determined

in accordance with the law of the State in which the employee is mainly employed; if the State in which the employee is mainly employed cannot be determined, the law to be applied shall be that of the State in which the employer has his place of business to which the employee is attached.

(2)   If two or more persons have made an invention independently of each other, the right to the European patent shall belong to the person whose European patent application has the earliest date of filing; however, this provision shall apply only if this first application has been published under Article 93 and shall only have effect in respect of the Contracting States designated in that application as published.

(3)   For the purposes of proceedings before the European Patent Office, the applicant shall be deemed to be entitled to exercise the right to the European patent.
. . .

Article 62   Right of the inventor to be mentioned
The inventor shall have the right, *vis-à-vis* the applicant for or proprietor of a European patent, to be mentioned as such before the European Patent Office.

Chapter III   Effects of the European patent and the European patent application

Article 63   Term of the European patent
(1)   The term of the European patent shall be 20 years as from the date of filing of the application.

(2)   Nothing in the preceding paragraph shall limit the right of a Contracting State to extend the term of a European patent under the same conditions as those applying to its national patents, in order to take into account a state of war or similar emergency conditions affecting that State.

Article 64   Rights conferred by a European patent
(1)   A European patent shall, subject to the provisions of paragraph 2, confer on its proprietor from the date of publication of the mention of its grant, in each Contracting State in respect of which it is granted, the same rights as would be conferred by a national patent granted in that State.

(2)   If the subject-matter of the European patent is a process, the protection conferred by the patent shall extend to the products directly obtained by such process.

(3)   Any infringement of a European patent shall be dealt with by national law.
. . .

Article 67   Rights conferred by a European patent application after publication
(1)   A European patent application shall, from the date of its publication under Article 93, provisionally confer upon the applicant such protection as is conferred by Article 64, in the Contracting States designated in the application as published.

(2)   Any Contracting State may prescribe that a European patent application shall not confer such protection as is conferred by Article 64. However, the protection attached to the publication of the European patent application may not be less than that which the laws of the State concerned attach to the compulsory publication of unexamined national patent applications. In any event, every State shall ensure at least that, from the date of publication of a European patent application, the applicant can claim compensation reasonable in the circumstances from any person who has used the invention in the said State in circumstances where that person would be liable under national law for infringement of a national patent.
. . .

(4)   The European patent application shall be deemed never to have had the effects set out in paragraphs 1 and 2 above when it has been withdrawn, deemed to be withdrawn or finally refused. The same shall apply in respect of the effects of the

European patent application in a Contracting State the designation of which is withdrawn or deemed to be withdrawn.

Article 68   Effect of revocation of the European patent
The European patent application and the resulting patent shall be deemed not to have had, as from the outset, the effects specified in Articles 64 and 67, to the extent that the patent hàs been revoked in opposition proceedings.

Article 69   Extent of protection
(1)   The extent of the protection conferred by a European patent or a European patent application shall be determined by the term of the claims. Nevertheless, the description and drawings shall be used to interpret the claims.

(2)   For the period up to grant of the European patent, the extent of the protection conferred by the European patent application shall be determined by the latest filed claims contained in the publication under Article 93. However, the European patent as granted or as amended in opposition proceedings shall determine retroactively the protection conferred by the European patent application, in so far as such protection is not thereby extended.

. . .

Chapter IV   The European patent application as an object of property

Article 71   Transfer and constitution of rights
A European patent application may be transferred or give rise to rights for one or more of the designated Contracting States.

Article 72   Assignment
An assignment of a European patent application shall be made in writing and shall require the signature of the parties to the contract.

Article 73   Contractual licensing
A European patent application may be licensed in whole or in part for the whole or part of the territories of the designated Contracting States.

Article 74   Law applicable
Unless otherwise specified in this Convention, the European patent application as an object of property shall, in each designated Contracting State and with effect for such State, be subject to the law applicable in that State to national patent applications.

PART III   APPLICATION FOR EUROPEAN PATENTS
Chapter I   Filing and requirements of the European patent application

Article 75   Filing of the European patent application
(1)   A European patent application may be filed:
   (a)   at the European Patent Office at Munich or its branch at The Hague, or
   (b)   if the law of the Contracting State so permits, at the central industrial property office or other competent authority of that State. An application filed in this way shall have the same effect as if it had been filed on the same date at the European Patent Office.

. . .

Article 78   Requirements of the European patent application
(1)   A European patent application shall contain:
   (a)   a request for the grant of a European patent;
   (b)   a description of the invention;
   (c)   one or more claims;
   (d)   any drawings referred to in the description or the claims;
   (e)   an abstract.

. . .

Article 79   Designation of Contracting States
(1)   The request for the grant of a European patent shall contain the designation of the Contracting State and States in which protection for the invention is desired.
. . .

Article 80   Date of filing
The date of filing of a European patent application shall be the date on which documents filed by the applicant contain:
    (a)   an indication that a European patent is sought;
    (b)   the designation of at least one Contracting State;
    (c)   information identifying the applicant;
    (d)   a description and one or more claims in one of the languages referred to in Article 14, paragraphs 1 and 2, even though the description and the claims do not comply with the other requirements of this Convention.

Article 81   Designation of the inventor
The European patent application shall designate the inventor. If the applicant is not the inventor or is not the sole inventor, the designation shall contain a statement indicating the origin of the right to the European patent.

Article 82   Unity of invention
The European patent application shall relate to one invention only or to a group of inventions so linked as to form a single general inventive concept.

Article 83   Disclosure of the invention
The European patent application must disclose the invention in a manner sufficiently clear and complete for it to be carried out by a person skilled in the art.

Article 84   The claims
The claims shall define the matter for which protection is sought. They shall be clear and concise and be supported by the description.

Article 85   The abstract
The abstract shall merely serve for use as technical information; it may not be taken into account for any other purpose, in particular not for the purpose of interpreting the scope of the protection sought not for the purpose of applying Article 54, paragraph 3.
. . .

Chapter II   Priority

Article 87   Priority right
(1)   A person who has duly filed in or for any State party to the Paris Convention for the Protection of Industrial Property, an application for a patent or for the registration of a utility model or for a utility certificate or for an inventor's certificate, or his successor in title, shall enjoy, for the purpose of filing a European patent application in respect of the same invention, a right of priority during a period of twelve months from the date of filing of the first application.
. . .

Article 89   Effect of priority right
The right of priority shall have the effect that the date of priority shall count as the date of filing of the European patent application for the purposes of Article 54, paragraphs 2 and 3, and Articles 60, paragraph 2.

PART IV   PROCEDURE UP TO GRANT

. . .

Article 91   Examination as to formal requirements

(1)   If a European patent application has been accorded a date of filing, and is not deemed to be withdrawn by virtue of Article 90, paragraph 3, the Receiving Section shall examine whether:

(a)   the requirements of Article 133, paragraph 2, have been satisfied;

(b) . the application meets the physical requirements laid down in the Implementing Regulations for the implementation of this provision;

(c)   the abstract has been filed;

(d)   the request for the grant of a European patent satisfies the mandatory provisions of the Implementing Regulations concerning its content and, where appropriate, whether the requirements of this Convention concerning the claim to priority have been satisfied;

(e)   the designation fees have been paid;

(f)   the designation of the inventor has been made in accordance with Article 81;

(g)   the drawings referred to in Article 78, paragraph 1(d), were filed on the date of filing of the application.

. . .

Article 92   The drawing up of the European search report

(1)   If a European patent application has been accorded a date of filing and is not deemed to be withdrawn by virtue of Article 90, paragraph 3, the Search Division shall draw up the European search report on the basis of the claims, with due regard to the description and any drawings, in the form prescribed in the Implementing Regulations.

(2)   Immediately after it has been drawn up, the European search report shall be transmitted to the applicant together with copies of any cited documents.

Article 93   Publication of a European patent application

(1)   A European patent application shall be published as soon as possible after the expiry of a period of eighteen months from the date of filing or, if priority has been claimed, as from the date of priority. Nevertheless, at the request of the applicant the application may be published before the expiry of the period referred to above. It shall be published before the expiry of the period referred to above. It shall be published simultaneously with the publication of the specification of the European patent when the grant of the patent has become effective before the expiry of the period referred to above.

(2)   The publication shall contain the description, the claims and any drawings as filed and, in an annex, the European search report and the abstract, in so far as the later are available before the termination of the technical preparations for publication. If the European search report and the abstract have not been published at the same time as the application, they shall be published separately.

Article 94   Request for examination

(1)   The European Patent Office shall examine, on written request, whether a European patent application and the invention to which it relates meet the requirements of this Convention.

. . .

Article 97   Refusal or grant

(1)   The Examining Division shall refuse a European patent application if it is of the opinion that such application or the invention to which it relates does not meet the requirement of this Convention, except where a different sanction is provided for by this Convention.

(2)   If the Examining Division is of the opinion that the application and the invention to which it relates meet the requirements of this Convention, it shall decide to grant the European patent for the designated Contracting States provided that:

(a)   it is established, in accordance with the provisions of the Implementating Regulations, that the applicant approves the text in which the Examining Division intends to grant the patent;

(b)   the fees for grant and printing are paid within the time limit prescribed in the Implementing Regulations;

(c)   the renewal fees and any additional fees already due have been paid.

...

Article 98   Publication of a specification of the European patent

At the same time as it publishes the mention of the grant of the European patent, the European Patent Office shall publish a specification of the European patent containing the description, the claims and any drawings.

PART V   OPPOSITION PROCEDURE

Article 99   Opposition

(1)   Within nine months from the publication of the mention of the grant of the European patent, any person may give notice to the European Patent Office of opposition to the European patent granted. Notice of opposition shall be filed in a written reasoned statement. It shall not be deemed to have been filed until the opposition fee has been paid.

...

Article 100   Grounds for opposition

Opposition may only be filed on the grounds that:

(a)   the subject-matter of the European patent is not patentable within the terms of Articles 52 to 57;

(b)   the European patent does not disclose the invention in a manner sufficiently clear and complete for it to be carried out by a person skilled in the art;

(c)   the subject-matter of the European patent extends beyond the content of the application as filed, or, if the patent was granted on a divisional application or on a new application filed in accordance with Article 61, beyond the content of the earlier application as filed.

Article 101   Examination of the opposition

(1)   If the opposition is admissible, the Opposition Division shall examine whether the grounds for opposition laid down in Article 100 prejudice the maintenance of the European patent.

...

Article 102   Revocation or maintenance of the European patent

(1)   If the Opposition Division is of the opinion that the grounds for opposition mentioned in Article 100 prejudice the maintenance of the European patent, it shall revoke the patent.

(2)   If the Opposition Division is of the opinion that the grounds for opposition mentioned in Article 100 do not prejudice the maintenance of the patent unamended, it shall reject the opposition.

(3)   If the Opposition Division is of the opinion that, taking into consideration the amendments made by the proprietor of the patent during the opposition proceedings, the patent and the invention to which it relates meet the requirements of this Convention, it shall decide to maintain the patent as amended ...

PART VI   APPEALS PROCEDURE

Article 106   Decisions subject to appeal

(1)   An appeal shall lie from decisions of the Receiving Section, Examining Divisions, Opposition Divisions and the Legal Division. It shall have suspensive effect.

. . .

Article 107   Persons entitled to appeal and to be parties to appeal proceedings
Any party to proceedings adversely affected by a decision may appeal. Any other parties
to the proceedings shall be parties to the appeal proceedings as of right.

. . .

PART VII   COMMON PROVISIONS
Chapter I   Common provisions governing procedure

. . .

Article 115   Observations by third parties
(1)   Following the publication of the European patent application, any person may
present observations concerning the patentability of the invention in respect of which
the application has been filed. Such observations must be filed in writing and must
include a statement of the grounds on which they are based. That person shall not be a
party to the proceedings before the European Patent Office.

(2)   The observations referred to in paragraph 1 shall be communicated to the
applicant for or proprietor of the patent who may comment on them.

. . .

Article 123   Amendments
(1)   The conditions under which a European patent application or a European
patent may be amended in proceedings before the European Patent Office are laid down
in the Implementing Regulations. In any case, an applicant shall be allowed at least one
opportunity of amending the description, claims and drawings of his own volition.

(2)   A European patent application or a European patent may not be amended in
such a way that it contains subject-matter which extends beyond the content of the
application as filed.

(3)   The claim of the European patent may not be amended during opposition
proceedings in such a way as to extend the protection conferred.

. . .

Article 125   Reference to general principles
In the absence of procedural provisions in this Convention, the European Patent Office
shall take into account the principles of procedural law generally recognised in the
Contracting States.

. . .

PART VIII   IMPACT ON NATIONAL LAW
Chapter I   Conversion into a national patent application

Article 135   Request for the application of national procedure
(1)   The central industrial property office of a designated Contracting State shall
apply the procedure for the grant of a national patent only at the request of the applicant
for or proprietor of a European patent, and in the following circumstances:

(a)   when the European patent application is deemed to be withdrawn pursuant to
Article 77, paragraph 5, or Article 162, paragraph 4;

(b)   in such other cases as are provided for by the national law in which the
European patent application is refused or withdrawn or deemed to be withdrawn, or the
European patent is revoked under this Convention.

(2)   The request for conversion shall be filed within three months after the European
patent application has been withdrawn or after notification has been made that the
application is deemed to be withdrawn, or after a decision has been notified refusing the

application or revoking the European patent. The effect referred to in Article 66 shall lapse if the request is not filed in due time.

. . .

Chapter II   Revocation and prior rights

Article 138   Grounds for revocation

(1)   Subject to the provisions of Article 139, a European patent may only be revoked under the law of a Contracting State, with effect for its territory, on the following grounds:

(a)   if the subject-matter of the European patent is not patentable within the terms of Articles 52 to 57;

(b)   if the European patent does not disclose the invention in a manner sufficiently clear and complete for it to be carried out by a person skilled in the art;

(c)   if the subject-matter of the European patent extends beyond the content of the application as filed or, if the patent was granted on a divisional application or on a new application filed in accordance with Article 61, beyond the content of the earlier application as filed;

(d)   if the protection conferred by the European patent has been extended;

(e)   if the proprietor of the European patent is not entitled under Article 60, paragraph 1.

(2)   If the grounds for revocation only affect the European patent in part, revocation shall be pronounced in the form of a corresponding limitation of the said patent. If the national law so allows, the limitation may be effected in the form of an amendment to the claims, the description or the drawings.

Article 139   Rights of earlier date or the same date

(1)   In any designated Contracting State a European patent application and a European patent shall have with regard to a national patent application and a national patent the same prior right effect as a national patent application and a national patent.

(2)   A national patent application and a national patent in a Contracting State shall have with regard to a European patent in which that Contracting State is designated the same prior right effect as they have with regard to a national patent.

(3)   Any Contracting State may prescribe whether and on what terms an invention disclosed in both a European patent application or patent and a national application or patent having the same date of filing or, where priority is claimed, the same date of priority, may be protected simultaneously by both applications or patents.

. . .

PROTOCOL ON THE INTERPRETATION OF ARTICLE 69 OF THE EUROPEAN PATENT CONVENTION

Article 69 should not be interpreted in the sense that the extent of the protection conferred by a European patent is to be understood as that defined by the strict, literal meaning of the wording used in the claims, the description and drawings being employed only for the purpose of resolving an ambiguity found in the claims. Neither should it be interpreted in the sense that the claims serve only as a guideline and that the actual protection conferred may extend to what, from a consideration of the description and drawings by a person skilled in the art, the patentee has contemplated. On the contrary, it is to be interpreted as defining a position between these extremes which combines a fair protection for the patentee with a reasonable degree of certainty for third parties.

CONVENTION RELATING TO THE DISTRIBUTION OF
PROGRAMME-CARRYING SIGNALS TRANSMITTED BY SATELLITE
Done at Brussels on 21 May 1974
(SATELLITE CONVENTION)

The Contracting States,

Aware that the use of satellites for the distribution of programme-carrying signals is rapidly growing both in volume and geographical coverage;

Concerned that there is no world-wide system to prevent distributors from distributing programme-carrying signals transmitted by satellite which were not intended for those distributors, and that this lack is likely to hamper the use of satellite communications;

Recognising, in this respect, the importance of the interests of authors, performers, producers of phonograms and broadcasting organisations;

Convinced that an international system should be established under which measures would be provided to prevent distributors from distributing programme-carrying signals transmitted by satellite which were not intended for those distributors;

Conscious of the need not to impair in any way international agreements already in force, including the International Telecommunication Convention and the Radio Regulations annexed to that Convention, and in particular in no way to prejudice wider acceptance of the Rome Convention of 26 October 1961, which affords protection to performers, producers of phonograms and broadcasting organisations,

Have agreed as follows:

Article 1

For the purposes of this Convention:

(i)   "signal" is an electronically-generated carrier capable of transmitting programmes;

(ii)   "programme" is a body of live or recorded material consisting of images, sounds or both, embodied in signals emitted for the purposes of ultimate distribution;

(iii)   "satellite" is any device in extraterrestrial space capable of transmitting signals;

(iv)   "emitted signal" or "signal emitted" is any programme-carrying signal that goes to or passes through a satellite;

(v)   "derived signal" is a signal obtained by modifying the technical characteristics of the emitted signal, whether or not there have been one or more intervening fixations;

(vi)   "originating organisation" is the person or legal entity that decides what programme the emitted signals will carry;

(vii)   "distributor" is the person or legal entity that decides that the transmission of the derived signals to the general public or any section thereof should take place;

(viii)   "distribution" is the operation by which a distributor transmits derived signals to the general public or any section thereof.

Article 2

(1)   Each Contracting State undertakes to take adequate measures to prevent the distribution on or from its territory of any programme-carrying signal by any distributor for whom the signal emitted to or passing through the satellite is not intended. This obligation shall apply where the originating organisation is a national of another Contracting State and where the signal distributed is a derived signal.

(2)   In any Contracting State in which the application of the measures referred to in paragraph (1) is limited in time, the duration thereof shall be fixed by its domestic law. The Secretary-General of the United Nations shall be notified in writing of such

duration at the time of ratification, acceptance or accession, or if the domestic law comes into force or is changed thereafter, within six months of the coming into force of that law or of its modification.

(3)   The obligation provided for in paragraph (1) shall not apply to the distribution of derived signals taken from signals which have already been distributed by a distributor for whom the emitted signals were intended.

Article 3
This Convention shall not apply where the signals emitted by or on behalf of the originating organisation are intended for direct reception from the satellite by the general public.

Article 4
No Contracting State shall be required to apply the measures referred to in Article 2(1) where the signal distributed on its territory by a distributor for whom the emitted signal is not intended

(i)   carries short excerpts of the programme carried by the emitted signal, consisting of reports of current events, but only to the extent justified by the informatory purpose of such excerpts, or

(ii)   carries, as quotations, short excerpts of the programme carried by the emitted signal, provided that such quotations are compatible with fair practice and are justified by the informatory purpose of such quotations, or

(iii)   carries, where the said territory is that of a Contracting State regarded as a developing country in conformity with the established practice of the General Assembly of the United Nations, a programme carried by the emitted signal, provided that the distribution is solely for the purpose of teaching, including teaching in the framework of adult education, or scientific research.

Article 5
No Contracting State shall be required to apply this Convention with respect to any signal emitted before this Convention entered into force for that State.

Article 6
This Convention shall in no way be interpreted to limit or prejudice the protection secured to authors, performers, producers of phonograms, or broadcasting organisations, under any domestic law or international agreement.

Article 7
This Convention shall in no way be interpreted as limiting the right of any Contracting State to apply its domestic law in order to prevent abuses of monopoly.

Article 8
(1)   Subject to paragraph (2) and paragraph (3), no reservation to this Convention shall be permitted.

(2)   Any Contracting State whose domestic law, on 21 May 1974, so provides may, by a written notification deposited with the Secretary-General of the United Nations, declare that, for its purposes, the words "where the originating organisation is a national of another Contracting State" appearing in Article 2(1) shall be considered as if they were replaced by the words "where the signal is emitted from the territory of another Contracting State."

(3)(a)   Any Contracting State which, on 21 May 1974, limits or denies protection with respect to the distribution of programme-carrying signals by means of wires, cable or other similar communications channels to subscribing members of the public may, by a written notification deposited with the Secretary-General of the United Nations, declare that, to the extent that and as long as its domestic law limits or denies protection, it will not apply this Convention to such distributions.

(b)   Any State that has deposited a notification in notify [sic] the States referred to in Article 9(1), as well as the accordance with subparagraph (a) shall notify the Secretary-General of the United Nations in writing, within six months of their coming into force, of any changes in its domestic law whereby the reservation under that subparagraph becomes inapplicable or more limited in scope.

. . .

TREATY ON INTELLECTUAL PROPERTY IN RESPECT OF INTEGRATED CIRCUITS
Done at Washington, DC, on 26 May 1989
(INTEGRATED CIRCUITS TREATY)

Article 1   Establishment of a Union

The Contracting Parties constitute themselves into a Union for the purposes of this Treaty.

Article 2   Definitions

For the purposes of this Treaty:

(i)   "integrated circuit" means a product, in its final form or an intermediate form, in which the elements, at least one of which is an active element, and some or all of the interconnections are integrally formed in and/or on a piece of material and which is intended to perform an electronic function,

(ii)   "layout-design (topography)" means the three-dimensional disposition, however expressed, of the elements, at least one of which is an active element, and of some or all of the interconnections of an integrated circuit, or such a three-dimensional disposition prepared for an integrated circuit intended for manufacture,

(iii)   "holder of the right" means the natural person who, or the legal entity which, according to the applicable law, is to be regarded as the beneficiary of the protection referred to in Article 6,

(iv)   "protected layout-design (topography)" means a layout-design (topography) in respect of which the conditions of protection referred to in this Treaty are fulfilled,

(v)   "Contracting Party" means a State, or an Intergovernmental Organisation meeting the requirements of item (x), party to this Treaty,

(vi)   "territory of a Contracting Party" means, where the Contracting Party is a State, the territory of that State and, where the Contracting Party is an Intergovernmental Organisation, the territory in which the constituting treaty of that Intergovernmental Organisation applies,

(vii)   "Union" means the Union referred to in Article 1,

(viii) "Assembly" means the Assembly referred to in Article 9,

(ix)   "Director General" means the Director General of the World Intellectual Property Organisation,

(x)   "Intergovernmental Organisation" means an organisation constituted by, and composed of, States of any region of the world, which has competence in respect of matters governed by this Treaty, has its own legislation providing for intellectual property protection in respect of layout-designs (topographies) and binding on all its member States, and has been duly authorised, in accordance with its internal procedures, to sign, ratify, accept, approve or accede to this Treaty.

Article 3   The Subject Matter of the Treaty

(1)   Obligation to Protect Layout-Designs (Topographies)

(a)   Each Contracting Party shall have the obligation to secure, throughout its territory, intellectual property protection in respect of layout-designs (topographies) in accordance with this Treaty. It shall, in particular, secure adequate measures to ensure the prevention of acts considered unlawful under Article 6 and appropriate legal remedies where such acts have been committed.

(b)   The right of the holder of the right in respect of an integrated circuit applies whether or not the integrated circuit is incorporated in an article.

(c)   Notwithstanding Article 2(i), any Contracting Party whose law limits the protection of layout-designs (topographies) to layout-designs (topographies) of semiconductor integrated circuits shall be free to apply that limitation as long as its law contains such limitation.

(2)   Requirement of Originality

(a)   The obligation referred to in paragraph (1)(a) shall apply to layout-designs (topographies) that are original in the sense that they are the result of their creators' own intellectual effort and are not commonplace among creators of layout-designs (topographies) and manufacturers of integrated circuits at the time of their creation.

(b)   A layout-design (topography) that consists of a combination of elements and interconnections that are commonplace shall be protected only if the combination, taken as a whole, fulfills the conditions referred to in subparagraph (a).

Article 4   The Legal Form of the Protection
Each Contracting Party shall be free to implement its obligations under this Treaty through a special law on layout-designs (topographies) or its law on copyright, patents, utility models, industrial designs, unfair competition or any other law or a combination of any of those laws.

Article 5   National Treatment
(1)   National Treatment

Subject to compliance with its obligation referred to in Article 3(1)(a), each Contracting Party shall, in respect of the intellectual property protection of layout-designs (topographies), accord, within its territory,

(i)   to natural persons who are nationals of, or are domiciled in the territory of, any of the other Contracting Parties, and

(ii)   to legal entities which or natural persons who, in the territory of any of the other Contracting Parties, have a real and effective establishment for the creation of layout-designs (topographies) or the production of integrated circuits, the same treatment that it accords to its own nationals.

(2)   Agents, Addresses for Service, Court Proceedings

Notwithstanding paragraph (1), any Contracting Party is free not to apply national treatment as far as any obligations to appoint an agent or to designate an address for service are concerned or as far as the special rules applicable to foreigners in court proceedings are concerned.

(3)   Application of Paragraphs (1) and (2) to Intergovernmental Organisations

Where the Contracting Party is an Intergovernmental Organization, "nationals" in paragraph (1) means nationals of any of the States members of that Organization.

Article 6   The Scope of the Protection
(1)   Acts Requiring the Authorisation of the Holder of the Right

(a)   Any Contracting Party shall consider unlawful the following acts if performed without the authorisation of the holder of the right:

(i)   the act of reproducing, whether by incorporation in an integrated circuit or otherwise, a protected layout-design (topography) in its entirety or any part thereof, except the act of reproducing any part that does not comply with the requirement of originality referred to in Article 3(2),

(ii)   the act of importing, selling or otherwise distributing for commercial purposes a protected layout-design (topography) or an integrated circuit in which a protected layout-design (topography) is incorporated.

(b)   Any Contracting Party shall be free to consider unlawful also acts other than those specified in subparagraph (a) if performed without the authorisation of the holder of the right.

(2)   Acts Not Requiring the Authorisation of the Holder of the Right

(a)   Notwithstanding paragraph (1), no Contracting Party shall consider unlawful the performance, without the authorisation of the holder of the right, of the act of reproduction referred to in paragraph (1)(a)(i) where that act is performed by a third party for private purposes or for the sole purpose of evaluation, analysis, research or teaching.

(b)   Where the third party referred to in subparagraph (a), on the basis of evaluation or analysis of the protected layout-design (topography) ("the first layout-design (topography)"), creates a layout-design (topography) complying with the requirement of originality referred to in Article 3(2) ("the second layout-design (topography)"), that third party may incorporate the second layout-design (topography) in an integrated circuit or perform any of the acts referred to in paragraph (1) in respect of the second layout-design (topography) without being regarded as infringing the rights of the holder of the right in the first layout-design (topography).

(c)   The holder of the right may not exercise his right in respect of an identical original layout-design (topography) that was independently created by a third party.

(3)   Measures Concerning Use Without the Consent of the Holder of the Right

(a)   Notwithstanding paragraph (1), any Contracting Party may, in its legislation, provide for the possibility of its executive or judicial authority granting a non-exclusive licence, in circumstances that are not ordinary, for the performance of any of the acts referred to in paragraph (1) by a third party without the authorisation of the holder of the right ("non-voluntary licence"), after unsuccessful efforts, made by the said third party in line with normal commercial practices, to obtain such authorisation, where the granting of the non-voluntary licence is found, by the granting authority, to be necessary to safeguard a national purpose deemed to be vital by that authority; the non-voluntary licence shall be available for exploitation only in the territory of that country and shall be subject to the payment of an equitable remuneration by the third party to the holder of the right.

(b)   The provisions of this Treaty shall not affect the freedom of any Contracting Party to apply measures, including the granting, after a formal proceeding by its executive or judicial authority, of a non-voluntary licence, in application of its laws in order to secure free competition and to prevent abuses by the holder of the right.

(c)   The granting of any non-voluntary licence referred to in subparagraph (a) or subparagraph (b) shall be subject to judicial review. Any non-voluntary licence referred to in subparagraph (a) shall be revoked when the conditions referred to in that subparagraph cease to exist.

(4)   Sale and Distribution of Infringing Integrated Circuits Acquired Innocently

Notwithstanding paragraph (1)(a)(ii), no Contracting Party shall be obliged to consider unlawful the performance of any of the acts referred to in that paragraph in respect of an integrated circuit incorporating an unlawfully reproduced layout-design (topography) where the person performing or ordering such acts did not know and had no reasonable ground to know, when acquiring the said integrated circuit, that it incorporates an unlawfully reproduced layout-design (topography).

(5)   Exhaustion of Rights

Notwithstanding paragraph (1)(a)(ii), any Contracting Party may consider lawful the performance, without the authorisation of the holder of the right, of any of the acts referred to in that paragraph where the act is performed in respect of a protected layout-design (topography), or in respect of an integrated circuit in which such a layout-design (topography) is incorporated, that has been put on the market by, or with the consent of, the holder of the right.

Article 7   Exploitation; Registration, Disclosure
(1)   Faculty to Require Exploitation
Any Contracting Party shall be free not to protect a layout-design (topography) until it has been ordinarily commercially exploited, separately or as incorporated in an integrated circuit, somewhere in the world.
(2)   Faculty to Require Registration; Disclosure
(a)   Any Contracting Party shall be free not to protect a layout-design (topography) until the layout-design (topography) has been the subject of an application for registration, filed in due form with the competent public authority, or of a registration with that authority; it may be required that the application be accompanied by the filing of a copy or drawing of the layout-design (topography) and, where the integrated circuit has been commercially exploited, of a sample of that integrated circuit, along with information defining the electronic function which the integrated circuit is intended to perform; however, the applicant may exclude such parts of the copy or drawing that relate to the manner of manufacture of the integrated circuit, provided that the parts submitted are sufficient to allow the identification of the layout-design (topography).
(b)   Where the filing of an application for registration according to subparagraph (a) is required, the Contracting Party may require that such filing be effected within a certain period of time from the date on which the holder of the right first exploits ordinarily commercially anywhere in the world the layout-design (topography) of an integrated circuit; such period shall not be less than two years counted from the said date.
(c)   Registration under subparagraph (a) may be subject to the payment of a fee.

Article 8   The Duration of the Protection
Protection shall last at least eight years.
. . .

Article 12   Safeguard of Paris and Berne Conventions
This Treaty shall not affect the obligations that any Contracting Party may have under the Paris Convention for the Protection of Industrial Property or the Berne Convention for the Protection of Literary and Artistic Works.

Article 13   Reservations
No reservations to this Treaty shall be made.
. . .

CONVENTION ON BIOLOGICAL DIVERSITY
of 5 June 1992, signed in Rio de Janeiro
(RIO CONVENTION)

PREAMBLE

The Contracting Parties,
Conscious of the intrinsic value of biological diversity and of the ecological, genetic, social, economic, scientific, educational, cultural, recreational and aesthetic values of biological diversity and its components,
Conscious also of the importance of biological diversity for evolution and for maintaining life sustaining systems of the biosphere,
Affirming that the conservation of biological diversity is a common concern of humankind,
Reaffirming that States have sovereign rights over their own biological resources,
Reaffirming also that States are responsible for conserving their biological diversity and for using their biological resources in a sustainable manner,

Concerned that biological diversity is being significantly reduced by certain human activities,

Aware of the general lack of information and knowledge regarding biological diversity and of the urgent need to develop scientific, technical and institutional capacities to provide the basic understanding upon which to plan and implement appropriate measures,

Noting that it is vital to anticipate, prevent and attack the causes of significant reduction or loss of biological diversity at source,

Noting also that where there is a threat of significant reduction or loss of biological diversity, lack of full scientific certainty should not be used as a reason for postponing measures to avoid or minimise such a threat,

Noting further that the fundamental requirement for the conservation of biological diversity is the *in-situ* conservation of ecosystems and natural habitats and the maintenance and recovery of viable populations of species in their natural surroundings,

Noting further that *ex-situ* measures, preferably in the country of origin, also have an important role to play,

Recognising the close and traditional dependence of many indigenous and local communities embodying traditional lifestyles on biological resources, and the desirability of sharing equitably benefits arising from the use of traditional knowledge, innovations and practices relevant to the conservation of biological diversity and the sustainable use of its components,

Recognising also the vital role that women play in the conservation and sustainable use of biological diversity and affirming the need for the full participation of women at all levels of policy-making and implementation for biological diversity conservation,

Stressing the importance of, and the need to promote, international, regional and global cooperation among States and intergovernmental organisations and the non-governmental sector for the conservation of biological diversity and the sustainable use of its components,

Acknowledging that the provision of new and additional financial resources and appropriate access to relevant technologies can be expected to make a substantial difference in the world's ability to address the loss of biological diversity,

Acknowledging further that special provision is required to meet the needs of developing countries, including the provision of new and additional financial resources and appropriate access to relevant technologies,

Noting in this regard the special conditions of the least developed countries and small island States,

Acknowledging that substantial investments are required to conserve biological diversity and that there is the expectation of a broad range of environmental, economic and social benefits from those investments,

Recognising that economic and social development and poverty eradication are the first and overriding priorities of developing countries,

Aware that conservation and sustainable use of biological diversity is of critical importance for meeting the food, health and other needs of the growing world population, for which purposes access to and sharing of both genetic resources and technologies are essential,

Noting that, ultimately, the conservation and sustainable use of biological diversity will strengthen friendly relations among States and contribute to peace for humankind,

Desiring to enhance and complement existing international arrangements for the conservation of biological diversity and sustainable use of its components, and

Determined to conserve and sustainably use biological diversity for the benefit of present and future generations.

Have agreed as follows:

Article 1   Objectives

The objectives of this Convention, to be pursued in accordance with its relevant provisions, are the conservation of biological diversity, the sustainable use of its components and the fair and equitable sharing of the benefits arising out of the utilisation of genetic resources, including by appropriate access to genetic resources and by appropriate transfer of relevant technologies, taking into account all rights over those resources and to technologies, and by appropriate funding.

Article 2   Use of terms

For the purposes of this Convention:

"Biological diversity" means the variability among living organisms from all sources including, *inter alia*, terrestrial, marine and other aquatic ecosystems and the ecological complexes of which they are part; this includes diversity within species, between species and of ecosystems.

"Biological resources" includes genetic resources, organisms or parts thereof, populations, or any other biotic component of ecosystems with actual or potential use or value for humanity.

"Biotechnology" means any technological application that uses biological systems, living organisms, or derivatives thereof, to make or modify products or processes for specific use.

"Country of origin of genetic resources" means the country which possesses those genetic resources in *in-situ* conditions.

"Country providing genetic resources" means the country supplying genetic resources collected from *in-situ* sources, including populations of both wild and domesticated species, or taken from *ex-situ* sources, which may or may not have originated in that country.

"Domesticated or cultivated species" means species in which the evolutionary process has been influenced by humans to meet their needs.

"Ecosystem" means a dynamic complex of plant, animal and micro-organism communities and their non-living environment interacting as a functional unit.

"*Ex-situ* conservation" means the conservation of components of biological diversity outside their natural habitats.

"Genetic material" means any material of plant, animal, microbial or other origin containing functional units of heredity.

"Genetic resources" means genetic material of actual or potential value.

"Habitat" means the place or type of site where an organism or population naturally occurs.

"*In-situ* conditions" means conditions where genetic resources exist within ecosystems and natural habitats, and, in the case of domesticated or cultivated species, in the surroundings where they have developed their distinctive properties.

"*In-situ* conservation" means the conservation of ecosystems and natural habitats and the maintenance and recovery of viable populations of species in their natural surroundings and, in the case of domesticated or cultivated species, in the surroundings where they have developed their distinctive properties.

"Protected area" means a geographically defined area which is designated or regulated and managed to achieve specific conservation objectives.

"Regional economic integration organisation" means an organisation constituted by sovereign States of a given region, to which its member States have transferred competence in respect of matters governed by this Convention and which has been duly authorised, in accordance with its internal procedures, to sign, ratify, accept, approve or accede to it.

"Sustainable use" means the use of components of biological diversity in a way and at a rate that does not lead to the long-term decline of biological diversity, thereby maintaining its potential to meet the needs and aspirations of present and future generations.

"Technology" includes biotechnology.

Article 3   Principle

States have, in accordance with the Charter of the United Nations and the principles of international law, the sovereign right to exploit their own resources pursuant to their own environmental policies, and the responsibility to ensure that activities within their jurisdiction or control do not cause damage to the environment of other States or of areas beyond the limits of national jurisdiction.

Article 4   Jurisdictional scope

Subject to the rights of other States, and except as otherwise expressly provided in this Convention, the provisions of this Convention apply, in relation to each Contracting Party:

(a)   In the case of components of biological diversity, in areas within the limits of its national jurisdiction; and

(b)   In the case of processes and activities, regardless of where their effects occur, carried out under its jurisdiction or control, within the area of its national jurisdiction or beyond the limits of national jurisdiction.

. . .

Article 8   *In-situ* conservation

Each Contracting Party shall, as far as possible and as appropriate:

. . .

(j)   Subject to its national legislation, respect, preserve and maintain knowledge, innovations and practices of indigenous and local communities embodying traditional lifestyles relevant for the conservation and sustainable use of biological diversity and promote their wider application with the approval and involvement of the holders of such knowledge, innovations and practices and encourage the equitable sharing of the benefits arising from the utilisation of such knowledge, innovations and practices;

. . .

Article 15   Access to genetic resources

1.   Recognising the sovereign rights of States over their natural resources, the authority to determine access to genetic resources rests with the national governments and is subject to national legislation.

2.   Each Contracting Party shall endeavour to create conditions to facilitate access to genetic resources for environmentally sound uses by other Contracting Parties and not to impose restrictions that run counter to the objectives of this Convention.

3.   For the purpose of this Convention, the genetic resources being provided by a Contracting Party, as referred to in this Article and Articles 16 and 19, are only those that are provided by Contracting Parties that are countries of origin of such resources or by the Parties that have acquired the genetic resources in accordance with this Convention.

4.   Access, where granted, shall be on mutually agreed terms and subject to the provisions of this Article.

5.   Access to genetic resources shall be subject to prior informed consent of the Contracting Party providing such resources, unless otherwise determined by that Party.

6.   Each Contracting Party shall endeavour to develop and carry out scientific research based on genetic resources provided by other Contracting Parties with the full participation of, and where possible in, such Contracting Parties.

7.   Each Contracting Party shall take legislative, administrative or policy measures, as appropriate, and in accordance with Articles 16 and 19 and, where necessary, through the financial mechanism established by Articles 20 and 21 with the aim of

sharing in a fair and equitable way the results of research and development and the benefits arising from the commercial and other utilisation of genetic resources with the Contracting Party providing such resources. Such sharing shall be upon mutually agreed terms.

Article 16   Access to and transfer of technology

1.   Each Contracting Party, recognising that technology includes biotechnology, and that both access to and transfer of technology among Contracting Parties are essential elements for the attainment of the objectives of this Convention, undertakes subject to the provisions of this Article to provide and/or facilitate access for and transfer to other Contracting Parties of technologies that are relevant to the conservation and sustainable use of biological diversity or make use of genetic resources and do not cause significant damage to the environment.

2.   Access to and transfer of technology referred to in paragraph 1 above to developing countries shall be provided and/or facilitated under fair and most favourable terms, including on concessional and preferential terms where mutually agreed, and, where necessary, in accordance with the financial mechanism established by Articles 20 and 21. In the case of technology subject to patents and other intellectual property rights, such access and transfer shall be provided on terms which recognise and are consistent with the adequate and effective protection of intellectual property rights. The application of this paragraph shall be consistent with paragraphs 3, 4 and 5 below.

3.   Each Contracting Party shall take legislative, administrative or policy measures, as appropriate, with the aim that Contracting Parties, in particular those that are developing countries, which provide genetic resources are provided access to and transfer of technology which makes use of those resources, on mutually agreed terms, including technology protected by patents and other intellectual property rights, where necessary, through the provisions of Articles 20 and 21 and in accordance with international law and consistent with paragraphs 4 and 5 below.

4.   Each Contracting Party shall take legislative, administrative or policy measures, as appropriate, with the aim that the private sector facilitates access to, joint development and transfer of technology referred to in paragraph 1 above for the benefit of both governmental institutions and the private sector of developing countries and in this regard shall abide by the obligations included in paragraphs 1, 2 and 3 above.

5.   The Contracting Parties, recognising that patents and other intellectual property rights may have an influence on the implementation of this Convention, shall cooperate in this regard subject to national legislation and international law in order to ensure that such rights are supportive of and do not run counter to its objectives.

Article 17   Exchange of information

1.   The Contracting Parties shall facilitate the exchange of information, from all publicly available sources, relevant to the conservation and sustainable use of biological diversity, taking into account the special needs of developing countries.

2.   Such exchange of information shall include exchange of results of technical, scientific and socio-economic research, as well as information on training and surveying programmes, specialised knowledge, indigenous and traditional knowledge as such and in combination with the technologies referred to in Article 16, paragraph 1. It shall also, where feasible, include repatriation of information.

Article 18   Technical and scientific cooperation

1.   The Contracting Parties shall promote international technical and scientific cooperation in the field of conservation and sustainable use of biological diversity, where necessary, through the appropriate international and national institutions.

2.   Each Contracting Party shall promote technical and scientific cooperation with other Contracting Parties, in particular developing countries, in implementing this

Convention, *inter alia*, through the development and implementation of national policies. In promoting such cooperation, special attention should be given to the development and strengthening of national capabilities, by means of human resources development and institution building.

3. The Conference of the Parties, at its first meeting, shall determine how to establish a clearing-house mechanism to promote and facilitate technical and scientific cooperation.

4. The Contracting Parties shall, in accordance with national legislation and policies, encourage and develop methods of cooperation for the development and use of technologies, including indigenous and traditional technologies, in pursuance of the objectives of this Convention. For this purpose, the Contracting Parties shall also promote cooperation in the training of personnel and exchange of experts.

5. The Contracting Parties shall, subject to mutual agreement, promote the establishment of joint research programmes and joint ventures for the development of technologies relevant to the objectives of this Convention.

Article 19   Handling of biotechnology and distribution of its benefits

1. Each Contracting Party shall take legislative, administrative or policy measures, as appropriate, to provide for the effective participation in biotechnological research activities by those Contracting Parties, especially developing countries, which provide the genetic resources for such research, and where feasible in such Contracting Parties.

2. Each Contracting Party shall take all practicable measures to promote and advance priority access on a fair and equitable basis by Contracting Parties, especially developing countries, to the results and benefits arising from biotechnologies based upon genetic resources provided by those Contracting Parties. Such access shall be on mutually agreed terms.

3. The Parties shall consider the need for and modalites of a protocol setting out appropriate procedures, including, in particular, advance informed agreement, in the field of the safe transfer, handling and use of any living modified organism resulting from biotechnology that may have adverse effect on the conservation and sustainable use of biological diversity.

4. Each Contracting Party shall, directly or by requiring any natural or legal person under its jurisdiction providing the organisms referred to in paragraph 3 above, provide any available information about the use and safety regulations required by that Contracting Party in handling such organisms, as well as any available information on the potential adverse impact of the specific organisms concerned to the Contracting Party into which those organisms are to be introduced.

. . .

Article 22   Relationship with other International Conventions

1. The provisions of this Convention shall not affect the rights and obligations of any Contracting Party deriving from any existing international agreement, except where the exercise of those rights and obligations would cause a serious damage or threat to biological diversity.

2. Contracting Parties shall implement this Convention with respect to the marine environment consistently with the rights and obligations of States under the law of the sea.

. . .

Article 27   Settlement of disputes

1. In the event of a dispute between Contracting Parties concerning the interpretation or application of this Covention, the parties concerned shall seek solution by negotiation.

2.   If the parties concerned cannot reach agreement by negotiation, they may jointly seek the good offices of, or request mediation by, a third party.

3.   When ratifying, accepting, approving or acceding to this Convention, or at any time thereafter, a State or regional economic integration organisation may declare in writing to the Depositary that for a dispute not resolved in accordance with paragraph 1 or paragraph 2 above, it accepts one or both of the following means of dispute settlement as compulsory:

(a)   Arbitration in accordance with the procedure laid down in Part I of Annex II;

(b)   Submission of the dispute to the International Court of Justice.

4.   If the parties to the dispute have not, in accordance with paragraph 3 above, accepted the same or any procedure, the dispute shall be submitted to conciliation in accordance with Part 2 of Annex II unless the parties otherwise agree.

5.   The provisions of this Article shall apply with respect to any protocol except as otherwise provided in the protocol concerned.

. . .

Article 37   Reservations
No reservations may be made to this Convention.

. . .

AGREEMENT ON TRADE-RELATED ASPECTS OF INTELLECTUAL PROPERTY RIGHTS (TRIPS AGREEMENT) 1994

Members,

Desiring to reduce distortions and impediments to international trade, and taking into account the need to promote effective and adequate protection of intellectual property rights, and to ensure that measures and procedures to enforce intellectual property rights do not themselves become barriers to legitimate trade;

Recognising, to this end, the need for new rules and disciplines concerning:

(a)   the applicability of the basic principles of GATT 1994 and of relevant international intellectual property agreements or conventions;

(b)   the provision of adequate standards and principles concerning the availability, scope and use of trade-related intellectual property rights;

(c)   the provision of effective and appropriate means for the enforcement of trade-related intellectual property rights, taking into account differences in national legal systems;

(d)   the provision of effective and expeditious procedures for the multilateral prevention and settlement of disputes between governments; and

(e)   transitional arrangements aiming at the fullest participation in the results of the negotiations;

Recognising the need for a multilateral framework of principles, rules and disciplines dealing with international trade in counterfeit goods;

Recognising that intellectual property rights are private rights;

Recognising the underlying public policy objectives of national systems for the protection of intellectual property, including developmental and technological objectives;

Recognising also the special needs of the least-developed country Members in respect of maximum flexibility in the domestic implementation of laws and regulations in order to enable them to create a sound and viable technological base;

Emphasising the importance of reducing tensions by reaching strengthened commitments to resolve disputes on trade-related intellectual property issues through multilateral procedures;

Desiring to establish a mutually supportive relationship between the WTO and the World Intellectual Property Organisation (referred to in this Agreement as "WIPO") as well as other relevant international organisations;

Hereby agree as follows:

PART I
GENERAL PROVISIONS AND BASIC PRINCIPLES

Article 1 Nature and Scope of Obligations

1. Members shall give effect to the provisions of this Agreement. Members may, but shall not be obliged to, implement in their law more extensive protection than is required by this Agreement, provided that such protection does not contravene the provisions of this Agreement. Members shall be free to determine the appropriate method of implementing the provisions of this Agreement within their own legal system and practice.

2. For the purposes of this Agreement, the term "intellectual property" referes to all categories of intellectual property that are the subject of Sections 1 through 7 of Part II.

3. Members shall accord the treatment provided for in this Agreement to the nationals of other Members.[1] In respect of the relevant intellectual property right, the nationals of other Members shall be understood as those natural or legal persons that would meet the criteria for eligibility for protection provided for in the Paris Convention (1967), the Berne Convention (1971), the Rome Convention and the Treaty on Intellectual Property in Respect of Integrated Circuits, were all Members of the WTO members of those conventions.[2] Any Member availing itself of the possibilities provided in paragraph 3 of Article 5 or paragraph 2 of Article 6 of the Rome Convention shall make a notification as foreseen in those provisions to the Council for Trade-Related Aspects of Intellectual Property Rights (the "Council for TRIPS").

---

[1] When "nationals" are referred to in this Agreement, they shall be deemed, in the case of a separate customs territory Member of the WTO, to mean persons, natural or legal, who are domiciled or who have a real and effective industrial or commercial establishment in that customs territory.

[2] In this Agreement, "Paris Convention" refers to the Paris Convention for the Protection of Industrial Property; "Paris Convention (1967)" refers to the Stockholm Act of this Convention of 14 July 1967. "Berne Convention" refers to the Berne Convention for the Protection of Literary and Artistic Works; "Berne Convention (1971)" refers to the Paris Act of this Convention of 24 July 1971. "Rome Convention" refers to the International Convention for the Protection of Performers, Producers of Phonograms and Broadcasting Organisations, adopted at Rome on 26 October 1961. "Treaty on Intellectual Property in Respect of Integrated Circuits" (IPIC Treaty) refers to the Treaty on Intellectual Property in Respect of Integrated Circuits, adopted at Washington on 26 May 1989. "WTO Agreement" refers to the Agreement Establishing the WTO

Article 2 Intellectual Property Conventions

1. In respect of Parts II, III and IV of this Agreement, Members shall comply with Articles 1 through 12, and Article 19, of the Paris Convention (1967).

2. Nothing in Parts I to IV of this Agreement shall derogate from existing obligations that Members may have to each other under the Paris Convention, the Berne Convention, the Rome Convention and the Treaty on Intellectual Property in Respect of Integrated Circuits.

Article 3 National Treatment

1. Each Member shall accord to the nationals of other Members treatment no less favourable than that it accords to its own nationals with regard to the protection[3] of intellectual property, subject to the exceptions already provided in, respectively, the Paris Convention (1967), the Berne Convention (1971), the Rome Convention or the

Treaty on Intellectual Property in Respect of Integrated Circuits. In respect of performers, producers of phonograms and broadcasting organisations, this obligation only applies in respect of the rights provided under this Agreement. Any Member availing itself of the possibilities provided in Article 6 of the Berne Convention (1971) or paragraph 1(b) of Article 16 of the Rome Convention shall make a notification as foreseen in those provisions to the Council for TRIPS.

2.   Members may avail themselves of the exceptions permitted under paragraph 1 in relation to judicial and administrative procedures, including the designation of an address for service or the appointment of an agent within the jurisdiction of a Member, only where such exceptions are necessary to secure compliance with laws and regulations which are not inconsistent with the provisions of this Agreement and where such practices are not applied in a manner which would constitute a disguised restriction on trade.

---

[3]   For the purposes of Articles 3 and 4, "protection" shall include matters affecting the availability, acquisition, scope, maintenance and enforcement of intellectual property rights as well as those matters affecting the use of intellectual property rights specifically addressed in this Agreement.

Article 4   Most-Favoured-Nation Treatment
With regard to the protection of intellectual property, any advantage, favour, privilege or immunity granted by a Member to the nationals of any other country shall be accorded immediately and unconditionally to the nationals of all other Members. Exempted from this obligation are any advantage, favour, privilege or immunity accorded by a Member:

   (a)   deriving from international agreements on judicial assistance or law enforcement of a general nature and not particularly confined to the protection of intellectual property;

   (b)   granted in accordance with the provisions of the Berne Convention (1971) or the Rome Convention authorising that the treatment accorded be a function not of national treatment but of the treatment accorded in another country;

   (c)   in respect of the rights of performers, producers of phonograms and broadcasting organisations not provided under this Agreement;

   (d)   deriving from international agreements related to the protection of intellectual property which entered into force prior to the entry into force of the WTO Agreement, provided that such agreements are notified to the Council for TRIPS and do not constitute an arbitrary or unjustifiable discrimination against nationals of other Members.

Article 5   Multilateral Agreements on Acquisition or Maintenance of Protection
The obligations under Articles 3 and 4 do not apply to procedures provided in multilateral agreements concluded under the auspices of WIPO relating to the acquisition or maintenance of intellectual property rights.

Article 6   Exhaustion
For the purposes of dispute settlement under this Agreement, subject to the provisions of Articles 3 and 4 nothing in this Agreement shall be used to address the issue of the exhaustion of intellectual property rights.

Article 7   Objectives
The protection and enforcement of intellectual property rights should contribute to the promotion of technological innovation and to the transfer and dissemination of technology, to the mutual advantage of producers and users of technological knowledge

and in a manner conducive to social and economic welfare, and to a balance of rights and obligations.

Article 8   Principles

1.   Members may, in formulating or amending their laws and regulations, adopt measures necessary to protect public health and nutrition, and to promote the public interest in sectors of vital importance to their socio-economic and technological development, provided that such measures are consistent with the provisions of this Agreement.

2.   Appropriate measures, provided that they are consistent with the provisions of this Agreement, may be needed to prevent the abuse of intellectual property rights by right holders or the resort to practices which unreasonably restrain trade or adversely affect the international transfer of technology.

PART II
STANDARDS CONCERNING THE AVAILABILITY, SCOPE AND USE OF INTELLECTUAL PROPERTY RIGHTS

SECTION 1:   COPYRIGHT AND RELATED RIGHTS

Article 9   Relation to the Berne Convention

1.   Members shall comply with Articles 1 through 21 of the Berne Convention (1971) and the Appendix thereto. However, Members shall not have rights or obligations under this Agreement in respect of the rights conferred under Article 6bis of that Convention or of the rights derived therefrom.

2.   Copyright protection shall extend to expressions and not to ideas, procedures, methods of operation or mathematical concepts as such.

Article 10   Computer Programs and Compilations of Data

1.   Computer programs, whether in source or object code, shall be protected as literary works under the Berne Convention (1971).

2.   Compilations of data or other material, whether in machine readable or other form, which by reason of the selection or arrangement of their contents constitute intellectual creations shall be protected as such. Such protection, which shall not extend to the data or material itself, shall be without prejudice to any copyright subsisting in the data or material itself.

Article 11   Rental Rights

In respect of at least computer programs and cinematographic works, a Member shall provide authors and their successors in title the right to authorise or to prohibit the commercial rental to the public of originals or copies of their copyright works. A Member shall be excepted from this obligation in respect of cinematographic works unless such rental has led to widespread copying of such works which is materially impairing the exclusive right of reproduction conferred in that Member on authors and their successors in title. In respect of computer programs, this obligation does not apply to rentals where the program itself is not the essential object of the rental.

Article 12   Term of Protection

Whenever the term of protection of a work, other than a photographic work or a work of applied art, is calculated on a basis other than the life of a natural person, such term shall be no less than 50 years from the end of the calendar year of authorised publication, or, failing such authorised publication within 50 years from the making of the work, 50 years from the end of the calendar year of making.

Article 13   Limitations and Exceptions

Members shall confine limitations or exceptions to exclusive rights to certain special cases which do not conflict with a normal exploitation of the work and do not unreasonably prejudice the legitimate interests of the right holder.

Article 14   Protection of Performers, Producers of Phonograms (Sound Recordings) and Broadcasting Organisations

1.   In respect of a fixation of their performance on a phonogram, performers shall have the possibility of preventing the following acts when undertaken without their authorisation: the fixation of their unfixed performance and the reproduction of such fixation. Performers shall also have the possibility of preventing the following acts when undertaken without their authorisation: the broadcasting by wireless means and the communication to the public of their live performance.

2.   Producers of phonograms shall enjoy the right to authorise or prohibit the direct or indirect reproduction of their phonograms.

3.   Broadcasting organisations shall have the right to prohibit the following acts when undertaken without their authorisation: the fixation, the reproduction of fixations, and the rebroadcasting by wireless means of broadcasts, as well as the communication to the public of television broadcasts of the same. Where Members do not grant such rights to broadcasting organisations, they shall provide owners of copyright in the subject matter of broadcasts with the possibility of preventing the above acts, subject to the provisions of the Berne Convention (1971).

4.   The provisions of Article 11 in respect of computer programs shall apply *mutatis mutandis* to producers of phonograms and any other right holders in phonograms as determined in a Member's law. If on 15 April 1994 a Member has in force a system of equitable remuneration of right holders in respect of the rental of phonograms, it may maintain such system provided that the commercial rental of phonograms is not giving rise to the material impairment of the exclusive rights of reproduction of right holders.

5.   The term of the protection available under this Agreement to performers and producers of phonograms shall last at least until the end of a period of 50 years computed from the end of the calendar year in which the fixation was made or the performance took place. The term of protection granted pursuant to paragraph 3 shall last for at least 20 years from the end of the calendar year in which the broadcast took place.

6.   Any Member may, in relation to the rights conferred under paragraphs 1, 2 and 3, provide for conditions, limitations, exceptions and reservations to the extent permitted by the Rome Convention. However, the provisions of Article 18 of the Berne Convention (1971) shall also apply, *mutatis mutandis*, to the rights of performers and producers of phonograms in phonograms.

SECTION 2:   TRADEMARKS

Article 15   Protectable Subject Matter

1.   Any sign, or any combination of signs, capable of distinguishing the goods or services of one undertaking from those of other undertakings, shall be capable of constituting a trademark. Such signs, in particular words including personal names, letters, numerals, figurative elements and combinations of colours as well as any combination of such signs, shall be eligible for registration as trademarks. Where signs are not inherently capable of distinguishing the relevant goods or services, Members may make registrability depend on distinctiveness acquired through use. Members may require, as a condition of registration, that signs be visually perceptible.

2.   Paragraph 1 shall not be understood to prevent a Member from denying registration of a trademark on other grounds, provided that they do not derogate from the provisions of the Paris Convention (1967).

3.   Members may make registrability depend on use. However, actual use of a trademark shall not be a condition for filing an application for registration. An application shall not be refused solely on the ground that intended use has not taken place before the expiry of a period of three years from the date of application.

4. The nature of the goods or services to which a trademark is to be applied shall in no case form an obstacle to registration of the trademark.

5. Members shall publish each trademark either before it is registered or promptly after it is registered and shall afford a reasonable opportunity for petitions to cancel the registration. In addition, Members may afford an opportunity for the registration of a trademark to be opposed.

Article 16 Rights Conferred

1. The owner of a registered trademark shall have the exclusive right to prevent all third parties not having the owner's consent from using in the course of trade identical or similar signs for goods or services which are identical or similar to those in respect of which the trademark is registered where such use would result in a likelihood of confusion. In case of the use of an identical sign for identical goods or services, a likelihood of confusion shall be presumed. The rights described above shall not prejudice any existing prior rights, nor shall they affect the possibility of Members making rights available on the basis of use.

2. Article 6*bis* of the Paris Convention (1967) shall apply, *mutatis mutandis*, to services. In determining whether a trademark is well-known, Members shall take account of the knowledge of the trademark in the relevant sector of the public, including knowledge in the Member concerned which has been obtained as a result of the promotion of the trademark.

3. Article 6*bis* of the Paris Convention (1967) shall apply, *mutatis mutandis*, to goods or services which are not similar to those in respect of which a trademark is registered, provided that use of that trademark in relation to those goods or services would indicate a connection between those goods or services and the owner of the registered trademark and provided that the interests of the owner of the registered trademark are likely to be damaged by such use.

Article 17 Exceptions

Members may provide limited exceptions to the rights conferred by a trademark, such as fair use of descriptive terms, provided that such exceptions take account of the legitimate interests of the owner of the trademark and of third parties.

Article 18 Term of Protection

Initial registration, and each renewal of registration, of a trademark shall be for a term of no less than seven years. The registration of a trademark shall be renewable indefinitely.

Article 19 Requirement of Use

1. If use is required to maintain a registration, the registration may be cancelled only after an uninterrupted period of at least three years of non-use, unless valid reasons based on the existence of obstacles to such use are shown by the trademark owner. Circumstances arising independently of the will of the owner of the trademark which constitute an obstacle to the use of the tradmark, such as import restrictions on or other government requirements for goods or services protected by the trademark, shall be recognised as valid reasons for non-use.

2. When subject to the control of its owner, use of a trademark by another person shall be recognised as use of the trademark for the purpose of maintaining the registration.

Article 20 Other Requirements

The use of a trademark in the course of trade shall not be unjustifiably encumbered by special requirements, such as use with another trademark, use in a special form or use in a manner detrimental to its capability to distinguish the goods or services of one undertaking from those of other undertakings. This will not preclude a requirement prescribing the use of the trademark identifying the undertaking producing the goods or services along with, but without linking it to, the trademark distinguishing the specific goods or services in question of that undertaking.

Article 21   Licensing and Assignment

Members may determine conditions on the licensing and assignment of trademarks, it being understood that the compulsory licensing of trademarks shall not be permitted and that the owner of a registered trademark shall have the right to assign the trademark with or without the transfer of the business to which the trademark belongs.

SECTION 3:   GEOGRAPHICAL INDICATIONS

Article 22   Protection of Geographical Indications

1.   Geographical indications are, for the purposes of this Agreement, indications which identify a good as originating in the territory of a Member, or a region or locality in that territory, where a given quality, reputation or other characteristic of the goods is essentially attributable to its geographical origin.

2.   In respect of geographical indications, Members shall provide the legal means for interested parties to prevent:

(a)   the use of any means in the designation or presentation of a good that indicates or suggests that the good in question originates in a geographical area other than the true place of origin in a manner which misleads the public as to the geographical origin of the good;

(b)   any use which constitutes an act of unfair competition within the meaning of Article 10bis of the Paris Convention (1967).

3.   A Member shall, ex officio if its legislation so permits or at the request of an interested party, refuse or invalidate the registration of a trade mark which contains or consists of a geographical indication with respect to goods not originating in the territory indicated, if use of the indication in the trademark for such goods in that Member is of such a nature as to mislead the public as to the true place of origin.

4.   The protection under paragraphs 1, 2 and 3 shall be applicable against a geographical indication which, although literally true as to the territory, region or locality in which the goods originate, falsely represents to the public that the goods originate in another territory.

Article 23   Additional Protection for Geographical Indications for Wines and Spirits

1.   Each Member shall provide the legal means for interested parties to prevent use of a geographical indication identifying wines for wines not originating in the place indicated by the geographical indication in question or identifying spirits for spirits not originating in the place indicated by the geographical indication in question, even where the true origin of the goods is indicated or the geographical indication is used in translation or accompanied by expressions such as "kind", "types", "style", "imitation" or the like.[4]

2.   The registration of a trademark for wines which contains or consists of a geographical indication identifying wines or for spirits which contains or consists of a geographical indication identifying spirits shall be refused or invalidated, ex officio if a Member's legislation so permits or at the request of an interested party, with respect to such wines or spirits not having this origin.

3.   In the case of homonymous geographical indications for wines, protection shall be accorded to each indication, subject to the provisions of paragraph 4 of Article 22. Each Member shall determine the practical conditions under which the homonymous indications in question will be differentiated from each other, taking into account the need to ensure equitable treatment of the producers concerned and that consumers are not misled.

4. In order to facilitate the protection of geographical indications for wines, negotiations shall be undertaken in the Council for TRIPS concerning the establishment of a multilateral system of notification and registration of geographical indications for wines eligible for protection in those Members participating in the system.

---

[4] Notwithstanding the first sentence of Article 42, Members may, with respect to these obligations, instead provide for enforcement by administrative action.

Article 24   International Negotiations; Exceptions

1. Members agree to enter into negotiations aimed at increasing the protection of individual geographical indications under Article 23. The provisions of paragraphs 4 through 8 below shall not be used by a Member to refuse to conduct negotiations or to conclude bilateral or multilateral agreements. In the context of such negotiations, Members shall be willing to consider the continued applicability of these provisions to individual geographical indications whose use was the subject of such negotiations.

2. The Council for TRIPS shall keep under review the application of the provisions of this Section; the first such review shall take place within two years of the entry into force of the WTO Agreement. Any matter affecting the compliance with the obligations under these provisions may be drawn to the attention of the Council, which, at the request of a Member, shall consult with any Member or Members in respect of such matter in respect of which it has not been possible to find a satisfactory solution through bilateral or plurilateral consultations between the Members concerned. The Council shall take such action as may be agreed to facilitate the operation and further the objectives of this Section.

3. In implementing this Section, a Member shall not diminish the protection of geographical indications that existed in that Member immediately prior to the date of entry into force of the WTO Agreement.

4. Nothing in this Section shall require a Member to prevent continued and similar use of a particular geographical indication of another Member identifying wines or spirits in connection with goods or services by any of its nationals or domiciliaries who have used that geographical indication in a continuous manner with regard to the same or related goods or services in the territory of that Member either (a) for at least 10 years preceding 15 April 1994 or (b) in good faith preceding that date.

5. Where a trademark has been applied for or registered in good faith, or where rights to a trademark have been acquired through use in good faith either:

(a) before the date of application of these provisions in that Member as defined in Part VI; or

(b) before the geographical indication is protected in its country of origin;

measures adopted to implement this Section shall not prejudice eligibility for or the validity of the registration of a trademark, or the right to use a trademark, on the basis that such a trademark is identical with, or similar to, a geographical indication.

6. Nothing in this Section shall require a Member to apply its provisions in respect of a geographical indication of any other Member with respect to goods or services for which the relevant indication is identical with the term customary in common language as the common name for such goods or services in the territory of that Member. Nothing in this Section shall require a Member to apply its provisions in respect of a geographical indication of any other Member with respect to products of the vine for which the relevant indication is identical with the customary name of a grape variety existing in the territory of that Member as of the date of entry into force of the WTO Agreement.

7. A Member may provide that any request made under this Section in connection with the use or registration of a trade mark must be presented within five years after the adverse use of the protected indication has become generally known in that Member or after the date of registration of the trademark in that Member provided that the

trademark has been published by that date, if such date is earlier than the date on which the adverse use became generally known in that Member, provided that the geographical indication is not used or registered in bad faith.

8. The provisions of this Section shall in no way prejudice the right of any person to use, in the course of trade, that person's name or the name of that person's predecessor in business, except where such name is used in such a manner as to mislead the public.

9. There shall be no obligation under this Agreement to protect geographical indications which are not or cease to be protected in their country of origin, or which have fallen into disuse in that country.

SECTION 4: INDUSTRIAL DESIGNS

Article 25   Requirements for Protection

1. Members shall provide for the protection of independently created industrial designs that are new or original. Members may provide that designs are not new or original if they do not significantly differ from known designs or combinations of known design features. Members may provide that such protection shall not extend to designs dictated essentially by technical or functional considerations.

2. Each Member shall ensure that requirements for securing protection for textile designs, in particular in regard to any cost, examination or publication, do not unreasonably impair the opportunity to seek and obtain such protection. Members shall be free to meet this obligation through industrial design law or through copyright law.

Article 26   Protection

1. The owner of a protected industrial design shall have the right to prevent third parties not having the owner's consent from making, selling or importing articles bearing or embodying a design which is a copy, or substantially a copy, of the protected design, when such acts are undertaken for commercial purposes.

2. Members may provide limited exceptions to the protection of industrial designs, provided that such exceptions do not unreasonably conflict with the normal exploitation of protected industrial designs and do not unreasonably prejudice the legitimate interests of the owner of the protected design, taking account of the legitimate interests of third parties.

3. The duration of protection available shall amount to at least 10 years.

SECTION 5:   PATENTS

Article 27   Patentable Subject Matter

1. Subject to the provisions of paragraphs 2 and 3, patents shall be available for any inventions, whether products or processes, in all fields of technology, provided that they are new, involve an inventive step and are capable of industrial application.[5] Subject to paragraph 4 of Article 65, paragraph 8 of Article 70 and paragraph 3 of this Article, patents shall be available and patent rights enjoyable without discrimination as to the place of invention, the field of technology and whether products are imported or locally produced.

2. Members may exclude from patentability inventions, the prevention within their territory of the commercial exploitation of which is necessary to protect *ordre public* or morality, including to protect human, animal or plant life or health or to avoid serious prejudice to the environment, provided that such exclusion is not made merely because the exploitation is prohibited by their law.

3. Members may also exclude from patentability:

---

[5] For the purposes of this Article, the terms "inventive step" and "capable of industrial application" may be deemed by a Member to be synonymous with the terms "non-obvious" and "useful" respectively.

(a) diagnostic, therapeutic and surgical methods for the treatment of humans or animals;

(b) plants and animals other than micro-organisms, and essentially biological processes for the production of plants or animals other than non-biological and microbiological processes. However, Members shall provide for the protection of plant varieties either by patents or by an effective *sui generis* system or by any combination thereof. The provisions of this subparagraph shall be reviewed four years after the date of entry into force of the WTO Agreement.

Article 28 Rights Conferred

1. A patent shall confer on its owner the following exclusive rights:

(a) where the subject matter of a patent is a product, to prevent third parties not having the owner's consent from the acts of: making, using, offering for sale, selling, or importing[6] for these purposes that product;

(b) where the subject matter of a patent is a process, to prevent third parties not having the owner's consent from the act of using the process, and from the acts of: using, offering for sale, selling, or importing for these purposes at least the product obtained directly by that process.

2. Patent owners shall also have the right to assign, or transfer by succession, the patent and to conclude licensing contracts.

---

[6] This right, like all other rights conferred under this Agreement in respect of the use, sale, importation or other distribution of goods, is subject to the provisions of Article 6.

Article 29 Conditions on Patent Applicants

1. Members shall require that an applicant for a patent shall disclose the invention in a manner sufficiently clear and complete for the invention to be carried out by a person skilled in the art and may require the applicant to indicate the best mode for carrying out the invention known to the inventor at the filing date or, where priority is claimed, at the priority date of the application.

2. Members may require an applicant for a patent to provide information concerning the applicant's corresponding foreign applications and grants.

Article 30 Exceptions to Rights Conferred

Members may provide limited exceptions to the exclusive rights conferred by a patent, provided that such exceptions do not unreasonably conflict with a normal exploitation of the patent and do not unreasonably prejudice the legitimate interests of the patent owner, taking account of the legitimate interests of third parties.

Article 31 Other Use Without Authorisation of the Right Holder

Where the law of a Member allows for other use[7] of the subject matter of a patent without the authorisation of the right holder, including use by the government or third parties authorised by the government, the following provisions shall be respected:

(a) authorisation of such use shall be considered on its individual merits;

(b) such use may only be permitted if, prior to such use, the proposed user has made efforts to obtain authorisation from the right holder on reasonable commercial terms and conditions and that such efforts have not been successful within a reasonable period of time. This requirement may be waived by a Member in the case of a national emergency or other circumstances of extreme urgency or in cases of public non-commercial use. In situations of national emergency or other circumstances of extreme urgency, the right holder shall, nevertheless, be notified as soon as reasonably practicable. In the case of public non-commercial use, where the government or contractor, without making a patent search, knows or has demonstrable grounds to know that a valid patent is or will be used by or for the government, the right holder shall be informed promptly;

(c)   the scope and duration of such use shall be limited to the purpose for which it was authorised, and in the case of semi-conductor technology shall only be for public non-conmercial use or to remedy a practice determined after judicial or administrative process to be anti-competitive;

(d)   such use shall be non-exclusive;

(e)   such use shall be non-assignable, except with that part of the enterprise or goodwill which enjoys such use;

(f)   any such use shall be authorised predominantly for the supply of the domestic market of the Member authorising such use;

(g)   authorisation for such use shall be liable, subject to adequate protection of the legitimate interests of the persons so authorised, to be terminated if and when the circumstances which led to it cease to exist and are unlikely to recur. The competent authority shall have the authority to review, upon motivated request, the continued existence of these circumstances;

(h)   the right holder shall be paid adequate remuneration in the circumstances of each case, taking into account the economic value of the authorisation;

(i)   the legal validity of any decision relating to the authorisation of such use shall be subject to judicial review or other independent review by a distinct higher authority in that Member;

(j)   any decision relating to the remuneration provided in respect of such use shall be subject to judicial review or other independent review by a distinct higher authority in that Member;

(k)   Members are not obliged to apply the conditions set forth in subparagraphs (b) and (f) where such use is permitted to remedy a practice determined after judicial or administrative process to be anti-competitive. The need to correct anti-competitive practices may be taken into account in determining the amount of remuneration in such cases. Competent authorities shall have the authority to refuse termination of authorisation if and when the conditions which led to such authorisation are likely to recur;

(l)   where such use is authorised to permit the exploitation of a patent ("the second patent") which cannot be exploited without infringing another patent ("the first patent"), the following additional conditions shall apply:

(i)   the invention claimed in the second patent shall involve an important technical advance of considerable economic significance in relation to the invention claimed in the first patent;

(ii)   the owner of the first patent shall be entitled to a cross-licence on reasonable terms to use the invention claimed in the second patent; and

(iii)   the use authorised in respect of the first patent shall be non-assignable except with the assignment of the second patent.

---

[7]   "Other use" refers to use other than that allowed under Article 30.

Article 32   Revocation/Forfeiture
An opportunity for judicial review of any decision to revoke or forfeit a patent shall be available.

Article 33   Term of Protection
The term of protection available shall not end before the expiration of a period of twenty years counted from the filing date.[8]

---

[8]   It is understood that those Members which do not have a system of original grant may provide that the term of protection shall be computed from the filing date in the system of original grant.

Article 34 Process Patents: Burden of Proof

1. For the purposes of civil proceedings in respect of the infringement of the rights of the owner referred to in paragraph 1(b) of Article 28, if the subject matter of a patent is a process for obtaining a product, the judicial authorities shall have the authority to order the defendant to prove that the process to obtain an identical product is different from the patented process. Therefore, Members shall provide, in at least one of the following circumstances, that any identical product when produced without the consent of the patent owner shall, in the absence of proof to the contrary, be deemed to have been obtained by the patented process:

(a)   if the product obtained by the patented process is new;

(b)   if there is a substantial likelihood that the identical product was made by the process and the owner of the patent has been unable through reasonable efforts to determine the process actually used.

2. Any Member shall be free to provide that the burden of proof indicated in paragraph 1 shall be on the alleged infringer only if the condition referred to in subparagraph (a) is fulfilled or only if the condition referred to in subparagraph (b) is fulfilled.

3. In the adduction of proof to the contrary, the legitimate interests of defendants in protecting their manufacturing and business secrets shall be taken into account.

SECTION 6:   LAYOUT-DESIGNS (TOPOGRAPHIES) OF INTEGRATED CIRCUITS

Article 35 Relation to the IPIC Treaty

Members agree to provide protection to the layout-designs (topographies) of integrated circuits (referred to in this Agreement as "layout-designs") in accordance with Articles 2 through 7 (other than paragraph 3 of Article 6), Article 12 and paragraph 3 of Article 16 of the Treaty on Intellectual Property in Respect of Integrated Circuits and, in addition, to comply with the following provisions.

Article 36 Scope of the Protection

Subject to the provisions of paragraph 1 of Article 37, Members shall consider unlawful the following acts if performed without the authorisation of the right holder:[9] importing, selling, or otherwise distributing for commercial purposes a protected layout-design, an integrated circuit in which a protected layout-design is incorporated, or an article incorporating such an integrated circuit only in so far as it continues to contain an unlawfully reproduced layout-design.

---

[9]   The term "right holder" in this Section shall be understood as having the same meaning as the term "holder of the right" in the IPIC Treaty.

Article 37 Acts Not Requiring the Authorisation of the Right Holder

1. Notwithstanding Article 36, no Member shall consider unlawful the performance of any of the acts referred to in that Article in respect of an integrated circuit incorporating an unlawfully reproduced layout-design or any article incorporating such an integrated circuit where the person performing or ordering such acts did not know and had no reasonable ground to know, when acquiring the integrated circuit or article incorporating such an integrated circuit, that it incorporated an unlawfully reproduced layout-design. Members shall provide that, after the time that such person has received sufficient notice that the layout-design was unlawfully reproduced, that person may perform any of the acts with respect to the stock on hand or ordered before such time, but shall be liable to pay to the right holder a sum equivalent to a reasonable royalty such as would be payable under a freely negotiated licence in respect of such a layout-design.

2.   The conditions set out in subparagraphs (a) through (k) of Article 31 shall apply *mutatis mutandis* in the event of any non-voluntary licensing of a layout-design or of its use by or for the government without the authorisation of the right holder.

Article 38   Term of Protection

1.   In Members requiring registration as a condition of protection, the term of protection of layout-designs shall not end before the expiration of a period of 10 years counted from the date of filing an application for registration or from the first commercial exploitation wherever in the world it occurs.

2.   In Members not requiring registration as a condition for protection, layout-designs shall be protected for a term of no less than 10 years from the date of the first commercial exploitation wherever in the world it occurs.

3.   Notwithstanding paragraphs 1 and 2, a Member may provide that protection shall lapse 15 years after the creation of the layout-design.

SECTION 7:   PROTECTION OF UNDISCLOSED INFORMATION

Article 39

1.   In the course of ensuring effective protection against unfair competition as provided in Article 10*bis* of the Paris Convention (1967), Members shall protect undisclosed information in accordance with paragraph 2 and data submitted to governments or governmental agencies in accordance with paragraph 3.

2.   Natural and legal persons shall have the possibility of preventing information lawfully within their control from being disclosed to, acquired by, or used by others without their consent in a manner contrary to honest commercial practices[10] so long as such information:

(a)   is secret in the sense that it is not, as a body or in the precise configuration and assembly of its components, generally known among or readily accessible to persons within the circles that normally deal with the kind of information in question;

(b)   has commercial value because it is secret; and

(c)   has been subject to reasonable steps under the circumstances, by the person lawfully in control of the information, to keep it secret.

3.   Members, when requiring, as a condition of approving the marketing of pharmaceutical or of agricultural chemical products which utilise new chemical entities, the submission of undisclosed test or other data, the origination of which involves a considerable effort, shall protect such data against unfair commercial use. In addition, Members shall protect such data against disclosure, except where necessary to protect the public, or unless steps are taken to ensure that the data are protected against unfair commercial use.

---

[10]   For the purpose of this provision, "a manner contrary to honest commercial practices" shall mean at least practices such as breach of contract, breach of confidence and inducement to breach, and includes the acquisition of undisclosed information by third parties who knew, or were grossly negligent in failing to know, that such practices were involved in the acquisition.

SECTION 8   CONTROL OF ANTI-COMPETITIVE PRACTICES IN CONTRACTUAL LICENCES

Article 40

1.   Members agree that some licensing practices or conditions pertaining to intellectual property rights which restrain competition may have adverse effects on trade and may impede the transfer and dissemination of technology.

2.   Nothing in this Agreement shall prevent Members from specifying in their legislation licensing practices or conditions that may in particular cases constitute an abuse of intellectual property rights having an adverse effect on competition in the

relevant market. As provided above, a Member may adopt, consistently with the other provisions of this Agreement, appropriate measures to prevent or control such practices, which may include for example exclusive grantback conditions, conditions preventing challenges to validity and coercive package licensing, in the light of the relevant laws and regulations of that Member.

3. Each Member shall enter, upon request, into consultations with any other Member which has cause to believe that an intellectual property right owner that is a national or domiciliary of the Member to which the request for consultations has been addressed is undertaking practices in violation of the requesting Member's laws and regulations on the subject matter of this Section, and which wishes to secure compliance with such legislation, without prejudice to any action under the law and to the full freedom of an ultimate decision of either Member. The Member addressed shall accord full and sympathetic consideration to, and shall afford adequate opportunity for, consultations with the requesting Member, and shall cooperate through supply of publicly available non-confidential information of relevance to the matter in question and of other information available to the Member, subject to domestic law and to the conclusion of mutually satisfactory agreements concerning the safeguarding of its confidentiality by the requesting Member.

4. A Member whose nationals or domiciliaries are subject to proceedings in another Member concerning alleged violation of that other Member's laws and regulations on the subject matter of this Section shall, upon request, be granted an opportunity for consultations by the other Member under the same conditions as those foreseen in paragraph 3.

PART III
ENFORCEMENT OF INTELLECTUAL PROPERTY RIGHTS

SECTION 1: GENERAL OBLIGATIONS

Article 41

1. Members shall ensure that enforcement procedures as specified in this Part are available under their law so as to permit effective action against any act of infringement of intellectual property rights covered by this Agreement, including expeditious remedies to prevent infringements and remedies which constitute a deterrent to further infringements. These procedures shall be applied in such a manner as to avoid the creation of barriers to legitimate trade and to provide for safeguards against their abuse.

2. Procedures concerning the enforcement of intellectual property rights shall be fair and equitable. They shall not be unnecessarily complicated or costly, or entail unreasonable time-limits or unwarranted delays.

3. Decisions on the merits of a case shall preferably be in writing and reasoned. They shall be made available at least to the parties to the proceeding without undue delay. Decisions on the merits of a case shall be based only on evidence in respect of which parties were offered the opportunity to be heard.

4. Parties to a proceeding shall have an opportunity for review by a judicial authority of final administrative decisions and, subject to jurisdictional provisions in a Member's law concerning the importance of a case, of at least the legal aspects of initial judicial decisions on the merits of a case. However, there shall be no obligation to provide an opportunity for review of acquittals in criminal cases.

5. It is understood that this Part does not create any obligation to put in place a judicial system for the enforcement of intellectual property rights distinct from that for the enforcement of law in general, nor does it affect the capacity of Members to enforce their law in general. Nothing in this Part creates any obligation with respect to the distribution of resources as between enforcement of intellectual property rights and the enforcement of law in general.

SECTION 2: CIVIL AND ADMINISTRATIVE PROCEDURES AND REMEDIES

Article 42   Fair and Equitable Procedures

Members shall make available to right holders[11] civil judicial procedures concerning the enforcement of any intellectual property right covered by this Agreement. Defendants shall have the right to written notice which is timely and contains sufficient detail, including the basis of the claims. Parties shall be allowed to be represented by independent legal counsel, and procedures shall not impose overly burdensome requirements concerning mandatory personal appearances. All parties to such procedures shall be duly entitled to substantiate their claims and to present all relevant evidence. The procedure shall provide a means to identify and protect confidential information, unless this would be contrary to existing constitutional requirements.

---

[11] For the purpose of this Part, the term "right holder" includes federations and associations having legal standing to assert such rights.

Article 43   Evidence

1.   The judicial authorities shall have the authority, where a party has presented reasonably available evidence sufficient to support its claims and has specified evidence relevant to substantiation of its claims which lies in the control of the opposing party, to order that this evidence be produced by the opposing party, subject in appropriate cases to conditions which ensure the protection of confidential information.

2.   In cases in which a party to a proceeding voluntarily and without good reason refuses access to, or otherwise does not provide necessary information within a reasonable period, or significantly impedes a procedure relating to an enforcement action, a Member may accord judicial authorities the authority to make preliminary and final determinations, affirmative or negative, on the basis of the information presented to them, including the complaint or the allegation presented by the party adversely affected by the denial of access to information, subject to providing the parties an opportunity to be heard on the allegations or evidence.

Article 44   Injunctions

1.   The judicial authorities shall have the authority to order a party to desist from an infringement, *inler alia* to prevent the entry into the channels of commerce in their jurisdiction of imported goods that involve the infringement of an intellectual property right, immediately after customs clearance of such goods. Members are not obliged to accord such authority in respect of protected subject matter acquired or ordered by a person prior to knowing or having reasonable grounds to know that dealing in such subject matter would entail the infringement of an intellectual property right.

2.   Notwithstanding the other provisions of this Part and provided that the provisions of Part II specifically addressing use by governments, or by third parties authorised by a government, without the authorisation of the right holder are complied with, Members may limit the remedies available against such use to payment of remuneration in accordance with subparagraph (h) of Article 31. In other cases, the remedies under this Part shall apply or, where these remedies are inconsistent with a Member's law, declaratory judgments and adequate compensation shall be available.

Article 45   Damages

1.   The judicial authorities shall have the authority to order the infringer to pay the right holder damages adequate to compensate for the injury the right holder has suffered because of an infringement of that person's intellectual property right by an infringer who knowingly, or with reasonable grounds to know, engaged in infringing activity.

2.   The judicial authorities shall also have the authority to order the infringer to pay the right holder expenses, which may include appropriate attorney's fees. In appropriate

cases, Members may authorise the judicial authorities to order recovery of profits and/or payment of pre-established damages even where the infringer did not knowingly, or with reasonable grounds to know, engage in infringing activity.

Article 46   Other Remedies

In order to create an effective deterrent to infringement, the judicial authorities shall have the authority to order that goods that they have found to be infringing be, without compensation of any sort, disposed of outside the channels of commerce in such a manner as to avoid any harm caused to the right holder, or, unless this would be contrary to existing constitutional requirements, destroyed. The judicial authorities shall also have the authority to order that materials and implements the predominant use of which has been in the creation of the infringing goods be, without compensation of any sort, disposed of outside the channels of commerce in such a manner as to minimise the risks of further infringements. In considering such requests, the need for proportionality between the seriousness of the infringement and the remedies ordered as well as the interests of third parties shall be taken into account. In regard to counterfeit trademark goods, the simple removal of the trademark unlawfully affixed shall not be sufficient, other than in exceptional cases, to permit release of the goods into the channels of commerce.

Article 47   Right of Information

Members may provide that the judicial authorities shall have the authority, unless this would be out of proportion to the seriousness of the infringement, to order the infringer to inform the right holder of the identity of third persons involved in the production and distribution of the infringing goods or services and of their channels of distribution.

Article 48   Indemnification of the Defendant

1.   The judicial authorities shall have the authority to order a party at whose request measures were taken and who has abused enforcement procedures to provide to a party wrongfully enjoined or restrained adequate compensation for the injury suffered because of such abuse. The judicial authorities shall also have the authority to order the applicant to pay the defendant expenses, which may include appropriate attorney's fees.

2.   In respect of the administration of any law pertaining to the protection or enforcement of intellectual property rights, Members shall only exempt both public authorities and officials from liability to appropriate remedial measures where actions are taken or intended in good faith in the course of the administration of that law.

Article 49   Administrative Procedures

To the extent that any civil remedy can be ordered as a result of administrative procedures on the merits of a case, such procedures shall conform to principles equivalent in substance to those set forth in this Section.

SECTION 3: PROVISIONAL MEASURES

Article 50

1.   The judicial authorities shall have the authority to order prompt and effective provisional measures:

(a)   to prevent an infringement of any intellectual property right from occurring, and in particular to prevent the entry into the channels of commerce in their jurisdiction of goods, including imported goods immediately after customs clearance;

(b)   to preserve relevant evidence in regard to the alleged infringement.

2.   The judicial authorities shall have the authority to adopt provisional measures *inaudita altera parte* where appropriate, in particular where any delay is likely to cause irreparable harm to the right holder, or where there is a demonstrable risk of evidence being destroyed.

3.   The judicial authorities shall have the authority to require the applicant to provide any reasonably available evidence in order to satisfy themselves with a sufficient degree of certainty that the applicant is the right holder and that the applicant's right is being infringed or that such infringement is imminent, and to order the applicant to provide a security or equivalent assurance sufficient to protect the defendant and to prevent abuse.

4.   Where provisional measures have been adopted *inaudita altera parte*, the parties affected shall be given notice, without delay after the execution of the measures at the latest. A review, including a right to be heard, shall take place upon request of the defendant with a view to deciding, within a reasonable period after the notification of the measures, whether these measures shall be modified, revoked or confirmed.

5.   The applicant may be required to supply other information necessary for the identification of the goods concerned by the authority that will execute the provisional measures.

6.   Without prejudice to paragraph 4, provisional measures taken on the basis of paragraphs 1 and 2 shall, upon request by the defendant, be revoked or otherwise cease to have effect, if proceedings leading to a decision on the merits of the case are not initiated within a reasonable period, to be determined by the judicial authority ordering the measures where a Member's law so permits or, in the absence of such a determination, not to exceed 20 working days or 31 calendar days, whichever is the longer.

7.   Where the provisional measures are revoked or where they lapse due to any act or omission by the applicant, or where it is subsequently found that there has been no infringement or threat of infringement of an intellectual property right, the judicial authorities shall have the authority to order the applicant, upon request of the defendant, to provide the defendant appropriate compensation for any injury caused by these measures.

8.   To the extent that any provisional measure can be ordered as a result of administrative procedures, such procedures shall conform to principles equivalent in substance to those set forth in this Section.

SECTION 4: SPECIAL REQUIREMENTS RELATED TO BORDER MEASURES[12]

Article 51   Suspension of Release by Customs Authorities
Members shall, in conformity with the provisions set out below, adopt procedures[13] to enable a right holder, who has valid grounds for suspecting that the importation of counterfeit trademark or pirated coyright goods[14] may take place, to lodge an application in writing with competent authorities, administrative or judicial, for the suspension by the customs authorities of the release into free circulation of such goods. Members may enable such an application to be made in respect of goods which involve other infringements of intellectual property rights, provided that the requirements of this Section are met. Members may also provide for corresponding procedures concerning the suspension by the customs authorities of the release of infringing goods destined for exportation from their territories.

---

[12] Where a Member has dismantled substantially all controls over movement of goods across its border with another Member with which it forms part of a customs union, it shall not be required to apply the provisions of this Section at that border.

[13] It is understood that there shall be no obligation to apply such procedures to imports of goods put on the market in another country by or with the consent of the right holder, or to goods in transit.

[14] For the purposes of this Agreement:

(a) "counterfeit trademark goods" shall mean any goods, including packiaging, bearing without authorisation a trademark which is identical to the trademark validly registered in respect of such goods, or which cannot be distinguished in its essential aspects from such a trademark, and which thereby infringes the rights of the owner of the trademark in question under the law of the country of importation;

(b) "pirated copyright goods" shall mean any goods which are copies made without the consent of the right holder or person duly authorised by the right holder in the country of production and which are made directly or indirectly from an article where the making of that copy would have constituted an infringement of a copyright or a related right under the law of the country of importation.

Article 52   Application

Any right holder initiating the procedures under Article 51 shall be required to provide adequate evidence to satisfy the competent authorities that, under the laws of the country of importation, there is *prima facie* an infringement of the right holder's intellectual property right and to supply a sufficiently detailed description of the goods to make them readily recognisable by the customs authorities. The competent authorities shall inform the applicant within a reasonable period whether they have accepted the application and, where determined by the competent authorities, the period for which the customs authorities will take action.

Article 53   Security or Equivalent Assurance

1.   The competent authorities shall have the authority to require an applicant to provide a security or equivalent assurance sufficient to protect the defendant and the competent authorities and to prevent abuse. Such security or equivalent assurance shall not unreasonably deter recourse to these procedures.

2.   Where pursuant to an application under this Section the release of goods involving industrial designs, patents, layout-designs or undisclosed information into free circulation has been suspended by customs authorities on the basis of a decision other than by a judicial or other independent authority, and the period provided for in Article 55 has expired without the granting of provisional relief by the duly empowered authority, and provided that all other conditions for importation have been complied with, the owner, importer, or consignee of such goods shall be entitled to their release on the posting of a security in an amount sufficient to protect the right holder for any infringement. Payment of such security shall not prejudice any other remedy available to the right holder, it being understood that the security shall be released if the right holder fails to pursue the right of action within a reasonable period of time.

Article 54   Notice of Suspension

The importer and the applicant shall be promptly notified of the suspension of the release of goods according to Article 51.

Article 55   Duration of suspension

If, within a period not exceeding 10 working days after the applicant has been served notice of the suspension, the customs authorities have not been informed that proceedings leading to a decision on the merits of the case have been initiated by a party other than the defendant, or that the duly empowered authority has taken provisional measures prolonging the suspension of the release of the goods, the goods shall be released, provided that all other conditions for importation or exportation have been complied with; in appropriate cases, this time-limit may be extended by another 10 working days. If proceedings leading to a decision on the merits of the case have been initiated, a review, including a right to be heard, shall take place upon request of the defendant with a view to deciding, within a reasonable period, whether these measures shall be modified, revoked or confirmed. Notwithstanding the above, where the suspension of the release of goods is carried out or continued in accordance with a provisional judicial measure, the provisions of paragraph 6 of Article 50 shall apply.

Article 56   Indemnification of the Importer and of the Owner of the Goods
Relevant authorities shall have the authority to order the applicant to pay the importer, the consignee and the owner of the goods appropriate compensation for any injury caused to them through the wrongful detention of goods or through the detention of goods released pursuant to Article 55.

Article 57   Right of Inspection and Information
Without prejudice to the protection of confidential information, Members shall provide the competent authorities the authority to give the right holder sufficient opportunity to have any goods detained by the customs authorities inspected in order to substantiate the right holder's claims. The competent authorities shall also have authority to give the importer an equivalent opportunity to have any such goods inspected. Where a positive determination has been made on the merits of a case, Members may provide the competent authorities the authority to inform the right holder of the names and addresses of the consignor, the importer and the consignee and of the quantity of the goods in question.

Article 58   Ex Officio Action
Where Members require competent authorities to act upon their own initiative and to suspend the release of goods in respect of which they have acquired *prima facie* evidence that an intellectual property right is being infringed:
    (a)   the competent authorities may at any time seek from the right holder any information that may assist them to exercise these powers;
    (b)   the importer and the right holder shall be promptly notified of the suspension. Where the importer has lodged an appeal against the suspension with the competent authorities, the suspension shall be subject to the conditions, *mutatis mutandis*, set out at Article 55;
    (c)   Members shall only exempt both public authorities and officials from liability to appropriate remedial measures where actions are taken or intended in good faith.

Article 59   Remedies
Without prejudice to other rights of action open to the right holder and subject to the right of the defendant to seek review by a judicial authority, competent authorities shall have the authority to order the destruction or disposal of infringing goods in accordance with the principles set out in Article 46. In regard to counterfeit trademark goods, the authorities shall not allow the re-exportation of the infringing goods in an unaltered state or subject them to a different customs procedure, other than in exceptional circumstances.

Article 60   *De Minimis* Imports
Members may exclude from the application of the above provisions small quantities of goods of a non-commercial nature contained in travellers' personal luggage or sent in small consignments.

SECTION 5: CRIMINAL PROCEDURES

Article 61
Members shall provide for criminal procedures and penalties to be applied at least in cases of wilful trademark counterfeiting or copyright piracy on a commercial scale. Remedies available shall include imprisonment and/or monetary fines sufficient to provide a deterrent, consistently with the level of penalties applied for crimes of a corresponding gravity. In appropriate cases, remedies available shall also include the seizure, forfeiture and destruction of the infringing goods and of any materials and implements the predominant use of which has been in the commission of the offence. Members may provide for criminal procedures and penalties to be applied in other cases of infringement of intellectual property rights, in particular where they are committed wilfully and on a commercial scale.

PART IV
ACQUISITION AND MAINTENANCE OF INTELLECTUAL PROPERTY
RIGHTS AND RELATED *INTER-PARTIES* PROCEDURES

Article 62
1.   Members may require, as a condition of the acquisition or maintenance of the intellectual property rights provided for under Sections 2 through 6 of Part II, compliance with reasonable procedures and formalities. Such procedures and formalities. Such procedures and formalities shall be consistent with the provisions of this Agreement.
2.   Where the acquisition of an intellectual property right is subject to the right being granted or registered, Members shall ensure that the procedures for grant or registration, subject to compliance with the substantive conditions for acquisition of the right, permit the granting or registration of the right within a reasonable period of time so as to avoid unwarranted curtailment of the period of protection.
3.   Article 4 of the Paris Convention (1967) shall apply *mutatis mutandis* to service marks.
4.   Procedures concerning the acquisition or maintenance of intellectual property rights and, where a Member's law provides for such procedures, administrative revocation and *inter partes* procedures such as opposition, revocation and cancellation, shall be governed by the general principles set out in paragraphs 2 and 3 of Article 41.
5.   Final administrative decisions in any of the procedures referred to under paragraph 4 shall be subject to review by a judicial or quasi-judicial authority. However, there shall be no obligation to provide an opportunity for such review of decisions in cases of unsuccessful opposition or administrative revocation, provided that the grounds for such procedures can be the subject of invalidation procedures.

PART V
DISPUTE PREVENTION AND SETTLEMENT

Article 63   Transparency
1.   Laws and regulations, and final judicial decisions and administrative rulings of general application , made effective by a Member pertaining to the subject matter of this Agreement (the availability, scope, acquisition, enforcement and prevention of the abuse of intellectual property rights) shall be published, or where such publication is not practicable made publicly available, in a national language, in such a manner as to enable governments and right holders to become acquainted with them. Agreements concerning the subject matter of this Agreement which are in force between the government or a governmental agency of a Member and the government or governmental agency of another Member shall also be published.
2.   Members shall notify the laws and regulations referred to in paragraph 1 to the Council for TRIPS in order to assist that Council in its review of the operation of this Agreement. The Council shall attempt to minimise the burden on Members in carrying out this obligation and may decide to waive the obligation to notify such laws and regulations directly to the Council if consultations with WIPO on the establishment of a common register containing these laws and regulations are successful. The Council shall also consider in this connection any action required regarding notifications pursuant to the obligations under this Agreement stemming from the provisions of Article 6*ter* of the Paris Convention (1967).
3.   Each Member shall be prepared to supply, in response to a written request from another Member, information of the sort referred to in paragraph 1. A Member, having reason to believe that a specific juicial decision or administrative ruling or bilateral agreement in the area of intellectual property rights affects its rights under this

Agreement, may also request in writing to be given access to or be informed in sufficient detail of such specific judicial decisions or administrative rulings or bilateral agreements.

4.   Nothing in paragraphs 1, 2 and 3 shall require Members to disclose confidential information which would impede law enforcement or otherwise be contrary to the public interest or would prejudice the legitimate commercial interests of particular enterprises, public or private.

Article 64   Dispute Settlement

1.   The provisions of Articles XXII and XXIII of GATT 1994 as elaborated and applied by the Dispute Settlement Understanding shall apply to consultations and the settlement of disputes under this Agreement except as otherwise specifically provided herein.

2.   Subparagraphs 1(b) and 1(c) of Article XXIII of GATT 1994 shall not apply to the settlement of disputes under this Agreement for a period of five years from the date of entry into force of the WTO Agreement.

3.   During the time period referred to in paragraph 2, the Council for TRIPS shall examine the scope and modalities for complaints of the type provided for under subparagraphs 1(b) and 1(c) of Article XXIII of GATT 1994 made pursuant to this Agreement, and submit its recommendations to the Ministerial Conference for approval. Any decision of the Ministerial Conference to approve such recommen-dations or to extend the period in paragraph 2 shall be made only by consensus, and approved recommendations shall be effective for all Members without further formal acceptance process.

PART VI

TRANSITIONAL ARRANGEMENTS

Article 65   Transitional Arrangements

1.   Subject to the provisions of paragraphs 2, 3 and 4, no Member shall be obliged to apply the provisions of this Agreement before the expiry of a general period of one year following the date of entry into force of the WTO Agreement.

2.   A developing country Member is entitled to delay for a further period of four years the date of application, as defined in paragraph 1, of the provisions of this Agreement other than Articles 3, 4 and 5.

3.   Any other Member which is in the process of transformation from a centrally-planned into a market, free-enterprise economy and which is undertaking structural reform of its intellectual property system and facing special problems in the preparation and implementation of intellectual property laws and regulations, may also benefit from a period of delay as foreseen in paragraph 2.

4.   To the extent that a developing country Member is obliged by this Agreement to extend product patent protection to areas of technology not so protectable in its territory on the general date of application of this Agreement for that Member, as defined in paragraph 2, it may delay the application of the provisions on product patents of Section 5 of Part II to such areas of technology for an additional period of five years.

5.   A Member availing itself of a transitional period under paragraphs 1, 2, 3 or 4 shall ensure that any changes in its laws, regulations and practice made during that period do not result in a lesser degree of consistency with the provisions of this Agreement.

Article 66   Least-Developed Country Members

1.   In view of the special needs and requirements of least-developed country Members, their economic, financial and administrative constraints, and their need for flexibility to create a viable technological base, such Members shall not be required to apply the provisions of this Agreement, other than Articles 3, 4 and 5, for a period of 10 years from the date of application as defined under paragraph 1 of Article 65. The

Council for TRIPS shall, upon duly motivated request by a least-developed country Member, accord extensions of this period.

2.   Developed country Members shall provide incentives to enterprises and institutions in their territories for the purpose of promoting and encouraging technology transfer to least-developed country Members in order to enable them to create a sound and viable technological base.

Article 67   Technical Cooperation
In order to facilitate the implementation of this Agreement, developed country members shall provide, on request and on mutually agreed terms and conditions, technical and financial cooperation in favour of developing and least-developed country Members. Such cooperation shall include assistance in the preparation of laws and regulations on the protection and enforcement of intellectual property rights as well as on the prevention of their abuse, and shall include support regarding the establishment or reinforcement of domestic offices and agencies relevant to these matters, including the training of personnel.

PART VII
INSTITUTIONAL ARRANGEMENTS; FINAL PROVISIONS

Article 68   Council for Trade-Related Aspects of Intellectual Property Rights
The Council for TRIPS shall monitor the operation of this Agreement and, in particular, Members' compliance with their obligations hereunder, and shall afford Members the opportunity of consulting on matters relating to the trade-related aspects of intellectual property rights. It shall carry out such other responsibilities as assigned to it by the Members, and it shall, in particular, provide any assistance requested by them in the context of dispute settlement procedures. In carrying out its functions, the Council for TRIPS may consult with and seek information from any source it deems appropriate. In consultation with WIPO, the Council shall seek to establish, within one year of its first meeting, appropriate arrangements for cooperation with bodies of that Organisation.

Article 69   International Cooperation
Members agree to cooperate with each other with a view to eliminating international trade in goods infringing intellectual property rights. For this purpose, they shall establish and notify contact points in their administrations and be ready to exchange information on trade in infringing goods. They shall, in particular, promote the exchange of information and cooperation between customs authorities with regard to trade in counterfeit trademark goods and pirated copyright goods.

Article 70   Protection of Existing Subject Matter
1.   This Agreement does not give rise to obligations in respect of acts which occurred before the date of application of the Agreement for the Member in question.

2.   Except as otherwise provided for in this Agreement, this Agreement gives rise to obligations in respect of all subject matter existing at the date of application of this Agreement for the Member in question, and which is protected in that Member on the said date, or which meets or comes subsequently to meet the criteria for protection under the terms of this Agreement. In respect of this paragraph and paragraphs 3 and 4, copyright obligations with respect to existing works shall be solely determined under Article 18 of the Berne Convention (1971), and obligations with respect to the rights of producers of phonograms and performers in existing phonograms shall be determined solely under Article 18 of the Berne Convention (1971) as made applicable under paragraph 6 of Article 14 of this Agreement.

3.   There shall be no obligation to restore protection to subject matter which on the date of application of this Agreement for the Member in question has fallen into the public domain.

4.   In respect of any acts in respect of specific objects embodying protected subject matter which become infringing under the terms of legislation in conformity with this Agreement, and which were commenced, or in respect of which a significant investment was made, before the date of acceptance of the WTO Agreement by that Member, any Member may provide for a limitation of the remedies available to the right holder as to the continued performance of such acts after the date of application of this Agreement for that Member. In such cases the Member shall, however, at least provide for the payment of equitable remuneration.

5.   A Member is not obliged to apply the provisions of Article 11 and of paragraph 4 of Article 14 with respect to originals or copies purchased prior to the date of application of this Agreement for that Member.

6.   Members shall not be required to apply Article 31, or the requirement in paragraph 1 of Article 27 that patent rights shall be enjoyable without discrimination as to the field of technology, to use without the authorisation of the right holder where authorisation for such use was granted by the government before the date this Agreement became known.

7.   In the case of intellectual property rights for which protection is conditional upon registration, applications for protection which are pending on the date of application of this Agreement for the Member in question shall be permitted to be amended to claim any enhanced protection provided under the provisions of this Agreement. Such amendments shall not include new matter.

8.   Where a Member does not make available as of the date of entry into force of the WTO Agreement patent protection for pharmaceutical and agricultural chemical products commensurate with its obligations under Article 27, that Member shall:

(a)   notwithstanding the provisions of Part VI, provide as from the date of entry into force of the WTO Agreement a means by which applications for patents for such inventions can be filed;

(b)   apply to these applications, as of the date of application of this Agreement, the criteria for patentability as laid down in this Agreement as if those criteria were being applied on the date of filing in that Member or, where priority is available and claimed, the priority date of the application; and

(c)   provide patent protection in accordance with this Agreement as from the grant of the patent and for the remainder of the patent term, counted from the filing date in accordance with Article 33 of this Agreement, for those of these applications that meet the criteria for protection referred to in subparagraph (b).

9.   Where a product is the subject of a patent application in a Member in accordance with paragraph 8(a), exclusive marketing rights shall be granted, notwithstanding the provisions of Part VI, for a period of five years after obtaining marketing approval in that Member or until a product patent is granted or rejected in that Member, whichever period is shorter, provided that, subsequent to the entry into force of the WTO Agreement, a patent application has been filed and a patent granted for that product in another Member and marketing approval obtained in such other Member.

Article 71   Review and Amendment

1.   The Council for TRIPS shall review the implementation of this Agreement after the expiration of the transitional period referred to in paragraph 2 of Article 65. The Council shall, having regard to the experience gained in its implementation, review it two years after that date, and at identical intervals thereafter. The Council may also undertake reviews in the light of any relevant new developments which might warrant modification or amendment of this Agreement.

2.   Amendments merely serving the purpose of adjusting to higher levels of protection of intellectual property rights achieved, and in force, in other multilateral agreements and accepted under those agreements by all Members of the WTO may be

referred to the Ministerial Conference for action in accordance with paragraph 6 of Article X of the WTO Agreement on the basis of a consensus proposal from the Council for TRIPS.

Article 72   Reservations
Reservations may not be entered in respect of any of the provisions of this Agreement without the consent of the other Members.

Article 73   Security Exceptions
Nothing in this Agreement shall be construed:

    (a) to require a Member to furnish any information the disclosure of which it considers contrary to its essential security interests; or

    (b) to prevent a Member from taking any action which it considers necessary for the protection of its essential security interests;

        (i) relating to fissionable materials or the materials from which they are derived;

        (ii) relating to the traffic in arms, ammunition and implements of war and to such traffic in other goods and materials as is carried on directly or indirectly for the purpose of supplying a military establishment;

        (iii) taken in time of war or other emergency in international relations; or

    (c) to prevent a Member from taking any action in pursuance of its obligations under the United Nations Charter for the maintenance of international peace and security.

WIPO COPYRIGHT TREATY
adopted by the Diplomatic Conference on 20 December 1996

PREAMBLE

The Contracting Parties,

Desiring to develop and maintain the protection of the rights of authors in their literary and artistic works in a manner as effective and uniform as possible,

Recognising the need to introduce new international rules and clarify the interpretation of certain existing rules in order to provide adequate solutions to the questions raised by new economic, social, cultural and technological developments,

Recognising the profound impact of the development and convergence of information and communication technologies on the creation and use of literary and artistic works,

Emphasising the outstanding significance of copyright protection as an incentive for literary and artistic creation,

Recognising the need to maintain a balance between the rights of authors and the large public interest, particularly education, research and access to information, as reflected in the Berne Convention,

Have agreed as follows:

Article 1   Relation to the Berne Convention
(1) This Treaty is a special agreement within the meaning of Article 20 of the Berne Convention for the Protection of Literary and Artistic Works, as regards Contracting Parties that are countries of the Union established by that Convention. This Treaty shall not have any connection with treaties other than the Berne Convention, nor shall it prejudice any rights and obligations under any other treaties.

(2) Nothing in this Treaty shall derogate from existing obligations that Contracting Parties have to each other under the Berne Convention for the Protection of Literary and Artistic Works.

(3) Hereinafter 'Berne Convention' shall refer to the Paris Act of July 24, 1971 of the Berne Convention for the Protection of Literary and Artistic Works.

(4)   Contracting Parties shall comply with Articles 1 to 21 and the Appendix of the Berne Convention.

Article 2   Scope of Copyright Protection
Copyright protection extends to expressions and not to ideas, procedures, methods of operation or mathematical concepts as such.

Article 3   Application of Articles 2 to 6 of the Berne Convention
Contracting Parties shall apply *mutatis mutandis* the provisions of Articles 2 to 6 of the Berne Convention in respect of the protection provided for in this Treaty.

Article 4   Computer Programs
Computer programs are protected as literary works within the meaning of Article 2 of the Berne Convention. Such protection applies to computer programs, whatever may be the mode or form of their expression.

Article 5   Compilations of Data (Databases)
Compilations of data or other material, in any form, which by reason of the selection or arrangement of their contents constitute intellectual creations, are protected as such. This protection does not extend to the data or the material itself and is without prejudice to any copyright subsisting in the data or material contained in the compilation.

Article 6   Right of Distribution
(1)   Authors of literary and artistic works shall enjoy the exclusive right of authorising the making available to the public of the original and copies of their works through sale or other transfer of ownership.

(2)   Nothing in this Treaty shall affect the freedom of Contracting Parties to determine the conditions, if any, under which the exhaustion of the right in paragraph (1) applies after the first sale or other transfer of ownership of the original or a copy of the work with the authorisation of the author.

Article 7   Right of Rental
(1)   Authors of:
   (i) computer programs;
   (ii) cinematographic works; and
   (iii)   works embodied in phonograms as determined in the national law of Contracting Parties,
shall enjoy the exclusive right of authorising commercial rental to the public of the originals or copies of their works.

(2)   Paragraph (1) shall not apply:
   (i)   in the case of computer programs where the program itself is not the essential object of the rental; and
   (ii)   in the case of cinematographic works, unless such commercial rental has led to widespread copying of such works materially impairing the exclusive right of reproduction.

(3)   Notwithstanding the provisions of paragraph (1), a Contracting Party that, on April 15, 1994, had and continues to have in force a system of equitable remuneration of authors for the rental of copies of their works embodied in phonograms may maintain that system provided that the commercial rental of works embodied in phonograms is not giving rise to the material impairment of the exclusive rights of reproduction of authors.

Article 8   Right of Communication to the Public
Without prejudice to the provisions of Articles 11(1)(ii), 11*bis*(1)(i) and (ii), 11*ter*(1)(ii), 14(1)(ii) and 14*bis*(1) of the Berne Convention, authors of literary and artistic works shall enjoy the exclusive right of authorising any communication to the public of their works, by wire or wireless means, including the making available to the

public of their works in such a way that members of the public may access these works from a place and at a time individually chosen by them.

Article 9   Duration of the Protection of Photographic Works
In respect of photographic works, the Contracting Parties shall not apply the provision of Article 7(4) of the Berne Convention.

Article 10   Limitations and Exceptions
(1)   Contracting Parties may, in their national legislation, provide for limitations of or exceptions to the rights granted to authors of literary and artistic works under this Treaty in certain special cases that do not conflict with a normal exploitation of the work and do not unreasonably prejudice the legitimate interests of the author.

(2)   Contracting Parties shall, when applying the Berne Convention, confine any limitations of or exceptions to rights provided for therein to certain special cases that do not conflict with a normal exploitation of the work and do not unreasonably prejudice the legitimate interests of the author.

Article 11   Obligations Concerning Technological Measures
Contracting Parties shall provide adequate legal protection and effective legal remedies against the circumvention of effective technological measures that are used by authors in connection with the exercise of their rights under this Treaty or the Berne Convention and that restrict acts, in respect of their works, which are not authorised by the authors concerned or permitted by law.

Article 12   Obligations Concerning Rights Management Information
(1)   Contracting Parties shall provide adequate and effective legal remedies against any person knowingly performing any of the following acts knowing or, with respect to civil remedies having reasonable grounds to know, that it will induce, enable, facilitate or conceal an infringement of any right covered by this Treaty or the Berne Convention:

(i)   to remove or alter any electronic rights management information without authority;

(ii)   to distribute, import for distribution, broadcast or communicate to the public, without authority, works or copies of works knowing that electronic rights management information has been removed or altered without authority.

(2)   As used in this Article, "rights management information" means information which identifies the work, the author of the work, the owner of any right in the work, or information about the terms and conditions of use of the work, and any number or codes that represent such information, when any of these items of information is attached to a copy of a work or appears in connection with the communiction of a work to the public.

Article 13   Application in Time
Contracting Parties shall apply the provisions of Article 18 of the Berne Convention to all protection provided for in this Treaty.

Article 14   Provisions on Enforcement of Rights
(1)   Contracting Parties undertake to adopt, in accordance with their legal systems, the measures necessary to ensure the application of this Treaty.

(2)   Contracting Parties shall ensure that enforcement procedures are available under their law so as to permit effective action against any act of infringement of rights covered by this Treaty, including expeditious remedies to prevent infringements and remedies which constitute a deterrent to further infringements.

. . .

Article 22   No Reservations to the Treaty
No reservation to this Treaty shall be admitted.

. . .

AGREED STATEMENTS CONCERNING THE WIPO COPYRIGHT TREATY
adopted by the Diplomatic Conference on 20 December 1996

Concerning Article 1(4)
The reproduction right, as set out in Article 9 of the Berne Convention, and the exceptions permitted thereunder, fully apply in the digital environment, in particular to the use of works in digital form. It is understood that the storage of a protected work in digital form in an electronic medium constitutes a reproduction within the meaning of Article 9 of the Berne Convention.

Concerning Article 3
It is understood that in applying Article 3 of this Treaty, the expression "country of the Union" in Articles 2 to 6 of the Berne Convention will be read as if it were a reference to a Contracting Party to this Treaty, in the application of those Berne Articles in respect of protection provided for in this Treaty. It is also understood that the expression "country outside the Union" in those Articles in the Berne Convention will, in the same circumstances, be read as if it were a reference to a country that is not a Contracting Party to this Treaty, and that "this Convention" in Articles 2(8), 2*bis* (2), 3, 4 and 5 of the Berne Convention will be read as if it were a reference to the Berne Convention and this Treaty. Finally, it is understood that a reference in Articles 3 to 6 of the Berne Convention to a "national of one of the countries of the Union" will, when these Articles are applied to this Treaty, mean, in regard to an intergovernmental organisation that is a Contracting Party to this Treaty, a national of one of the countries that is member of that organisation.

Concerning Article 4
The scope of protection for computer programs under Article 4 of this Treaty, read with Article 2, is consistent with Article 2 of the Berne Convention and on a par with the relevant provisions of the TRIPS Agreement.

Concerning Article 5
The scope of protection for compilations of data (databases) under Article 5 of this Treaty, read with Article 2, is consistent with Article 2 of the Berne Convention and on a par with the relevant provisions of the TRIPS Agreement.

Concerning Articles 6 and 7
As used in these Articles, the expressions "copies" and "original and copies", being subject to the right of distribution and the right of rental under the said Articles, refer exclusively to fixed copies that can be put into circulation as tangible objects.

Concerning Article 7
It is understood that the obligation under Article 7(1) does not require a Contracting Party to provide an exclusive right of commercial rental to authors who, under that Contracting Party's law, are not granted rights in respect of phonograms. It is understood that this obligation is consistent with Article 14(4) of the TRIPS Agreement.

Concerning Article 8
It is understood that the mere provision of physical facilities for enabling or making a communication does not in itself amount to communication within the meaning of this Treaty or the Berne Convention. It is further understood that nothing in Article 8 precludes a Contracting Party from applying Article 11*bis* (2).

Concerning Article 10
It is understood that the provisions of Article 10 permit Contracting Parties to carry forward and appropriately extend into the digital environment limitations and excep-

tions in their national laws which have been considered acceptable under the Berne Convention. Similarly, these provisions should be understood to permit Contracting Parties to devise new exceptions and limitations that are appropriate in the digital network environment.

It is also understood that Article 10(2) neither reduces nor extends the scope of applicability of the limitations and exceptions permitted by the Berne Convention.

Concerning Article 12

It is understood that the reference to "infringement of any right covered by this Treaty or the Berne Convention" includes both exclusive rights and rights of remuneration.

It is further understood that Contracting Parties will not rely on this Article to devise or implement rights management systems that would have the effect of imposing formalities which are not permitted under the Berne Convention or this Treaty, prohibiting the free movement of goods or impeding the enjoyment of rights under this Treaty.

WIPO PERFORMANCES AND PHONOGRAMS TREATY
adopted by the Diplomatic Conference on 20 December 1996

PREAMBLE

The Contracting Parties,

Desiring to develop and maintain the protection of the rights of performers and producers of phonograms in a manner as effective and uniform as possible,

Recognising the need to introduce new international rules in order to provide adequate solutions to the questions raised by economic, social, cultural and technological developments,

Recognising the profound impact of the development and convergence of information and communication technologies on the production and use of performances and phonograms,

Recognising the need to maintain a balance between the rights of the performers and producers of phonograms and the larger public interest, particularly education, research and access to information,

Have agreed as follows:

CHAPTER I
GENERAL PROVISIONS

Article 1   Relation to Other Conventions

(1)   Nothing in this Treaty shall derogate from existing obligations that Contracting Parties have to each other under the International Convention for the Protection of Performers, Producers of Phonograms and Broadcasting Organisations done in Rome, October 26, 1961 (hereinafter the "Rome Convention").

(2)   Protection granted under this Treaty shall leave intact and shall in no way affect the protection of copyright in literary and artistic works. Consequently, no provision of this Treaty may be interpreted as prejudicing such protection.

(3)   This Treaty shall not have any connection with, nor shall it prejudice any rights and obligations under, any other treaties.

Article 2   Definitions

For the purposes of this Treaty:

(a)   "performers" are actors, singers, musicians, dancers, and other persons who act, sing, deliver, declaim, plan in, interpret, or otherwise perform literary or artistic works or expressions of folklore;

(b)   "phonogram" means the fixation of the sounds of a performance or of other sounds, or of a representation of sounds other than in the form of a fixation incorporated in a cinematographic or other audiovisual work;

(c) "fixation" means the embodiment of sounds, or of the representations thereof, from which they can be perceived, reproduced or communicated through a device;

(d) "producer of a phonogram" means the person, or the legal entity, who or which takes the initiative and has the responsibility for the first fixation of the sounds of a performance or other sounds, or the representations of sounds;

(e) "publication" of a fixed performance or a phonogram means the offering of copies of the fixed performance or the phonogram to the public, with the consent of the rightholder, and provided that copies are offered to the public in reasonable quantity.

(f) "broadcasting" means the transmission by wireless means for public reception of sounds or of images and sounds or of the representations thereof; such transmission by satellite is also "broadcasting"; transmission of encrypted signals is "broadcasting" where the means for decrypting are provided to the public by the broadcasting organisation or with its consent;

(g) "communication to the public" of a performance or a phonogram means the transmission to the public by any medium, otherwise than by broadcasting, of sounds of a performance or the sounds or the representations of sounds fixed in a phonogram. For the purposes of Article 15, "communication to the public" includes making the sounds or representations of sounds fixed in a phonogram audible to the public.

Article 3 Beneficiaries of Protection under this Treaty

(1) Contracting Parties shall accord the protection provided under this Treaty to the performers and producers of phonograms who are nationals of other Contracting Parties.

(2) The nationals of other Contracting Parties shall be understood to be those performers or producers of phonograms who would meet the criteria for eligibility for protection provided under the Rome Convention, were all the Contracting Parties to this Treaty Contracting States of that Conventino. In respect of these criteria of eligibility, Contracting Parties shall apply the relevant definitions in Article 2 of this Treaty.

(3) Any Contracting Party availing itself of the possibilities provided in Article 5(3) of the Rome Conventions or, for the purposes of Article 5 of the same Convention, Article thereof 17 shall make a notification as foreseen in those provisions to the Director General of the World Intellectual Property Organisation (WIPO).

Article 4 National Treatment

(1) Each Contracting Party shall accord to nationals of other Contracting Parties, as defined in Article 3(2), the treatment it accords to its own nationals with regard to the exclusive rights specifically granted in this Treaty and to the right to equitable remuneration provided for in Article 15 of this Treaty.

(2) The obligation provided for in paragraph (1) does not apply to the extent that another Contracting Party makes use of the reservations permitted by Article 15(3) of this Treaty.

CHAPTER II
RIGHTS OF PERFORMERS

Article 5 Moral Rights of Performers

(1) Independently of a performer's economic rights, and even after the transfer of those rights, the performer shall, as regards his live aural performances or performances fixed in phonograms have the right to claim to be identified as the performer of his performances, except where omission is dictated by the manner of the use of the performance, and to object to any distortion, mutilation or other modification of his performances that would be prejudicial to his reputation.

(2) The rights granted to a performer in accordance with paragraph (1) shall, after his death, be maintained, at least until the expiry of the economic rights, and shall be

exercisable by the persons or institutions authorised by the legislation of the Contracting Party where protection is claimed. However, those Contracting Parties whose legislation, at the moment of their ratification of or accession to this Treaty, does not provide for protection after the death of the performer of all rights set out in the preceding paragraph may provide that some of these rights will, after his death, cease to be maintained.

(3) The means of redress for safeguarding the rights granted under this Article shall be governed by the legislation of the Contracting Party where protection is claimed.

Article 6 Economic Rights of Performers in their Unfixed Performances

Performers shall enjoy the exclusive right of authorising, as regards their performances:

    (i) the broadcasting and communication to the public of their unfixed performances except where the performance is already a broadcast performance; and

    (ii) the fixation of their unfixed performances.

Article 7 Right of Reproduction

Performers shall enjoy the exclusive right of authorising the direct or indirect reproduction of their performances fixed in phonograms, in any manner or form.

Article 8 Right of Distribution

(1) Performers shall enjoy the exclusive right of authorising the making available to the public of the original and copies of their performances fixed in phonograms through sale or other transfer of ownership.

(2) Nothing in this Treaty shall affect the freedom of Contracting Parties to determine the conditions, if any, under which the exhaustion of the right in paragraph (1) applies after the first sale or other transfer of ownership of the original or a copy of the fixed performance with the authorisation of the performer.

Article 9 Right of Rental

(1) Performers shall enjoy the exclusive right of authorising the commercial rental to the public of the original and copies of their performances fixed in phonograms as determined in the national law of Contracting Parties, even after distribution of them by, or pursuant to, authorisation by the performer.

(2) Notwithstanding the provisions of paragraph (1), a Contracting Party that, on April 15, 1994, had and continues to have in force a system of equitable remuneration of performers for the rental of copies of their performances fixed in phonograms, may maintain that system provided that the commercial rental of phonograms is not giving rise to the material impairment of the exclusive rights of reproduction of performers.

Article 10 Right of Making Available of Fixed Performances

Performers shall enjoy the exclusive right of authorising the making available to the public of their performances fixed in phonograms, by wire or wireless means, in such a way that members of the public may access them from a place and at a time individually chosen by them.

CHAPTER III
RIGHTS OF PRODUCERS OF PHONOGRAMS

Article 11 Right of Reproduction

Producers of phonograms shall enjoy the exclusive right of authorising the direct or indirect reproduction of their phonograms, in any manner or form.

Article 12 Right of Distribution

(1) Producers of phonograms shall enjoy the exclusive right of authorising the making available to the public of the original and copies of their phonograms through sale or other transfer of ownership.

(2) Nothing in this Treaty shall affect the freedom of Contracting Parties to determine the conditions, if any, under which the exhaustion of the right in paragraph (1) applies after the first sale or transfer of ownership of the original or a copy of the phonogram with the authorisation of the producer of phonograms.

Article 13   Right of Rental

(1) Producers of phonograms shall enjoy the exclusive right of authorising the commercial rental to the public of the original and copies of their phonograms, even after distribution of them by or pursuant to authorisation by the producer.

(2) Notwithstanding the provisions of paragraph (1), a Contracting Party that, on April 15, 1994, had and continues to have in force a system of equitable remuneration of producers of phonograms for the rental of copies of their phonograms, may maintain that system provided that the commercial rental of phonograms is not giving rise to the material impairment of the exclusive rights of reproduction of producers of phonograms.

Article 14   Right of Making Available of Phonograms

Producers of phonograms shall enjoy the exclusive right of authorising the making available to the public of their phonograms, by wire or wireless means, in such a way that members of the public may access them from a place and at a time individually chosen by them.

CHAPTER IV
COMMON PROVISIONS

Article 15   Right to Remuneration for Broadcasting and Communication to the Public

(1) Performers and producers of phonograms shall enjoy the right to a single equitable remuneration for the direct or indirect use of phonograms published for commercial purposes for broadcasting or for any communication to the public.

(2) Contracting Parties may establish in their national legislation that the single equitable remuneration shall be claimed from the user by the performer or by the producer of a phonogram or by both. Contracting Parties may enact national legislation that, in the absence of an agreement between the performer and the producer of a phonogram, sets the terms according to which performers and producers of phonograms shall share the single equitable remuneration.

(3) Any Contracting Party may in a notification deposited with the Director General of WIPO, declare that it will apply the provisions of paragraph (1) only in respect of certain uses, or that it will limit their application in some other way, or that it will not apply these provisions at all.

(4) For the purposes of this Article, phonograms made available to the public by wire or wireless means in such a way that members of the public may access them from a place and at a time individually chosen by them shall be considered as if they had been published for commercial purposes.

Article 16   Limitations and Exceptions

(1) Contracting Parties may, in their national legislation, provide for the same kinds of limitations or exceptions with regard to the protection of performers and producers of phonograms as they provide for, in their national legislation, in connection with the protection of copyright in literary and artistic works.

(2) Contracting Parties shall confine any limitations of or exceptions to rights provided for in this Treaty to certain special cases which do not conflict with a normal exploitation of the performance or phonogram and do not unreasonably prejudice the legitimate interests of the performer or of the producer of phonograms.

Article 17   Term of Protection

(1)   The term of protection to be granted to performers under this Treaty shall last, as least, until the end of a period of 50 years computed from the end of the year in which the performance was fixed in a phonogram.

(2)   The term of protection to be granted to producers of phonograms under this Treaty shall last, at least, until the end of a period of 50 years computed from the end of the year in which the phonogram was published, or failing such publication within 50 years from fixation of the phonogram, 50 years from the end of the year in which the fixation was made.

Article 18   Obligations concerning Technological Measures

Contracting Parties shall provide adequate legal protection and effective legal remedies against the circumvention of effective technological measures that are used by performers or producers of phonograms in connection with the exercise of their right under this Treaty and that restrict acts, in respect of their performances or phonograms, which are not authorised by the performers or the producers of phonograms concerned or permitted by law.

Article 19   Obligations concerning Rights Management Information

(1)   Contracting Parties shall provide adequate and effective legal remedies against any person knowingly performing any of the following acts knowing or, with respect to civil remedies, having reasonable grounds to know that it will induce, enable, facilitate or conceal on infringement of any right covered by this Treaty:

(i)   to remove or alter any electronic rights management information without authority;

(ii)   to distribute, import for distribution, broadcast, communicate or make available to the public, without authority, performances, copies of fixed performances or phonograms knowing that electronic rights management information has been removed or altered without authority.

(2)   As used in this Article, "rights management information" means information which identifies the performer, the performance of the performer, the producer of the phonogram, the phonogram, the owner of any right in the performance or phonogram, or information about the terms and conditions of use of the performance or phonogram, and any numbers or codes that represent such information, when any of those items of information is attached to a copy of a fixed performance or a phonogram or appears in connection with the communication or making available of a fixed performance or a phonogram to the public.

Article 20   Formalities

The enjoyment and exercise of the rights provided for in this Treaty shall not be subject to any formality.

Article 21   Reservations

Subject to the provisions of Article 15(3), no reservations to this Treaty shall be permitted.

Article 22   Application in Time

(1)   Contracting Parties shall apply the provisions of Article 18 of the Berne Convention, *mutatis mutandis*, to the rights of performers and producers of phonograms provided for in this Treaty for that Party.

Article 23   Provisions on Enforcement of Rights

(1)   Contracting Parties undertake to adopt, in accordance with their legal systems, the measures necessary to ensure the application of this Treaty.

(2)   Contracting Parties shall ensure that enforcement procedures are avaialble under their law so as to permit effective action against any act of infringement of rights

covered by this Treaty, including expeditious remedies to prevent infringements and
remedies which constitute a deterrent to further infringements.
. . .

AGREED STATEMENTS CONCERNING
THE WIPO PERFORMANCES AND PHONOGRAMS TREATY
adopted by the Diplomatic Conference on 20 December 1996

Concerning Article 1
It is understood that Article 1(2) clarifies the relationship between rights in phonograms
under this Treaty and copyright in works embodied in the phonograms. In cases where
authorisation is needed from both the author of a work embodied in the phonogram and
a performer or producer owning rights in the phonogram, the need for the authorisation
of the author does not cease to exist because the authorisation of the performer or
producer is also required, and vice versa.

It is further understood that nothing in Article 1(2) precludes a Contracting Party
from providing exclusive rights to a performer or producer of phonograms beyond those
required to be provided under this Treaty.

Concerning Article 2(b)
It is understood that the definition of phonogram provided in Article 2(b) does not
suggest that rights in the phonogram are in any way affected through their incorporation
into a cinematographic or other audiovisual work.

Concerning Articles 2(e), 8, 9, 12, and 13
As used in these Articles, the expressions "copies" and "original and copies", being
subject to the right of distribution and the right of rental under the said Articles, refer
exclusively to fixed copies that can be put into circulation as tangible objects.

Concerning Article 3
It is understood that the reference in Articles 5(a) and 16(a)(iv) of the Rome
Convention to "national of another Contracting State" will, when applied to this
Treaty, mean, in regard to an intergovernmental organisation that is a Contracting Party
to this Treaty, a national of one of the countries that is a member of that organisation.

Concerning Article 3(2)
For the application of Article 3(2), it is understood that fixation means the finalisation
of the master tape ("bande-mère").

Concerning Articles 7, 11 and 16
The reproduction right, as set out in Articles 7 and 11, and the exceptions permitted
thereunder through Article 16, fully apply in the digital environment, in particular to the
use of performances and phonograms in digital form. It is understood that the storage
of a protected performance or phonogram in digital form in an electronic medium
constitutes a reproduction within the meaning of these Articles.

Concerning Article 15
It is understood that Article 15 does not represent a complete resolution of the level of
rights of broadcasting and communication to the public that should be enjoyed by
performers and phonogram producers in the digital age. Delegations were unable to
achieve consensus on differing proposals for aspects of exclusivity to be provided in
certain circumstances or for rights to be provided without the possibility of reservations,
and have therefore left the issue to future resolution.

Concerning Article 15
It is understood that Article 15 does not prevent the granting of the right conferred by this Article to performers of folklore and producers of phonograms recording folklore where such phonograms have not been published for commercial gain.

Concerning Article 16
The agreed statement concerning Article 10 (on Limitations and Exceptions) of the WIPO Copyright Treaty is applicable *mutatis mutandis* also to Article 16 (on Limitations and Exceptions) of the WIPO Performances and Phonograms Treaty.

Concerning Article 19
The agreed statement concerning Article 12 (on Obligations concerning Rights Management Information) of the WIPO Copyright Treaty is applicable *mutatis mutandis* also to Article 19 (on Obligations concerning Rights Management Information) of the WIPO Performances and Phonograms Treaty.

INDEX